AMERICAN EDUCATION

THE NATIONAL EXPERIENCE

1783–1876

By the same author

The American Common School: An Historic Conception

The Transformation of the School: Progressivism
   in American Education, 1876–1957

The Genius of American Education

The Wonderful World of Ellwood Patterson Cubberley: An
   Essay in the Historiography of American Education

American Education: The Colonial Experience, 1607–1783

Public Education

Traditions of American Education

AMERICAN EDUCATION

THE NATIONAL EXPERIENCE

1783–1876

Lawrence A. Cremin

1817

HARPER & ROW, PUBLISHERS, New York
Cambridge, Hagerstown, Philadelphia, San Francisco
London, Mexico City, São Paulo, Sydney

FIRST EDITION

Designer: Sidney Feinberg

Library of Congress Cataloging in Publication Data

Cremin, Lawrence Arthur, 1925–
  American education, the national experience, 1783–1876
  Bibliography: p.
  Includes index.
  1. Education—United States—History. I. Title.
LA215.C74   370'.973   79-3387
ISBN 0-06-010912-2

---

80 81 82 83 10 9 8 7 6 5 4 3 2 1

For Jody and David

Children can scarcely be fashioned to meet with our
likes and our purpose.
Just as God did us give them, so must we hold
them and love them,
Nurture and teach them to fullness and leave them
to be what they are.

GOETHE

CONTENTS

Part IV. An American Education

PREFACE

The present work is a continuation of the effort begun in *American Education: The Colonial Experience, 1607–1783* (New York: Harper & Row, 1970) to present a comprehensive scholarly account of the history of American education. In that volume, I traced the origins of American education to the European Renaissance, depicting the transplantation of educational institutions to the New World as part of the colonizing efforts of the seventeenth and eighteenth centuries, describing the gradual modification of those institutions under novel social and economic circumstances, and explicating the role of those institutions in the movement for independence. The present volume carries the account to 1876, portraying the development of an authentic American vernacular in education that proffered a popular *paideia* compounded of evangelical pieties, democratic hopes, and utilitarian strivings, and indicating the role of that *paideia* in the creation of a unified American society, on the one hand, and in the rending of that society by civil conflict, on the other. A subsequent volume will carry the account to the present, emphasizing the transformation and proliferation of American educational institutions under the influence of industrialization, urbanization, technological innovation, and transnational expansion.

As in the first volume, I have defined education broadly, as the deliberate, systematic, and sustained effort to transmit, evoke, or acquire knowledge, values, attitudes, skills, or sensibilities, as well as any learning that results from the effort, direct or indirect, intended or unintended. And I have paid special heed to the changing configurations of education in nineteenth-century America—particularly the growing significance of schools, newspapers, and voluntary associations—and to the various ways in which different individuals interacted with those configurations. The more general theory underlying all this is set forth in

Public Education (New York: Basic Books, 1976). As in the first volume, too, I have given substantial attention to ideas about education, not as disembodied notions in their own right or as mere rationalizations of existential reality, but rather as moving forces that compete for attention and that profoundly influence what people believe is possible and desirable in the realm of education. Similarly, I have dealt extensively with institutions, though one should bear in mind that educational institutions remained small and loosely structured during the nineteenth century and that individuals made their own way through these institutions, as often as not irregularly, intermittently, and indeterminately. Finally, I have tried steadfastly to avoid the related sins of Whiggishness and anachronism: what happened during the first century of national life was not leading inexorably to some foreordained present, and it should not be understood and judged solely in the terms of the present.

One or two technical comments about style may be of interest. I have tried to keep footnotes to a minimum, as a rule documenting only quotations (except where they are meant to indicate commonplaces) and direct assertions involving statistics or statutes. Also, given the choice between citing an original source or referring to some more easily accessible accurate reprint, I have ordinarily chosen the latter; thus, the well-known Yale Report of 1828 is quoted, not from the *American Journal of Science,* where it was printed the year it appeared, but rather from the excellent collection of documents in Richard Hofstadter and Wilson Smith, eds., *American Higher Education: A Documentary History* (2 vols.; Chicago: University of Chicago Press, 1961). I have discussed most of the secondary and tertiary literature on which the work rests in the bibliographical essay; hence, those interested in the sources for a particular section should read that essay in conjunction with the text and the notes. I should add that in developing the bibliography I have not tried to be exhaustive—that would have doubled the length of an already lengthy book; I have merely tried to enable the reader to retrace my steps and then to proceed independently. Particularly in instances where an authoritative synthesis with a competent bibliography is available, I have kept my own citations to a minimum. As in the first volume, I have expanded, modernized, and Americanized all spelling and some punctuation in quoted passages; in the case of titles of written works, I have made only those alterations required to follow modern typographical convention.

The overall project of which the present volume is part originated

from an invitation in 1964 by W. Stull Holt, then secretary of the
American Historical Association; Francis Keppel, then United States
Commissioner of Education; and John Gardner, then president of the
Carnegie Corporation of New York, to prepare a comprehensive scholarly history of American education in connection with the centenary of
the United States Office of Education in 1967. I agreed at the time to
produce three volumes in seven years and have managed to produce two
in fifteen. The sponsoring organizations have been consistently patient
and encouraging, however, especially the Carnegie Corporation, which,
under the leadership of Alan Pifer, has provided additional funds to
sustain the effort. It is a pleasure once again to state my gratitude to
the Association, the Office, and the Corporation for their kindness in
furthering the work and at the same time to absolve them of any responsibility for the outcome: characteristically, Messrs. Holt, Keppel,
Gardner, and Pifer arranged for all matters of content to rest wholly
and finally in my hands.

No one engaged in a work of comprehensive scholarship can fail to
be aware of the infinite variety of kindnesses that contribute at every
point to the progress of the enterprise. Librarians and archivists at a
score of research centers in the United States and Europe have been pa-
tiently generous with their time and expertise; they are the unsung heroes and heroines of historical inquiry. I am also fortunate to have had
the assistance of a number of able associates during the course of the
endeavor: Steven L. Schlossman helped me with the research on the
configurations of education in Lowell, Massachusetts, Sumter District,
South Carolina, and Macoupin County, Illinois, presented in chapter
12; Toni Thalenberg helped me with the research on the educational
biographies of Lucy Larcom and Jacob Stroyer presented in chapter
13; Judith F. Suratt made any number of valuable suggestions on matters of style and substance; and Ellen Condliffe Lagemann collaborated
closely with me in every aspect of the latter stages of the effort, from
the canvassing of relevant literatures to the drafting and redrafting of
text, the verification of data, and the tracking down of elusive documents—she has been, in the truest meaning of the phrase, a colleague.
Tim Oliver and Dianne D. Marcucci typed the manuscript with intelligence and care. To these and others is owed a good deal of whatever
merit the book may possess; responsibility for its shortcomings is most
assuredly mine.

The work on the volume began during a year of residence at the
Center for Advanced Study in the Behavioral Sciences in 1971–72, and

it has proceeded both at the Center and at Teachers College, Columbia University, during the period since. The Center is an incomparable setting for reflection and writing, and I am grateful to O. Meredith Wilson, Gardner Lindzey, Preston S. Cutler, and their associates for their gracious hospitality. Teachers College has nurtured the project since its inception, and it is a pleasure to acknowledge the many kindnesses and continuing encouragement of the trustees of the college and of my faculty and student colleagues. Through the generosity of the University of Wisconsin, I had the opportunity to present the principal theses of the volume in the 1976 Merle Curti Lectures, which were subsequently published as *Traditions of American Education* (New York: Basic Books, 1977).

Finally, there is my incalculable debt to my beloved wife and children, who assisted me from time to time with the work itself and whose devotion and understanding have been, as always, unfailing.

L.A.C.

Teachers College, Columbia University
September, 1979

AMERICAN EDUCATION

The National Experience
1783–1876

INTRODUCTION

> We have changed our forms of government, but it remains yet to effect
> a revolution in our principles, opinions, and manners, so as to accom-
> modate them to the forms of government we have adopted.
>
> BENJAMIN RUSH

"I think it one of the most important revolutions that has ever taken
place in the world," the English Nonconformist Richard Price wrote to
Benjamin Rush in the summer of 1783. "It makes a new opening in
human affairs which may prove an introduction to times of more light
and liberty and virtue than have yet been known." For Rush, who was
fond of reminding his countrymen that the war was over but the revolution had yet to be accomplished, the challenge and the opportunity of
that "new opening" were prodigious. "We have changed our forms of
government," he later remarked to Price, "but it remains yet to effect a
revolution in our principles, opinions, and manners, so as to accommo-
date them to the forms of government we have adopted. This is the
most difficult part of the business of the patriots and legislators of our
country. It requires more wisdom and fortitude than to expel or to reduce armies into captivity. I wish to see this idea inculcated by your
pen."[1]

Price never responded to Rush's invitation, apparently content with
the counsel of his *Observations on the Importance of the American Revolution* (1784), where he set forth the typical Dissenter plea for an education aimed at shielding the mind from traditional orthodoxies ("Its
business should be to teach *how* to think, rather than *what* to think").

---

1. Richard Price to Benjamin Rush, June 26, 1783 (Rush mss., Library Company of Philadelphia); and Benjamin Rush to Richard Price, May 25, 1786, in *Letters of Benjamin Rush,* edited by L. H. Butterfield (2 vols.; Princeton, N.J.: Princeton University Press, 1951), I, 388.

But Rush and his compatriots worked indefatigably at the task, spinning endless versions of the political and educational arrangements that alone could "render the American Revolution a blessing to mankind." They were men who sensed themselves standing at the edges of history; yet for all their tendency to millennialism, they held a tough-minded regard for the lessons of the past, arguing as often by example as by exhortation and drawing upon the full range of the Western tradition, from ancient Babylonia to contemporary Britain. They quarreled incessantly, over everything from the reform of spelling to the redemption of criminals, for they knew with Aristotle that it was in the nature of politics for men to disagree over the ends and means of education. Yet there was a characteristic cast about their discussions, a characteristic agenda and rhetoric, that holds the key to much of what they proposed and eventually wrought.[2]

In the first place, they insisted with Montesquieu that the laws of education be relative to the forms of government; hence, while monarchies needed an education to status that would fix each class of the citizenry to its proper place in the social order, republics needed an education to virtue that would motivate all men to choose public over private interest. By "virtue," of course, Americans in the 1780's and 1790's implied some proper combination of piety, civility, and learning, with the definitions ranging from Thomas Paine's rationalistic humanitarianism through Benjamin Rush's Scottish moralism to Timothy Dwight's Puritan orthodoxy. And by "education" they meant the full panoply of institutions that had a part in shaping human character—families and churches, schools and colleges, newspapers, voluntary associations, and, most important perhaps in an era of constitution making, the laws. Yet they saw no simple relationship between people and politics, recognizing on the one hand that republics could not thrive in the absence of widespread public virtue and on the other hand that no system of government could in the last analysis stake its existence on the assumption of public virtue. And, being practical men, they proceeded on more than one front, establishing educational arrangements that would nurture piety, civility, and learning in the populace at large at the same time as they erected a political system through which the inevitable conflicts of self-interest might be reconciled.

Second, they argued for a truly American education, purged of all

2. Richard Price, *Observations on the Importance of the American Revolution, and the Means of Making It a Benefit to the World* (Boston: Powars and Willis, 1784), p. 50; and Benjamin Rush to Richard Price, May 25, 1786, in *Letters of Benjamin Rush*, I, 389.

vestiges of older monarchical forms and dedicated to the creation of a cohesive and independent citizenry. Decrying the widespread mimicry of European ways, they urged the deliberate fashioning of a new republican character, rooted in the American soil, based on an American language and literature, steeped in American art, history, and law, and committed to the promise of an American culture. In part, of course, this implied a conscious rejection of Europe, a turning away from what was widely perceived as a thousand-year tradition of feudalism, despotism, and corruption. More importantly, it implied a conscious act of creation, for the American character had yet to be defined, and the health and safety of the new nation depended on its proper definition. Rush spoke enthusiastically about a uniform system of education that would convert men into "republican machines"—a vision that must have seemed unassailable when first advanced in 1786 but that doubtless gave pause as time passed. And Noah Webster wrote boldly of national pride as one of the nobler human passions. "Unshackle your minds and act like independent beings," he exhorted his countrymen. "You have been children long enough, subject to the control and subservient to the interest of a haughty parent. You have now an interest of your own to augment and defend: you have an empire to raise and support by your exertions and a national character to establish and extend by your wisdom and virtues. To effect these great objects, it is necessary to frame a liberal plan of policy and build it on a broad system of education."[3]

Third, they urged a genuinely useful education, pointedly addressed to the improvement of the human condition. At its heart would be the new sciences, through which citizens might come to know the immutable laws governing nature and humankind and on the basis of which they might build a society founded on reason and conformity to moral truth. Through botany, chemistry, and geology, Americans would unlock the secrets of their virgin continent, with incalculable gain to agriculture, trade, and industry. Through economics, politics, and ethics, they would discover the customs of peoples and nations, with consequent benefit to the conduct of domestic and foreign affairs. And, through the systematic application of science to every realm of living, they would learn in countless ways to enhance the dignity and quality

3. Benjamin Rush, *A Plan for the Establishment of Public Schools and the Diffusion of Knowledge in Pennsylvania; to Which Are Added, Thoughts upon the Mode of Education, Proper in a Republic* (1786), in Frederick Rudolph, ed., *Essays on Education in the Early Republic* (Cambridge, Mass.: Harvard University Press, 1965), p. 17; and Noah Webster, *On the Education of Youth in America* (1790), in *ibid.*, p. 77.

of their daily existence, via smokeless chimneys, tougher seeds, purer metals, more productive silkworms, and better-tasting wines. It was a view best symbolized, perhaps, by the American Philosophical Society, whose *Transactions* reported the members' disposition to limit their studies "to such subjects as tend to the improvement of their country, and advancement of its interest and prosperity."[4]

Finally, they called for an exemplary education, through which America would instruct the world in the glories of liberty and learning. Possessed by the sense that they were acting not merely for themselves but "for all mankind," they deeply believed that their republican experiment would "excite emulation through the kingdoms of the earth, and meliorate the condition of the human race." And as part of that belief they came naturally to assume that their churches, schools, colleges, museums, academies, and institutions would be widely imitated by other peoples in other places—with all the burden of responsibility implicit in such an expectation. It was not merely a matter of pride, though pride they exhibited in abundance; it was rather a sense of being "subservient to the great designs of Providence," of having been chosen by God to lead the way to a millennium of truth, knowledge, love, peace, and joy. The charge doubtless moved individuals to extraordinary zeal at the same time as it filled them with fervid self-righteousness.[5]

Amidst all this enthusiasm there was ambivalence, to be sure, for some already saw in the emerging tendencies of American education qualities that could only be deplored. Thus, John Pickering perceived Noah Webster's effort to Americanize the language as a capricious surrender to colloquialism, while Josiah Quincy ridiculed the program of the American Philosophical Society as trivial and visionary. And Samuel Miller, whose *Brief Retrospect of the Eighteenth Century* was surely one of the most perceptive commentaries of its time, excoriated those who tended to assign a kind of "intellectual and moral omnipotence" to education. Never before was there an age, he noted, when knowledge of various kinds had been so popular and widely diffused: the public mind had been awakened, the masks of ignorance and corruption had been

4. *Transactions of the American Philosophical Society,* I (2d ed., corrected, 1789), xvii.

5. Thomas Jefferson to Joseph Priestley, June 19, 1802, in *The Writings of Thomas Jefferson,* edited by Paul Leicester Ford (10 vols.; New York: G. P. Putnam's Sons, 1892–1899), VIII, 159; Joel Barlow, *An Oration, Delivered at the North Church in Hartford, at the Meeting of the Connecticut Society of the Cincinnati, July 4th, 1787* (Hartford, Conn.: Hudson and Goodwin, 1787), p. 20; and Jonathan Elliot, ed., *The Debates in the Several State Conventions, on the Adoption of the Federal Constitution* (1836; 5 vols.; Philadelphia: J. B. Lippincott Company, 1941), II, 529.

lifted, and the love of freedom had been advanced. But in the wake of these improvements had come superficiality, infidelity, materialism, and, worst of all, hubris. God would show little mercy, he warned, to a society that ignored human limitation.[6]

Withal, it was an age of exuberant faith in the power and possibility of education, as men such as Rush and Webster set out to define a *paideia* appropriate to the aspirations of the young nation. The goal was nothing less than a new republican individual, of virtuous character, abiding patriotism, and prudent wisdom, fashioned by education into an independent yet loyal citizen. Without such individuals, the experiment in liberty would be short-lived at best. The Revolution, Noah Webster observed, had gained for Americans independence of government, and hence the opportunity to build a future. But the Revolution had in no way guaranteed that future. Only as Americans could awaken and nurture a corresponding independence of manners and opinion would the Revolution be completed and a proper foundation for the Republic established. The task of erecting and maintaining that foundation became the task of American education.

II

The Revolution, Price once observed, had opened a new prospect in human affairs: it had created a *republic* more liberal and equitable than any other in history; it had provided a place of *refuge* for oppressed peoples everywhere; and it had laid the foundations of an *empire* wherein liberty, science, and virtue would flourish and in due course spread throughout the world. Next to the introduction of Christianity itself, Price judged, the Revolution had been the single most salutary event in the history of human improvement. Republic, Refuge, and Empire—the three symbols and the aspirations they embodied interacted in the thought and experience of the Revolutionary generation in ways that profoundly affected the development of American education.

Politically, the Republic was defined in the drafting of the state and federal constitutions. In this realm more than others, Americans had undergone extended mutual instruction. They had studied and debated the political writings of the British Enlightenment—indeed, they had fought the war itself on a platform of political principle, and they had

6. Samuel Miller, *A Brief Retrospect of the Eighteenth Century* (2 vols.; New York: T. and J. Swords, 1803), II, 295.

come to certain broad agreements on such matters as the sovereignty of the people, the separation of powers, mixed government, and representation. Yet, for all the clarity of the political definitions implicit in an emerging constitutional law, there were important unclarities concerning the nature of the American people and the character and extent of their domain.

Who, after all, were the people who had made a successful revolution and thereby won the right to sovereignty? In one sense, they were simply the residents of the colonies. Legally, the Continental Congress resolved on June 24, 1776 (in an effort to define who might be charged with treason), that "all persons residing within any of the United Colonies, and deriving protection from the laws of same, owe allegiance to the said laws, and are members of such colony." Once independence was asserted (in the Declaration) and acknowledged (in the Treaty of Paris), the United States became free and sovereign, rendering the inhabitants of the colonies subject to the authority of the states in which they resided (though it is interesting to note that there was argument in the British courts as late as 1808 over whether the acknowledgment of independence by the King actually deprived the former colonists of their rights as British subjects). The Articles of Confederation guaranteed to the free inhabitants of each state (paupers, vagrants, and fugitives excepted) "all privileges and immunities of free citizens in the several states"; and the federal Constitution provided in similar language that "the citizens of each state shall be entitled to all privileges and immunities of citizens in the several states." At first glance, then, the citizenry of the Republic comprised the free inhabitants of the several states.[7]

Yet the matter was more complicated. For one thing, from the very beginning the status of blacks and Indians was ill defined. However anomalous the situation of a republic countenancing chattel slavery, the fact remains that slavery was openly acknowledged by the federal Constitution and explicitly provided for by state codes, though some states did begin to move toward abolition in the 1780's and others drastically curtailed the slave traffic. As a result, most blacks continued in slavery, and even those who were free ended up neither citizens nor aliens and in fact without the rights and privileges of either. The situation of the Indians was equally confused; they were considered alien members of

7. *Journals of the Continental Congress, 1774–1789*, edited by Worthington Chauncey Ford *et al.* (34 vols.; Washington, D.C.: Government Printing Office, 1904–1937), V, 475–476; The Articles of Confederation, in Henry Steele Commager, ed., *Documents of American History* (9th ed.; 2 vols.; New York: Appleton-Century-Crofts, 1973), I, 111; and The Constitution of the United States, in *ibid.*, I, 144.

their respective tribes, with which the United States negotiated treaties, but they were accorded few of the traditional prerogatives of aliens.

To complicate the matter further, the civil status of women differed from that of men. According to English common law, women surrendered all civil rights upon marriage. They could not control their property, whether dowered or earned; they could not sign contracts; and they did not hold legal guardianship of their own children. American practice, however, had come to diverge somewhat from the common law. Women did, in fact, exercise rights they did not legally possess; and, because a number of state constitutions did not explicitly deny them the right of suffrage, women in a few isolated instances voted in town elections during the early years of the Republic. Nevertheless, the principle of "feme covert," embodying the notion that a married woman was one and the same as her husband, governed the civil status of most women, while the rights of unmarried, widowed, and divorced women remained at best ambiguous. In actuality, then, the initial citizenry of the Republic comprised the free white male population of the several states.

Beyond this, there was the question of receptivity to immigrants, and here too, for all the talk of refuge and asylum, there was widespread ambivalence. On the one hand, for almost a century a policy of openness prevailed, despite bitter disagreements in Congress, frequent manifestations of public xenophobia, and occasional local efforts to bar particular groups, such as California's laws against the Chinese. On the other hand, commencing with the Naturalization Act of 1790, citizenship itself was proffered only to free white aliens, after a period of residence in the United States (the period varying significantly during the 1790's and early 1800's) and upon certification of good behavior and willingness to take an oath of allegiance. Almost from the beginning, then, there were limitations on the inclusiveness of America as refuge. Yet, granted this, the American population diversified as it increased (from just under 4 million in 1790 to almost 40 million in 1870), with immigrants arriving in large numbers from various regions of northwestern Europe, notably the British Isles, Germany, Alsace and Lorraine, Switzerland, and Scandinavia, and in smaller numbers from Africa via the West Indies and from China.

As education assumed a role in creating the American Republic, it inevitably became involved in defining the American people. Indeed, in the minds of many, education became subsidiary to citizenship and dependent upon it. Thus, Thomas Jefferson's Bill for the More General

Diffusion of Knowledge (1779) proffered public education to free, white children only; Benjamin Rush's *Thoughts upon Female Education* (1787) stressed subjects that would prepare women for their special responsibilities in guarding the property of their husbands and forming the character of their sons; and Robert Coram's *Political Inquiries* (1791), with its powerful argument for compulsory schooling, alluded to the Indians only as sources of data on the character of men living in a state of nature. Moreover, any number of commentators warned that if the immigrants were not to turn the American people into "a heterogeneous, incoherent, distracted mass"—the words as well as the fears were Jefferson's—they would have to be properly instructed, even more vigorously than the native-born, perhaps, since they would need to slough off the ways of the Old World before they could learn those of the New. Education would be popularized, then, but in the process it would also be politicized, and its obligations and commitments would vary from one segment of the population to another according to civic status and possibility.[8]

A nation is in one respect a people, in another respect a place—an identifiable territory the people may call their own. That eighteenth-century Americans saw their nation as an empire—even an empire of liberty—was of profound consequence. For an empire is in its very nature imperial: empire connotes the assertion of sovereignty and power over a vast domain. Americans may have perceived their empire as benevolent, virtuous, and committed to the service of the Lord, but there was no escaping the expansiveness implicit in their view. "Hail Land of light and joy!" sang a young Yale tutor named Timothy Dwight; "Thy power shall grow / Far as the seas, which round thy regions flow; / Through earth's wide realms thy glory shall extend, / And savage nations at thy scepter bend."[9]

Actually, one of the first questions the Continental Congress had to deal with was the nature and size of the national domain, and it was a thorny question on several counts. In the first place, there were the stubborn conflicts between the so-called landed and landless states, those like Virginia and New York, which asserted historic claim to territories extending as far west as the Mississippi, and those like Maryland and Pennsylvania, which had fairly well defined western bound-

8. Thomas Jefferson, *Notes on the State of Virginia* (1785), in *Writings of Thomas Jefferson*, edited by Ford, III, 188.
9. [Timothy Dwight], *America: or, A Poem on the Settlement of the British Colonies; Addressed to the Friends of Freedom, and Their Country* (1780), in *The Major Poems of Timothy Dwight* (Gainesville, Fla.: Scholars' Facsimiles and Reprints, 1969), p. 11.

aries and which demanded that most of the land west of the Appalachians become the property of the nation as a whole. Then there were the claims of the several Indian tribes, which insisted that the western lands were theirs to begin with. And, finally, there were the persistent disagreements over how to develop the western lands in any case, whether as quasi-colonies to be exploited for the benefit of the older eastern settlements or as self-governing territories to be brought eventually into some sort of equal partnership with the older states.

Congress stated a clear policy in the autumn of 1780, resolving that such unappropriated lands as might be ceded to the United States by any of the particular states would "be settled and formed into distinct republican states, which shall become members of the Federal Union, and shall have the same rights of sovereignty, freedom and independence, as the other states." Subsequently, in three far-reaching land ordinances, Congress specified the process by which government would be established in the newer territories. An ordinance of 1784, initially drafted by Jefferson, provided that the western lands be divided into states, that the initial settlers of these states be authorized to establish temporary governments based on the constitution and laws of any of the original states, and that, whenever the population of any state reached that of the smallest of the original states, it could be admitted to the Union on an equal basis, provided it consent forever to remain a part of the United States, carry its share of the federal debt, and maintain a republican form of government. An ordinance of 1785 provided that the western lands be parceled into towns six miles square and the towns into lots one mile square, that the lots be sold at public auction for not less than one dollar per acre, and that one lot in each town be reserved for the maintenance of public schools. And, finally, the Northwest Ordinance of 1787, revoking the ordinance of 1784, provided that initial government in the Northwest Territory be not by the inhabitants themselves but rather by a governor, secretary, and three judges appointed by Congress, that whenever there were five thousand free male inhabitants in the district they could create an assembly (which could pass laws subject to the veto of the governor), and that eventually three to five new states could be defined and whenever any of these states achieved a population of sixty thousand it could enter the Union on an equal basis. In addition, the Northwest Ordinance explicitly extended the rights of free worship, legislative representation, habeus corpus, trial by jury, and the inviolability of contracts to inhabitants of the territory; pointedly prohibited slavery; and further stipulated in an oft-quoted proviso: "Religion, morality, and knowledge, being necessary to good government and the happiness of mankind, schools and the means of education shall forever be encouraged."[10]

Much has been made in the historiography of education of these mandates concerning education in general and schooling in particular: they prefigured, in the words of one enthusiastic commentator, "the ideal of republican institutions" and "the gospel of American democracy." Yet far more important than the particular provisions regarding schools were the more general procedures for extending American governmental forms and for incorporating vast new regions into the nation on terms of equal participation in the polity. With the cession by the several original states of their western lands between 1782 and 1802, with the wresting of additional lands from the Indians, with the additions of Louisiana, Florida, Texas, Oregon, the Mexican cession, and California, the American empire spanned the continent, realizing what many came shrilly to proclaim as its "manifest destiny." In the course of this growth, land speculation, political conflict, and sheer accident interacted in ways that made the movement across the continent anything but tranquil. Yet in the long run the principles articulated by Jefferson in the ordinance of 1784 did prevail: the continental empire ended up an expanding metropolis rather than a metropolis with colonies. To the extent that the law educates, a common education prevailed.[11]

The Jeffersonian solution, however, was not without its problems, for what happened in effect was that many of the strains and tensions that would ordinarily have appeared between a metropolis and its colonies in the development of an empire were in the American experience encountered within the confines of the metropolis itself. The ill-defined political status of blacks and Indians was translated in spatial terms into the conflicts between the slaveholding and the nonslaveholding states and territories and into the distinction between enclaves "reserved" for Indians and their environs occupied by whites. The inevitable tendency to confuse political with cultural hegemony led to innumerable confrontations between religious and ethnic minorities, none more exemplary than the persistent harrying of the Mormons by local, state, and federal authorities. And the future problems that an expan-

10. *Journals of the Continental Congress,* XVIII, 915; and The Northwest Ordinance, in Commager, ed., *Documents of American History,* I, 131.
11. A. D. Mayo, "Public Schools During the Colonial and Revolutionary Periods in the United States," in U.S., Bureau of Education, *Report of the United States Commissioner of Education for 1893–94,* I, 738.

sive empire would encounter when its influence reached beyond its continental limits were readily apparent in missionary efforts to Asia, Africa, and the Middle East, and in military engagements with Mexico.

Yet, withal, an expanding national domain meant not merely wealth and power but spaciousness, movement, and, above all, opportunity. On the one hand, the notion of empire carried with it an educational imperative—in effect, the obligation to extend civilization over a vast continent at the same time as new experience was codified so that it could be passed along to succeeding generations. On the other hand, the vastness of the continent meant that there would be room for diversity, for different versions of civilization to compete and for different codifications of experience to flourish. In the counterpoint between the force of empire and the fact of diversity lay some of the central themes of the national experience in education.

III

The American Revolution confirmed and initiated, in education as in politics. It gathered together developments tending toward the popularization of education that had been in the making for at least a generation, and it invested those developments with new and important meaning. It set in motion significant innovations in educational theory and practice that were widely thought of as essential to the survival and prosperity of the Republic. And it lent new urgency to the discussion of educational affairs, there being widespread agreement that in republics the nurturance of morality and intellect in the citizenry at large is a matter of the highest public responsibility. In the process, there emerged during the first century of national life an authentic vernacular in education that stands in retrospect—granting its flaws, its imperfections, and even its several tragic shortcomings—among the two or three most significant contributions the United States has made to the advancement of world civilization.

The processes by which this vernacular was formed were clearly continuous with those of the provincial era, as during the nineteenth century transplantation, adaptation, imitation, and invention interacted to lend a distinctive character to American education. New groups of immigrants came in unprecedented numbers, bringing with them time-honored ideas and institutions from Europe, Africa, and Asia: the Irish brought a particular form of the Roman Catholic church; the Angolese brought a particular form of the matriarchal family; the Chinese brought a particular form of the mutual benefit society. As in earlier times, some of these institutions flourished essentially as they came; others evolved more or less rapidly into essentially different forms; still others passed into oblivion. Native-born Americans, in turn, reached out to other countries for ideas and institutions that seemed to promise educational advance—to England for the Sunday school and the lyceum, to Switzerland for more liberal methods of childrearing and classroom instruction, to Prussia for modes of school and university organization, to France for models of military training (all these too were quickly transformed amidst the diverse conditions of American life). Simultaneously, autochthonous institutions came into being as the deliberate fruits of human invention: Charles Willson Peale's museum, Benjamin H. Day's penny newspaper, Jonathan Baldwin Turner's agricultural college, and Joseph Smith's Mormon family.

In all of this, the confrontation with novelty remained a central phenomenon. As in the provincial era, educational institutions were forced to contend with new and changing circumstances in three related ways. For one thing, they were obliged to modify their formal structures to meet the demands of altered social and economic conditions: churches developed missionary arms to rebuild their dwindling congregations, and colleges arranged denominational affiliations to replenish their empty treasuries. For another, they were obliged to make the substance of their teaching conform to the realities that surrounded them: schools developed more "practical" curricula to prepare their students for "life," and newspapers broadened their notions of the "news" to satisfy the curiosity of expanding clienteles. And, as these sorts of shifts occurred, the relationships among educational institutions also changed: families spent less time systematically teaching reading as it was increasingly assumed that schools of one sort or another would do so, and apprenticeships in law and medicine carried less of an educational burden as law schools and medical schools became more widely available. The result was a kind of formlessness about American education, deriving in part from the sheer rapidity of change but also from the extraordinary extent of innovation, formal and informal, temporary and permanent.

In all of this, too, a developing and often strident nationalism invested institutions and programs of education with a significance that extended far beyond their immediate clienteles. The missionary efforts of the Congregational church were promoted not merely as saving particular souls but as vouchsafing civilization in the Ohio Valley; and the burgeoning common school systems of the several states were promoted not merely as imparting literacy to the oncoming generation but as guaranteeing the health and safety of the Republic. It was surely a form of what Daniel J. Boorstin has called "booster talk," but it was surely more as well. For it imparted a millennial tone to the rhetoric of American education that profoundly influenced its politics, reinforcing a relationship between the fortunes of education and the future of the Republic that would endure for several generations.[12]

In all of this, finally, Americans became the exporters as well as the importers of educational ideas and institutions (indeed, educational agencies were actually developed for the express purpose of being exported). Thus, Horace Mann studied Prussian and English methods of infant schooling during his European travels of 1843, but the Prussians and the English became equally interested in the pedagogical experiments of A. Bronson Alcott. And not a few of the European visitors to America during the first decades of the nineteenth century included substantial sections on education in their published observations. Later, a number of European countries actually sent individuals and commissions officially to study American churches, schools, colleges, factories, and rehabilitative institutions; and numerous American missionaries in turn took it upon themselves to carry the benefits of American culture to Africa, Asia, and the Middle East. In sum, the vernacular in education that emerged during the nineteenth century flourished as a national phenomenon with transnational implications. In education as elsewhere, nationhood did not mean a retreat from the world but rather a new relationship with it.

12. Daniel J. Boorstin, *The Americans: The National Experience* (New York: Random House, 1965), pp. 296-298.

PART I

THE KINGDOM OF GOD

———————————

It was the opinion of Edwards, that the millennium would commence in America. When I first encountered this opinion, I thought it chimerical; but all providential developments since, and all the existing signs of the times, lend corroboration to it.

LYMAN BEECHER

INTRODUCTION

When it came time to design a seal for the new nation, it is said that Franklin wanted it to portray Moses bringing down the waters upon Pharoah, while Jefferson would have preferred a rendering of the children of Israel in the wilderness, with a cloud leading them by day and a pillar of fire by night. Neither of these prevailed, however, and the Great Seal that finally issued from the hands of Charles Thomson and William Barton showed the familiar eagle holding the olive branch and arrows, and on the obverse a pyramid watched over by the eye of Providence, with the mottoes *Annuit coeptis* (He has favored our undertaking) and *Novus ordo seclorum* (A new order of the ages has begun).

A new era, under the watchful eye of Providence, proclaimed in Virgilian rhetoric—nothing could be more representative of the way in which Americans thought about themselves and their destiny as a people. The Biblical metaphors were neither ornamental nor even prudently didactic, they were of the essence. It was in the language and substance of religion that nineteenth-century Americans pondered the meaning of their individual and public experience. What in fact did it mean to be an American? The Frenchman Michel Guillaume Jean de Crèvecoeur wrote in the 1780's that to be an American simply meant leaving behind old prejudices and manners and receiving new ones from a new mode of life and a new government. But American preachers, mindful of their historic responsibility for articulating and celebrating the common values of their society, were not content to let the matter rest there. Rather, they took it as their fundamental obligation to fashion a *paideia* appropriate to the special role that the new nation would play in human and divine history. If America was to be the set-

17

ting for the building of God's kingdom on earth, the values and aspirations that Americans needed to share could not be left to chance; they would have to be carefully defined and vigorously nurtured.[1]

These tasks of definition and nurturance, essentially tasks of education, were taken as a first order of business by preachers of every kind and persuasion during the early decades of nationhood. In a torrent of sermons, tracts, learned disquisitions, and utopian proposals, they attempted to determine the moral substance of American citizenship and to devise the educational arrangements that would prepare a responsible citizenry. As one would expect in a pluralistic society that had quickly moved to disestablish religion, there were bitter conflicts: the conservative Timothy Dwight inveighed against the "infidel" Thomas Paine; the evangelical Lyman Beecher inveighed against the "heretic" William Ellery Channing; and the inspired Joseph Smith inveighed against the entire gentile world. What is more remarkable, however, was the degree to which substantial agreements were achieved. By the 1840's and 1850's, a generalized Protestant piety had become an integral part of the American vernacular, and the responsibility for teaching that piety to all Americans had become the central task of a newly constructed configuration of educative institutions. The piety that emerged was an embracing one, popular in character and millennial in orientation; and its substance and spirit were shared by an extraordinary variety of sects, denominations, and utopian communities.

The language of this early discussion of the philosophy and politics of education can be deceptive to present-day Americans—the concerns seem narrowly theological to the contemporary ear. To nineteenth-century Americans, however, the rhetoric was not only appropriate but absolutely essential. For two thousand years, the public values of the West had been thought about and articulated via the language and categories of religion; it should scarcely be surprising that a people who saw themselves charged by God to create "a new order of the ages" would continue to use such rhetoric as they defined who they were and hoped to become.

---

1. Michel Guillaume Jean de Crèvecoeur, *Letters from an American Farmer* (1782; New York: E. P. Dutton & Co., 1957), p. 39.

Chapter 1

BENEVOLENT PIETIES

It is the only true idea of Christian education, that the child is to grow up in the life of the parent, and be a Christian, in principle, from his earliest years.

HORACE BUSHNELL

"I know not whether any man in the world has had more influence on its inhabitants or affairs for the last thirty years than Tom Paine," John Adams wrote to his friend Benjamin Waterhouse on October 29, 1805. "There can be no severer satire on the age," Adams went on to say. "For such a mongrel between pig and puppy, begotten by a wild boar on a bitch wolf, never before in any age of the world was suffered by the poltroonery of mankind, to run through such a career of mischief. Call it then the Age of Paine." The fury of Adams's rhetoric, even in a private letter, tells us something of contemporary civility. But it also tells us a good deal about Paine, not only as seen by Adams, but as seen by an entire generation.[1]

It was indeed an age of Paine, in the first place, because Paine gave voice to so much that was commonplace; in effect, he interpreted the age to itself. It was an age of Paine, too, because of the sharpness of Paine's pen, because of his extraordinary ability to grasp issues and define them in elemental terms. And it was an age of Paine, finally, because of the pervasiveness of Paine's thought, on both sides of the Atlantic, in France and Great Britain as well as in the United States. "My country is the world, and my religion is to do good," Paine proclaimed. In doing good he inspired, he provoked, he frightened, and he antagonized, but ultimately he taught: the conflicts he engendered—and

1. John Adams to Benjamin Waterhouse, October 29, 1805, in Worthington Chauncey Ford, ed., *Statesman and Friend* (Boston: Little, Brown, 1927), p. 31.

19

they were ubiquitous—afforded his contemporaries the opportunity to educate themselves.[2]

Paine had been well equipped by his own arduous self-education to create that opportunity for his fellow men. Born in England in 1737 to the modest circumstances of a Quaker corset maker's household, he had attended a local grammar school for seven years, before being apprenticed at the age of thirteen to his father's trade. He fretted in the work, however, and soon resolved to make his own way in the world, initially at sea and subsequently in a variety of occupations—as exciseman, teacher, preacher, and tobacconist-grocer. More importantly, perhaps, he resolved to make his own way intellectually, reading widely and systematically in contemporary writings on science and philosophy and carrying forward a variety of his own mechanical and mathematical investigations. He managed his personal affairs poorly, however, and toward the end of 1774 he decided to emigrate to Philadelphia, where he took up work as a journalist. Fourteen months after his arrival, *Common Sense* appeared as an anonymous pamphlet and wrought its extraordinary effect throughout the colonies. Paine's authorship soon became known, and the reputation deriving from that effort as well as from *The American Crisis* won him an honored—if temporary—place among the Revolutionary leadership.

Paine himself observed that soon after the appearance of *Common Sense* he came to recognize "the exceeding probability that a revolution in the system of government would be followed by a revolution in the system of religion" and that "man would return to the pure, unmixed, and unadulterated belief in one God, and no more." As the twin revolutions unfolded in Paine's writings, they emerged as a popularized version of the Newtonian and Lockean philosophies, affirming the existence of an ordered universe set in motion by a benevolent God and inhabited by reasonable men who could know God's law and live according to its dictates. We have little knowledge of whether Paine had actually read Newton or Locke or the other Enlightenment thinkers whose ideas so closely prefigured his own; Harry Hayden Clark and others have traced many of his root concepts to the lectures of Benjamin Martin and James Ferguson, which Paine had attended in London between 1757 and 1759. More significantly, perhaps, Paine could easily have imbibed Newton and Locke, Collins and Toland, Rousseau and Condorcet, without ever having read a word of them. Like others of his

2. *Rights of Man* (1791, 1792), in *The Writings of Thomas Paine*, edited by Moncure Daniel Conway (4 vols.; New York: G. P. Putnam's Sons, 1894–1896), II, 472.

generation, he received his Enlightenment affirmations from newspapers and magazines, from informal study groups and itinerant lecturers, from conversations in taverns and disputes in coffeehouses. And, like others of his generation, he mulled them, argued them, and translated them into his own terms, producing a new and powerful version that was at the same time coarse and clear, simple and persuasive, audacious and reasonable. Leslie Stephen once observed that Paine's uniqueness consisted in the freshness with which he came upon old discoveries and the vehemence with which he asserted them. True enough, though, to the self-educated who were his audience, his affirmations were a revelation.[3]

Paine's two great works of popularization, following the immensely successful *Common Sense*, were the *Rights of Man*, styled as a reply to Edmund Burke's attack on the French Revolution, and *The Age of Reason*, which was for all intents and purposes Paine's attempt to formulate a "religion of humanity." The *Rights of Man* set forth a republican theory of government, based on the social contract, constitutionalism, popular sovereignty, and political representation. Monarchy and aristocracy were declared anathema; and mankind in general and Englishmen in particular were urged to overthrow their hereditary rulers and establish republican pieties. A republican theory of education was patently implied—though Paine talked only briefly of educational institutions per se, in a plan whereby the poor would be given child subsidies and enjoined to send their children to school, the local ministers to certify that they had complied. Rather, republican education was defined in the broadest terms, as an individual's lifelong quest for wisdom and understanding.

The Age of Reason set forth the deistic piety Paine obviously saw as complementary to republican civility. Essentially Newtonian, it began with a profession of faith in "one God, and no more" and proceeded baldly to attack the most cherished teachings of contemporary Christianity: the divinity of Christ, the authenticity of Scripture, and the authority of the Church. It then called for a redirection of religion in which men would be taught to contemplate the power, the wisdom, and the benignity of God as revealed in his works. Only as men sought to conform their own lives and institutions to the immutable, universal,

---

3. *The Age of Reason* (1794, 1796), in *ibid.*,IV, 22; Harry Hayden Clark, "An Historical Interpretation of Thomas Paine's Religion," *University of California Chronicle*, XXXV (1933), 56–87; and Leslie Stephen, *History of English Thought in the Eighteenth Century* (1876; 2 vols.; New York: Harcourt, Brace & World, 1962), I, 390.

and eternal laws of nature would the new world of equality, justice, and happiness portended by the revolutions in America and France come forth on truly permanent foundations. Once again, a theory of education was patently implied, though in this instance Paine stated much of it explicitly. Preachers would need to become philosophers, and churches, schools of science. More fundamentally, individuals would have to be taught to pursue knowledge on their own, for ultimately self-education was the truest education. "Every person of learning is finally his own teacher," Paine counseled. In the last analysis, the pious man was one who had used his God-given reason to study God's own creation, therein to discover the standards by which all must be judged. Not surprisingly, Paine saw himself as the supreme exemplar of his own piety.[4]

There is a fairly common portrayal of the course of American deism, in which deism rises steadily during the 1770's and 1780's, peaks during the 1790's—especially in the colleges, where *The Age of Reason* became something of an "atheist's bible" to the young—and then declines precipitously in the face of the Second Awakening. The account needs substantial modification. In the first place, deism was no luxury of the learned; along with Volney's *Ruins*, which had been translated by Thomas Jefferson and Joel Barlow, and the writings of Elihu Palmer, John Fitch, John Fellows, and Ethan Allen, *The Age of Reason* was read, pondered, and discussed by a wide spectrum of Americans, including farmers, artisans, and shopkeepers. Bishop Meade found Parson Weems hawking the book during an election-day gathering at the Fairfax (Virginia) Courthouse (along with Richard Watson's reply to Paine), while a Massachusetts circuit rider complained that the volume was "highly thought of by many who knew neither what the age they lived in, or reason, was."[5]

Beyond this, though deism may have been overshadowed by early nineteenth-century revivalism, it by no means disappeared. It flourished in sometime deistical societies in New York, Pennsylvania, Connecticut, and Massachusetts, which seemed to draw most of their recruits from the ranks of lower-class radicals; it manifested itself in ephemeral newspapers with such titles as the *Temple of Reason,* the *Prospect, or*

4. *Age of Reason*, in *Writings of Thomas Paine*, IV, 21, 194, 64.

5. Bishop William Meade, *Old Churches, Ministers and Families of Virginia* (2 vols.; Philadelphia: J. B. Lippincott & Co., 1900), II, 235; and J. E. A. Smith, *The History of Pittsfield, Massachusetts, from the Year 1800 to the Year 1876* (Springfield, Mass.: C. W. Bryan, 1876), pp. 145–146.

View of the New Moral World, the *Theophilanthropist,* and the *Correspondent;* and it regularly reappeared in alliance with other reformist movements, finding support from a Universalist congregation in one place, a Masonic lodge in another, a utopian community in another, or a workingmen's association in yet another. Deism waxed and waned during the early decades of the Republic, but it never died; and its continued existence as an undercurrent of American intellectual life is an important factor in understanding the reception accorded some of the more secular communitarian reform movements of the 1830's and 1840's.

Finally, it is important to recognize that although the more militant American deists wrote few treatises on education—the anonymous utopian *Equality—A Political Romance* (1802), in which a people espousing reason as its only guide manages to achieve universal happiness, is perhaps the leading example—deism was no marginal piety in respect to education. Indeed, its advocates made bold to establish it as the *paideia* of the early Republic, and they succeeded to a more than modest degree. Franklin and Jefferson may have been more prudent than Paine in their public utterances, but they were no less deistic in their fundamental orientation. And, insofar as their design was inextricably intertwined with their widely known educational proposals, it had influence beyond their immediate milieux. Moreover, Paine himself may well have taken some of his educational ideas from Jefferson, though the question of originality is less important than the fact of their essential agreement on the proposition that self-government is a chimera in the absence of universal education. However that may be, the fact is that the early Republic could boast few self-proclaimed deists, but deism had considerable popular appeal. And its impact must be sought in the self-confidence of ordinary men who thought they could plumb the mysteries of the universe and govern themselves accordingly, rather than in the circulation figures of the *Theophilanthropist* or in the attendance records of the Society of Free Enquirers.

II

Paine once remarked toward the end of his life that one of the objects of his religious writings had been to impress upon his fellow men a sense of trust, confidence, and consolation in their Creator. However radical his own solution may have been, he was certainly addressing himself to the central problem of the generations that had fallen heir to Locke's epistemological doctrines. How far could reason go in testing faith before it ultimately subverted faith? Could a true and effective piety be founded on natural law, rationally known, by reason unaided? Such questions could scarcely be avoided during what Adams had called "the Age of Paine"; indeed, Paine's very popularity made them the more pressing and insistent.

One who wrestled with such questions all his life—and in the process inevitably ended up wrestling with Paine—was Samuel Stanhope Smith, John Witherspoon's successor at the College of New Jersey. The son of a distinguished Presbyterian clergyman-educator, Smith had been at Nassau Hall at precisely the time Witherspoon had arrived to do battle with the regnant Berkeleyan idealism, brandishing the weapons of Scottish common-sense realism. Witherspoon's triumph had been complete, and his influence on Smith, profound and permanent. Smith was graduated valedictorian of his class (at Witherspoon's first commencement), and then proceeded to advanced studies in theology, first at his father's academy at Pequea, Pennsylvania, and then at Princeton with Witherspoon. Licensed to preach in 1773, he went off as a missionary to Virginia, where he played a key role in the establishment of Hampden-Sydney College as a southern replica of Princeton. He returned to Princeton in 1779 as professor of moral philosophy and remained for the rest of his life, acting as second-in-command to Witherspoon until the latter's death in 1794 (he had married Witherspoon's daughter in 1775), acceding to the presidency in 1795, resigning under pressure in 1812, and dying in 1819.

It would have been difficult to follow Witherspoon in any event; but Smith was simply not the executive his father-in-law was, and what might have been a distinguished presidency was increasingly marred after 1804 by political conflict and personal ill health. Yet, for all his problems as president, Smith exerted a profound intellectual influence on his own and subsequent generations. He refashioned the Scottish common-sense realism he had learned from Witherspoon, liberalizing it, extending it, and further adapting it to the American situation, and in the process made it the most significant school of systematic philosophy to appear in the United States between the Revolution and the Civil War.

At the heart of Smith's thought was the concept of man as a reasonable creature, actively using reason to guide his conduct and search for happiness. Sharing with Paine a post-Newtonian commitment to observation, induction, and generalization, he insisted that the methods of

moral philosophy be entirely conformable to those which had proved so
fruitful and liberating in natural philosophy. Yet Smith did not see reason going so far as to question those essential truths about man and society that could not be readily demonstrated by ordinary empirical
methods, and it was at this point that he parted company with Paine.
Building on the arguments of contemporary Scottish realism, Smith
contended that there are certain fundamental intuitions about the world
that can be grasped directly by the understanding and that make up
what must be deemed the "common sense" of mankind. We know
these, he reasoned, by "the testimony of our senses, and of all our simple perceptions," and they "ought to be admitted as true, and no ulteri-
or evidence be required of the reality, or the nature of the facts which
they confirm." Once perceived, these "perfectly simple" truths become
the "first elements" of our knowledge, and indeed are "intended to be
ultimate." Thus, via the route of intuition, Smith attempted to steer a
course between the Scylla of an older dogmatism and the Charybdis of
an unacceptable deism. By joining intuition to induction he was able to
put forward a piety that was consonant both with Locke's epistemology
and with the more traditional truths of Christianity.[6]

Smith was by no means uncritical in the way he drew upon his
Scottish contemporaries. In one of his major essays, for example, he
took sharp issue with the Scottish jurist Lord Kames on the sensitive
question of the nature and origin of human diversity. Kames had argued in his *Sketch of the History of Man* (1774) that the races of mankind were descended from various pairs of parents, each especially fitted for the climate and circumstance in which God had set it down
during the dispersal following the catastrophe of Babel. Smith maintained on the contrary that all men were descended from a single original stock and that any discernible racial differences could be attributed
to variations in climate and "the state of society." Now, the essential
environmentalism here had obvious bearing on Smith's ideas about education: after all, a human nature susceptible to modification is by definition educable; and the basic equalitarianism with respect to race was
momentous at a time when a new nation was being defined out of a
vastly heterogeneous society. But, more to the point, Smith ended up

6. Samuel Stanhope Smith, *The Lectures, Corrected and Improved, Which Have Been Delivered for a Series of Years, in the College of New Jersey; on the Subjects of Moral and Political
Philosophy* (2 vols.; Trenton, N.J.: Daniel Fenton, 1812), I, 23; and William H. Hudnut III,
"Samuel Stanhope Smith: Enlightened Conservative," *Journal of the History of Ideas*, XVII
(1956), 545, 548.

once again simultaneously affirming Christianity as traditionally taught and asserting that observable phenomena could "on proper investigation, be accounted for by the ordinary laws of nature."[7]

Smith's immersion in Scottish common-sense philosophy during this most fertile stage in its development made him easily one of the most interesting educational theorists of the post-Revolutionary generation. He echoed contemporary British-American rhetoric about education and liberty, arguing that an "enlightened people cannot easily be enslaved"; and he urged not only a general arrangement for the "common education" of the entire citizenry but also ample provision for the cultivation of the "sublime sciences" and the "liberal arts." Beyond these, he argued for that saving and sustaining virtue that would derive from the universal teaching of true religion. To such commonplaces of the 1780's and 1790's he joined rigorous expositions of the nature and function of human communication (derived largely from Thomas Reid), powerful arguments for the advancement of the several sciences, notably physics and chemistry, and fascinating discussions of such fundamental pedagogical problems as the nature of perception and the role of intellect. Ultimately, he saw education as the enterprise par excellence for the formation of human personality and the shaping of national character; and he tried his best to make Princeton exemplary of the unique combination of piety, civility, and learning he had fashioned during his lifelong encounter with the Scottish moralists.[8]

In the end, Smith's views proved more workable in theory than in practice. A just philosophy, he once contended, would always be "coincident with true theology." Yet one person's coincidence is often another person's heresy; and, in much the same way that Smith judged Paine infidel, there were those who judged Smith infidel. His younger brother, John Blair Smith, who followed him in the presidency of Hampden-Sydney College, is reputed to have charged him once with preaching, not "Jesus Christ and him crucified, but Sam Smith and him dignified." And, while the remark itself may well have been apocryphal, the charge was not. The delicate balance that Smith had wrought between the God-centered theology of Calvinism and the man-centered ethics of the Scottish philosophers proved unacceptable to the

7. Samuel Stanhope Smith, *An Essay on the Causes of the Variety of Complexion and Figure in the Human Species* (Philadelphia: Robert Aiken, 1787), p. 2.

8. *Sermons of Samuel Stanhope Smith* (2 vols.; Philadelphia, S. Potter, 1821), II, 31; and *Lectures*, II, 306.

more orthodox wing of American Presbyterianism, and amidst accusations that ranged from Arminianism to rakishness Smith was forced to resign.[9]

Smith's influence, however, extended far beyond the confines of Princeton; and, ironically, that influence was intimately bound up with the very synthesis of philosophy and theology that ultimately proved his political undoing. Smith's students were among the foremost college administrators of the early 1800's, including Frederick Beasley of the University of Pennsylvania, Joseph Caldwell of the University of North Carolina, and Philip Lindsley of the University of Nashville. All were innovators, and all espoused the same breadth and modernity in matters curricular that Smith had taught at Princeton. Indeed, it is not too much to argue that Smith's thought contributed significantly to the remarkable vitality of the Presbyterians in establishing new institutions of higher learning during the early decades of the nineteenth century, a vitality, incidentally, that was less and less noticeable at Princeton itself under Smith's immediate successors.

Even more significant, perhaps, was the pervasive influence of the Scottish philosophy in American colleges during virtually the entire span of the nineteenth century. Woodbridge Riley once remarked that Scottish realism "overran the country" during the Revolutionary era "and had an exclusive and preponderant influence well beyond the centennial of the country's independence." His assertion is surely too sweeping, though it would be accurate to say that the philosophy did overrun the colleges and then extended considerably beyond them through the informal networks of the educated. The vehicle for the triumph was the culminating course in moral philosophy that was ordinarily offered to seniors under the personal tutelage of the president. During Smith's own era, the dominant textbook was William Paley's *The Principles of Moral and Political Philosophy* (1785), a standard English work setting forth a bland utilitarian view in the context of nonsectarian New Testament Christianity. Yet, even in Smith's time, the works of such Scottish theorists as Thomas Reid, Adam Smith, Dugald Stewart, and Adam Ferguson were increasingly assigned and discussed—and not merely in Presbyterian institutions. With the appearance of Francis Wayland's *The Elements of Moral Science* (1835),

9. Smith, *Essay*, p. 109; and John Maclean, *History of the College of New Jersey, from Its Origin in 1746 to the Commencement of 1854* (2 vols.; Philadelphia: J. B. Lippincott & Co., 1877), II, 133.

however, Paley was decisively replaced by a textbook located squarely within the Scottish tradition (and authored, interestingly, by a Baptist clergyman). For fully a generation the higher learning in America bore a distinctly Scottish flavor.[10]

Riley, in a revealing aside, went on to muse over what might have happened in American philosophy had Jefferson founded an institution like the French Academy or the English Royal Society. Jefferson did not, of course, and the result was the Scottish triumph, at least among the learned. Riley saw the outcome as a catastrophic victory for conservatism, which held American philosophy in check for a century. Yet it is important to note that, during its initial phases in both Europe and America, the Scottish philosophy was far more liberating than constraining. In the hands of Smith, at least, it provided a version of the Enlightenment genuinely acceptable to the faithful—or at least to some of the faithful. Years later it would become arid and formalistic, but that should not obscure its profound effect upon several generations of American leaders during the first part of the nineteenth century.

III

Samuel Stanhope Smith was easily the most distinguished alumnus of Princeton's class of 1769, though there were others among his classmates who went on to considerable success in the politics and professions of the early Republic. Thomas Melville was for years naval officer of the port of Boston; John Beatty and John Henry were members of the Continental Congress; James Linn was secretary of state for New Jersey; and Mathias Burnet, John Davenport, Peter Dewitt, Samuel Niles, and Elihu Thayer ministered to various congregations in New England and the Middle Atlantic states. Probably the most noteworthy after Smith himself, however, was a young Rhode Islander named William Channing, who went from Nassau Hall to read law with Oliver Arnold in Providence and then set up practice in his native city of Newport, serving first as attorney general of the state and then, after the adoption of the federal Constitution, as United States attorney for Rhode Island. In 1773 Channing married Lucy Ellery, the daughter of a fellow Newport lawyer who had attended Harvard; and their

10. Woodbridge Riley, *American Thought: From Puritanism to Pragmatism and Beyond* (New York: Henry Holt and Company, 1915), p. 119. Smith cited Paley respectfully in his *Lectures;* see, for example, I, 321, and II, 18.

fourth child and third son was William Ellery Channing, born in 1780.[11]

William Ellery's childhood was spent amid the stimulating intellectual atmosphere one would expect of a Channing-Ellery household: beyond the associations with his parents and maternal grandparents, there were close ties with the Reverend Ezra Stiles, the family minister (later to be president of Yale), whose moderate Calvinism proved an important influence in William Ellery's early development, and with the Reverend Samuel Hopkins, a family friend, whose concept of "disinterested benevolence" would later prove immensely attractive to Channing as a young divinity student. After an indifferent schooling, the boy was sent at the age of twelve to prepare for Harvard with his uncle Henry Channing, a New London pastor. The following year William Channing died unexpectedly, leaving the boy for all intents and purposes under the intellectual guardianship of his uncle and his maternal grandfather. He completed his preparation in time to enter Harvard in 1794, electing to live at the home of another uncle, Chief Justice Francis Dana of Massachusetts, who resided in Cambridge.

Young Channing arrived at Harvard at precisely the time Paine's *Age of Reason* was first beginning to circulate; and, though he would later recall that poverty, well-chosen friends, and a zeal for intellectual improvement had saved him from the worst of contemporary skepticism, there is little doubt that the young Rhode Islander got caught up along with everyone else in the debates over faith versus reason. The corporation manifested its concern by furnishing a copy of Richard Watson's *An Apology for the Bible* to each undergraduate as soon as it became available in 1796; and the Dudleian lecturer for that year added his warning that Paine was little more than a "daring insurgent," whose prime concern was the disruption of public order. But it was Richard Price rather than Richard Watson who ultimately shaped Channing's ideas, along with Francis Hutcheson, Adam Ferguson, and the other Scottish liberals systematically taught by Professor David Tappan. Channing observed in his later years that it was Price's writings more than any others that had molded his philosophy into permanent form; and indeed, as Arthur W. Brown has pointed out, Price's doctrine of an innate moral sense, his emphasis on disinterested benevolence, his commitment to liberty, and his belief in the possibility of hu-

11. Samuel Davies Alexander, *Princeton College During the Eighteenth Century* (New York: Anson D. F. Randolph & Company, 1872), pp. 127–133.

man progress bear such striking resemblance to the doctrines that would become paramount in Channing's life that the recollection must be taken as more than the ordinary eulogistic sentiment.[12]

Channing completed his undergraduate work at Harvard with a vocation to the ministry and embarked upon a five-year program of reading and reflection that culminated in his ordination and installation at the Federal Street Church in Boston in 1803. He remained there for the rest of his life, using the Federal Street pulpit to define and articulate many of the most characteristic doctrines of American Unitarianism. The story is a familiar one: the split in New England Congregationalism between traditional and New Light Calvinists on the one hand and the more liberal critics of Calvinism on the other; the crisis occasioned by the death of David Tappan in 1803 and the vacancy thereby created in the Hollis Professorship of Divinity at Harvard; the appointment of the Reverend Henry Ware, Sr., a liberal, as Tappan's successor in 1805; the subsequent forging of an Old Light–New Light coalition by the Reverend Jedidiah Morse and the founding of Andover Theological Seminary in 1808 as a conservative bastion against Harvard infidelity; and the deepening theological rift that followed. By 1815 Boston Congregationalists were engaged in open theological warfare, with charges of hypocrisy and heresy rampant; and when in that year Morse published a pamphlet accusing the liberals of secretly embracing Unitarianism, events quickly came to a head. It fell to Channing to prepare what would be the manifesto of a new liberal faith, and he delivered it in the form of a sermon on the occasion of Jared Sparks's ordination as minister of a professedly liberal congregation in Baltimore. Out of that sermon grew a new denomination and, even more important, a new version of the Christian *paideia* in America.

The emergence of the new denomination was a significant development for education, however restricted its influence may have been. The oft-repeated quip that Unitarian preaching was limited to the fatherhood of God, the brotherhood of man, and the neighborhood of Boston has always been more clever than true: a considerable number of Unitarian congregations appeared in the South and West, many of

12. *Memoir of William Ellery Channing*, edited by William M. Channing (3 vols.; London: John Chapman, 1848), I, 60-61, 65; Nathan Fiske, *A Sermon Preached at the Dudleian Lecture, in the Chapel of Harvard College, September 7, 1796* (Boston: Manning & Loring, 1796), p. 16; and Arthur W. Brown, *Always Young for Liberty: A Biography of William Ellery Channing* (Syracuse, N.Y.: Syracuse University Press, 1956), p. 22.

them centers of intellectual vitality, and the great Unitarian controversies of the 1850's testify to the continuing importance of theological and doctrinal questions within the fold. The fact is some of the most influential families of Jacksonian America educated themselves and their children in Unitarian congregations, and that in itself was of no small significance. Yet it was rather as a broader cultural movement with its source in the Boston-Cambridge region than as a particular religious doctrine with its source in a limited number of churches that Unitarianism influenced American education. It was a movement that united the best of eighteenth-century British rationalism with the moral fervor of New England Puritanism, and in so doing it spoke profoundly to the social predicament of nineteenth-century America. In the development of that movement, Channing was the pivotal figure.

Unlike Samuel Stanhope Smith, Channing was neither a scholar nor a critic but rather an activist whose ideas flowed piecemeal in sermons, addresses, pamphlets, and letters. Yet there were leading themes that resounded through everything he said, which lent a certain coherence to his philosophy. Like others of his generation, he began with the problem of faith and reason that had been posed by Locke, wrestled with by the Scottish moralists, and carried to one logical extreme by Paine. And, like many liberals within the New England Congregationalist fold, he was deeply influenced by the Arminianism of Jonathan Mayhew and Charles Chauncy. The solution he eventually proposed represented a precarious balance between what he deemed essential in Christian revelation and what he saw as the minimal demands of reason. In formulations reminiscent of Locke's *Essay Concerning Human Understanding* and *The Reasonableness of Christianity,* Channing told Americans that they could determine the essentials of Christianity from an attentive and unbiased search of Scripture and that they would find nothing essential to Christianity contrary to reason. And, in controversies also reminiscent of Locke's, Channing was forced to contend on the one hand with those who considered a reasoned interpretation of Scripture to be apostasy and on the other hand with those who were ready to abandon revelation in its entirety. Thus, Moses Stuart of Andover Theological Seminary saw Unitarianism as little more than a halfway house to infidelity, while Theodore Parker saw it as full of compromise with the ultimate demands of reason. Channing's affectionate—if qualified—sympathy with Parker's spiritual quest suggests that Unitarianism probably represented the farthest advance of rationalism within a recognizable Christian framework to develop during the early national era. It was essentially Lockean latitudinarianism with a nineteenth-century American flavor.

Frederic Henry Hedge, Channing's Transcendentalist contemporary and friend, once remarked in an analysis of Channing's immense influence that there were two closely related foci in Channing's thought—the goodness of God and the dignity of man—and that all else was corollary. The goodness of God implied the possibility of universal salvation, the perfectibility of man, the spiritual efficacy of good works, and the anticipation of progress. Beyond these it implied a spiritual link between God the father and all mankind that conferred an ultimate dignity upon each and every human being. "The idea of God," Channing observed in 1828, "sublime and awful as it is, is the idea of our own spiritual nature, purified and enlarged to infinity. In ourselves are the elements of the Divinity. God, then, does not sustain a figurative resemblance to man. It is the resemblance of a parent to a child, the likeness of a kindred nature."[13]

This sense of an inextricable link between God and man and of the idea of God as the idea of man's spiritual nature purified and enlarged pointed to an expansive and noble concept of education and its purpose. "The child is not put into the hands of parents alone," Channing taught. "It is not born to hear but a few voices. It is brought at birth into a vast, we may say an infinite, school. The universe is charged with the office of its education." The purpose of that education was to energize the child, to set in motion a lifelong effort toward self-culture, or the harmonious growth and cultivation of all the human faculties in the direction of their divine manifestations. Insofar as the teacher had responsibility for assisting and encouraging such effort and the knowledge and ability to do so, he was entitled to the highest possible respect from society—his office being "the noblest on earth," more important even than the minister's or the statesman's. Further, insofar as growth toward the divine was the end in life for every individual, all associations and institutions were to be judged by the extent to which they stimulated such growth and reformed so that they could advance it.[14]

13. *Services in Memory of Rev. William E. Channing* (Boston: John Wilson and Son, 1867), p. 27; and *The Works of William E. Channing* (new ed.; Boston: American Unitarian Association, 1886), p. 293.

14. *Works of William E. Channing*, pp. 117–118, 119–120, 14–15.

Now, for all the breadth of his view of education, Channing was no utopian dreamer. He was aware that families educate, as do churches and lyceums and lectures and literature. Indeed, he saw the highest responsibility of the minister as teaching a healthful, well-proportioned, and all-comprehending piety that would widen the range of human thought, feeling, and enjoyment; and his remarks on the impact of a national literature upon national character anticipated many of Emerson's better-known observations in "The American Scholar." In the end, however, Channing realized that in his own time schools and schoolteachers would carry the greatest burden of popular education, and he campaigned for an expanded common school system in which better-trained teachers would employ more benevolent methods to encourage self-help and self-culture.

The question is often raised as to whether Channing was a Transcendentalist and, if so, to what extent he foreshadowed and in fact articulated the characteristic views of Transcendentalism. There is evidence on both sides, though there can be no denying that, however much Channing publicly dissented from many of the ideas that the Transcendentalists preached, he tended to support them personally and intellectually. They in turn most assuredly joined Emerson in seeing him, despite his strictures, as their "bishop." Yet, as important as that issue may be in its own right, there is a more central question with respect to Channing's larger influence on American education, namely, his relation to the broader intellectual movement that Van Wyck Brooks called "the flowering of New England." Brooks himself saw Channing as "the great awakener," who harrowed the ground for literature by first harrowing the ground for life. Certainly the same was true in education. The liberal Christian *paideia* we associate with Channing's Unitarianism was more than a matter of particular churches or a particular philosophy. It manifested itself rather in the broader cultural efflorescence that made the Boston-Cambridge region the moral and cultural hub of the Republic for at least a generation and that made the Unitarian and Transcendentalist intellectuals the teachers of the Republic for an even longer period of time. Emerson's essays, Longfellow's poetry, Alcott's novels, and Sparks's histories were all part of it; they penetrated to the farthest reaches of American society, imparting a view of man and the world that had an enduring effect on education. In its more formal sense, Unitarianism was essentially an elite religion; but it provided the moral epicenter of a far more popular *paideia,* which exercised incalculable influence on the ideals and aspirations of nineteenth-century Americans.[15]

IV

The advance of Unitarianism was observed by the orthodox with a curious mixture of fear, disdain, and resistance. It was not so much that orthodoxy felt its power waning, though the disestablishment of the Congregational church in Connecticut in 1818 did give the orthodox pause, as did the defection of some eighty-one Massachusetts Congregational churches to Unitarianism after an 1820 court decision placing the selection of ministers in the hands of the voters of the several parishes. It was rather that Unitarianism was seen as a genuine threat to the body politic and hence deserving of opposition on the basis of national as well as religious loyalties. "We feel the danger of allowing the Unitarian heresy too much popular headway," the Reverend Lyman Beecher wrote to his young friend Elias Cornelius in 1821, "lest the stress, like toleration, once running, should defy obstruction, and sweep foundations and superstructure in a promiscuous ruin. An early and decided check followed up will turn back this flood, and save the land from inundation."[16]

By 1821, Beecher had already committed himself to turning back the flood and thereby saving the land. Connecticut born and reared, the son and grandson of blacksmiths, Beecher had attended Yale during the time of its shift from Ezra Stiles's liberalism to Timothy Dwight's orthodoxy. From Dwight, Beecher had imbibed an implacable opposition to "French infidelity" in all its forms, an unshakable belief in America's God-ordained future, and an unswerving confidence in the power of evangelical preaching to bring that future to pass. "A new day was dawning as I came on the stage," Beecher later remarked of Dwight's influence on him, "and I was baptized into the revival spirit." In pastorates at East Hampton, Long Island, and Litchfield, Connecticut, Beecher had preached a new version of Calvinism that taught at one and the same time God's ultimate sovereignty and man's freedom to choose. All the glory of God, Beecher argued in an 1808 sermon,

15. Elizabeth Palmer Peabody, *Reminiscences of Rev. Wm. Ellery Channing, D.D.* (Boston: Roberts Brothers, 1880), p. 371; and Van Wyck Brooks, *The Flowering of New England, 1815–1865* (new and rev. ed.; New York: E. P. Dutton & Co., 1936), pp. 109–110.

16. Lyman Beecher to Elias Cornelius, January 23, 1821, in *The Autobiography of Lyman Beecher* (1864), edited by Barbara M. Cross (2 vols.; Cambridge, Mass.: Harvard University Press, 1961), I, 326.

"depends wholly upon the fact, that men, though living under the government of God, and controlled according to his pleasure are still, entirely free, and accountable for all the deeds done in the body." Revivals became Beecher's instrument for ensuring that men would use their freedom well, and at both East Hampton and Litchfield reports of "exertions for the revival of religion" were commonplace and continuous.[17]

What became clear as Beecher's war with the Unitarians progressed was that revivals were merely one weapon in a larger arsenal that included sermons, tracts, organizations of the clergy, moral improvement societies, and properly staffed Sunday schools, colleges, and seminaries. The war was ultimately an educational conflict, with not only the souls of individual men and women at stake but the soul of the nation itself. It had its political aspects, to be sure: Beecher was not above alluding to Unitarian reliance on "strategem," "duplicity," "wealth," and "favor," in "laying sacrilegious hands on chartered institutions, and funds dedicated to Christ and the church [Harvard and those eighty-one Congregational pulpits]." But, at bottom, it was a conflict over the nature of man and his institutions. If God was indeed benevolent and man essentially rational, as Channing had argued, then reason and Scripture were man's truest guides to that slow but steady moral and civic improvement that would facilitate his progress toward perfection. If, however, God was just and man corrupt, as Beecher argued, then conversion and regeneration were man's surest guides to salvation. True, Beecher and his close friend Nathaniel Taylor of Yale tried to soften the evangelical view by arguing that man did have moral agency—man could choose the way of righteousness. Yet that did not in fact alter the demands of righteousness, or the awesome alternative that awaited the unregenerate.[18]

As Beecher saw it, the same choice faced the nation. The disestablishment of the churches had created a new opportunity in human affairs. The older monopolies of power had been superseded by the suffrages of freemen and the older prescription of creed by the emancipation of conscience. The stage had thereby been set for one of the great experiments of human history, determining whether under proper moral persuasion a free people would choose voluntarily to consecrate themselves to God. "If it had been the design of heaven," Beecher maintained, "to establish a powerful nation, in the full enjoyment

17. Ibid., 45; Lyman Beecher, Sermons Delivered on Various Occasions (Boston: T. R. Marvin, 1828), p. 10 (italics removed); and Autobiography, I, 189.
18. Quarterly Christian Spectator, II (1820), 595.

of civil and religious liberty, where all the energies of man might find scope and excitement, on purpose to show the world by experiment, of what man is capable; and to shed light on the darkness which should awake the slumbering eye, and rouse the torpid mind, and nerve the palsied arm of millions; where could such an experiment have been made but in this country, and by whom so auspiciously as by our fathers, and by what means so well adapted to that end, as by their institutions?" If Americans chose wisely in their freedom, they would surely usher in the millennium.[19]

Whatever Beecher's effect on the Unitarians, he found an interested audience among the orthodox; and, when a new orthodox congregation was formed in connection with the Hanover Street Church in Boston in 1825, it seemed only natural to invite Beecher as spiritual leader. He accepted the call the following year, arriving in Boston at the peak of his powers and moving quickly to the center of a revival movement that at least one contemporary likened in influence to the Great Awakening of the 1740's. It was during his tenure at Hanover Street that he effected his much publicized rapprochement with the revivalist preacher Charles Grandison Finney over the appropriateness of Finney's "new measures" for the saving of souls; and it was during the Hanover period, too, that he delivered his first public lectures on the incompatibility of republicanism and Roman Catholicism—lectures that surely helped fire the animosities that eventually led to the sacking of the Ursuline convent at Charlestown. Despite his growing influence in Boston, however, Beecher became increasingly restless, and his attention was soon drawn to the West by the prospect of a new Presbyterian institution on the outskirts of Cincinnati called Lane Seminary, dedicated to producing ministers for the evangelization of the wilderness. "The moral destiny of our nation," Beecher wrote his daughter Catharine in the summer of 1830, "and all our institutions and hopes, and the world's hopes, turns on the character of the West, and the competition now is for that of preoccupancy in the education of the rising generation, in which Catholics and infidels have got the start of us."[20]

From an initial interest in fundraising for Lane, Beecher rapidly developed a personal commitment to the institution, and after considerable vacillation he accepted the presidency in 1832, moving to Cincinnati in the latter part of that year. And it was at Lane, amid continuing

19. Lyman Beecher, The Memory of Our Fathers (Boston: T. R. Marvin, 1828), pp. 13-14.

20. Lyman Beecher to Catharine Beecher, July 8, 1830, in Autobiography, II, 167.

controversy over the validity of his religious orthodoxy (the question concerned Beecher's resolution of man's inherent sinfulness with his ability to choose salvation) and over the translation of his orthodoxy into political commitments (the question concerned Beecher's stand on the evils of slavery and the efficacy of abolitionism), that Beecher gave fullest statement to his belief in the millennial future of the Republic and to the role of education in bringing that future to pass. The essentials of his view were enunciated in sermons delivered on various occasions—most of them fundraising meetings for Lane—and received widest circulation in two publications that first appeared in 1835, *A Plea for the West* and *A Plea for Colleges*.

A Plea for the West went through several printings and reached interested audiences in many regions of the country. Beginning with a restatement of Beecher's faith that the millennium would commence in America, the pamphlet sounded a clarion call to action: "If this nation is, in the providence of God, destined to lead the way in the moral and political emancipation of the world, it is time she understood her high calling, and were harnessed for the work." An epochal battle was in the making, Beecher continued, and it was plain that the battle would be fought in the West and would concern education. "The conflict which is to decide the destiny of the West," Beecher argued, "will be a conflict of institutions for the education of her sons, for purposes of superstition, or evangelical light; of despotism, or liberty." Hence, there was need for "permanent, powerful, literary and moral institutions [like Lane, of course], which, like the great orbs of attraction and light, shall send forth at once their power and their illumination." These literary and moral institutions would educate an autochthonous ministry trained in the use of pedagogical weaponry—tracts, Bibles, missions, families, Sabbath schools, common schools, churches, colleges, and seminaries. It was this ministry that would win the West to true religion and genuine republicanism.[21]

The conflict Beecher portrayed in *A Plea for the West* was not with the ephemeral forces of darkness embedded in the hearts and souls of individuals; it was with the tangible forces of darkness incarnate in the clergy and parishioners of the Roman Catholic church. Beecher sketched the awesome threat of waves of immigrants from the despotic monarchies of Europe flooding the West, there to be manipulated by

21. Lyman Beecher, *A Plea for the West* (2d ed.; Cincinnati: Truman & Smith, 1835), pp. 11, 12, 10.

Catholic priests, who would maintain over them in the land of strangers and unknown tongues an ascendancy as absolute as they had been able to maintain in Europe. His solution lay partly in the checking of immigration and partly in the restriction of naturalization, but it lay most fundamentally in education. "The education of the nation," Beecher perorated, "the culture of its intellect—the formation of its conscience, and the regulation of its affection, heart, and action, is of all others the most important work, and demands the supervision of persons, of wise and understanding hearts—consecrated to the work, and supported and highly honored in accordance with their self-denying, disinterested, and indispensable labors." [22]

A Plea for Colleges was in many respects complementary to A Plea for the West, elaborating the special demands that the preparation of America for her destiny would exert on literary institutions. Here, Beecher focused on those literary institutions which would "qualify the portion of mind which is destined to act upon mind, for the various spheres of professional instruction, and moral and religious cultivation." The colleges, he insisted, were "the intellectual manufactories and workshops" of the nation: they broke up monopolies of knowledge; they proffered true equality to rich and poor to compete for learning and wealth; and they united the nation by mixing all classes in a "constant communion of honor and profit." But their very importance to the nation's future (and the West's) made it crucial that they be stable and orderly institutions of discipline, removed from the passions of political controversy (abolitionism) and insulated from the thrusts of journalists and students (his critics at Lane). The whole tendency of educating institutions, Beecher concluded, of families, churches, and schools alike, was toward "an unsubdued spirit of republican independence" that threatened to overthrow law, authority, and virtue; hence, only as the tendency could be reversed and the rising generation trained to habits of subordination and spontaneous obedience to law would freedom flourish and the nation survive. Again, in Beecher's view, the crisis would surely be resolved in the West.[23]

Beecher resigned from the presidency of Lane in 1850, thereafter returning to Boston for a time and finally retiring to Brooklyn Heights, where his son Henry Ward Beecher held a pulpit. He suffered a lin-

22. Ibid., p. 187.
23. Lyman Beecher, A Plea for Colleges (2d ed.; Cincinnati: Truman & Smith, 1836), pp. 13, 15, 16, 91.

gering decline, and finally died in 1863. His life had spanned the two cataclysmic events of the nation's history: he had been born during the early months of the Revolution and he had died in the middle of the Civil War. Ironically, he had spent much of that life wrestling with the very problems of national identity that the first war had spawned and the second war would test. His nationalism was strident and unyielding, and inextricably tied to evangelical Protestantism; to advance his version of the Protestant *paideia*, he had enlisted every major cultural institution, including the public school, which during his lifetime was rapidly becoming the crux of the American educational system.

V

"Beecherism," as Beecher's special combination of theological views and revival techniques came to be referred to within the Congregational and Presbyterian folds, was widely perceived by Old-School ministers as a corrosive and disorganizing force within the churches. They never tired of lamenting the ecclesiastical schisms, the doctrinal heresies, and the general emotional excesses that seemed unfailingly to follow in its wake. But, by the mid-1830's, when Beecher himself was sermonizing across the country on behalf of Lane and the crusade to save the West, the orthodox were already aware of an even greater threat on the horizon. It was no longer Beecher, or even his erudite Yale friend Nathaniel Taylor, who represented the most serious challenge to Christian truth; it was now an unlettered preacher from western New York named Charles Grandison Finney. "Mr. Finney . . . of all others," charged the editor of the Andover-based *Literary and Theological Review*, "has taught the New Haven theology in its greatest purity and has ventured to push its principles to their legitimate results."[24]

Finney's rise in the theological firmament of Jacksonian America had been nothing short of meteoric. Born in Warren, Connecticut, in 1792 of an old New England family, he had grown up in Oneida County, New York, and attended the common schools there, then went back to Warren for his secondary education, and then prepared himself for the law in the office of Benjamin Wright in Adams, New York. An able and promising advocate, little interested in matters religious, he had turned to Scripture in pursuing a number of legal allusions to Mo-

24. *Literary and Theological Review*, V (1838), 70n.

saic institutions. What began as a marginal interest, however, soon turned into a major preoccupation; and there followed a period of intensive study culminating in a conversion that entailed a commitment to preach. Finney promptly deserted the law and embarked directly upon his new work, carrying the word to all who would hear him and at the same time undertaking a program of systematic theological preparation under the supervision of his pastor, the Reverend George W. Gale. Finney was licensed to preach by the St. Lawrence Presbytery in March, 1824, and ordained a few months thereafter, but not before a succession of disagreements with Gale that patently foreshadowed what would be Finney's fundamental attack on the old divinity.

As recounted in Finney's memoirs, Gale tenaciously held to the Old-School doctrine of original sin, insisting that people were morally depraved and hence utterly unable to believe, repent, or do anything that God required of them. All were therefore eternally damned, with the exception of the elect, for whom Christ had died; these were saved by grace on the principle of justice (since Christ had suffered their punishment), not by any act of contrition or repentance of their own. Such views, so far as Finney was concerned, caught Gale in a doctrinal strait jacket: "If he preached repentance, he must be sure before he sat down, to leave the impression on his people that they could not repent. If he called them to believe he must be sure to inform them that, until their nature was changed by the Holy Spirit, faith was impossible to them. And so his orthodoxy was a perfect snare to himself and to his hearers. I could not receive it. I did not so understand my Bible; nor could he make me see that it was taught in the Bible."[25]

Finney on his side asserted that Christ had died to remove the burden of original sin from everyone, thereby disposing of an insurmountable obstacle to God's forgiveness and rendering it possible for him to proclaim a "universal amnesty," inviting people to repent, to believe in Christ, and to accept salvation. "I insisted upon the voluntary total moral depravity of the unregenerate," Finney recalled; "and the unalterable necessity of a radical change of heart by the Holy Ghost, and by means of truth." Most important, perhaps, he insisted that the radical change of heart was open to all—that God stood willing and ready and that the giving of themselves to him was theirs to decide.[26]

Human agency—that was the nub of Finney's optimistic reformula-

25. Memoirs of Rev. Charles G. Finney (New York: A. S. Barnes & Co., 1870), pp. 59–60.
26. Ibid., pp. 50, 77.

tion of Calvinism. It was not that God was declared benign and hell expunged, as Channing had preached; the fires of hell burned as brightly as ever in Finney's theology. It was rather that God, through Christ, had granted man freedom to partake of his "universal amnesty." Those who accepted it could achieve everlasting life; those who rejected it were quite properly condemned.

During the initial years after his ordination, Finney labored as an itinerant minister in upstate New York, first under the auspices of the Female Missionary Society of the Western District of the State of New York and later as a member of a ministerial cooperative called the Oneida Evangelical Association. It was in the course of these activities that he perfected his revival techniques, achieving a phenomenal number of conversions and gaining a reputation that soon extended far beyond the so-called burned-over district of New York to the older coastal cities, where it elicited a variety of responses ranging from utter horror to genuine acclaim. The conservatives in Boston sent Lyman Beecher and his friend Asahel Nettleton to meet with Finney in an effort to persuade him to tone down his preaching, but the result (at the famous New Lebanon convention of 1827) was at best a stand-off. On the other hand, the revivalist forces in New York City leased the Chatham Theatre, converted it into a chapel, and established the Second Free Presbyterian Church there, with Finney as pastor. He remained at Chatham for three immensely productive years, during which he published his most important work on education, the *Lectures on Revivals of Religion*.

Finney's lectures were essentially a pedagogical handbook for the revival movement. If salvation was available to all men and women, it was the minister's role as teacher to persuade them to seek it. And what Finney purported to furnish were the substance and the means for doing so. He began by naturalizing the revival. "It is not a miracle, or dependent on a miracle, in any sense. It is a purely philosophical result of the right use of the constituted means—as much so as any other effect produced by the application of means." Once naturalized, once removed from some domain where it could be initiated only by God, the revival became subject to the same laws of cause and effect as plowing and planting and harvesting. It remained only for Finney to set forth the techniques best suited for activating them.[27]

27. Charles Grandison Finney, *Lectures on Revivals of Religion* (1835), edited by William G. McLoughlin (Cambridge, Mass.: Harvard University Press, 1960), p. 13.

In the lectures, there was a substantial discussion of the design and management of prayer meetings: "The prayers should always be very short"; "The time should be fully occupied"; "A great deal of singing often injures a prayer meeting." There were also instructions for preachers: "A minister ought to know the religious opinions of every sinner in his congregation"; "If a minister means to promote a revival, he should be very careful not to introduce controversy"; "Preaching should be parabolical. . . . The illustrations should be drawn from common life, and the common business of society." The variety of forms a revival might take were amply explicated, with the "anxious meeting" (for the purpose of holding personal conversations with anxious sinners), the "protracted meeting" (for the purpose of making a more powerful impression of divine things upon the minds of people), and the "anxious seat" (for the purpose of enabling the anxious to be addressed particularly and made the subjects of prayer) all being fully described. And the instruction of young converts, the problem of backsliders, and the evidence of growth in grace were each accorded a chapter. "All ministers should be revival ministers," Finney urged, "and all preaching should be revival preaching; that is, it should be calculated to promote holiness." So Finney counseled his fellow teachers. They had not only the right but the high obligation to adopt new measures for successful evangelization. To do otherwise would be to fail in their responsibilities to their parishioners and to God.[28]

As might be expected, this codification of Finney's theology and the pedagogy associated with it made him the target for the full wrath of the orthodox. "We tender him our thanks," wrote the Reverend Albert Baldwin Dod, a mathematics professor at Princeton, whose mordant pen was often called upon by Old-School Presbyterians to do battle with heterodoxy, "for the substantial service he has done the church by expounding the naked deformities of the New Divinity." And, so far as Dod was concerned, the charge of naked deformity was as justly pressed against Beecher and his friend Nathaniel Taylor as it was against Finney. All three men, and indeed the New Divinity men in general, had in the purest and simplest terms affirmed the ancient heresy of Pelagianism: they had exalted the ability and agency of man at the expense of the sovereignty and omnipotence of God. In so doing, they had not only sinned against God and misled their fellow men, they

28. *Ibid.*, pp. 128, 129, 133, 199, 201, 209.

had loosed upon the churches and the world every manner of excitement, fanaticism, and demagoguery.[29]

But the "demagoguery" of the New Divinity men, as William G. McLoughlin has persuasively argued, expressed nothing more than the optimistic individualism of Jacksonian America, while the "fanaticism" they excited, blending as it did the awesomeness of Calvin's God with Arminian notions of universal salvation, was in the last analysis little more than a democratized pietism that promised to provide the moral basis of the emerging republican society. It was a philosophy that moved easily across creedal and organizational lines to appeal directly to the common people, and as such it seemed to conservatives subversive of existing institutions. Yet it was less antinomian in its essential form than it was reformist, for its goal was not the obliteration of institutions but rather their transformation.[30]

The character of the New Divinity is especially clear in Finney's own career. Shortly after he delivered the lectures on revivals, he accepted a post as professor of theology at the recently founded Oberlin Institute. There, as fate would have it, he found himself cast once again as Lyman Beecher's antagonist. A group of students at Lane Seminary, in the face of firm trustee opposition, had taken a strong position favoring immediate abolitionism, with the result that the leaders had been expelled. Beecher, whose own inclinations were toward moderation on both the substantive question and the issue of academic freedom, attempted to effect a compromise, with the result that the preponderance of students simply withdrew from Lane and subsequently migrated to Oberlin. The issue itself, and the arrival of the Lane students, enabled Oberlin to attract Finney, who, like Beecher, had long wanted to train an army of inspired evangelists to battle for the Lord in the West. Once at Oberlin, Finney breathed life into that faltering institution, developing with President Asa Mahan the special version of Christian sanctification known as "Oberlin perfectionism," serving as president himself from 1851 to 1866, and in some forty years of service making the institution for all intents and purposes the embodiment of his vision of the evangelical Christian community. When Finney died in 1875, evangelicism had become the characteristic form of Protestant Christianity in America, and surely the most pervasive version of the Protestant American *paideia*.

29. *Biblical Repertory and Theological Review*, VII (1835), 527.
30. William G. McLoughlin, "Introduction," in Finney, *Lectures*, pp. ix–x.

VI

However settled Finney was during the years after his removal to Oberlin, he remained an itinerant at heart, preaching from time to time in New York and New England and on at least two extended occasions in the British Isles as well. It was in the course of one such itineration, during the winter of 1851–52, that he found himself in Hartford, Connecticut—an extraordinary city, he later noted in his memoir, not merely for the intelligence and erudition of its laity but for the fastidiousness and propriety of its clergy. Indeed, Finney went on to remark, his own mission had almost foundered on that fastidiousness, since at least two of Hartford's leading ministers were in "an unhappy state of disagreement" on theological matters and were initially quite unprepared to come "fraternally together" in the cause of the revival. The two ministers were Joel Hawes and Horace Bushnell, whose ostensible disagreement was over Bushnell's Christology in *God in Christ* (1849) but whose deeper disagreement doubtless reflected the gap between Hawes's revivalist propensities and Bushnell's more traditional approach. The two men were finally—if uneasily—reconciled by Finney's arrival, and in subsequent dialogues they appeared to find a modicum of agreement. In addition, Bushnell came to have considerable affection for Finney. "I know not how it is," he wrote to his wife a year after Finney's visit, "but I feel greatly drawn to this man, despite the greatest dissimilarity of tastes and a method of soul, whether in thought or feeling, wholly unlike."[31]

"Wholly unlike" may have been too strong, but the dissimilarities were indeed substantial. True, both men shared an active interest in social reform, and certainly neither was by temperament or training a traditionalist. Both vehemently denounced the evils of slavery and sought at the very least to prevent its extension into new territories. Yet there was a fundamental difference in their theologies that profoundly affected virtually everything they believed and taught. Whereas Finney believed that true Christian living began with a change of heart—with the conversion experience itself—Bushnell believed that it began in Christian nurture and was only confirmed in an "inward discovery" of God's infinite spirit, a discovery that was intuitive, direct, and immediate.[32]

31. *Memoirs of Rev. Charles G. Finney* (New York: A. S. Barnes & Co., 1876), p. 415; and Horace Bushnell to Mary Apthorp Bushnell, December 3, 1852, in *Life and Letters of Horace Bushnell,* edited by Mary Bushnell Cheney (New York: Harper & Brothers, 1880), p. 275.
32. Horace Bushnell, *Sermons on Living Subjects* (centenary ed.; New York: Charles Scribner's Sons, 1908), p. 127.

Bushnell's progress toward that belief provides one of the exemplary intellectual odysseys of early nineteenth-century America. Born to a Connecticut farm family, he grew up under the early tutelage of his mother, a remarkable woman to whom he later attributed extraordinary wisdom and prudence. After attending the local public schools, he entered Yale in 1823, already considerably more mature than most of his classmates (he was by then twenty-one) and yet in many respects almost a caricature of a yokel. He did well at Yale and upon graduation successively tried schoolteaching, journalism, and the law. But a religious revival during the winter of 1831 turned his interest to religion, and the following fall he entered Yale's Divinity School, where he came under the prodigious influence of Nathaniel Taylor. Bushnell was less than wholly persuaded by the New Divinity, however, in part because of a characteristic tendency to take "t'other side" when confronted with what seemed to him overly mechanical doctrines or formulae, and in part because of a fascination with Samuel Taylor Coleridge's *Aids to Reflection* (1825), which he had studied earlier and continued to ponder (he later remarked that he was more indebted to Coleridge than to any other extra-Scriptural author). In any case, he went from Yale to the pulpit of the North Church in Hartford, where he remained until his retirement in 1861.[33]

Bushnell's earliest writings, the substance of which is embodied in a volume entitled *Discourses on Christian Nurture* (1847), transformed the terms of the theological debate that had been raging for a quarter-century. The traditional Calvinists had proclaimed the overwhelming and total depravity of man, while their Unitarian critics had insisted instead upon man's inherent goodness. Meanwhile, partisans of the New Divinity had located themselves strategically in between, granting man's depravity but at the same time affirming man's ability with God's help to seek (and, for Finney, to achieve) sanctification. All three schools of thought, Bushnell maintained, had erred by viewing the individual in isolation. If one considered him instead in relation to those who nurture him, notably parents, one saw immediately that all questions of depravity and virtue were inextricably tied to the multifarious relations between parents and children, that there was no such thing as an initial depravity (nor, for that matter, an initial goodness) wholly the child's and no such thing as a clear-cut time of moral agency when a decision for Christ would suddenly produce virtue. Taking an essentially pedagogical approach, Bushnell set out to alter the terms of the

33. *Life and Letters of Horace Bushnell*, p. 62.

theological argument. "What is the true idea of Christian education?" he asked.

I answer in the following proposition, which it will be the aim of my argument to establish, viz.: That the child is to grow up a Christian. In other words, the aim, effort, and expectation should be, not, as is commonly assumed, that the child is to grow up in sin, to be converted after he comes to a mature age; but that he is to open on the world as one that is spiritually renewed, not remembering the time when he went through a technical experience, but seeming rather to have loved what is good from his earliest years.[34]

Bushnell's assertions evoked a storm of criticism. Bennet Tyler, a strident spokesman for traditional Calvinism, issued an open letter accusing Bushnell of misconceiving both depravity and regeneration. Several orthodox periodicals picked up Tyler's charge, in one instance referring to the issuance of the *Discourses* "as a sort of libel on the evangelical community." The Sabbath School Society, which had actually published the *Discourses* (after close scrutiny and review), suspended circulation immediately, eliciting in turn from Bushnell a lengthy defense of his reasoning in which he argued—quite correctly—that his theories were not dissimilar from those of the early New England Puritans. Shortly thereafter, Bushnell reissued the *Discourses*, which along with the defense and a number of additional papers became the tract entitled *Views of Christian Nurture, and of Subjects Adjacent Thereto* (1847). In the months that followed, the storm seemed to subside, though not before Tyler returned to charge that Bushnell was teaching "fatal delusion." Bushnell himself continued to elaborate his argument and reissued the work yet again, in expanded form, in 1861, this time under the title *Christian Nurture*. It was destined to circulate for years, exerting a more profound influence on the theory of Christian education than any other contemporary work.[35]

Barbara M. Cross pointed out in her incisive biography of Bushnell the extent to which he confronted during his tenure at North Church

34. Horace Bushnell, *Views of Christian Nuture, and of Subjects Adjacent Thereto* (Hartford, Conn.: Edwin Hunt, 1848), p. 6 (*Views* brought together the *Discourses* and other writings). In the classic edition of *Views*, published in 1861, Bushnell added the phrase "and never know himself as being otherwise" to the proposition "that the child is to grow up a Christian."
35. Bennet Tyler, "Letter to Dr. Bushnell on Christian Nurture" (East Windsor Hill, Conn.: no publisher, June 7, 1847); "Discourses on Christian Nurture," *Christian Observatory*, I (1847), 326; Horace Bushnell, *An Argument for Discourses on Christian Nurture, Addressed to the Publishing Committee of the Massachusetts Sabbath School Society* (Hartford, Conn.: Edwin Hunt, 1847); Bennet Tyler, *Letters to the Rev. Horace Bushnell, D.D., Containing Strictures on His Book Entitled "Views of Christian Nurture, and of Subjects Adjacent Thereto"* (Hartford, Conn.: Brown & Parsons, 1848), p. 64.

all the complex problems of an urbanizing mercantile America, particularly as seen through the eyes of an upper middle-class congregation. Moreover, she indicated, poignantly, the extent to which he considered himself a failure, particularly in light of Joel Hawes's revival harvests of the 1830's, 1840's, and 1850's. Given Bushnell's resultant insecurity, it would be tempting to see his emphasis on household nurture as a reversion to the remembered warmth of his mother's tutelage during what he came to refer to as "the age of homespun." But that assumption is too simple. The fact is there were larger intellectual tendencies in Jacksonian America—tendencies to view the child as innocence incarnate and the mother as protector of that innocence—that must surely have encouraged Bushnell's halcyon recollections, on the one hand, and his social and educational aspirations, on the other. If the child was to be the hope and the savior of society—and certainly that is what the sentimental revolution of the thirties and forties proclaimed—then his proper nurturance in the face of ubiquitous evil was the answer at one and the same time to harsh revivalism and bland Unitarianism.[36]

Bushnell stressed the household, but he by no means confined his attention there. In 1847, the very year the Christian nurture controversy raged, he published, under the sponsorship of the American Home Missionary Society, *Barbarism the First Danger,* in which he argued that the leading danger to the body politic had always been barbarism rather than Catholicism (and this from an active member of the anti-Romanist Christian Alliance). And, to resist the descent into barbarism, especially in the West, education was desperately needed. That education would come with railroads and telegraphy ("the sooner we have railroads and telegraphs spinning into the wilderness, and setting the remotest hamlets in connexion and close proximity with the east, the more certain it is that light, good manners and Christian refinement, will become universally diffused"); it would derive from schools and colleges; and it would flow from Christian ministers sponsored by the Home Missionary Society. Bushnell even went so far as to argue, in contradiction to what had become a cliché in the Protestant community by that time, that Protestants might make common cause with Roman Catholics in the work: "Earnest for the truth," he concluded, "we must also remember, that truth itself is catholic and comprehensive. We must shun that vapid liberalism, which instead of attracting us into unity,

36. Barbara M. Cross, *Horace Bushnell: Minister to a Changing America* (Chicago: University of Chicago Press, 1958).

will only dissolve us into indifference, and yet we must be willing to stretch our forbearance and charity even to Romanists themselves, when we clearly find the spirit of Jesus in their life."[37]

Six years later, he turned his attention to common schools, in an essay that stands as a classic exposition of the common-school philosophy in the midst of the so-called common-school revival. The common school, Bushnell maintained, is "an integral part of the civil order." It exists because society requires a place where children of all classes can come together early in their lives to acquaint themselves with one another, "to be exercised together on a common footing of ingenuous rivalry; the children of the rich to feel the power and do honor to the struggles of merit in the lowly, when it rises above them; the children of the poor to learn the force of merit, and feel the benign encouragement yielded by its blameless victories." As such, the common school is not a Protestant school, but a Christian school; more important, perhaps, it is an American school, indispensable to American institutions. It is the responsibility of Protestants to do all they can to render it acceptable to Roman Catholics, and the responsibility of Roman Catholics to respond by joining in the common venture instead of demanding their own schools. "Let us draw our strange friends as close to us as possible," Bushnell urged his parishioners, "not in any party scramble for power, but in a solemn reference of duty to the nation and to God."[38]

Perhaps as much as any educator of his time, Bushnell understood the range and variety of institutions that educate and sought to turn all to a common purpose—the service of the nation. He was remarkable for the primacy he assigned to the family and the church at precisely the time his contemporaries were moving the school to the forefront of the educational configuration. And yet he had no narrow or isolated notion of education. Indeed, the very power of Bushnell's educational analysis derived from the larger organic view of society on which it rested, and on his conception of the loyalty vital to sustain that society. Particularly after the sectional tensions of the 1850's had exploded into civil war, Bushnell saw the future of the nation as ultimately dependent upon loyalty. And, insofar as he conceived of loyalty as a moral rather than a legal obligation, wholly voluntary and not subject to civil coer-

37. Horace Bushnell, *Barbarism the First Danger: A Discourse for Home Missions* (New York: American Home Missionary Society, 1847), pp. 27, 31–32.

38. Horace Bushnell, *Common Schools: A Discourse on the Modifications Demanded by the Roman Catholics* (Hartford, Conn.: Case, Tiffany and Co., 1853), pp. 6, 7, 24.

cion (in the last analysis truly governed by God), the burden of education became awesome. If the centrifugal forces of selfishness (individualism) were to be countered, it would not be through governmental constraint but rather through voluntary acquiescence in the laws of God. The good citizen was the individual dedicated to God, and the good society was simply a society composed of such individuals. Only as a brotherhood of man under the fatherhood of God would the United States fulfill its God-given purpose in history. And the creation of that brotherhood was the task of education.

Chapter 2

THE EVANGELICAL CRUSADE

The Gospel of Christ, brought in contact with the mind and heart of
our entire population, is the only influence to which we can safely en-
trust the destiny of this country.

THE REVEREND ANDREW L. STONE,
IN A REPORT TO THE AMERICAN
HOME MISSIONARY SOCIETY

Like its predecessor movement of the provincial era, the so-called second awakening of the early national period was a reaction to the conditions of American life, to the incessant social and geographical movement that marked the American scene and to the resultant insecurity
that touched every segment of the American population. Like its predecessor movement, the second awakening was also profoundly influenced
by transatlantic ideas and relationships—by the romanticism of a Coleridge and a Schleiermacher as well as by the organizational machinery
of the British Clapham Sect and the Methodists. And, like its predecessor movement, the second awakening partook of the denominational
character of American Protestantism, both reflecting and advancing the
idea of the churches as purposive, voluntary, and evangelical. Whether
there was actually a sufficient hiatus between the earlier and the later
movements to warrant the concept of a *second* awakening remains
moot; that there was indeed an era of intensive revival activity beginning during the later 1790's and continuing through the middle of the
nineteenth century is undeniable.

Historians have frequently noted the simultaneous and dramatic
upsurge of evangelical ardor in several widely separated regions of the
country. In Connecticut, for example, revivals began at Yale under the
determined leadership of Timothy Dwight, who succeeded Ezra Stiles

in the presidency in 1795. Deeply suspicious of the ideological mischief he saw spewing forth from Europe and threatening to engulf the young Republic, Dwight personally undertook a crusade against infidelity, with Yale as the headquarters of a new army of Christ. Within a decade, the college had been transformed from "a sink of moral and spiritual pollution" into "a nursery of piety and virtue," and a corps of the converted was reaching out to proselytize New England, the West, and the world. In Kentucky, the renewal began in the backwater region of Logan County, in response to the fiery preaching of James McGready, a Scots-Irish Presbyterian trained at John McMillan's academy at Canonsburg, Pennsylvania, and subsequently tempered by revivalist activity in Virginia and North Carolina. Sparked initially in 1797 by McGready's eloquent sermons to his three congregations near the Gaspar, Red, and Muddy rivers in Logan County, the revival spread and intensified until it burst forth at the epochal Cane Ridge gathering of early August, 1801, which was attended by a crowd of enthusiastic worshipers that may well have numbered in the thousands. As the Holy Spirit manifested itself during that extraordinary week, preachers shouted, women fainted, men shrieked, and children wailed; and the distinctive American institution of the large-scale, carefully planned camp meeting emerged in its full flowering. In New York, the renewal began in the westernmost part of the state in a series of scattered localized outpourings that may have been less tumultuous than those in Kentucky but no less intense; at least one, at Pittstown under the leadership of the Methodist itinerant Lorenzo Dow, yielded a hundred new converts in a single day. And, in Georgia, the renewal began among blacks under the inspired preaching of the Baptist George Liele of Savannah. The revivals quickly spread from these and a dozen other early sources, sending sparks in every direction and creating innumerable "burned-over" neighborhoods, urban as well as rural, where the fires of enthusiasm waxed and waned for a generation. In the process, evangelicism solidified its hold on the forms and institutions of American Protestantism.[1]

In much the same way that the eighteenth-century awakenings can be viewed as a large-scale educational movement that markedly affected every conceivable aspect of the church as a teaching institution, so must these later revivals be seen as having an essentially educational charac-

1. Matthew Rice Dutton, "Reflections of the Life and Character of Doct. Dwight," Yale misc. ms. no. 1 (Manuscript and Archives Department, Sterling Memorial Library, Yale University, New Haven).

ter. At the least, as Charles Grandison Finney made clear in his *Lectures on Revivals of Religion* (1835)—and we must bear in mind that Finney's *Lectures* was but one treatise among many on the subject—enthusiastic preaching was profoundly different from both traditional Calvinist preaching and liberal Unitarian preaching. It reached out to the unchurched in a vigorous, colorful, and popular rhetoric that dramatically portrayed the threat of damnation and set beside it the possibility of everlasting life. Its aim, in Finney's analysis, was not merely to fill people with doctrine but to move them to action. The good minister was the successful minister, and the successful minister won souls to Christ; any pedagogical measures he used in the struggle, so long as he maintained decency and decorum, were justified. "We must have exciting, powerful preaching, or the devil will have the people," Finney warned. And his message was not lost on his contemporaries, even in staid New England.[2]

Beyond preaching, and indeed beyond the immediacies of religious observance in any form, revival meetings provided educational opportunity in a much larger and more varied sense. Particularly in the sparsely settled regions of the frontier, the revival meeting became an extraordinary opportunity for expanded social intercourse, the exchange of information and intelligence, the discussion of social and political as well as theological issues, and the consideration of a potpourri of propaganda and salesmanship. A family at a three- or four-day camp meeting could make new acquaintances and renew old ones, listen to lectures on the meaning of the American Revolution, sign teetotal pledges, subscribe to book series, compare everything from methods of growing corn to recipes for cooking it, and sample a vast range of culinary delights, while simultaneously experiencing a variety of preaching styles and exhortatory messages. Like the church itself, the revival meeting was a commons, a forum, a marketplace, and a fair. Its explicit purpose was to shape and influence via systematic religious instruction, but in affording direct acquaintance with alternative ways of living and thinking it also educated in a more general sense.

For all the drama of the revival meetings themselves, however, there were deeper currents in the early national awakenings that merit attention. Like the frontier brush fires that provide the dominant metaphors of evangelical history, revivals ignited, flared, and died with extraordi-

2. Charles Grandison Finney, *Lectures on Revivals of Religion* (1835), edited by William G. McLoughlin (Cambridge, Mass.: Harvard University Press, 1960), p. 273.

nary rapidity, so that to study them as isolated events is to miss their relationship to the churches that set them and fanned them and indeed were warmed and even occasionally consumed by them. Revivalism profoundly affected the denominational structure of the churches, splitting some (like the Presbyterians), fusing others (like the Christians and the Disciples of Christ), and transforming still others into essentially new entities (like the Mormons) that little resembled the institutions from which they had derived. Revivalism also affected the communities into which it propelled the revived. To have a conversion experience is one thing, but to continue to take it seriously is quite another; the "new life" that is ecstatically celebrated in the conversion must be more routinely confirmed in a religious community. The very presence of the revived inevitably heightened the educational role of churches themselves.

To shift from the experience of conversion to the structures for maintaining it is to confront the most important popular religious phenomenon of the early Republic, the development of American Methodism. At the time of the signing of the Treaty of Paris in 1783, the Methodists were a small community of 82 preachers and 13,740 members, with a precarious future as an organization. Dependent upon English Methodism for leadership and upon the Anglican clergy for the sacraments, the community had been bitterly torn during the Revolution by conflicting political and ecclesiastical loyalties. Some Methodists, like Thomas Rankin, had returned to England; others, like Francis Asbury, had gone into seclusion; others, like Freeborn Garrettson, had suffered persecution at the hands of the revolutionaries. In general, a taint of Toryism had marked the community as a whole. Then, in a series of crucial conferences held during 1784, the community reorganized. Under the auspices of John Wesley and the leadership of Francis Asbury and Thomas Coke, the Methodist Episcopal Church was formed, a clergy was ordained, and a discipline, a doctrine, and a liturgy were adopted. Energetically evangelical and charismatically led, the new church prospered: by 1840 the Methodists could boast some 10,000 preachers and just over 850,000 members located in every section of the country; and, even granting the internal schisms that appeared as early as the 1790's, they were still far and away the largest American denomination.[3]

3. Robert Baird, *Religion in the United States of America* (Glasgow: Blackie and Son, 1844), p. 568.

At bottom, this remarkable growth testified to three important characteristics that made Methodism quintessentially appropriate to the American scene: its democratic theology, its flexible organization, and its effective use of the instruments of popular education. Methodism proclaimed free grace for all in a form of evangelical Arminianism that stood between the perceived extremes of deism and Unitarianism on the one hand and traditional or even New Divinity Calvinism on the other. Primarily a devotional religion, concerned with the practice of a relatively simple piety and the living of a relatively uncomplicated version of the good life, Methodism asserted the equalitarian doctrine that each and every individual was capable of achieving salvation. What is more, though Methodists were not wholly free of race prejudice, the first conference did proclaim that slavery was contrary to the laws of God, man, and nature; the first discipline did insist that masters free their slaves; and the first ministry in the United States did include black preachers.

Beyond that, Methodism exploited techniques that had been developed earlier with the disinherited of England to organize and minister to the mobile American population. It reached out vigorously to the unchurched and sought to draw them into "Christian connection with each other." It embraced various levels of organization, from small local classes overseen by indigenous leaders to circuits composed of classes and ministered to by itinerant circuit riders to conferences composed of circuits and overseen by elders and superintendents. It encouraged various degrees of leadership and membership, depending on the depth, length, and intensity of an individual's commitment. A local class leader could be a relatively new member with a flair for leadership and a call to preach; a circuit rider might be a local leader who had enjoyed unusual success in preaching and had come to the attention of the elders (he was most often unmarried and was long paid an annual stipend of under $100). New classes were organized and new leaders selected as needed; new circuits were formed by dividing old ones when they became too large. And, with respect to the society in general, the only clear distinction between the larger congregation to which any preacher might address himself and the smaller group of more committed (and more disciplined) members-in-society was the issuance of membership tickets to the latter that gained them entry to the love feasts, which were quasi-sacramental occasions for the display of fraternal love through prayer, singing, and testimony.

Finally, Methodism made remarkably effective use of the instruments of popular education. Beyond the camp meetings designed to at-tract new converts and reawaken old ones, the Methodists established elementary schools, secondary schools, and especially Sunday schools (and later colleges and theological seminaries for the training of a pas-toral leadership); they founded the Methodist Book Concern and sup-ported a network of agents to distribute its books, tracts, and periodi-cals; they sponsored a missionary program to work among groups as varied as the Roman Catholics of New Orleans, the Chippewa Indians of eastern Mississippi, the German ragpickers of New York City, and the Afro-Americans of Liberia; they organized innumerable clubs, soci-eties, and associations for every age group and for both sexes in connec-tion with their local congregations; and they collaborated in a host of social causes ranging from temperance to abolitionism (and antiaboli-tionism). In these activities, as in all Methodist educational endeavors, there were few certificatory distinctions between preacher and class, with the result that there was the possibility of easy alternation be-tween the roles of teacher and learner and a widespread participation in the kind of teaching that itself facilitates learning on the part of the individual engaged in the process.

No single individual articulated, led, and exemplified the vigor and promise of early American Methodism more eloquently than Francis Asbury. He was, from the first American Conference in 1773 until his death in 1816, the living embodiment of the Methodist Episcopal Church. Converted at the age of fourteen in the "back country" near Birmingham, England, where he grew up, and formed in the crucible of early English Methodism, Asbury came to America in 1771 to serve as a missionary, beginning a career of preaching that he pursued inde-fatigably for almost a half-century, with but one period of respite—an enforced sojourn in Delaware during the Revolution. In a church in which itineracy was the standard pattern, Asbury was the itinerant par excellence: he never settled, traveling more than a quarter of a million miles under the most trying physical and personal conditions; and he insisted, wisely it would seem, that if his colleagues wished success in evangelizing the world they must never settle either. He preached a pi-ety much in the spirit of Richard Baxter, John Bunyan, and Philip Doddridge, all of whom he had read and pondered, and he familiarized himself with the teaching of Jonathan Edwards and the example of David Brainerd. In place of systematic treatises on theology, he left as his enduring literary monument a journal, less inwardly searching than

George Fox's and less polished than John Wesley's, though as revealing as both with respect to a life of spiritual growth in teaching the
word.

The Methodists, then, used an evangelical Arminianism to attract
the unconverted and a flexible organization to draw them into Christian connection with one another, and they radically popularized the
structure, the pedagogy, the curriculum, and the teaching corps of the
church. Furthermore, as T. Scott Miyakawa and Donald G. Mathews
have persuasively argued, they decisively shaped the character and outcome of the early national awakening, channeling the enormous energy
of the revivals into their own disciplined educational organizations and
teaching not only other denominations but whole communities to do
likewise. In an aggressively competitive society, the very success of the
Methodists made the Methodist spirit contagious: the Baptists used
Methodist techniques to organize new congregations, though perhaps a
bit more informally, while the Presbyterians and the Congregationalists
used them to revitalize old ones. There was much ridicule within the
older denominations of unschooled Methodist preachers abusing "new
measures" with a vengeance, but there was also a grudging acknowledgment that the same preachers always seemed to reach the unchurched before anyone else. Finney doubtless spoke for more than a
few when he remarked that "a Methodist preacher, without the advantages of a liberal education, will draw a congregation around him
which a Presbyterian minister, with perhaps ten times as much learning, cannot equal." In other words, the ridicule may have been as nervous as it was derisive, and the more traditional clergy may well have
been glancing over their shoulders as they scoffed.[4]

I I

Revivalism filled the churches with new communicants during the early
years of the Republic, patently heightening the denominational rivalry
that had been a salient feature of American Protestantism at least since
the awakenings of the 1730's and 1740's. At precisely the same time,
ironic as it may seem, revivalism also advanced the cause of Christian
unity. The very same popularized divinity and generalized piety that

4. T. Scott Miyakawa, *Protestants and Pioneers: Individualism and Conformity on the Amer-
ican Frontier* (Chicago: University of Chicago Press, 1964); Donald G. Mathews, "The Second
Great Awakening as an Organizing Process, 1780–1830: An Hypothesis," *American Quarterly*,
XXI (1969), 23–43; and Finney, *Lectures*, p. 273.

reached out to the unchurched provided a context within which groups of denominations could mount collaborative programs with a minimum of abrasion and discord. The phenomenon was scarcely new, for during much of the eighteenth century denominational cooperation had been the obverse of denominational competition, initially via the moral reformation societies of the 1690's and early 1700's and subsequently via missions to the Indians, educational programs for new immigrants, and charitable ventures among the poor. Now, during the nineteenth century, as one principal outcome of the revival movement, such cooperative efforts broadened and intensified and, in the process, profoundly affected the institutions of education.

Behind the burst of new interdenominational activity lay a view of the new nation and its prospects that assumed an inextricable link between Protestantism and patriotism. It was a view widely held by the most diverse of clerical theorists, from an orthodox Congregationalist like Jedidiah Morse to a New Divinity man like Lyman Beecher, from an Old-School Presbyterian like Samuel Miller to a mainstream Baptist like Luther Rice. In essence, it saw the new nation incarnating the aspirations of God and the hopes of mankind for a purified society that would live according to the dictates of Scripture. The millennium was possible in America if America would but attend to her divine destiny. To do that, however, was no simple matter. Human nature was weak, and Satan's efforts were already manifest in the incessant quarreling of factions, the ubiquitous race for power, and the cacophonous noise of idolatry. The only way for the great experiment in liberty to succeed would be under the watchful eyes of a virtuous citizenry. And the only way to nurture a virtuous citizenry would be via the beneficent influence of evangelical Protestantism. To realize America's promise Americans would have to choose; only as they chose God's way, individually and collectively, would they fulfill God's plan for the nation. Thus did nationalism, millennialism, and evangelicism converge in an ideology of civic piety and pious civility.

To advance this ideology and thereby ensure the nation's destiny, evangelical Protestants organized on the local, state, regional, and national levels a complex of overlapping and often interlocking organizations that has been aptly referred to as the "evangelical united front." The local and state societies appeared earliest, concentrated principally but by no means exclusively in the older eastern cities. The First Day Society was organized in Philadelphia in 1790 by a group that included a Universalist of Presbyterian background, a Roman Catholic, and the

Protestant Episcopal bishop of Pennsylvania. The New York Missionary Society was formed in 1796 by a group of Presbyterian, Baptist, Dutch Reformed, and Associate Reformed clergymen and laymen, for the purpose of seeking the conversion of the Indians. The Missionary Society of Connecticut appeared the following year, with a somewhat broader commitment to the evangelizing of the frontier, while the Massachusetts Missionary Society appeared in 1799, with similar goals. During the decade that followed, a plethora of interdenominational organizations sprang up in Pennsylvania, New York, and New England, with purposes that varied from the distribution of Bibles and tracts to the establishment of Sunday schools to the advancement of temperance or peace.

In 1810 the first of the national organizations appeared in the form of the American Board of Commissioners for Foreign Missions, established initially as a regional arm of the Congregational churches of Massachusetts and Connecticut but broadened soon thereafter by the addition of Presbyterian board members from New York, New Jersey, and Pennsylvania. In 1815 the American Education Society was founded in Boston to assist in "educating pious youth for the gospel ministry." In 1816 the American Bible Society was formed at a convention of representatives of state Bible societies that included such clerical luminaries as Jedidiah Morse of Massachusetts; Lyman Beecher and Nathaniel W. Taylor of Connecticut; Gardiner Spring, Eliphalet Nott, and John Griscom of New York; and John Holt of Virginia. In 1824 the American Sunday-School Union was organized to publish moral and religious works for children, and in the following year the American Tract Society, to undertake similar work especially for adults. And in 1826 the American Home Missionary Society was established to subsidize indigent pastors, especially in the newly settled regions of the West.[5]

Then, in an interesting next stage, the regional and national organizations began in turn to form (or to confederate) local auxiliaries or affiliates. The Education Society, for example, maintained a far-flung network of town, county, state, and regional affiliates, many of which, like the numerous women's charitable societies of Massachusetts and Connecticut, were of ephemeral character, though some, like the Western Education Society, were more effectively organized and endured for

---

5. The original and official name of the American Education Society was The American Society for Educating Pious Youth for the Gospel Ministry. See Natalie Ann Naylor, "Raising a Learned Ministry: The American Education Society, 1815–1860" (doctoral thesis, Teachers College, Columbia University, 1971), pp. 44–45.

a considerable period. The Education Society also worked out an arrangement with the Presbyterian Education Society that made that denominational group for a time a branch of the national organization. Similarly, the Sunday-School Union, the Bible Society, and the Tract Society made widespread use of local affiliates; indeed, they were initially founded as confederations or consolidations of local, state, regional, and denominational efforts, and from the beginning they devoted a good deal of their energy to coordinating activities. Thus, many of the so-called national interdenominational societies frequently remained more regional than national and more "Presbygational" than interdenominational, and many were paralleled by denominational societies dedicated to similar ends. As a result, the tensions between cooperation and competition were heightened, and, however fuzzy the edges of denominations ended up, they by no means disappeared.

All of the national organizations were voluntary, raising their own funds from membership fees, individual contributions, and church collections. All were nonecclesiastical and interdenominational in character—or indeed paradenominational, as Natalie Naylor has suggested, to indicate the extent to which they stood alongside the denominations and occasionally competed with them, most often with a strong core of Congregational and Presbyterian leadership working in collaboration with a smaller number of Episcopalians, Methodists, Baptists, and Friends. All tended to draw their leadership from an alliance of well-to-do landowners and businessmen (Stephen Van Rensselaer of the American Bible Society); politicians and statesmen, mostly of conservative proclivities (Theodore Frelinghuysen of the American Tract Society, the American Bible Society, the American Sunday-School Union, and the American Board of Commissioners for Foreign Missions); renowned clerics (Eliphalet Pearson of the American Education Society); upward-mobile young men of affairs (James Milnor of the American Tract Society); and energetic women who found in the societies an alternative or complement to domesticity and schoolteaching (Joanna Graham Bethune of the American Sunday-School Union). Each was aware of the others' efforts: William Cogswell observed in an 1833 book about the societies, significantly entitled *The Harbinger of the Millennium*, that the organizations "have an interest in each other, depend upon each other, and assist each other." All were explicitly, self-consciously, and overwhelmingly in the business of education.[6]

6. *Ibid.*, p. 16; and William Cogswell, *The Harbinger of the Millennium* (Boston: Pierce and Parker, 1833), p. iii

In preaching the ideology of civic piety (or of pious civility), the united front of evangelical organizations employed a fascinating panoply of organizational techniques and pedagogical strategies. The goal was a general uniformity of belief and commitment across the length and breadth of the nation—what Lyman Beecher referred to as "a sameness of views, and feelings, and interests, which would lay the foundation of our empire upon a rock." Moreover, the ways of achieving this goal would be as patently interlocking as the organizations themselves. The American Education Society would stimulate the training of enterprising evangelical ministers who would establish "institutions of homogeneous influence"—schools, academies, colleges, youth groups, discussion circles, every manner of formal and informal educating agency. The American Home Missionary Society would maintain these men in the newer and poorer regions of the country, while the American Board would do likewise in needful regions elsewhere in the world. And the American Bible Society, the American Tract Society, and the American Sunday-School Union would publish the literature required for the effort and organize the networks of clergymen and laypeople to distribute it.[7]

With this larger design very much in mind, each society developed its own organizations and systems of influence. The Bible Society, the Tract Society, and the Sunday-School Union, for example, adopted the organizational plan of the English evangelist C. S. Dudley, who pioneered the use of the women's auxiliary as a device for organizing and canvassing a rural region or an urban neighborhood. Dudley's *An Analysis of the System of the Bible Society* (1821)—which his critics referred to as "Bible Society craft, made easy to the meanest capacity"—described in detail the establishment of an auxiliary, the election of officers, the organization of teams of canvassers and their assignment to particular districts, and the procedures by which the canvassers were to visit homes, query the residents, sell subscriptions, collect funds, and generally serve as the organization's direct representatives to the public at large. Obviously, the initial sale of a Bible to a household labeled it as a potential market for Sunday-school and Tract Society literature and as a potential source of Sunday-school students and church members. Once the labeling had occurred, the household became a natural target for the propaganda of the temperance, peace, mission, and anti-

7. Lyman Beecher, *On the Importance of Assisting Young Men of Piety and Talents in Obtaining an Education for the Gospel Ministry* (New York: Dodge & Sayre, no date), p.16.

slavery movements. Not surprisingly, the manifold opportunities offered to women in the course of these evangelical activities proved enormously attractive in a world in which teaching, writing, and charity work were virtually the only other alternatives to domestic duties as outlets for female energy and expertise. In fact, the evangelical auxiliaries themselves became important institutions in the education of nineteenth-century women.[8]

In a quite different way, the American Education Society, in the course of sponsoring ministerial training, also promoted all sorts of other educational endeavors. It vigorously supported the manual labor programs that developed during the 1820's, publicizing them in its *Quarterly Register,* offering financial aid to fledgling institutions that featured them (for example, the Oneida Institute, a progenitor of Oberlin College, and Lane Seminary), and encouraging students to enroll in such institutions. Interestingly, it was equally vigorous in its support of Latin and Greek in school and college curricula, particularly for theology students, and indeed when Oberlin College dropped the "heathen classics" from its program in the 1830's, the Society refused to give further aid to students who went there (the classics slowly returned to Oberlin over the next quarter-century). During a time of collegiate boosterism on a scale unprecedented in history, the Society served as a regulative agency of limited, though significant, power.

All of these organizational and pedagogical strategies came into full flower during the great campaign of the 1830's to evangelize the West. The American Home Missionary Society was formed in 1826, for the express purpose of subsidizing ministers in the new states and territories so that Christianity could combat the powerful forces of frontier dissolution. Two years later, the American Tract Society set out to extend its influence in the Mississippi Valley, appointing the able corresponding secretary of the Boston branch, the Reverend Orman Eastman, general agent for the West; and the following year the American Bible Society and the American Education Society joined the effort, the former by pledging to supply every family in the West (indeed, in the nation) with a free or low-cost Bible, the latter by organizing a special western branch in Cincinnati under the Reverend Franklin Y. Vail as secretary. Then in 1830 the American Sunday-School Union unanimously resolved at its annual convention that it would "within two years, estab-

8. William Jay, *A Letter to the Right Reverend Bishop Hobart* (New York: John P. Haven, 1832), p. 73.

lish a Sunday school in every destitute place where it is practicable, throughout the valley of the Mississippi." During roughly the same period, under the vigorous leadership of Bible, tract, and Sunday-school societies and their women's auxiliaries, efforts quickened in Boston, New York, Philadelphia, Charleston, Cincinnati, St. Louis, and Pittsburgh systematically to disseminate the evangelical message to every family that could be reached.[9]

The immediate goal was to proffer the word in the hope of gaining the conversions that would guarantee political stability; and in the pursuit of that goal the united front exploited all the pedagogical techniques of the evangelical movement, from the revival meeting to the Dudley system of distributing literature. The Tract Society organized networks of colporteurs that rivaled the most effective sales organizations of the era; the Home Missionary Society appointed state and regional supervisors who performed functions not unlike bishops in the more hierarchical churches; while the Sunday-School Union embarked upon a full-fledged program of teacher training to create a nationwide Sunday-school system literally *ex nihilo*. People like John R. McDowall (who served in New York City as a volunteer missionary for the American Tract Society), George H. Atkinson (the first missionary sent to Oregon by the American Home Missionary Society), and Stephen Paxson (who started over a thousand Sunday schools in the service of the American Sunday-School Union) vividly displayed every aspect of boosterism in education, their interests and efforts spilling into every manner of organizational and instructional activity. As a result, millions of Americans who had hitherto been untouched by formal programs of education were reached by the evangelical message. Whatever else the great campaign of the 1830's may have accomplished, it did popularize education.

As the campaign proceeded, however, a number of unintended and unanticipated outcomes became apparent. First, the more the crusade succeeded, the more the crusaders became acquainted with the lives and problems of the unchurched, especially the impoverished unchurched, whom they were trying to save. In the process, the crusaders themselves were sifted and winnowed by experience, and those who remained ended up knowing a good deal about an America very different from the one with which they themselves were most familiar. Second, as the cru-

9. *Sixth Annual Report of the American Sunday-School Union* (1830), p. 4.

saders learned about the conditions of poverty, especially in the cities, they broadened their purview by attempting to alleviate poverty through charity as well as conversion. Thus, the dispensers of tracts began to bring food, money, and clothing as well as pamphlets into the slums, and some even set out to find jobs for the unemployed. In the process, piety became tied, not merely to the promotion of patriotism, but also to the alleviation of poverty, and education became tied to both. Finally, the more the crusaders learned about poverty, the more they learned that prayers and tracts and Sunday schools alone would not save the nation. Unfortunately, however, they learned this with only one compartment of their minds. The millennial rhetoric and the behaviors associated with it persisted, perhaps even increased, as over the years the frustration born of seemingly intractable problems and seemingly overwhelming difficulties steadily mounted.

III

There was a widespread sense among early nineteenth-century Americans that voluntary societies themselves would be the great crucible of American republicanism and that participation in their affairs would serve as an important instrument of social integration. Yet, however significantly the evangelical crusade educated, in and of itself, its more permanent and far-reaching influence came through a vast spiritualizing of the educational institutions of the country and a resultant institutionalizing of the evangelical spirit that was destined to transcend the immediacies of the 1820's and 1830's. In its drive for a Christian America, the front established some institutions, cooperated in the establishment of others, and captured others; but it sought to influence all. In the struggle with Satan there could be no neutral ground; what was not already Christ's had to be won for Christ, or it remained in continuing danger of going to the Devil.

One of the first institutions the front sought to evangelize was the family. Viewed historically as the principal unit of social organization and the most important agency of education, the family had been the subject of an unbroken line of literature extending back to the English Renaissance. For centuries, authors of every stripe had counseled both parents and children on their awesome responsibilities and obligations. Americans initially had imported English devotional manuals in large numbers, and in the 1800's John Bunyan, Philip Doddridge, Isaac

Watts, and Daniel Defoe, with their explicit and implicit counsel about how to live and what to teach, could still be found beside the Bible in many a household. Next to them, a somewhat smaller variety of native products might also be found, for instance, Enos Hitchcock's *The Parent's Assistant* or John Witherspoon's *A Series of Letters on Education*. While each of these volumes had its own special approach to family nurture, they all tended to teach the Renaissance paradigm of the household as a patriarchal system corresponding to the church and the state and serving as the nursery of both, with the father as divine ruler, the mother as his aid, and the children as subjects, and with their relations defined by a set of mutual obligations that could be derived from the Fifth Commandment.

The evangelizing of the family in the 1820's, 1830's, and 1840's loosed on parents a flood of advice in direct descent from this earlier literature. That the advice came at a time when the incessant mobility of Americans, from region to region and from farm to city, appeared to be loosening the bonds of the family only made the advice shriller and more insistent; that it came at a time of increasing immigration made it more monolithic, especially to the immigrants; and that it came at a time of the rapid expansion of American publishing made it certainly more voluminous and indeed more regionally based in the newly developing centers of book publishing in Boston, New York, and Cincinnati. Some of the new advice simply reiterated earlier dicta in the language of the nineteenth century: Heman Humphrey's book *Domestic Education* (1840), for example, preached in classic Puritan homiletic style that the key to the reform of society was the reassertion of parental discipline under the absolute authority of the father, who was accountable to no earthly power. And, while the pedagogical methods Humphrey proposed were moderated by the more humane precepts of the nineteenth century in general and the American scene in particular, his concept of the family and its educative function was quite traditional. Some of the advice, however, departed from the traditional in at least two respects. First, it began to regard the household as a haven from the world instead of merely a preparation for it, within which the character of children and adults alike might be fashioned and fortified for subsequent encounters with harsh reality. "Our hope is not in schools," the Reverend Matthew Hale Smith counseled, "but in [the] home; in the power of parental love and discipline." His opinion clearly connected with Horace Bushnell's in *Views of Christian Nurture*. Where would the truest Christian nurture take place? In the organic Christian family, where the light of Christ would lead and the life of God would perpetually reign.[10]

A second change from the traditional in the new literature on child-rearing involved the vastly expanded responsibilities of the mother. From an earlier role as aid and adjunct, she became the dominant figure of the family, creating with her strength, devotion, piety, and knowledge the ambience within which proper nurture could proceed. Technically, the mother's authority remained subsidiary to the father's, but now, in actuality, he too would be succored and ennobled within the orbit of her influence. "When our land is filled with virtuous and patriotic mothers, the Reverend John S. C. Abbott perorated in his widely read treatise *The Mother at Home*, "then will it be filled with virtuous and patriotic men. She who was first in the transgression, must be yet the principal earthly instrument in the restoration." Building on similar assumptions, Catharine Beecher, Lyman Beecher's eldest daughter, wrote a whole series of textbooks and manuals designed to instruct the new American woman in her responsibilities. The pious mother, she believed, could do well only as the instructed mother, steeped in wisdom about health, cookery, clothing, the economy of time, the care of the sick, and the management of the household—in short, in the wisdom of domestic economy.[11]

In all of this, the goal was "to prepare the child for its heavenly home" by facilitating conversion—whether earlier in life, as in the theology of Bushnell, or later in life, as in the theology of Finney. And, in pursuing this end, the evangelical movement saw the family as closely linked to other local nurturing institutions, notably the church, the Sunday school, and the common school. The several institutions, of course, were in quite different stages of development and therefore demanded quite different strategies on the part of the united front. Whereas the family and church were historic institutions being revivified and recalled to their age-old functions in the face of perceived threats to public piety, the Sunday school and the common school were

10. Heman Humphrey, *Domestic Education* (Amherst, Mass.: J. S. & C. Adams, 1840); Matthew Hale Smith, *Counsels Addressed to Young Women, Young Men, Young Persons in Married Life, and Young Parents* (Washington, D.C.: Blair and Rives, 1846), p. 115; and Horace Bushnell, *Views of Christian Nurture, and of Subjects Adjacent Thereto* (Hartford, Conn.: Edwin Hunt, 1848).

11. John S. C. Abbott, *The Mother at Home; or, the Principles of Maternal Duty Familiarly Illustrated*, revised and corrected by Daniel Walton (London: John Mason, 1834), p. 166; and Catharine E. Beecher, *A Treatise on Domestic Economy, for the Use of Young Ladies at Home, and at School* (Boston: Marsh, Capen, Lyon, and Webb, 1841). It should be noted that, especially in urban areas, the father was out of the home for a good part of the day in any case.

newer institutions, far less universal in their scope and not as well defined in their function.

The Sunday school was first developed in England in the 1780's and imported to the United States during the twenty years thereafter by groups of citizens in Philadelphia, Boston, and Pawtucket. During the first decades of the nineteenth century, it was merely one among many forms of American school, including church schools, charity schools, public schools, private entrepreneurial schools, and incorporated schools of every sort and variety. Its special purpose was to offer the rudiments of reading and writing to children who worked during the week, with the added benefit of keeping them off the streets on the Sabbath; given its limited scope, it could also easily be used to educate special segments of the population—especially blacks, free and enslaved. The Bible was commonly its textbook, partly because that seemed prudent for a school that met on the Sabbath and partly because the Bible was commonly a reading text in any case; and religious authorities were frequently involved as sponsors, partly because that, too, seemed prudent for a Sabbath venture and partly because the clergy were characteristically active in charitable and educational ventures of all kinds. The Sunday school, then, was not initially seen as an adjunct to the religious work of the churches and was not intended to help seek conversions; the united front, however, in its effort to organize, develop, and extend the Sunday school, was largely successful in capturing it and converting it to evangelical purposes. Whereas in 1815 Sunday schools were scattered institutions that catered to a small number of children from lower-class homes, by 1830 they had become widely available to a larger number of children from homes of all sorts. Moreover, by that time their initially practical purpose had been superseded by more religious concerns: they had become institutions primarily for the nurturance of piety.

The Sunday school often preceded the common school in a new community, and when the common school was organized it often complemented the Sunday school. "Let Sabbath schools be established wherever it is practicable," suggested the Indiana Sabbath School Union in 1827. "They will answer the double purpose of paving the way for common schools, and of serving as a substitute till they are generally formed." Not surprisingly, the same local evangelical group that originally organized a Sunday school was often in due course the prime mover in the establishment of a common school, in the process overseeing the selection of teachers, the organization of curricula, and the choice of textbooks. In the older, settled regions, where common schools were already in existence or being formed out of older private or eleemosynary institutions, the evangelical movement sought to shape or influence or even take them over through a variety of strategems: by supplying textbooks and libraries, by seeking overlapping membership on school committees or in professional associations, and by exerting pressure via parent and civic associations espousing temperance or peace or Sabbatarianism. The common school has traditionally been portrayed as a product of secular forces acting in contradistinction to the evangelical movement, but that portrayal is at best a half-truth: just as the evangelical leaders saw Christianity and republicanism as mutually supportive and dependent upon one another, so did they see the common school, teaching a truth properly grounded in evangelical doctrine, as an instrument of their movement and a bulwark of the Republic.[12]

The same must be said of the academies, colleges, and seminaries that multiplied with such rapidity during the age of Jackson: as Beecher and Bushnell had eloquently stated it in paeans to a West saved from barbarism by the timely intervention of Christianity, such institutions were considered nurseries of piety and manufactories of republicanism. The colleges especially were seen as centers of a vigorous religious life amid hostile or at least indifferent environments: they were, as the rhetoric went, schools of the prophets from which would issue the pious ministers that would be God's instruments for the conversion of the world. We have no idea of precisely how many colleges and seminaries of various sorts were actually founded during the first half of the nineteenth century; though, given the ease of organizing such institutions and even of arranging charters for them, the number probably ran into the hundreds. Certain it is, though, that the evangelical movement influenced many of them, in some instances by subsidizing students and programs, in others by recommending presidents and professors, in still others by sponsoring and organizing student groups. Public and private institutions were touched equally, especially the newer ones, and it was only the older and more liberal institutions like Harvard or the University of Pennsylvania, or the newer, specialized institutions like the military academy at West Point or Rensselaer Institute, that resisted with any success.

Family, church, school, and college, then, were wrought into configurations of nurturing institutions by the evangelical movement, no

12. *First Annual Report of the Indiana Sabbath School Union* (1827), p. 14.

matter what their origin or their sponsorship—or at least the attempt
was made. And, in purpose and pedagogical style, these configurations
became mutually supportive and mutually confirming. Moreover, to
them must be added any number of other institutions that attached
themselves to the configurations in supportive or complementary roles.
A library, for example, carefully chosen by officers of the Sunday-
School Union or the Tract Society, or perhaps by a religious publishing
house, was often available in the Sunday school or the common school
or some other public or quasi-public building: at midcentury, for example, more than half the libraries designated "public" in the United
States were located physically in Sunday schools. Publishing houses
were maintained by several of the societies and denominations and, the
market being what it was, commercial houses were quite ready to shape
their products to evangelical audiences. Youth and adult groups were
organized on the local level, in collaboration with churches or colleges
or the societies themselves, and in the traditional fashion of the moral
reformation societies these, too, became educative. And in 1851 the
Young Men's Christian Association was organized in Boston, following
an earlier British model, as "a social organization of those in whom the
love of Christ has produced love to men; who shall meet the young
stranger as he enters our city, . . . introduce him to the church and Sabbath school, bring him to the rooms of the Association, and in every
way throw around him good influences, so that he may feel that he is
not a stranger, but that noble and Christian spirits care for his soul."
Finally, evangelical organizations created and assisted houses of refuge,
almshouses, penitentiaries, and asylums of various sorts—custodial institutions explicitly designed to rehabilitate (reeducate) deviant and dependent individuals. Indeed, even the factory was seen as an agency capable of being spiritualized and of nurturing spirituality. Though the
workers who were to be nurtured by such programs soon became aware
of their paternalistic—and sometimes utterly cynical—aspects, the programs nevertheless went forward for a time and occasionally, as in the
early phases of the much publicized experiment at Lowell, Massachusetts, even led to periods of intense revivalism.[13]

In sum, the configurations formed by the evangelical movement
were complex, far-reaching, and influential. Obviously not all families
or schools or libraries were touched. Obviously those that were touched

13. William B. Whiteside, *The Boston Y.M.C.A. and Community Need: A Century's Evolution, 1851–1951* (New York: Association Press, 1951), p. 21.

felt the weight of influence in varying forms and degrees: families were perfunctorily pious, schools went through curricular motions, libraries shelved a host of books that never circulated, and publishers made a good deal of money. The spiritualizing of institutions meant different things in different places. Yet there is no denying that new institutions were formed and old ones transformed, that a considerable apparatus of education propagated the ideas of evangelicism via the rhetoric of evangelicism, and that, long after the united front itself collapsed in the face of renewed denominationalism during the 1840's and 1850's, its spirit continued to be reflected and its program continued to be purveyed by the configurations that had emerged as a result of its influence. In the extent to which the nation's educational institutions had been spiritualized, the evangelical spirit, as seen by the movement, had been institutionalized.

IV

The pedagogy of evangelization was personal: mothers, ministers, schoolteachers, librarians, superintendents of houses of refuge, and volunteer distributors of tracts were all seen by the united front as directly involved in purveying the word. In the purveying, however, they had at their disposal, to a degree unprecedented in history, printed materials mass-produced by the burgeoning American publishing industry. Some of these were directly sponsored by the voluntary societies themselves; others derived from commercial sources. Their circulation during the first two-thirds of the nineteenth century was extraordinary. The American Sunday-School Union, for example, published its first book in 1817, an American edition of Mary Butt Sherwood's *Little Henry and His Bearer* (a sorrowful story in which an English orphan in India dies while teaching the Bible to his bearer, Boosy). By 1830 the organization had issued over 6 million copies of similar works, specifically chosen or prepared for Sunday-school students. The American Tract Society, established in 1825, published 3 million tracts during the first five years of its operation. By 1865 it had circulated 20 million bound volumes, each including a dozen or more tracts, as well as some 250 million individual pamphlets. And, between 1836 and 1870, some 47 million copies of books in the so-called McGuffey series of readers (a prime example of independently produced material) were sold, mostly though not entirely for use in common-school instruction. Along with the Bible, these texts and tracts were among the most widely read materials in the United States; and, being both similar and complementary in purpose, substance, and pedagogical design, they played a significant role in articulating and shaping the attitudes, values, tastes, and sensibilities of the American people.[14]

The principal purpose of the McGuffey series, of course, was to provide a comprehensive system of reading instruction. There were six graded readers and a primer preceding them, and as time passed there were charts, spellers, and other pedagogical paraphernalia. The lessons in each volume were arranged in a logical sequence, becoming more difficult linguistically, more sophisticated in content, and more demanding of previously acquired information. Significantly, the publications of the American Tract Society and the American Sunday-School Union were also designed as systems of reading instruction. Both organizations issued primers, and both included in their offerings publications quite as graded in linguistic and substantive difficulty as the McGuffey series. In addition, there was a sustained effort in all these materials to cultivate a taste for good books—good books being, as McGuffey explained in a lesson on the value of time and knowledge, "an effectual preservative from vice" and, next to the "fear of God," the best possible "safeguard to character." Indeed, it would have been impossible for the evangelical mind to distinguish between the teaching of reading skills and the cultivation of literary taste.[15]

The goal of all these systems was the creation of a literate American public. This meant in the first place a public prepared in all the arts of language. Thus, the McGuffey readers built training in elocution and in public speaking systematically into their instructional format, alongside the exercises in spelling and comprehension. Notes on pronunciation as well as on inflection, articulation, and gesture were prominently featured throughout the series, with the early volumes prefacing lessons with rules, such as "Read this story exactly as if you were telling it to someone," and the later volumes including orations of such well-known figures as Daniel Webster and soliloquies from such classic authors as Shakespeare. Similarly, the publications of the American

14. Edwin Wilbur Rice, *The Sunday-School Movement and the American Sunday-School Union, 1780–1917* (Philadelphia: American Sunday-School Union, 1917), p. 146; Harvey George Neufeldt, "The American Tract Society, 1825–1865: An Examination of Its Religious, Economic, Social, and Political Ideas" (doctoral thesis, Michigan State University, 1971), p. 38. The figures on sales of the McGuffey readers are the estimates of Louis M. Dillman, who was president of the American Book Company (latter-day publishers of the readers) from 1914 to 1931, as reported in Harvey C. Minnich, *William Holmes McGuffey and the Peerless Pioneer McGuffey Readers* (Oxford, Ohio: Miami University, 1928), p. 92.

15. *New Fifth Eclectic Reader* (Cincinnati: Sargent, Wilson & Hinkle, 1857), p. 92.

Tract Society and the American Sunday-School Union included sermons and other materials that were clearly intended to be read aloud,
for example, a pamphlet of "Anecdotes for the Family and Social Circle." This stress on oral English along with spelling and reading comprehension was scarcely new, given that reading had for centuries been
a social phenomenon and indeed that most reading had been carried on
aloud and in groups. What was new was the quite explicit effort to
prepare poeple for active participation in public speaking and debate.[16]

A literate public would also be an awakened public, one inspired by
tales of the virtue of personal sacrifice and correspondingly warned
against the hazards of worldly life. The publications of the American
Tract Society and the American Sunday-School Union, like the Mc-
Guffey texts, were replete with "authentic narratives" intended to appeal to the reader's emotions and powers of emulation. Thus, the tract
"Life of William Kelley" told of "an habitual drunkard" who became a
new man and thereafter "delightfully exemplified the Christian character"; while the story "George's Feast" described a boy who would have
enjoyed eating some strawberries he had found but instead saved them
for his sick mother. The simple parable dominated, and there was no
mistaking the message of tales entitled "An Appeal in Behalf of the
Christian Sabbath" or "Beware of Bad Books."[17]

Finally, a literate public would be a public capable of self-instruction, one that might be expected to turn to literature for guidance on all
questions. The publications of the American Sunday-School Union,
with *The Union Bible Dictionary* serving "to connect" other works in
the various libraries, offered the reader "A Complete Biblical Cyclope-
dia"; the McGuffey readers proffered a similarly comprehensive curriculum, including history, literature, theology, and natural science; and
the catalogues of the American Tract Society implied that they would
make available all the world's worthwhile writing: missionary memoirs,
the "Standard Works of the Seventeenth Century," Paley's *Natural
Theology*, Aubigné's *History of the Reformation*, and innumerable didactic narratives and sermons. Some of the material appeared in foreign
language editions; some of it addressed specific age groups, for example, Burder's *Sermons to the Aged* or Pike's *Persuasives to Early Piety*;

16. William H. McGuffey, *Newly Revised Eclectic Third Reader* (New York: Clark, Austin, and Smith, 1848), p. 30; and *Circulation and Character of the Volumes of the American Tract
Society* (New York: American Tract Society, 1848), pp. 104–105.

17. *Sketch of the Origin and Character of the Principal Series of Tracts of the American
Tract Society* (New York: American Tract Society, 1859), pp. 5, 24, 23; and William H. McGuffey, *Newly Revised Eclectic Second Reader* (Cincinnati: Winthrop B. Smith, 1853), pp. 92–94.

and some of it deliberately interwove practical knowledge with moral injunctions—the *Christian Almanac,* for example, provided a lunar calendar and advice on planting intermixed with quotations from Scripture and the sayings of Benjamin Franklin.[18]

In pedagogical design, then, the evangelical literature was popular, didactic, and comprehensive. From it, one could obtain a complete and continuing Christian education. Through it, the educative influence of the united front would be extended throughout all ranks of society and across the entire United States. As the McGuffey readers became increasingly the textbooks of the nation, they would bring scattered schools into closer relationship, permit children to move from school to school without interruption or loss of time, and purvey through all parts of the nation a common curriculum. Similarly, as the publications of the American Tract Society were passed from hand to hand, they would, on the one hand, bring the basic elements of that common curriculum to all who had not been able to attend school and, on the other hand, continue that curriculum for those who had completed their schooling. The evangelicals sought nothing less than to harness the intellectual energies of the entire populace to the task of creating a unified, orderly, and righteous society.

The substance of the effort, the content of the common curriculum, was surely a popularized version of a Protestant *paideia.* In fable, history, prayer, hymn, and essay, the evangelical literature joined Biblical commandment to Franklinian preachment. Legh Richmond's *The Dairyman's Daughter,* widely distributed by both the Tract Society and the Sunday-School Union, taught by example the crucial importance of living a life "rich in faith," while the Tract Society's *Illustrated Family Christian Almanac* urged youngsters to "Work! Work!" Constant injunctions to diligence notwithstanding, the moral in this literature was invariably to be satisfied with one's station in life. The Tract Society's periodical *The Child's Paper* advised that "To each a daily task is given / A labor that shall fit for heaven," and Legh Richmond was quick to point out that, even if the dairyman's daughter was the poor child of a poor man, the riches deriving from her faith were heavenly riches and far more valuable than worldly wealth and comfort.[19]

18. *The Union Bible Dictionary for the Use of Schools, Bible Classes, and Families* (Philadelphia: American Sunday-School Union, 1855), p. 3; *Circulation and Character of the Volumes of the American Tract Society,* passim; and *The Christian Almanac for the Year of Our Lord and Saviour Jesus Christ 1824* (New York: American Tract Society and the Religious Tract Society of New York, 1824).

19. Legh Richmond, "The Dairyman's Daughter," in *Favorite Narratives for the Christian*

The message conveyed by the McGuffey readers was virtually identical, although the special genius of the readers was to combine this advice with lessons drawn from the American context. The heroes of American history were portrayed as exemplars of industriousness, honesty, and intelligence and assigned the stature of Biblical heroes: George Washington, for example, was often compared to Moses. The events of American history were portrayed as developments in a holy design, Columbus having been guided by the hand of Providence and the Revolution having been brought to a successful conclusion by the intervention of God. And the significance of American history was equated with "the divine scheme for moral government."[20]

In myriad ways, then, the evangelical literature expounded a complete moral and ethical system involving an orderly complex of relationships among man, God, and nation. To be sure, the explication of such relationships was as old as Protestant casuistry, but in the special *paideia* articulated by the nineteenth-century evangelicals there was an emphasis on human will that set it apart from earlier visions of God's purpose for humankind. Within a benevolent universe, Americans were to make themselves. The possibility of righteousness was present in all people at birth, and, given proper nurture and instruction, children and adults alike could be persuaded, indeed formed, to eschew greed, idleness, and ignorance in favor of generosity, diligence, and truth. It was these beliefs that led the evangelicals to promote the skills and habits of literacy, so that people of all ages and "classes of mind" might voluntarily choose to instruct themselves in useful, elevating, and disciplining knowledge, and thereby create a nation in which the millennium would surely be achieved.

Household (London: T. S. Nelson, 1864), p. 39; *The Illustrated Family Christian Almanac for the United States for the Year of Our Lord and Saviour Jesus Christ 1852* (New York: American Tract Society, 1852), p. 27; and *Child's Paper*, II (1853), 33.

20. William H. McGuffey, *Eclectic Fourth Reader* (Cincinnati: Truman & Smith, 1837), p. 245.

Chapter 3

MODES OF SECTARIANISM

Education's all.
A. BRONSON ALCOTT

The descant to evangelicism during the early decades of the Republic was sectarianism. The evangelist went out into the world and attempted to reform it through charismatic persuasion; the sectarian withdrew from the world and attempted to reform it by charismatic example. Both were, in their very nature, committed to education. The evangelist taught centrifugally, systematically expounding the meaning and significance of Christian doctrine for all men. The sectarian taught centripetally, creating and maintaining the kind of perfected society that nurtured the good within at the same time as it exemplified the good without. The evangelist sought the conversion of individuals, one by one. The sectarian sought the conversion of whole communities. Both, in the end, sought nothing less than the regeneration of the entire world.

The very forces that revitalized evangelicism during the latter years of the eighteenth century revitalized sectarianism as well. Perfectionism, disinterested benevolence, and millennialism—in their European as well as in their American versions—marked the utopian experiments of the time quite as characteristically as they marked the broader interdenominational revivals. And they made their influence felt within a common context of incessant social movement and chronic psychological instability. Beyond that, the sectarian experiments manifested their own organizational pattern that, again, was quite as characteristic a response to the conditions of American life as were the interdenominational organizations of the evangelical movement. Arthur Bestor has aptly referred to that pattern as "communitarianism" (the term itself

74

dates from the 1840's), to suggest a system of social reform based on the exemplary influence of small "lighthouse" communities. The number of such communities to appear on the American scene during the early decades of the nineteenth century was impressive, representing every conceivable combination of social mix and ideological thrust: there were the Shakers and the Rappites and the Moravians; there were the followers of Jemima Wilkinson and of William Miller and of John Humphrey Noyes; and there were the infinitely varied forms of socialist and communist endeavor. Each community tried in its own way to construct some perfect configuration of education in which no institution would be at cross-purposes with any other. All remain of interest because of their influence on the educational outlook of nineteenth-century Americans.[1]

Three of these communities, each of which incarnated a profoundly different view of education, are particularly worthy of note: the Owenite community at New Harmony, Indiana; the Transcendentalist community at Fruitlands, Massachusetts; and the Mormon community of Utah. They are in no way representative of all the other communitarian experiments—no group of communities could be. New Harmony and Fruitlands failed, as did most utopias of the time (and of all times). The Mormon community succeeded, perhaps even more dramatically than all but a few of the early leaders might have predicted. But all three exercised an influence on American education that extended far beyond their boundaries and, in the case of the failures, well beyond their demise.

II

New Harmony had its origins in the English reformer Robert Owen's aspirations to create a "new moral world," where truth and goodness would prevail in public affairs and every individual would have the opportunity to achieve his fullest potential as a human being. Owen, the self-made son of a Welsh saddler, had first come to public attention during the early years of the nineteenth century, when he made of New Lanark, Scotland, a village of some two thousand people, a model industrial community in which textile mills were operated at a profit at the same time as the living and working conditions of the mill

---

1. Arthur Eugene Bestor, Jr., *Backwoods Utopias: The Sectarian and Owenite Phases of Communitarian Socialism in America, 1663–1829* (Philadelphia: University of Pennsylvania Press, 1950).

hands were significantly improved. Owen himself later maintained that the effort at New Lanark had been a limited one at best, representing merely an attempt to alleviate "the worst evils of a fundamentally erroneous system." Yet the reforms he had achieved were sufficient in the eyes of his contemporaries to attract attention throughout Europe and North America. More importantly, Owen's own reading and intellectual associations had steeped him in the thought of the Scottish and Continental Enlightenments, from which he had derived a fundamentally environmentalist outlook on human nature; and he found himself moved to articulate the principles underlying the New Lanark innovations in terms that joined this environmentalism to a sense of infinite possibility concerning the rational organization and conduct of human affairs. One result, between 1812 and 1816, was a plethora of essays, addresses, letters, and pamphlets—four of the essays appeared as a book under the title *A New View of Society* (1816)—that not only lent impressive significance to the work at New Lanark but actually projected an even more radical vision promising nothing less than the achievement of the millennium.[2]

Several persistent themes sounded through these documents, none more central than the ultimate dependence of all social arrangements on proper modes of education. Owen argued the point forcefully in an 1816 address inaugurating New Lanark's Institution for the Formation of Character. Intended as a facility for all age groups and classes of the population, the Institution included a day-care center for toddlers ("By this means many of you, mothers of families, will be enabled to earn a better maintenance or support for your children"), a general classroom for the teaching of reading, writing, arithmetic, sewing, and knitting to children under ten, an evening school for youngsters employed in the factory, a reading and recreation center for the adults of the community, and various special accommodations for dancing and music, vocational training, nature study, and self-instruction. In Owen's view, the value of the Institution would extend far beyond the direct benefits of those who used it, for it would serve as an example to other industrial communities of the substantial advantages to be derived from an educated work force at the same time as it alerted the British Parliament to

2. Robert Owen, *The Book of the New Moral World* (1842–1844; reprint ed; 7 parts; New York: Augustus M. Kelly, 1970), I, xvii–xviii; *The Life of Robert Owen, Written by Himself* (2 vols.; London: Effingham, Wilson, 1857–58), I, 79.

the possibilities that might be universally achieved through appropriate legislation.[3]

Perhaps the most interesting aspect of Owen's Institution was its attempt to embody the reformist pedagogy of the Swiss educators Johann Heinrich Pestalozzi and Philipp Emanuel von Fellenberg. Owen had become personally acquainted with the two men during a tour of Europe, in the course of which he had pronounced Fellenberg's schools at Hofwyl (an estate near Berne) as "two or three steps in advance of any I had seen yet in England or on the continent." So great was his enthusiasm that he subsequently entered his two eldest sons, Robert Dale and William, in the academy at Hofwyl, under Fellenberg's "especial care and direction." In his later recollections, Owen, characteristically, made much of the improvements he had been able to suggest to Fellenberg as a result of his experience at New Lanark. But in actuality the influence was mostly in the other direction, and the Institution at New Lanark was profoundly affected by Fellenberg's commitment to the integration of mental, moral, and manual education, to the pursuit of a beneficent and "natural" pedagogy, and to the maintenance of a warm and mutually tolerant relationship among the children of various social classes.[4]

As much as Owen prized the work of the Institution, he thought it at best a partial effort. Ultimately, he believed it was life at large that formed character and therefore life at large that would have to be altered if permanent human progress was to be achieved. In a series of oft-repeated propositions, Owen maintained that character was formed *for* and not *by* individual human beings and that with the application of rational principles any community could be arranged "in such a manner, as not only to withdraw vice, poverty, and, in a great degree, misery, from the world, but also to place *every* individual under circumstances in which he shall enjoy more permanent happiness than can be given to *any* individual under the principles which have hitherto regulated society." Beyond the partial education of the infant school, the primary classroom, and the recreation center, there lay the larger education of growing up and living in a particular community. If this larger education could be made right—by which Owen meant if all social

3. Robert Owen, "Address Delivered at New Lanark on Opening the Institution for the Formation of Character, on the 1st of January, 1816," in Owen, *A New View of Society and Other Writings,* edited by G. D. H. Cole (London: J. M. Dent & Sons, 1927), p. 98.

4. *Life of Robert Owen,* I, 178, 179.

arrangements in family, church, mill, and community could be so structured as gradually to withdraw the sources of anger, hatred, and discord and to substitute the nurturance of charity, kindness, and philanthropy—the truly good society would emerge. "What ideas individuals may attach to the term millennium I know not," Owen rhapsodized in a burst of chiliastic rhetoric; "but I know that society may be formed so as to exist without crime, without poverty, with health greatly improved, and with little, if any, misery, and with intelligence and happiness increased a hundred-fold; and no obstacle whatsoever intervenes at this moment, except ignorance, to prevent such a state of society from becoming universal." Not surprisingly, Owen soon expanded the partial education of the Institution into the total education of a utopia; and, in a report published in 1817 by the Parliamentary Committee on the Poor Law, he sketched for the first time what came to be known as his educational parallelogram—a wholly planned, self-supporting community of some five hundred to fifteen hundred persons living in a quadrangular compound embracing family living quarters, children's dormitories, communal dining rooms, chapels, and schools, and surrounded by the stables, farms, and factories that would support the population.[5]

It was the larger view symbolized by this parallelogram that propelled Owen beyond the confines (and hard realities) of New Lanark and launched him on a quest for perfection. And it was this same larger view that lay behind New Harmony. Frustrated in his efforts to obtain parliamentary action (he actually stood for Parliament in 1819 and lost), impatient with partial approaches, and increasingly under fire for his outspoken criticisms of organized religion, Owen began to search for an opportunity to create a perfect society *ex nihilo* as an example to the world. When Frederick Rapp, the leader of an experimental religious community at Harmony, Indiana, decided during the winter of 1823–24 to sell Harmony and relocate with his brethren in Pennsylvania, Owen resolved to purchase the community's assets and undertake his experiment under the name New Harmony.

The actual story of New Harmony is one of noble social visions joined to ill-conceived social arrangements. During the initial months after Owen acquired title to New Harmony on January 3, 1825, hundreds of applicants crowded into the community, bearing with them a vast muddle of conflicting hopes and expectations: some thought they

5. Owen, "Address Delivered at New Lanark," in *New View of Society and Other Writings*, pp. 110, 106; and "Report to the Committee of the Association for the Relief of the Manufacturing and Labouring Poor, March, 1817," in *Life of Robert Owen*, II, 53–64.

would work for Owen; others presumed they would live off his bounty; while still others actually sought to form their own experimental communities, using his resources. Nothing Owen said or did ever really clarified the confusion. The first of a succession of constitutions went into effect on May 1, 1825, but it provided high-sounding principles instead of practical guidelines. Owen himself was absent much of the time, propagandizing for the millennium in the East and in Europe, while his son William remained in charge of local arrangements. The younger man was competent enough; but, considering the conflicting expectations of the settlers and the vague directions of the founder, it would have taken more than mere competence to establish viable living and working arrangements.

The entry of an able partner onto the scene in 1826, the scientist William Maclure, seemed to make little difference in the overall course of the experiment. Maclure was a Scotsman who had amassed a fortune at business in Europe and had then immigrated to the United States to undertake a second career in the worlds of science, education, and social reform. Settling in Philadelphia, he had embarked upon an extensive geological survey of the United States at the same time as he had entered vigorously into the activities of the American Philosophical Society and the Academy of Natural Sciences of Philadelphia. Equally important, given his later role at New Harmony, he had come quite independently upon the work of Pestalozzi and Fellenberg and had personally persuaded Pestalozzi's colleague Joseph Neef to come to Philadelphia and establish a school on Pestalozzian principles. Later, he had also provided the wherewithal by which at least two other Pestalozzian teachers from Paris, Marie Duclos Fretageot and Guillaume Sylvan Casimir Phiquepal d'Arusmont, had been enabled to transfer their activities to Philadelphia. Finally, he had familiarized himself with the work at New Lanark, having visited that community in the summer of 1824 and having remarked upon "the vast improvement in society effected by Mr. Robert Owen's courage and perseverance in spite of an inveterate and malignant opposition." Indeed, it was only shortly after Maclure's visit that Owen had decided to purchase New Harmony. When Maclure's friends and associates in Philadelphia—Neef, Fretageot, and Phiquepal, as well as the scientists Thomas Say, Gerard Troost, John Speakman, and Charles-Alexandre Lesueur—heard of the projected community, they found themselves immediately drawn to the possibilities; and they not only made their own plans to participate but also set about persuading Maclure to join them. Anything but an enthusiast, Maclure resisted for a time; but a personal conference with Owen in Philadelphia decided the matter and Maclure was won over.[6]

The arrival of Maclure and his colleagues—known affectionately as the "boatload of knowledge" because they had embarked on the last leg of their journey to New Harmony aboard a keelboat named *Philanthropist*— brought a burst of hope to New Harmony, but precious little progress toward utopia. A new constitution setting up the permanent Community of Equality (the instrument of 1825 had established the Preliminary Society, or "halfway house") was adopted on February 5, 1826, placing the general management of affairs in the hands of a small executive council. But, on the crucial question of how much by way of goods and services each individual would contribute and be entitled to, the new constitution was even vaguer than its predecessor. To make matters worse, several members of the Preliminary Society refused to go along with the new constitution and instead organized a subcommunity of their own named Macluria.

It was only a matter of days before the unworkability of the new constitution became apparent, and on February 19 the executive council asked the elder Owen to assume direction of the community for a year. Owen accepted, and the uncertainty subsided—though not the difficulties. Other subcommunities were founded; factionalism intensified; and economic problems mounted as cash payments under the agreement with Frederick Rapp fell due. Reorganization followed upon reorganization, but nothing stemmed the tide of disintegration.

Within this context, Maclure felt obliged at the least to obtain an arrangement that would permit him and his friends to carry forward the educational work they had projected and begun. In May, 1826, therefore, Maclure proposed the division of New Harmony into a number of relatively separate communities—one of which would be an education community—that would exchange goods and services with one another but remain fairly autonomous in calculating the value of the labor contributed by each member (there had been disparaging remarks about the comparative value of mental and manual labor). The proposal was accepted, and what was left of New Harmony was reorganized into three subcommunities—the Education Society, the Agricultural and Pastoral Society, and the Mechanic and Manufacturing Society— to be coordinated by a unit called the Board of Union. The problems of

---

6. William Maclure to Mme. Fretageot, August 25, 1824, in A. E. Bestor, Jr., ed., "Education and Reform at New Harmony: Correspondence of William Maclure and Marie Duclos Fretageot, 1820–1833," *Publications of the Indiana Historical Society*, XV (1948), 307.

New Harmony were not one mite alleviated by the arrangement, but Maclure and his associates were at least freed to advance their plans. The decision was a fateful one; for, though New Harmony failed dismally as a practical exemplar of the "new moral world," its Education Society developed some of the most interesting innovations of the nineteenth century, however short-lived they may have been and however limited their direct and immediate impact.

Essentially, Maclure's enterprise joined a program much like the one at New Lanark's Institution for the Formation of Character to an industrial school, a variety of embryonic library and museum collections, and a publishing venture featuring serious scientific books and a didactic periodical for young people. The infant and higher schools were assertively Pestalozzian in character: they maintained a pedagogical ambience of benevolence and affection and sought in their instruction to proceed from the simple and concrete to the complex and abstract. Unlike the schools at New Lanark, however, they were conceived—and for a time conducted—as boarding institutions that would receive all children of the community as soon as they could walk and keep them for up to ten years. The goal, of course, was to eradicate those age-old vices that had afflicted mankind for generations by interrupting their transmission within the household once and for all. The adult school, following the pattern of the mechanics' institutes in England and in the American East, was expanded from the informal reading center at New Lanark into the "Society for Mutual Instruction," designed to "communicate a general knowledge of the arts and sciences to those persons who have hitherto been excluded from a scientific or general education by the erroneous and narrow-minded policy of colleges and public schools." The Society itself was short-lived, but it did lay the groundwork for the permanent Workingmen's Institute and Library that Maclure established in 1837, toward the end of his life.[7]

The industrial training school taught the trades after the fashion of Fellenberg's Institute at Hofwyl and was expected after a preliminary period to become self-supporting through the sale of its products. At one time or another it offered instruction in taxidermy, carpentry, blacksmithing, cabinetmaking, shoemaking, agriculture, cooking, sewing, housekeeping, and millinery, but its pride and joy was its curriculum in printing, binding, and engraving. The publishing venture combined the efforts of the industrial school's printshop with the output of

7. William Maclure, *Opinions on Various Subjects, Dedicated to the Industrious Producers* (3 vols.; New Harmony, Ind.: printed at the school press, 1831–1838), I, 78–86.

New Harmony's scientists and literati and managed to issue some extraordinary books, including Maclure's own *Opinions on Various Subjects* (1831–1838) and Say's *American Conchology* (1830–1834), and a magazine called the *Disseminator of Useful Knowledge*, edited, printed, and published, it was claimed, by the pupils of the industrial school but actually edited by Say. Finally, there was for a time another school, the Orphans' Manual Training School, at which a few children twelve years of age and older were instructed in "all useful knowledge as well as in the useful arts." In all these efforts, benevolently but contentiously overseen by Neef and his wife, Phiquepal, Fretageot, Say, Troost, and Lesueur, a primary goal was to offer equal opportunity to female as well as male students and especially to equip young women to enter crafts and professions that had traditionally been closed to them.[8]

If any date can be given for the demise of New Harmony as a would-be utopia, it was probably May 27, 1827, when Owen, on the eve of his return to Europe, delivered himself of a parting counsel to the "ten social colonies of equality and common property on the New-Harmony estate." The address was full of the usual enthusiasm: industry, economy, beauty, and order were surely gaining ground, and there was no doubt but that a right understanding of principle would lead to the ultimate achievement of common objectives. "When I return, I hope to find you prosperous, and in Harmony together," Owen concluded. But in actuality the experiment was in shambles. Only two of the so-called social colonies of equality and common property were really functioning, and one of these was the Education Society, which itself was torn by internal strife. Yet, in the end, it would be the work of the Education Society (though not the Society itself) that would continue more durably than anything else in the experiment.[9]

Neither the innovativeness of the infant and the industrial schools nor the longevity of the Workingmen's Institute, however, holds the key to New Harmony's significance in the history of American education. Both were important in their own right, to be sure, as was the very real goal of providing equal educational opportunity for young women. But more important than any of these was the intellectual impact of New Harmony, which lay rather in the force of Owenite ideas than in the example of Maclurean institutions. In the end Maclure endowed the

8. *New-Harmony Gazette*, II (1827), 268.

9. *Ibid.*, II (1827), 279. See also Owen's address of May 6, 1827, in *ibid.*, II (1827), 254–255.

Institute as well as a novel system of public libraries extending across Indiana and into Illinois. But, for all the permanence of these institutions, their influence remained essentially local or at best regional. Owenite ideas, on the other hand, profoundly influenced American ways of thinking and talking about education. Owenism was for all intents and purposes a secular version of Protestant evangelicism, maintaining that education could enable man to transcend the historic limitations of his nature and thereby achieve the millennium. Untroubled by a continuing vacillation between education as partial (the perfect school) and education as total (the perfect community), Owenism ended up insisting that education could not only itself be perfect but also lead on to larger social perfection. In so doing, it invested education with a chiliastic potential that lent it immense popular appeal. One sees the phenomenon in Robert Dale Owen's subsequent pronouncements on behalf of the New York labor movement during the years immediately after the collapse of the New Harmony experiment and later in the Indiana legislature and the United States Congress. Even more importantly, one sees it in the larger discussion of popular education in its relation to democratic society, particularly as carried on by deistic and workingmen's societies during the 1830's and 1840's. Quite apart from the realities of New Harmony, Owenite rhetoric about New Harmony (and other Owenite communities) infused the more general American rhetoric about education with a lofty sense of individual and social possibility. And it was in that way that Owenism exercised its most significant influence on the American scene.

II

Bronson Alcott first read Robert Owen's *A New View of Society* in the summer of 1826, at about the time he had begun the systematic study of such popular pedagogical works as the Edgeworths' *Practical Education,* Joseph Neef's *Sketch of a Plan and Method of Education,* and the anonymously compiled *Hints to Parents on the Cultivation of Children, in the Spirit of Pestalozzi's Method.* Alcott was much taken with Owen's views, finding their benevolent humanitarianism much to his liking and doubtless drawing inspiration from Owen's emphasis on education as the crucial factor in any hoped-for progress of humankind. Some months later, he wrote a summary of Owen's philosophy in his journal, concluding, "The philosophy of his system we know to be true.

And we look forward to the day when society in general may partake of its benefits."[10]

Alcott and Owen did not actually meet until 1842, when Alcott visited England to reside for a time at Alcott House, a kind of lay monastery with a school attached that had taken as its mission the advancement of Alcott's philosophy. The British reformer was still preaching the gospel of millennialism, with a reconstructed society founded on a new view of education as the heart of his program. Alcott, however, had changed radically. No less a millennialist than Owen, he had nevertheless turned his back on Owen's principle that any general character could be given to any community by the application of proper means, and had espoused instead the view that education is essentially the self-realization of individuals, each sacred, each a part of the being of God, each with a divine mission to seek the highest expression of his own unique nature. Only by assisting every man, woman, and child— each in his own way—to seek self-knowledge and spiritual advancement, Alcott maintained, would the foundations of the good society be laid on any permanent basis.

Alcott's intellectual odyssey, from essential agreement with Owen to radical opposition, forms a critical chapter in the history of American Transcendentalism and patently establishes Alcott, in Ernest Sutherland Bates's apt phrase, as "the most transcendental of the Transcendentalists." Born in 1799, the son of a mechanic-farmer, Alcott grew up near Wolcott, Connecticut, as part of a large family within a close-knit community called Spindle Hill, made up largely of kin and neighbors of long standing. He attended the local schools; perused more than the usual number of books, including *The Pilgrim's Progress*, which apparently affected him profoundly; tried his hand at writing, clock making, and peddling (he liked to peddle books, so that he could read as he traveled); and eventually, during the winter of 1823–24, embarked upon a career as a teacher in the region where he had spent his boyhood.[11]

Very soon, his neighbors realized that they had employed no ordinary schoolmaster. Taking as his motto "Education's all," Alcott set out to teach, as he himself put it, "with reference to eternity." Attempting to proceed "in imitation of the Saviour," he tried to substitute encour-

10. Bronson Alcott Journals, October, 1827, pp. 122–124 (Alcott family mss., Houghton Library, Harvard University, Cambridge, Mass.). By permission of the Houghton Library.

11. Ernest Sutherland Bates, "Amos Bronson Alcott," *Dictionary of American Biography* (24+ vols.; New York: Charles Scribner's Sons, 1928–   ), I, 139.

agement for competition, explanation for memorization, persuasion for coercion. Seeking to adapt his instruction "to the genius and habits of the young mind," he moved from the simple to the difficult, from the known to the unknown, and from the concrete to the abstract, stressing always short steps, plain language, and "allusion to familiar objects and occurrencies." And, scrupulously eschewing all "sinister, sectarian, or oppressive principles," he tried to carry on his work with independence and imagination, avoiding "veneration of antiquity" on the one hand and "excess of novelty" on the other. To these ends, he purchased (with his own funds) scores of new textbooks for the youngsters and a wide range of professional literature for himself, much of it oriented toward the reformist philosophies of Locke, Watts, and Pestalozzi. Out of it all came a torrent of innovative exercises, approaches, and devices for use in the classroom.[12]

Not surprisingly, public reaction was mixed. Whereas Alcott quickly attracted the admiration of fellow teachers throughout New England, parental skepticism in and around Wolcott ran high. "Wretched indeed is the public sentiment in reference to education in this village . . . ," he noted in his journal in 1827. "The public sentiment needs enlightening; the prejudices of men dissipated; intelligence diffused; precedent rendered ridiculous; and what is worse than all to effect, avarice liberalized. This is a work which requires the talent and temper of a true reformer to accomplish. I am not that one." The words were prophetic. A true reformer was patently needed, and Alcott's disclaimer was probably correct. But he did give his life to the task.[13]

Alcott moved from school to school after the winter of 1827–28, teaching for a time in Boston, then shifting his efforts to Germantown and Philadelphia, and then returning to Boston in 1834 to found the Temple School, his best-known venture. It was in this period of some six or seven years that the remarkable transformation of his thought occurred—if indeed there was a transformation, since what may have happened was that he simply came to see the disjunction between the writings he admired and his own deepest beliefs. However that may be, the Alcott of 1827 perceived himself to be in agreement with Locke and Owen—in fact, in the enthusiastic journal entry he wrote that year he foresaw the triumph of the Owenite system throughout the world. Over the next few years, however, he became progressively disenchanted with

12. Alcott's pedagogical "maxims" appear at the beginning of his journal for 1826–27 (Alcott family mss.).

13. Journals, May 11, 1827 (Alcott family mss.).

Owenism, partly because of Owen's vitriolic attacks on organized Christianity, but more fundamentally because of the distance Alcott increasingly perceived between the Owenite (and Lockean) view of character as essentially malleable via the senses and his own view of character as a spiritual emergence touched by the divine. Doubtless Alcott's more deeply held view of human nature was strengthened by his reading of the Pestalozzian literature. But, as with many of his contemporaries, it was decisively confirmed by his study of the writings of Samuel Taylor Coleridge. As Alcott observed in his journal for 1832, "In Coleridge in particular, there are passages of surpassing beauty and deep wisdom. He seems to have studied man more thoroughly, and to understand him better, than any previous poetic writer, unless it be Wordsworth; and his prose writings are full of splendid ideas clothed in the most awful and imposing imagery. There is in this man's soul a deep well of wisdom, and it is a wisdom not of earth. No writer ever benefited me more than he has done. The perusal of 'Aids to Reflection' and 'The Friend' forms a new era in my mental and psychological life." Significantly, earlier that year Alcott had reviewed what he had written about Owen in the journal for 1827 and had then commented, "Want of discrimination!"[14]

Beyond his teaching and his reading, Alcott's role as a father during these years furnished yet another opportunity for the refinement of his educational ideas. He had married Abigail May in the spring of 1830, and the arrival of Anna Bronson Alcott the following year, during the family's residence in Germantown, gave Alcott the chance to launch an experiment that he had been considering for some time. Through systematic observation and judicious recording, he would try to ascertain the essential nature of the child, to the end that any who would undertake the work of education could proceed "in due accordance and harmony with the laws of its constitution." Once a cooperation of nature and nurture had been achieved, educators would come to know the truest reaches of human potential. It was a bracing idea for a reformer, and Alcott set about the work assiduously. By the end of Anna's first year, he had filled more than three hundred pages; by 1836, with not only Anna but Louisa May (1832) and Elizabeth Sewall (1835) to observe, he had filled almost twenty-five hundred. As might be expected, the "Observations" are fascinating in their own right, constituting as they do the first known records of their kind systematically compiled in

14. Journals, October, 1827, and October, 1832 (Alcott family mss.). The final quotation is penned and dated at the conclusion of the October, 1827, sketch of Owen's philosophy.

the United States; they are replete with data about the children's own development and about the Alcotts' efforts to influence that development. But, even more importantly, they are immensely revealing of Alcott. However much he sought "objective" data about the children, he found beyond all else confirmation of his own views—that the infant mind is filled with "dimly-perceived anticipations" of all that is "elevated in intellect, pure in affections, lofty in anticipation, and happy in remembrance"; that a "conscious and intelligent soul" can begin to be discerned at around the age of two months; that the infant's sense of self-reliance flourishes best under a regimen marked by affection and gentleness ("The child must be treated as a free, self-guiding, self-controlling being"); and that the key to the progressive development of the individual is self-control, of the passions by the soul. Alcott himself was quite aware of his tendency to find what he was looking for, and he even tried to correct for it; but the "Observations" bear the unmistakable stamp of the observer, and their primary value in their own time was doubtless to confirm Alcott's own emerging view of the nature of individuality.[15]

By the time Alcott inaugurated the Temple School in Boston in 1834, his professed views and deeply held beliefs were one, and by then quintessentially Transcendental, though that term had not yet come into fashion. He began the school—so-called because it was conducted in the Masonic Temple on Tremont Street—under the benign patronage of William Ellery Channing and with the able assistance of Elizabeth Palmer Peabody, the clientele being some thirty children (most of them under ten years of age) from the most prominent families of the city. The physical layout provided for individual work space, equipped with individual desks and blackboards, at the same time as it allowed for the possibility of groupings around the master. A large Gothic window dominated the room, with a bas-relief of Christ and busts of Socrates, Plato, Shakespeare, Milton, and Sir Walter Scott gazing down upon the children. In Alcott's view, education proceeded in part via example, and his aim was to furnish the room "with such forms as would address and cultivate the imagination and the heart."[16]

Much of the work was conventional, though it was pursued with the kind of verve, thoughtfulness, and commitment that in and of them-

---

15. Alcott, "Observations on the Life of My First Child (Anna Bronson Alcott) during her First Year," pp. 27, 23, 10, 46 (Alcott family mss.).

16. [Elizabeth Palmer Peabody], *Record of a School* (2d ed.; Boston: Russell Shattuck, 1836), p. 1.

selves made the school unusual. But the larger philosophical approach that underlay the studies in reading, spelling, writing, arithmetic, geography, and drawing made the school unique. The grand object of the curriculum was not learning in the traditional sense but rather self-knowledge—that understanding of the true idea of one's own being that permits one to use one's God-given endowments for the growth and perfection of one's spirit. To attain that object, Alcott introduced two pedagogical devices that soon became the hallmarks of the school: the journal and the conversation. The aim of the journal, which was kept on a continuing basis by the student himself (vide Bunyan, and of course Alcott himself), was to occasion the kind of introspection and self-analysis that would lead the youngster to the truth of his own nature. In daily exercises, each child was encouraged to write reflectively in his notebook as a means of bringing all his studies into relation around his own individuality and of thereby providing unity to his own being. Paralleling these exercises, some of the journals were read aloud, the purpose being to determine the extent to which each child approached the ideal life as lived by Jesus; once again, the effort was to teach via example. The aim of the conversation, which went hand in hand with the journal, was to employ the dialectical method that Alcott saw at the heart of the pedagogy of Socrates, Plato, and Jesus. Alcott would group the children around his desk and begin with a question—on some event from everyday life, on some well-known fable or episode from *The Pilgrim's Progress*, or, best of all, on some passage from the Gospels. In the discussion that followed, he would lead, explain, comment, and question, evoking ideas from the farthest reaches of the children's minds. His hoped-for outcome was nothing less than the awakening of the genius of the soul.

There were really two periods in the life of the Temple School, one of considerable public acceptance, marked by the appearance of Elizabeth Peabody's *Record of a School* in two editions (1835, 1836), the other of sharp public rejection, marked by the appearance of Alcott's own *Conversations with Children on the Gospels* (1836, 1837). Scarcely a politician by temperament, Alcott was wholly unprepared for the storm that greeted the latter work; indeed, he had confided in his journal that its publication might well "date a new era in the history of education, as well as a prophecy of the renovation of philosophy and of Christianity." Amid charges of indecency, obscenity, and heresy, the school in general and the conversational method in particular quickly became the foci of a city-wide controversy, in the wake of which enrollment fell off sharply. By the spring of 1838 there were only three children left, and Alcott decided to close the institution. He did make a final effort to continue the work in his own home later that year, but the admission of a black child turned most of the white parents against him and forced him to abandon the venture entirely (though he steadfastly refused to expel the black child). In June, 1839, Alcott left schoolteaching for the last time.[17]

In one of those ironies that often marks the career of a reformer, at precisely the low ebb of his fortunes at home, Alcott's reputation abroad began to tide. A group of mystics and reformers gathered around the English educator James Pierrepont Greaves, who had worked personally with Pestalozzi at Yverdon, had become interested in Alcott's work as reported in *Record of a School* and *Conversations with Children on the Gospels* and had decided to correspond with the man whom they regarded as the American Pestalozzi. Later, when they founded a small community and school at Ham Common, near Richmond, they named the establishment Alcott House and invited their mentor to visit them. Alcott's friend Emerson, hoping that such a visit might lift Alcott from the despondency into which he had slipped after the failure of the Temple School, encouraged him to go and offered to advance the necessary funds. Alcott accepted, spending the period from early June through late September, 1842, in England. It was a heady experience for the visionary schoolmaster, from which he returned bearing nothing less than the plan for a new Eden that would regenerate the world. The outcome was Fruitlands, easily one of the most interesting and certainly one of the most short-lived of the pre-Civil War utopias.

For all intents and purposes, Fruitlands was the creation of three individuals: Charles Lane, a reformist editor whom Alcott first met at Alcott House; Henry Gardiner Wright, the gifted schoolmaster of Alcott House (who stayed only briefly with the experiment); and Alcott himself. The vision developed in England, compounded partly of a strange eugenicism that Greaves had injected into the Alcott community (and which outlived Greaves, who died shortly after Alcott's arrival), partly of Lane's asceticism, and partly of Alcott's personalism. As set forth formally by Lane and Alcott in a communication to the *Herald of Freedom,* the purpose of the experiment was to demonstrate, first, that "the evils of life are not so much social, or political, as personal, and a

17. Journals, first week of January, 1837 (Alcott family mss.).

personal reform only can eradicate them" and, second, that the family situation is the one in which the reformed life can be best exemplified and best transmitted. The locale was a ninety-acre farm in the village of Harvard, Massachusetts, which Lane purchased in the spring of 1843. The principal participants, beyond the founders, Lane's son, and Alcott's family, were Samuel Bower, Joseph Palmer, and Isaac Hecker, essentially seekers pursuing their respective visions of the good (Palmer wore a long beard when beards were out of fashion and actually suffered a brief imprisonment for that fact in Worcester, Massachusetts), and a sprinkling of others.[18]

The experiment was formally launched on June 14, 1843, when the Alcotts and the Lanes moved onto the newly purchased farm; seven months later, it ended in failure. In the interim, the participants lived the stuff of comedy, tragedy, high principle, and low foolishness. The establishment was named Fruitlands, because fruit, which was to be home grown, was seen as the main staple of daily life. Characteristically, no orchard was ever planted, and a crop of cereals and vegetables was put in too late for a reasonable return. It was also decided that domestic animals would be liberated from enslavement to human needs, but the members of the community never quite decided what might replace them, involved as they were in perpetual conversations plumbing the depths of human understanding. There was a steady procession of interested visitors—Emerson and Channing, Theodore Parker and George Ripley, Nathaniel Hawthorne and Henry David Thoreau—and there was an unceasing stream of experiment and innovation, in diet and clothes, matters of health and articles of belief. Alcott's children, from Anna, aged twelve, to Abby May, aged three, participated as fully as they could, with time out for an impoverished school conducted by Anna for the other three.

For a while excitement, hope, and aspiration were dominant; then, as the novelty of the venture wore off, the struggle that would prove the undoing of Fruitlands broke into the open. Lane and Alcott had both seen the family as the heart of any viable program of reform. But for the ascetic Lane it was the celibate, consociate family as exemplified by the religious community, while for the paternal Alcott it was an expanded nuclear family as exemplified by the Alcotts themselves. By autumn, Lane and Abigail Alcott were at war within the household, Lane seeing her relationship with Alcott as a distortion and compromise of

---

18. Clara Endicott Sears, ed., *Bronson Alcott's Fruitlands* (Boston: Houghton Mifflin Company, 1915), p. 45.

the experiment, she herself viewing the relationship as its essence. In the end, Abigail Alcott won, but the experiment collapsed. Early in January, 1844, Lane and his son went off to live at a nearby Shaker village, whose consociate family was more to Lane's liking, and on January 14 the Alcotts left Fruitlands for new lodgings in the nearby village of Still River. As Louisa May Alcott later remarked in "Transcendental Wild Oats," "The world was not ready for Utopia yet, and those who attempted to found it only got laughed at for their pains."[19]

It is tempting to mock the foolishness that was Fruitlands. Yet the experiment did teach in its own way, for there was a principle at stake that would not down. Transcendentalism actually gave birth to three models of millennial reform: Brook Farm, which even before it entered its Fourierist phase was more like New Harmony than not, in that it sought change through social restructuring; Walden, which proclaimed the Transcendentalist's resistance to the shams, delusions, and complexities of modern life in the form of a hermitage convenient to occasional visitors and well stocked with selected classics; and Fruitlands, which assigned the crucial role in the quest for a better life to neither a restructured society nor an isolated individual but instead to a self-conscious family presided over by a Socratic father-teacher. In a sense all three failed—even Walden, since Thoreau did eventually return as a sojourner within civilization. Two of the three occasioned manuals of instruction, however, that remained available to seekers everywhere. Thoreau left *Walden* as a guide to those who would discover their essential natures in solitude and then try to live by their discoveries. The Alcotts left *Little Women,* which preached the values of Fruitlands long after the reality had passed. However decisively Fruitlands failed as a community, it generated an idea against which at least two generations of Americans would measure the quality of their family life and education.

III

Owen's vision was of a new moral world so perfectly ordered and organized as to educe only decency and intelligence in the individuals who inhabited it. Alcott's vision was of transcendent individuals so perfect of being and spirit as to constitute in their collectivity a new moral world. Interestingly, it was in 1827, the very year when Owen's vision

19. Louisa May Alcott, "Transcendental Wild Oats" (1876), in Sears, ed., *Alcott's Fruitlands,* p. 169.

was dissolving in the disorder of New Harmony, that Alcott's vision was first taking visible form in the exhilarating work in Connecticut. And ironically, given the ultimate failure of the Owen and Alcott experiments, it was during that same year that Joseph Smith, an unknown young man of uncertain character, is reputed to have dug up the golden plates on which were engraved the Book of Mormon. Smith's vision was also of a new moral world, in this instance rendered regenerate by the true church of Christ restored to earth. And, while Smith did not live to see his vision realized, it did ultimately inspire the single most successful gathering of Zion in nineteenth-century America, the Great Basin kingdom that became the state of Utah.

Joseph Smith had by his own account slipped into vice and folly by the time the angel Moroni first informed him that he had been chosen by God to resurrect the true church in America. Born in 1805 to a New England farm family, he had spent his boyhood drifting from place to place with his luckless parents, finally settling in Palmyra, a fair-sized community of four thousand in western New York on the projected route of the Erie Canal. There he had gotten caught up in the pervasive instability of a frontier boomtown—the comings and goings of migrants, the frenzied speculation, and the shrill warnings of self-styled seers and prophets. Smith was able to cleanse himself, however, and on September 11, 1827, the angel Moroni permitted him to dig up the plates and carry them to his home. He spent the next three years translating them, producing in the process an extraordinary compound of myths and precepts that drew freely upon the prevailing doctrines of contemporary evangelical Protestantism. On April 6, 1830, Smith founded the Church of Jesus Christ of Latter-day Saints, the initial converts being his own kith and kin; and three months later the Book of Mormon was published.

During the next fourteen years, until his brutal murder in 1844 at the hands of a Carthage, Illinois, lynch mob, Smith, in concert with such trusted lieutenants as Sidney Rigdon, W. W. Phelps, Heber C. Kimball, and Brigham Young, slowly worked out the piety and policy of the new church. Assertively perfectionist, restorationist, and millennial in its theology, it was conceived as a gathered community withdrawn from the gentile world and living according to the ideals of economic communalism, theocratic government, and plural marriage. In Kirtland, Ohio, Independence and Far West, Missouri, and Nauvoo, Illinois, Smith skillfully employed principle, pragmatism, and revelation to develop the blueprint for a new utopia. And, when the Saints, in the aftermath of his death, finally did make their epochal trek to the Great Basin west of the Rockies, that blueprint had already been tried and tested, and waited only for a chance to be realized, away from the interference of hostile neighbors.

Mormonism's earliest appeal was to the disinherited, Yankee and Yorker farmers caught up in the multifarious enthusiasms of the day, many of them former Methodists, Baptists, or sectarian come-outers. Mormonism offered them the perfectionism they so fervently yearned for, but it joined that perfectionism to a highly traditional theology revolving around a personal, omnipotent God standing once again at the center of time and the universe. In place of liberalism, Mormonism preached orthodoxy; in place of individualism, it preached discipline; and, in place of progress, it preached restoration. And its instrument for the realization of these goals would be the model Zion, the perfect community that would educate its citizens to virtue at the same time as it exemplified virtue to an unregenerate world.

There is much to be written about Mormon theology, particularly as it reflected and incorporated certain characteristic values of Jacksonian America. It is not without significance, for example, that Mormonism located Eden as well as Zion within the continental limits of the United States. It was there that the drama of creation and redemption was destined to be played out. It was there that God would work his wonders, via the personal day-by-day efforts of his chosen people. It was there that individual human beings, choosing, aspiring, striving, and achieving, would, like the ancient Hebrews, live under God's law in an eternal covenant with him. It was there that Christ would reappear to preside everlastingly over the city of the Saints. The sacred and the secular would once again be united, each infusing the other with ever richer meaning.

The concept of the faithful gathered out of the bosom of Babylon became a cardinal principle of Mormon doctrine. As Father Lehi had proclaimed in *The Book of Mormon:* "Yea, the Lord hath covenanted this land unto me, and to my children forever, and also all those who should be led out of other countries by the hand of the Lord." And, as Smith himself proclaimed in revelations handed down in 1830 and 1831, the Lord, having sent forth truth in the form of *The Book of Mormon,* had decided to gather his elect to build the New Jerusalem, to which the city of Enoch would one day descend from heaven in millennial greeting. Moreover, the New Jerusalem was to be the American West, and the portal to that New Jerusalem the town of Kirtland,

Ohio, to which the faithful were to repair so that Zion might be chosen and then promptly and everlastingly secured.[20]

It was initially at Kirtland, and then at Independence and Far West, Missouri, and at Nauvoo, Illinois, that Smith, largely in collaboration with Sidney Rigdon, worked out the law of consecration and stewardship, the basis for the Mormons' economic communism. Rigdon, a Campbellite preacher who had been converted to Mormonism along with his entire congregation, had familiarized himself with the Owenite experiment at New Harmony, and had actually organized his congregation at Kirtland as a communistic colony. When he fell out with his fellow Campbellites on the rightness of holding "all things in common," he persuaded Smith to consider the Kirtland congregation as the core of the Mormon gathering there and to adopt the communism of Christ's early disciples as the basis of Mormon living. As Smith formulated the doctrine in a revelation handed down on February 9, 1831, the faithful were obliged to "consecrate" all their property to the presiding bishop and his counselors, who would then assign a "stewardship" to every family on the basis of its needs and just wants, while retaining the remainder for the poor, for general church purposes, and for the building of the New Jerusalem. Once the stewardship had been assigned, it was up to the individual family to determine how and in what ways it would be utilized, which rendered Mormon communism quite different from the several varieties of contemporary Owenism.[21]

In any case, the arrangement did not work, in part for many of the same reasons as bedeviled New Harmony, in part because of the unrelenting opposition of gentile neighbors. By 1838, in a revelation handed down in Far West, Missouri, Smith announced the beginning of tithing among the Mormons, and at about that time, too, several groups of Saints undertook to form cooperative enterprises known as "United Firms," which applied the laws of consecration and stewardship on a much more limited basis. When Zion shifted to Nauvoo, Illinois, the following year, there was no effort to reinstitute the original plan of Kirtland days. But tithing and cooperation, not only with respect to wealth and property, but also with respect to personal time and effort, became integral to Mormon life and remained signal characteristics of the Mormon community from that time forward.[22]

20. *The Book of Mormon*, translated by Joseph Smith, Jr. (Salt Lake City, Utah: The Church of Jesus Christ of Latter-day Saints, 1973), 2 Nephi, 1, 5 (p. 50); and *The Doctrine and Covenants of the Church of Jesus Christ of Latter-day Saints* (Salt Lake City, Utah: The Church of Jesus Christ of Latter-day Saints, 1970), sec. 37, 3; sec. 39, 13–15; sec. 42, 8–9 (pp. 54, 58, 61).
21. *Doctrine and Covenants*, sec. 42, 30–35 (p. 62).
22. *Ibid.*, sec. 119, 1–3 (p. 212).

Joseph Smith once wrote that his inclination in government was toward "theo-democracy," by which he meant that the revealed will of Almighty God, as made known by his prophet, was law and that the priesthood administered the law, though individuals retained free will in accepting or rejecting the law and in approving those who administered it. In actuality, "theo-democracy" took the form of a fascinating combination of autocracy and widespread participation. There were two lay priesthoods, the Aaronic and the Melchizedek, the first declared as a result of the vision of 1829 that led to the founding of the church, the latter declared as a higher priesthood in an 1831 revelation handed down at the initial general conference of the church in Kirtland. Every male convert to Mormonism was a priest (with the exception of blacks, who could be members but who were barred from the priesthood), and most in due course earned some special responsibilities, as deacons, teachers, and elders, which they carried in addition to the regular work that earned them their living. Only elders, however, "regularly ordained by the heads of the church," were permitted to preach. Smith early designated himself First Elder and later took the title President of the High Priesthood (a revealing combination of republican and Biblical terminology). Together with two personally chosen counselors, he formed the First Presidency of the Church.[23]

Essentially, church government was hierarchical, all officers being appointed by their superiors with the consent of the constituency involved—a consent that soon became for all intents and purposes a formality. During the 1830's, a series of five councils oversaw affairs in various domains and all five were presumed to be co-equal; in reality, however, the Council—or Quorum, as it was called—of the Twelve Apostles, which worked closely with the President and subsequently filled vacancies in the Presidency, was supreme. The President, as God's spokesman on earth, promulgated doctrine and oversaw the affairs of the kingdom; all acts, appointments, and appropriations within the church were carried out in his name. In addition, there was the Presiding Bishop of the Church, who oversaw its financial affairs but who worked within policies set by the Presidency and the Quorum.

During the 1830's and early 1840's, the spiritual and temporal affairs of the kingdom were seen as one, and local church congregations, each presided over by a resident bishop, concerned themselves with a wide range of activities, from the religious instruction of the young to the care of the aged and infirm. By 1844, however, Smith and his asso-

23. Journal History of the Church of Latter-day Saints, April 15, 1844 (ms. collections, Church Historian's Office, Salt Lake City, Utah); and *Doctrine and Covenants*, sec. 42, 11 (p. 61).

ciates saw the need to solve the problem that every Zion that permits the unregenerate to live within its bounds must sooner or later confront, namely, the devising of some governmental arrangement that will secure a reasonable degree of consent. Their response was the creation of the Council of Fifty, a mixed group of Mormons and gentiles entrusted with regulating the affairs of the community (in this instance, of Nauvoo). The Quorum of the Twelve Apostles served as ex-officio members, and the president of the church was the president of the Council—once again indicating the unity of the religious and political kingdoms of God. In the period following Smith's death in 1844, it was Brigham Young's ability to win the confidence of the Quorum and the Council of Fifty and to govern through them as President of the High Priesthood that decisively established his leadership in the exodus to the Great Basin and the establishment of the new Zion there.

By the 1840's, the gathered community withdrawn from the world and living under God's law according to the principles of consecration, stewardship, and theo-democracy had become the essence of Mormonism. But, to many contemporaries, all these features were secondary to the principle of plural marriage. There is evidence to the effect that Joseph Smith had prepared a revelation on polygamy as early as 1831, but none was published at that time. And there is also indication in the autobiographies of Orson Pratt and W. W. Phelps that the prophet had discussed the idea from time to time during the later 1830's. But it was in the Nauvoo period that the principle of plural marriage was first set forth in detail. Essentially, it maintained that souls exist through eternity, that only the most infinitesimal part of that existence is spent on earth (although the actions of souls on earth powerfully affect existence through eternity), that an earthly marriage sealed in the temple is a covenant for time and eternity and hence celestial in character, that the married state for time and eternity is more blessed and godlike than the unmarried state, and that plural marriage, insofar as it provides physical bodies for the innumerable souls awaiting earthly tabernacles, is in the last analysis a fulfillment of the Lord's commandment, "Be fruitful, and multiply, and replenish the earth."[24]

It should be noted that only a small number of Mormons, principally Smith and his closer associates, undertook plural marriage during the 1840's and that it was not until the removal to the Great Basin and the relative isolation there that any significant number of Mormons ever did. Even then, there probably never was a time when more than a

24. Genesis 1:28.

fifth or a sixth of the families in Utah were polygamous. In effect, therefore, whatever its theological sanction and justification, plural marriage was always a minority practice within the Mormon community, though it was a practice of the more highly prestigious element.

In 1833, in connection with the planting of the Mormon community in Jackson County, Missouri, the prophet designed a plan for the City of Zion that was to exercise considerable influence during the ensuing half-century. It was conceived as a square mile in size and intended for a population of some fifteen to twenty thousand. Three central blocks were set aside for public buildings, with the remainder of the city laid out on a grid pattern with designated areas for commercial and residential use. The city was to be circumscribed by farm lands and thereby limited with respect to expansion. "When this square is thus laid off and supplied," Smith wrote, "lay off another in the same way, and so fill up the world in these last days; and let every man live in the city for this is the City of Zion." Far West, Missouri, was developed according to the plan, and then Nauvoo, Illinois, and then Winter Quarters in the Nebraska Territory, where the Saints encamped temporarily during the exodus of 1847, and finally Salt Lake City and a dozen other communities in the territory of Utah.[25]

Within this carefully planned physical layout, doubtless representing Smith's version of the square Biblical cities described in Leviticus and Numbers, the Mormons developed the particular constellation of institutions that gave social embodiment to their religious aspirations. The characteristic Mormon community assumed its early form in Missouri, was further developed in Nauvoo, and reached its full flowering in Salt Lake City, where, ironically, at the very peak of its development, it encountered the forces that would later engulf it and reintegrate it into the gentile world. Three elements were critical in sustaining this community: the particular complex of values that Thomas O'Dea has aptly characterized as "the transcendentalism of achievement"; the configuration of mutually supportive educative institutions devoted to transmitting and nurturing those values; and a relative isolation from competing values and social systems.[26]

The Mormon conception of the universe as evolving, developing, and advancing, and of each individual's choices on earth as ultimately

25. John W. Reps, *The Making of Urban America: A History of City Planning in the United States* (Princeton, N.J.: Princeton University Press, 1965), pp. 466–472. Reps notes that Smith's city was intended for a population of fifteen to twenty thousand persons and had only around a thousand house lots, indicating that the average hosuehold size was expected to be between fifteen and twenty.

26. Thomas F. O'Dea, *The Mormons* (Chicago: University of Chicago Press, 1957), p. 150.

decisive with respect to his lot in eternity, placed immense emphasis on personal agency, activity, and achievement. Moreover, Smith's millennialist prophecies of "last days," of the need to prepare for Christ's literal return that would mark the miraculous restoration of the earth to its first glory, placed a tremendous premium on the prudent use of earthly time by those free to choose the Lord's way. Taken together, these precepts combined possibility and urgency into an immensely powerful work ethic: whether in farming the land, or building the temple, or studying the Scriptures, or caring for the infirm, the Mormon was simultaneously assisting God in gaining mastery over the universe and advancing himself in likeness to God.

These values were purveyed, realized, and celebrated within a configuration of interacting and complementary educative institutions that touched every aspect of life in the Mormon community. Despite the practice of polygamy on the part of a segment of the population, Mormon households tended to remain separate and patriarchal; hence, though polygamy patently altered and extended kin relationships and surely placed greater stress and obligation on the mothers of plural families, it does not appear to have radically altered contemporary patterns of childrearing. Fathers and mothers of monogamous and polygamous families alike transmitted the achievement ethic, and they were encouraged and assisted in this endeavor by numerous local officials in the two priestly orders and by the formal rituals of the local congregation and the central temple. Beyond the education of family and church, the values and outlooks of Mormonism were reinforced by a school system; a university (which derived from the School of the Prophets first organized by Smith himself in 1833); a plethora of books, pamphlets, newspapers, and magazines; a profusion of public lectures; and a wide variety of clubs, societies, and associations—all sponsored, controlled, or influenced in one way or another by church authorities. And, beyond all these, there was the critically important education implicit in participation: in the lay priesthoods, in church conferences, in missionary activities, in the Nauvoo Legion (the Mormon militia), in the Women's Relief Society, in economic cooperatives, and in other community organizations. Mormonism was not only activist in its organization, it invited—nay required—extensive participation in its programs.

Finally, given these integrative activities within the community, there was the advantage of isolation. It was never complete isolation, of course. The California gold rush sent a steady stream of travelers through the Promised Land, though here as elsewhere in the economic realm the Mormons turned a problem into an advantage and saw to it that Salt Lake City became an important (and lucrative) way station on the road to California. The railroad turned that stream into a river, and here, too, the Mormons gained economically by investing in the roads and the trade they made possible. Certainly during the years of Brigham Young's ascendancy, though there was continuing conflict with the United States government, especially over polygamy, the Mormon kingdom prospered as an enclave within the American commonwealth. By the time of Young's death in 1877, there must have been some 150,000 Mormons in Utah and its environs, testifying eloquently to the vitality of Mormon educational institutions (both at home and abroad, for the Mormon ranks had been significantly enlarged by thousands of converts who had come from Europe after having been won over by Mormon missionaries) and surely establishing the Mormon kingdom as the most fruitful millennialist community in nineteenth-century America.

In a sense, Mormonism represents all the sectarian communities that retreated from the world with a design for perfection and succeeded, at least in that elemental definition of success that assumes, at the minimum, survival. Some of these communities, like the Shakers, survived with their ideals intact and continued essentially in the image projected by their founders. Others, like the Mennonites, survived while undergoing subtle and significant transformations deriving from their location within the American society. Still others, like the Oneida community, survived in their projected form for a time and then underwent radical alteration. For all these ventures, there were persistent problems of education. In the first place, there was the problem of transmitting essential values, which was especially difficult in those communities which could perpetuate themselves only by recruitment, as was the case with the Shakers, but by no means simple even in communities that did not practice celibacy. Second, there was the problem of interpreting or contravening the outside educational influences that entered the community through trade, or preaching, or literature, or, toward the end of the century, compulsory schooling. And, finally, there was the problem of maintaining consent amidst the incessant internal squabbles over doctrine and the constant defections to the external world. Yet the communities persisted, forming social, cultural, and educational enclaves within the larger American society, inevitably sharing many of its patterns and values while at the same time rejecting others, and in the end creating composite rather than homogeneous cultural entities. In persisting, though they failed to convert the larger society, they did teach it, in such varied realms as productive craftsmanship, economic cooperation, social discipline, and millennial hope.

John Humphrey Noyes, who founded the Oneida community after being converted to Charles Grandison Finney's earlier perfectionism, observed in his *History of American Socialisms* (1870) that religion had to be at the base of any successful communitarian venture, by which he meant an integrating value system that controlled "all external arrangements." Noyes was probably correct, though his observation implied as well that the value system, to be successful in its disciplining of power, had to be shared by contemporaries if the community was to function and by future generations if the community was to survive. In the absence of education, the most deeply held religion would be ephemeral, and the most sectarian of communities transitory, as countless charismatic leaders learned to their bitter disappointment in the crucible of nineteenth-century America.[27]

27. John Humphrey Noyes, *History of American Socialisms* (1870; New York: Hillary House, 1961), p. 655. See also Charles Nordhoff, *The Communistic Societies of the United States* (1875; New York: Schocken Books, 1965), p. 408.

PART II

THE VIRTUOUS REPUBLIC

Promote then as an object of primary importance, institutions for the general diffusion of knowledge. In proportion as the structure of government gives force to public opinion, it is essential that public opinion should be enlightened.

GEORGE WASHINGTON

INTRODUCTION

No theme was so universally articulated during the early decades of the Republic as the need of a self-governing people for universal education. The argument pervaded the discourse of the Revolutionary generation. Washington included it in the farewell address that marked his decision not to stand again for the presidency in 1796. "It is substantially true," he observed, "that virtue or morality is a necessary spring of popular government. The rule indeed extends with more or less force to every species of free government. Who that is a sincere friend to it can look with indifference upon attempts to shake the foundation of the fabric? Promote then as an object of primary importance institutions for the general diffusion of knowledge. In proportion as the structure of a government gives force to public opinion, it is essential that public opinion should be enlightened." John Adams proffered similar advice in his inaugural address, despite his growing disenchantment by the 1790's with his earlier hopes for the perfectibility of mankind. And Jefferson and Madison sounded the theme again and again in their public speeches and private correspondence, as indeed did countless governors, legislators, stump speakers, and Fourth of July orators in every region of the country. By the 1820's, the need of a self-governing people for universal education had become a familiar part of the litany of American politics.[1]

Yet, beneath the rhetoric of high aspiration concerning the need, there were major disagreements concerning the means. Washington, for example, never elucidated what he meant by institutions for the general diffusion of knowledge, though there is evidence that what he most de-

---

1. *The Writings of George Washington from the Original Manuscript Sources, 1745-1799,* edited by John C. Fitzpatrick (39 vols.; Washington, D.C.: Government Printing Office, 1931-1944), XXXV, 229-230.

sired in 1796 as an instrument for enlightening public opinion was a national university located in the capital city. Jefferson, on the other hand, spelled out quite explicitly in his several bills of 1779 what he meant by institutions for the general diffusion of knowledge: they included public primary schools, quasi-public grammar schools, a publicly controlled college (the College of William and Mary), and a great public reference library at Richmond. But Jefferson as president doubted that Congress had the power under the Constitution to establish a national university, and in 1806 he actually suggested that a constitutional amendment would be required before Congress could properly consider the possibility. John Adams continued to believe in the role of the churches in nurturing the public discipline required for the successful operation of a free society; Jefferson and Madison, on the contrary, led the campaign for disestablishment in Virginia that culminated in the 1786 Statute for Religious Freedom. And Adams never really forgave the press for its calumnious attacks on his administration and his person during the hard-fought election of 1800; but Jefferson, who suffered similar attacks, continued to view the press as an agency whose capacity for enlightening the public exceeded even that of the schools.

Granted the depth and intensity of these disagreements—and they reflected even more extensive disagreements among ordinary citizens—Americans did develop a degree of consensus during the early decades of the nineteenth century concerning what a broad public education in the arts of self-government might be. That education would center in three essential components: popular schooling, for the purpose of conveying literacy along with a certain common core of knowledge, morality, and patriotism; a free press, to give voice to multiple views on important public issues and thereby to help form an enlightened public opinion; and a host of voluntary associations, ranging from civic organizations to political parties to the agencies of government itself. Equipped by schooling with the skills of literacy and by newspapers with up-to-date information, a free American citizenry would learn the business of self-government by governing, by actually experiencing the formulating, debating, legislating, and carrying out of public policies. It was a heady vision of a new world in the making, in which men and, somewhat differently, women of every social background—rich and poor, German and French, Protestant and Catholic— would take part in the great experiment as to whether a people could manage its own affairs.

Rich and poor, German and French, Protestant and Catholic—but not black and red. For all the talk of refuge and asylum, American notions of citizenship managed to transcend the barriers of class, ethnicity, religion, and even—with persisting unclarities—gender, but not the barriers of race. Blacks and Indians were excluded from citizenship and hence from education for self-government. They were subjected instead to a demeaning education by the dominant white community that barred them from participating in public affairs. In the treatment they were accorded, the virtue of the Republic was sorely tested, and found wanting.

Chapter 4

REPUBLICAN CIVILITIES

It may be an easy thing to make a republic, but it is a very laborious thing to make republicans.

HORACE MANN

In 1823, at the ripe age of seventy-seven, Thomas Jefferson set out to "make some memoranda, and state some recollections of dates and facts concerning myself, for my own more ready reference, and for the information of my family." The autobiography that resulted was spare and unrevealing at best and broke off abruptly with Jefferson's arrival in New York during the spring of 1790 to take up his post as secretary of state in the new administration. But, in the fragment that was completed, Jefferson did take the opportunity to reflect on the revisal of the laws of Virginia that he had pressed with such vigor during the years between 1776 and 1779. In retrospect, four of the bills in particular had seemed to him to form a system "by which every fibre would be eradicated of ancient or future aristocracy; and a foundation laid for a government truly republican." The repeal of the laws of entail and primogeniture would prevent the accumulation of wealth in select families and remove the feudal distinctions that rendered one member of a family rich and the rest poor. The Bill for Religious Freedom would relieve the people of the odious burden of supporting a religion not theirs. And the Bill for the More General Diffusion of Knowledge would qualify them to "understand their rights, to maintain them, and to exercise with intelligence their parts in self-government."[1]

Actually, for all the vigor of his leadership during the early phases of the revisal, Jefferson was in France during much of the time the

1. "Autobiography," in *The Writings of Thomas Jefferson,* edited by Paul Leicester Ford (10 vols.; New York: G. P. Putnam's Sons, 1891–1899), I, 1, 68, 69.

bills were before the legislature. Those abolishing entail and primogeniture were passed in 1785, and the one establishing religious freedom was finally enacted in 1786, though only after Patrick Henry's alternative Bill for Religious Assessments had been defeated under the
skillful leadership of James Madison (Henry's bill had justified tax
support for the Christian religion generally on the ground of the state's
right to diffuse knowledge). The Bill for the More General Diffusion
of Knowledge, however, which Jefferson saw as the most important in
the whole code, fared less well (as did its companion measures to
amend the charter of the College of William and Mary and to establish
a major public library in Richmond—both of which received cursory
consideration at best and ultimately failed to pass in either house). The
bill came before the House of Delegates in 1778 and again in 1780,
and was actually passed by the House in 1785, but it failed in the Senate. Writing from France, Jefferson urged his friend George Wythe,
who had served with him on the original committee of revisers, to re-
double his efforts on behalf of the measure. "Preach, my dear sir, a
crusade against ignorance; establish and improve the law for educating
the common people. Let our countrymen know . . . that the tax which
will be paid for this purpose is not more than the thousandth part of
what will be paid to kings, priests and nobles who will rise up among
us if we leave the people in ignorance." But it was to no avail. The
measure came before the House in 1786 and was again rejected. "The
necessity of a systematic provision on the subject was admitted on all
hands," Madison wrote from Virginia, informing Jefferson of the failure. But apparently the cost of the program and the difficulty of carrying it out, given the sparseness of population in many areas, had kept
the requisite support from materializing. Ten years later, when the
matter came again to the fore, the legislature approved that part of the
bill which provided for elementary schools, but inserted a local option
clause empowering the county courts to determine whether and when to
institute the program. It was Jefferson's belief that the clause effectively emasculated the bill, since the local justices, being generally men of
wealth, had little interest in being taxed for the education of the poor.[2]

Jefferson gave only passing attention to education during his tenure
as vice-president and president of the United States. He continued his

2. Thomas Jefferson to George Wythe, August 13, 1786, in *The Papers of Thomas Jefferson*,
edited by Julian P. Boyd *et al.* (19+ vols.; Princeton, N.J.: Princeton University Press, 1950–   ),
X, 245; and James Madison to Thomas Jefferson, February 15, 1787, in *The Writings of James
Madison*, edited by Gaillard Hunt (9 vols.; New York: G. P. Putnam's Sons, 1900–1910), II, 308.

correspondence with friends such as Joseph Priestley and Pierre Samuel Du Pont de Nemours concerning the proper system of schooling for a republic. He noted in his second inaugural address that the federal government might soon have a surplus of revenues and urged that the Constitution be amended to permit the excess to go to the states for the development of "rivers, canals, roads, arts, manufactures, education, and other great objects within each state." And he did press forward his interest in a national university, encouraging Joel Barlow to develop plans for such an institution and recommending to the Congress in 1806 that the necessary legislation (and Constitutional amendment) be adopted. But the efforts were half-hearted at best and eventually came to naught; indeed, on the matter of the surplus revenues he may even have changed his opinion by the time of his retirement. Once back in Monticello as a private citizen, however, Jefferson again focused his concern on the question of education in Virginia.[3]

The legislation of 1796 had changed nothing, since no county court had exercised its prerogative of initiating the program. Thus the problem in Jefferson's view was still to erect a comprehensive system that would at the same time provide a general education for the electorate at large and afford additional educational opportunity to potential leaders. In an oft-cited letter to his nephew Peter Carr in 1814, he divided the citizenry into two general classes, the laboring and the learned, and then specified the establishment of elementary schools for all white children and the opportunity for further schooling in "general schools" (the academies of the bill of 1779) and "professional schools" for those headed toward positions of political, social, and intellectual leadership. Three years later he sent to his trusted lieutenant, Joseph Carrington Cabell, a package of bills providing for local elementary schools, district colleges (again, the academies of the bill of 1779), and a university to be erected on the foundation of Central College in Jefferson's own home county of Albemarle. The elementary schools were to be supported by local taxation, while the district colleges and the university were to be partially financed by income from the state literary fund, an endowment that had been established in 1810 for the purpose of aiding specified educational causes. The program came into conflict with an alternative arrangement put forward by Charles Fenton Mercer, a Federalist spokesman for the western interests of the state, which

3. Second Inaugural Address, March 4, 1805, in Saul K. Padover, ed., *The Complete Jefferson* (New York: Tudor Publishing, 1943), p. 411.

would have assigned the burden of income from the literary fund to the primary schools and which would have located the state university in the Shenandoah Valley. The result was that neither proposal attracted the necessary votes for passage. A substitute measure was enacted, providing only for the education of the poor in such elementary schools as were available, and it was onto that measure that Cabell "engrafted" the provision for a university. The hastily wrought legislation turned Jefferson decisively—though never solely—to the consideration of higher education.[4]

Cabell's provision stipulated that the governor appoint a commission to meet at Rockfish Gap on August 1, 1818, to determine a site for the university and sketch a plan for its organization, its program, and its buildings. Twenty-one commissioners duly met from August 1 through 4, elected Jefferson chairman, selected Charlottesville (the location of Central College) as the site of the university, and adopted as their own a report on organization and program that Jefferson had drafted the previous June. The document is immensely revealing of Jefferson's larger view of education and for that reason bears close scrutiny. The objects of primary education, Jefferson suggested, were as follows:

> To give every citizen the information he needs for the transaction of his own business;
> To enable him to calculate for himself, and to express and preserve his ideas, his contracts and accounts, in writing;
> To improve, by reading, his morals and faculties;
> To understand his duties to his neighbors and country, and to discharge with competence the functions confided to him by either;
> To know his rights; to exercise with order and justice those he retains; to choose with discretion the fiduciary of those he delegates; and to notice their conduct with diligence, with candor, and judgment;
> And, in general, to observe with intelligence and faithfulness all the social relations under which he shall be placed.

The subjects Jefferson thought would achieve these goals were reading, writing, arithmetic, mensuration, geography, and history—essentially the list included in the bill of 1779, with mensuration and geography added.[5]

---

4. Thomas Jefferson to Peter Carr, September 7, 1814, in *The Writings of Thomas Jefferson*, edited by Andrew A. Lipscomb and Albert Ellery Bergh (20 vols.; Washington, D.C.: Thomas Jefferson Memorial Association, 1903–1904), XIX, 211–221; and Joseph C. Cabell to Thomas Jefferson, February 20, 1818, in *Early History of the University of Virginia as Contained in the Letters of Thomas Jefferson and Joseph C. Cabell* (Richmond: J. W. Randolph, 1856), p. 125.

5. Report of the Commissioners for the University of Virginia, August 1–4, 1818, in Padover, ed., *Complete Jefferson*, p. 1097.

Similarly, the objects of higher education were:

To form the statesmen, legislators and judges, on whom public prosperity and individual happiness are so much to depend;

To expound the principles and structure of government, the laws which regulate the intercourse of nations, those formed municipally for our own government, and a sound spirit of legislation, which, banishing all arbitrary and unnecessary restraint on individual action, shall leave us free to do whatever does not violate the equal rights of another;

To harmonize and promote the interests of agriculture, manufactures and commerce, and by well-informed views of political economy to give a free scope to the public industry;

To develop the reasoning faculties of our youth, enlarge their minds, cultivate their morals, and instill into them the precepts of virtue and order;

To enlighten them with mathematical and physical sciences, which advance the arts, and administer to the health, the subsistence, and comforts of human life;

And, generally, to form them to habits of reflection and correct action, rendering them examples of virtue to others, and of happiness within themselves.

The subjects Jefferson thought would achieve these goals were ancient languages (Latin, Greek, Hebrew), modern languages (French, Spanish, Italian, German, Anglo-Saxon), pure mathematics (algebra, fluxions, geometry, architecture), physico-mathematics (mechanics, statics, dynamics, pneumatics, acoustics, optics, astronomy, geography), natural philosophy (chemistry and mineralogy), botany (including zoology), anatomy (including medicine), government (political economy, the law of nature and nations, and history), municipal law, and ideology (grammar, ethics, rhetoric, belles-lettres, and the fine arts). Divinity, incidentally, was nowhere mentioned, its substance having been left in part to the professor who would teach ideology and in part to the several sects, which were invited to provide, "as they think fittest, the means of further instruction in their own peculiar tenets."[6]

The entire scheme, Jefferson maintained, was founded upon the view that human nature was not fixed, that man was essentially improvable, and that education was the chief means of effecting that improvement. "Education . . . engrafts a new man on the native stock," Jefferson asserted, "and improves what in his nature was vicious and perverse into qualities of virtue and social worth. And it cannot be but that each generation succeeding to the knowledge acquired by all those who preceded it, adding to it their own acquisitions and discoveries, and handing the mass down for successive and constant accumulation,

6. *Ibid.*, p. 1098.

must advance the knowledge and well-being of mankind, not *infinitely,* as some have said, but *indefinitely,* and to a term which no one can fix and foresee." It was an optimistic philosophy, though not romantically optimistic. "My theory has always been," he wrote to the Marquis de Barbé-Marbois, "that if we are to dream, the flatteries of hope are as cheap, and pleasanter than the gloom of despair."[7]

The report was presented to the legislature in December and adopted the following month. But it would be another six long years before the buildings would be ready, the faculty recruited, and a genuine university erected on the foundations of Central College. During that time, with Jefferson serving as rector (chairman of the board of visitors), the principle of election—or choice among schools—was introduced, the ten chairs originally envisioned (one for each of the major subject areas) were reduced to eight (law and government were combined and phys-ico-mathematics was dropped), and the various Christian denominations were invited to establish theological seminaries on the "confines" (borders) of the university. But, in the main, the Rockfish Gap report proved decisive in the shaping of the institution. For all the genuine contributions of others, notably Joseph C. Cabell, James Madison, and Francis Gilmer, the university was, in Emerson's phrase, the "lengthened shadow of one man."[8]

By the time of Jefferson's death in 1826, a substantial portion of his program for education had come to pass. The church had been disestablished and its teaching relegated to a more private—though not wholly private—sphere; a university had been founded under public auspices; and a press that had consistently extended its freedom despite its ever-sharpening attacks on leading public figures, including Jefferson, was daily performing its vital—if cacophonous—function of public enlightenment. But the great library at Richmond had not been built, and neither had the small circulating libraries Jefferson had recommended for each county of the state in 1809. More importantly, perhaps, the system of free primary schools envisioned in the Bill for the More General Diffusion of Knowledge had not been established. Opinion has been divided concerning Jefferson's own culpability in the latter failure. There can be no denying his steadfast commitment to popular

7. *Ibid.,* p. 1099; Thomas Jefferson to M. de Barbé-Marbois, June 14, 1817, in *Writings of Thomas Jefferson,* edited by Lipscomb and Bergh, XV, 131.

8. Report of the Rector and Visitors of the University of Virginia, October 7, 1822, in *Early History of the University of Virginia,* p. 474; and Ralph Waldo Emerson, "Self-Reliance," in *The Complete Works of Ralph Waldo Emerson* (12 vols.; Boston: Houghton Mifflin and Company, 1903–1904), II, 61.

schooling: he reiterated it time and again during the years following 1809 and even went so far as to remark to Cabell in 1823 that, if forced to choose between the university and the primary schools, he would choose the latter. Nevertheless, the fact remains that by 1823 he had made a choice, and his choice had been the university. His preference may well have been the reflection of an inveterate elitism under all the rhetoric, as some have claimed. But it was more likely the reflection of a stubborn popularism joined to a characteristic localism. From the beginning, Jefferson had viewed the "hundreds" (later "wards")—subdivisions of counties roughly six square miles in area—that would have responsibility for the primary schools as the basic units of local government, miniature republics where every man might enjoy direct participation in public affairs, caring not only for education but also for police protection, roads, the poor, the militia company, and other immediate concerns. In Jefferson's mind, the primary schools and the hundreds were inseparable. When Charles Fenton Mercer's bill of 1817 proposed a state-sponsored system of primary schools along with state-aided academies and colleges *and* a state university somewhere in the Shenandoah Valley, Jefferson (through Cabell) opposed it. The immediate reasons were pragmatic—Jefferson did not think the literary fund could or should support all the endeavors simultaneously and he wanted the state university at Charlottesville first. But the deeper reasons were ideological—Jefferson had come to see an inextricable connection between education and politics at the local level that was quite as significant to him as the general need for an educated electorate and a wise leadership, and that connection proved decisive as he chose among the political options available after 1809. His choices may not have been wise or prudent but they were at the least considered.[9]

Finally, Jefferson's popularism itself, though radical for its time, was also subject to limitations characteristic of the time. He wanted the slaves emancipated and even educated, but only so that they could return to Africa. He wanted the Indians amalgamated, but ended up concurring as president in the policy of Indian removal. He cared deeply about the education of his daughters, but wrote to Nathaniel Burwell in 1818 that he had never thought systematically about the education of females, although he did comment on the advantages of teaching them dancing, drawing, music, household economy, and French literature

9. Thomas Jefferson to Joseph C. Cabell, January 13, 1823, in *Early History of the University of Virginia*, p. 267; and Thomas Jefferson to Major John Cartwright, June 5, 1824, in *Writings of Thomas Jefferson*, edited by Lipscomb and Bergh, XVI, 46.

and alerting them to the danger of novels. Granted his abiding concern with the education of the people, he defined the people in political terms—as free white males.

However that may be, the influence of Jefferson's educational thought, during the nineteenth century and into the twentieth, was powerful and pervasive. The University of Virginia became the model of the American state university from the time of its founding through the passage of the Morrill Act in 1862, and Jeffersonian disciples such as Philip Lindsley, Augustus B. Woodward, and Thomas Cooper were for a generation in the forefront of movements to extend higher education. Similarly, the Bill for Religious Freedom became the model statute for other states seeking to disestablish the Christian religion, while Jeffersonian rhetoric about the indispensability of a free press —"Where the press is free, and every man able to read, all is safe"— became the rhetoric of editors everywhere, and of the judges who defended them. Most important, perhaps, despite the failure of the primary school effort, the Jeffersonian program for popular schooling, with its assertions about the inextricable ties between education and freedom, was acknowledged in every region, by reformers as different as Henry W. Collier in Alabama, Robert Dale Owen in New York, and Horace Mann in Massachusetts. The prophet unarmed in Virginia proved triumphant everywhere else and became in effect the patron saint of American popular education.[10]

I I

Jefferson passed from the scene with a profound sense of his role as author of the Declaration of Independence; his friend Benjamin Rush lived his life with an equally profound sense of his role as a signer. For Rush, who was present in the Congress as a representative of Pennsylvania, the events surrounding the creation of the Republic marked nothing less than a turning point in the course of human history. "I was animated constantly," he reflected in later years, "by a belief that I was acting for the benefit of the whole world, and of future ages, by assisting in the formation of new means of political order and general happiness."[11]

10. Thomas Jefferson to Colonel Charles Yancey, January 6, 1816, in *Writings of Thomas Jefferson,* edited by Ford, X, 4.

11. *The Autobiography of Benjamin Rush,* edited by George W. Corner (Princeton, N.J.: Princeton University Press, 1948), p. 161.

REPUBLICAN CIVILITIES 115

The self-justifying reminiscences of an old man, perhaps. Yet there is abundant evidence of their legitimacy, for Rush's republicanism was scarcely new in 1776. A native of Pennsylvania, he had been educated at Samuel Finley's academy at Nottingham (Finley was his uncle), then at the College of New Jersey, where he remained only briefly from the spring of 1759 through September, 1760, having been admitted to the junior class, then via an apprenticeship with Dr. John Redman of Philadelphia, during which he attended the lectures of John Morgan and William Shippen at the College of Philadelphia, and then at the University of Edinburgh, with clinical work at Middlesex and St. Thomas hospitals in London (after the fashion of John Morgan). While in Europe he was introduced to Whig radicalism, first by his fellow student John Bostock, who directed him to Locke and Sydney ("Never before had I heard the authority of kings called in question. I had been taught to consider them nearly as essential to political order as the sun is to the order of our solar system"), and then by the circle around Catharine Macaulay, which included James Burgh, John Sawbridge, and Adam Ferguson. He returned from Europe to a professorship of chemistry at the College of Philadelphia—the first formal chair of its kind in America—and proceeded to build a thriving practice, something of an accomplishment since he was a Presbyterian Whig in a city whose middling and upper classes included large numbers of Anglican and Quaker Tories.[12]

It was as one of Philadelphia's most promising young professionals, then, that Rush greeted the great and near-great as they gathered for the First Continental Congress in 1774. For a while it seemed as if he was everywhere and knew everyone. He helped welcome John Adams and Robert Treat Paine to the city. He entertained George Washington, John and Samuel Adams, Thomas Mifflin, and Charles Lee in his home. He inoculated Patrick Henry against smallpox. He encouraged Thomas Paine in his pamphleteering and actually suggested the title of *Common Sense*. And, by way of culmination, he was himself elected to the Congress in 1776, in good time to sign the Declaration and take part in the establishment of the Confederation. Yet politics was not Rush's forte. He labored indefatigably but tactlessly as a congressman, managing to make as many enemies as friends, and was not returned in 1777. He then accepted a commission in the medical department of the army, only to find himself appalled by conditions in the military hospi-

12. *Ibid.,* p. 46.

tals and thereafter quarreling incessantly with his superiors, including Washington. He resigned his commission in 1778, embittered but not defeated, and spent the next three years on the margins of the Revolution. It was only after Yorktown that he seemed to come into his own, laboring ceaselessly in the cause of the more fundamental revolution he saw yet to be accomplished—the revolution that would bring the principles, morals, and manners of the citizenry into conformity with republican modes of government.

During the next decade, Rush carried on what Lyman H. Butterfield has aptly called "a one-man crusade to remake America." He devoted himself with seemingly inexhaustible energy to campaigns for free schools, a national university, prison reform, free postage for newspapers, churches for blacks, temperance, emancipation, the education of women, and the abolition of capital punishment. At the heart of it all was a vast and comprehensive program of popular education. So far as Rush was concerned, the Revolution had ushered in more than another new society; it had quite literally heralded the millennium. "Republican forms of government are the best repositories of the Gospel," he wrote to the Universalist theologian Elhanan Winchester; "I therefore suppose they are intended as preludes to a glorious manifestation of its power and influence upon the hearts of men." But the hearts of men needed to be formed, inspired, and prepared for the millennium, and that was a task for the educator who, in a post-Revolutionary age, could teach the truths of republicanism and Christianity confident in the knowledge that they were overlapping and inextricably interwoven with one another.[13]

"The business of education has acquired a new complexion by the independence of our country," Rush proclaimed in 1786. "The form of government we have assumed, has created a new class of duties to every American. It becomes us, therefore, to examine our former habits upon this subject, and in laying the foundations for nurseries of wise and good men, to adapt our modes of teaching to the peculiar form of our government." What might such an adaptation involve? In Pennsylvania, at least, it meant the development of a three-level system of schooling, comprising free district or township schools that would teach reading, writing, arithmetic, and the English and German languages, four

13. *Letters of Benjamin Rush,* edited by L. H. Butterfield (2 vols.; Princeton, N.J.: Princeton University Press, 1951), I, lxviii; and Benjamin Rush to Elhanan Winchester, November 12, 1791, in *ibid.,* I, 611.

colleges in various regions of the state, where young men might be instructed in mathematics and the higher branches of science, and a university at Philadelphia that would offer courses in law, medicine, and divinity, politics, economics, and natural philosophy. By such an arrangement, Rush argued, the whole state would be "tied together by one system of education. The university will in time furnish masters for the colleges, and colleges will furnish masters for the free schools, while the free schools, in their turns, will supply the colleges and the university with scholars, students and pupils. The same systems of grammar, oratory and philosophy, will be taught in every part of the state, and the literary features of Pennsylvania will thus designate one great, and equally enlightened family."[14]

The emphasis on a single system, and the notions of uniformity associated with it, are worthy of note; for, although they were enunciated within the context of Pennsylvania's variegated culture, they were in many ways characteristically republican. "Our schools of learning," Rush argued, "by producing one general, and uniform system of education, will render the mass of people more homogeneous, and thereby fit them more easily for uniform and peaceable government." It was a theme that ran throughout the republican literature on education, namely, the need for some minimal core of shared knowledge and values that seemed essential to the functioning of popular government. Jefferson expressed it in his *Notes on the State of Virginia* (1785) when he asked, concerning immigration, whether the heterogeneity that would derive from the notion of America as asylum ("They [the immigrants] will infuse into it their spirit, warp and bias its directions, and render it a heterogeneous, incoherent, distracted mass") was compatible with the needs of America as a republic ("It is for the happiness of those united in society to harmonize as much as possible in matters which they must of necessity transact together").[15]

Each republican, of course, had his own ideas about the substance of the core of shared values. For Rush, it was a characteristic mixture of Christianity and Enlightenment liberalism. In the lower schools, youngsters would be nurtured in the doctrine of the New Testament.

14. Benjamin Rush, *Essays, Literary, Moral and Philosophical* (2d ed.; Philadelphia: Thomas and William Bradford, 1806), pp. 6–7, 4.
15. Rush, *Essays*, pp. 7–8. By "system" Rush meant a curriculum, not the organization of the schools. Thomas Jefferson, *Notes on the State of Virginia* (1785), in *Writings of Thomas Jefferson*, edited by Ford, III, 190, 189.

"Without this there can be no virtue, and without virtue there can be no liberty, and liberty is the object and life of all republican governments." Beyond religion they would be taught the duties and principles of republicanism and the necessary bonds of affection for their fellow citizens. And, by way of facilitating such instruction, they would be subjected to a temperate diet, intermittent manual labor, moderate sleep, and regular solitude, the last being especially important to Rush in light of his dubiety about the standard practice of crowding youngsters together in large groups for purposes of instruction. "From these observations that have been made," Rush concluded, "it is plain, that I consider it is possible to convert men into republican machines. This must be done, if we expect them to perform their parts properly, in the great machine of the government of the state." Once again the leitmotif was harmony—the harmony of the Newtonian machine, running according to God's rational law, dispensing throughout society the benefits of peace and prosperity.[16]

For those who proceeded on to the colleges, Rush urged an emphasis on English rather than the classical languages ("Too much pains cannot be taken to teach our youth to read and write our American language with propriety and elegance"), with concomitant attention to French and German. In addition, he thought young men should study rhetoric, history (especially the history of ancient republics), political economy ("I consider its effects as next to those of religion in humanizing mankind"), chemistry (Rush's own subject), and "all the means of promoting national prosperity and independence, whether they relate to improvements in agriculture, manufactures, or inland navigation." Interestingly, he omitted the usual moral philosophy course, thinking that it had become in American colleges "a regular system of instruction in practical deism."[17]

In connection with his views on liberal education, Rush's efforts on behalf of Dickinson College bear special mention. He must certainly be

16. Rush, *Essays*, pp. 8, 14. As Donald J. D'Elia has pointed out, Rush's views on education were founded on a new science of the mind, derived from the associational psychology of David Hartley, and constituted a kind of "mental physics of social reform—the ultimate science of the Enlightenment." See D'Elia, "Benjamin Rush, America's Philosopher of Revolutionary Education," in *The Boyd Lee Spahr Lectures in Americana* (York, Pa.: York Composition Co., 1970), IV (1962–1969), 82.

17. Rush, *Essays*, pp. 15, 17, 18; and Rush, "A Lecture [circa 1795]," in Harry G. Good, *Benjamin Rush and His Services to American Education* (Berne, Ind.: Witness Press, 1918), p. 241.

denominated the founder of that institution: he took part in the initial conversations of 1781 or 1782 that projected it; he was a leader in developing the petition for its charter in 1783; and he remained an active partisan of its cause for the rest of his life. It is Rush's conception of Dickinson, however, that merits scrutiny, for it was different from Jefferson's conception of higher education, yet equally republican. Rush saw Dickinson as possibly "the best bulwark of the blessings obtained by the Revolution." And he saw it as such because he deemed colleges "true nurseries of power and influence" and believed that only as every religious society sponsored one would its representation in government be preserved. The Presbyterians, he argued, had suffered from a want of power under the pre-Revolutionary government of Pennsylvania, had then gained an excess of power in the Revolutionary government, and were almost certain to be reduced to their pre-Revolutionary state as a result of the jealousies thereby excited. Only as they—and all the other major denominations—provided through the training offered in a college a kind of balance wheel for their power would a larger balance in the machinery of government be preserved. The argument was partly self-serving—Rush had had a falling out with the leaders of the newly created University of the State of Pennsylvania (formerly the College of Philadelphia) and wanted to establish an academic counterweight to its influence—but it was also firmly rooted intellectually in his Christian republicanism.[18]

Like Jefferson, Rush concentrated his attention on the development of a state system of education; but, unlike Jefferson, he also saw the need for a national component in the form of a federal university. "To conform the principles, morals and manners of our citizens to our republican forms of government," he wrote in the essay *On the Defects of the Confederation* (1787), "it is absolutely necessary that knowledge of every kind, should be disseminated through every part of the United States." To this end he proposed a federal university that would teach "everything connected with government" and to which young men would come after they had completed their studies in the colleges and universities of their respective states. Beyond its courses, the university would send its abler students on research missions to collect and trans-

18. *Freeman's Journal: or The Weekly North American Intelligencer*, February 23, 1785; and "Hints for Establishing a College at Carlisle in Cumberland County, Pennsylvania, September 3, 1782," in Good, *Benjamin Rush*, p. 102.

mit to their professors up-to-date information on inventions and improvements abroad and on natural resources at home. And, after thirty years, if the experiment proved successful, Congress might consider legislation mandating a degree from the federal university for every person seeking election or appointment to public office. "We require certain qualifications in lawyers, physicians and clergymen, before we commit our property, our lives or our souls to their care," Rush reasoned. "Why then should we commit our country, which includes liberty, property, life, wives and children, to men who cannot produce vouchers of their qualifications for the important trust?"[19]

Unlike many of his contemporaries, Rush did not think solely about the education of young men. He believed that female education also "should be accommodated to the state of society, manners, and government of the country, in which it is conducted." And, given the particular needs and conditions of American life, this required careful attention to the systematic training of young women as wives and mothers, so that they might assist their husbands in the advancement of their fortunes, prepare their daughters for the tasks of motherhood, and instruct their sons in the principles of liberty and government. However limited the roles he projected, he did sketch a fairly broad curriculum, including the reading, writing, and grammar of the English language; arithmetic and bookkeeping; geography and history; the elements of astronomy, chemistry, and natural philosophy; vocal music; dancing; and the Christian religion. Rush's ideas were scarcely original, deriving as they did from François Fénelon's essay of 1687. But, in a society that was increasingly tying its educational schemes to the responsibilities of active citizenship, his formulations concerning the education necessary to prepare women for their indirect civic responsibilities were both noteworthy and influential.[20]

Rush's plans for schooling by no means exhausted his thinking about education, though the degree to which they dominated it is characteristic of the time. He wrote much—though often by indirection—about the centrality of the home in the nurture of republicans; and he thought young people would be better quartered with their families

19. "On the Defects of the Confederation," in Dagobert D. Runes, ed., *The Selected Writings of Benjamin Rush* (New York: Philosophical Library, 1947), p. 29; and "Plan for a Federal University," in *ibid.*, p. 104. In connection with Rush's advocacy of educational certification, it is interesting to consider Thomas Jefferson's support for a literacy test for voters as included in his draft of a comprehensive education bill for Virginia in 1817. See An Act for Establishing Elementary Schools, in Padover, ed., *Complete Jefferson*, p. 1075.

20. Rush, *Essays*, p. 75.

than in residential schools, for they learned their vices more readily from one another than from adults. He recommended the establishment of a post office that would extend "the living principle of government" to every hamlet in the nation and urged that it distribute newspapers free of charge, as "vehicles of knowledge and intelligence" and "sentinels of the liberties of our country." He urged the ministers of all denominations to collaborate in their efforts to promote the objects of the Christian religion and he also campaigned for undenominational Sunday schools. He protested against corporal punishment in the schools, espoused treatment rather than incarceration for the insane, and advocated a penal system committed to rehabilitation rather than punishment, capital or otherwise. And he denounced slavery, pointing to its pernicious effects on the communities that practiced it and proclaiming the equal potential of blacks given equal opportunities. At the bottom of all these opinions, plans, and campaigns was a vision of human beings as perfectible through education, of social institutions capable of perfecting them, and of a society dedicated to the enhancement of their dignity. It was, in effect, the vision of the millennium that in Rush's view the American Revolution had heralded.[21]

III

There was a decided shift in the character of Rush's career during the 1790's, a retreat from public life that made him far more a spectator than the mover and shaper he had been. One can only speculate as to the causes—a weariness with controversy, disappointment at having been passed over for a post in Washington's administration, perhaps a simple shift in interest. Whatever the reasons, Rush devoted himself after 1792 increasingly to the teaching and practice of medicine. The withdrawal, however, was not complete. In 1795 he served as president of a national convention of abolition societies and in 1797 he accepted John Adams's invitation to be treasurer of the United States Mint. Equally significant, perhaps, he assumed a more active role in the affairs of the American Philosophical Society, appearing frequently at its meetings and serving as its vice-president from 1797 to 1801.

The Society had enjoyed a varying reputation since its revitalization during the years immediately preceding the Revolution. The first vol-

21. "An Address to the People of the United States" (1787), in Hezekiah Niles, *Republication of the Principles and Acts of the Revolution in America* (New York: A. S. Bourne & Co., 1876), p. 235.

ume of its *Transactions* had been well received, and for a time the Society had seemed to incarnate the fullest promise of colonial science. In the period during and following the Revolution, however, both its vitality and its fortunes had waned; and, while the appearance of the second volume of its *Transactions* in 1786 was certainly a sign of new life, the quality of the volume (and the response to it) left much to be desired. Yet it was at precisely that time that Benjamin Franklin, recently returned from Europe, was able to assume a more active presidency of the Society; and, under Franklin's leadership and subsequently under David Rittenhouse's, the organization began again to thrive. By the mid-nineties, it had regained much of its pre-Revolutionary eminence; and, although it now shared the scene with a number of rivals, notably the New England-based American Academy of Arts and Sciences, its activities patently exemplified early federal intellectual life at its best.

In 1795, the Society announced seven essay contests, each concerning a different subject of "useful knowledge," to wit, the most economical means of warming rooms; the best methods of preserving peaches from premature decay; the most expedient means of calculating longitude from lunar observations; the best construction of lamps, especially for lighting streets; the most effective methods of producing dyes from American vegetables; the best improvements of ships' pumps (or at least the ones most likely to be adopted by seamen); and the best "system of liberal education and literary instruction, adapted to the genius of the government, and best calculated to promote the general welfare of the United States:—comprehending also, a plan for instituting and conducting public schools in this country on principles of the most extensive utility." The prizes varied from $50 to $100, with the largest single premium designated for the winning essay on education.[22]

Whether out of interest or avarice, the education contest elicited more contributions than any of the others—some eight in all. Each essay was scrutinized with the greatest care and seriousness, and two were judged the winners and ordered published, the authors to share equally in the prize. When the sealed envelopes were opened, revealing the names of the contestants, it was discovered that the first was written by the Reverend Samuel Knox, an alumnus of the University of Glasgow who had settled as a Presbyterian minister in Bladensburg, Maryland, and the second by Samuel Harrison Smith, an alumnus of the

22. "Early Proceedings of the American Philosophical Society," *Proceedings of the American Philosophical Society,* XXII (1885), part III, pp. 229, 231.

University of Pennsylvania who had only recently launched a Jeffersonian newspaper in Philadelphia called the *Universal Gazette*.[23]

Knox's essay was divided into two parts, a prefatory section addressed quite explicitly to the educational problems of Maryland and a principal section projecting an educational system for the nation as a whole. The two parts were coincident and complementary, though the section on Maryland dealt specifically with the needs of institutions such as the recently chartered Washington College and undertook specific comparisons with neighboring states such as Pennsylvania and Virginia. Knox's concern, like Rush's before him (there is no indication that Knox was familiar with Rush or his work), was for a "uniform system of national education" that would bring local parish schools, county academies, state colleges, and a national university into a comprehensive organization under a board of national education. The board, with representatives in each state (assisted in turn by county rectors), would assume responsibility for seeing to it that identical curricula, identical textbooks, and identical standards prevailed throughout the nation. "The *uniformity* of this plan of public instruction," Knox concluded, "would, it is presumed, contribute highly to its success and, at the same time, conduce much both to the improvement and embellishment of society. It might also, in no small degree, be productive of not only harmony of sentiments, unity of taste and manners, but also the patriotic principles of genuine federalism amongst the scattered and variegated citizens of this extensive Republic."[24]

Smith's essay was remarkably similar, projecting a comprehensive system of national education along Jeffersonian lines (again, there is no evidence that Smith was familiar with Jefferson's writings on education) that would include two levels of primary education (classes for youngsters between the ages of five and ten and classes for those between ten and eighteen), a number of colleges, and a national university. A national board of literature and science was called for, whose duty it would be to "form a system of national education" by choosing text-

23. The eight that can be discerned from extant copies and the minutes of the Society are labeled as follows: "Essay on Education" [Samuel Knox], "Remarks on Education" [Samuel Harrison Smith], "Academicus," "Hiram," "Letter to the A.P.S.," "Hand," "Freedom," and "Pieces." The "Pieces" that was ordered returned to Alex. Moore, Tavern-Keeper, on December 15, 1797, may or may have not been one of the latter six. There are four manuscript essays in the library of the Society, one by "Academicus," one by "Hiram," and two anonymous productions that may or may not be identical with two of the latter four.

24. Samuel Knox, *An Essay on the Best System of Liberal Education, Adapted to the Genius of the Government of the United States* (1799), in Frederick Rudolph, ed., *Essays on Education in the Early Republic* (Cambridge, Mass.: Harvard University Press, 1965), pp. 311, 368.

books, appointing teachers, and generally overseeing all details of instruction at every level. "By calling into active operation the mental resources of a nation," Smith observed, "our political institutions will be rendered more perfect, ideas of justice will be diffused, the advantages of the undisturbed enjoyment of tranquillity and industry will be perceived by everyone, and our mutual dependence on each other will be rendered conspicuous. The great result will be harmony. Discord and strife have always proceeded from, or risen upon, ignorance and passion. When the first has ceased to exist and the last shall be vigorously directed, we shall be deprived of every source of misunderstanding."[25]

The similarity of the two prize essays is striking enough, though in the last analysis it may merely testify to the consistency of the judges. But, when the prize essays are laid alongside the others that were submitted (or at least the four others that are extant), and when the six from the contest are laid alongside some half-dozen other contemporary plans for American education, a broader similarity emerges that is immensely significant. It testifies to a certain consensus of assumptions and aspirations marking a republican style of educational thought that was far more pervasive than has hitherto been recognized, a style that cut across partisan lines in politics and religion, that surely transcended regional boundaries, and that may even have transcended social class boundaries. It was not universally concurred in, of course—few styles are; but neither was it narrowly Republican, nor even avant-garde. It was widely articulated and widely accepted, and it provided a context of value and aspiration within which the educational controversies of the era were fought.[26]

What were the elements of the style? Essentially, they inhered in the following propositions: that the success—nay, the salvation—of the Republic lay in education; that education consisted of the diffusion of knowledge, the nurturance of virtue (including patriotic civility), and the cultivation of learning; that the best means of providing education on the massive scale required were schools and colleges; and that the most effective way of obtaining the number and kind of schools and col-

25. Samuel Harrison Smith, *Remarks on Education: Illustrating the Close Connection Between Virtue and Wisdom* (1798), in Rudolph, ed., *Essays on Education*, pp. 213, 219.

26. I have characterized here the six extant plans from the American Philosophical Society contest, along with the roughly contemporary plans of Benjamin Rush, Noah Webster, Robert Coram, Amable-Louis-Rose de Lafitte du Courteil, and Simeon Doggett (all of which are reprinted in Rudolph, ed., *Essays on Education*), and Pierre Samuel Du Pont de Nemours, *National Education in the United States of America*, translated by B. G. Du Pont (1800; Newark, Del.: University of Delaware Press, 1923).

leges needed was via some *system* ultimately tied to the polity. Most of
these propositions, of course, had been argued in one form or another
during the 1760's and 1770's, by men such as William Douglass, John
Adams, and Thomas Jefferson. What was essentially new in the republican style was the dual emphasis on system and on relationship to the
polity. "System" was used in at least two different but related senses;
first, to refer to a regular method of progress through one of the standard subjects of the curriculum or through the curriculum itself (a system of arithmetic or a system of instruction); and, second, to refer to a
pattern of institutional organization that allowed progress from one level to another (from primary school to academy to college to university)
as well as some coordination of the whole via a board of well-qualified,
public-spirited individuals. As for relationship to the polity, it could
take various forms, ranging from public support of one sort or another
to direct or indirect oversight by public officials, or both. The discussion
of system employed terms like "harmony," "machine," and "uniformity," and there were doubtless some who would have colored all citizens
with the same dye, in the fashion of Plato in the *Republic*. But for
many others the terms were Newtonian and implied a desire to create a
"more perfect union." Similarly, the discussion of relationship with the
polity employed phrases like "public schooling," and there were doubtless some, like Knox, who anticipated latter-day systems of publicly
supported, publicly controlled institutions. But for others the point was
to contrast "public," or extrafamilial, instruction with "private," or in-
trafamilial, instruction, after the fashion of John Locke. Thus, when
Smith remarked in his essay, "This, then, appears to be the era, if ever,
of public education," he meant that it was the era of schooling.[27]

One more element in the style is crucial, namely, a conception of
the ideal citizen. Smith articulated it as well as anyone: "The citizen,
enlightened, will be a free man in its truest sense. He will know his
rights, and he will understand the rights of others; discerning the connection of his interest with the preservation of these rights, he will as
firmly support those of his fellow men as his own. Too well informed
to be misled, too virtuous to be corrupted, we shall behold man consistent and inflexible. Not at one moment the child of patriotism, and at
another the slave of despotism, we shall see him in principle forever the
same. Immutable in his character, inflexible in his honesty, he will feel
the dignity of his nature and cheerfully obey the claims of duty." It was

27. Smith, *Remarks on Education,* in Rudolph, ed., *Essays on Education,* p. 207.

the statement of a Jeffersonian journalist, but it could just as well have
been made by a Federalist journalist like Noah Webster, a Presbyterian
moralist like Samuel Stanhope Smith, a deistic radical like Thomas
Paine, a cosmopolitan landholder like Thomas Jefferson, or a simple
farmer like William Manning.[28]

Within the broad area of consensus implicit in the republican style
of educational thought, there were several debates that raged well into
the first decades of the nineteenth century. For one thing, there were
the time-honored controversies over precisely what knowledge needed to
be diffused and precisely what learning needed to be cultivated—controversies that dated at least from the battles between the "ancients"
and the "moderns" during the seventeenth century. What was interesting about the controversies during the early federal period, as Linda K.
Kerber has incisively observed, was the extent to which they took on
political overtones. Thus, for example, as the lines were drawn around
the person and the preferences of Thomas Jefferson, his support for the
modern rather than the ancient languages in the curriculum (had he
not, after all, persuaded the College of William and Mary to discard
the ancient languages as requirements for admission) and his interest in
natural history rather than natural philosophy became matters of the
sharpest political exchange. "I would as soon think of closing all my
window shutters, to enable me to see, as of banishing the classics, to
improve republican ideas," John Adams wrote to Benjamin Rush in
1789. And fifteen years later his son John Quincy Adams suggested
that if James Madison had known his classics better he would have behaved more sensibly in the proceedings of Marbury versus Madison. As
for the several natural sciences, natural history early became identified
with the American Philosophical Society, which was perceived as Republican (after the fashion of its president, Jefferson), while natural
philosophy was identified with the American Academy of Arts and Sciences, which was perceived as Federalist. And, although the classification breaks down if pushed too far, it does indicate the way in which
educational debate became tied to regional and political competition.[29]

Second, there were the profound differences over the extent to
which the national government should be involved in education. Thus,
for example, Samuel Knox's essay sketched what was for all intents

28. *Ibid.*, pp. 220–221.
29. Linda K. Kerber, *Federalists in Dissent: Imagery and Ideology in Jeffersonian America*
(Ithaca, N.Y.: Cornell University Press, 1970), chaps. iii–iv; John Adams to Benjamin Rush, June
19, 1789, in *Letters of Benjamin Rush*, I, 518; and *Port Folio*, December 8, 1804.

and purposes a federal educational system, from primary school through the university; George Washington proposed a national university as an antidote to sectionalism (and actually contemplated endowing such an institution) but said little about any more general federal role; while Roger Sherman, one of Connecticut's representatives at the Constitutional Convention, opposed the effort of James Madison and Charles Pinckney to persuade the Convention to empower Congress "to establish a university, in which no preferences or distinctions should be allowed on account of religion," contending that the power to establish universities should be exercised by the states in their "separate capacities." While the range of variation persisted, there were patent shifts in the weight of opinion, from the early 1780's, when only a handful of avant-garde theorists conceived of a significant federal role in education, to the time of the Convention, when a significant minority of the delegates were willing to support the Madison-Pinckney motion, to the period from the 1790's through the War of 1812, when there was considerable public discussion of a federal role in education, to the years after the Treaty of Ghent, when the idea of such a federal role declined in the face of rising sectional sentiment. James Monroe was the last president to seek Constitutional authority that would have given Congress the power to "institute . . . seminaries of learning"; John Quincy Adams considered the possibility but gave it half-hearted attention; and Andrew Jackson and his successors confined their discussion of a federal role in education largely to the debates over the uses of the Smithson legacy. Otherwise, congressional policy toward education was expressed largely in the form of land grants to the several states for the development of schools and universities and the return of surplus revenues for education and other internal improvements.[30]

Finally, there were the significant differences over the extent to which public funds should be expended on education, with opinion ranging again from that of Samuel Harrison Smith, whose essay actually proposed tax support for the entire system in order that it gain "a fair trial," to those of Jefferson and Rush, who envisioned particular combinations of public and private support for particular levels of education, to the views of those who opposed spending public money for any sort of education. While this controversy, like the one between the

30. *Writings of James Madison*, IV, 453–454; *The Debates and Proceedings in the Congress of the United States*, 1st Congress, 2nd Session, II, 1551; and *A Compilation of the Messages and Papers of the Presidents, 1789–1908* (11 vols.; Washington, D.C.: Government Printing Office, 1896–1899), II, 18.

"ancients" and the "moderns," dated at least from the seventeenth century, and particularly from the Commonwealth period, during which plans for the reform of education abounded, it was given new form and impetus by Adam Smith's observations in *An Inquiry into the Nature and Causes of the Wealth of Nations*. First published in 1776, Smith's *Inquiry* became increasingly familiar to Americans during the closing years of the eighteenth century, both directly and through a number of derivative works, exerting a prodigious influence on the way in which they defined the public good and conceived of their options for attaining it.[31]

IV

Adam Smith probably began the systematic drafting of *The Wealth of Nations* in 1766, though there are manuscripts dating from the winter of 1750–51 that give evidence of thinking later incorporated into the volume. Smith had been early steeped in the traditions of Scottish moral philosophy, having been a student of Francis Hutcheson at Glasgow, and had then taught moral philosophy at Glasgow from 1751 through 1763—directing his first attention to political economy as a branch of that field. From 1764 to 1766 he had traveled in Europe as tutor to the young Duke of Buccleuch and had come to know a number of the leading French economists, notably François Quesnay, chief theorist of the Physiocratic school, and A. R. J. Turgot, the able intendant of Limoges, who had tried to put into practice most (though not all) of Quesnay's doctrines. Thus, when Smith returned to Scotland to devote himself to the development of a comprehensive system of moral philosophy, he had imbibed the best of the Scottish and French traditions and was prepared to unite them in a new and original formulation. What emerged after a decade of labor was *The Wealth of Nations*, initially projected as merely one section of a much larger work, but sufficiently broad in scope and rich in knowledge to be absolutely definitive in its own right.

Smith's treatise was divided into five parts, dealing respectively with the division of labor and problems of value, capital, the economic differences among nations (really a discourse on economic history), the various systems of political economy (notably mercantilism), and public expenditures and taxes; and it was under the last heading that he dis-

31. Smith, *Remarks on Education,* in Rudolph, ed., *Essays on Education,* p. 216.

cussed education, as one of the public institutions and works "which, though they may be in the highest degree advantageous to a great society, are, however, of such a nature, that the profit could never repay the expense to any individual or small number of individuals, and which it therefore cannot be expected that any individual or small number of individuals should erect or maintain."[32]

Smith began with a searing attack on publicly endowed higher education, contending that exertion was always proportional to its necessity and that endowments had removed the necessity for exertion and hence affected the quality of education. Conversely, those aspects of education that were not conducted by publicly endowed institutions, for example, the instruction given in writing or fencing schools or in households (hence, virtually all female education), were the most effective. He readily granted that what the universities had traditionally taught badly would probably not have been taught at all in their absence, which amounted to a grudging acknowledgment of their utility; but his sympathies were patently with private entrepreneurial or familial instruction, where the motivation for effort and hence for effectiveness was both clear and direct.

With respect to popular education, Smith was of another mind. Contending openly against the views of the Dutch-born English moralist Bernard Mandeville, whose *Essay on Charity, and Charity-Schools* (1723) had maintained that schooling diverted the poor from useful labor, educated them above their stations, and left them ill-prepared for the unpleasant work society needed and they had to do, Smith asserted that the state had a responsibility to educate the common people at public expense if for no other reason than to prevent them from slipping into the torpor and stupidity that so often attended simple and routinized labor. An instructed and intelligent people, he reasoned (also *contra* Mandeville), was invariably more decent and orderly than an ignorant and stupid one; and hence in free societies the state's responsibility for the education of the common people became even greater, since the safety of the government "depends very much upon the favorable judgment which the people may form of its conduct" and "it must surely be of the highest importance that they should not be disposed to judge rashly or capriciously concerning it."[33]

---

32. Adam Smith, *An Inquiry into the Nature and Causes of the Wealth of Nations*, edited by Edwin Cannan (New York: Random House, 1937), p. 681. Interestingly, Smith also discussed defense, the administration of justice, and the instruments of commerce (roads, bridges, canals, and harbors) in the last section.

33. *Ibid.*, p. 740.

Smith then went on to discuss popular education as carried on by the various churches, concluding that it was the reformed and evangelical sects that had tended to be most successful, since they had not been able to depend on public support or endowments and had therefore had to count on their own exertions and persuasiveness in winning support and clientele. Where churches did gain the support of the state, Smith argued, such support should be sufficient to attract able individuals to the clergy, yet modest enough to discourage them from idleness and vanity. The entire cost of the Church of Scotland, he observed, could not have exceeded eighty or eighty-five thousand pounds a year, and "the most opulent church in Christendom does not maintain better the uniformity of faith, the fervor of devotion, the spirit of order, regularity, and austere morals in the great body of the people, than this very poorly endowed church." Interestingly, at this point he was one with Mandeville, who had contended that compulsory attendance of the poor at church on Sundays would furnish them with all the education they needed and also leave them free for labor on weekdays.[34]

The ambivalence reflected here is significant: on the one hand, Smith wanted the common people saved from a bovine stupidity; on the other hand, he wanted them formed to habits of decency and order, instrumentally through schools (an instructed and intelligent people is a decent and orderly people) and directly through churches. The ambivalence was destined to resound through nineteenth-century discussions of public policy for education, with the emphasis going one way or another, depending on the times, the individuals, and the circumstances, but with neither concern ever absent for very long.

Smith's doctrines slowly made their way in America, initially among the intelligentsia such as Franklin, Jefferson, Hamilton, and the Philadelphia physician George Logan, later among a larger audience created by American editions of The Wealth of Nations (Philadelphia, 1789, 1796, 1817; Hartford, 1804, 1818) as well as through formal courses in political economy at several of the American colleges, notably the College of William and Mary. By the early 1800's, they had become the common property of the educated and professional classes. With the appearance in 1821 of Jean Baptiste Say's A Treatise on Political Economy (1803) in an American edition of the English translation, Smith's doctrines were further popularized. Jefferson found Say's treatise "a succinct, judicious digest of the tedious pages of Smith," partly, perhaps, because Say's discussion of public institutions unre-

34. *Ibid.*, p. 765.

servedly praised science ("Every advance of science is followed by an increase of social happiness") and omitted Smith's lengthy acknowledgment of the social benefits of an inexpensive religious establishment. In any case, Say repeated Smith's argument for public primary schooling (for youngsters of both sexes) and even went so far as to add that first-class textbooks in the several fields of knowledge should also be encouraged, since "the reputation and profit of a good book in this class do not indemnify the labor, science, and skill, requisite to its composition" (the English translator took pains to disagree, noting that in England, "works of instruction are probably amongst the most profitable to the authors").[35]

A considerable American pamphlet literature on economic policy also helped to popularize the doctrines of political economy, though, as is often the case in policy debates, the same reference was often enlisted both for and against the same cause. The first formal American textbook on political economy was Daniel Raymond's *Thoughts on Political Economy,* initially published in 1820 and reissued in an enlarged edition three years later under the title *The Elements of Political Economy.* Raymond, a Baltimore lawyer of Federalist propensities who had prepared for the bar at Judge Tapping Reeve's Litchfield, Connecticut, law school, was roundly critical of Adam Smith for failing to distinguish between public and private wealth. In Smith's view, he argued, the wealth of a nation was the totality of the private property of its individuals (and Say, he charged, construed it the same way, though Say's formulations were "vastly inferior"). Yet, so far as Raymond was concerned, the wealth of a nation went far beyond mere private accumulation to comprise its "capacity for acquiring the necessaries and comforts of life," a capacity dependent upon the extent of its natural resources, the diligence of its people, the degree of perfection of its arts and sciences, and the vigor of its commerce. Raymond did not go on to describe in detail the modes of nurturing diligence and perfecting the arts and sciences. Had he done so, he might well have made a significant contribution to contemporary educational theory. As it was, his shift in the definition of wealth was significant, and pamphleteers and scholars alike were quick to seize upon it.[36]

35. Thomas Jefferson to Joseph C. Cabell, January 31, 1814, in *Writings of Thomas Jefferson,* edited by Lipscomb and Bergh, XIV, 82; Jean Baptiste Say, *A Treatise on Political Economy,* translated by C. R. Prinsep (Philadelphia: J. B. Lippincott and Co., 1832), pp. 432–433, 436, 434–435.

36. Daniel Raymond, *The Elements of Political Economy* (2d ed.; 2 vols.; Baltimore: F. Lucas, Jr., and E. J. Coale, 1823), I, 173, 47.

There is no indication that Stephen Simpson, a Philadelphia journalist who dabbled in politics as a Jacksonian during the 1820's and then switched to run for Congress on the Federal Republican ticket in 1830, ever read Raymond's treatise; but his thought ran in many of the same directions and both he and Raymond ended up vigorous proponents of the American system. In an intriguing tract called *The Working Man's Manual: A New Theory of Political Economy, on the Principle of Production the Source of Wealth* (1831), Simpson sharply attacked Smith as "the foremost of these apologists of tyranny" and Say as a "recondite" rationalist and called for a characteristically American system of political economy that would help the new nation realize the moral promise of the Revolution. He founded his system on a plan for the education of the common man and dedicated it to "the shade of Jefferson." Not surprisingly, Simpson became the major theorist of the Philadelphia workingmen's movement and a prime influence in the definition of its social program.[37]

"Nothing is so essentially connected with the wealth of nations, and the happiness of the people," Simpson maintained, "as the proper cultivation, expansion, and discipline of the popular mind. Upon this depends not only the amount of public virtue and happiness—but the aggregate of industry, ingenuity, temperance, economy, and vigor." From this assertion, Simpson moved easily to the proposal for a "*general system of popular education,* reaching beyond the mere attainment of reading and writing," as a matter of right in common schools rather than as a matter of almsgiving in charity schools. Given such a system, vice and crime would vanish ("A reading and intellectual people were never known to be sottish"), sobriety and civility would flourish, and inventiveness and industry would "change the whole face of society into one radiant smile of content and enjoyment." Most important, perhaps, there would be "redress of that perverted system of society, which dooms the producer to ignorance, to toil, and to penury, to moral degradation, physical want, and social barbarism." The New World had begun with a system of education "devised in the midnight of the dark ages" and wholly inappropriate for a free people; now, that system was slowly giving way to a genuine system of popular education. In a new *American* economic system, founded on a new *American* education system, the Revolution would be completed.[38]

37. Stephen Simpson, *The Working Man's Manual: A New Theory of Political Economy, on the Principle of Production the Source of Wealth* (Philadelphia: Thomas L. Bonsal, 1831), pp. 45, 47.
38. *Ibid.,* pp. 199, 205, 214–215, 37.

Simpson's tract was doubtless read in the circles of the Philadelphia and New York workingmen and their intellectual supporters, and indeed Simpson was even thought of by some as a kind of American William Cobbett. Together with Robert Dale Owen, Frances Wright, and Thomas Skidmore, he played a significant role in placing public schooling at the forefront of the workingmen's demands. But there is no evidence that his treatise was seriously considered by political economists or moral philosophers. Their attention was drawn rather to a textbook by Francis Wayland, the redoubtable president of Brown University. Entitled *The Elements of Political Economy* (1837), it went through at least twenty-three editions before 1876 and must have sold over 50,000 copies, for all intents and purposes dominating the field. Wayland claimed to have written the text as "an American, a Christian, and a gentleman," though at least one reviewer criticized the work for "its want of American character." There was no question, however, about the discussion of education having been thoroughly Americanized. Located, in the fashion of Adam Smith, under the heading of public consumption or expenditure, it asserted the economic advantages of the cultivation and diffusion of knowledge, especially scientific knowledge; advised that education be popularized via district schools, which would elicit community interest at the same time that they diffused knowledge; and insisted that religious worship be divorced from the civil authority and permitted to flourish freely under the aegis of voluntary associations. The discussion was laconic, direct, and unambiguous, and must certainly have assisted the campaigns for public schooling in the various states of the Northeast and West during the middle third of the nineteenth century.[39]

V

So far as we know, Horace Mann first encountered *The Wealth of Nations* in his senior year at Brown, probably in connection with the moral philosophy course taught by President Asa Messer. There is no record of his reaction to the work, merely the stark evidence of his having withdrawn it from the library. Yet Mann was a diligent student, and it is not likely that he left the pages unturned. And, if the treatise did have an influence, it was almost surely in the direction of strengthening

39. Francis Wayland, *The Elements of Political Economy* (Boston: Gould and Lincoln, 1837), p. v; and Francis Bowen, Review of *The Elements of Political Economy, Christian Examiner*, XXIV (1838), 57.

Mann's already buoyant optimism about the future of mankind in general and the United States in particular. Like Daniel Raymond, Mann would Americanize the doctrines of political economy and convert the concept of capital into human terms. A quarter-century later, he would argue that the richest mines of Massachusetts were not deposits of gold and silver but rather the developed intellectual capabilities of its population.[40]

The years at Brown were pivotal in Mann's career. Born to modest circumstances in Franklin, Massachusetts, in 1796, he had been educated primarily at home and in church, preparing himself academically through a characteristic combination of intermittent schooling, occasional tutoring, and systematic self-study in the Franklin town library. Admitted to the sophomore class at Brown in 1816, he had worked assiduously at his studies and at the correlative activities of the United Brothers, a Republican-oriented literary and debating society, seeing academic honor as the open sesame to a lucrative career in business or the law. He more than achieved his goal, graduating as valedictorian of his class in 1819 and subsequently winning the hand of President Messer's daughter Charlotte.

Following graduation, Mann served as an apprentice in the law office of Josiah J. Fiske, a Wrentham attorney and former member of the United Brothers, then returned to Brown for several years as a tutor in Latin and Greek, then attended Litchfield Law School in Connecticut for a year of systematic training, and then completed his apprenticeship in Dedham, where he won admission to the bar in 1823 and settled into his own practice. He applied himself there with the same assiduousness as at Brown, attracting growing numbers of clients, entering enthusiastically into the social and civic life of the town, and in due course winning a seat in the state legislature. He served in the House from 1827 to 1833, espousing a variety of causes ranging from railroad development to better care for the insane, and then, having moved to Boston after the tragic death of his wife in 1832, he was elected to the Senate in 1834. It was as president of that body in 1837 that he helped push through a measure that would drastically alter his career: it was a bill to establish a state board of education.

The movement for the board tells much about the ambiguous resolution of the tensions implicit in the republican style of educational

40. *Tenth Annual Report of the Board of Education, Together with the Tenth Annual Report of the Secretary of the Board* (1846), p. 235.

thought. Massachusetts had accepted the propositions that the success of the Republic depended upon education; that education consisted of the diffusion of knowledge, the nurturance of virtue (including patriotic civility), and the cultivation of learning; and that the best means of providing education on the massive scale required were schools and colleges. Indeed, the three propositions had been embodied in chapter v of the Constitution of 1780 and in the several laws subsequently enacted in response to its mandates. Yet that fact alone indicates one element in the ambiguity, for what was clearly perceived as a national need—given the character of the nation as a Republic—was attended to at the state level. And there were even those in 1780 and in the years thereafter who maintained that education was no business of the state in any case but rather the business of the towns, whose inhabitants were held to be "the properest judges of what schools are the most suitable."[41]

With respect to the matter of an educational system, however, and any relation it might bear to the polity, there were at best sporadic and conflicting proposals. New York, for example, had established the comprehensive University of the State of New York in 1784 and 1787, designed to encourage and coordinate colleges, academies, and schools throughout the state, and it had then established beside it in 1795 and 1812 a state common-school system under the general oversight of a superintendent of common schools. Various European countries, notably Prussia and France, had developed national systems of school and university education (the French had organized a Napoleonic university in 1806 that in many ways resembled the earlier comprehensive university in New York), and a number of commentators during the 1820's and 1830's had begun to publicize these systems in the United States and point to the challenge they posed for republican institutions. And, in Massachusetts itself, men such as James G. Carter had for more than a decade been calling for an educational renaissance based on a reassertion of state authority with respect to the schools and on the establishment of a public teacher-training institution as part of a comprehensive public school system.

Not surprisingly, it was Carter who led the initiative that culminated in the establishment of the board. As a member of the Massachusetts House of Representatives (and chairman of its Committee on Education), he advocated (unsuccessfully) the creation of a state superinten-

41. Oscar and Mary Handlin, eds., *The Popular Sources of Political Authority: Documents on the Massachusetts Constitution of 1780* (Cambridge, Mass.: Harvard University Press, 1966), p. 29.

dency of common schools in 1836 and then drafted the bill that created the state board of education in 1837. The board was granted little authority: each year it was to prepare for the legislature an abstract of the state's school returns along with a report on the condition and efficacy of the school system and the best means of improving it. But the governor, Edward Everett, who had joined with Carter in advocating the board, appointed an influential membership, including (besides himself and Lieutenant-Governor George Hull, who were designated members ex officio by the statute) Jared Sparks, the president of Harvard; Robert Rantoul, Jr., a leading Democrat in the legislature; Edmund Dwight, a wealthy Boston businessman; Edward A. Newton, a Pittsfield merchant and banker; Emerson Davis and Thomas Robbins, prominent Congregational ministers; and Carter and Mann. It was Dwight who first approached Mann with the suggestion that he assume the secretaryship of the board, the one paid office established by the legislation. Mann's initial response was disbelief—"I never had a sleeping nor a waking dream, that I should ever think of myself, or be thought of by any other, in relation to that station," he wrote in his diary. But over the next six weeks Dwight prevailed, and on June 29, 1837, Mann was appointed to the post.[42]

Probably the most important single thing about the position, at least in retrospect, is that it had no power; for in the absence of power Mann was forced to rely on his wit. What followed during the twelve years of his incumbency was a statewide (and in time nationwide) campaign of public education about public education. Mann lectured and wrote voluminously, meeting ceaselessly with groups of interested citizens and teachers to air his views, using his annual reports as occasions for the systematic discussion of educational theory and policy, and editing a monthly journal as a vehicle for the exchange of educational opinion and practice. Beginning with no formal knowledge of education— shortly after his appointment he hurriedly read James Simpson's *The Necessity of Popular Education* (1834) and Thomas Brown's *Lectures on the Philosophy of the Human Mind* (1820) and turned through the back issues of the *American Journal of Education* (1826–1830)—he soon became one of the leading educational statesmen of his time. And, in the process, he articulated a characteristic American theory of education that was destined to prevail for more than a century.

In essence, Mann accepted the propositions of the republican style

42. Horace Mann, Journal, May 6, 1837, p. 4 (Mann mss., Massachusetts Historical Society, Boston, Mass.). By permission of the Massachusetts Historical Society.

of educational thought and recast them in the forms of nineteenth-century nondenominational Protestantism. Like Jefferson, he believed that a nation could not long remain ignorant and free—hence the need for universal popular education. But for Mann the problem went beyond mere knowledge to become a question of moral elevation. "Never will wisdom preside in the halls of legislation," he warned, "and its profound utterances be recorded on the pages of the statute book, until common schools . . . create a more far-seeing intelligence and a purer morality than has ever yet existed among communities of men." If the Republic was to survive, moral rectitude would have to be universally diffused among the people, and the quintessential instrument for achieving that end would be the school.[43]

Like Jefferson, too, Mann believed that schooling would lay the foundation for the responsible exercise of citizenship in a free society, but only a particular kind of schooling, publicly supported, publicly controlled, and open to all. *"The common school,"* he once remarked in typical hyperbole, *"is the greatest discovery ever made by man.* In two grand, characteristic attributes, it is supereminent over all others: —first, in its universality;—for it is capacious enough to receive and cherish in its parental bosom every child that comes into the world; and second, in the timeliness of the aid it proffers;—its early, seasonable supplies of counsel and guidance making security antedate danger. Other social organizations are curative and remedial; this is a preventive and an antidote; they come to heal diseases and wounds; this to make the physical and moral frame invulnerable to them. Let the common school be expanded to its capabilities, let it be worked with the efficiency of which it is susceptible, and nine tenths of the crimes in the penal code would become obsolete; the long catalogue of human ills would be abridged; men would walk more safely by day; every pillow would be more inviolable by night; property, life, and character held by strong tenure; all rational hopes respecting the future brightened." The millennialism of these assertions—and they are entirely representative of his rhetoric as secretary—holds the key to Mann's reformulation of the Jeffersonian ideal. From an institution that would "illuminate, as far as practicable, the minds of the people at large," the school had become an institution that would brighten "all rational hopes respecting the future."[44]

43. *Twelfth Annual Report of the Board of Education, Together with the Twelfth Annual Report of the Secretary of the Board* (1848), p. 84.
44. *Common School Journal,* III (1841), 15.

Finally, like Jefferson, Mann believed in a system of schooling under the beneficent aegis of the state. In the initial lecture Mann delivered during his first "great circuit" through the towns of Massachusetts in the summer and autumn of 1837, he was sharply critical of the lack of organization in the educational institutions of the state, depicting a congeries of isolated local ventures conducted by men and women who were "strangers and aliens to each other." Only as Massachusetts organized a true system of common schools would improvements be rapidly diffused, uniformities properly insisted upon, and economies appropriately realized. For Mann, pedagogical system and organizational system merged and the advance of one became dependent upon the advance of the other.[45]

Mann's ideal common school embodied all the elements he deemed essential to education in a republic. It would be common, not as a school for the common people—the Prussian Volksschule, for example—but rather as a school common to all people. It would be open to all and supported by tax funds. It would be for rich and poor alike, the equal of any private institution. And, by receiving children of all creeds, classes, and backgrounds (on the matter of race, Mann, who would be an uncompromising abolitionist when he served in Congress after 1848, was mute), it would kindle a spirit of amity and mutual respect that the conflicts of adult life could never destroy. In consonance with the republican style, he saw social harmony as a prime goal of popular education.

But, beyond social harmony, there was the elevated morality that Mann considered crucial to the future of the Republic. A half-century after Rush, the Revolution was still incomplete. "Revolutions which change only the surface of society, can be effected in a day," Mann observed; "but revolutions working down among the primordial elements of human character; taking away ascendancy from faculties which have long been in subjection;—such revolutions cannot be accomplished by one convulsive effort, though every fibre in the nation should be strained to the endeavor." The political convulsion of the 1770's had substituted liberty for the restraints that had historically held men under oppression; but that same liberty had afforded free reign to human passion. Unless passion was controlled by morality, unless moral force replaced physical force, the fruits of liberty would be worse than the ills of tyranny ("The slave of the vilest tyrant is less debased than the

45. Horace Mann, Journal, November 15, 1837, p. 61 (Mann mss.); and Horace Mann, *Lectures on Education* (Boston: Ide & Dutton, 1855), p. 19.

thrall of his own passions"). What was required was a revolution in character, in which the great ideas of justice, truth, benevolence, and reverence would be enthroned in the hearts of the people and made ascendant over conduct. That revolution was the mission of the schools, and on their ability to carry it out would depend "the worth or worthlessness of our free institutions." This was one inescapable link between schooling and politics that Mann sought to establish during the twelve years of his campaign: "As 'the child is father to the man,' " he taught, "so may the training of the schoolroom expand into the institutions and fortunes of the state."[46]

The similarity, of course, to what Lyman Beecher was preaching during the great Valley campaigns of the 1830's is patent, though with a special twist. Following the disestablishment of Connecticut Congregationalism in 1818, Beecher had made a virtue of necessity: the voluntary church, he maintained, would be the moral gyroscope of the free society, both in its own right and in the education it provided the citizenry via the configuration of educative institutions it controlled. Mann, who had heard Beecher's preaching at Litchfield in 1822 and had even found himself responding to it, was willing to advance the same general substantive principles, but, like Jefferson a half-century earlier, he assigned to the school what others would rather have left to the church. By the 1830's and 1840's, with schools already outnumbering churches in some regions, the shift was more subtle, but none the less profound. And, as a civic institution able to draw upon public resources in a rapidly developing society, the school derived immense strength from the sense of vital connection with a coming political millennium that Mann was able to conjure.

One other aspect of Mann's design is relevant here—the mechanism of public control. Through state legislatures and local boards of education, popularly elected representatives rather than professional schoolmen would exercise ultimate oversight. The manifest reason, of course, was that public supervision must follow public support (though as a politician Mann also knew that public interest must precede it). Yet the relationship went far deeper, for through the mechanism of lay control the public would be entrusted with the continuing definition of the public philosophy (elevated morality!) taught its children. *"Upon the people,"* Mann wrote, "will rest the great and inspiring duty of prescribing to the next generation what their fortunes shall be, by deter-

46. *Ninth Annual Report of the Board of Education, Together with the Ninth Annual Report of the Secretary of the Board* (1845), p. 69; and *Twelfth Annual Report,* p. 43.

mining in what manner they shall be educated." And by "the people" in this instance he meant citizens in their localities. Like Beecher, he was making a virtue of necessity: as secretary of a board with no power his political device was to awaken, and he used all the rhetorical techniques of the evangelical movement in doing so. One outcome, perhaps unintended, was a sense of parental control over the destinies of children that enabled parents to travel the route of public schooling. And in the mechanisms for the exercise of that control lay the means for a continuing redefinition of what would be taught.[47]

For all his battles with the evangelical clergy of Massachusetts, Mann's definition of what should be taught came remarkably close to the evangelical conceptions of the day—a common piety rooted in Scripture, a common civility revolving around the history and the state documents of a Christian Republic, and a common intellectual culture conveyed via reading, writing, spelling, arithmetic, English grammar, geography, singing, and some health education. His pedagogical ideas were wholly derivative—a potpourri of contemporary liberalism rooted in phrenology, Pestalozzianism, Scottish common-sense philosophy, and Boston Unitarianism according to Channing. But he was wise enough to recognize that children differ in temperament, ability, and interest and that lessons should be adapted to these differences; that the discipline of a free society must be self-discipline and not, Mann was fond of arguing, blind obedience on the one hand or anarchic willfulness on the other; and that equal opportunity for all precludes a too-early classification and streaming. And he was prudent enough to grant that only as competent teachers could be attracted to the schools and prepared for service within them would such principles be honored and applied in the day-to-day life of classrooms. In the end, however, all was subsidiary to the need for moral elevation. "Above all others," he wrote,

must the children of a Republic be fitted for society, as well as for themselves. As each citizen is to participate in the power of governing others, it is an essential preliminary, that he should be imbued with a feeling for the wants, and a sense of the rights, of those whom he is to govern; because the power of governing others, if guided by no higher motive than our own gratification, is the distinctive attribute of oppression;—an attribute whose nature and whose wickedness are the same, whether exercised by one who calls himself a republican, or by one born an irresponsible despot. In a government like ours, each individual must think of the welfare of the state as well as of the welfare of his

47. Mann, *Lectures on Education*, p. 13. For Mann's own view of his "evangelism," see Horace Mann to Elizabeth Peabody, August 4, 1837 (Mann mss.).

own family; and therefore, of the children of others as well as of his own. It becomes then, a momentous question, whether the children in our schools are educated in reference to themselves and their private interests only, or with a regard to the great social duties and prerogatives that await them in afterlife. Are they so educated that when they grow up, they will make better philanthropists and Christians, or only grander savages?—for, however loftily the intellect of man may have been gifted, however skillfully it may have been trained, if it be not guided by a sense of justice, a love of mankind and a devotion to duty, its possessor is only a more splendid, as he is a more dangerous barbarian.[48]

Unlike many of the articulators of the republican style of educational thought, Mann gave little attention to higher education. Whereas Rush, Knox, Smith, and even Jefferson designed systems of education in the abstract, Mann's wisdom was prudential, deriving from the crucible of daily political experience. Actually, a contemporary like John D. Pierce, who was Michigan's superintendent of schools between 1836 and 1841 and thereby responsible for a system of education constitutionally defined as extending from the primary school through the university, worked out formulations far more comprehensive in scope than Mann, who saw the state's responsibility ending at the secondary level. But Mann was more profound in his recognition of the inextricable tie between education and freedom and more insistent in his delineation of priorities. Jefferson, it will be recalled, maintained that if forced to choose between universal primary education for the citizenry and a state university for leaders he would choose the former. But, when the former was politically blocked and the latter became politically possible, he chose the latter. Mann was in the very nature of his work able to act more consistently. Believing that in a republic the leaders could never far surpass the general level of intelligence, he maintained that the important thing was the education given the great body of the people. If the people were wise, the problem of leadership would take care of itself. "By a natural law," he maintained, "like that which regulates the equilibrium of fluids, elector and elected, appointer and appointee, tend to the same level. It is not more certain that a wise and enlightened constituency will refuse to invest a reckless and profligate man with office, or discard him if accidentally chosen, than it is that a foolish or immoral constituency will discard or eject a wise man." His concern was with the greatest general proficiency of average students—the gen-

48. *Ninth Annual Report*, pp. 64–65.

eral progress of all rather than the remarkable progress of a few. And by a doctrine of first things first he gave himself wholly to the problems of universal primary schooling.[49]

Mann resigned the secretaryship in 1848 to take the seat of former president John Quincy Adams in Congress. There followed a stormy period in which his abolitionist sympathies projected him to the forefront of national politics. Then, having been defeated for the Massachusetts governorship in 1852, he accepted the presidency of Antioch College, recently founded by the Christian denomination with a commitment to coeducation, nonsectarianism, and equal opportunity for blacks. There, amid the usual crises attendant upon the launching of a new institution, he finished out his years, succumbing to ill health in the summer of 1859.

By then, Mann was already universally acknowledged as the commanding figure of the public school movement; and a quarter-century of lionizing by surviving contemporaries, notably Henry Barnard, decisively confirmed his reputation. It was a fame richly deserved, given the influence of his ideas. His writings, particularly the annual reports to the board, were cited, quoted, reprinted, and plagiarized, throughout the United States as well as in Great Britain, Germany, and Argentina; and he was incessantly consulted by schoolmen, boards of education, politicians, and philanthropists. At a time when schooling was rapidly expanding in the United States, Mann not only accelerated the movement but gave it its essential meaning, both in educational terms and in broader political terms. When the *Edinburgh Review,* not given to an easy adulation of things American, received his tenth annual report, it asserted what must have been the judgment of many of his contemporaries: "The volume is, indeed, a noble monument of civilized people; and, if America were sunk beneath the waves, would remain the fairest picture on record of that ideal commonwealth."[50]

VI

For all the range and profundity of his discussions, one looks in vain through Mann's annual reports for any extended commentary on women's education—something of a puzzle in light of his own comparatively liberal views on the matter. It may have been simple prudence—

49. *Twelfth Annual Report,* p. 77.
50. *Edinburgh Review,* CLXXXVIII (1850), 355.

Mann was loath to raise questions that might have endangered the fragile coalition he had put together in favor of the schools; though it was more likely a failure to see any real issue at stake so far as the responsibilities of a board of public education might be concerned. Girls were of course to be educated in the common schools alongside boys, as they had been in New England for several generations, and then encouraged to assume their crucial roles as mothers of the coming generation of citizens. "The rulers of our country need knowledge (God only knows how much they need it!)," Mann declared in 1853, "but mothers need it more; for they determine, to a great extent, the very capacity of the rulers' minds to acquire knowledge and to apply it." Even these fairly mild assertions, however, were moot for Mann's generation, with the lines of opposition running from those who flatly opposed any education for females on the grounds that it was harmful and wasteful, to those who opposed the education of females at public expense since they would not exercise the prerogatives of citizenship, to those who opposed any education of females that went beyond the fundamentals.[51]

Mann's beliefs on "the woman question" were progressive enough, though scarcely avant-garde. With the publication of Mary Wollstonecraft's *A Vindication of the Rights of Women* (1792), which was reprinted in Philadelphia as early as 1794, every American woman who was moved to ponder the time-honored inequalities of gender had a bible to guide her thought. There was nothing natural about the subjugation of women, Wollstonecraft maintained, it was simply a matter of injustice. Women were the natural equals of men, in rights, liberties, and abilities, and a proper education (and employment) would render them equals in actuality. For a people who had justified a revolution on the basis of natural rights and had then gone on to articulate the heady rhetoric of equality, the question of women's rights was unavoidable, and indeed there were voices of protest early in the nineteenth century against the "civil death" associated with traditional marriage, the religious inequity implicit in an all-male ministry, and the political impotence resulting from disenfranchisement. Whatever the particular concern of any protester, however, the question of education was inevitable: unless women were afforded opportunity in that realm, all else would fail.

There were a number of women—and even a few men—who spoke

51. Horace Mann, "A Few Thoughts on the Powers and Duties of Woman," in *Lectures on Various Subjects* (New York: Fowler and Wells, 1864), p. 65.

out in favor of the reform of women's education during the 1820's and 1830's: one thinks of Hannah Crocker, Emma Willard, Mary Lyon, Sarah and Angelina Grimké, Sarah Josepha Hale, Thomas Gallaudet, John J. Shipherd, and Theodore Weld. But none was more influential on the general course of popular education than Catharine E. Beecher. Born in 1800, the first child of Lyman and Roxana Beecher, she had received her most important education from the various members of the Beecher family and then, after her father gave up his pulpit at East Hampton, Long Island, for one at Litchfield, Connecticut, from the teachers and other students at Miss Pierce's School. Betrothed in 1821 to a gifted Yale professor who died tragically in a shipwreck off the Irish coast the following year, she had never married, devoting herself wholly to a career of teaching and writing. She opened a school for young women in Hartford in 1823 in cooperation with her sister Mary—it subsequently became the celebrated Hartford Female Seminary—and she published a moral philosophy textbook in 1831, the first of a long succession of didactic works that would profoundly influence American life and thought.

The mere fact of the Hartford Female Seminary was significant in its own right, since the opportunities for advanced education for women in the 1820's were severely limited. From the very beginning, in their rented room above a harness shop, Catharine and Mary Beecher between them taught grammar, geography, rhetoric, philosophy, chemistry, ancient and modern history, arithmetic, algebra, geometry, moral philosophy, natural theology, and Latin; and, though they were often themselves only a few pages ahead of their students in the textbooks being used, they did not in that respect differ much from the standard practice of the time. What was even more significant, however, was the series of justifications Beecher used in promoting the seminary, for here were sounded the themes that would mark her efforts all the rest of her life. "It is to *mothers,* and to *teachers,*" she wrote in 1829,

that the world is to look for the character which is to be enstamped on each succeeding generation, for it is to them that the great business of education is almost exclusively committed. And will it not appear by examination that neither mothers nor teachers have ever been properly educated for their profession. What is *the profession* of a *woman?* Is it not to form immortal minds, and to watch, to nurse, and to rear the bodily system, so fearfully and wonderfully made, and upon the order and regulation of which, the health and well-being of the mind so greatly depends?

To form immortal minds in home and school—that was the unique and vital role of women in a republic.[52]

It was in connection with her father's campaign to save the West from barbarism that the full significance of Catharine Beecher's formulation became apparent. She went to Cincinnati with him in 1832 and organized a school there called the Western Female Institute, modeled, not surprisingly, after the earlier venture at Hartford. But her own role in the actual conduct of the institute was far less central than it had been at Hartford, for her attention was on larger matters. In the configuration of institutions that her father and his associates were counting on to win the West for Christ, she considered the common schools to be crucial, and she saw her own task as one of awakening the nation to the need for a sufficient corps of female teachers to staff these institutions. In the far-flung network of the united evangelical front, there were societies to train and support ministers, to print and distribute Bibles and tracts, and to organize, staff, and supply Sunday schools. But there was no society to advance common schools. Hence, Beecher focused her attention there, and in the process legitimatized the common school movement as an aspect of the evangelical crusade, while also helping to create a new vocation for American women.

Beecher first set forth her plan for a nationwide effort on behalf of common schools in the West in *An Essay on the Education of Female Teachers* (1835), which was initially delivered as a lyceum address in New York and then published both in New York and Cincinnati. The proposal combined various elements from other evangelical efforts in the Ohio Valley. Subsidized by eastern money, a group of endowed teacher-training seminaries would be established at key locations in the West, with the express purpose of preparing female teachers for the common schools. Those seminaries would offer a curriculum equal in character and quality to the colleges for men, with special emphasis on moral and undenominational religious instruction; and each seminary would have a model primary school attached. The best of the alumnae would go on to form additional regional seminaries, the others would serve as model teachers in the schools. Finally, during the period when the seminaries were being developed, a vast recruiting effort would be undertaken in the East for women willing to serve as missionary teachers in western schools. "Meantime," Beecher assured her audience with

52. Catharine E. Beecher, *Suggestions Respecting Improvements in Education, Presented to the Trustees of the Hartford Female Seminary* (Hartford, Conn.: Packard & Butler, 1829), p. 7.

appropriate urgency, "proper efforts being made by means of the press, the pulpit, and influential men employed as agents for this object, the interest of the whole nation can be aroused, and every benevolent and every pious female in the nation, who has the time and qualifications necessary, can be enlisted to consecrate at least a certain number of years to this object. There is not a village in this nation that cannot furnish its one, two, three, and in some cases ten or even twenty, laborers for this field."[53]

It was an ingenious plan, which, like so many contemporary evangelical efforts, demanded leadership, organization, and money. Beecher provided the first in enthusiastic abundance. She set out to make her Western Female Institute a model for the seminaries she described, and when that failed and a similar school developed at Milwaukee, Wisconsin, she helped organize the American Women's Education Association to sustain it and other institutions like it. She traveled widely through the East seeking funds to support an agency (in the fashion of the leading interdenominational organizations) that could coordinate the work of locating western schools in need of teachers, enlisting eastern women willing to serve, and making the necessary arrangements to bring the two together. For a time she actually had the services of former governor William Slade of Vermont in this capacity; but she and Slade fell out with one another and he went on to organize the Board of National Popular Education, which, alas, also failed. In the end, however, leadership, even the vigorous leadership proffered by Beecher and the members of her family, could not substitute for organization and money; and, for reasons both personal and political—the Beechers were not universally loved, especially after the explosion at Lane Seminary—organization did not succeed and money was not forthcoming, with the result that the plan of 1835 failed.

But in many respects the cause of evangelization on behalf of common schools, particularly common schools taught by female teachers, succeeded massively. Horace Mann devoted his second annual lecture as secretary of the board to the preparation of teachers and included a significant section on the special qualifications of females; characteristically, he spoke of "a divinely appointed ministry" in the "sacred temple of education." And, when the first public normal schools were organized in Massachusetts in the years 1839 and 1840, it was generally as-

---

53. Catharine E. Beecher, *An Essay on the Education of Female Teachers* (New York: Van Nostrand & Dwight, 1835), p. 19.

sumed that they would be attended by females. Obviously, Beecher cannot be credited for the assumption, but her work both reflected and advanced it. Later, when Beecher was organizing the effort that would subsequently attract Slade, she enlisted the interest and cooperation not only of Mann but also of Henry Barnard, Samuel Lewis, and Catharine Sedgwick, individuals who were not by temperament and outlook likely to make common cause with the Beechers. Most important, perhaps, was the moral force that Beecher's campaign generated on behalf of common schools. It brought what was essentially a civic movement within the scope of a broad Protestant consensus and in the process won for it untold support. Of course, Beecher's efforts also helped to Protestantize the common school during the period of its modern definition and thereby created one of the political problems it would persistently encounter from that time forward.[54]

In the course of her campaign to save the West, Beecher published a succession of essays, addresses, and manuals, each of which in its own way pointed to a new American consensus concerning female roles that she herself was helping to shape. "In civil and political affairs," she wrote in A Treatise on Domestic Economy (1841), "American women take no interest or concern, except so far as they sympathize with their family and personal friends. . . . In matters pertaining to the education of their children, in the selection and support of a clergyman, in all benevolent enterprises, and in all questions relating to morals or manners, they have a superior influence." Primarily through the home and the school, women had a crucial responsibility in the new Republic to create the elevated morality and social unity on which the successful operation of republican institutions ultimately depended. Women were by nature divinely ordained and equipped for that responsibility, and a proper education would enable them to carry it out. "Let the women of a country be made virtuous and intelligent, and the men will certainly be the same," Beecher perorated. "If this be so, as none will deny, then to American women, more than to any others on earth, is committed the exalted privilege of extending over the world those blessed influences, that are to renovate degraded men, and 'clothe all climes with beauty.' "[55]

54. Mann, Lectures on Education, p. 73.
55. Catharine E. Beecher, A Treatise on Domestic Economy, for the Use of Young Ladies at Home, and at School (Boston: Marsh, Capen, Lyon, and Webb, 1841), pp. 9, 13.

Chapter 5

SYSTEMS OF SCHOOLING

It shall be the duty of the general assembly, as soon as circumstances will permit, to provide, by law for a general system of education, ascending in regular gradation from township schools to state university, wherein tuition shall be gratis, and equally open to all.

INDIANA CONSTITUTION OF 1816

The republican style in American education was compounded of four fundamental beliefs: that education was crucial to the vitality of the Republic; that a proper republican education consisted of the diffusion of knowledge, the nurturance of virtue (including patriotic civility), and the cultivation of learning; that schools and colleges were the best agencies for providing a proper republican education on the scale required; and that the most effective means of obtaining the requisite number and kind of schools and colleges was through some system tied to the polity. The colonists had long manifested a commitment to education as an instrument of individual and social development, and they had increasingly expressed that commitment during the provincial era in their support and patronage of schools and colleges. What was fresh in the republican style (though scarcely fresh in the history of Western thought) was the emphasis on system, on a functional organization of individual schools and colleges that put them into regular relationship with one another and with the polity. The very novelty of the idea bespoke a variety of approaches, and indeed one leading theme in the history of American education during the first century of the Republic is the remarkable multiplicity of institutional ways and means by which states and localities moved to the creation of public school systems.

New York, for example, created a board of regents in 1784 and charged it with oversight of Columbia College (King's College redivivus) and such other schools and colleges as the regents might choose to establish in other parts of the state. But the single comprehensive system envisioned in the legislation of 1784 was not to be. Within twenty-five years the regents were overseeing colleges and secondary schools, but the legislature and the several towns of the state were overseeing common schools; while in New York City the Common Council, having assigned a portion of its state subsidy to the local charity schools, was overseeing no schools because it had simply failed to establish any. Massachusetts made room for a similar comprehensive design in its Constitution of 1780, which enjoined the legislature to "cherish" all seminaries of learning, especially the university at Cambridge, the public schools, and the grammar schools. The legislature in due course provided for elementary and secondary schools (though interestingly there were no public primary schools in Boston until 1818), and under the leadership of Horace Mann the state did develop a model school system; but the legislature also concluded that cherishing Harvard did not mean continuing that institution's traditional financial subsidies, with the result that from 1830 on Harvard became more and more a private institution. Virginia tried repeatedly to establish a comprehensive system along Jeffersonian lines, but for decades the most notable result remained the state university. All effort to go beyond a patchwork quilt of public, quasi-public, religious, and pauper schools on the elementary and secondary levels failed until Reconstruction, and even then the venture was viewed by many as a Yankee imposition. Michigan, by contrast, moved early and decisively to establish a comprehensive public system extending from the elementary school through the state university, and indeed for a time that state was actually inhospitable to various forms of nonpublic schooling.

Variegation, then, was the rule, and with it improvisation, imitation, trial and error—whatever historical development there was ended up anything but uniform and linear. Yet, by the 1850's and 1860's, visitors from abroad could clearly discern an American public school system as an autochthonous institutional creation, while Americans on their side tended to view that system as an inspired bequest handed down to them directly from their Puritan ancestors. The passage of the Morrill Act in 1862, with its provision of federal assistance for the establishment of public colleges of agriculture and the mechanic arts, created additional opportunities to ponder the design of the system, as state legislatures were required to decide where the new institutions would be located and what their relationship would be to the schools and colleges already in existence.

All of this went forward via a political process that was informed by the arguments of the Jeffersons, the Manns, and the Beechers, but never wholly dependent upon them. For one thing, the expansion of schooling had begun in the provincial era and clearly antedated the rise of public school systems. For another, the development of public school systems was frequently tied to other political agenda: the sponsors of public schooling in Massachusetts in the 1830's included Whigs who strongly favored internal improvements (Horace Mann wanted a railroad system as well as a public school system), and the sponsors of the Morrill Act in the 1860's included Republicans who sought a land policy that would unite the industrializing North with the agricultural West. Finally, the shifting coalitions that in the end created unitary comprehensive public school systems may well have opted for a political program that was strongly preferred by an articulate few but that was at best acceptable to a decisive majority. Once the majority had achieved its goal, the articulate few who had originally urged that goal proceeded to develop a substantial rhetoric of justification. In doing so, they imposed a larger social meaning on what had been accomplished and thereby furnished a continuing basis of ideological support for the enterprise.

II

The creation of the University of the State of New York was an extraordinary event in the life of the early Republic, in both the breadth of its aspiration and the artistry of its design. The initial legislation of 1784 sought to attend to two immediate concerns: the continuation of King's College in some cleansed post-Revolutionary form and the more general promotion of literature and learning throughout the state. The instrument wrought for the task was a university designed not as a teaching institution but rather as an administrative system for a number of teaching institutions at various academic levels, governed by a board of regents with broad supervisory powers. The first board was dominated by King's College men and devoted itself almost exclusively to the affairs of that institution (the legislation renamed it Columbia College). Not surprisingly, pressure developed for a more representative political apparatus, with the result that revised legislation in 1787 created the university anew, this time primarily as a comprehensive administrative organization. There has been some debate over the origins of the revised law, but the evidence seems to point to the key role of three regents, James Duane, Ezra L'Hommedieu, and Alexander Hamilton, and the influence of the English Commonwealth tradition, as articulated by William Livingston and his associates during the 1750's in the *Independent Reflector*.

Whatever the hopes of those who conceived the university as some single comprehensive organization that would coordinate the development of the state's schools and colleges, the drift of affairs was otherwise. After several years of urging from both the regents and Governor George Clinton, the legislature in 1795 passed an act for the encouragement of schools, which provided for annual appropriations of two thousand pounds for a period of five years, the money to be apportioned among towns demonstrating a willingness to tax themselves for the maintenance of schools. Specific provision was made whereby New York City could use part of its portion for the support of "the several charity schools" of that city; and in the end it was the schools for poor children conducted by various churches and benevolent societies that received the city's entire share. Thus, the legislation of 1795 neither expanded the regents' system nor created an alternative system; it simply encouraged schools.[1]

The program of 1795 was not renewed when it expired in 1800. But the pressure for expanded schooling under civil auspices persisted. In 1805 the legislature created a permanent school fund, but made no provision for the expenditure of the interest. And then in 1811 Governor Daniel D. Tompkins appointed a commission to draft for the next session of the legislature "a system for the organization and establishment of common schools." The commission duly reported on February 14, 1812 (in a document marvelously representative of the republican style), and the legislature acted the following June. Unlike its predecessor of 1795, the new law was patently intended to erect a system. Its very first provisions created a state superintendency of schools and defined as among the responsibilities of the office the development of plans for the better management of schools and their resources. Subsequent provisions established a three-tiered organization of the system, with local districts (created by the towns) responsible for the maintenance of school buildings, the towns responsible for the employment and oversight of schoolteachers, and the state responsible for assisting local effort via the diffusion of information and the distribution of interest from the permanent school fund. One supplementary bill enacted in 1813 named the Common Council of New York City the custodian of that city's share of the annual state appropriation and authorized the

---

1. An Act for the Encouragement of Schools, April 9, 1795, in Thomas E. Finegan, ed., *Free Schools: A Documentary History of the Free School Movement in New York State* (Albany: The University of the State of New York, 1921), p. 29.

apportionment of the appropriation among such groups as the Free School Society (later the Public School Society), the Orphan Asylum Society, and the Manumission Society (which ran the African Free Schools), and the various religious societies that conducted charity schools in the city. Another supplementary bill enacted in 1814 authorized localities to make up any deficits in annual school budgets by a tax on the parents of schoolchildren, provided that poor and indigent families were exempted (the assessments were called "rate bills" and were levied according to the number of children a family had at school).[2]

The intent of the legislation of 1812–1814 was clear and explicit. It created a school system, but it was a system that stood alongside the university rather than within it. Moreover, as the various institutions comprised by the two systems evolved, there were further divisions within the systems themselves. Thus, Columbia College and then Union College (chartered in 1795) and Hamilton College (chartered in 1812), and the dozen-odd additional colleges chartered before the Civil War, were entitled to their own boards of trustees under the university legislation of 1787, and these boards found it increasingly difficult to obtain funds from the state—after 1812 the legislature consistently favored the common schools. As a result, though they were technically constituent parts of the university system, the colleges went their own separate ways, guided largely by presidents, trustees, and patrons.

In a quite different realm, the regents incorporated over three hundred academies between 1787 and 1876 (not all of which flourished) and oversaw their general development as college preparatory institutions, the goal being systematically to articulate them with the colleges. Nevertheless, there were also academies chartered by the legislature as well as academies that were never chartered at all, and in addition there were high schools under local control that grew up as part of the public school system. Finally, there was the special case of New York City, which for all intents and purposes went its own way, accepting the schools of the Public School Society along with a number of other eleemosynary and denominational institutions as its public school system until the creation of a public board of education in 1842. Over and over again, as the development of schools went forward, hopes for a single comprehensive system gave way to alternative arrangements.

For all the power of the drive toward systematization, then, the result in New York was several systems and subsystems, each comprising institutions of varying degrees of publicness. Variegation was the rule,

2. Finegan, ed., *Free Schools*, p. 37.

and it remained the rule even after the great legislative battles of the 1840's, 1850's, and 1860's had made the common school generally tax supported and free of tuition. As for higher education, whatever the hopes and fears of the regents at different times in their history, New York would have no state university as a teaching institution (apart from the Morrill Act colleges at Cornell) until after World War II.

Massachusetts also moved toward systematization, but with no such grand design as the University of the State of New York. The Constitution of 1780 made broad provision for the advancement of education, charging legislators and magistrates to cherish seminaries of learning (especially the university at Cambridge, the public schools, and the grammar schools in the towns); to encourage institutions for the promotion of agriculture, arts, sciences, commerce, trade, and manufactures; and to inculcate the principles of humanity, benevolence, charity, industry, honesty, punctuality, and sincerity in the population at large. With respect to schools, the legislature decided in 1789 to codify into a single law the various practices that had become standard during the provincial era. By its provisions, towns having fifty or more families were required to furnish six months of schooling (distributed among one or more schools) during the course of the year, while towns which had grown to two hundred families were also required to support a grammar school. In addition, the practice of school districting, which had grown up in the eighteenth century as one response to the continuing settlement of the rural areas, was formally sanctioned (though districts were not granted the power to tax until 1800). There was little debate over the measure insofar as it merely codified the commonplace; and, though the legislature recognized a three-tiered organization of school governance, with the state mandating and encouraging, the towns serving as prime agents, and the districts coming into being as surrogates for the towns in certain functions, there was no attempt to systematize beyond the general requirement that teachers at all levels (including those at Harvard) nurture piety, patriotism, and virtue and that ministers and selectmen in the several towns regularly visit and inspect the schools and inquire into the maintenance of discipline and the proficiency of the scholars.

As for the university at Cambridge, the legislature was initially generous in subsidizing faculty salaries, but then denied all requests for assistance until 1814, when it divided the proceeds of a bank tax among Harvard, Williams (chartered in 1793), and Bowdoin (chartered in 1794). Meanwhile, the legislature altered Harvard's charter from time to time to make it more or less responsive to changing legislative opinion. Finally, the legislature incorporated some thirty-six academies by 1820, beginning with the Phillips Academy at Andover in 1780. Once again, however, there was no attempt to organize these various institutions into a system.

The attempt to systematize really began during the 1820's with the efforts of James G. Carter, a young teacher and journalist who had settled in Lancaster after his graduation from Harvard in 1820. Carter's views appeared in the Boston press from time to time between 1821 and 1826, but his influence and reputation stemmed largely from two widely circulated pamphlets that gathered his ideas together and tied them to specific recommendations—*Letters to the Hon. William Prescott, LL.D. on the Free Schools of New England, with Remarks on the Principles of Instruction* (1824) and *Essays upon Popular Education* (1826). The thrust of the pamphlets was twofold, first, to lament what Carter perceived as a dangerous decline in public concern for schooling, and, second, to spark a revival of public interest at the state level. "If the policy of the legislature, in regard to free schools, for the last twenty years be not changed," Carter warned, "the institution, which has been the glory of New England will, in twenty years more, be extinct. If the states continue to relieve themselves of the trouble of providing for the instruction of the whole people, and to shift the responsibility upon the towns, and the towns upon the districts, and the districts upon individuals, each will take care of himself and his own family as he is able, and as he appreciates the blessing of a good education." Carter's immediate proposal was for the establishment of a public teacher-training seminary as part of the state's free school system. But more important, perhaps, was the leitmotif that sounded through *Essays upon Popular Education*, namely, that the legislature take the lead in strengthening and encouraging the towns to remedy the inequities of the districts. Centralization—and with it systematization—was Carter's answer to the lamentable decline of schooling he perceived in Massachusetts.[3]

One can draw a direct line from Carter's efforts of the 1820's to the establishment of the Massachusetts board of education in 1837. As has been indicated, Carter himself played an influential role in the creation of the board, though the instrument that actually resulted from his efforts was granted comparatively little power by the legislature. The board's principal responsibilities were to gather data from the towns (which the towns were required to furnish under an 1834 law estab-

3. James G. Carter, *Essays upon Popular Education* (Boston: Bowles & Dearborn, 1826), p. 41.

lishing a permanent school fund and providing for distribution of the income) and to report annually on the condition and efficacy of the schools; and even its paid secretary was entrusted primarily with the task of collecting and diffusing information on "the most approved and successful methods of arranging the studies and conducting the education of the young." Yet, in the end, Horace Mann turned powerlessness into a virtue, using the secretaryship as a lectern from which to educate not only the legislature but teachers, school committees, reformers in other states, and the political leaders of a half-dozen foreign countries.[4]

Mann sounded the theme of systematization early and powerfully in his lectures and reports. "In this Commonwealth," he remarked in his lecture of 1837, "there are about three thousand public schools, in all of which the rudiments of knowledge are taught. These schools, at the present time, are so many distinct, independent communities; each being governed by its own habits, traditions, and local customs. There is no common, superintending power over them; there is no bond of brotherhood or family between them. They are strangers and aliens to each other. The teachers are, as it were, imbedded, each in his own school district; and they are yet to be excavated and brought together, and to be established, each as a polished pillar of a holy temple. As the system is now administered, if any improvement in principles or modes of teaching is discovered by talent or accident, in one school, instead of being published to the world, it dies with the discoverer. No means exist for multiplying new truths, or even for preserving old ones."[5]

The observations hold one key to Mann's conception of system. He continued to insist that he was not concerned with putting forth a series of perfect models to which there would be universal conformity. Rather, he wished to promulgate widely those general principles on which intelligent educational choice inevitably depended. Systematization, he would have argued, meant rationality, not uniformity. Still, the call for uniformity also sounded through his reports—uniformity of textbooks, uniformity of curricula, uniformity of library collections, uniformity of methods, and uniformity of discipline. Here as elsewhere Mann faced the paradox of all reformers. What he saw as irrefutable truth, his opponents saw as partisan doctrine, with the result that an effort conceived as being above party or faction—for the good of the commonweal—became enmeshed in political controversy. Mann persisted, though, ever convinced that uniformities were minima required in the

4. Massachusetts, *Laws of the Commonwealth of Massachusetts* (1837), chap. ccxli, sec. 2.

5. Horace Mann, *Lectures on Education* (Boston: Ide & Dutton, 1855), p. 19.

cause of equity. And, when critics such as Edward A. Newton or Matthew Hale Smith or the Boston schoolmasters suggested that no ephemeral equity could ever justify a strongheaded uniformity, Mann was uncomprehending. However that may be, Mann weathered the political storms and systematization was advanced, bringing, along with a measure of equity, an increasingly politicized concern for education.

Mann at several points during his secretaryship undertook to explicate what he liked to refer to as "the theory of the Massachusetts free school system." In every instance he pointed with pride to the district schools open to all as well as to the more advanced schools of the larger towns open to those marked by "a peculiar destination, or an impelling spirit of genius"; and after 1839 he was also wont to include the public normal schools as well. But he was always careful to note that at the conclusion of the town secondary schools "seminaries for higher learning, academies and universities, should stand ready to receive, at private cost, all whose path to any ultimate destination may lie through their halls." This, Mann went on to explain, was "the paternal and comprehensive theory of our institutions." For all intents and purposes, Mann was merely reflecting the situation as it had developed in Massachusetts by the 1830's. By that time, Harvard, Williams, and Amherst (chartered in 1825) and the hundred-odd incorporated academies had drifted toward "privateness" in theory and in fact; and, though the drift did not prevent them from perpetually seeking public subsidies, they received such subsidies only occasionally and increasingly grudgingly. By the time Mann left office in 1848, they were not only considered to be outside the public school system, they were actually viewed by some as hostile to the public school system and, in the case of the academies, essentially competitive with it.[6]

Finally, it is important to note that Mann constantly inveighed against parental indifference to schooling, but at no point recommended a compulsory attendance policy. Rather, he advocated regulations that would require children either to attend regularly or not at all. The point was to awaken parents, not to compel attendance. And indeed, when Massachusetts actually enacted the first general compulsory school attendance statute in 1852 (requiring every child between eight and fourteen, with certain stipulated exceptions, to attend some public or other school for at least twelve weeks each year, six weeks to be consecutive), it was neither Mann, nor Mann's successor, Barnas Sears,

6. *First Annual Report of the Board of Education, Together with the First Annual Report of the Secretary of the Board* (1837), pp. 55–56.

nor the board, nor the teaching profession, nor the local town school committees that pushed through the law. It was rather organized labor and reform groups concerned about youthful idleness on the one hand and youthful exploitation on the other, that pressed its enactment. While the legislation had little immediate effect, owing to indifferent enforcement, it did lead ultimately to a momentous shift in the configuration of American education.

Virginia tried repeatedly to create a comprehensive school system along Jeffersonian lines, but proponents of the various plans submitted proved unable to put together the necessary political coalitions. Indeed, on at least one occasion when a comprehensive program had passed the House of Delegates, none other than Jefferson himself helped defeat it in the Senate. The occasion, of course, was the session of 1816–17, and the sponsor of the measure that failed was Charles Fenton Mercer.

Mercer is an interesting figure in the history of American education, and the failure of his program reveals a good deal about the politics of education during the early national period. A native of Fredericksburg, Mercer had attended the College of New Jersey (Princeton), graduating in 1797 at the head of his class, and had then gone on to read law, winning admission to the bar in 1802. He entered politics in 1810 as a member of the Virginia House of Delegates (from Loudoun County in the northern part of the state) and remained there until 1817, when he went on to a seat in Congress. And it was as a Federalist member of the House of Delegates that he led in efforts to develop Virginia's economy via a program of internal improvements, one component of which would be education. For Mercer, as for Mann during his subsequent career in the Massachusetts lower house, economic development involved the expansion of opportunity for schooling at all levels.

Virginia had established a literary fund in 1810, the interest from which was to be appropriated "to the sole benefit of a school or schools, to be kept in each and every county . . . subject to such orders and regulations as the general assembly shall hereafter direct." The fund was not large—in its first year it yielded an income of approximately a thousand dollars—and the legislature voted in 1811 to contribute the entire proceeds to the education of the poor, "an object equally humane, just and necessary, involving alike the interests of humanity and the preservation of the constitution, laws and liberty of the good people of this commonwealth." In 1816, however, under the leadership of Mercer, the fund was designated the repository of substantial rebates and debt obligations of the federal government to Virginia, with the result that, for the first time in its history as a state, Virginia appeared in a position to have a comprehensive system of public schooling (which was widely desired) without a substantial program of local taxation (which was widely opposed).[7]

It was in this context that Mercer introduced a bill "providing for the establishment of primary schools, academies, colleges, and a university." As has been mentioned, it proposed a state-sponsored system of primary schools along with state-aided academies and colleges and a state university somewhere in the Shenandoah Valley; and it also provided for a state board of public instruction with responsibility for creating a comprehensive system of public instruction that would have co-opted a number of extant schools, academies, and colleges, while establishing a significant number of new institutions, among them a new university. Mercer's program succeeded in the House but was defeated in the Senate by a substantial coalition of eastern elitists and Jeffersonian Republicans. The fact is that every partisan of every educational scheme in Virginia, contemplated or already in operation, had his eye on the income from the augmented literary fund, and Mercer simply could not garner the support required.[8]

There were two more major efforts to legislate a comprehensive system of public schooling before the Civil War, one in 1829 and one in 1846. But the general thrust of the legislation that resulted was to make publicly supported schooling for the poor mandatory and publicly supported schooling for everyone else subject to local option (and local taxation). The legislation of 1846 did make obligatory the establishment of county boards of school commissioners and the election of county superintendents of schools by those boards; but, except in the case of the handful of counties that opted for tax-supported primary schools open to all whites, the boards and the superintendents oversaw only schools for the poor. In the end, on the pre-university level, Virginia systematized only pauper schooling in the era before the Civil War.

On the university level, of course, the story was quite different. The legislature for all intents and purposes adopted the report of the Rockfish Gap commissioners, which Jefferson wrote in 1818, and in a bill

7. Virginia, *Acts Passed at a General Assembly of the Commonwealth of Virginia* (1809), chap. xiv, p. 15; Virginia, *Acts Passed at a General Assembly of the Commonwealth of Virginia* (1810), chap. viii, sec. 5.

8. The bill is given in A. J. Morrison, *The Beginning of Public Education in Virginia, 1776–1860* (Richmond: State Board of Education, 1917), pp. 32–34.

enacted during the first weeks of 1819 created a new university on the foundation of Central College in Charlottesville. The act provided for a board of visitors appointed by the governor to oversee the institution and for an annuity of fifteen thousand dollars to support the institution. In effect, neither the provision for the board nor the grant of the public subsidy was substantially different from what the Massachusetts legislature was doing vis-à-vis Harvard at about the same time. But the spirit of the new university, as articulated by Jefferson, as well as the sources and timing of its establishment made the differences profound. Whereas Harvard within a generation was to be one model of the private American university, Virginia was destined to be the archetype of the public state university.

The Civil War wrought havoc with Virginia's schools and colleges: the literary fund was diverted; students and teachers went off to military service; and educational facilities were in some instances destroyed and in others converted into hospitals, barracks, and headquarters. And after Appomattox there was not only the impoverishment of defeat but the widespread feeling that free schools and school systems were an accursed Yankee invention designed to promote racial mixing. For the very reason of bestowing full citizenship on the newly emancipated blacks, however, Reconstruction conventions and legislatures were insistent upon the establishment of free schools, with the result that the Virginia Constitution of 1870 mandated the creation of a "uniform system of free public schools" by 1876, and the 1870 Act to Establish and Maintain a System of Public Free Schools called for a statewide system of free primary schools under a three-tiered arrangement for governance that included school districts, county superintendents, a state board of education, and a state superintendent of public instruction. The university was also revived with its traditional state subsidy; but interestingly, in light of its Jeffersonian heritage, it was unable to win for itself the funds that accrued to the state under the Morrill Act, and instead Virginia's Morrill Act programs in agriculture and the mechanic arts were established at Hampton Institute and at a new A & M college at Blacksburg.[9]

Education was nowhere mentioned in the federal Constitution, with the result that it remained among the powers that the Tenth Amendment reserved "to the states respectively, or to the people." The several

9. Virginia Constitution of 1870, Article VIII, in *The Federal and State Constitutions, Colonial Charters, and Other Organic Laws,* edited by Francis Newton Thorpe (7 vols.; Washington, D.C.: Government Printing Office, 1909), VII, 3892.

states therefore felt free by tradition and by law to go their own particular ways in education, though from the very beginning they taught
one another and borrowed freely back and forth. Horace Mann was
wont to cite the experience of New York State where it seemed to him
in advance of Massachusetts; New York in turn circulated Mann's
Common School Journal to its local school districts and actually reprinted Mann's Fifth Annual Report at public expense. Similarly, Charles
Fenton Mercer cited the experience not only of New York and Massachusetts but also of Rhode Island, Connecticut, and New Hampshire in
pressing his program of 1817, alluding to the "humiliation" Virginians
must have felt as their youngsters went North for an education. In the
newer states, with bequeathed traditions depending on the origins of
their settlers, imitation combined with innovation to form patterns that
varied from the familiar to the bizarre. The early experience of Michigan is illustrative, though in the West as in the East the states continued to go their separate ways.[10]

The territory that became Michigan initially fell within the Northwest Territory and was therefore formally governed under the land ordinances of 1785 and 1787. The township system of settlement was ordained, and the sixteenth section of each township was reserved "for
the maintenance of public schools within the said township"; and, in
the interest of religion, morality, and good government, schools and
the means of education were forever to be encouraged. As in most of
the newly settled regions, the population was sparse and survival was
the first order of business, with the result that education devolved upon
the family and whatever ad hoc arrangements groups of families could
make with ministers, schoolteachers, or their surrogates. The formal
creation of the territory of Michigan in 1805 brought a variety of laws
concerning schooling, none of which was particularly well carried out;
but surely the most interesting and far reaching of these was the law
creating the Catholepistemiad, or University of Michigania, in 1817.[11]

The story of the Catholepistemiad is inseparable from the story of
the man who conceived it, Augustus B. Woodward, chief justice of the
Supreme Court of the Michigan Territory. Born and raised in New
York, Woodward had attended Columbia College from 1789 to 1793.
Thereafter he had taught for a time at Liberty Hall Academy in Lexington, Virginia, and probably simultaneously read law (the details of
his legal education are ephemeral, though there is clear evidence that

10. The Constitution of the United States, in Henry Steele Commager, ed., *Documents of American History* (9th ed.; 2 vols.; New York: Appleton-Century-Crofts, 1973), I, 146.
11. Land Ordinance of 1785, in *ibid.*, I, 124.

he was practicing law in the spring of 1799). It was also during his residence in Virginia that he became a regular visitor to Monticello, beginning what would be a lifelong discipleship to Jefferson. During the first years of Jefferson's presidency, Woodward settled in Washington and participated actively in the politics of that city. Several years later, Jefferson appointed him to the Michigan judgeship.

The powers of the governor and judges were considerable, and for the next three decades Woodward did everything from holding court for the purpose of settling land titles to laying out a plan for the city of Detroit. Sometime in 1817, he turned his attention to the establishment of a comprehensive system of education for the territory. The plan he developed was an amalgam of sound ideas expressed in bizarre Greco-Roman neologisms. It called for a university (Catholepistemiad) of thirteen departments (didaxia) covering the full gamut of scholarly studies. The governing body would consist of the president and professors (didactors), and support would come from general taxes, state lotteries (two were actually drawn), and voluntary contributions (the city of Detroit raised three thousand dollars). So far, the Catholepistemiad was a university described in quaint language. But it went far beyond the thirteen professorships, for the plan also called for a subordinate apparatus of colleges, academies, schools, libraries, museums, athenaeums, and botanical gardens. In other words, the Catholepistemiad came fully equipped with feeder and associated institutions and comprised for all intents and purposes a complete system of education.

What were the sources of Woodward's remarkable plan? The Napoleonic university? Jefferson's vision of the University of Virginia (the two men might have discussed such ideas during Woodward's visits to Monticello)? The University of the State of New York, which was new and full of hope when Woodward attended Columbia College? There is no way of knowing, though Woodward's scheme did embody elements similar to all three. In any case, the Catholepistemiad was duly legislated into existence and actually began operation in 1817 or 1818, but only at the primary and secondary levels. Though later judicial decisions would trace the formal legal origins of the University of Michigan to the enactment of 1817, the Catholepistemiad never offered instruction at the exalted level envisioned by Woodward.

There is a significance about the Catholepistemiad, however, that should not be ignored, for it introduced a notion of comprehensiveness into the discussion of educational affairs in Michigan that remained operative throughout the formative period of the state. The Constitution of 1835 included one of the most inclusive articles on education to appear in any of the early state constitutions. Probably prepared by John D. Pierce and Isaac Crary, two New Englanders who had immigrated to the territory during the 1830's, the article created a state superintendency of public instruction, charged the legislature with providing for a system of common schools and town libraries, and also enjoined it to exert the utmost care in managing the lands set aside for the support of the university. When Pierce, an alumnus of Brown University who had settled in Michigan under the aegis of the American Home Missionary Society, was appointed the first superintendent of public instruction, he considered his responsibility to be the entire system, from the primary schools through the university. Later, the Constitution of 1850 confirmed the early commitment to comprehensiveness, repeating the major provisions of 1835 and adding provisions for an elected board of regents to oversee the University of Michigan; for an agricultural school to promote intellectual, scientific, and agricultural improvements; and for special institutions for the deaf, the dumb, and the blind. It took time for these constitutional mandates to be translated into law, and as a matter of fact the district schools of Michigan did not actually become free until 1870. But the systematization inherent in a centralized comprehensive scheme was present from the beginning.[12]

One additional point is worthy of note. It was in Michigan that the right of local school districts (in the particular instance, union school districts) to operate free high schools capable of preparing young people for the university was legally tested and established. The question was an interesting one, since by mid-century there were two related but quite different thrusts present in the state school system, one more practicalist in orientation and embodied in free primary schools supplemented by free secondary schools in the towns (recall Horace Mann's argument concerning the theory of the Massachusetts free school system) and the other more academic in orientation and embodied in a public university with a feeder apparatus of public primary and secondary schools (recall Woodward's Catholepistemiad). In the merging of the two into a single comprehensive system, it was almost certain that there would be controversy around the precise definition of secondary schooling, and such was indeed the case, with Kalamazoo, Michigan, as the locale.

12. In a memoir written many years later, Pierce recounted that he and Crary had discussed at length Victor Cousin's report on the Prussian school system (the thrust of which was decidedly in favor of centralization) and drawn from it the "fundamental principles" they deemed essential to the proper development of education in the new state; the most fundamental of these was a well-supported comprehensive system of public schooling. See John D. Pierce, "Origins and Progress of the Michigan School System," *Michigan Pioneer Collections*, I (1877), 37–45.

The facts were fairly simple. For many years Kalamazoo had sent those of its youngsters wishing to prepare for the university to the preparatory department of Kalamazoo College (chartered in 1855). But in 1858 Kalamazoo created a union high school, with one Daniel Putnam as superintendent. The school carried on its work for several years amid growing controversy, teaching not only advanced English subjects but also the classical languages, mathematics, and natural sciences required for entry into the university. In 1873, a number of prominent citizens filed suit to restrain the school board from spending public money on the high school. The local circuit judge who initially heard the case decided against the complainants, affirming the right of the board to maintain a high school with tax funds. When the case was appealed, the Michigan Supreme Court unanimously upheld the lower court. Judge Thomas M. Cooley and his associates pointed to the two traditions of secondary schooling that had emerged in the state, one deriving from the university legislation of 1817 and the provision for public academies, the other deriving from the Constitution of 1835 and the provision for free public primary schooling (which had then been extended to include high schools). The melding of the two, the opinion held, provided ample precedent for the actions of the Kalamazoo school board: "If these facts do not demonstrate clearly and conclusively a general state policy, beginning in 1817 and continuing until after the adoption of the present constitution [1850], in the direction of free schools in which education, and at their option the elements of classical education, might be brought within the reach of all the children of the state, then, as it seems to us, nothing can demonstrate it."[13]

Ultimately, what the Michigan Supreme Court had confirmed was the unitary as well as the comprehensive character of the Michigan (and the American) school system. There would not be in Kalamazoo, as was the case in contemporary Europe, two secondary school systems, one for those desiring a practical education and one for those aiming toward the university. It was an immensely influential decision, widely cited in other states; and, as often happened in nineteenth-century America, the holding of a state court took on important national overtones.

III

As had long been true, significant numbers of Americans during the nineteenth century continued to pursue their education entirely within

13. *Charles E. Stuart and others* v. *School District No. 1 of the Village of Kalamazoo and others,* 30 Michigan (1874), 84.

families and churches or through more informal means. For some, the alternative represented a choice; for others, it was imposed by physical or social circumstance. Nevertheless, as schooling became increasingly prevalent (as the century progressed, greater numbers of people had some schooling) and as one state after another adopted compulsory school attendance legislation (whose initial effect in the aggregate seems to have been to hold youngsters already enrolled in school to somewhat better records of attendance), the line separating those who had had some schooling from those who had not became more clearly etched. What had once been commonplace became increasingly a departure from the commonplace.

The boundary between public and private schooling also took on new prominence, though here, too, the distinctions were in process of becoming and therefore unclear and inconsistent. In 1813, for example, when New York City used its share of the state's public school subsidy to assist the charity schools maintained by the various denominations of the city, those charity schools were doubtless perceived by most as public or common schools. Later, in the 1820's and 1830's, when the Free School Society (renamed the Public School Society in 1826) insisted that denominational schools ought not to get money appropriated for the support of common schools, the city council was forced to wrestle with the definition of a common school. And then, in the 1840's, when Roman Catholics in New York accused the state-chartered but nongovernmental Public School Society of maintaining a Protestant bias and demanded that they be given a share of tax support for their own schools or that a public board be created to replace the Society, the task of definition fell to the state legislature. The legislature resolved the issue by passing an act "To Extend to the City and County of New York the Provisions of the General Act in Relation to Common Schools." In due course, the Public School Society went out of existence and the Roman Catholics set out to expand their own parochial school system.[14]

A similar process of definition took place in the realm of higher education, with even more tortuous twists and turns and even less clarity. The simple fact of being chartered gave an institution an aura of publicness during the last years of the eighteenth and first years of the nineteenth centuries, and almost as if to symbolize this publicness a charter frequently brought a public subsidy. A half-century later, after charters had been widely associated with the world of competitive busi-

14. New York (State), *Laws of the State of New-York* (1842), chap. cl.

ness, the publicness of a chartered institution was less clear. Compounding the shift was the changing relationship of the colleges and the churches. Before the disestablishment of the Congregational church in Massachusetts in 1833, to take but one example, the Congregational church was public, and so for all intents and purposes were Harvard College, Williams College, and Amherst College. The simple legislating of disestablishment did not change those perceptions overnight. In Michigan, on the other hand, where the first eighteen years of statehood witnessed what was for all intents and purposes a war between the state university and the aspiring denominational colleges, the distinctions were established early and clearly. In Massachusetts, they remained unclear through much of the nineteenth century.

Finally, the issue of publicness inevitably extended to the academy, which since the provincial era had overlapped both the primary school and the college as a characteristically general American institution. For fully a century in the life of the Republic the academy was the prevalent form of secondary education, until its decline in favor of the public high school during the 1880's and 1890's. While it prevailed, it came in every size, shape, and form, and under every variety of sponsorship. Many were chartered, many more were not. Some were the ephemeral enterprises of particular teachers, some had corporate boards that transcended particular teachers. Some were tied to local communities, some to church assemblies, some to government agencies. Some were supported by endowments, some by taxes, some by subscriptions, some by tuition rates, and most by some combination of the four. In New York, under the aegis (and subvention) of the regents, the state actually organized academies into a "system" for a time, with special responsibility for the training of teachers. They seemed infinitely adaptable to particular needs and opportunities, and, indeed, in 1845 Edward Hitchcock, the president of Amherst College, celebrated the academy as a quintessentially American institution: it breathed the American spirit of liberty from government restraint; it incarnated American individualism; and its form and traditions made it ideal for experiment.[15]

Definitions of public and private, then, were neither precise nor static during the nineteenth century; they were rather in process of evolution. And Edward Hitchcock could look upon the academies of Mas-

15. John Walter Gifford, *Historical Development of the New York State High School System* (Albany: J.B. Lyon, 1922); and Edward Hitchcock, *The American Academy System Defended: An Address Delivered at the Dedication of the New Hall of Williston Seminary, in Easthampton, January 28, 1845* (Amherst, Mass.: J.S. & C. Adams, 1845).

sachusetts as no less *American* than the common schools were to Horace Mann. Moreover, though systematization advanced, isolated, idiosyncratic institutions persisted, as indeed did the possibility (though not the prevalence) of education entirely devoid of schooling. And, to compound the range of alternatives even further, there were not only school systems under government auspices, there were school systems under church auspices as well. In fact, the development of the church systems was in many ways a response to sharpening definitions of public schooling.

The fastest growing and best organized of the church systems was the Roman Catholic. Catholic efforts in the diocese of New York have already been alluded to, and they are worthy of elaboration because of their influence elsewhere. The first Roman Catholic school in New York was established in connection with St. Peter's Church in 1801 and the second in connection with St. Patrick's in 1815; both schools received a share of the city's state school subsidy (along with the Free School Society, the Manumission Society, the Orphan Asylum Society, and several other sponsors of denominational schools). After 1825, however, the Common Council voted to restrict allocations from the state subsidy to nondenominational institutions, with the result that the two parish schools as well as two others maintained by the Sisters of Charity were barred from governmental assistance. The Roman Catholic clergy in the city objected strenuously, contending that the so-called undenominational schools of the Public School Society, which continued to receive aid as common schools, were not undenominational at all but in effect Protestant. They taught morality apart from religion (which the Catholics saw as a Protestant delusion) or they taught it in connection with Protestant doctrine (which the Catholics saw as blatant sectarianism), and in either case they conveyed hostility to Catholic history and culture. On any or all of these grounds, they were unacceptable for Catholic children. But there seemed no recourse, so Catholics continued to build their own schools—there were eight parish free schools by 1840 as well as a number of tuition schools—at the same time that they voiced their dissatisfaction with the prevailing government arrangement.

The smoldering controversy of the 1830's broke into open political conflict in 1840 when Governor William H. Seward included in his inaugural address the recommendation that immigrant groups be permitted to have public schools presided over by teachers of their own language and faith. "The children of foreigners," Seward argued, found in great numbers in our populous cities and towns, and in the vicinity of our public works, are too often deprived of the advantages of our system of public education, in consequence of prejudices arising from difference of language or religion. It ought never to be forgotten that the public welfare is as deeply concerned in their education as in that of our own children. I do not hesitate, therefore, to recommend the establishment of schools in which they may be instructed by teachers speaking the same language with themselves and professing the same faith. There would be no inequality in such a measure, since it happens from the force of circumstances, if not from choice, that the responsibilities of education are in most instances confided by us to native citizens, and occasions seldom offer for a trial of our magnanimity by committing that trust to persons differing from ourselves in the language or religion. Since we have opened our country and all its fullness to the oppressed of every nation, we should evince wisdom equal to such generosity by qualifying their children for the high responsibilities of citizenship.[16]

Encouraged by the governor, a number of the city's Catholic churches petitioned the Common Council for a share of the school fund. Learning of the petition, several other religious groups in the city—the Scotch Presbyterian Church and several Hebrew congregations—indicated that in the event the Catholic request was granted they, too, would want a pro rata share of the common school fund; while the trustees of the Public School Society entered a remonstrance contending that the state funds in question had been set aside for the support of common schools open to all on an equal basis and that to use such funds to assist sectarian institutions would be improper and unconstitutional. With the lines thus drawn, both sides marshaled their forces. The vigorous young coadjutor bishop of New York, John Hughes, assumed personal command of the Catholic effort, while the able lawyers of the Public School Society, Theodore Sedgwick and Hiram Ketchum, led the opposition. There were meetings and petitions and newspaper exchanges during the summer and fall, and on October 29 there was a full dress debate between Hughes, Sedgwick, and Ketchum before the Common Council. Early in 1841, the council reached a decision denying the Catholic petition.

Having lost in the council, the Catholics carried the matter to the state legislature, which deferred action until the following year. In the meantime, the local elections of 1841 were held, and in New York City they were dominated by the school issue. Neither the Democrats nor

16. *State of New York: Messages from the Governors,* edited by Charles Z. Lincoln (11 vols.; Albany: J. B. Lyon Company, 1909), III, 768.

the Whigs would provide the public assurances Hughes demanded: the issue, after all, was an explosive one, with the result that Hughes and his confreres eventually put forward their own ticket. The Democrats won by a landslide, and there is a good deal of evidence to the effect that Catholic endorsement made the difference in a number of instances. Yet, in the end, neither Hughes nor the Public School Society prevailed. Rather, the legislature acted to bring the city within the general provisions of the state school system, establishing a public board of education, placing the schools of the Public School Society and the other nongovernmental agencies enjoying public assistance under the jurisdiction of the board, and enjoining that no school "in which any religious sectarian doctrine or tenet shall be taught, inculcated, or practiced" receive public money under the terms of the act.[17]

Hughes claimed victory, but it was a Pyrrhic victory at best. Shortly afterward, he abandoned the effort to obtain public funds for the parochial schools or to bring about reforms that would make the common schools more acceptable for Catholic children and turned instead to the building up of a parochial school system under church auspices. "How are we to provide for the Catholic education of our children?" he asked in a widely published letter. "I answer: Not by agitating the questions of the constitutionality, legality, or expediency of state schools. Let us leave these points to be settled by politicians, legislators, political economists, philosophers, and denominations out of the church. . . . Let us then leave the public schools to themselves." The following year, in a Circular Letter to the diocese, he set forth what was in time to become American Catholic policy with respect to schooling:

It may not be out of place to urge upon you the necessity of providing for the primary education of your children, in connection with the principles of our holy religion. I think the time is almost come when it will be necessary to build the schoolhouse first, and the church afterwards. Our fellow citizens have adopted a system of general education which I fear will result in consequences, to a great extent, the reverse of those which are anticipated. They have attempted to divorce religion, under the plea of excluding the sectarianisms from elementary education and literature. There are some who seem to apprehend great mischief to the state, if the children in our public schools should have an opportunity of learning the first elements of the Christian doctrine in connection with their daily lessons. Happily they require of us only to contribute our portion of the expense necessary for the support of this system. This, as good citizens, we are bound to do; especially as we are not compelled

17. New York (State), *Laws of the State of New-York* (1842), chap. cl, sec. 14.

to send our children to such schools, to receive the doubtful equivalent which is to be given for the taxes collected. I hope that the friends of education may not be disappointed in their expectations of benefits from this system, whilst for myself, I may be allowed to say that I do not regard it as suited to a *Christian* land, whether Catholic or Protestant, however admirably it might be adapted to the social condition of an enlightened paganism.[18]

Within the New York archdiocese, new pastors were instructed to proceed upon the principle that in America, at least for the time being, the school would be before the church. Meanwhile, the First Plenary Council of Baltimore in 1852 urged bishops to see to it that schools be established in connection with the churches of their dioceses, an admonition repeated by the Second Plenary Council in 1866. There was a testing period as bishops in Michigan, Pennsylvania, Ohio, Massachusetts, Iowa, Alabama, and Virginia made their own efforts to obtain public funds for Catholic schools and then one by one adopted similar policies. Finally, the Third Plenary Council in 1884 made the policy mandatory and universal, requiring that, within two years of the promulgation of the Council, a parochial school be erected near each Catholic church (unless one was already in operation) and ordering Catholic parents to send their children to Catholic schools unless released from that obligation by the bishop or ordinary of the diocese.

It was really the Third Plenary Council, with its decrees concerning parochial schools, Catholic high schools, academies, and colleges, diocesan boards of education, and a Catholic University of America crowning the enterprise, that established a Catholic school system in the United States. But, well before the promulgations of that Council were put into effect, there was a nascent systematization of Catholic schools that flowed from the systematization of the Catholic church itself—from the authoritative promulgation of doctrine, the diocesan regulation of churches, the hierarchical organization of the clergy, and the social cohesiveness of the teaching orders. One must not read into that systematization the monolithic character imputed by contemporary or latter-day critics: pastors could be curmudgeons, teaching orders could and did ignore diocesan policies, and doctrine was incessantly debated. But it was a systematization that doubtless imposed a measure of order upon a congeries of schools, academies, and colleges conducted by pas-

18. Hughes's first letter, which was signed "Inquirer," appeared in several newspapers, including the *New York Freeman's Journal*, December 15, 1849. The Circular Letter is given in Lawrence Kehoe, ed., *Complete Works of the Most Rev. John Hughes* (2 vols.; New York: Lawrence Kehoe, 1865), II, 715.

tors, bishops, teaching orders, and laypersons of diversified backgrounds and abilities.

Catholics, of course, were not alone in their determination to develop an alternative system of schools. The Presbyterian Church, U.S.A. (Old School), for example, expressing dual concern over the general secularizing of the public schools and the aggressive determination of the Roman Catholics to build up their own parochial school system, also established a substantial system of parochial schooling between 1846 and 1870. The initial impetus came from the General Assembly during the 1840's, which gradually concluded under the intellectual leadership of James Waddel Alexander, Cortlandt Van Rensselaer, and Charles Hodge that Presbyterians in the United States could no longer "safely rely" on state common schools for proper religious training. On May 31, 1847, the Assembly adopted a resolution expressing conviction "that the interests of the church and the glory of our Redeemer, demand that immediate and strenuous exertions should be made, as far as practicable, by every congregation to establish within its bounds one or more primary schools, under the care of the session of the church, in which together with the usual branches of secular learning, the truths and duties of our holy religion shall be assiduously inculcated." Implementation of the policy was placed in the hands of the Assembly's board of education (under the leadership of Van Rensselaer), which was granted three thousand dollars to subsidize the work. To qualify for assistance, a school had to be under the care of a particular session and subject to the general supervision of the presbytery; it had to use the Bible as a textbook for daily instruction in religion; it had to be under the direction of a member of the Presbyterian church; and it had to report annually to the board. Van Rensselaer was unflagging in his efforts, and for the first seven years there was continued growth, with approximately a hundred schools flourishing in some twenty-six states and the District of Columbia between 1850 and 1855. Thereafter a decline set in: pastors lost interest or complained of the burden of maintaining schools; money was hard to raise; parents seemed insufficiently dissatisfied with the public schools; and a significant number of the parochial schools already in existence were seeking more advanced students, transforming themselves in the process into academies or even colleges. By 1870 the movement was really at an end, and the new constitution of the board of education adopted by the General Assembly that year carried no mention of parochial schools.[19]

The Presbyterian "system" was really a victim of the success of the public school system. But such was not uniformly the case with Protestant alternative systems. Thus, for example, the Evangelical Lutheran Synod of Missouri, Ohio, and Other States, organized in 1847, early settled on a policy of a parochial school for every congregation, and indeed among the early conditions of admission and retention for congregations were the stipulations that there be "Christian schooling of the children of the congregation" and that the curriculum be rooted in orthodox books, readers, hymnals, and catechisms. In addition, the Synod undertook on its own to oversee the effort, to assist with funds, to train pastors and teachers, to publish appropriate materials, and to sponsor a "college" (really a combined seminary and gymnasium to train pastors, teachers, and other professionals). Under the leadership of C.F.W. Walther, probably the most important early figure in the Synod, these policies were aggressively pursued, and during the first generation at least they received widespread adherence. But there was an additional factor that had not pertained in the Presbyterian effort, namely, the factor of language and culture. The Old-School Presbyterians were probably as dissatisfied with the common schools as the Evangelical Lutherans, but the Lutheran dissatisfaction on religious grounds was compounded by their desire to retain a religious-cultural-linguistic tradition. And that as much as anything contributed to the tenacity of the leadership in pursuing the policy and to the willingness of congregations to abide by it.[20]

IV

As has been suggested, the formal legal movement toward systems of public schooling was at best uneven and fluctuant. Constitutions would proclaim principles, which legislatures would then interpret or ignore. Thus, Indiana's constitution of 1816 made it the duty of the general assembly "as soon as circumstances will permit, to provide, by law for a general system of education, ascending in regular gradation from township schools to state university, wherein tuition shall be gratis, and equally open to all." Circumstances apparently did not "permit" for

19. *Minutes of the General Assembly of the Presbyterian Church in the U.S.A.* (1846), p. 118; and *Minutes of the General Assembly of the Presbyterian Church in the U.S.A.* (1847), p. 3.
20. *Lutheraner*, January 3, 1847.

more than three decades. In state after state, laws would be passed, only to be repealed a year or two later: Illinois went through the experience in 1825 and 1826, as did New Jersey between 1829 and 1831. In other states, elaborate permissive systems would be designed, to which few localities would pay heed—recall Virginia's experience during the 1840's. And occasionally there would simply be unflagging resistance, as in South Carolina. Finally, where efforts were successful, they were frequently piecemeal. Thus, the New England states—and especially Massachusetts—led the movement for public primary schools, but among them only Vermont also created a state university before the Civil War. Similarly, many of the southeastern states—Georgia, the Carolinas, Virginia, and Maryland—created state universities of one sort or another before the Civil War, but only North Carolina also developed a state primary school system of any comprehensiveness and vigor. In the West, the several components were more frequently joined, as in Michigan, Wisconsin, Indiana, and, for a time, Louisiana.[21]

Within systems, there was considerable variation from community to community and from school to school. For one thing, there was the infinite mixing of private, quasi-public, and public forms of support and control. For another, there was the interweaving of forms occasioned by the varying social compositions of different communities. Thus, Lowell, Massachusetts, experimented during the 1840's with an arrangement whereby certain Roman Catholic parochial schools attended by Irish-Catholic students and taught by Irish-Catholic teachers were actually incorporated into the public school system and reported as public schools. Similarly, Pennsylvania, Ohio, and Wisconsin boasted public schools during the 1850's attended overwhelmingly by German-speaking Lutheran students and taught largely by German-speaking Lutheran teachers. Then there were the urban situations in which high concentrations of impoverished immigrant families struck the fear of social disorder into the hearts of city fathers, leading them to establish public schools more than usually concerned with discipline and regulation, of the sort that Daniel Webster once referred to as "a wise and liberal system of police, by which property, and life, and the peace of society are secured." New York and Boston contended massively with such problems during the 1840's, owing to the unprecedented influx of Germans and Irish during those decades. And in the realm of

21. Indiana Constitution of 1816, Article II, in *Federal and State Constitutions, Colonial Charters, and Other Organic Laws,* II, 1069.

higher education, granted all the influence of the University of Virginia as a model of the enlightened Jeffersonian university capping a state system of public education, most state universities during the pre-Civil War era were no more public, or enlightened, or university-like in character than the dozens of denominational colleges that surrounded them and competed with them for students.[22]

Along with these emerging but ill-defined structures, a new politics of education developed, quite different in character and tone from the politics of the provincial era. At the state level, there were the coalitions of interests necessary to gain enactment of school legislation. Traditional analyses of the "friends of education," as public school promoters liked to style themselves, have tended to portray them as a collection of democratic altruists, aspiring workingmen, liberal Protestants, and urban progressives. In actuality, the coalitions that pressed for public schools and universities were shifting, occasionally unstable, and frequently unique to particular times and regions. Thus, organized labor and organized Roman Catholicism played a significant role in the politics of New York education during the 1830's and 1840's; neither was a significant factor in Virginia or Michigan. The presence of New Englanders in a region appears to have had a positive effect on the development of public schooling, but the converse was not necessarily true, as witness pre-Civil War North Carolina and Louisiana. A Whig governor in Massachusetts, Edward Everett, helped establish a state board of education and generally supported an aggressive program of undenominational Protestant public schooling; a Whig governor in New York, William H. Seward, proposed that Roman Catholic schools receive a measure of state aid. And, when the Ohio legislature established a state superintendency of public schools early in 1837, the measure passed by the barest majority in the House of Representatives, with nineteen Whigs and sixteen Democrats voting yes and fifteen Whigs and nineteen Democrats voting no. Workingmen appear to have supported the upward extension of public schooling in New York City in the 1830's; they appear to have opposed the upward extension of public schooling in Beverly, Massachusetts, in the 1860's. Presbyterians appear to have opposed public schooling in New Jersey during the 1840's but to have supported it during the same decade in North Carolina, Tennessee, and Ohio. Ethnic politics appears to have been a significant element in Pennsylvania school affairs, but an unimportant element in South

22. *The Great Speeches and Orations of Daniel Webster,* edited by Edwin P. Whipple (Boston: Little, Brown, & Co., 1895), p. 47.

Carolina, where class politics remained in the ascendancy.

The fact is that public school legislation was often pushed through state legislatures by coalitions expressly created for the purpose. As Howard Mumford Jones once remarked of Horace Mann, his genius was to promise something to everyone: he managed simultaneously to appeal to the aspirations and hurt pride of the workingmen, the frugality of the wealthy, the self-interest of industrialists, the timidity of the cultured who saw the Boston Latin School as a bulwark against the immigrant hordes, the altruism of reformers, and the nostalgia of the old. A similar coalition could not be sustained in neighboring Connecticut, where the state board of education, modeled after that of Massachusetts, was abolished in 1842, only four years after its establishment. And in Virginia, no alliance of the "friends of education" during the pre-Civil War era was able to prevail against the relentless opposition of eastern landowners, who refused to be taxed for a public school system, and western populists, who were not at all certain they needed one. Public schooling as a cause may have been nonpartisan insofar as the coalitions that supported it did not ordinarily follow formal party lines—the 1837 vote in the Ohio House of Representatives on the state superintendency of schools was typical—but public schooling as a cause was anything but nonpolitical. The leaders of that cause may have traditionally been celebrated for their ideological verve and rhetorical skill, but their ability to create and maintain the coalitions that established and extended state systems of public schooling was as significant as their ability to articulate the justifications for doing so.[23]

Three additional points concerning the new politics of public schooling bear comment. First, the development of state systems must be seen in a nineteenth-century context of localism: neither the ideology nor the technology of political control at the state level had been developed to the point where it was seen as a replacement for political control at the district, town, or county level. Even in Massachusetts, where the vigor of Horace Mann's secretaryship made the authority of the state seem more visible and more forceful than elsewhere, that authority was never conceived to be more than stimulatory and supportive in character; at one point Mann used the metaphor of a "flesh-brush" that would excite the "torpid circulation" of localities to describe his role as secretary of the Massachusetts board of education. And in other states, however imperative the wording of legislation mandating the establishment of schools, it was usually the carrot, in the form of state

23. Howard Mumford Jones, "Horace Mann's Crusade," in Daniel Aaron, ed., *America in Crisis* (New York: Alfred A. Knopf, 1952), pp. 91–107.

subsidies, rather than the stick, in the form of state fines, that moved recalcitrant localities to action. As for the localities, they experienced a different politics of schooling, even less structured along party lines than state politics and even more concerned with the level of immediate pocketbook issues that regularly pitted parents against the childless, community boosters against traditional individualists, the schooled against the unschooled, and the well-to-do against the impoverished.[24]

Second, given the millennialist rhetoric that suffused debates over educational policy, the new politics of public schooling was as likely to revolve around symbolic issues as real issues and was therefore more than usually volatile. The real issues—the levying of taxes, the allocation of public money, the appointment of public officials, and the award of public contracts—were divisive enough; but the symbolic issues could be even more explosive. Thus, Horace Mann's sharpest battles during his tenure as secretary were fought with conservative clergymen over what piety would be taught in the schools and with conservative schoolmasters over how discipline would be maintained—issues on which there was probably a substantial measure of agreement among Massachusetts legislators and state board members (as indeed among similar officials in other states), but which nevertheless provoked intense controversy. And, on the local level, the redrawing of a school district boundary or the situating of a new schoolhouse could generate quite as much political heat as a proposed increase in the school tax rate.

Third, the development of state school systems created growing numbers of amateurs, semiprofessionals, and professionals associated with schooling who in the very nature of their enterprise became partisans of more schooling. By the 1840's and 1850's, many of them were well known to one another: James G. Carter and Horace Mann in Massachusetts; Henry Barnard in Connecticut; J. Orville Taylor in New York: Charles Fenton Mercer and Henry Ruffner in Virginia; Calvin H. Wiley in North Carolina; Caleb Mills in Indiana; Calvin Stowe, Albert Picket, Samuel Lewis, and Catharine Beecher in Ohio; Ninian Edwards and John Mason Peck in Illinois; John D. Pierce and Isaac Crary in Michigan; Robert Breckinridge in Kentucky; William F. Perry in Alabama; John Swett in California; and George Atkinson in Oregon. They organized into associations like the American Institute of Instruction, the Western Literary Institute and College of Professional Teachers, and, more nationally, the American Lyceum, and enlisted as many recruits as they could attract, not only from the teaching

24. Horace Mann to Cyrus Pierce, May 7, 1845 (Mann mss., Massachusetts Historical Society, Boston, Mass.).

profession, but also from politics and public life. They published and edited numerous periodicals like the *American Journal of Education* (1826–1830, William Russell, ed.) and its successor, the *American Annals of Education* (1830–1839, W.C. Woodbridge, ed. [1831–1838]), the *Common School Assistant* (1836–1840, J. Orville Taylor, ed.), the *Common School Advocate* (1837–1841, E.D. Mansfield, L. Harding, and Alexander McGuffey, eds.), the *Journal of Education* (1838–1840, John D. Pierce, ed.), the *Connecticut Common School Journal* (1838–1842, Henry Barnard, ed.), the *Common School Journal* (1839–1852, Horace Mann and William B. Fowle, eds.), and the *American Journal of Education* (1855–1881, Henry Barnard, ed.), along with the various state common school journals that began to serve the burgeoning teaching profession. They were the prime movers at the public school conventions that assembled in the several states and that often facilitated the coalescing of opinion that eventuated in legislation; they organized the coalitions that enacted the legislation; and they frequently ended up the political leaders and professional managers of the public school systems that resulted. In effect, they spearheaded the public school movement, articulating its ideals, publicizing its goals, and instructing one another in its political techniques; indeed, in the absence of a national ministry of education, it was their articulating, publicizing, and mutual instruction in politics that accounted for the spread of public education across the country.

Many though not all of the self-styled "friends of education" practiced one or another of the professions: Mann, Barnard, Mercer, Wiley, Lewis, Edwards, Crary, and Perry were attorneys; Ruffner, Mills, Stowe, Lewis, Peck, Breckinridge, and Atkinson were clergymen; Carter, Ruffner, Stowe, Beecher, Breckinridge, and Swett were teachers; and Barnard and Picket were editors. Most were Congregationalists or Presbyterians, though Mann was a Unitarian; Barnard, an Episcopalian; Lewis, a Methodist; and Peck, a Baptist. But what distinguished them as "friends of education" was the extent to which they shared a common belief in a millennialist Christian republican political economy in which education would play a central role, and a common ability to use the strategies of voluntarism and political collaboration as demonstrated by the evangelical movement. They drew freely on each other for intellectual sustenance and political support, reprinting one another's essays and reports, corresponding regularly, and exchanging lectures. Interestingly, when a United States Bureau of Education was finally created in 1867, with Henry Barnard and then John Eaton as the first two commissioners of education, one of its most significant latent functions was to facilitate and intensify that process of communication and mutual support.

The "friends of education" appeared in every state before the Civil War; and, if they did not prevail everywhere, they prevailed in a sufficient number of instances to make the public school movement the most enduringly successful of all the pre-Civil War reforms. "In universal education," Horace Mann wrote in 1847, "every 'follower of God and friend of humankind' will find the only sure means of carrying forward that particular reform to which he is devoted. In whatever department of philanthropy he may be engaged, he will find that department to be only a segment of the great circle of beneficence, of which *universal education* is center and circumference; and that it is only when these segments are fitly joined together, that the wheel of progress can move harmoniously and resistlessly onward." It was the singular accomplishment of the "friends of education" that they built their reform coalitions in such a way as to incarnate Mann's principle: public schooling became the reform on which the largest majority of reformers would continue to collaborate.[25]

One final observation is worthy of note. Although the "friends of education" appeared throughout the South during the 1850's, they did not prevail in that region to the same extent that they did elsewhere. They were fond of citing Jefferson in support of their programs, and they drew frequent comparisons between the "progress" of public schooling in New England and New York and their own lagging efforts. Yet in most cases—North Carolina was the notable exception—they were unable to muster the political support necessary for the development of public school systems along northern lines. Indeed, the very "northernness" of public schooling made it increasingly suspect in the South during the 1850's and 1860's, and when Reconstruction governments imposed public schools after Appomattox the suspicion was confirmed. Thus, while the politics of persuasion and voluntarism goes far in explaining the spread of public schooling through the United States, it does not tell the whole story; public schooling was imposed on some regions as part of a political and military occupation. Yet there is an irony about that imposition that tells much about the politics of public schooling; for the imposed systems eventually needed revitalization to make them truly effective, and when that revitalization did come, during the last years of the nineteenth century and first years of the

25. *Eleventh Annual Report of the Board of Education, Together with the Eleventh Annual Report of the Secretary of the Board* (1848), p. 135.

twentieth, a latter-day generation of "friends of education" was again at the heart of the movement.

V

With the advance of the public school movement, enrollments rose, especially at the primary level, though some of the gains in public school enrollment were more apparent than real insofar as they involved the shift of students from private to public schools rather than the recruitment of new students who might not have attended school at all. Yet the movement did stimulate enrollment increases in various ways. It prodded uninterested or reluctant localities to establish schools, using an array of lures ranging from subsidies to threats of compulsion. It provided a standard organizational and administrative technology for maintaining and conducting schools; one need only think of the paradigmatic curricula and schoolhouse plans carried in the numerous common school journals of the era. And it created a body of people—teachers, administrators, and school board members—who in the very nature of the situation became a continuing lobby for schooling. Most important, perhaps, it created a framework for expansion and, with it, an expectancy.

It is important to bear in mind, however, that the popularization of schooling antedated the public school movement. What is clear, though the statistics remain fragmentary, is that there was already a considerable amount of school-going during the last decades of the eighteenth and first decades of the nineteenth centuries, especially in New England, and that the greatest gains in school-going in relation to population after 1820 came not in New England but rather in the Midwest and the South, owing partly to the fact that these regions had significantly lower rates of school-going to begin with and partly to the substantial immigration to New York and Massachusetts of European ethnic groups lacking traditions of school attendance. Further, it is also clear that, while the public school movement ordinarily brought taxation and other forms of public support, the movement did not immediately and invariably make schools free or even cheap.

In this regard, it is interesting to note that aggregate national school enrollment rates for whites between the ages of five and nineteen rose from approximately 35 percent in 1830 to 38.4 percent in 1840, to 50.4 percent in 1850, to 57.7 percent in 1860, to 61.1 percent in 1870. The greatest gains were in the West and the South. In the West they stemmed largely from the public school movement, but in the South

TABLE I
School Enrollment Rates: 1840–1870

	1840	1850	1860	1870
Total number of students: primary, secondary, and higher	2,025,636	3,642,694	5,477,037	7,209,938
Total population	17,069,453	23,191,876	31,443,321	38,558,371
Total number of students divided by total population	.119	.157	.174	.187
Total population, 5 to 19 years of age	——	8,661,689	11,253,475	13,641,490
Total number of students divided by total population, 5 to 19 years of age	——	.421	.487	.529
White population, 5 to 19 years of age	5,275,479	7,234,973	9,494,432	11,799,212
Total number of students divided by white population, 5 to 19 years of age	.384	.504	.577	.611

they occurred under conditions of mixed public and private support and in the relative absence of taxation for public schooling. Indeed, as late as 1850, though over 90 percent of the school and college enrollment was in institutions defined by the United States Census as public (the definition included schools "receiving their support in whole or in part from taxation or public funds"), less than half of the $16.1 million expended for schools and colleges that year derived from taxation or interest from state permanent school funds. It was not until the later 1860's and the 1870's, with the ending of the rate-bill system in a number of northern and western states and the establishment of public school systems in the South, that significantly more than half the total outlay for schools and colleges derived from public funds, primarily taxes. Even then, as indicated by the Census of 1870, the variations remained tremendous, with Georgia spending $1,250,299 for schooling, of which $114,626, or 9 percent, derived from public funds, and Iowa spending $3,570,093 for schooling, of which $3,347,629, or 94 percent, derived from public funds. In the end, what proved decisive in the enrollment gains was that total school and college expenditures rose substantially in all regions, from $16,162,000 in 1850 to $94,402,726 in 1870, an increase of almost 600 percent in reported dollar values and of roughly 400 percent in constant dollar values (if one takes account of the significant inflation during the Civil War years), as contrasted with a 170 percent increase in the total population and a 160 percent increase in the population between five and nineteen years of age.[26]

For the nation as a whole, then, schooling was established in those areas where it had been nonexistent, regularized in those areas where it had been intermittent, and systematized and extended in those areas where it had already been prevalent. Yet these generalizations are subject to significant qualifications. First, there were the regional differences already alluded to: the increases in public schooling were substantial in the northern and Middle Atlantic states, spectacular in the Midwest, and at best modest in the South, though the South continued to spend considerable sums on those who actually did attend school. Moreover, even within regions, there were differences in the length of the school term and in the availability of schooling beyond the primary level. Second, there were significant racial, ethnic, and religious differences in access to schooling and in the use of available schooling. Irish Catholics and German Lutherans sent their children to parochial schools in large numbers. Blacks in the South were generally prevented from attending school, while blacks in the North were generally consigned to separate schools. Sects like the Amish and the Mennonites tended to hold their children out of schools to protect them from the "corrupting" influences of the larger society. And, though females enjoyed a rough equality of access to primary schooling and were sometimes in the majority among those who continued on to grammar and secondary schooling, they were at a decided disadvantage in access to colleges and universities. Finally, there were the differences in teacher qualifications that made a year of schooling in one institution or locality quite another thing from a year of schooling in another. Taken together, such variations led to profound disparities in the schooling that was actually available to any given American in the 1870's and in the perception of that schooling as it was considered, utilized, and evaluated.

26. Albert Fishlow, "The American Common School Revival: Fact or Fancy?" in Henry Rosovsky, ed., *Industrialization in Two Systems: Essays in Honor of Alexander Gerschenkron* (New York: John Wiley & Sons, 1966), pp. 42–46; J. D. B. De Bow, ed., *Statistical View of the United States . . . , Being a Compendium of the Seventh Census* (Washington, D.C.: A. O. P. Nicholson, 1854), p. 141; and Francis A. Walker, ed., *A Compendium of the Ninth Census* (Washington, D.C.: Government Printing Office, 1872), pp. 8, 487, 492. The expenditure figures cited here do not represent the total investment in schooling, since they do not include estimates of foregone earnings on the part of students. See Albert Fishlow, "Levels of Nineteenth-Century American Investment in Education," *Journal of Economic History*, XVI (1966), 418–436. See also Tables II and III on pp. 182–85 *infra*. I have used the total population figure given in the Census of 1870 (it was subsequently adjusted to 39,818,449 to take account of underenumeration in the southern states) in order to preserve the consistency of the proportions.

The same caution must be used in discussing the outcomes of schooling. Schools performed many functions, ranging from the elementary training in reading given in an Illinois rural district school to the sophisticated training in ancient and modern languages given at Harvard. At their most pervasive level, they provided youngsters with an opportunity to become literate in an increasingly standard American English. They offered youngsters a common belief system combining undenominational Protestantism and nonpartisan patriotism. They afforded youngsters a modest familiarity with simple arithmetic, bits and pieces of literature, history, geography, and some rules of life at the level of the maxim and proverb. They introduced youngsters to an organized subsociety other than the household and church in which such norms as punctuality, achievement, competitiveness, fair play, merit, and respect for adult authority were generally observed. And they laid before youngsters processes of reasoning, argument, and criticism—indeed, processes of learning to learn—that were more or less different from thought processes proffered earlier and elsewhere. It should not, of course, be assumed that youngsters necessarily learned these things or learned them in the same way, for children came to school with their own temperaments, their own histories, and their own agenda, having been educated by other institutions before entering school and continuing to be educated by other institutions while attending school.

Whatever was learned and however well, schools sought to prepare youngsters for several kinds of adult experience. Schools tended to ease the way of youngsters into productive work outside the household, where literacy and punctuality, adherence to rules and procedures, and the ability to cooperate with people of varying ages who were not kin would be expected. Schools enabled them to make various uses, and misuses, of printed material, from its uncritical consumption as propaganda to its intelligent employment as an instrument of deliberate self-instruction. And schools taught some of the elementary skills needed for participation in the voluntary associations that sprang up in such large numbers during the early nineteenth century as vehicles for everything from mutual consciousness-raising to systematic political lobbying. Again, not all of these things were learned or learned in the same way; but the prevalence of schooling occasioned their widespread nurturance in the population at large, enhancing the readiness of Americans to participate in a larger public education that was rapidly coming into being during the early decades of the Republic.

TABLE II*   Schooling 1850

	Aggregate Population	Aggregate Population 5–19	Number of Schools	Number of Teachers	Number of Pupils	Total Income	Income from Endowment	Income from Public Funds	Income from Other Sources
United States	23,191,876	8,661,689	87,257	105,858	3,642,694	$16,162,000	$923,763	$7,590,117	$7,648,120
Alabama	771,623	313,209	1,323	1,630	37,237	521,022	9,916	62,421	448,685
Arkansas	209,897	86,855	446	495	11,050	74,800	1,720	9,209	63,871
California	92,597	9,610	8	7	219	17,870	6,600	70	11,200
Connecticut	370,792	116,676	1,862	2,172	79,003	430,826	33,119	195,931	201,776
Delaware	91,532	34,913	261	324	11,125	108,893	1,425	42,176	67,292
District of Columbia	51,687	18,456	71	196	4,720	122,272	2,300	12,640	107,332
Florida	87,445	33,226	103	122	3,129	35,475	1,900	250	33,325
Georgia	906,185	372,387	1,483	1,667	43,299	396,644	29,617	39,179	327,848
Illinois	851,470	337,442	4,141	4,443	130,411	403,138	27,011	231,744	144,383
Indiana	988,416	403,914	4,964	5,154	168,754	421,337	25,340	208,716	187,281
Iowa	192,214	76,492	775	878	30,767	61,472	2,700	35,627	23,145
Kentucky	982,405	395,574	2,579	3,006	86,014	595,930	51,053	108,633	436,244
Louisiana	517,762	170,556	812	1,211	30,843	619,006	74,000	316,397	228,609
Maine	583,169	213,211	4,176	5,793	199,745	380,623	12,571	313,819	54,233
Maryland	583,034	212,393	1,142	1,585	44,923	564,091	16,554	162,801	384,736
Massachusetts	994,514	306,562	4,066	5,049	190,292	1,424,873	88,599	977,630	358,644
Michigan	397,654	152,025	2,754	3,324	112,382	206,753	7,960	143,158	55,635

Minnesota	6,077	1,751	1	1	12	140	0	0	140
Mississippi	606,526	241,919	964	1,168	26,236	370,276	14,520	71,911	283,845
Missouri	682,044	273,057	1,783	2,053	61,592	383,469	30,178	78,701	274,590
New Hampshire	317,976	104,359	2,489	3,214	81,237	221,146	12,659	156,938	51,549
New Jersey	489,555	174,234	1,702	2,076	88,244	523,080	10,373	141,486	371,221
New Mexico	61,547	22,775	1	1	40	0	0	0	0
New York	3,097,394	1,053,585	12,481	17,269	727,156	2,431,247	73,178	1,384,929	973,140
North Carolina	869,039	345,438	2,934	3,162	112,430	386,912	28,822	140,314	217,776
Ohio	1,980,329	767,267	11,893	13,540	502,826	1,018,258	50,985	631,197	336,076
Oregon	13,294	4,525	32	48	922	24,815	0	2,527	22,288
Pennsylvania	2,311,786	842,766	9,606	11,063	440,743	2,164,578	189,184	1,367,959	607,435
Rhode Island	147,545	45,993	463	604	24,881	136,729	10,660	93,730	32,339
South Carolina	668,507	258,718	934	1,115	26,025	510,879	21,350	79,099	410,430
Tennessee	1,002,717	418,125	2,944	3,284	114,773	415,792	24,395	113,008	278,389
Texas	212,592	83,206	448	504	11,500	84,472	0	0	84,472
Utah	11,380	4,076	27	0	0	13,562	0	8,200	5,362
Vermont	314,120	108,647	2,854	4,460	100,785	246,604	15,164	156,531	74,909
Virginia	1,421,661	552,667	3,252	3,617	77,764	708,787	49,525	194,802	464,460
Wisconsin	305,391	105,080	1,483	1,623	61,615	136,229	385	108,384	27,460

*The data for Tables II and III are drawn from J. D. B. De Bow, ed., *Statistical View of the United States . . . , Being a Compendium of the Seventh Census* (Washington, D.C.: A. O. P. Nicholson, 1854), pp. 40, 141–144; Francis A. Walker, ed., *A Compendium of the Ninth Census* (Washington, D.C.: Government Printing Office, 1872), pp. 8, 487, 492; and U.S., Bureau of the Census, *The Vital Statistics of the United States, . . . Compiled from the Original Returns of the Ninth Census* (1870), pp. 563–564, 575–576.

TABLE III SCHOOLING 1870

	Aggregate Population	Aggregate Population 5–19	Number of Schools	Number of Teachers	Number of Pupils	Total Income	Income from Endowment	Income from Public Funds	Income from Other Sources
United States	38,558,371	13,641,490	141,629	221,042	7,209,938	$95,402,726	$3,663,785	$61,746,039	$29,992,902
Alabama	996,992	387,617	2,969	3,364	75,866	976,351	39,500	471,161	465,690
Arizona	9,658	1,856	1	7	132	6,000	0	0	6,000
Arkansas	484,471	187,971	1,978	2,297	81,526	681,962	7,300	555,331	119,331
California	560,247	153,354	1,548	2,444	85,507	2,946,308	59,057	1,669,464	1,217,787
Colorado	39,864	10,274	142	188	5,033	87,915	0	73,375	14,540
Connecticut	537,454	159,410	1,917	2,926	98,621	1,856,279	140,887	1,227,889	487,503
Dakota	14,181	3,805	35	52	1,255	9,284	0	8,364	920
Delaware	125,015	45,041	375	510	19,575	212,712	0	120,429	92,283
District of Columbia	131,700	40,815	313	573	19,503	811,242	23,000	476,929	311,313
Florida	187,748	72,243	377	482	14,670	154,569	6,750	73,642	74,177
Georgia	1,184,109	460,016	1,880	2,432	66,150	1,253,299	66,560	114,626	1,072,113
Idaho	14,999	1,968	25	33	1,208	19,938	0	16,178	3,760
Illinois	2,539,891	922,599	11,835	24,056	767,775	9,970,009	252,569	6,027,510	3,689,930
Indiana	1,680,637	640,481	9,073	11,652	464,477	2,499,511	50,620	2,126,502	322,389
Iowa	1,194,020	443,095	7,496	9,319	217,654	3,570,093	63,150	3,347,629	159,314
Kansas	364,399	122,253	1,689	1,955	59,882	787,226	19,604	678,185	89,437
Kentucky	1,321,011	510,675	5,149	6,346	245,139	2,538,429	393,015	674,992	1,470,422
Louisiana	726,915	254,918	592	1,902	60,171	1,199,684	34,625	564,988	600,071
Maine	626,915	202,250	4,723	6,986	162,636	1,106,203	98,626	841,524	166,053
Maryland	780,894	277,321	1,779	3,287	107,384	1,998,215	21,697	1,134,347	842,171
Massachusetts	1,457,351	430,351	5,726	7,561	269,337	4,817,939	383,146	3,183,794	1,250,999

Michigan	1,184,059	405,898	5,595	9,559	266,627	2,550,018	81,775	2,097,122	371,121
Minnesota	439,706	157,913	2,479	2,886	107,266	1,011,769	20,000	903,101	106,668
Mississippi	827,922	315,315	1,564	1,728	43,451	780,339	11,500	167,414	601,425
Missouri	1,721,295	648,039	6,750	9,028	370,337	4,340,805	57,567	3,067,449	1,215,789
Montana	20,595	2,438	54	65	1,745	41,170	0	30,434	10,736
Nebraska	122,993	38,790	796	840	17,614	207,560	0	186,435	21,125
Nevada	42,491	6,253	53	84	2,373	110,493	0	84,273	26,220
New Hampshire	318,300	91,655	2,542	3,355	64,677	574,898	59,289	396,991	118,618
New Jersey	906,096	298,204	1,893	3,889	129,800	2,982,250	49,000	1,499,550	1,433,700
New Mexico	91,874	33,494	44	72	1,798	29,886	0	1,200	28,686
New York	4,382,759	1,400,809	13,020	28,918	862,022	15,936,783	674,732	9,151,023	6,111,028
North Carolina	1,071,361	408,360	2,161	2,692	64,958	635,892	9,160	232,104	394,628
Ohio	2,665,260	959,640	11,952	23,589	790,795	10,244,644	222,074	8,634,815	1,387,755
Oregon	90,923	32,521	637	826	32,593	248,022	24,500	135,778	87,744
Pennsylvania	3,521,951	1,222,697	14,872	19,522	811,863	9,628,119	539,496	7,187,700	1,900,923
Rhode Island	217,353	64,727	561	951	32,596	565,012	31,535	348,656	184,821
South Carolina	705,606	264,393	750	1,103	38,249	577,953	51,506	282,973	243,474
Tennessee	1,258,520	484,513	2,794	3,587	125,831	1,650,692	79,100	629,461	942,131
Texas	818,579	319,233	548	706	23,076	414,880	760	15,230	398,890
Utah	86,786	33,367	267	408	21,067	150,447	0	4,151	146,296
Vermont	330,551	103,107	3,084	5,160	62,913	707,292	13,046	523,970	170,276
Virginia	1,225,163	447,818	2,024	2,697	60,019	1,155,582	47,586	120,148	987,851
Washington	23,955	7,060	170	197	5,499	48,305	800	30,326	17,176
West Virginia	442,014	169,428	2,445	2,838	104,949	698,062	15,300	598,124	84,637
Wisconsin	1,054,670	396,408	4,943	7,955	344,014	2,600,310	32,953	2,027,876	539,481
Wyoming	9,118	1,097	9	15	305	8,376	0	2,876	5,500

Chapter 6

EDUCATION BY COLLISION

It has been well said, that the collision of opposite opinions, produces
the spark which lights the torch of truth.

PATRIOTIC SOCIETY OF NEWCASTLE COUNTY,
DELAWARE

William Manning perceived himself as a patriot and a thorough-going
republican. Born in 1747, he had spent his entire life working the
North Billerica farm his great grandfather had carved out of the wilderness during the early days of the Massachusetts Bay Colony. He
had served with the minutemen at Concord, had imbibed the heady idealism of the Revolution, and, after the war, had been twice elected a se-
lectman of the town. Untraveled, unlettered, and for all intents and
purposes unschooled ("I never had the advantage of six months schooling in my life"), he had nevertheless thought profoundly about "men &
measures" and, as he put it, about "Liberty & a free Government."
And in 1797 Manning was deeply troubled about the future of his
country—so troubled, in fact, that he painfully put his thoughts to paper and sent them to the editor of the *Independent Chronicle,* Boston's
sole Jeffersonian newspaper. The document, which he called "The Key
of Libberty. Shewing the Causes why a free government has Always
Failed, and a Remidy against it," was never published in its time—in
fact, the editor was shortly to be imprisoned under the despised Sedition Act—but its plain-spoken assertions tell us much about the indis-
soluble link between education and politics as perceived by one citizen
of the early Republic.[1]

1. William Manning, *The Key of Libberty,* edited by Samuel Eliot Morison (Billerica,
Mass.: The Manning Association, 1922), p. 3.

What troubled Manning was the relentless drift he perceived on the part of the Federalist leadership away from the ideals of the Revolution and in the direction of militarism and monarchy. He saw the financial policies of Hamilton and the diplomatic policies of Adams as utterly misguided, and he was genuinely alarmed by talk of tough laws to deal with aliens (read Frenchmen) and sedition (read republicanism). The cause of it all, he pointed out, was the age-old tendency of the few, who wish to live without labor, to dominate the many, who must earn their bread by the sweat of their brows. And the chief weapon of the few was to keep the many in ignorance. By associating together for their own selfish ends, by opposing cheap schools and making newspapers as expensive as possible, and by using every mechanism of government and banking for their own advantage, the few were slowly subverting the rights and liberties of the many. "They cant bare to be on a leavel with their fellow cretures," Manning observed, "or submit to the determinations of a Lejeslature whare (as they call it) the Swinish Miltitude are fairly represented, but sicken at the eydea, & are ever hankering & striving after Monerca or Aristocracy whare the people have nothing to do in maters of government but to seport the few in luxury & idlenes."[2]

What was the "remidy" Manning proposed? Essentially, it was for the many to beat the few at their own game. The many needed to associate for their own larger purposes; they needed to see to it that accurate knowledge was put into the hands of the people via inexpensive publications that could be counted on to speak the truth; and they needed thereby to make government once again responsive to their needs. For all the quaintness of his phrasing and the inaccuracy of his spelling, Manning's political prescience was impressive. In an age when learned leaders of all persuasions saw associations as deleterious to the common good and newspapers as rabble-rousing scandal sheets, a plain-spoken farmer who "neaver was 50 Miles from whare I was born in no direction" could see the shape of things to come. In association and in a truly popular press, he saw the promise of republicanism fulfilled.[3]

I I

Manning's observations concerning the press must be placed in context for one to understand fully his criticisms of contemporary newspapers

2. *Ibid.*, p. 18.
3. *Ibid.*, p. 3.

and his proposals regarding a genuinely republican periodical voice. There were some two hundred newspapers in the United States at the time Manning wrote, most of them weeklies or semiweeklies with circulations in the neighborhood of six or seven hundred. A few prestigious journals, like Boston's *Columbian Centinal* or Philadelphia's *Porcupine's Gazette* could boast national audiences that ran in the thousands, but most newspapers served local or at best regional clienteles.

While only a dozen of the pre-Revolutionary newspapers actually survived into the last years of the eighteenth century, there was a striking resemblance between the newspapers of the 1790's and their earlier counterparts. Hand produced on wooden presses that imprinted one side of one sheet at a time, they featured foreign news commonly gleaned from English and Continental newspapers; national affairs (a speech by the president or the text of an important treaty or bill, more often than not taken from some other domestic newspaper); literary productions excerpted from published works or specially prepared by local authors (usually under some pretentious pseudonym such as "Publius," "Lucullus," or "Cato"); and, all important to a practical-minded readership, advertising, shipping schedules, and general news of local commerce. Interestingly, though the newspapers tended to cater to local or regional clienteles, they offered little local or regional news beyond that relating to commerce, the assumption being that people would scarcely be willing to pay for news they could procure via word of mouth. Subscription rates for the weeklies and semiweeklies varied from $1.50 to $5.00 per year, with the mean ranging between $2.00 and $3.00, while subscription rates for the score of dailies that had begun to appear in the larger cities varied from $6.00 to $10.00. The papers were distributed via the stagecoaches and postriders of the United States postal system at a fixed cost of a cent per paper (up to a distance of one hundred miles), with free exchange of papers among editors and liberal franking privileges. It was the exchange system that in effect subsidized the establishment of a national news network, by enabling editors, who were in the habit of freely borrowing from one another, to dispense national news to local clienteles.

It is difficult to determine how many readers actually perused each newspaper, though given the tradition of reading aloud in households, taverns, coffeehouses, and reading rooms, and given the practice of saving and exchanging newspapers, it is reasonable to assume fifteen, twenty, or more readers per copy circulated. In any case, as early as

1793, Noah Webster, as usual not disinterested, asserted in the *American Minerva:* "Most of the citizens of America are not only acquainted with letters and able to read their native language; but they have a strong inclination to acquire, and properly to purchase, the means of knowledge. Of all these means of knowledge, newspapers are the most eagerly sought after, and the most generally diffused. In no other country on earth, not even in Great Britain, are newspapers so generally circulated among the body of the people, as in America." And in 1801 the prospectus of Alexander Hamilton's *New York Evening Post* (with William Coleman as editor) announced: "The design of this paper, is to diffuse among the people correct information on all interesting subjects; to inculcate just principles in religion, morals, and politics; and to cultivate a taste for sound literature."[4]

Already in the provincial era, the press had played a critical role in bringing publics into being and, with them, public opinion, public affairs, and the drift toward a new politics. Particularly in the business of fomenting the Revolution, printers had developed a formidable arsenal of popularizing techniques designed to reach the widest possible audiences with the greatest possible impact. Thus, along with reasoned political argument, the 1760's and 1770's had witnessed the emergence of the satirical essay, the inflammatory editorial, the hortatory letter, the atrocity story, the calumnious attack, the pointed cartoon, the blaring headline, the provocative engraving, the inspirational poem, and the propagandistic song. All these remained available to the printers and editors of the early Republic, and indeed they were used with calculated verve in an era that was in its very essence political.

What was new, however, was the formal association of particular newspapers with particular points of view and eventually with particular parties or factions. Thus, in 1789 a Boston schoolteacher named John Fenno founded the *Gazette of the United States* for the express purpose of exhibiting "the people's own government, in a favorable point of light—and to impress just ideas of its administration, by exhibiting facts." Two years later, as the rift between Jefferson and Hamilton deepened, a poet and journalist named Philip Freneau was brought to Philadelphia (and given a job in the State Department by Jefferson) to edit the *National Gazette* as the organ of an emerging Republican opposition. Later, after the demise of the *National Gazette,* Benjamin Franklin Bache (Franklin's grandson, known irreverently as "Lightning Rod Junior") made the *General Advertiser and Political, Com-*

4. *American Minerva,* December 9, 1793; and *New York Evening Post,* November 16, 1801.

mercial, Agricultural and Literary Journal, a Philadelphia newspaper that also bore the name *Aurora,* into a similar organ of Republicanism; while William Cobbett's *Porcupine's Gazette* was founded in 1797 as an outspoken advocate of the Federalists. Other editors—though by no means all editors—also decided to align themselves with one side or the other of the developing controversy; and, with few traditional canons of civility, ethics, and even law to guide them, the exchange of views all too often became an exchange of scurrility, vituperation, and falsehood. In the process, however, there began an education for Americans that came to constitute an essential element of public affairs.[5]

As Richard Hofstadter pointed out, the idea of a legitimate political opposition was one of the significant inventions of the early years of the Republic. The idea sprang up neither full-blown nor overnight. Indeed, during most of the 1790's, the assumptions on both sides of the deepening Federalist-Republican controversy were that parties were evil, that the Republic could not long endure them, and that the outcome of the controversy would be the incorporation of one faction by the other. Not surprisingly, the incumbent Federalists, increasingly irritated by the barbs of their Republican critics, set about hastening the incorporation with all the power at their command. One of their devices was the ill-fated Sedition Law of 1798. Enacted in the heat of passion surrounding the publication of the so-called XYZ dispatches, along with two new Alien Laws and a law toughening the requirements for naturalization, the Sedition Law had two central provisions, one punishing conspiracies and other unlawful combinations "with intent to oppose any measure or measures of the government of the United States," the other punishing individuals for "any false, scandalous and malicious writing or writings against the government of the United States, or either house of Congress . . . , or the President . . . , with intent to . . . bring them into contempt or disrepute." There was no doubt in anyone's mind concerning the aim of the statute, namely, to silence the Republican opposition in general and the Republican press in particular. In all, fourteen indictments were handed down under the Sedition Law, with the majority coming to trial during the spring of 1800, just in time to influence the presidential contest between Adams and Jefferson. The prosecutions did pose a threat to the Republican press, with some editors going to jail and some actually ceasing to publish. But in the end the effort failed to stem the "Revolution of 1800." The Republicans, using measures like the Kentucky and Virginia Resolutions, actually turned

5. *Gazette of the United States,* April 27, 1791.

the Sedition Act against the Federalists, making it a prime issue in the election; Jefferson won the presidency and eventually pardoned all those condemned under the law; and by its own provision the statute itself expired in 1801.[6]

The threat of prosecution for seditious libel did not disappear with the election of Jefferson, but it did wane considerably. And the ensuing six decades were remarkable for the simple proliferation of newspapers of every sort and variety. There were some 200 papers in 1801, including some 20 dailies; there were some 1,200 papers in 1833, including some 65 dailies; and there were some 5,871 papers in 1870, including 574 dailies. But these are merely benchmark statistics indicating a fairly steady growth; they convey no sense of the extraordinary number of papers that started up, flourished for a time, and then died. Most newspapers served particular localities; some served particular clienteles, especially religious, political, or commercial clienteles; and a few, such as the *New York Weekly Tribune* or the *Springfield Republican*, served regional or even national clienteles. By 1833 the United States could boast as large a number of newspapers and as impressive an aggregate circulation as any nation in the world, the chief contender being England. Moreover, as the English commentator Thomas Hamilton was moved to remark in that year, newspapers in the United States penetrated "to every crevice of the Union." The four-page sheets were well nigh ubiquitous and important beyond measure, even before the substantial popularization set in motion by the rise of the penny press. The widespread sense that it was an "age of newspapers" reflected actuality as much as it shaped it.[7]

The penny press itself was made possible by many changes: technological innovations in papermaking and printing, which sharply reduced the cost of paper and permitted as many as 4,000 impressions an hour in the 1820's and 20,000 impressions an hour by the 1850's; the expansion of the federal postal system and the continued subsidizing of newspaper circulation via low postal rates (more than 90 percent of the mail consisted of newspapers during the early 1830's, but only one-ninth of the postal revenue derived from them); the extension of literacy; the development of a vigorous two-party politics; and the general

6. Richard Hofstadter, *The Idea of a Party System: The Rise of Legitimate Opposition in the United States, 1780–1840* (Berkeley: University of California Press, 1969); and The Sedition Act, July 14, 1789, in Henry Steele Commager, ed., *Documents of American History* (9th ed.; 2 vols.; New York: Appleton-Century-Crofts, 1973), I, 177–178.

7. Thomas Hamilton, *Men and Manners in America* (2 vols.; reprint ed.; New York: Augustus M. Kelley, 1968), II, 74.

TABLE IV*   NEWSPAPERS 1850

	Aggregate Population	Total Number of Newspapers	Total Circulation	Daily Newspapers	Daily Circulation	Weekly Newspapers	Weekly Circulation	Number of Other Newspapers	Circulation of Other Newspapers
United States	23,191,876	2,526	5,142,177	254	758,454	1,902	2,944,629	370	1,439,094
Alabama	771,623	60	34,282	6	2,804	48	29,020	6	2,458
Arkansas	209,897	9	7,250	0		9	7,250	0	0
California	92,597	7	4,619	4	2,019	3	2,600	0	0
Connecticut	370,972	46	52,670	7	5,654	30	40,716	9	6,300
Delaware	91,532	10	7,500	0	0	7	6,900	3	600
District of Columbia	51,687	18	100,073	5	19,836	8	72,489	5	7,748
Florida	87,445	10	5,750	0	0	9	5,550	1	200
Georgia	906,185	51	64,155	5	3,504	37	50,188	9	10,463
Illinois	851,470	107	88,050	8	3,615	84	68,768	15	15,667
Indiana	988,416	107	63,138	9	3,720	95	56,168	3	3,250
Iowa	192,214	29	22,500	0	0	25	17,750	4	4,750
Kentucky	982,405	62	79,868	9	7,237	38	58,712	15	13,919
Louisiana	517,762	55	80,288	11	32,088	37	31,667	7	16,533
Maine	583,169	49	63,439	4	3,110	39	55,887	6	4,442
Maryland	583,034	68	124,779	6	50,989	54	60,887	8	12,903
Massachusetts	994,514	209	718,221	22	130,640	126	391,752	61	195,829
Michigan	397,654	58	52,690	3	4,039	47	32,418	8	16,233
Minnesota	6,077	0	0	0	0	0	0	0	0
Mississippi	606,526	50	30,555	0	0	46	28,982	4	1,573
Missouri	682,044	61	70,235	5	10,905	45	46,280	11	13,050
New Hampshire	317,976	38	60,226	0	0	35	58,426	3	1,800

New Jersey	489,555	51	44,521	6	7,017	43	36,544	2	960
New Mexico	61,547	2	1,150	0	0	1	400	1	750
New York	3,097,394	428	1,624,756	51	206,222	308	753,960	69	664,574
North Carolina	869,039	51	35,252	0	0	40	29,427	11	5,825
Ohio	1,980,329	261	389,463	26	46,083	201	256,427	34	86,953
Oregon	13,294	2	1,134	0	0	2	1,134	0	0
Pennsylvania	2,311,786	310	984,777	24	162,635	261	526,142	25	296,000
Rhode Island	147,545	19	24,472	5	5,705	12	18,525	2	242
South Carolina	668,507	46	53,743	7	16,357	27	27,190	12	10,196
Tennessee	1,002,717	50	67,672	8	14,218	36	41,147	6	12,307
Texas	212,592	34	18,205	0	0	29	14,837	5	3,368
Utah	11,380	0	0	0	0	0	0	0	0
Vermont	314,120	35	45,961	2	555	30	41,206	3	4,200
Virginia	1,421,661	87	87,768	15	16,104	55	48,434	17	23,230
Wisconsin	305,391	46	33,015	6	3,398	35	26,846	5	2,771

* The data for Tables IV and V are drawn from Francis A. Walker, ed., *A Compendium of the Ninth Census* (Washington, D. C.: Government Printing Office, 1872), pp. 510–513.

TABLE V   Newspapers 1870

	Aggregate Population	Total Number of Newspapers	Total Circulation	Daily Newspapers	Daily Circulation	Weekly Newspapers	Weekly Circulation	Number of Other Newspapers	Circulation of Other Newspapers
United States	38,558,371	5,871	20,842,475	574	2,601,547	4,295	10,594,643	1,002	7,646,285
Alabama	996,992	89	91,165	9	16,420	76	71,175	4	3,570
Arizona	9,658	1	280	0	0	1	280	0	0
Arkansas	484,471	56	29,830	3	1,250	48	26,280	5	2,300
California	560,247	201	491,903	33	94,100	140	298,603	28	99,200
Colorado	39,864	14	12,750	4	2,200	9	9,550	1	1,000
Connecticut	537,454	71	203,725	16	35,730	43	107,395	12	60,600
Dakota	14,181	3	1,652	0	0	3	1,652	0	0
Delaware	125,015	17	20,860	1	1,600	12	13,600	4	5,660
District of Columbia	131,700	22	81,400	3	24,000	12	41,900	7	15,500
Florida	187,748	23	10,545	0	0	20	9,425	3	1,120
Georgia	1,184,109	110	150,987	15	30,800	73	88,837	22	31,350
Idaho	14,999	6	2,750	0	0	4	1,900	2	850
Illinois	2,539,891	505	1,722,541	39	166,400	364	890,913	102	665,228
Indiana	1,680,637	293	363,542	20	42,300	233	239,342	40	81,900
Iowa	1,194,020	233	219,090	22	19,800	196	187,840	15	11,450
Kansas	364,399	97	96,803	12	17,570	78	71,393	7	7,840
Kentucky	1,321,011	89	197,130	6	31,900	68	137,930	15	27,300
Louisiana	726,915	92	84,165	7	34,395	75	39,970	10	9,800
Maine	626,915	65	170,690	7	10,700	47	114,600	11	45,390
Maryland	780,894	88	235,450	8	82,921	69	127,314	11	25,215
Massachusetts	1,457,351	259	1,692,124	21	231,625	153	899,465	85	561,034
Michigan	1,184,059	211	253,774	16	27,485	174	192,889	21	33,400
Minnesota	439,706	95	110,778	6	14,800	79	79,978	10	16,000

State								
Mississippi	827,922	111	71,868	3	2,300	92	60,018	16	9,550
Missouri	1,721,295	279	522,866	21	86,555	225	342,361	33	93,950
Montana	20,595	10	19,580	3	6,980	6	12,200	1	400
Nebraska	122,993	42	31,600	7	6,850	30	22,400	5	2,350
Nevada	42,491	12	11,300	5	7,500	5	2,850	2	950
New Hampshire	318,300	51	173,919	7	6,100	37	75,819	7	92,000
New Jersey	906,096	122	205,500	20	38,030	95	120,670	7	46,800
New Mexico	91,874	5	1,525	1	225	4	1,300	0	0
New York	4,382,759	835	7,561,497	87	780,470	518	3,388,497	230	3,392,530
North Carolina	1,071,361	64	64,820	8	11,795	44	43,325	12	9,700
Ohio	2,665,260	395	1,388,367	26	139,705	299	923,502	70	325,160
Oregon	90,923	35	45,750	4	6,350	26	30,400	5	9,000
Pennsylvania	3,521,951	540	3,419,765	55	466,070	385	1,214,395	100	1,739,300
Rhode Island	217,353	32	82,050	6	23,250	19	43,950	7	14,850
South Carolina	705,606	55	80,900	5	16,100	42	44,000	8	20,800
Tennessee	1,258,520	91	225,952	13	34,630	65	117,022	13	74,300
Texas	818,579	112	55,250	12	3,500	89	45,300	11	6,450
Utah	86,786	10	14,250	3	2,700	3	8,400	4	3,150
Vermont	330,551	47	71,390	3	3,190	43	56,200	1	12,000
Virginia	1,225,163	114	143,840	16	24,099	69	75,488	29	44,253
Washington	23,955	14	6,785	1	160	10	4,525	3	2,100
West Virginia	442,014	59	54,432	4	5,192	48	42,390	7	6,850
Wisconsin	1,054,670	190	343,385	14	43,250	160	266,000	16	34,135
Wyoming	9,118	6	1,950	2	550	4	1,400	0	0

growth of population. But the most important factor, perhaps, was the great editors of the 1830's, 1840's, and 1850's, among them William Cullen Bryant of the *New York Evening Post,* Benjamin H. Day of the *New York Sun,* James Gordon Bennett of the *New York Herald,* William M. Swain and A. S. Abell of the *Philadelphia Public Ledger* and the *Baltimore Sun,* Henry J. Raymond of the *New York Times,* and Horace Greeley of the *New York Tribune.* Each of these men had his own style and his own conception of the popular press. Bryant and Raymond were the most dedicated to literary quality and dispassionate reporting; Bennett was easily the most flamboyant and contentious; Greeley was probably the most nationally influential. Yet all had notions, both implicit and explicit, of the press as educator of the populace, and all demonstrated these notions in ways that set the style of American journalism for decades to come.

By the 1830's and 1840's it was a commonplace in the United States for newspapers to assert the people's need for knowledge and the special role of the press in serving that need. Every editor professed the litany and then went about his business according to his own best lights, expressing in his paper's substance the particular set of assumptions that guided his work. "A good portion of knowledge among the citizens of a free republic," Noah Webster observed in the first issue of the *American Minerva,* "is . . . the ultimate resort for a correction of the evils incident to the best systems of government. It is an important fact in the United States that the best informed people are the least subject to passion, intrigue and a corrupt administration. The utility of newspapers is therefore most clearly ascertained in republican governments; like schools, it should be a main point to encourage them; like schools, they should be considered as the auxiliaries of government, and placed on a respectable footing; they should be the heralds of truth; the protectors of peace and good order." Webster then went on to school his readers in portions of knowledge with a decidedly Federalist flavor. Four decades later, the editorial page of the *Sun,* the first successful penny newspaper in the United States, spoke of having "done more to benefit the community by enlightening the minds of the common people than all the other papers together." Of course, Benjamin H. Day, the *Sun's* editor, had enlightened his readers mainly in police court proceedings and murder trials. Day's contemporary James Gordon Bennett, never reticent with rhetoric, talked of the newspaper as the chief regenerator of society. "What is to prevent a daily newspaper from being made the greatest organ of social life?" he asked. "Books have had their day—the theatres have had their day—the temple of religion has had its day. A newspaper can be made to take the lead of all these in the great movements of human thought and of human civilization. A newspaper can send more souls to Heaven, and save more from Hell, than all the churches or chapels in New York—besides making money at the same time." Thus, Bennett, too, had his view of the newspaper's function and styled the *New York Herald* accordingly. Like Day, Bennett also schooled his readers in crime news and social gossip, though he did serve them more generous portions of political knowledge than Day did in the *Sun*.[8]

It was Horace Greeley, perhaps, who more than any other editor of his time joined profession and performance to fashion the most influential version of the new popular journalism. The son of a New England farmer, Greeley combined an intermittent schooling with voracious reading of the few volumes in the family library and any other printed matter he could obtain. His career as a journalist began in 1826, at the age of fifteen, when he apprenticed himself to Amos Bliss, editor of the *Northern Spectator* in East Poultney, Vermont. When the *Spectator* failed four years later, Greeley returned home for a time and then made his way to New York City, where he worked at a variety of printing jobs and then, in 1834, started his own weekly called the *New Yorker* in collaboration with Jonas Winchester. The magazine flourished but lost money, and Greeley was forced to support himself by writing for the *Daily Whig* and other journals, a practice that brought him to the attention of Whig party leaders in New York. After simultaneously editing two Whig weeklies, while continuing his oversight of the *New Yorker*, Greeley decided to found his own daily, as an organ of Whig opinion that would fall in character somewhere between Bennett's more flamboyant *Herald* and Bryant's more stodgy *Evening Post*, both, incidentally, Democratic papers. The first issue of the *New York Tribune* appeared on April 10, 1841, with a promise from Greeley to produce a "cheap daily, devoted to literature, intelligence, and the open and fearless advocacy of Whig principles and measures." After a period of uncertainty during which circulation rose steadily but not sufficiently rapidly to overtake expenses, the paper was established on a sound basis. Greeley served it as editor until his death in 1872, and during much of that time was indistinguishable in the public mind from the newspaper itself.[9]

Emerson once remarked to Thomas Carlyle that Horace Greeley

---

8. *American Minerva*, December 9, 1793; Frank M. O'Brien, *The Story of the Sun* (1917; new ed.; New York: D. Appleton, 1928), p. 81; and *New York Herald*, August 19, 1836.
9. *New York Tribune*, April 10, 1841.

did all the thinking and theorizing for America's midwestern farmers at $2.00 a year. He was referring, of course, to the enormous influence during the 1840's and 1850's of the weekly version of the *Tribune* (made up of gleanings from the daily), which Greeley began several months after establishing the daily and which circulated most heavily in New England and among transplanted New Englanders in the Midwest. What was the nature of this extraordinary influence, and whence did it derive? Once again, the explicitly stated aims were formulated in the rhetoric of popular education. "The Tribune—whether in its daily or weekly edition," Greeley declared in the prospectus for the weekly, "will be what its name imports—an unflinching supporter of the people's rights and interests, in stern hostility to the errors of superficial theorists, the influences of unjust or imperfect legislation, and the schemes and sophistries of self-seeking demagogues.... The proceedings of Congress will be carefully recorded; the foreign and domestic intelligence early and lucidly presented; and whatever shall appear calculated to promote morality, maintain social order, extend the blessings of education, or in any way subserve the great cause of human progress to ultimate virtue, liberty and happiness, will find a place in our columns." The *Tribune*, to state it simply, would nurture virtuous character, abiding patriotism, and prudent wisdom.[10]

Part of Greeley's influence, in Emersonian terms, doubtless derived from his ability to articulate clearly and decisively what his audience sensed at best vaguely and inchoately—essentially the influence of the "great man" as Emerson conceived him. Over the years, Greeley favored prohibition, internal improvements, protective tariffs, western expansion, scientific farming, and antislavery—all solid planks in the Whig platform of the 1840's and 1850's. But Greeley also favored the organization of labor, the ten-hour day, women's rights, and Fourierism—programs scarcely calculated to attract Whig, or even farmer, support. Thus, even if much of Greeley's influence can be seen as leading his readers in the directions in which they were already tending, the Emersonian explanation is on its own insufficient. Greeley gave his readers what they wanted up to a point, but beyond that he gave them what he thought they needed, and he did so with a style and verve and indomitability unprecedented in American journalism. In the end, it was Greeley's pedagogy that held the key to his power.

In testifying before a committee of the House of Commons in 1851, Greeley averred that it was the news presented in the *Tribune* rather

10. *Ibid.*, September 14, 1841.

than its editorials that formed the basis of its effects on public opinion. There is no denying that the *Tribune*'s staff was indefatigable and resourceful in its newsgathering and that the paper's willingness to eschew—or at least to downplay—the sensationalism of crime, scandal, and vice gave its readers as much political and social news of moment as any large popular audience in pre-Civil War America. But, granted this, it was the *Tribune*'s editorials that were the chief instrument of its pedagogy. By the 1850's Greeley had developed a characteristic editorial style that was instantly recognizable and immensely persuasive. The elements of that style become apparent as one follows the editorials on a particular issue, say, the Kansas-Nebraska Bill of 1854. What one notes is a clear sense of purpose; an artistic synthesis of form, rhetoric, and substance; and a skillfully contrived use of symbols. Greeley's sense of purpose involved a definite idea of mission and a definite idea of audience. With respect to mission, Greeley believed that "public opinion is the great instrument for all civil and social good" and that "educated men" should "keep this public opinion pure, sound, healthy, and vigorous." Educated men do this, he contended, by persuading the people of the rightness of certain "truths" or "principles," the key to persuasion being the appeal to popular "common sense." Once the truth had been properly explicated, as Greeley saw it, the people would act according to its dictates. Essentially, Greeley was aiming at an audience of white, native-born, literate males—the "common men" and "free laborers" who constituted the enfranchised citizenry of the Republic.[11]

Throughout the pages of the *Tribune,* Greeley combined form, rhetoric, and substance in such a way as to enhance teachability via print. With a clear idea of mission and audience, he made the editorial the heart of the paper, placing editorials on a center page especially designed to look serious and dignified, summarizing the important news nearby, using headlines that tersely encapsulated the argument, and embroidering both with correspondence (much of it written by Greeley) supporting the paper's positions. The general vigor, clarity, and simplicity of Greeley's writing have often been noted. What has not been remarked is the equally vigorous presentation of Greeley's arguments— a tripartite presentation that commonly began with an account of the facts under discussion, then proceeded to an opinion by Greeley, and finally concluded with an effort to connect that opinion with the past

11. Greeley's testimony is quoted at length in Frederic Hudson, *Journalism in the United States, from 1690 to 1872* (New York: Harper & Brothers, 1873), pp. 540–548. His mission is especially clear in *New York Tribune,* October 10, 1843. The several quoted phrases are commonplaces in Greeley's writing.

(the Tribune's previous position) and the future (some prophecy as to consequences for the nation). As a homiletic device, the technique placed emphasis on the beginning and the end, thereby stressing "objective truth" rather than personal opinion. And, when the device was joined to the constant personifying of issues—the Kansas-Nebraska Bill, for example, was "Douglas's Bill," the Dred Scott Decision was "Taney's Decision" (with "Douglas" and "Taney" often spelled in capital letters)—its kinship to contemporary teaching and preaching comes through with striking clarity.[12]

Finally, there was the special symbol system Greeley used to connect national political issues with the personal world of the reader. Greeley conceived of his audience as made up of intelligent, honest, independent, civically minded farmers and laborers. These were the real Americans to and for whom the Tribune spoke, as contrasted with the "Reverends, Doctors, Honorables, Generals" and sundry other "titled shams" who had "imbibed the humanities" at some college or other. "Truth," "freedom," and "justice" were associated with "mechanics," "laborers," and "tillers of the soil"; "dishonesty," "error," and "injustice" were proffered and perpetrated by "mischievous rascals," "barroom politicians," and "little Northern Judas Iscariots" (those who supported Calhoun). And Greeley as editor was the moralist-teacher who explicated the truth so that the people would know what was right and therefore how to act. Through a continuing use of democratic rhetoric, agrarian imagery, and a concomitant appeal to traditional virtues, Greeley set out to persuade his readers that he spoke the truth because he was, after all, just like them. And, to a considerable degree, he managed to persuade them.[13]

Ultimately, Greeley was representative, not because his style was widely imitated (it was really sui generis) and not even because his editorials were widely reprinted (though they were), but rather because of the special editor's role he conceived and exemplified. In an age when Emerson was defining the vocation of letters, Greeley defined the vocation of editor. Both roles were forms of public teaching. In effect, it was the educative power and responsibility of the editor that Greeley taught his fellow newspapermen, and the country at large.

12. New York Tribune, January 10, 1854; March 3, 1854; March 9, 1857; and March 10, 1857.

13. Ibid., February 14, 1854; and February 8, 1854. Again, the several quoted phrases are commonplaces in Greeley's writing.

III

Obviously, newspapers were not the only media for the publicizing of information in the early Republic; magazines, broadsides, pamphlets, and books continued to circulate in ever increasing numbers, and in the process served similar functions. But, given their ready availability and low cost, their favored treatment by postal authorities, and their frequency and regularity of appearance, newspapers became the chief vehicles for the conversion of foreign and domestic news into public intelligence, and thereby one of the crucial factors in the continuing evolution of public affairs. Once again, however, it is important to bear in mind that both the phenomenon of public affairs and the public perception of that phenomenon underwent considerable development during the Revolutionary and early national eras; and, notwithstanding the fact that the Revolution itself derived from a newly self-conscious public and its participation in a newly emerging public affairs, there was no instant comprehension, even on the part of the actors, as to what in fact was taking place. At the very time voluntary associations of every conceivable sort were coming into being at accelerating rates, commentators of all political persuasions were lamenting the curse of factionalism and looking forward to the restoration of consensus.

In the political realm, the appearance of the so-called democratical societies of the early 1790's marked an interesting convergence of the phenomenon of association with public awareness of the phenomenon. The first such society was probably the one the Philadelphia Germans organized during the spring of 1793, to direct the attention of their countrymen to public affairs and to exchange opinions on the administration of government. The "mother club" of the movement, however, appears to have been the Democratic Society of Pennsylvania, also organized in Philadelphia in 1793 by a brilliant array of public luminaries, including David Rittenhouse, the scientist; Charles Biddle, the merchant; Dr. George Logan, the physician and legislator; and Alexander J. Dallas, an associate of Governor Thomas Mifflin. The Democratic Society circularized the country during the summer of 1793, urging the formation of similar groups in every locality, with the result that by the end of 1794 there were at least thirty-five such organizations in communities as widely scattered as Lexington, Kentucky; Charleston, South Carolina; Ulster County, New York; New Haven, Connecticut; and

Portland, Maine; and there may well have been more. The societies convened frequently; formulated resolutions on the salient issues of the day; publicized their views via correspondence, broadsides, pamphlets, and newspapers; convened meetings for the discussion of public policy; attended in force the meetings they did not convene; and generally attempted to arouse and shape public opinion and bring the weight of opinion to bear politically.[14]

The societies were clearly linked by overlapping membership with such earlier radical organizations as the Sons of Liberty and the Committees of Correspondence and of Safety, and they tended to use many of the propagandizing techniques that had been developed and popularized by those organizations during the Revolutionary era. They were also well aware of kindred movements in other countries, notably the Constitutional Societies in England and the Jacobin Clubs in France, and indeed saw themselves involved in a worldwide struggle for the rights of man, testifying on the one hand to obvious similarities of social and political orientation, which have often been remarked, and on the other hand to certain more general trends in the political development of Western political culture, which may well have been the more fundamental. The societies played a significant role in the emergence of the Republican Party, which subsequently formed around Jefferson, though on the whole they tended not to concern themselves with the details and mechanics of party organization. Rather, and this is perhaps the most interesting point to be made about them, they concentrated on education. Thus, the New York Democratic Society declared ignorance "the irreconcilable enemy of liberty" and spoke of the role of associations like itself in "the promotion of useful knowledge, and the dissemination of political information." The Essex County (New Jersey) Democratic Society warned that it would be necessary to erect institutions especially directed to the political instruction of the people. The Addison County (Vermont) Democratic Society declared its intention "to study the Constitution, to avail ourselves of the journals, debates and laws of Congress—reports and correspondence of secretaries, and such other publications as may be judged necessary to give information on the proceedings of Congress and the departments of government." And the Republican Society of Norwalk (Connecticut) stated as its objects: "To support the laws and constitutions of this and the United States, even at the hazard of lives if called thereto. To exercise the right

14. William Playfair [William Cobbett], *The History of Jacobinism: Its Crimes, Cruelties and Perfidies* (2 vols.; Philadelphia: printed for William Cobbett, 1796), II, Appendix 18.

of speech, and freedom of debate, recognized by the Constitution. To perpetuate the equal rights of man, to propagate political knowledge, and to revive the republican spirit of '76." In sum, as a contemporary observer put it, the societies saw themselves as "schools of political knowledge," dedicated to forming public opinion on public affairs.[15]

The initial flurry of democratic associations waned in late 1794—after Washington branded them "self-created societies" intent upon destroying the government. For a time, the number of new societies declined and many of the extant societies lapsed into inactivity. Yet even so loyal an ally of Washington as John Adams sensed that "political clubs must and ought to be lawful in every free country"; and in fact the role of the societies in forming and articulating public opinion had not been lost on either the Republicans or the Federalists. During the later 1790's, as David Hackett Fischer has pointed out, a new group of political associations began to appear that combined benevolence, mutual financial aid, and political education. On the Republican side, they took the form of the Tammany Societies or the more loosely bound groups that called themselves "Friends of the People." On the Federalist side, they took the form of the Washington Benevolent Societies, the first of which was organized in Alexandria, Virginia, in 1800, about a month after the general's death. Furthermore, as the Republicans consolidated their power after 1801, a number of Federalists began to see in such organizations one answer to Republican successes at the polls. As Hamilton put the issue in 1802, "We must consider whether it be possible for us to succeed, without, in some degree, employing the weapons which have been employed against us." Surely one such "weapon" was the weapon of political education, and to this end Hamilton sketched an elaborate plan for what he called the Christian Constitutional Society, with state and local branches, dedicated to diffusing information via newspapers and pamphlets, promoting the election of *"fit* men" to office, and advancing institutions of a charitable and useful nature "in the management of Federalists." Hamilton's plan received little attention, but over the next decade and a half scores of Washington Benevolent Societies were established, principally in New England but also in New York, New Jersey, Pennsylvania, Maryland, Virginia, and Ohio. They published political literature, organized public celebra-

---

15. *Greenleaf's New York Journal & Patriotic Register,* May 31. 1794; *Farmer's Library; or, Vermont Political & Historical Register,* September 9, 1794; *New London Bee,* April 4, 1798; and Ebenezer Bradford, *The Nature of Humiliation, Fasting and Prayer Explained, A Sermon* (Boston: Adams & Larkin, 1795), p. 32.

tions and ceremonials, and generally assisted the more formal Federalist party organization with money, influence, and expertise. And, though it may have been ironic, just as the democratic societies of the 1790's had been branded "self-created" by Washington in the wake of the Whiskey Rebellion (1794), so were the Washington Benevolent Societies branded as "malevolent" in the wake of the Hartford Convention (1814-15).[16]

During the interim between 1794 and 1815, however, much had been learned on both sides. The partisan voluntary society committed to political education had linked with the partisan newspaper also committed to political education, and as a result of that linking a welter of conflicting opinion had come to be seen as the essence of public affairs. Whereas Washington's generation had seen such conflict as destructive of good government, Jackson's generation saw it as valuable to the health of government. Political parties were increasingly viewed as organs for the gathering and articulation of opinion, and indeed it was widely assumed that in the end the public mind would actually be enlightened by the resulting competition. As the Patriotic Society of Newcastle (Delaware) had put it as early as 1795, "The collision of opposite opinions, produces the spark which lights the torch of truth." And so in fact it did, for in the conflict of political opinion that was the essence of public affairs lay an education for the American public.[17]

In the realm of religion, there was a kindred development in much the same direction. Here, too, there had been an earlier assumption that divisive partisanship was destructive of true faith and that consensus was the ideal to be achieved; indeed, that assumption had historically been at the heart of establishmentarianism. But, given the heterogeneous character of the American people, dissent had arisen, then toleration, and then the assertion of the right of free exercise; and, given the evangelical character of American Protestantism, the right of free exercise had implied the right to proselytize and teach. Out of it all

16. George Washington to Burges Ball, September 25, 1794, in *The Writings of George Washington from the Original Manuscript Sources, 1745-1799*, edited by John C. Fitzpatrick (39 vols.; Washington, D. C.: Government Printing Office, 1931-1949), XXXIII, 506; John Adams to Abigail Adams, December 14, 1794, in *Letters of John Adams, Addressed to His Wife*, edited by Charles Francis Adams (3 vols.; Boston: Chas. C. Little and James Brown, 1841), II, 171; David Hackett Fischer, *The Revolution of American Conservatism: The Federalist Party in the Era of Jeffersonian Democracy* (New York: Harper & Row, 1965), chap. vi; Alexander Hamilton to James A. Bayard, April, 1802, in *The Works of Alexander Hamilton*, edited by Henry Cabot Lodge (12 vols.; New York: G. P. Putnam's Sons, 1904), X, 432-437; and *Pittsfield Sun*, April 1, 1813.

17. The Patriotic Society of Newcastle County, in the State of Delaware, Circular: To the Patriotic Societies Throughout the United States (1795) (mss. collections, Delaware Historical Society, Wilmington, Del.).

had come the theory of denominationalism, asserted as early as 1752 by
the New Light pastor Gilbert Tennent, who spoke of a common Christianity within which the various churches were "but several branches
(more or less pure in minuter points) of one visible kingdom of the
Messiah." Obviously inherent in the idea of denominationalism was the
idea of several churches proffering competing—or at least alternative—
versions of the truth; and obviously, too, there was the idea of each distinct church as a voluntary society, freely formed and maintained by
Christians covenanting with God and one another. Beyond this generic
voluntarism implicit in the concept of denominationalism, there was the
particular form of voluntarism associated with the Methodist class,
which became so prevalent during the great organizing campaigns of
the late eighteenth and early nineteenth centuries. In the very process
of Methodist proselytizing, there was an essential voluntarism readily
visible to those who participated and those who observed from without.[18]

Most importantly, perhaps, voluntarism was the basis for the vast
proliferation of church-related organizations that constituted the evangelical united front—the congeries of Bible and tract societies, Sunday-
school associations, youth and adult education groups, and missionary
agencies erected largely by the Congregationalists and Presbyterians of
the New England and Middle Atlantic states but with counterparts in
almost all the other denominations and regions. As in the realm of politics, these organizations appeared on the local, state, regional, and national levels and were linked by overlapping membership, common
sources of funds, and a similar ideological commitment, that is, the
commitment to public teaching via newspapers, pamphlets, magazines,
and books. Once again, the technologies of organization were joined to
the instruments of publicity to create a far-flung apparatus of public
education. When the Presbyterian clergyman and educator Robert
Baird claimed in 1844 that the voluntary principle had influenced the
character and habits of the American people in ways that a legally established church could not, he was obviously alluding to the churches
and their networks of related organizations as agencies of moral nurturance and social control; but his claim also applied in the realm of
participation, in the public affairs of churches and church-related organizations as well as in public discourse about religion.[19]

    18. Gilbert Tennent, *The Divine Government over All Considered* (Philadelphia: William
Bradford, 1752), p. 45.
    19. Robert Baird, *Religion in the United States of America* (Glasgow: Blackie and Son,
1844).

Finally, there was a similar movement toward voluntary organization in what might broadly be referred to as the "social realm." Whether or not political and religious groups were the most decisive nonfamilial associations in the lives of their members, they were surely the most comprehensive in the range and extent of their concerns. Yet, along with these more generally oriented organizations, there arose a vast number of groups reflecting more limited or particular concerns. There were, for example, the associations that grew up around the interests and activities of specific economic pursuits or occupations: the consociations of the clergy, the bar associations, and the physicians' societies that dated from the Revolutionary era; the local chambers of commerce and manufacturers' associations and the unions of craftsmen and artisans that dated from the last years of the eighteenth and first years of the nineteenth centuries; and the more general trade unions of mechanics and factory operatives that expanded rapidly during the 1830's to a nationwide membership of 300,000 before the panic of 1837 drastically curtailed their enrollment and vitality. There were also the numerous civic, benevolent, and charitable associations that established and maintained special community services, such as fire companies, hospitals, almshouses, and schools, or that arranged for mutual economic and social benefits ranging from insurance and burial services to the maintenance of particular Old World customs and ties. There were the various reform organizations devoted to causes that varied from international peace to women's rights to temperance to abolition. Some of these at one time or another managed to spark nationwide crusades involving hundreds of thousands of participants in every region of the country. The Sons of Temperance, for example, grew in six years from a single association to one boasting 600 units and 200,000 dues-paying members, all pledged to total abstinence. And the American Anti-Slavery Society, founded in Philadelphia by a small number of committed individuals in 1833, not only proliferated to a point where at its peak it involved 2,000 societies with some 200,000 members, but made its views prevail in the Republican Party, through which its program became even more broadly influential. Lastly, there were the infinitely diverse literary, scientific, and educational societies committed to everything from the advancement of agriculture to the promotion of the fine arts. Here, too, at least one such society, the American Lyceum, became for all intents and purposes a national adult education association, with affiliates in hundreds of localities concentrated in New England, the Middle Atlantic states, and the Midwest that not only sponsored lecture programs and community entertainment aimed at general cultural and moral uplift but also lobbied in various legislatures for public schools and libraries.

It would be impossible to determine with any precision the actual number of such voluntary societies in the United States at different periods of the nineteenth century. We do know, from Richard D. Brown's research on Massachusetts, that there were 114 such societies founded during the 1780's and 852 founded during the 1820's, and there is every reason to believe that the exponential growth persisted for several decades (the multiplications of lyceums and academies alone would account for a good deal of the growth). It is clear, too, that, as in the case of political development, the increase in voluntary societies varied from region to region, and that the phenomenon appeared somewhat later and less vigorously in the South. Yet for the nation as a whole there was a quantum leap in the number and variety of voluntary associations during the first half-century of the Republic.[20]

Obviously, the character of the groups varied significantly, and with it the education they afforded to members. Some, like the trade unions, offered opportunity for fairly full and vigorous political participation; some, like the lyceums, offered opportunity primarily to listen to lectures arranged for by others; some, like the temperance societies, offered the opportunity to make a dramatic personal gesture (sign the pledge), reap the social benefits of that gesture (in symbolic middle-class status), and then try to hew to the agreed-upon behaviors, with greater or less support from fellow members. Obviously, the nature and strength of the influence on members varied from individual to individual, from association to association, and from community to community. Yet participation in nonfamilial groups did teach skills, attitudes, and values less easily conveyed within a small coterie of kin; and hence, whatever the specific outcomes for particular individuals, the expansion of voluntary associations and the growing involvement of the public in their affairs inevitably enlarged the educational opportunities available to nineteenth-century Americans.

Beyond the education of the participants themselves, there was also a significant effect on outside audiences. To an extent, all of the associations, but especially those interested in reform, advertised their programs and sought sympathy, if not adherents. The fire company discreetly proclaimed the benefits of fire protection; the society for the promotion of agriculture published pamphlets on scientific farming, and in the process discreetly proclaimed the benefits of agriculture. The temperance and abolitionist crusades were more direct and more vociferous, proffering their views to the public via newspapers, broadsides, pamphlets, books, mass meetings, marches, ceremonials, and political lobbying. The outcome was at the least a cacophony of address and, as often as not, political conflict. No one could be against fire protection or the advantages of agriculture, though one could ignore fire protection and the advantages of agriculture. More people were ready to oppose temperance and abolition with equal vociferousness. The outcome was a new kind of education that went forward in the arena of public affairs, with some as participants, exemplifying, espousing, and instructing, and others as observers, ignoring, attending, considering, combating, or agreeing. It was an education born of conflict and collision that sought at the least attention and ultimately persuasion or conversion. And, if its effects on individual consciousness and concern were various, it did tend to increase awareness of and interest in public affairs.

Emerson's famous description of the Chardon Street Convention of the Friends of Universal Reform has often been quoted: "If the assembly was disorderly, it was picturesque. Madmen, madwomen, men with beards, Dunkers, Muggletonians, Come-outers, Groaners, Agrarians, Seventh-Day Baptists, Quakers, Abolitionists, Calvinists, Unitarians, and Philosophers,—all came successively to the top, and seized their moment, if not their hour, wherein to chide, or pray, or preach, or protest." Chide, or pray, or preach, or protest—in a sense, the convention was a microcosm of early national America. Every shade of opinion was broadcast to the populace in the hope that it would be heard and end up persuasive. In the conflict and contentiousness lay a new form of popular education.[21]

IV

When the young French nobleman Alexis de Tocqueville came to the United States in 1831 to observe the workings of the new democracy, he was already persuaded that aristocracy was dying throughout the world and that equality would be the moving force of subsequent gen-

21. Ralph Waldo Emerson, "The Chardon Street Convention (1842)," in *The Complete Works of Ralph Waldo Emerson* (12 vols.; Boston: Houghton, Mifflin and Company, 1903–1904), X, 374.

erations. Indeed, it was that very belief that had motivated him and his friend Gustave de Beaumont to travel to America, ostensibly to study the prison system, but actually to undertake a more fundamental analysis of democracy as a working principle of society and government. Yet the belief itself posed one of the central dilemmas that later appeared at the heart of Tocqueville's masterwork, *Democracy in America* (1835, 1840).

Aristocracy, Tocqueville maintained, was on the decline; but aristocracy had over the centuries performed certain vital functions for European civilization. Aristocratic societies had been marked by a pervasive sense of permanence and continuity that derived from fixed positions of social status; aristocratic institutions had served to bind men to one another in a web of acknowledged mutual relations that had called forth self-sacrifice, devoted service, and even genuine affection. The relentless drift toward equality, however, accelerated as it had been by the great revolutions of the late eighteenth and early nineteenth centuries, had on the one hand swept away the sense of permanence and continuity and on the other hand torn asunder the web of acknowledged mutual relations. The result was a rampant individualism—and recall that it was Tocqueville who coined the word "individualism"— that initially sapped the virtues associated with public life and in the long run destroyed all virtue, leaving a society of isolated individuals consumed with self-love and vulnerable to tyranny from within and without. Tocqueville's dilemma, given the relentless progress of equality in the world, was how to retain the virtues of equality without suffering the vices of individualism. And what he discovered in the United States was that the Americans had sought to resolve the dilemma through two closely related institutions, newspapers and voluntary associations.

When men are no longer united among themselves by firm and lasting ties, it is impossible to obtain the cooperation of any great number of them unless you can persuade every man whose help you require that his private interest obliges him voluntarily to unite his exertions to the exertions of all the others. This can be habitually and conveniently effected only by means of a newspaper; nothing but a newspaper can drop the same thought into a thousand minds at the same moment. A newspaper is an adviser that does not require to be sought, but that comes of its own accord and talks to you briefly every day of the common weal, without distracting you from your private affairs.

Newspapers therefore become more necessary in proportion as men become more equal and individualism more to be feared. To suppose that they only serve to protect freedom would be to diminish their importance; they maintain civilization. I shall not deny that in democratic countries newspapers frequently lead the citizens to launch together into very ill-digested schemes; but if there were no newspapers there would be no common activity. The evil which they produce is therefore much less than that which they cure.

So far as Tocqueville was concerned, newspapers were the beacons that attracted isolated individuals to one another and the media through which those individuals communicated with one another once they had made common cause. Beyond that, they provided the common stock of information that permitted citizens to manage their own affairs on the local level, formally via government and informally via associations.[22]

As for voluntary associations, they were the chief social institutions that mediated between the individual and his government.

As soon as several of the inhabitants of the United States have taken up an opinion or a feeling which they wish to promote to the world, they look out for mutual assistance; and as soon as they have found one another out, they combine. From that moment they are no longer isolated men, but a power seen from afar, whose actions serve for an example and whose language is listened to. . . .

Nothing, in my opinion, is more deserving of our attention than the intellectual and moral associations of America. The political and industrial associations of that country strike us forcibly; but the others elude our observation, or if we discover them, we understand them imperfectly because we have hardly ever seen anything of the kind. It must be acknowledged, however, that they are as necessary to the American people as the former, and perhaps more so. In democratic countries the science of association is the mother of science; the progress of all the rest depends upon the progress it has made.

Among the laws that rule human societies there is one which seems to be more precise and clear than all others. If men are to remain civilized or to become so, the art of associating together must grow and improve in the same ratio in which the equality of conditions is increased.

Once again, so far as Tocqueville was concerned, it was association that empowered individuals and caused them to look beyond their narrower selves to the broader notion of self-interest that is implicit in public life. Moreover, association begat association. Having joined together in great political causes, individuals would learn to join together in minor political causes. Once acquainted, they could always meet again in social and cultural causes. "Political associations may therefore be considered as

22. Alexis de Tocqueville, *Democracy in America,* edited by Phillips Bradley (2 vols.; New York: Alfred A. Knopf, 1945), II, 111.

large free schools," Tocqueville maintained, "where all the members of the community go to learn the general theory of association." Once learned, "the art of association" would serve as the quintessential energizing force in democratic society; it would be "the mother of action, studied and applied by all."[23]

Finally, Tocqueville's analysis included a recognition of the vital relationship between associations and newspapers. The very concept of audience implied association and vice versa. "Newspapers make associations," he concluded, "and associations make newspapers; and if it has been correctly advanced then associations will increase in number as the conditions of men become more equal, it is not less certain that the number of newspapers increases in proportion to that of associations."[24]

Now, there was doubtless a quality of exaggeration about all this in which Tocqueville ended up romanticizing the newspapers and voluntary associations of the Jacksonian era. It simply taxes the imagination to think of the insistently vituperative *Washington Globe* (speaking for the Democratic Party) as a beacon of light or the relentlessly anti-Catholic Protestant Reformation Society (speaking through the *American Protestant Vindicator*) as a large free school for instruction in the theory of association. Yet there can be no denying Tocqueville's insights into the larger processes of public education that were coming into being in connection with the new politics. What he perceived more clearly than most of his contemporaries was not only the political role of newspapers and voluntary associations but their educative role as well. And in this respect the educational metaphors that marked his rhetoric—the characterization of newspapers as "advisers" concerning the "common weal" and of associations as "large free schools"—went far beyond the commonplace didacticisms of his day. What he saw at the heart of the emerging phenomenon of public affairs was a new process of public education, which not only ushered public affairs into being but was itself enhanced by the dynamics of public affairs. In the reciprocal relationship between the two lay the inescapable tie between democratic politics and democratic education.

That said, other questions present themselves. Tocqueville, as was his wont, presented the historical phenomena of Jacksonian America as a theoretical model of liberal democracy. But what, at bottom, were the actual historical sources of voluntary association? They were surely

23. *Ibid.*, II, 109-110, 116, 117.
24. *Ibid.*, II, 112.

traceable in part to the intellectual outlooks of republican politics and evangelical religion. Republican politics located sovereignty in the people—it was the key element in what the eighteenth-century Whigs had called "public (or political) liberty"—and the people in turn granted specified powers to legitimate representatives. Since the aggrandizement of power was natural and ubiquitous among humankind, the maintenance of liberty depended upon eternal vigilance. The exercise of that vigilance demanded at the least interest and scrutiny and, beyond interest and scrutiny, actual participation in the political process via the instruction of representatives and via representation itself. Similarly, evangelical Protestantism located moral agency in individuals and urged believing Christians, in the spirit of disinterested benevolence, to promote the Kingdom of God by active missionary work among their fellow human beings, cooperating with one another where possible, yet always bearing individual witness in conduct and belief. Given these fundamental motivations in the form of pervasive self-images, and given the availability of organizational techniques derived from eighteenth-century sources as varied as English Methodism and home-grown revolutionary activism, Americans turned easily to voluntary association and the mutual education it invariably entailed.

If republican politics and evangelical religion provided the motivating outlooks, necessity provided a substantial context. The large-scale migrations westward during the early decades of the Republic provided an experience in the lives of thousands of Americans in which communities had to be created in the absence of established structures of leadership and conjoint activity. The absence of such structures put a premium on voluntary communal effort. It evoked both the sense of individual agency implicit in republican politics and evangelical religion and the commitment to conjoint activity necessitated by tasks beyond the capacity of isolated individuals or even isolated families. In the process, the habits of association and communication were encouraged and nurtured.

Yet, granted the sources of voluntary association, it was experienced variously in different communities. In a relatively new and homogeneously Protestant town like Quincy, Illinois, the vast majority of the adult population appears to have been involved in a host of missionary, benevolent, and reform organizations, most of which offered outlets for participation in social and political activities at the same time as they provided a form of persuasive social discipline for their members and for others not affiliated. In a more heterogeneous community like Cin-

cinnati, Ohio, the rate of participation appears to have been considerably lower. There, well under a quarter of the city's male householders
seem to have been involved, most of them native-born middle- or up-
per-class Yankees or Ohioans who used the local voluntary associations
as an informal network to manage the communal affairs of the city.
And, in an even more heterogeneous community like New York City,
there were several networks of voluntary organizations: roughly half
the city's Protestants appear to have participated in a congeries of religious and benevolent associations that sought through educational and
welfare activities to "uplift" (for which read a range of efforts from
outright social control to the alleviation of ill health) the lower-class
black and immigrant population, while an indeterminate percentage of
the city's lower-class black and immigrant population were involved in
comparable associations seeking to advance their own political interests
and to maintain their own cultural identity. However generalized Tocqueville's portrayal of the phenomenon, then, association was in actuality less than universal and served a variety of functions beyond the articulation of public opinion, including the assignment of social status,
the exercise of community leadership, and the exertion of social control.[25]

It is also important to note that an expanding experience with
schooling played a significant mediative role in the development of voluntary associations. Tocqueville himself discussed schooling as one of
the chief "causes which tend to maintain democracy" in America, along
with custom, religion, and the laws. And he took special note of the
middling state of learning on the part of the population: if there were
few individuals who could be described as learned, he also believed
there were fewer illiterates than anywhere else in the world. Most citizens, he maintained, received at least the elements of knowledge, religion, and civics, and the outcome contributed powerfully to the support
of the Republic. Put otherwise, schooling bestowed literacy and thereby
prepared people to read and appreciate newspapers; and schooling
taught the norms of social institutions beyond the family and thereby
prepared people for participation in voluntary associations.[26]

The outcomes of public education for and through public affairs

25. This paragraph draws on the analyses of Quincy and New York in Gregory H. Singleton, "Protestant Voluntary Organizations and the Shaping of Victorian America," *American
Quarterly*, XXVII (1975), 549–560, and on the analysis of Cincinnati in Walter S. Glazer, "Participation and Power: Voluntary Associations and the Functional Organization of Cincinnati in
1840," *Historical Methods Newsletter*, V (1972), 151–168.
26. Tocqueville, *Democracy in America*, II, chap. xvii.

were manifold. The Ohio jurist Frederick Grimke discussed them at length in *The Nature and Tendency of Free Institutions* (1848, 1856), an extraordinary treatise that has been somewhat ignored by American scholars over the years because of Grimke's acquiescence in slavery and the right of secession. For one thing, Grimke noted, both newspapers and voluntary associations contributed in the long run to what he called a politics of restraint. At the least, they implied a commitment in the political system to persuasion rather than the exercise of raw power, in ways that complemented the more direct system of checks and balances introduced via constitutional means. Beyond that, they implied a commitment to choice, for matters under widespread public debate would no longer be readily determinable by reference to custom on the one hand or by the fiat of the few on the other. And, finally, they implied a commitment to toleration and indeed to the idea of a legitimate political opposition.

Grimke saw the most profound and abiding outcome of all, however, in the continued civilizing—or educative—influence on the populace. "Party spirit," he noted, "at bottom is but the conflict of different opinions, to each of which some portion of truth almost invariably adheres; and what has ever been the effect of this mutual action of mind upon mind, but to sharpen men's wits, to extend the circle of their knowledge, and to raise the general mind above its former level. Therefore it is that an era of party spirit, whether religious, philosophical, or political, has always been one of intellectual advancement." Further along in the treatise, Grimke portrayed schooling, voluntary associations, and newspapers as complementary aspects of a national system of popular education. "What we ordinarily term a plan of popular instruction," Grimke argued, "is one adapted to the minds of youth, but, if this is not followed up by a system which confers independence of thought in after life, the faculties and knowledge which were acquired at schools and academies will become inert and fruitless."[27]

Perhaps the most important function served by public education for and through public affairs was to nurture a heightened sense of community at various levels. At first glance, of course, the very idea of a multitude of voluntary associations purveying a multitude of messages via a multitude of newspapers scarcely conjures images of community. One rather imagines confusion, collision, and cacophony, all rendered the more intense by the private selfishness of leaders, representatives,

27. Frederick Grimke, *The Nature and Tendency of Free Institutions*, edited by John William Ward (Cambridge, Mass.: Harvard University Press, 1968), pp. 173, 664–665.

and editors. Yet voluntary associations performed a significant integrating function in both older and newer communities that was often masked by social and political bickering. They frequently had overlapping membership; they often provided bridges across sect, party, and social class; and in instances where they were joined in regional and national federations they facilitated the transfer of status from one community to another. In addition, the participation they made possible in its very nature taught the skills of participation, which were readily transferable from one organization to another.

As for the press, it is important to bear in mind that the purveying of messages—of news, information, and opinion—became increasingly efficient during the early national era. When George Washington died in the winter of 1799, it took seven days for the news to reach New York City and twenty-four days for the news to reach Cincinnati. When William Henry Harrison died in 1841, the news traveled from Washington to New York in about twenty hours, from New York to Cincinnati in about seven days, and from New York to the Mississippi cities in seven to fifteen days. During the four decades that separated the two events, improvements in the gathering of news, the production of newspapers, and the distribution of printed materials via the postal system had significantly improved communication among cities in the various regions of the country and in the process had enhanced a sense of cosmopolitan community among these cities and more generally among the hinterlands they served. With the invention of the electromagnetic telegraph in 1844, the time required for the dissemination of news decreased sharply, and by the end of the Polk administration Washington had been connected by telegraph with all the major cities of the country, including St. Louis and New Orleans.

Given the steady improvement in the efficacy and rapidity of communication and the consequent growth of the audiences reached, an extraordinary fund of common knowledge was disseminated. Certainly there was much by way of information—the results of elections, the substance of legislation and judicial decisions, the comings and goings of heads of state, the transaction of commerce, the development of new technology, and the occurrence of natural and man-made catastrophes. Beyond information, there was the constant flow of opinion—speeches reported, editorials proffered, letters conveyed, affirmed, and rebutted, and advertisements tendered. The line between fact and opinion was rarely clear and often deliberately blurred, there being no clear canons among journalists concerning the wisdom or the need to separate them;

but the advance by way of enlightenment, in whatever measure, beyond the diurnal mixture of word-of-mouth information and opinion, was doubtless significant. At the least, the concept of public affairs was projected beyond the immediate locality.

This projection beyond the locality, and at the same time beyond the immediacies of ethnic, religious, and class parochialism, is perhaps the most interesting point to be made about the popular education offered by nineteenth-century newspapers. Virtually all the papers were local in character, sponsorship, and principal circulation, yet virtually all nurtured a sense of community that extended beyond the locality. The key to the seeming paradox lies in contemporary notions of what constituted the news; for the fact is that, apart from local advertisements, local announcements of commercial interest (prices, bank-note tables, and arrivals and departures of ships and shipments), local reports of marriages and deaths, and local expressions of editorial opinion, most of the discretionary material that filled the columns of pre-Civil War newspapers consisted of national and international news and literary matter taken from other newspapers, principally though not wholly New York dailies (their superiority as sources derived from the preeminence of New York as the chief port of entry for foreign news as well as from its key location in the network of American postal routes).

Given the multiplicity of newspapers, many of them flagrantly partisan to some contentious political or religious interest, the phenomenon of borrowing created less a uniformity of opinion than a measure of agreement on the items and issues concerning which one might have an opinion, that is, on the agenda of public affairs. And in that agreement lay the roots of a developing sense of state, regional, and national community. The newspapers in their own way created Rhode Islanders, Wisconsinites, South Carolinians, New Englanders, midwesterners, southerners, and Americans. They did not create them *ex nihilo*, for the issues and affairs around which such identities were formed had a patent objective reality. Later, when editors such as Benjamin H. Day of the *New York Sun*, James Gordon Bennett of the *New York Herald*, George Roberts and William H. Garfield of the *Boston Daily Times*, and William M. Swain of the *Philadelphia Public Ledger* pioneered the concept of local news, drawing substantially on crime reports, the comings and goings of the wealthy, and sensational happenings both true and fabricated, a tension grew up between the local and the extralocal, but it was a tension rather than a displacement, with borrowed national and international news and literary material continually in evidence.

The community of public affairs created by the press was scarcely identical in character and intensity to the community of face-to-face discourse and direct participation that was rooted in the experience of the locality; it was a more transient, more ephemeral, and more marginal phenomenon in the lives of its members. But it was a community nonetheless, and doubtless contributed significantly to feelings of sectionalism and nationality during the first century of the Republic as well as to the conflicts and complementarities these feelings induced in particular individuals of particular ethnic, religious, and social-class backgrounds.

Chapter 7

OUTCASTS

> "Now," said he, "if you teach that nigger (speaking of myself) how to read, there would be no keeping him. It would forever unfit him to be a slave. He would at once become unmanageable, and of no value to his master. As to himself, it could do him no good, but a great deal of harm. It would make him discontented and unhappy."
>
> FREDERICK DOUGLASS

The politics of discussion—and the intellectual quickening that political theorists like Grimke and Tocqueville saw as its correlates—presupposed a society of free individuals who could express themselves openly on matters of public interest and freely organize into associations of the like-minded. It assumed citizens who were prepared, able, and at liberty to state their opinions and act on their preferences, at the ballot box, in public office, and in the more general realm of civil and cultural affairs. To the extent that American society during the first decades of the Republic actually comprised such individuals, analyses such as Grimke's and Tocqueville's were more or less pertinent.

Yet there were profound anomalies, as both men recognized. Grimke was well aware that the essential thrust of his argument in *The Nature and Tendency of Free Institutions* held that individuals were best educated to freedom by being given the experience of freedom. Yet he drew back from the logic of that argument when it came to blacks and Indians, maintaining that they belonged to races decidedly inferior to the whites and hence would not profit from the experience (the contradiction doubtless reflecting views pervasive among his countrymen). And Tocqueville, assuming a more detached stance, observed in a chapter on blacks and Indians in *Democracy in America* that their situation was typically American but decidedly undemocratic. "These

218

two unhappy races," he remarked, "have nothing in common, neither birth, nor features, nor language, nor habits. Their only resemblance lies in their misfortunes. Both of them occupy an equally inferior position in the country they inhabit; both suffer from tyranny; and if their wrongs are not the same, they originate from the same authors." Enforced servitude, he continued, would deny civilization to the enslaved blacks, while enforced segregation would deny it to the freed blacks; and a self-chosen "barbarous independence" would deny it to the Indians. In the absence of civilization, neither race could ever assimilate to the American community. The prospect for the Indians, as Tocqueville saw it, was outright destruction, while the prospect for the blacks, even in the event of an emancipation freely granted or forcibly wrested, was nothing but calamity.[1]

In the dilemma associated with the social status of the two races, education was deeply involved, in both the teaching proffered to blacks and Indians by the dominant white society and the teaching blacks and Indians conducted for and among themselves. If there were educational correlates of freedom that were central to the life of the young Republic, there were also education correlates of oppression—the latter constituting a tragic contradiction in light of the society's professed values and its hopes of serving as a virtuous example to the world.

II

The situation of American blacks changed perceptibly from decade to decade during the years following the Revolution. Initially, there was widespread sentiment favoring emancipation and equal rights. States revoked their laws prohibiting manumission, and large numbers of slaves were freed and in some cases even enfranchised. For a time it seemed as if the problem of slavery might gradually solve itself through suspension of the slave trade and gradual emancipation. But revolutionary aspirations were soon dashed on the shoals of economic reality, and the Constitution ratified in 1788 acquiesced in slavery as a fact of American life, without, incidentally, ever mentioning the term.

The impulse to gradual emancipation persisted, kept alive by Quaker organizations, the nascent abolitionist movement, and growing

---

1. Frederick Grimke, *The Nature and Tendency of Free Institutions,* edited by John William Ward (Cambridge, Mass.: Harvard University Press, 1968), p. 234; and Alexis de Tocqueville, *Democracy in America,* edited by Phillips Bradley (2 vols.; New York: Alfred A. Knopf, 1945), I, 332, 334.

numbers of black Methodist and Baptist congregations led by newly self-conscious black preachers. But, with the development of the northern cotton industry and the expansion of southern cotton production that followed the invention and diffusion of the cotton gin, hope for gradual emancipation waned, giving way in the South to a solidly entrenched slave system and in the North to an increasingly strident abolitionist movement. A few Americans tried to find what they saw as a middle way in proposals to educate blacks for colonization abroad; but the blacks themselves showed no enthusiasm for such schemes, and their own uninterest was compounded by southern suspicions that they would not depart in any case and northern recognition that colonization was in truth a compromise with equality.

By 1830, of a total population of almost 13 million, there were some 2 million slaves, all but a handful of whom lived in the South, principally in the states of Virginia (469,757), South Carolina (315,401), North Carolina (245,601), Georgia (217,531), Kentucky (165,213), and Tennessee (141,603). In addition, there were some 319,599 free blacks, most of them concentrated in the cities of the North and the upper South. The free blacks were really quasi-free at best—largely disenfranchised, rigidly segregated, and relentlessly discriminated against. Yet their freedom was far from meaningless and did serve in significant ways to challenge the dominant white ethos of black racial inferiority.[2]

The 2 million slaves lived under quite varied conditions. The vast majority lived on the land, and of these roughly half lived on farms and half on plantations (a plantation being defined in contemporary terms as a unit of twenty slaves or more). Among white southerners, only a fraction (averaging around a quarter) lived in households directly involving slave ownership, and of these roughly half were involved with fewer than five slaves. Even these proportions, however, differed considerably from region to region. Delaware and North Carolina, for example, tended to have larger than average percentages of slaveowners holding only a single slave; South Carolina and Louisiana, on the other hand, tended to have larger than average percentages of slaveowners holding a hundred or more slaves. Similarly, Delaware tended to have smaller than average percentages of whites holding any slaves at all, while South Carolina tended to have larger than average percentages of whites involved in slaveholding. Once these differences are further com-

2. J. D. B. De Bow, ed., *Statistical View of the United States . . . , Being a Compendium of the Seventh Census* (Washington, D.C.: A. O. P. Nicholson, 1854), pp. 82, 63.

pounded by differences within states and localities and by differences owing to individual temperament, the full range of variation becomes clear. Yet, however much the life circumstances of any given slave may have differed from region to region and from locality to locality, the essential fact of entrapment in a system of racial oppression and domination remained. And, just as that system was most blatantly in evidence on larger plantations with sizable slave populations, so, too, was it on those plantations that the various components of an education rooted in the social implications of race became most apparent.

While plantations varied in size and character, the status of the two races was implicit in the spatial design common to most of them, namely, that of a large farmstead, either concentrated in a single unit or dispersed into several large units within walking distance of one another. The farm was owned and managed by a white household, made up of the immediate family and kin of the resident owner (most though not all slaveowners were resident) and of white employees such as overseers, tutors, and occasional preachers, and worked by a labor force of slaves, who lived in the slave quarters and constituted the "quarter community." The slave group ordinarily included a large proportion of field hands and a smaller proportion of skilled and semiskilled craftsmen, a varying complement of midwives, preachers, healers, parent-surrogates, others with special roles (often persons either handicapped or too old to work in the fields), and the very young. The quarter community was organized into families, who maintained identifiable residential space in the huts, cottages, or larger structures in which the quarter community resided. Finally, there were usually a few slaves who lived in the so-called Big House as houseservants, coachmen, or hostlers for the white family and who maintained varying relationships of distance from the quarter community.

Within the plantation system, slaves held a clear place. They were the unfree chattels of their master, and the pedagogy emanating from the Big House was designed to transmit the lessons correlative to that status. Some of these lessons were intended to convey the skills and manners required for the proper fulfillment of a slave's particular task. But all were expected to nurture in slaves the attitudes of perfect submission, the goal being absolute obedience and subordination to the master in particular and to white people in general. The entire white household was involved in carrying out this teaching—not only the slaveowners themselves, but also their wives, their children, and their hired surrogates—and, although the means they employed varied, it

was the whip and the Bible that served as the two most important pedagogical instruments in instructing blacks in the white version of their
place in the world.

As one former Maryland slave recalled, "We were all afraid of
master: when I saw him coming, my heart would jump up into my
mouth as if I had seen a serpent." Not knowing when the master or,
worse yet, the overseer might appear, or what that arrival might bring,
slaves lived in constant fear. Some were able to surmount the fright engendered by the precariousness of their situation, others were not. But
fear was an emotional state that whites encouraged in order to achieve
their pedagogical ends. The masters themselves may have been less
harsh than their overseers; yet, in terms of pedagogical effect, the differences mattered little. It was the constant threat of punishment, purposefully and implicitly exemplified by each slave subjected to the lash,
that ultimately secured cooperative behavior. As one contemporary observer explained the underlying principle, " 'Breaking their spirit' is a
phrase as frequently used with regard to slaves as to horses. Sometimes
a slave must be killed, that the mastery of a hundred others may be secured."[3]

To be sure, slaveowners varied as much in their behavior as the
slaves themselves, with "good masters" genuinely eager to treat their
slaves in as kindly a fashion as possible and "bad masters" more inclined to sadism than paternalistic benevolence. Yet, whatever the differences deriving from temperament, slaveowners tended (for economic
as well as humane reasons) to find gentler pedagogical devices more to
their liking than the whip. Consequently, along with fear, affection,
and even gratitude were emotions that whites used for their own purposes. As Governor John Henry Hammond of South Carolina once put
it, in exchange for obedience, fidelity, and industry, slaves had the right
to expect from their masters peace, plenty, and security; and in the
teaching of this equation the whites used religion as a prime pedagogical tool.[4]

On some plantations, slaves were allowed to attend church services
with the whites; on others, white preachers were brought to the plantation to deliver sermons on carefully chosen passages from Scripture; on
still others, black preachers were hired by the whites to instruct the
slaves in the duties and obligations of Christianity. The purpose of this

3. Benjamin Drew, *The Refugee; or, the Narratives of Fugitive Slaves in Canada* (1856; reprint ed.; New York: Negro Universities Press, 1968), p. 42; and M.D. Conway. *Testimonies
Concerning Slavery* (London: Chapman and Hall, 1864), p. 10.
4. John Henry Hammond to L. Tappan, August 1, 1845 (John H. Hammond mss., Manuscript Division, Library of Congress, Washington, D.C.).

preaching was to familiarize the slaves with those parts of the Bible that were believed to sanction their servile status and to provide them with the minimal Scriptural knowledge required for salvation. Told that they were the descendants of Ham who had been brought to America in bondage at God's command, the blacks were expected to learn that their servitude was sacred, the result of a racial inferiority ordained by God and therefore not to be violated in any way. Told also that they would go to heaven if they were good, the slaves were expected to learn and accept what goodness demanded. Relentlessly, then, though the rhetoric was religious and the illustrations were Biblical, slaves were subjected to a litany that supported white oppression. As one former slave remembered, "The niggers didn't go to the church building; the preacher came and preached to them in their quarter. He'd just say, 'Serve your master. Don't steal your master's turkey. Don't steal your master's chickens. Don't steal your master's hawgs. Don't steal your master's meat. Do whatsoever your master tells you to do.' Same old thing all the time."[5]

Despite widespread awareness that religious instruction could undermine white domination as well as support it, some slaveowners were honestly concerned that their slaves experience conversion. And it was this sentiment, promoted by a growing literature emanating from ministers of evangelical persuasion, that led some masters to permit white missionaries to hold Sabbath schools and evening meetings on their plantations. Using special curricula, for example, the Reverend Charles Colcock Jones's *A Catechism for Colored Persons* (1834) or Bishop William Meade's *Sermons, Dialogues and Narratives for Servants, To Be Read to Them in Families* (1836), supplemented by devices such as Scripture cards carrying illustrations for the Bible, the missionaries managed to gain significant numbers of converts. Between 1846 and 1861, for example, the Methodists increased their roster from 118,904 to 209,836, while the Baptists increased theirs from approximately 200,000 to 400,000. But, if the double-edged message feared by the whites was conveyed by the teaching of these missionaries, their curricular materials were certainly not designed to have that effect. Rather, they were purposefully constructed to synthesize religious instruction and exhortation concerning obedience and place.[6]

On the antebellum plantation, then, whites sought to educate blacks

5. George P. Rawick, ed., *The American Slave: A Composite Autobiography* (19 vols.; Westport, Conn.: Greenwood Publishing Company, 1972–1974), VIII, part 1, p. 35.

6. The statistics on Methodist and Baptist church membership are given in Albert J. Raboteau, *Slave Religion: The "Invisible Institution" in the Antebellum South* (New York: Oxford University Press, 1978), pp. 175–176.

to a particular status in a particular social and economic system and, as part of that status, to an acceptance of inherent racial inferiority. Yet, despite persistent white efforts to prevent countervailing teaching of any kind, blacks were simultaneously exposed to a second pedagogy, one that sought to impart the lessons necessary to the slaves' survival as a people, as human beings rather than property. And, in the transmission of this pedagogy, the pedagogy of the quarter community itself, two institutions were crucial—the family and the clandestine religious congregation.

The two-parent family, while not omnipresent, was common among slaves of the antebellum period; and within the quarters it was parents, complemented by grandparents, aunts, uncles, and other kin, who were the primary educators of their children. Eager to protect their children so far as was humanly possible, as well as to prepare them for the reality they would confront when they went to work (usually sometime between seven and ten years of age), slave parents offered their children affection, discipline, traditional wisdom, and training in useful skills. Mothers and fathers told their children stories and sang them to sleep at night. They insisted that they respect and obey their elders and punished them when they did not. If the jobs they were assigned by the master permitted, they encouraged their children to observe them and to assist them in their activities, and in the evening, after work, they shared with their youngsters the activities they assumed of their own volition—gardening, hunting and fishing, quilting, sewing, and cooking. More importantly, perhaps, by setting examples of loyalty to family, a loyalty that often endured despite imposed physical separation, and by assigning their children family names (sons were often named after their fathers and both sons and daughters frequently carried the name of some dead relative), they sought to confer upon their children an identity that could transcend the immediacies of time and place and to develop their capacity to recognize distance between themselves, their family, and the black community, on the one hand, and the master, his household, and the white world, on the other.

For the adults of the quarter community, the clandestine religious congregation fulfilled several crucial educative functions. Usually gathered around a black preacher, an informal religious leader, or, in the absence of a single leader, a group of community elders, the congregation met several nights a week in secret places called "hush-harbors" that were located in woods or swamps adjacent to the quarters. Revolving around "preaching by the brethren" and then "praying and singing all around," the congregation's meetings provided adult slaves with emotional release and a sense of camaraderie and community support similar to that afforded to children by the peer group with whom they spent a good part of the day. At such meetings, as one former slave explained, "the slave forgets all his sufferings, except to remind others of the trials during the past week, exclaiming: 'Thank God I shall not live here always!'" Beyond that, however, the very existence of a slave-controlled group, convened in secrecy and often including slaves from neighboring plantations, provided a focal point for black resistance, not only to the rules of the master, but also to the religious practices of white Christianity. In the safety of a "hush-harbor," away from the eyes of the white world, slaves were able to express openly the more physical and emotional aspects of their religious faith and to articulate their yearning for freedom. Finally, because the clandestine congregation assumed a variety of benevolent functions and constantly sought the conversion of the unconverted, it helped to maintain a sense of group identity and mutual support.[7]

The pedagogy of the family, though not insignificant for adult slaves, was primarily directed to the children of the quarters, while that of the congregation was addressed to adults. Yet the two institutions were mutually supportive, and the themes underlying their more specific curricula—the themes of personal dignity and pride, family and community solidarity, resistance to white oppression, and the aspiration to freedom and salvation—were reinforced for children and adults alike by the more general mores and customs of the quarter community. In the quarters, for example, it was common practice to address all older slaves as "aunt" and "uncle," and the terms conveyed a number of significant messages. They provided group support for parental insistence on obedience and respect; they underscored a sense of communal kinship; and, serving as substitutes for the terms "Mr." and "Mrs.," which the whites forbade the slaves to use in addressing one another, they represented a subtle form of resistance to bondage. In somewhat different ways, the practice of magic additionally reinforced and extended the more purposeful teaching of families and congregations. Conjurers could be found on almost all antebellum plantations. And their spells and trances not only instilled courage and assuaged despair, they also helped to maintain order in the quarters (slaves who were left in charge of the children by day often carried rabbits' feet and dead

7. Peter Randolph, *Sketches of Slave Life; or, Illustrations of the Peculiar Institution* (2d ed.; Boston: published by the author, 1835), pp. 30–31.

turtles to place spells on the children if they refused to behave) and served to remind slaves that there were certain kinds of supernatural power that could not be exercised by whites.

Beyond all else, however, it was through music and stories that the culture of the quarters was maintained, modified, and transmitted from one generation to the next; in fact, since the very existence of that culture was denied, misunderstood, and abhorred by whites, its perpetuation in itself constituted a central educational message. Spirituals and folk tales served many purposes in the quarters. Meetings of the clandestine congregation were announced in song ("I take my text in Matthew, and by de Revelation, I know you by your garment, Dere's a meeting here tonight. Dere's a meeting here tonight, [Brudder Tony,] Dere's a meeting here tonight, [Sister Rina,] Dere's a meeting here tonight, I hope to meet again"); cooperative projects such as the felling of a tree were organized according to the words and rhythms of spirituals, with everyone chopping together when the last line of the refrain began; and, most important in terms of education, traditional beliefs were preserved and taught through both songs and stories. Deprived of books and in most cases of literacy, slaves used songs and stories to transmit information, educate the young, and share inspiration. At times, songs and stories were invented to meet an immediate need, for example, to express the community's support for brethren in trouble. Thus, in discussing the functions of spirituals, a former slave explained: "My master call me up and order me a short peck of corn and a hundred lash. My friends see it and is sorry for me. When dey come to de praise meetin' dat night dey sing about it. Some's very good singers and know how; and dey work it in, work it in, you know; till dey git it right; and dat's de way." At times, songs and stories were repeated in essentially the same form for generations. At once, then, the major instruments of the slaves' oral tradition helped to unify members of the community, to maintain their connections with the past, and to establish a common future in which their suffering would be left behind.[8]

Spirituals, which were more likely than stories to center on explicitly religious themes, often detailed the slaves' miseries. Yet, through Biblical metaphors and descriptions of more immediate pleasures, they almost always added the triumphs that would transcend those miseries. Even a song such as "When We Do Meet Again," which clearly re-

8. William Francis Allen, Charles Pickard, and Lucy McKim Garrison, eds., *Slave Songs in the United States* (New York: A. Simpson & Co., 1867), p. 9; and "Negro Songs," *Dwight's Journal of Music*, X (1862), 148-149.

flected the pain of separation from family and friends, included the line, "When we do meet again, 'Twill be no more to part." Not all messages of triumph and deliverance involved escape from slavery, however, though that theme in various forms was virtually ubiquitous in trickster stories like the Brer Rabbit tales as well as in the spirituals. Indeed, the moral implicit in many slave stories had more to do with surmounting human failings than with the need to escape the bondage imposed by whites. Lawrence W. Levine has pointed out the degree to which slave moralizing tales dealt with everyday personal relationships. The examples abound: an eagle soaring higher in the sky than other birds but who still had to return to earth for food taught the importance of humility and kindness; a chicken devoured by a hawk because he had not listened to his mother's warning taught the dangers of disobedience; and a hawk who claimed he did not need the Lord's help and died soon thereafter as he crashed into a stump he had mistaken for a chicken taught the importance of dependence upon God. The analogy should not be pressed too far, for there are obvious differences, but the slaves' songs and stories were in their own way a curricular system as all-encompassing and purposefully didactic as the printed libraries purveyed by the American Sunday-School Union and the American Tract Society. And it was through the messages they imparted, concerning relationships between blacks and blacks, blacks and whites, man and God, parents and children, and individuals and communities, as well as through the instruction proffered in the family and at "hush-harbor" religious gatherings, that slaves learned to negotiate the world and to comprehend its meaning in their own terms.[9]

In some respects, there was an obvious overlap, mirroring, and complementarity between the two pedagogies of the plantation. The metaphors associated with both were often the same, with slaveowners using familial imagery to portray their relationship with slaves and slaves using the same imagery to portray their relationships with one another and with God. Similarly, the pedagogical instruments used by the whites were often adopted by the blacks, religion as well as naming along kinship lines being significant in both systems of instruction. The same teachers, in some instances, could simultaneously serve the purposes of the master and the needs of the slaves, as when a black preacher offered a sermon pleasing to both whites and blacks. Indeed, the

9. Allen *et al.,* eds., *Slave Songs,* p. 41; and Lawrence W. Levine, *Black Culture and Black Consciousness: Afro-American Folk Thought from Slavery to Freedom* (New York: Oxford University Press, 1977), chap. ii.

pedagogical techniques of one group were often used on the other, as, for example, when the fear instilled in blacks by white cruelty was turned around and blacks purposefully instilled fear in the master or overseer to establish the parameters of their acquiescence. And, though the derivative effects could be quite different, whites and blacks at times shared immediate educational aims, as, for example, when the mastery of a skill would engender pride in both slave and master and for each represent a lesson achieved.

In other respects, however, there was dissonance and opposition in the two pedagogies of the plantation. Indeed, however ironic, the most fundamental relationship between the two pedagogies derived from the extent to which each augmented, intensified, and even necessitated the other. The continuing effort to nurture pride, resistance, and community solidarity within the quarters required the countervailing effort on the part of whites to nurture submission; conversely, the continuing effort by whites to instill fear and dependence demanded the countervailing effort by blacks to instill courage and independence. In many respects, these dynamics were the result of the slave system itself, which, by definition, pitted master against servant. Yet the discordant education of the plantation had an influence well beyond both its geographic boundaries and the era during which slavery held sway.

In 1830 there were roughly 319,599 free blacks in the United States. In 1860 there were roughly 488,070. Living primarily in the cities of the North and the upper South, these men and women, though free from enforced servitude, could not fully escape the bondage of caste. Increasingly excluded from white institutions or discriminated against within white institutions, free blacks sought to establish their own churches, schools, and benevolent associations. And, as the number of such agencies increased, white hostility and fear also increased, locking both groups into a cycle of teaching and counterteaching not dissimilar to the one that existed on the plantation. Thus, free blacks, like their enslaved counterparts, though able to travel, hold property, and go to school, were subjected, on the one hand, to white efforts to teach inferiority and, on the other hand, to black efforts to teach pride, resistance, and community solidarity.[10]

As was true on the plantation, the family and the church were the chief institutions used by free blacks for their own education, with the church serving the additional function of establishing and maintaining

10. Francis A. Walker, ed., *A Compendium of the Ninth Census* (Washington, D.C.: Government Printing Office, 1872), pp. 14–15.

schools. Beginning ordinarily with a Sunday school and occasionally supplementing that with a day school, the churches found their resources severely strained by the demands of their congregations for schooling. Yet in this realm, too, the discord engendered by the two pedagogies of the plantation was in evidence, with whites seeking to prevent the spread of black schooling and in some instances actually forbidding blacks by law to open schools, and blacks pressing forward with the effort. For fifteen years after Georgia had prohibited the attendance of free blacks at school, Julian Troumontaine, a free black schoolteacher, successfully held clandestine classes. Like their enslaved brethren—among whom, according to W. E. B. Du Bois's estimate, some 5 percent could read in 1860, despite all the provisions of the slave codes prohibiting the teaching of literacy—free blacks equated learning with liberation. And for them, as for the slaves, the power of that equation derived at least in part from white attention to literacy (and its prohibition) as well as from the whites' constant display of their own reliance on the words of a book, namely, the Bible.[11]

Frederick Douglass once remarked that "no colored man was really free while residing in a slave state. He was ever more or less subject to the conditions of his slave brother. In his color was his badge of bondage." And Tocqueville went even further to observe that no Negro could really be free and reside anywhere in the United States, for even freed he was "alien" to whites, who retained the prejudices associated with race and color. Such observations point to the inescapable realities of the quasi-free status of the so-called free blacks. North and South alike, though even more so in the South, they were subject to sharp restriction and rigid segregation, in education, in employment, and in social services. Yet there was a difference in the white education of the North that is worthy of note. To be sure, white families, white churches, white schools and colleges, and white spokesmen for innumerable voluntary associations repeated the litanies of savage origins, Biblical stigma, and biological inferiority. By contrast, however, some elements of the white community taught otherwise. Often, the instruction was at best conflicting: the same teacher or preacher would assert the equality of all persons before God in one paragraph and the inferiority of the Negro before his fellow human beings in another; or, the teacher or preacher would assert the principle of equality and practice

11. W. E. Burghardt Du Bois, *Black Reconstruction: An Essay Toward a History of the Part Which Black Folk Played in the Attempt to Reconstruct Democracy in America, 1860–1880* (Philadelphia: Albert Saifer, 1935), p. 638.

the behavior of inequality—even the Quakers maintained segregation in their meeting halls. Granted the prevalence of such conflicts, however, there were some white families, congregations, schools, and organizations that preached and practiced true equality. At best, they constituted a small, articulate minority, even in the North, but many abolitionists did teach and live the principles of equality. As a consequence, the education proffered by the white communities in which they resided became more cacophonous and less internally coherent, with the result that it demeaned less decisively at the same time as it afforded powerful examples of genuine alternatives that could not be wholly ignored.[12]

III

As with the blacks, the situation of the Indians also changed perceptibly from decade to decade during the years following the Revolution. Initially, there was widespread sentiment favoring their assimilation into the Anglo-American community. The federal government mounted a variety of programs designed to induce the tribes to abandon their traditional culture and adopt the ways of the American farmer, and the churches lent their assistance through missionary endeavors. The assumption was that once they were offered the benefits of civilization the Indians would immediately seize the opportunity and enter into the mainstream of American life. The War of 1812, however, brought a major change of view. The Indian tribes, long angered by the relentless westward movement of the whites and the concomitant seizure of their lands, tended to side with the British, occasioning fundamental questions on the part of the whites concerning the desire and even the ability of the Indian to adapt. In place of the older assumption of ready assimilation, a new view came into fashion, maintaining that more time would be needed for the civilizing process to work and that the only way of obtaining the additional time would be to remove the tribes to a protected environment west of the Mississippi where they could effect the transition at their own pace. Assimilation would remain the ultimate goal, but removal would be the immediate instrument. The outcome was that a generally benevolent aim ended up justifying harsh and violent means. Such was the stuff of Indian policy from the age of Jackson through Reconstruction.

12. Frederick Douglass, *Life and Times of Frederick Douglass* (rev. ed. of 1892; reprint ed.; New York: Collier Books, 1962), p. 208; and Tocqueville, *Democracy in America*, I, 358.

In actual numbers, the Indian population was much smaller than the black population. To be sure, as the United States acquired territory, it also acquired Indians. But the Indian population did not increase naturally at rates comparable to those of the white and black populations, owing mainly to the effects of disease, war, and continuing social and physical dislocation. And there were also the reductions in population that derived from Indians formerly included within the formal confines of the United States being relocated beyond the pale. Yet, quite apart from numbers, the fate of the Indians remained important to white Americans: there was a continuing recognition of their original occupancy of the land and an abiding sense that their fate was a matter of national conscience and concern. As the Reverend Edward D. Griffin put it in an annual missionary sermon before the General Assembly of the Presbyterian Church in 1805, "We are living in prosperity on the very lands from which the wretched pagans have been ejected; from the recesses of whose wilderness a moving cry is heard, *When it is well with you, think of poor Indians.*"[13]

During the golden period of revolutionary aspiration in the 1780's and 1790's, when many white Americans hoped for the emancipation of the blacks even though they considered the blacks to be essentially inferior, there was widespread belief that the Indian was equal as a human being and needed only to be taught the ways of civilization to take his place in the mainstream of American life. Jefferson articulated this view as systematically as any of his contemporaries. He observed in *Notes on the State of Virginia* (1785) that the physical stature of the Indian was generally equal to that of the European and argued that further study would probably demonstrate that the Indians were "formed in mind as well as body, on the same module with the 'Homo sapiens Europeaus' "—this, all too ironically, while suggesting that blacks really lacked the mental ability ever to achieve true equality. Moreover, Jefferson believed that the best solution for both whites and Indians would be a total amalgamation of the two peoples—once again while suggesting that the blacks could never be amalgamated and should therefore be resettled elsewhere. "In truth," Jefferson wrote of the Indians in 1803, "the ultimate point of rest and happiness for them is to let our settlements and theirs meet and blend together, to intermix, and become one people. Incorporating themselves with us as citizens of the United States, this is what the natural progress of things will of course

13. Edward D. Griffin, *The Kingdom of Christ: A Missionary Sermon* (Philadelphia: Jane Aitken, 1805), p. 27.

bring on, and it will be better to promote than retard it."[14]

Believing with Jefferson in the educability of the Indians, Americans of the early national era set about developing a program of activities that would lead them to "civilization," the stage of social evolution at which they would be ready for amalgamation. During Washington's presidency, Indian affairs were assigned to the War Department, with the result that Henry Knox became responsible for the initial development of an Indian policy. Since the various tribes were considered independent foreign powers and since there had been continuing friction along the borders of settlement, pacification became the decisive element in policymaking. But Washington and Knox were not unmindful of the eventual goal of civilization, and they repeatedly urged the Indian to adopt the white man's modes of agriculture and stock raising, viewing these as preliminary steps in the civilizing process. To this end, Washington in 1791 asked Congress to undertake "rational experiments" for imparting to the Indian the "blessings of civilization"; and Congress responded over the next few years with a series of "trade and intercourse acts" authorizing the president to furnish goods and money in order "to promote civilization among the friendly Indian tribes, and to secure the continuance of their friendship"; to appoint agents to reside among the Indians and to assist in civilizing them by means of agriculture and the domestic arts; to establish and maintain factories, or trading houses, whereby the government might assist the Indians in obtaining a variety of supplies and manufactured products at cost; and to arrange for the licensing of individuals wishing to trade with the Indians. The aim of these efforts was to secure for the Indians what was perceived to be the "discipline" of private ownership of property and the pursuit of agriculture, while at the same time furnishing them with protection against exploitation at the hands of sharp or illegal traders.[15]

Surrounding all these activities, however, and coloring every element of policy was the unquenchable hunger of white Americans for Indian lands. The hope that the shift to agriculture would eventually civilize the Indians was integrally connected with the expectation that the shift would also make them less dependent upon the large tracts of commonly owned land they needed to support a hunting and trapping

14. Thomas Jefferson, *Notes on the State of Virginia* (1785), in *The Writings of Thomas Jefferson*, edited by Paul Leicester Ford (10 vols.; New York: G. P. Putnam's Sons, 1892–1899), III, 155; and Thomas Jefferson to Benjamin Hawkins, February 18, 1803, in *ibid.*, VIII, 214.

15. *A Compilation of the Messages and Papers of the Presidents, 1789–1899*, edited by James D. Richardson (11 vols.; Washington, D.C.: Government Printing Office, 1896–1899), I, 105; and U.S., *Statutes at Large*, I, 331, 472, 746–747, II, 143.

economy. In the more gentle version of the scenario, Indians who
farmed would be more ready to sell or cede their holdings; in the
harsher version, they would be less apt to defend their holdings to the
death. However that may be, some states, such as Georgia, did not even
wait to see what the outcome of the civilizing policy would be, but rather went about immediately assigning vast tracts of Indian land to squatters, speculators, and land companies. By 1799 the latent purpose of the
policy was manifest in the order to the army to handle squatters "with
all the humanity which the circumstances will possibly permit."[16]

The Washington-Knox program probably helped achieve the short-
term goal of pacification, though there is no way to determine its larger
effects; at least it did no harm. The Adams administration continued
the program, despite Adams's own skepticism concerning the Indians'
ability ever to achieve civilization. It was Jefferson, however, who
shaped the program into the form it would assume through the next
twenty years. He persuaded Congress to renew those elements of the
Washington program that had expired and obtained authorization for
the expenditure of $15,000 annually toward the civilizing of the Indi-
ans; and he was much more direct and explicit than his predecessors
about the goal of separating the Indian from his land. By 1802, he was
suggesting that the government trading factories encourage the Indians
to purchase beyond their means in the hope that they would eventually
accrue debts sufficient to force them to cede their lands; and in his con-
fidential message to Congress in 1803 he put forward a plan for a buff-
er zone of white settlements along the Mississippi and proposed the
mounting of an expedition to explore the Missouri River "even to the
western ocean," with a view to finding out more about the region itself
and the Indians who inhabited it. When the purchase of Louisiana was
arranged, Jefferson actually drafted a constitutional amendment to le-
gitimatize the transaction, a major provision of which would have set
aside the territory above the thirty-first parallel for the Indians in exchange for their lands east of the Mississippi. Though the amendment
was never adopted, the Louisiana territory was thereafter perceived as
a place for the removal of those Indians who seemed unwilling to abandon the ways of the hunter or, in the Jeffersonian euphemism, unwilling to become civilized.[17]

16. U.S., *Statutes at Large*, I, 748.
17. *The Writings of Thomas Jefferson*, edited by Andrew Lipscomb and Albert Ellery Bergh
(20 vols.; Washington, D.C.: Thomas Jefferson Memorial Association, 1903–1904), III, 493; and
Draft of an Amendment to the Constitution, July, 1803, in *Writings of Thomas Jefferson* edited by
Ford, VIII, 241–249.

In their efforts to civilize the Indians, the Jeffersonians collaborated closely with the missionary arms of the several Christian churches. Indian missionaries under various sorts of denominational and interdenominational sponsorship had been working among the tribes throughout the seventeenth and eighteenth centuries—ever since the efforts of Alexander Whitaker and John Eliot during the earliest years of settlement. With the organization of the American Board of Commissioners for Foreign Missions by the Presbyterians and Congregationalists in 1810, however, the missionary movement took on new vigor. The Board sent Eleazer Williams, himself a descendant of an Iroquois chief, to labor among the Iroquois in northern New York and Vermont, Cyrus Kingsbury to organize missions among the Cherokees in Tennessee and the Choctaws in Mississippi, and Cephas Washburn and Alfred Finney to work among the Cherokees in Arkansas. The efforts of these missionaries were explicitly intended to create Indians who would be "English in their language, civilized in their habits, and Christian in their religion." Their instruments would be schools, some of them day schools located among the tribes to carry on the initial work, others of them boarding schools located in the older, more settled white regions, where the most apt pupils could be brought to the point where they were ready for complete amalgamation. Along with their formal classroom instruction, the missionaries were expected to work with the adults, on the one hand teaching them the reading and religion that would prepare them for conversion and on the other hand teaching them the ways of contemporary white agriculture and domestic economy. The tie that had existed in the minds of the colonial missionaries between piety and civility, between the ways of Christian belief and the ways of Anglo-American civilization, persisted into the national era.[18]

Actually, a good deal of the money that Jefferson obtained from Congress to civilize the Indians went toward the partial support of missionary efforts. Later, in 1819, Congress formally established the Civilization Fund of $10,000 a year to subsidize such efforts; but the federal funds merely supplemented the much larger sum of money that was raised by the Board and the several denominations to support the work among the tribes. Similarly, when the government after 1820 began to specify that certain treaty annuities be designated specifically for educational purposes, that money also went toward partial support for missionaries. In effect—and paradoxically, given the Jeffersonian penchant

18. *Report of the American Board of Commissioners for Foreign Missions; Compiled from Documents Laid Before the Board at the Seventh Annual Meeting* (1816), p. 11.

for secularism—the government ended up in patent partnership with the several Christian denominations. Jefferson himself was always ambivalent about the partnership, and as late as 1822 he refused an invitation from American Board member Jedidiah Morse to join a contemplated society for the civilization and improvement of the Indian tribes, maintaining that in light of the government's effort in that realm the society was unnecessary. As for Madison and Monroe, they were simply less concerned than Jefferson with the entire Indian problem. Madison indicated in his inaugural address that he would continue the effort to civilize the Indian, but there is no evidence that he took much interest in the matter. And Monroe clearly reflected the disenchantment that arose in light of the widespread Indian collaboration with the British in the War of 1812. He began his presidency believing that only coercion would ever civilize the tribes and ended it dubious even about the promise of coercion.

Probably the most successful single example of the civilization policy in operation during the early decades of the nineteenth century was with the Cherokees, a tribe numbering approximately seventeen thousand, organized into some forty villages in a region covering parts of Georgia, the western Carolinas, and Tennessee. Various missionaries had worked with the tribe during the latter half of the eighteenth century; and indeed the Treaty of Holston (1791) between the federal government and the tribe had made funds available for assisting in the transition from a hunting to an agricultural economy. In 1796 Washington addressed an explicit invitation to the tribe to accept farming as a way of life; and one of the ablest of the early Indian agents, Return J. Meigs, had worked with the tribe in the effort to accomplish that end. The result was an unusual readiness among the Cherokees—and in some quarters actually a determination—to adopt agricultural ways and assimilate to Anglo-American-Christian culture.

Both the Moravians and the Presbyterians had established schools among the Cherokees with tribal permission during the first years of the nineteenth century; but it was really the decision of the American Board to concentrate a considerable portion of its effort on the Cherokees after 1816 that enabled the tribe to develop what was probably the most extensive system of schooling to be found in any Indian community. In 1817 a Cherokee delegation actually went to Washington to ask for governmental assistance in educating the children of the tribe; and in response the authorities agreed to construct a schoolhouse and quarters for a teacher and to purchase a supply of plows, hoes, spinning wheels, and other equipment for the teaching of agriculture and the domestic arts, assuming that the Board would provide the services of a teacher and that the tribal leaders would lend their political and financial support. The result was a jointly sponsored venture at Chickamauga, Georgia, subsequently named the Brainerd Mission (after the eighteenth-century missionary David Brainerd), which became the model and the motherhouse for most of the additional schools subsequently established among the Cherokees.

Brainerd Mission conducted a program explicitly designed to prepare Indian youngsters for rapid and complete assimilation into the dominant white society. Within a year, the institution included, in addition to the schoolhouse and teacher's quarters, five dormitories, a kitchen, a dining hall, a gristmill, a sawmill, a barn, a stable, and fifty acres of land under cultivation—in other words, it had become a self-sustaining community (the American Board referred to it as an "education family"). English was the language of instruction, and indeed upon entering the school each of the pupils was assigned a new English name to take the place of his or her Indian name, usually the name of some church leader or benefactor of the institution. The Lancasterian system of instruction was used, with the teacher drilling the older children, who in turn became the monitors who drilled the younger children. The regimen was full and stringent, with the school day extending from 5:30 A.M. to 9 P.M., and in those hours not assigned to classroom instruction the boys cut wood and worked in the fields while the girls sewed, knitted, cooked, and spun. Evenings were regularly devoted to discussions of religious doctrine. Finally, the Brainerd Mission served as a church for those Indians who had undergone conversion to Christianity and as a propagating agency for adult Indians who were ready to hear the Gospel. Other mission schools similar to Brainerd were established among the Cherokees during the 1820's, and by the end of the decade there were eight of them in all, enrolling 180 students. In addition, through the efforts of Thomas L. McKenney, who was Superintendent of Indian Trade at the time, Brainerd became a national model for other tribes in other regions of the country.

Meanwhile, in 1821, an illiterate, self-educated Cherokee named Sequoyah managed to devise a Cherokee alphabet: it was phonetic in nature, consisting of eighty-six characters, each representing a sound in the oral language, with the result that it took only a few weeks for a person who had facility with the spoken language to learn to read it. In 1825, the tribal council voted fifteen hundred dollars toward the acquisition of a press and a font of type in Sequoyah's characters, and additional funds were sought through the First Presbyterian Church in Philadelphia. The press and type were duly acquired and sent forth a steady flow of tracts and hymns, and eventually a Bible in Cherokee. And in 1828 a newspaper called the *Cherokee Phoenix* was begun, under the editorship of Elias Boudinot, a Cherokee graduate of the Board's school for "heathen youth" in Cornwall, Connecticut. While the schools themselves never reached a large proportion of the Cherokee population, the printed material that issued from the press went far in advancing literacy and a knowledge of Anglo-American-Christian ways among members of the tribe.[19]

By the end of the 1820's the Cherokees had devised a written constitution modeled after the American Constitution, proclaimed their nation a republic after the model of the United States, and claimed sovereignty over their tribal land in Georgia, North Carolina, Tennessee, and Alabama. An agricultural way of life was slowly being adopted, schools had been established, and literacy was spreading; in a word, the "civilizing process" was advancing apace. But, alas, the values of the dominant white society had shifted. During the same period when the Cherokees were advancing toward civilization, Americans were becoming increasingly skeptical concerning the government's civilizing policies and the Indian's capacity for the assimilation process in general. Some simply hungered for land and wanted the Indians moved elsewhere, whatever their state of civilization. Others recognized the mixed results of continuing contact between Indian and white civilizations: as literacy, agriculture, and Christianity advanced, so did drunkenness, disease, and demoralization. The civilizing process would take longer than expected, they reasoned, and while it proceeded the Indians required a place where they could be spared the disadvantages of contact with white society at the same time as they profited from the benefits of white education. Moreover, the acquisition of the Louisiana territory for the first time made such a policy not only advisable but also feasible: the land was there to be used for beneficent purposes. Finally, there were the mixed results of civilization itself: the Cherokees, after all, had moved a long way toward civilization, but the cohesive force of tribal society had persisted, with the result that civilization had not brought amalgamation.

During the 1820s a variety of proposals appeared in Congress intended to create a designated Indian territory west of the Mississippi,

19. *Ibid.*, p. 9.

with various arrangements for the tribes still residing in the East. Then, in 1827, when the Cherokee Nation proclaimed itself independent and claimed sovereignty over its territory, the state of Georgia countered by asserting the authority of the state and its laws over the Cherokee lands. As Georgia proceeded to press its claim, the Indians appealed to Andrew Jackson, but to no avail. Citing the constitutional provision against erecting any new state within the territory of an existing state without the existing state's approval, Jackson advised the Cherokees to surrender or to immigrate to the West. In addition, he obtained Congressional authorization in the Removal Act of 1830 to grant lands west of the Mississippi to tribes ready to cede lands which they occupied east of the Mississippi. The provisions of the act were entirely permissive, to be sure, but a new policy had been cast. For the next half-century, removal rather than incorporation, or, put more euphemistically, removal looking toward eventual incorporation, was the official policy of the federal government.

The remaining tribes in the East were relentlessly removed to the West, some via persuasion, as with the Chickasaws in Mississippi, others via trickery, as with the Seminoles in Florida, and still others via coercion, as with the Cherokees themselves. The last constituted what may have been the supreme educational irony of the early Republic. For, as the Cherokees themselves pointed out again and again, the federal authorities had sent plows and hoes and urged them to take up farming and the ways of civilization. Having done so in an exemplary fashion, they were being forcibly removed from their ancestral homes. The apparent reward for their readiness to assimilate was ejection.

Meanwhile, the federal government, through the Indian Act of 1834 (establishing the Office of Indian Affairs and making provision for the regulation of trade in the new Indian territory west of the Mississippi), continued the very complex of policies that had earlier been designed to bring the Indian to civilization. The verbal justification of removal was that the goal of incorporation continued to prevail, but that the process would simply take longer than had been anticipated. In the reserved territories west of the Mississippi (the term "reservation" did not come into fashion until after the Civil War), the Indians were to be protected from the demoralizing effects of white civilization by being kept from contact with whites at the same time as they were educated in the ways of agriculture and the domestic arts, private ownership of property, and Anglo-American-Christian belief. The instruments of that education, as earlier, would be institutions variously patterned after the Brainerd Mission, partially subsidized by the federal government, partially supported by tribal funds derived from removal treaties with the federal government, and partially financed by the various Christian denominations. Some, like Brainerd itself, would be boarding schools; others, day schools. Some would operate under the aegis of tribal councils; others would be run directly by the missionary agencies themselves. Whatever the details, however, the thrust of the schools would be essentially similar.

Significantly, even in the new environment the effect of the schools was severely limited. The missionary-teachers carried on their instruction with dedication and verve, but white traders who brought whiskey, guns, and horses to sell to the Indians also conveyed educational messages, as did the white farmers who squatted on Indian lands. Hence, the missionaries' teaching was often contravened by the behavior of exploitative traders and farmers and on occasion by marauding armies; and, even when it was not, it was paralleled by the powerful diurnal education in tribal ways carried on by the Indians themselves—by parents, kin, chiefs, and medicine men. As was true for blacks, especially on large plantations, the education of Indians involved two discordant pedagogies.

Indian tribes varied significantly in their social organization: among the Iroquois and the Cheyennes the matrifocal extended family prevailed; among the Comanches it was the individual polygynous family; among the River Yumans, it was the patrifocal extended family. Yet in all tribes the family carried important educative responsibilities. In general, there was a fairly clear division of labor between the sexes, with the women undertaking the planting, cultivation, and harvesting of crops, the preparation of foods, and the making of clothing, while the men undertook the hunting or the fishing or, on occasion, the making of war. The training of the young went forward essentially through a continuing process of exemplification, explanation, and imitation, with particular teaching roles assigned to particular kin (the mother's brother, for example, as disciplinarian) or tribal officials (medicine men) and with the young often undergoing instruction in age cohorts (thus, the ethnologist Henry Rowe Schoolcraft's observation that the children of the Dakotas were explicitly taught to use the spear and the bow and arrow and began to hunt large game at the age of twelve). Most tribes relied upon praise, reward, and prophecy rather than physical punishment to stimulate the mastery of skills, and competition was often included as an additional spur. Thus, the Natchez of the lower Mississippi held frequent shooting contests for boys, with the best and second best marksmen being awarded ceremonial titles, while the Noskas of the Northwest made public predictions of the good things young braves were expected to accomplish and thereby provided the incentive of publicity. And, as precursors of the ridicule commonly employed to encourage and sustain appropriate behavior in adults, teasing and shaming were also widely used as pedagogical devices. Among the Blackfeet, for example, boys going to war for the first time were assigned demeaning nicknames that could only be dropped after some clear demonstration of courage and skill, for example, the killing of an enemy or the stealing of a horse.[20]

Beyond the continuing training in knowledge and skills, the tribes imposed meaning on the world through songs, stories, dances, and ceremonies. Schoolcraft reported at length on the myths of creation that were perpetuated in various oral traditions, with the Iroquois tracing their origins to Atahentsic, the Woman of Heaven; the Osages maintaining that the first man of their nation emerged from a shell and met with the Great Spirit, who gave him a bow and arrows and commanded him to hunt; and the Pottawatomies believing that there were two Great Spirits governing the world, one good and the other evil, with the first having made the world and called all things into being. And the artist George Catlin provided vivid descriptions and colorful illustrations of the various dances performed by the Mandans of the upper Missouri: the sham scalp dance, in which boys between the ages of seven and fifteen were divided into companies and taught the arts of war (each company, Catlin explained, was headed by an experienced warrior, "who leads them on, in the character of a teacher"); the bull dance, in which boys arriving at the age of manhood were subjected to ordeals of privation and torture in *rites de passage* marking the beginning of adulthood; and the buffalo dance, which, beyond its mythic function, galvanized the tribe to action at times when food was scarce and a successful hunt was necessary.[21]

In addition, there were the didactic stories and trickster tales handed down from generation to generation in which men, women, and animals exemplified important lessons about life: the story of the sun-snar-

20. Henry R. Schoolcraft, *Information Respecting the History, Conditions and Prospects of the Indian Tribes of the United States* (5 vols.; Philadelphia: Lippincott, Grambo & Co., 1853–1856), IV, 61.

21. *Ibid.*, I, 316–320; and George Catlin, *Illustrations of the Manners, Customs, and the Condition of the North American Indians with Letters and Notes* (2 vols.; 10th ed.; London: Henry G. Bohn, 1866), I, 131.

er, for example, in which the mouse, among all the animals who tried, released the sun from the death grip of an angry boy; or the trickster tale of the hero Manabozho getting even with a buzzard who had carried him in flight and then purposely dropped him, by pulling off his scalp and neck feathers and condemning him to stink of the carrion he ate. Schoolcraft actually witnessed such stories being used among the Chippewas "to convey instruction, or impress examples of courage, daring, or right action."[22]

Given the power of such a pedagogy, the impact of a Brainerd curriculum taught by white "outsiders" was at best weak, at worst disruptive, and most often meaningless. Thomas Hartley Crawford, who was Commissioner of Indian Affairs from 1838 to 1845, stated the problem poignantly in one of his annual reports: "They must at the least be taught to read and write, and have some acquaintance with figures," he observed; "but if they do not learn to build and live in houses, to sleep on beds; to eat at regular intervals; to plow, and sow, and reap; to rear and use domestic animals; to understand and practice the mechanic arts; and to enjoy, to their gratification and improvement, all the means of profit and rational pleasure that are so profusely spread around civilized life, their mere knowledge of what is learned in the school room proper will be completely valueless." Crawford's effort during his tenure was to institute a much more wide-ranging program of education among the tribes, centered in clan or neighborhood schools but including adjoining farms and shops that would teach, not only agriculture, the mechanic arts, and "housewifery," but also the entire way of life of white Christian Americans.[23]

Not surprisingly, Crawford failed. In the absence of political and economic supports outside the school to confirm the view of civilization taught by the school, the education proffered by the whites was essentially unrealistic. Indians who had learned agriculture in the East often ended up having to hunt in the West simply to get enough food for their families. Moreover, where they were able to practice the arts of agriculture in their new western homes, they were often warred upon by their huntsmen neighbors, who saw them as intruders despite their removal treaties with the white men in Washington. In the Far West, the so-called civilizing process frequently became a device for teaching the English language and Protestant doctrine to western Indians who

22. Henry R. Schoolcraft, *Personal Memoirs of a Residence of Thirty Years with the Indian Tribes of the American Frontiers* (Philadelphia: Lippincott, Grambo, & Co., 1851), p. 196.
23. U.S., Congress, Senate Documents, 28th Congress, 2d sess., 1844, 449, 1, 313.

had already been "civilized" to the Spanish language and Roman Catholic doctrine. Ultimately, cut off from their own history, shunned by their fellow Indians, and regarded with hostility by surrounding whites, the Indians who "accepted" civilization ended up strangers in several worlds and at home in none. The outcome of their education was not civilization but rather confusion, disappointment, and disintegration.

IV

There was a dilemma at the heart of both black and Indian education that called to the fore the very nature of the way in which Americans conceived their own society during the nineteenth century. From the beginning, the black was considered unassimilable. Even emancipated, he was deemed a person apart. "Educate him," the Connecticut Colonization Society declared in 1828, "and you have added little or nothing to his happiness—you have unfitted him for the society and sympathies of his degraded kindred, and yet you have not procured for him and cannot procure for him any admission into the society and sympathy of white men." Twenty years later, Frederick Grimke put it even more crassly: "It seems impossible to train this emasculated race to the hardy and vigorous industry of the white man. To have made slaves of them originally was a deep injustice. To introduce them into the society of whites and to leave them to contend with beings so greatly their superior is a still more flagrant injustice." That the black could not be assimilated was a common nineteenth-century sociopolitical assumption to which educational correlates attached. The alternatives for those who shared the assumption were slavery (or quasi-slavery), on the one hand, or colonization abroad (removal), on the other.[24]

Much the same was true of the Indian. While post-Revolutionary rhetoric pronounced him assimilable, post-Revolutionary behavior argued otherwise. The facts were nowhere better demonstrated than in the demise of the Foreign Mission School that the American Board of Commissioners for Foreign Missions established for heathen youth from all over the world in Cornwall, Connecticut, in 1817. In 1823 one of the Cherokee students there married Sara Northrup, daughter of the

24. An Address to the Public by the Managers of the Colonization Society of Connecticut (New Haven: Treadway and Adams, 1828), p. 5; and Frederick Grimke, The Nature and Tendency of Free Institutions, edited by John William Ward (Cambridge, Mass.: Harvard University Press, 1968), p. 428.

institution's steward, and in 1824 another Cherokee, Elias Boudinot, married Harriet Gold, daughter of a local family. For all the talk about assimilation, there was an outburst of public criticism in the town that eventually contributed to the closing of the academy. And, on a larger scale, the proclamation of the independent Cherokee Nation in 1827 and the events that followed in its wake indicate that the notion of unassimilability was shared on both sides. Once again, there was a common sociopolitical assumption to which educational correlates attached. The alternatives for those who shared this view were destruction or removal to the territory west of the Mississippi.

The educational correlates reflected the intractability of the problem. As the American Colonization Society stressed in its literature, if blacks were to remain in their subservient situation, they had best be kept "in the lowest state of degradation and ignorance," lest education raise their hopes for privileges they could never attain. Properly educated, they would only be suited for removal. The Indians, on the other hand, confronted a profound irony. They were invited to undergo education for "civilization" that would prepare them for assimilation to the American community, but when the invitation was accepted and the education was successful, as among the Cherokees, assimilation was ultimately barred by the very community that had extended the invitation. They were forcibly removed to what were for all intents and purposes colonies west of the Mississippi and told that they should subject themselves to the same education for "civilization," but there appeared to be no realistic anticipation that they would ever be accepted by the white society that had sent them there, and the probability was that the education itself would ill prepare them for the lives they would lead in their own territories.[25]

The resultant dilemmas highlighted the more general problem of assimilation during the first century of national life. The effort of the dominant white Anglo-American-Christian community to educate the blacks and the Indians produced one of many forms of a discordant education—an education in which at least two conflicting configurations of education sought to inculcate in the same individuals quite different sets of values and attitudes via quite different pedagogies. The overall impact of such a discordant education on any given black or Indian depended on a variety of factors, any one of which might prove de-

25. *A View of Exertions Lately Made for the Purpose of Colonizing the Free People of Colour, in the United States, in Africa, or Elsewhere* (Washington, D.C.: Jonathan Elliott, 1817), p. 7.

cisive. But surrounding the entire process was the hard reality of assumed unassimilability. In the end, depending on the particulars of communities, configurations of education, and individual temperaments, the result could range from the complete adoption of a white Anglo-American-Christian identity in a situation of partial acceptance or total nonacceptance by whites, to the complete rejection of the proffered Anglo-American-Christian identity in favor of some assertive version of a black Afro-American or a tribal identity.

The dynamics of a discordant education were present in numerous other subcommunities during the nineteenth century, but with a difference, of course. The Irish-Catholic families of New York City during the 1850's and 1860's, crowded as they were into increasingly homogeneous immigrant neighborhoods, developed their own configurations of Irish households, Irish churches, Irish schools, Irish benevolent societies and Irish newspapers; while New York City, in turn, offered public schools, dozens of alternative churches and newspapers, a variety of social services conducted by benevolent organizations representing the missionary thrust of the evangelical united front, and a dazzling array of social and vocational apprenticeships, most of which, however, were unavailable to the Irish. For children and adults alike, the pull and haul of conflicting loyalties, divergent ambitions, and alternative opportunities was incessant; and, once again, the overall impact of that discordant education on any given Irish Catholic depended upon a complex variety of factors, one of which was invariably luck.

Much the same might be said for the German Lutherans who settled in Lancaster, Pennsylvania, though the range of alternative churches, newspapers, social services, and vocational opportunities there was infinitesimal in comparison with that of New York, and indeed for a time the German leaders of Lancaster actually hoped that the county would remain a German enclave within the larger American community. Much the same might also be said for the Norwegian or Swedish Reformed immigrants who settled on the farmlands of Wisconsin and Minnesota, and later for the Mexican immigrants who settled in the towns of Texas and for the Chinese and Japanese immigrants who settled in the cities of California and Washington.

Given the prevalence of discordant education, the crucial variable was race. The assumption of the dominant white community with respect to the Irish Catholics, the German Lutherans, and the Norwegian and Swedish Reformed was that they needed to be and could be Americanized—Americanization being a concept that was widely used to imply some combination of learning English, understanding the Constitution, living productively within the law according to middle-class standards, and accepting the values of an undenominational Protestant *paideia*. Put otherwise, the assumption was that white ethnic immigrants were assimilable and indeed needed to be assimilated as rapidly as possible. Clearly, however, the assumption of the dominant white community with respect to blacks and Indians, and indeed with respect to all peoples of color, was that they were essentially unassimilable. There was, to be sure, an area of overlap and confusion. Mulattoes and light-skinned Indians of mixed blood were occasionally permitted to "pass" if they were culturally similar, while swarthy white immigrants from Mexico were not. The Fourteenth Amendment to the federal Constitution did pointedly bestow citizenship upon "all persons born or naturalized in the United States, and subject to the jurisdiction thereof." But the blacks were held apart from the larger community and denied the rights and privileges of citizenship, while the Indians were judged subject to the jurisdiction, not of the United States, but of their tribal "nations." And the first generation of Chinese and Japanese immigrants were flatly denied naturalization. In the end, whatever the unclarities, the prevailing assumption was clear: people could be educated to transcend the barriers of ethnicity and religion in order to become full-fledged members of the American community, but they could not be educated to transcend the barriers of race.[26]

26. The Constitution of the United States, Article XIV, in Henry Steele Commager, ed., *Documents of American History* (9th ed.; 2 vols.; New York: Appleton-Century-Crofts, 1973), I, 147.

PART III

THE PRUDENT SOCIETY

When sobered by experience I hope our successors will turn their attention to the advantages of education. I mean education on the broad scale, and not that of the petty *academies,* as they call themselves, which are starting up in every neighborhood, and where one or two men, possessing Latin, and sometimes Greek, a knowledge of the globes, and the first six books of Euclid, imagine and communicate this as the sum of science. They commit their pupils to the theatre of the world with just taste enough of learning to be alienated from industrious pursuits, and not enough to do service in the ranks of science.

THOMAS JEFFERSON

INTRODUCTION

"An useful American education," Jefferson liked to call it; and he would then proceed to adumbrate its constituent elements—the classics, mathematics, ethics, politics, civil history, zoology, anatomy, surgery, medicine, commerce, law, agriculture, modern languages (especially French, Spanish, and Italian), natural history (including botany), natural philosophy (including chemistry), and in fact every branch of science in its "highest degree." "Have you ever turned your thoughts . . . ," he asked John Adams during the extraordinary correspondence they carried on after Benjamin Rush had repaired the estrangement that had occurred after the election of 1800, to "the particular sciences of real use in human affairs, and how they might be so grouped as to require so many professors only as might bring them within the views of a just but enlightened economy?" Adams replied by return mail:

Grammar, rhetoric, logic, ethics, mathematics cannot be neglected; classics, in spite of our friend Rush, I must think indispensable. Natural history, mechanics, and experimental philosophy, chemistry etc. at least their rudiments, cannot be forgotten. Geography, astronomy, and even history and chronology, though I am myself afflicted with a kind of Pyrrhonism in the two latter, I presume cannot be omitted. Theology I would leave to Ray, Derham, Nieuwentyt and Paley, rather than to Luther, Zinzendorf, Swedenborg, Wesley, or Whitefield, or Thomas Aquinas or Wollebius. Metaphysics I would leave in the clouds with the Materialists and Spiritualists, with Leibnitz, Berkeley, Priestley, and Edwards, and I might add Hume and Reid, or if permitted to be read, it would be with romances and novels. What shall I say of music, drawing, fencing, dancing, and gymnastic exercises? What of languages

249

oriental or occidental? Of French, Italian, German, or Russian? Of Sanskrit or Chinese?[1]

Adams's list, not suprisingly, was the more conventional; but there was an unmistakable bent toward the practical in the proposals of both men that typified the Revolutionary generation. It derived in part from a preoccupation with the immediacies of life that had inevitably characterized the provincial situation in which they had come of age, but it derived from a considered prudence as well. They saw the traditional education of Europe as archaic and of little relevance to the needs of a free people led by a "natural aristocracy" of virtue and talent, and they sensed a consequent obligation to create in its place a genuinely useful American education that would enhance the quality of the common life in the young Republic. It would be a broad and all-encompassing education, but its focus would be on the immediate, the concrete, and the scientific, with metaphysics, in Adams's good-humored phrase, consigned to "the clouds with the Materialists and Spiritualists."

Granted a shared bent toward the practical, there were vigorous disagreements over detail. There was the question, for example, of how far to carry utilitarianism in the first place. Rush, as Adams mentioned, wanted to abolish Latin and Greek for all but a handful of youngsters who planned to go on to the higher learning; Adams believed the lack would be grievous. Similarly, Noah Webster wanted to revise all spelling and pronunciation in the interest of linguistic simplicity; the Boston clergyman John Sylvester John Gardiner excoriated the results as colloquial barbarisms. There was, in addition, the bickering over precisely which sciences should be stressed. Jefferson and his colleagues in the American Philosophical Society placed great stock in natural history, which Jefferson himself had set at the heart of his *Notes on the State of Virginia* (1785); Adams and his colleagues in the American Academy of Arts and Sciences much preferred natural philosophy. And, finally, there were the inevitable controversies over questions of popularization: if a free society demanded a widespread diffusion of knowledge, what

1. The phrase "an useful American education" is from Thomas Jefferson to John Bannister, Jr., October 15, 1785, in *The Papers of Thomas Jefferson*, edited by Julian P. Boyd *et al.* (19+ vols.; Princeton, N.J.: Princeton University Press, 1950–), VIII, 635. The list is a composite of the subjects mentioned in the letter to Bannister cited above and in Thomas Jefferson to Joseph Priestley, January 18, 1800, in *The Writings of Thomas Jefferson*, edited by Paul Leicester Ford (10 vols.; New York: G. P. Putnam's Sons, 1892–1899), X, 429. Thomas Jefferson to John Adams, July 5, 1814, in *The Adams-Jefferson Letters: The Complete Correspondence Between Thomas Jefferson and Abigail and John Adams*, edited by Lester J. Cappon (2 vols.; Chapel Hill: University of North Carolina Press, 1959), II, 434; and John Adams to Thomas Jefferson, July 16, 1814, in *ibid.*, 438–439.

knowledge in particular would be diffused to whom and by what means? would all receive a common education or would there be distinctions? and, if distinctions, on what basis?

Both the shared utilitarianism of the Revolutionary era and the educational tensions associated with it persisted into the nineteenth century. Within the schools and colleges, there were endless debates over which studies would be available and which studies would be required; while, outside the schools and colleges, a host of educational agencies ranging from libraries to lyceums to museums competed for funds and clienteles by proffering curricula representing ever-shifting balances of attractiveness and worth. And all of this proceeded within a context of continuing social and economic development that severely tested notions of what would be useful to whom. In the end, as Francis Wayland, the leading moral philosopher of the time, thought they should be, curricular offerings of every kind were judged in the marketplace—a marketplace that weighed claims of educational merit on the ability to attract clients and patronage. It was a harsh discipline that in its very nature wrought continuing transformations in what was actually defined as education and in how it was laid before the public.

Chapter 8

PRUDENT LEARNING

Whenever an institution is established in any part of our country, our first inquiry should be, what is the kind of knowledge (in addition to that demanded for all) which this portion of our people needs, in order to perfect them in their professions, give them power over principles, enable them to develop their intellectual resources and employ their talents to the greatest advantage for themselves and for the country? This knowledge, whatever it may be, should be provided as liberally for one class as for another.

FRANCIS WAYLAND

The story of Benjamin Franklin's *Autobiography* is a familiar one. He began the work as a memoir of instruction to his son, William (and ultimately to all his "posterity"), during a sojourn at Twyford, England, in the summer of 1771. The writing apparently went swiftly and well, to an outline also produced at Twyford, with the result that in two weeks he was able to carry the account to 1730 and the organization that year of the subscription library at Philadelphia. There followed an interruption of more than a decade, during which the colonies won their independence from England and Franklin was appointed their representative to the court of France. Then, in 1782, the Quaker merchant Abel James, who had come into possession of the initial segment as well as the outline of what was to follow, wrote Franklin from Philadelphia urging him to complete the project. Franklin was clearly intrigued by the possibility, for he promptly sent James's letter along with a copy of the outline to his friend and confidant Benjamin Vaughan, with a request for advice on whether to proceed. Vaughan replied enthusiastically, arguing that Franklin's life was at the same time a model of self-education and a mine of information on the affairs and prospects of the new Republic. "All that has happened to you is also connected with the detail of the manners and situation of *a rising people*," Vaughan observed; "and in this respect I do not think that the writings of Caesar and Tacitus can be more interesting to a true judge of human nature and society." Accordingly, Franklin produced a second segment in 1784, at Passy, France, and a third and a fourth segment between 1788 and 1789 at his home in Philadelphia, probably completing the final revisions of the manuscript during the last few months before his death on April 17, 1790.[1]

The result was a remarkable document by any standard. It presented in a disarmingly ingenuous style the rise of a tallowmaker's son from "poverty and obscurity" to "a state of affluence and some degree of reputation in the world," and portrayed education as the chief element in the odyssey. From his very first recollections of perusing Plutarch and Defoe in his father's household, through the account of his successive apprenticeships in Boston, to the description of his various enterprises of the Philadelphia years, the story recounted a series of self-consciously designed projects, all of them intended to develop and refine qualities Franklin admired. Nowhere was the essential teaching of the work better revealed than in what Franklin described as "the bold and arduous project of arriving at moral perfection," more commonly known as "the art of virtue." Having concluded during his late twenties that he "wished to live without committing any fault at any time," Franklin set out systematically to nurture in himself "a steady and uniform rectitude of conduct." He began by listing thirteen virtues and the precepts that would give them meaning in everyday life:

1. TEMPERANCE.

Eat not to dullness.
Drink not to elevation.

2. SILENCE.

Speak not but what may benefit others or yourself. Avoid
trifling conversation.

3. ORDER.

Let all your things have their places. Let each part of
your business have its time.

<hr>

1. *The Autobiography of Benjamin Franklin,* edited by Leonard W. Labaree, Ralph L. Ketcham, Helen C. Boatfield, and Helene H. Fineman (New Haven: Yale University Press, 1964), pp. 43, 135.

4. RESOLUTION.

Resolve to perform what you ought. Perform without fail
what you resolve.

5. FRUGALITY.

Make no expense but to do good to others or yourself:
i.e., waste nothing.

6. INDUSTRY.

Lose no time. Be always employed in something useful.
Cut off all unnecessary actions.

7. SINCERITY.

Use no harmful deceit.
Think innocently and justly; and, if you speak, speak
accordingly.

8. JUSTICE.

Wrong none, by doing injuries or omitting the benefits
that are your duty.

9. MODERATION.

Avoid extremes. Forbear resenting injuries so much as
you think they deserve.

10. CLEANLINESS.

Tolerate no uncleanness in body, clothes or habitation.

11. TRANQUILITY.

Be not disturbed at trifles, or at accidents common
or unavoidable.

12. CHASTITY.

Rarely use venery but for health or offspring; never
to dullness, weakness, or the injury of your own
or another's peace or reputation.

13. HUMILITY.

Imitate Jesus and Socrates.

He then created a system of moral bookkeeping whereby he could concentrate on the practice of a particular virtue each week, scrutinize his behavior for lapses and record them, traverse the entire series of virtues in thirteen weeks, and by repeating the process as soon as it was completed go through the full cycle four times a year. To give effect to the arrangements, he created a little book with a page devoted to each virtue and crossed columns representing the days of the week and the thirteen virtues. By a system of symbols indicating offenses against the several virtues, he could mark the development of his behavior, as he attempted to keep the various lines free of demerits. The goal was a clean book after thirteen weeks of daily examination.[2]

FORM OF THE PAGES

TEMPERANCE							
Eat not to dullness. *Drink not to elevation.*							
	S	M	T	W	T	F	S
T							
S	••	•		•		•	
O	•	•	•		•	•	•
R			•		•		
F		•					
I			•				
S							
J							
M							
Cl.							
T							
Ch.							
H							

Having sketched the project, Franklin proceeded to recount his own experience with it—his initial surprise at finding himself so much "fuller of faults" than he had imagined, his satisfaction at seeing them diminish, his incorrigibility with respect to order, and his advances with respect to temperance, sincerity, justice, industry, frugality, and humility. "On the whole," he concluded, "though I never arrived at the perfection I had been so ambitious of obtaining, but fell far short of it, yet I was by the endeavor a better and happier man than I otherwise should have been, if I had not attempted it; as those who aim at perfect writing by imitating the engraved copies, though they never reach the

2. *Ibid.*, pp. 43, 148, 157, 148–150.

wished for excellence of those copies, their hand is mended by the endeavor, and is tolerable while it continues fair and legible."[3]

Now, all of this, along with the numerous other projects reported in the *Autobiography*, instructed on several levels. It provided in the first place a revealing source for the actualities of provincial education. Whether or not Franklin ever really pursued his system of moral bookkeeping, the *Autobiography* did afford nineteenth-century Americans the sense of an indigenous educational history. In it were recounted the beginnings of the mutual improvement society, the subscription library, the American Philosophical Society, the Academy at Philadelphia, the didactic newspaper and almanac, and a host of other eighteenth-century creations. In addition, it offered Franklin's idealized portrayal of the education of a "rising people," a vade mecum of the pedagogical principles that had set Americans on the course of independence. And finally, in the ancient tradition of the exemplary biography and the memoir of advice to a son, it conveyed a series of preachments ranging from the more homely precepts scattered through the account ("After getting the first hundred pounds, it is more easy to get the second: money itself being of a prolific nature") to the more general depiction of life as a series of educational projects.[4]

The *Autobiography* appeared initially in a French edition, in 1791, and then in an English edition, in 1793, though only the first segment, written at Twyford, was included in these early publications. The second and third segments did not become generally known until 1818, while the fourth was not published until 1828, and then only in a French translation. Yet, once available, the document quickly took on a life of its own, going through scores of printings during the decades preceding the Civil War, often in combination with *The Way to Wealth* and *Advice to a Young Tradesman*. And, beyond the original, there were numerous variant versions: Parson Weems bowdlerized it in the biography he published in 1815, making of Franklin an even more pious example to the young; Noah Webster abridged it for the sketch he included in *Biography for the Use of Schools* in 1832; and Peter Parley paraphrased it for the life he published in 1832. Whatever the form in which it was read, however, its most fundamental teaching lay in the example of an ambitious individual using education for his own purposes; and, whatever it may have taught about a historical person named Benjamin Franklin, it doubtless helped to introduce an activist educative style into the American vernacular and to give the self-educa-

3. *Ibid.*, pp. 152, 156.
4. *Ibid.*, pp. 135, 181.

tion and self-determined education of the self-made individual a central place in the American imagination. In the end, it affected the very way in which nineteenth-century Americans would focus experience in their own autobiographies, namely, as the larger education of the individual in the active leading of American life.

There has long been an ambivalence about the *Autobiography* on the part of latter-day American commentators, owing in no small measure to the various ways in which Franklin's ideas were refracted through the lenses of the nineteenth century. The work, after all, can be read as both a triumph of crabbed practicality and moral obtuseness and a celebration of life fully and genially lived; but, however it is read, one cannot deny the wit, the serenity, and the urbanity of the life it describes and the doctrines it proffers. Even *The Way to Wealth,* for all the assertiveness of its preachments concerning sobriety, industry, and thrift, ends with a counsel against the sin of worldly pride: "This doctrine, my friends, is reason and wisdom: But after all, do not depend too much upon your own industry and frugality, and prudence, though excellent things; for they may all be blasted without the blessing of Heaven; and therefore, ask that blessing humbly, and be not uncharitable to those that at present seem to want it, but comfort and help them."[5]

As often occurs, however, nineteenth-century proponents of self-education and the self-made individual stressed one or another of the elements in Franklin's doctrine, but abstracted these elements from the more general context in which they had been embedded. The Transcendentalists, for example, spiritualized the concept of self-education— or "self-culture," as they preferred to call it—and placed it at the heart of the process by which individuals achieve humanness and societies achieve progress. "He ... who does all he can to unfold all his powers and capacities," William Ellery Channing explained in his lecture *Self-Culture* (1838), appropriately delivered as an introduction to the seventh series of Franklin Lectures in Boston, "especially his nobler ones, so as to become a well proportioned, vigorous, excellent, happy being, practises self-culture." Self-culture, Channing went on to elucidate, combined moral elements (It illuminated the conflict between conscience and appetite), intellectual elements (Its essential process was the search for truth), social elements (It transformed the emotions from instincts into principles), and practical elements (It fitted individuals for action). It drew upon books, newspapers, public schools, association

5. Benjamin Franklin, *The Way to Wealth* (Worcester, Mass.: Isaiah Thomas, 1790), p. 19.

with exemplary personalities, and the experience of diurnal labor and participation in public affairs. And it pertained to men and women of all classes. "You have many and great deficiencies to be remedied," Channing perorated to his audience of merchants and artisans; "and the remedy lies, not in the ballot box, not in the exercise of your political powers, but in the faithful education of yourselves and your children." If Franklin secularized education and turned it to the advancement of the ordinary individual in the ordinary business of life, Channing respiritualized it, contending that education ultimately nurtured the divinity inherent in every human being.[6]

Less lofty, perhaps, but doubtless more powerful in their didactic influence, were the innumerable conduct-of-life books that spewed from the presses of the burgeoning publishing industry. Proposing varying combinations of Christian piety and secular preachment, they all taught in one way or another the Franklinian virtue of self-education. William Andrus Alcott's score of guides for the young provide excellent examples of the genre. A lecturer and author with experience as a schoolmaster and physician (he studied medicine at Yale), Alcott was steeped in the reformist thinking of his day, especially in the realms of pedagogy and hygiene. *The Young Man's Guide,* which was published in 1838 and which went through eighteen editions by 1846, was typical of the material that flowed prolifically from his pen. It ranged in substance from "The Importance of High Character" to "Criminal Behavior" and included a reprint of the Constitution, to be "thoroughly studied and understood by all young men who would become the intelligent and useful citizens of a free country." The recommendations throughout were explicit, detailed, and practical. A substantial section, "The Improvement of the Mind," proffered counsel on habits of observation, rules of conversation, methods of digesting books, maps, and newspapers, and the advantages of participation in some appropriately respectable lyceum or debating society. A broad curriculum of self-study was suggested, including not only reading, writing, and arithmetic but also history, geography, botany, geology, and, only second to the three R's, chemistry. Readers were advised to pursue history and geography in connection with references to events and places in the daily newspapers and to sharpen their arithmetic skills via calculations deriving from the shipments reported therein; they were admonished to avoid periodicals that sneered at religion or concerned themselves with "depravity"; and they were urged to keep a daily journal as a record of their progress—

6. William E. Channing, *Self-Culture* (Boston: Dutton and Wentworth, 1838), pp. 15, 80-81.

and provided with sample pages. In a sequel entitled *Letters to a Sister; or, Woman's Mission,* which appeared in 1849, Alcott sounded the same themes, contending that "the great work of woman is the education of her household" and then going on to recommend self-study in the fields of botany, geology, hygiene, languages, and, of course, chemistry. Not surprisingly, when Alcott published *Tall Oaks from Little Acorns; or, Sketches of Distinguished Persons of Humble Origin* in 1856, he included a sketch of Benjamin Franklin, pointing out to the reader that Franklin was not as "elevated" in a moral sense as Johann Friedrich Oberlin, Martin Luther, or John Harvard, but that he was a great man in many respects nonetheless.[7]

Even more powerful and pervasive in their didactic influence were the countless works of fiction that taught the virtues of self-education in plots that were as predictable as the sunrise. The most typical examples of this genre, of course, were the 108 novels of the New England minister-author Horatio Alger. From the first success of the Ragged Dick series in 1867 until the years following World War I, when public interest waned, the novels may have sold upwards of a hundred million copies. Much has been written of the stereotyped Alger hero and his rise from rags to riches via the Franklinian regimen of thrift, industry, and sobriety. Actually, if one analyzes the works themselves, the rise is more accurately described as from rural impoverishment to urban respectability, via the virtues and good fortune Franklin alluded to in *The Way to Wealth.* But the Franklinian virtue of self-education is also central. Ragged Dick, it will be remembered, attended the Sunday-school classes of Mr. Greyson, his benefactor; he was tutored in his boardinghouse room by his friend Henry Fosdick, in reading, writing, arithmetic, grammar, and geography; and, after he had progressed as far as Fosdick could take him, the two of them spent a portion of every evening together in uplifting reading and conversation, and the continuing study of French, mathematics, and, of course, Scripture. In the end, education was as critical as hard work and good luck in the success of the Alger hero. The Franklinian virtues were apparent even in the most popular of nineteenth-century literary forms, and in this way they were taught to Franklin's countrymen fully a century after he had articulated them for his posterity, that they might "find some of them suitable to their own situations, and therefore fit to be imitated."[8]

7. William A. Alcott, *The Young Man's Guide* (18th ed.; Boston: T.R. Marvin, 1846), pp. 5, 221, and *Letters to a Sister; or, Woman's Mission* (Buffalo: G.H. Derby and Co.; 1849), p. 73.
8. *Autobiography,* p. 43.

II

Noah Webster first met Benjamin Franklin in Philadelphia during the winter of 1785–86. Characteristically, the ambitious young lawyer, who was lecturing on the need for a purified American language, sought out the most prestigious citizens of the community—the physician Benjamin Rush; the attorney general, Andrew Bradford; the president of the university, John Ewing; and, of course, Benjamin Franklin, just returned from his triumphant tour as ambassador to France. Characteristically, too, Webster asked Franklin for an endorsement of his recently published *Grammatical Institute, of the English Language,* in order to facilitate its introduction to the American public. The endorsement was never forthcoming, though Franklin did take the opportunity to press upon Webster his own long-held interest in an augmented, phonetically precise English alphabet. In any case, Webster's lectures were well received, and on March 22 he wrote to his publishers, "I am diffusing useful knowledge and supporting the honor of New England. Even the Philadelphians, who are much inclined to find fault, acknowledge that my remarks are new and my design laudable." Eager, energetic, and ambitious for an influence on literature, Webster felt himself "beginning to make a bustle."[9]

Born in 1758 in West Hartford, Webster had attended Yale College, served in the Connecticut militia during the Revolution, and then, following the common pattern of the era, read law while he taught to earn a living, gaining admission to the bar in 1781. It was while conducting schools in Sharon, Connecticut, and Goshen, New York, during the period between Cornwallis's surrender at Yorktown and the signing of the Treaty of Paris, that Webster conceived his plan for a radically new "system of instruction" that would pointedly address the educational needs of the new nation. The earliest fruits of his labors—his "star" that would cast its benevolent beams upon all ranks of society— was a three-part work published between 1783 and 1785 with the high-sounding title *A Grammatical Institute, of the English Language, Comprising, an Easy, Concise, and Systematic Method of Education, Designed for the Use of English Schools in America.*[10]

9. Noah Webster to Hudson & Goodwin, March 22, 1786, in *Letters of Noah Webster,* edited by Henry R. Warfel (New York: Library Publishers, 1953), p. 45.

10. Noah Webster, *A Grammatical Institute, of the English Language, Comprising, an Easy, Concise, and Systematic Method of Education, Designed for the Use of English Schools in America. In Three Parts,* part I (3d ed.; Hartford, Conn.: Hudson & Goodwin, 1784), preface, p. i; and Noah Webster to John Canfield, January 6, 1783, in *Letters of Noah Webster,* p. 4.

The first part was a speller, based substantially on two contemporary English textbooks, Thomas Dilworth's *A New Guide to the English Tongue* (1740) and Daniel Fenning's *The Universal Spelling Book; or, a New and Easy Guide to the English Language* (1756). In the classic mode of primers since the Reformation, it began with the alphabet and proceeded through a syllabarium and lists of words of increasing syllabic length before turning to the actual material to be read. The substance of the material consisted of the usual maxims and aphorisms (many of them adapted from Dilworth and Fenning), along with a compendium of useful geographical information (including some about the United States and a disproportionate amount about Connecticut) and a brief chronology of "remarkable events in America" from 1492 to 1783. Finally, there was an emphasis throughout upon orthodox pronunciation, Webster's hope being "to destroy the provincial prejudices that originate in the trifling differences of dialect and produce reciprocal ridicule." In all these respects, the speller was at best a variant of standard contemporary fare. What made it truly remarkable was the aim stated in the preface, in which Webster announced the goal of cultural independence for the new nation: "American glory begins to dawn at a favorable period, and under flattering circumstances. We have the experience of the whole world before our eyes; but to receive indiscriminately the maxims of government, the manners and the literary taste of Europe and make them the ground on which to build our systems in America, must soon convince us that a durable and stately edifice can never be created upon the mouldering pillars of antiquity. It is the business of *Americans* to select the wisdom of all nations, as the basis of her constitutions,—to avoid their errors,—to prevent the introduction of foreign vices and corruptions and check the career of her own,—to promote virtue and patriotism,—to embellish and improve the sciences,—to diffuse a uniformity and purity of *language*,—to add superior dignity to this infant Empire and to human nature."[11]

Parts two and three of the *Grammatical Institute* consisted, respectively, of a grammar and a reader. Like the speller, the grammar was based on a contemporary English work, in this instance, Robert Lowth's *A Short Introduction to English Grammar* (1762). And, for all Webster's insistence that children would learn to read with greater facility if they were taught a grammar directly derived from contempo-

11. Webster, *A Grammatical Institute, of the English Language*, part I (1st ed.; Hartford, Conn.: Hudson & Goodwin, [1783]), p. 118; part I (3d ed., 1784), preface, pp. vii–viii; and part I (1st ed.), preface, pp. 14–15.

PRUDENT LEARNING 263

rary English usage, his grammar ended up wholly traditional, emphasizing both the topics and the methods that had dominated Latin textbooks since the era of Donatus. Webster's reader, on the other hand, which he explained, "completes the system I had proposed to publish for the use of schools," was essentially original, including among its selections excerpts from "The Vision of Columbus" by Joel Barlow, "The Conquest of Canaan" by Timothy Dwight, *The American Crisis* by Thomas Paine, and other writings growing out of the American experience. "In the choice of pieces," he observed in the preface to the reader, "I have not been inattentive to the political interests of America. Several of those masterly addresses of Congress, written at the commencement of the late revolution, contain such noble, just and independent sentiments of liberty and patriotism, that I cannot help wishing to transfuse them into the breasts of the rising generation."[12]

The moral of the *Grammatical Institute,* namely, the inseparability of cultural and political independence, was the moral Webster attempted to teach his countrymen over the next half-century. His first elaboration of the theme beyond the prefaces of the *Grammatical Institute* came in a forty-eight–page pamphlet entitled *Sketches of American Policy,* which he wrote early in 1785 to expose the weaknesses of the Confederation and to make the case for a strong central government. Arguing the need for "a supreme power at the head of the union, vested with authority to make laws that respect the states in general and to compel obedience to these laws"—always the Connecticut booster, he characteristically analogized to Connecticut's relationship with its towns—he went on to the concomitant need for an education that would "confirm the union of these states" by laying the basis for social harmony. "Education or a general diffusion of knowledge among all classes of men, is an article that deserves peculiar attention," he counseled. "Science liberalizes men and removes the most inveterate prejudices. Every prejudice, every dissocial passion is an enemy to a friendly intercourse and the fuel of discord." Even more important, he continued, was the development of a national character appropriate to an independent empire. "Nothing," he concluded, "can be more ridiculous, than a servile imitation of the manners, the language, and the vices of foreigners. For setting aside the infancy of our government and our inability to support the fashionable amusements of Europe, nothing can

12. Noah Webster, *A Grammatical Institute, of the English Language,* part III (Hartford, Conn.: Barlow & Babcock, 1785), preface, p. 5.

betray a more despicable disposition in Americans, than to be the apes of Europeans. An American ought not to ask what is the custom of London and Paris; but what is proper for us in our circumstances and what is becoming our dignity."[13]

Two years later, at precisely the time the Constitution was being debated in the several states, Webster further developed his ideas in a series of six unsigned essays prepared for the *American Magazine,* which he was then editing. "I am not vain enough to suppose I can suggest any new ideas upon so trite a theme as education in general," he observed in an uncharacteristic burst of modesty; "but perhaps the manner of conducting the youth in America may be capable of improvement. Our constitutions of civil government are not yet firmly established; our national character is not yet formed; and it is an object of vast magnitude that systems of education should be adopted and pursued which may not only diffuse a knowledge of the sciences but may implant in the minds of the American youth the principles of virtue and liberty and inspire them with just and liberal ideas of government and with an inviolable attachment to their own country."[14]

With respect to the knowledge that would implant the principles of virtue and liberty, Webster was essentially utilitarian, in the mode of Franklin. Every American child, he believed, should be taught to speak, read, and write the English language correctly; all should have a working knowledge of arithmetic and a fundamental acquaintance with the history, geography, and politics of their native land. Beyond that, they should study what would assist them in preparing for life: those destined for farming should learn practical husbandry; those destined for business should have a chance to take up modern languages, mathematics, and the principles of trade and commerce; those aiming at the learned professions should immerse themselves in the classics; and women should have special opportunities to learn poetry and belles-lettres. Webster sharply attacked the traditional preoccupation with Latin and Greek as the bases of advanced study, contending that the effort ordinarily expended on those languages was scarcely worth the superficial results. He also criticized the historic reliance on the Bible as a school textbook, arguing, on the one hand, that overfamiliarity inevi-

13. Noah Webster, *Sketches of American Policy* (Hartford, Conn.: Hudson & Goodwin, 1785), pp. 31, 44, 47.
14. Noah Webster, "On the Education of Youth in America," in Frederick Rudolph, ed., *Essays on Education in the Early Republic* (Cambridge, Mass.: Harvard University Press, 1965), pp. 44–45.

tably bred contempt and, on the other hand, that textbooks specially prepared for American children would do more to advance a uniquely American education. Finally, Webster advocated rigorous character training (in the form of strict discipline) as a necessary adjunct to all academic instruction.

How would this education be conveyed? Partly by attentive parents, partly by public newspapers, partly by travel through the various regions of the United States, whereby "young gentlemen" would complete their liberal studies by "examining the local situation of the different states—the rivers, the soil, the population, the improvements and commercial advantages of the whole—with an attention to the spirit and manners of the inhabitants, their laws, local customs, and institutions." Mostly, however, the essentials of Webster's version of a truly American education would be given in local public schools (once again, on the Connecticut model), conducted at least four months a year by the most respected and best informed men of the community. "Here children should be taught the usual branches of learning, submission to superiors and to laws, the moral or social duties, the history and transactions of their own country, the principles of liberty and government. Here the rough manners of the wilderness should be softened and the principles of virtue and good behavior inculcated."[15]

Throughout the essays, the emphasis was on America's uniqueness, on the need to create a new education for a new people, an education that would reject historic (and corrupt) European values, manners, and institutions. "Americans, unshackle your minds and act like independent beings," Webster perorated. "You have been children long enough, subject to the control and subservient to the interest of a haughty parent. You have now an interest of your own to augment and defend: you have an empire to raise and support by your exertions and a national character to establish and extend by your wisdom and virtues. To effect these great objects, it is necessary to frame a liberal plan of policy and build it on a broad system of education."[16]

Curiously, beyond his remarks concerning the classical languages, Webster had little to say in his essays about the problems of higher education. Indeed, it was not until many years later, after he himself had undergone a religious conversion, relocated to Massachusetts in order to live more frugally, and there taken part in the founding of Am-

15. *Ibid.*, pp. 77, 67.
16. *Ibid.*, pp. 77.

herst College, that Webster gave any sort of sustained attention to the higher learning. By then it was an older and more conservative man who spoke. In place of the republican rhetoric of the *Sketches,* one now heard the evangelical rhetoric of the Yale revival. Thus, at a ceremony marking the laying of a cornerstone at Amherst in 1820, Webster observed: "The object of this institution . . . is to second the efforts of the apostles themselves, in extending and establishing the Redeemer's empire—the empire of truth. It is to aid in the important work of raising the human race from ignorance and debasement; to enlighten their minds; to exalt their character; and to teach them the way to happiness and to glory." The college, established explicitly to provide a liberal education for aspiring ministers of the gospel, was wholly orthodox in character and curriculum; in fact, Webster and the other founders had high hopes that it would play a significant role in checking "the progress of errors which are propagated from Cambridge"—by which, of course, they referred to Unitarian Harvard. However that may be, it would be an error to view that orthodoxy as wholly discontinuous with Webster's earlier concern for a unique American education. For a man caught up in the revival in New England, nothing could have been more characteristically American, more surely supportive of the foundations of freedom, than the evangelical college. It united the discipline of inspired Christianity with the substance of classical learning to form a truly liberal education. If the founding of the University of Virginia climaxed Jefferson's version of a republican education, the founding of Amherst as surely climaxed Webster's.[17]

Like Jefferson, Webster conceived of public education broadly, as a process that extended far beyond the schools. In fact, in defining the verb "to educate" in his 1828 dictionary, he made no mention of schooling but indicated instead that to educate means "to instill into the mind principles of arts, sciences, morals, religion and behavior. To *educate* a child well is one of the most important duties of parents and guardians." And, though he clearly relished his role as an attorney—he loved signing his name Noah Webster, Esq.—he saw himself essentially as an educator and used every pedagogical instrument available to him in pressing his various causes with his countrymen. He served as a classroom teacher. He wrote a variety of school textbooks, not only the *Grammatical Institute* in numerous revisions, but also the *Elements of*

17. Noah Webster, *A Collection of Papers on Political, Literary, and Moral Subjects* (New York: Webster & Clark, 1843), p. 246; Noah Webster to William Leffingwell, September 27, 1820, in *Letters of Noah Webster,* p. 402.

Useful Knowledge (1801–1812), comprising volumes on history, geography, and zoology; *Biography for the Use of Schools* (1830); *A History of the United States* (1832); *The Teacher* (1836), designed as a supplement to the spelling book; and *A Manual of Useful Studies* (1839), essentially a one-volume home encyclopedia. He edited a variety of periodicals, including the *American Magazine* (1787–1788), the *American Minerva* (1793–1797), the *Herald* (1794–1797), the *Commercial Advertiser* (1797–1803), and the *Spectator* (1797–1803). He issued a steady stream of essays, addresses, articles, and lectures—some of the best and most popular were collected in *The Prompter* (1791), a commonplace book modeled after the sayings of Poor Richard. And he helped found the Connecticut Academy of Arts and Sciences in 1799. All of these were insistently didactic in purpose and character: whether acting in the capacity of schoolmaster, attorney, journalist, or politician, Webster was incessantly teaching; and what he taught was that the American Republic required a distinctively American culture and that the good citizen was a person who had been properly nurtured in that culture.[18]

The capstone of Webster's lifelong work as an educator was his dictionary. Indeed, that this was so tells us much about his conception of the central purposes and processes of education. For Webster, a common language was not only the key to culture, it was also the essence of community and the foundation of nationality. Thus, in his *Dissertations on the English Language* (1789), he wrote:

A sameness of pronunciation is of considerable consequence in a political view; for provincial accents are disagreeable to strangers and sometimes have an unhappy effect upon the social affections. All men have local attachments, which lead them to believe their own practice to be the least exceptionable. Pride and prejudice incline men to treat the practice of their neighbors with some degree of contempt. Thus small differences in pronunciation at first excite ridicule—a habit of laughing at the singularities of strangers is followed by disrespect—and without respect friendship is a name, and social intercourse a mere ceremony.

These remarks hold equally true, with respect to individuals, to small societies and to large communities. Small causes, such as a nick-name, or a vulgar tone in speaking, have actually created a dissocial spirit between the inhabitants of the different states, which is often discoverable in private business and

18. *An American Dictionary of the English Language* (2 vols.; New York: S. Converse, 1828), I. On the importance of familial education, see also Noah Webster to John Brooks, May–June, 1819, in *Letters of Noah Webster*, pp. 397–398.

public deliberations. Our political harmony is therefore concerned in a uniformity of language.

As an independent nation, our honor requires us to have a system of our own, in language as well as government.[19]

In light of these sentiments, it was far from fortuitous that Webster's first published work had been a spelling book and even more fitting that very soon after the appearance of that work he had begun to entertain the thought of "compiling a dictionary, which should complete a system for the instruction of the citizens of this country in the language." It was not until 1800, however, that Webster was able to turn in earnest to the preparation of such a work, the first fruits of his lexicographical effort appearing in 1806 as *A Compendious Dictionary of the English Language.* The dictionary contained five thousand more words than Dr. Johnson's great dictionary of 1755 (at the time still the principal reference book in the Anglo-American world), and many of them were American neologisms. It undertook a moderate reform of orthography, dropping the *k* in words like *musick* and the *u* in words like *honour,* and using the *er* instead of the *re* in words like *theater.* And it sought to advance a uniformity of pronunciation, taking as a standard "the common unadulterated pronunciation of the New England gentlemen." Webster also announced in the preface to the *Compendious Dictionary* his intention to compile yet another work, "which shall exhibit a far more correct state of the language than any work of this kind." That additional work appeared twenty-two years later as *An American Dictionary of the English Language,* a massive two-volume work comprising some seventy-thousand entries and over thirty-thousand definitions, many of both addressed to the particular forms, laws, customs, ideas, and institutions of the United States. Sounding again the theme of the need for purity and uniformity of language if the Republic was to survive, Webster presented the work to his fellow citizens, with his "ardent wishes for their improvement and their happiness; and for the continued increase of the wealth, the learning, the moral and religious elevation of character, and the glory of my country." It was surely his magnum opus, embodying in form and substance as well as interest everything he believed as an educator.[20]

19. Noah Webster, *Dissertations on the English Language* (Boston: Isaiah Thomas, 1789), pp. 19–20.

20. *An American Dictionary,* I, preface; and *A Compendious Dictionary of the English Language* (Hartford, Conn.: Hudson & Goodwin, 1806), preface, pp. xvi, xviii.

At least two major contradictions in Webster's educational writings bear comment in assessing the influence of his ideas. First, there was the disjunction between Webster's professed aim of developing a wholly new and uniquely American culture and his actual practice of borrowing the best from Europe in general and from England in particular. He himself, of course, never suggested that American culture would develop *ex nihilo*. He repeatedly advised his countrymen to canvass the entire available wisdom of the world, to take what appeared valuable, and to adapt it to their own situation. What he opposed was not borrowing but mindless imitation. Yet there is no denying the fact that Webster's scholarship was heavily informed by European precedents: the substance of his dictionaries, the principles of his grammars, the content of his textbooks, indeed, the very essence of his educational outlook rested on contemporary British sources. Second, there was the obvious evolution of Webster's own thought over a long and active career, from the radicalism of his youth to the conservatism of his old age. Yet, as has already been suggested, the shift that came with maturity was scarcely as profound as some have suggested. Like many Federalists of his generation, Webster saw the health and safety of the Republic as being entirely dependent upon the ability of its citizens to reconcile their individual wants with the larger social good and upon its ability to reconcile internal conflicts through a strong central government. And from beginning to end he saw education as a crucial force in bringing about the sense of community—he preferred the term "uniformity"— that would render both sorts of reconciliation possible.

Whatever the inconsistencies of Webster's ideas, their impact was ubiquitous. The speller sold by the millions throughout much of the nineteenth century, in every region of the nation and among every quarter of the population. Even Sequoyah, when he turned to the task of creating a Cherokee alphabet and a written language, used the speller as a model. As for the *American Dictionary,* it imposed its standards not only on the Americans but on the British as well, refracting back across the Atlantic the very scholarship from which it had derived. Yet, for all the triumph of his medium, Webster's message proved more ephemeral. A common and purified language may well have assisted in unifying the nation, but the cement it provided proved less durable than Webster had supposed. It did not prevent the persistence of a vigorous localism or the development of a contentious sectionalism; and thirty-three years after the *American Dictionary* first appeared a fratricidal war was fought by people equally steeped in the orthography, pronunciation, and definitions it had helped to render standard.

III

Noah Webster was one of the two or three moving spirits behind the founding of Amherst Academy and its subsequent conversion into a collegiate institution, though he resigned as president of the board of trustees in 1821, some four years before a formal charter was granted and the institution received the right to confer degrees. There is every indication that he remained in touch with the college, however, welcoming the students to his home from time to time and retaining both personal and intellectual association with the faculty as he pursued his own lexicographical studies. For Webster as for Jefferson, the college was the child of his old age.

Once chartered, Amherst developed rapidly under the leadership of Heman Humphrey, who served as president from 1823 to 1845, and such faculty members as Edward Hitchcock, the geologist, who held the professorship of chemistry and natural history; Nathan W. Fiske and Solomon Peck, who taught the classics; Samuel Worcester, the rhetorician, who also oversaw the library; and Jacob Abbott, who specialized in mathematics and the sciences. In fact, despite the aura of orthodoxy that surrounded its establishment, the college moved boldly to the forefront of reform during the later 1820's, introducing new curricula and new courses that for a brief time excited considerable interest among contemporary institutions of higher learning.

The impetus for reform, interestingly enough, came from the faculty, largely under the prodding of Abbott, though there is no doubt that a rapid increase in the number of students and the diversification that came as a consequence added to the pressures for change. What the faculty contended, in fairly direct terms, was that higher education had not kept pace with the social and economic transformations that had followed in the wake of the Treaty of Ghent. They had no cavil, they maintained, against the traditional classical and scientific curriculum, nor indeed against the assumption that most students would profit from pursuing that curriculum. Their objection was rather against the continuing insistence that all students, regardless of social or vocational aspiration, pursue that curriculum. And they warned implicitly that unless the college took account of a new class of students who were arriving in growing numbers, students destined not for the learned professions but rather for business, commerce, and agriculture, it would soon be deserted by potential benefactors in the community as well as by the students themselves.

What the faculty proposed, in an effort to meet the challenge of "the rapid march of improvement," was a mix of continuity and innovation. The requirements for admission for all students would be left as they had been, with emphasis on competence in Greek and Latin, and the four-year classical and scientific course leading to the bachelor's degree would continue in its traditional form. But a new program would be instituted, distinguished from the regular course "by a more modern and national aspect" and by a "better adaptation to the taste and future pursuits of a large class of young men, who aspire to the advantages of a liberal education." It would substitute French and German for Greek and Latin; it would stress English literature, modern history, civil and political law, and the natural sciences; and it would be equivalent in quality to the classical and scientific course, although it would not lead to a degree. In addition, a new department of the science and art of teaching would be organized, with an initial concern for the training of schoolmasters; and a department of theoretical and practical mechanics would also be created, which would not only "afford exercise and amusement to many of the students" but also be profitably employed "in keeping all the buildings and furniture in constant repair."[21]

The trustees accepted the faculty's proposals, making the creation of the two new departments contingent upon the obtaining of additional funds; and the parallel course was announced in the catalogues of 1827 and 1828. There was an initial burst of student interest, and for a time the excitement of reform pervaded the Amherst community. But the interest soon subsided as students realized that a diploma attesting completion of even the most modern curriculum was not quite the equivalent of a degree, and in the summer of 1829 the trustees abandoned the experiment. The one lasting innovation was the work in French, which became a permanent part of the curriculum.

All the elements in the Amherst drama of the 1820's—the arguments in favor of reform, the particular curricular proposals advanced, the mixture of principle and prudence in the action of the trustees, and the eventual failure of the innovation—were characteristic of American

21. *The Substance of Two Reports of the Faculty of Amherst College, to the Board of Trustees, with the Doings of the Board Thereon* (Amherst, Mass.: Carter and Adams, 1827), pp. 6, 10, 20.

higher education during the pre-Civil War era. The spirit of reform was ubiquitous. The higher learning, the argument ran, required adaptation to the needs of a developing republican society. Reform programs, inspired by an influx of ideas and models from contemporary European universities, ranged from the modification of traditional courses, to the introduction of parallel programs, to the organization of new departments, to the creation of new faculties, to the founding of entirely new institutions. In fact, the 1820's were in many ways the watershed of the movement, the decade witnessing Jefferson's innovations at the University of Virginia, whereby students were given the opportunity to choose among the eight schools that constituted the university; George Ticknor's innovations at Harvard, organizing the curriculum into departments and permitting students some choice among subjects; Eliphalet Nott's innovations at Union College, instituting a parallel course emphasizing the modern languages and the natural sciences; and James Marsh's innovations at the University of Vermont, beginning the move toward departmentalization and again permitting students some choice among subjects. Even those who saw themselves as conservatives resisted reform in the name of reform. Thus, the much cited Yale Report of 1828, prepared by President Jeremiah Day and Professor James L. Kingsley, argued for gradual rather than radical changes in the college curriculum, contending that the object of a college was *"to lay the foundation of a superior education"* and that it could best accomplish that end through a uniform course concentrating on the classics, mathematics, and the natural sciences. Of course, the report insisted upon intellectual culture—in Day's phrasing, upon expanding the powers of the mind and storing it with knowledge—but it must be recalled that Day and Kingsley were arguing for a foundation upon which further practical and professional studies in law, medicine, or theology, or indeed in "mercantile, mechanical, or agricultural concerns," would rest.[22]

As so often happens, moderate reform prevailed. In the end, it was the Yale Report that dominated curriculum making at the college level: the more durable innovations of the 1830's, 1840's, and 1850's came either within the substance of the established liberal arts subjects themselves or in institutions other than the four-year liberal arts colleges— the scientific and technical institutes, the professional schools, the scientific societies, and the host of special-purpose agencies such as Peale's

22. The Yale Report of 1828, in Richard Hofstadter and Wilson Smith, eds., *American Higher Education: A Documentary History* (2 vols.; Chicago: University of Chicago Press, 1961), I, 278.

Museum in Philadelphia or the Lowell Institute in Boston or the Smithsonian Institution in Washington. Yet, if the Yale Report had a decisive, moderating influence on reform, it neither dampened the persistent pressure for innovations at particular institutions nor prevented the development of more general plans for the reform of academic learning. "The march of mind," as it was put in the contemporary phrasing, demanded that every aspect of higher education be brought "to the test of practical utility," and the variety of interpretations of that phrase as well as the schemes for realizing it were myriad.[23]

Perhaps the most comprehensive reform proposals of the era were those advanced by Francis Wayland, who presided over Brown University for more than a quarter-century. Wayland was born in New York City in 1796 and brought up in various other parts of New York State, his father having been a currier turned Baptist minister who moved successively to pastorates in Poughkeepsie, Albany, Troy, and Saratoga Springs. He attended Union College during the early years of Eliphalet Nott's administration and became a lifelong favorite and disciple of Nott; he then went on to study medicine, first via an apprenticeship with the Doctors Moses Hale and Eli Burritt of Troy and then more formally via lectures in New York City. He never practiced medicine, however, experiencing a conversion and a call to the ministry in 1816 that led him to the Andover Theological Seminary, where he studied for a year under the guidance of Moses Stuart. Wayland returned to Union as a tutor in 1817 and remained until 1821, when he accepted pastoral charge of the First Baptist Church in Boston (it was as the minister there that he joined the board of trustees of the newly chartered Amherst College in 1825). He returned once again to Union College in 1826, but stayed less than a year. In 1827, partly on the basis of his reputation as a Baptist preacher and partly also on the recommendation of Nott, Stuart, and others, Wayland succeeded Asa Messer as president of Brown, remaining in that post for twenty-eight years until his retirement in 1855.

Based largely on what he had learned from Nott at Union, Wayland began his presidency essentially as a pedagogical reformer. His

23. The phrases are from the Reverend James M. Mathews's opening remarks to the gathering of "literary and scientific gentlemen," who convened in New York City in the fall of 1830 to discuss the contemplated University of the City of New York (New York University). What was striking about the four days of lectures, papers, and discussion was the extent to which Mathews's criterion of utility was accepted by traditionalists and reformers alike. See *Journal of the Proceedings of a Convention of Literary and Scientific Gentlemen, Held in the Common Council Chamber of the City of New York, October, 1830* (New York: Jonathan Leavitt and G. & C. H. Carvill, 1831), p. 18 and *passim*.

predecessor, Asa Messer, had experienced growing difficulties in the realm of student discipline during the final period of his administration: the exaggerated pranks of the years following the War of 1812 had escalated to full-blown riots during the 1820's, the latter doubtless exacerbated by the doctrinal heterodoxy that ultimately occasioned Messer's resignation. Wayland took immediate steps to restore order, redrawing the laws of the college to require that members of the faculty live within the college and regularly visit the students in their quarters to exercise oversight. All absences and infractions were reported immediately to the president, who had the power to dismiss an erring student forthwith and so notify his parents. Wayland's new residence policy, incidentally, wrought havoc with the medical faculty, who were reluctant to abandon their lucrative practices in Providence, with the result that the medical school was literally destroyed.

Beyond restoring discipline, Wayland sought to invigorate the academic program by increasing the number of daily recitations required of each student and by banning textbooks from the classroom in all subjects except the "learned languages," the point being to require faculty members and students alike to master the textual material on their own and to use classroom time for comment and discussion in their own words and phrases. "Let us never forget that the business of an instructor begins where the office of a book ends," Wayland once observed. "It is the action of mind upon mind, exciting, awakening, showing by example the power of reasoning and the scope of generalization, and rendering it impossible that the pupil should not think; this is the noble and the ennobling duty of an instructor." In addition, Wayland went to great lengths to expand the library, which consisted of a mere six thousand books when he assumed office, and also to develop a system of cumulative daily grades so that parents might be informed of the performance and standing of their sons at the conclusion of each term.[24]

In all of this, Wayland led by the sheer force of example, much in the fashion of his mentor, Nott. He was ubiquitous: he held forth to the entire college body in the chapel, lectured the seniors in the moral philosophy course, and visited the students in their quarters. As one of Wayland's students during the early years of his presidency recalled: "The personal example and influence of Dr. Wayland at once infused a new spirit into the university. The power of a great mind, and the

24. *The Introductory Discourse and Lectures Delivered in Boston, Before the Convention of Teachers, and Other Friends of Education, Assembled to Form the American Institute of Instruction* (Boston: Hilliard, Gray, Little and Wilkins, 1831), p. 19.

energy of a controlling will, were immediately felt. He taught without a textbook, encouraged discussion and inquiry, introduced the important element of analysis, and imparted a novel interest to every recitation which he conducted."[25]

From the beginning, however, Wayland went beyond matters of pedagogy and discipline to a more fundamental consideration of the nature of learning. As he himself recalled concerning the earliest days of his presidency:

> At this time, the beginning of my independent labors as an instructor, I was deeply impressed with the importance of two things: first, of carrying into practice every science which was taught in theory, and secondly, of adopting the course of instruction, as far as possible, to the wants of the whole community. The first seemed to me all-important as a means of intellectual discipline. The abstract principles of a science, if learned merely as disconnected truths, are soon forgotten. If combined with application to matters of actual existence, they will be remembered. Nor is this all. By uniting practice with theory, the mind acquires the habit of acting in obedience to law, and thus is brought into harmony with a universe which is governed by law.
>
> In the second place, if education is good for one class of the community, it is good for all classes. Not that the same studies are to be pursued by all, but that each one should have the opportunity of pursuing such studies as will be of the greatest advantage to him in the course of life which he has chosen.[26]

Starting thus with clear notions of the proper connection between theory and practice and of the extended range of studies required for a truly universal education, Wayland developed over the twenty-eight years of his administration an unprecedentedly broad conception of the learning requisite for a newly industrializing republic. While the elements of this conception can be gleaned from his annual reports and other fugitive writings, they were brought together most comprehensively in three documents: his *Thoughts on the Present Collegiate System of the United States,* published in 1842 after an extended visit to France, England, and Scotland; the report he prepared in 1850 to the trustees of Brown as chairman of a committee to assess "proposed alterations in the course of study"; and an address entitled "The Education Demanded by the People of the United States," delivered in 1854 at Union College to mark the fiftieth anniversary of Nott's presidency.[27]

25. Francis Wayland and H. L. Wayland, *A Memoir of the Life and Labors of Francis Wayland* (2 vols.; New York: Sheldon and Company, 1867), I, 226.

26. *Ibid.,* I, 206.

27. [Francis Wayland], *Report to the Corporation of Brown University on Changes in the System of Collegiate Education* (Providence: George H. Whitney, 1850), p. 5.

Wayland's proposals were firmly rooted in an analysis of the political economy of the New England region. He took note of two fundamental transformations that had occurred in the period since the Revolution, the growth of political freedom and the development of commerce and industry. "Every man among us is the architect of his own fortune," he observed. "In asserting the privileges, he also assumes the responsibilities of a free man. Hence every man is desirous for himself and especially for his children, of that knowledge which is most essential to success in the field which is placed before him." Beyond that, Wayland continued, the rapid economic development of New England and of Providence (where Brown was located) was creating a new class of individuals with very special educational needs. "It is manifest to the most casual observer," he continued, "that the movement of civilization is precisely in the line of the useful arts. Steam, machines and commerce, have built up a class of society which formerly was only of secondary importance. The inducements to enter the learned professions have become far less, and those to enter upon the active professions, vastly greater." In Wayland's view, these changes had occasioned a crisis in education, the preeminent symptom of which was that enrollment in the colleges of New England was not keeping pace with the growth of population. And it was in the effort to come to grips with the crisis that he worked out his comprehensive series of proposals.[28]

In the realm of general elementary learning, Wayland accepted the prevalent New England outlook of the 1830's and 1840's. "It may I suppose be taken for granted that the settled policy of the United States is to furnish the means for obtaining a common English education to every citizen, and to improve that education from time to time without any assignable limit. It may be hoped that within a short time every American citizen will be able to read, write, and keep accounts, and that at no very distant period he will also be familiar with all the more important branches of elementary knowledge." That said, however, he went on to make two additional points. First, he argued that well-chosen and properly trained schoolteachers could become a force for untold good in their neighborhood communities, exerting an influence for cultural uplift extending far beyond the classroom.

I by no means suppose the whole duty of a teacher to be fulfilled by the performance of the labors of the school room. If a suitable person be engaged for this office, and if the station be rendered permanent and sufficiently attrac-

28. *Ibid.*, pp. 13, 21.

tive by the social consideration which properly belongs to it, a multitude of indirect benefits will naturally follow. Such an instructor would be the friend and companion of his pupils after the relation of master and scholar had terminated. He would encourage and direct the studies of those who wished to pursue their investigations by themselves. He would cultivate science and stimulate his neighbors to literary acquisition by the delivery of lectures, the formation of libraries and every other means of popular improvement. In this manner a class of professional men would be raised up among us whose influence would be felt most benignly over every class of society, and of whose labors the benefit would be incalculable.[29]

In addition, he argued that the very prevalence of education would create a demand for more education, as raw talents hitherto unnoticed and uncultivated came to the fore and literally cried out for further development. Hence, he saw the need for a far more extensive system of higher education, one that would provide for every man able to avail himself of it "that *kind* of education which will be of the greatest use to him in the prosecution of useful industry." It was at this point that Wayland leveled his sharpest criticism against the traditional curriculum. Both in Europe and the United States, it had catered to those preparing for the learned professions (law, medicine, divinity, and teaching), he argued, and in the process it had ignored the needs of a large numbers of individuals destined for the "productive professions."[30]

What would a collegiate institution look like that sought to adapt its instruction "to the wants of the whole community"? Wayland proposed a series of interrelated reforms that would drastically alter the character of higher education. The fixed curriculum leading to the bachelor's degree—the four years of study in the classics, mathematics, and natural and moral philosophy, with everyone progressing through the same subjects at the same pace—would be abandoned. In its place there would be an expanded curriculum embracing various courses of various lengths, including, alongside the traditional subjects, work in chemistry, physics, and geology, English language and rhetoric, political economy, history, law, the science of teaching, the principles of agriculture, the application of chemistry to the arts, and the application of science to the arts, all so arranged that, "in so far as it is practicable, every student might study what he chose, all that he chose, and nothing but what he chose." All students would be entitled to certificates of proficiency in

29. Francis Wayland, *Thoughts on the Present Collegiate System in the United States* (Boston: Gould, Kendall & Lincoln, 1842), pp. 3, 5.

30. [Wayland], *Report to the Corporation*, pp. 56–57, 51.

the courses they had pursued, and the faculty and trustees would retain the right to define those particular courses and combinations of courses that would lead to degrees.[31]

There were three essential principles to Wayland's plan, then: first, to broaden the curriculum to embrace the intellectual needs of all classes of society; second, to make all classes of society welcome at the college; and, third, to proffer choice among programs, courses, and educational goals to those who came. If equality of access to the higher learning was to become a reality, it would have to be accompanied by an expanded conception of the higher learning that embraced the intellectual principles, or sciences, underlying all activities of life and that extended choice to clients as to what studies they would pursue. Wayland concluded:

It would seem ... that, in devising a system of higher education for our country, we should commence with the self-evident maxim, that we are to labor not for the benefit of one but of all; not for a caste, or a clique, but for the whole community. Proceeding upon this ground, we should provide the instruction needed by every class of our fellow-citizens. Wherever an institution is established in any part of our country, our first inquiry should be, what is the kind of knowledge (in addition to that demanded for all) which this portion of our people needs, in order to perfect them in their professions, give them power over principles, enable them to develop their intellectual resources and employ their talents to the greatest advantage for themselves and for the country? This knowledge, whatever it may be, should be provided as liberally for one class as for another. Whatever is thus taught, however, should be taught, not only with the design of increasing knowledge, but also of giving strength, enlargement and skill to the original faculties of the soul. When a system of education formed on these principles shall pervade this country, we may be able to present to the world the legitimate results of free institutions; by pursuing any other career we may render them a shame and a by-word.[32]

One final element of Wayland's reform program deserves mention. If colleges were to become truly popular institutions, they would have to reach out to the community at large. Taking Boston's Lowell Institute as his model, he pictured colleges, not merely as offering a broader curriculum to all who came, but also as diffusing the best that had been thought, said, and discovered to the populace at large. Like the elementary schoolteacher, who would reach beyond the walls of the classroom

31. *Ibid.*, p. 51.
32. Francis Wayland, *The Education Demanded by the People of the United States* (Boston: Phillips, Sampson, and Company, 1855), pp. 26–27.

to become a force for cultural uplift in the neighborhood, each college would become "the grand center of intelligence to all classes and conditions of men, diffusing among all the light of every kind of knowledge, and approving itself to the best feelings of every class of the community." And, lest his comment be misunderstood, Wayland took pains to explain what he meant by "popular": not stylishness or modishness or an undue sensitivity to popular convention but rather the aspiration to high quality. "Popularity is valuable when it follows us, not when we run after it," he counselled; "and he is most sure of attaining it, who, caring nothing about it, honestly and in simplicity, and kindness earnestly labors to render his fellow men wiser, and happier, and better."[33]

Wayland's program was the best known of several comprehensive proposals for the reform of higher education that appeared during the quarter-century preceding the Civil War. Philip Lindsley at the University of Nashville, for example, issued a steady stream of addresses and essays envisioning a complete system of formal education for the state of Tennessee, from infant schools through colleges, universities, and special professional schools of law, divinity, medicine, military and naval science, agriculture, and architecture, in which, at all levels, a boundless curriculum would be purveyed. In Lindsley's plan, the common schools would teach, not only reading, writing, arithmetic, grammar, geography, and history, but literally every other branch of learning a well-trained teacher might be capable of teaching—physics, astronomy, mechanics, rural economy, perhaps even ethics, rhetoric, political economy, geology, chemistry, mineralogy, and botany. And the university would possess "the means of teaching all the sciences, and everything, indeed, which it is desirable for any man to know." Its libraries would contain "one or more copies of every valuable book extant in any language, ancient or modern"; and its laboratories would include "specimens, living or preserved, of every vegetable and animal and mineral, peculiar to the earth, the air and the waters of our planet." In addition, it would boast its own botanical gardens, astronomical observatories, models of machines and useful inventions; and works of the noblest artists (or well-executed copies). Similarly, Henry Philip Tappan, a student of Nott's who assumed the presidency of the University of Michigan in 1852, proffered a vision of a comprehensive system of formal education for the state of Michigan, based more on a Prus-

33. Wayland, *Thoughts on the Present Collegiate System*, pp. 156, 149.

sian model than Lindsley's (which drew freely, as did Wayland's, on a knowledge of contemporary European and American systems) but equally concerned with providing "all branches of human learning," with affording students choice among curricula, and with gathering together in one great center of learning the resources of libraries, laboratories, observatories, museums, and galleries of fine arts, each assisting and complementing the efforts of the others to extend the boundaries of human knowledge and understanding.[34]

Like Wayland's proposals, Lindsley's were essentially practicalist in emphasis; the central difference between them was that Lindsley conceived of a comprehensive education system entirely within the public sector while Wayland believed higher education should justify itself in the free market. Tappan's proposals, by contrast, were essentially intellectualist. Yet all three pressed for an extension of the boundaries of learning. None of the three succeeded within his own institution in his own time: Wayland's reforms, adopted by the Brown Corporation in 1851, were abandoned by his successor, Barnas Sears, as too visionary; Lindsley was never able to raise the funds even to introduce his innovations, though he did advance the cause of higher education in Tennessee; and Tappan was forced to resign in 1863 after a series of nasty political encounters with the regents. Yet, the fact that reform did not win out in the colleges and universities does not imply that there was no reform. Change did come via two important roads. First, it came as the extant courses of the colleges, particularly the offerings in languages, the sciences, and moral philosophy, continued to broaden. And, second, it came through the development of special-purpose institutions that were only later brought within the orbit of the universities—schools of engineering, law, medicine, and agriculture; museums; botanical gardens; libraries; and scientific societies. The colleges were partly altered, but higher education was dramatically transformed. The two movements remained relatively separate until the decades of the 1880's and 1890's, when the great architects of modern higher education—men like Daniel Coit Gilman, Charles W. Eliot, Nicholas Murray Butler, and William Rainey Harper—brought them together into comprehensive universities.

34. *The Works of Philip Lindsley,* edited by Le Roy J. Halstead (3 vols.; Philadelphia: J. B. Lippincott & Co., 1864–66), I, 133, 407–408; and Henry P. Tappan, "The University: Its Constitution and Its Relations, Political and Religious" (1858), in Hofstadter and Smith, eds., *American Higher Education,* II, 528.

IV

During the summer of 1838, at the direction of President Martin Van Buren, Secretary of State John Forsyth addressed a letter of inquiry to a number of the nation's leading college presidents, professors, and men of affairs. "By the will of James Smithson, late of London, deceased," the letter began, "property to a considerable amount was bequeathed to the United States, for the purpose, and expressed in the language of the will, of 'founding at Washington, under the name of the Smithsonian Institution, an establishment for the increase and diffusion of knowledge among men.'" The letter then continued:

The United States having, under the authority of an act of Congress, approved the 1st of July, 1836, accepted the legacy, pledged their faith for the performance of the trust, in such manner as Congress may hereafter direct, and recovered the proceeds of the bequest, to the amount of about one hundred thousand pounds sterling, the President is anxious, in presenting the subject to Congress for their consideration and action upon it, to aid his judgment by consulting the views of persons versed in science and in matters relating to public education, as to the mode of applying the proceeds of the bequest, which shall be likely at once to meet the wishes of the testator, and prove most advantageous to mankind.[35]

One of the first to reply the following autumn was Francis Wayland. Maintaining that there was no additional need for colleges or professional schools in the United States, Wayland argued for the creation of an institution that would occupy "the space between the close of a collegiate education and a professional school." Its aim would be to carry both classical and philosophical education beyond the point at which the college had left it and to offer instruction in "the broad and philosophical principles of a professional education." The curriculum would be much like that of the college, only "far more generously taught—that is, taught to men, and not to boys"; it would include, in addition to the "philosophical principles of law and medicine," Latin, Greek, Hebrew, and the Oriental languages; all modern languages of use to the scholar; mathematics; astronomy, civil and military engineering; the art of war "beginning where it is left at West Point"; chemistry, geology, mining; rhetoric and poetry; political economy; intellectual

35. William J. Rhees, ed., *The Smithsonian Institution: Documents Relative to Its Origin and History* (Washington, D.C.: The Smithsonian Institution, 1879), p. 837.

philosophy; physiology; anatomy; history; and the laws of nations. There would be a growing clientele for such an institution, Wayland continued (always the political economist), owing to the general tendency of young men to take a year off between their graduation from college and their entry upon professional studies.[36]

Less than a month later, Forsyth received a quite different response from John Quincy Adams, the former president who was then serving in the House of Representatives. Under no circumstances, Adams argued, should the Smithsonian funds be applied to any school, college, university, or ecclesiastical establishment, or, for that matter, to any institution whatever for the education of youth, "for that is a sacred obligation, binding upon the people of this Union themselves, at their own expense and charge, and for which it would be unworthy of them to accept an eleemosynary donation from any foreigner whomsoever." Rather, the money should be applied to the founding and maintenance of a great astronomical observatory "upon the largest and most liberal scale"—one comparable to the Greenwich Observatory in England or the Bureau des Longitudes in France—and for the publication of data gathered at the observatory as well as an annual nautical almanac based on those data.[37]

And less than a month after Adam's communications arrived—Adams, characteristically, had sent not one letter but two—Forsyth received yet another communication, this one from Richard Rush, the lawyer-diplomat who had been the chief figure in moving Smithson's estate through the English chancery court and then bringing the bequest to the United States. In Rush's view, too, the support of a college or university in the ordinary sense, or of any institution engaged in primary education or the general instruction of youth, would be an inappropriate use of the Smithson legacy. Rather, Rush envisioned an institution to which Americans residing in every corner of the globe would send seeds and plants, to be reproduced and diffused throughout the country, and where distinguished scholars from all over the country and the world—scholars appointed by the president and Senate—would deliver lectures open to all comers, which would then be published by a press attached to the institution and circulated as widely as possible.[38]

Other letters came to Forsyth, both solicited and unsolicited, pro-

36. Francis Wayland to John Forsyth, October 2, 1838, in *ibid.*, p. 840.
37. John Quincy Adams to John Forsyth, October 8, 1838, and October 11, 1838, in *ibid.*, pp. 844, 848.
38. Richard Rush to John Forsyth, November 6, 1838, in *ibid.*, pp. 849–856.

posing other schemes; letters appeared in newspapers and magazines advancing still other schemes; organizations framed memorials urging one plan or another; and individual senators and congressmen worked out their own proposals. In fact, interest was such that a full-scale national debate developed, centered in Congress, concerning what sort of "establishment for the increase and diffusion of knowledge among men" might best meet the provision of James Smithson's will and the needs of the American people. Politics—sectional, social, and personal—was surely involved in the process, but so also were conflicting ideas of what knowledge would be of most worth to the young Republic. The full range of proposals between 1838, when substantive consideration first came up in Congress, and 1846, when a bill creating the Smithsonian Institution was finally enacted, was extraordinary, extending from Senator George M. Keim's suggestion in 1838 that a professor of the German language be included in any contemplated institution, to Congressman Isaac E. Morse's suggestion in 1846 that the funds be used to create prizes for the best-written entries in a national essay contest, the winning submissions to be printed and widely distributed among institutions of learning in the United States and abroad. Throughout the debate, there were those who insisted with Senator John C. Calhoun that the legacy was an insult to the new nation and that the funds should be returned. In the end, four essential models of the institution were put forward, and the final enactment was for all intents and purposes a compromise.

The first model was that of a national university, more or less along the lines of the one envisioned by Wayland. Such a proposal was advanced in 1838 by Senator Asher Robbins of Rhode Island. Robbins connected his idea with the historic movement for a national university that dated at least from the days of George Washington's presidency; but, aware of the conflict that had surrounded the project for almost a half-century, he was content merely to allude to the precedent. In effect, he proposed an independent institution that Congress would help to support and maintain. The faculty would be composed of world-renowned master-scholars. The curriculum would combine science and literature with all their appropriate arts. "As to science," Robbins observed,

they [the studies] should be restricted to science properly so called—to pure original science—with some of the practical branches thereof not necessary now to be indicated, excluding professory learning altogether. As to literature, the studies should be given to select models of a perfect literature, and to all those arts by which that perfect literature has been produced and may be reproduced, accompanied by all those exercises, regularly and ardently pursued, by which power and skill is [sic] given in those arts. The preliminary studies to qualify for admission should also be prescribed. I would have a model school for this preparation annexed to this institution and made a part of the establishment.[39]

The second model was that of a national agricultural school. It, too, was put forward early in the debate, in a memorial by Charles Lewis Fleischmann transmitted by a select committee of the House, under the chairmanship of John Quincy Adams, which had been charged with developing proposals for the proper use of the Smithson legacy. The object of Fleischmann's institution would be "to show how to gain the highest clear and permanent profit from agriculture, under any circumstances." Its primary departments would concern themselves with agronomy, agriculture, vegetable production, animal husbandry, and rural economy, and it would have ancillary departments of the veterinary arts, agricultural technology, forestry, agricultural architecture, and agricultural engineering, as well as chemistry, natural philosophy, mineralogy and geology, botany, zoology, meterology, mathematics, and drawing. Finally, it would have an experimental farm, a botanical garden, a library, a chemistry laboratory, and a museum with agricultural implements, the skeletons of domestic animals, insect specimens, and seeds. There would be no more than one hundred students at the institution during the initial period, all to be at least fourteen years of age and of sufficient strength to perform the work required on the farm.[40]

Robbins and Fleischmann put forward models of what were essentially teaching institutions. Robbins's embraced the whole spectrum of literature and the sciences; Fleischmann's concentrated on the practical sciences and arts of agriculture. Obviously, Adams's proposals for an observatory envisioned an institution of vastly differing character. In a report to the House in 1840, on behalf of the select committee on the Smithson bequest, Adams set forth two principles that the committee considered fundamental in the development of any appropriate recommendation. First, the capital resources of the Smithson bequest should be preserved in perpetuity and only the interest expended. "The increase and diffusion of knowledge," Adams explained, "is, in its nature, progressive to the end of time. An institution which should exhaust in

39. William Jones Rhees, ed., *The Smithsonian Institution: Documents Relative to Its Origin and History, 1835–1899* (2 vols.; Washington, D.C.: Government Printing Office, 1901), I, 168.
40. *Ibid.*, p. 157.

its first establishment and organization the whole, or the principal part of the bequest, would necessarily be confined within limits exceedingly narrow, compared with the vast design of increasing and diffusing knowledge." Second, by way of repeating the recommendation in his letter to Forsyth, no part of the fund, principal or interest, should be appropriated to any school, college, university, institute of education, or ecclesiastical establishment. "The ultimate object of them all," Adams explained, "is instruction—the communication of knowledge already possessed—and not the discovery of new truths or the invention of new instruments for the enlargement of human power." It was on the basis of this latter principle, Adams continued, that the committee was recommending the establishment of an observatory, with provision for continuing investigation of the phenomena of the heavens and for periodic publication of the results of the investigations. Yet even an observatory would be only a beginning. "A botanical garden, a cabinet of natural history, a museum of mineralogy, conchology, or geology, a general accumulating library—all institutions of which there are numerous examples among the civilized Christian nations, and of most of which our own country is not entirely destitute; all are undoubtedly included within the comprehensive grasp of Mr. Smithson's design." No "branch or department of human knowledge" would be excluded from its equitable share of the benefaction; but no one science was as needful of immediate assistance as "practical astronomy."[41]

Somewhat akin to Adam's proposal was the one envisioned in a bill presented by Senator Benjamin Tappan of Ohio on December 12, 1844. What Tappan envisioned as the Smithsonian Institution was a center for scientific research and inquiry, with emphasis on "the productive and liberal arts of life, improvements in agriculture, in manufactures, in trades, and in domestic economy." There would be a professor of agriculture, horticulture, and rural economy (who would also serve as superintendent), whose duty it would be "to determine the utility and advantage of new modes and instruments of culture, to determine whether new fruits, plants, and vegetables may be cultivated to advantage in the United States." There would be a professor of chemistry, who would "make experiments on the various modes of improving and enriching the several kinds of soil found within the United States." And there would be a professor of natural history, who would lecture on the nature and habits of beneficial and deleterious insects and ani-

41. *Ibid.*, pp. 191, 195.

mals. Similarly, a professor of geology would emphasize the working
and exploration of mines, a professor of architecture would emphasize
the practical phases of rural and domestic architecture, and a professor
of astronomy would emphasize the arts of practical navigation. The
faculty would regularly lecture in their several fields, with free admission to all qualified students; and they would also prepare popular
tracts, which the board of managers would offer for sale "at the lowest
rates that will repay the actual expenses of publication." Finally, the
institution would include a library, a chemistry laboratory, an experimental farm or botanical garden, and a museum, the latter two to
house whatever collections of natural history, plants, and mineralogical
or geological specimens that were in the possession of the United States.
Tappan's own model, interestingly enough, was the Jardin des Plantes
in Paris, where Smithson himself had spent considerable time during
the years he had lived on the Continent.[42]

Also akin to Adams's proposal was the plan advanced by Senator
Rufus Choate of Massachusetts in 1845, which would have created the
Smithsonian Institution in the form of a great national library. The
Smithson will, Choate maintained, directed that the new establishment
"increase and diffuse knowledge among men." "And do not the judgments of all the wise," he continued, "does not the experience of all enlightened states, does not the whole history of civilization concur to de-
clare that a various and ample library is one of the surest, most
constant, most permanent, and most economical instrumentalities to increase and diffuse knowledge?" If such a library could also house a
program of lectures "upon literature, science, and art, and the application of science and art," then in Choate's view both the letter and the
spirit of Smithson's injunction would be satisfied.[43]

Finally, there was the composite model envisioned in the bill Congressman Robert Dale Owen of Indiana submitted in 1845, when for
all intents and purposes he replaced Adams in the leadership of the
House's select committee on the Smithson legacy. Owen's plan incorporated those provisions of Tappan's proposal calling for a museum and
other facilities to house the scientific collections of the United States
government; for the employment of scholars who would emphasize the
sciences and arts of practical agriculture; for the publication of popular
reports of their investigations, as well as other brief works "for the dis-

42. *Ibid.*, p. 279.
43. *Ibid.*, p. 287.

semination of information among the people"; and for instruction to be gratis to students admitted to the institution. It also embraced the provision of Choate's plan calling for a library, though of considerably reduced proportion. To these Owen added a provision calling for the development of a pedagogical branch of the institution, designed to "qualify young persons as teachers of common schools, and to give to others a knowledge of an improved common school system."[44]

The legislation that was finally adopted on August 10, 1846, made provision for an institution that would comprise a museum of natural history, including a geological and mineralogical cabinet, a chemistry laboratory, and a gallery of art, the museum and cabinet to receive the collections of specimens of natural history and philosophy owned by the United States in Washington; a library "composed of valuable works pertaining to all departments of human knowledge"; and lecture rooms. In the end, it was a modified version of the Adams model that prevailed: the Smithsonian Institution would concentrate on the increase of knowledge in the sciences and the arts, via a conglomeration of those very institutions outside the colleges and universities where the expansion of learning was proceeding apace—the library, the laboratory, and the museum. Adams himself considered the establishment of the Institution in its final form one of the signal accomplishments of his generation.[45]

The first Board of Regents of the Smithsonian, as the governing board was styled, met on September 7, 1846. Three months later, at its December meeting, the Board elected Joseph Henry of the College of New Jersey to be secretary and thereby chief executive officer of the Institution. It was a fateful decision that went far in confirming the essential thrust of the legislation. Henry, who was about to turn forty-nine at the time of his appointment, was probably the most remarkable creative scientist that the United States produced during the first half of the nineteenth century, having pursued pioneering inquiries into the phenomena of electromagnetism at roughly the same time as Michael Faraday. Essentially self-taught in the sciences, he had served as professor of mathematics and natural philosophy at the Albany Academy in New York from 1826 until 1832 and had then gone on to become professor of natural philosophy at Princeton.

The fact that the regents chose a gifted investigator as their first

44. *Ibid.*, pp. 326, 325.
45. *Ibid.*, pp. 429–434.

secretary had prodigious consequences for the subsequent development of the Institution. Henry tersely set forth his interpretation of "the increase and diffusion of knowledge" in a "Programme of Organization" that the regents adopted as their own on December 17, 1847: to increase knowledge, he proposed "to stimulate men of talent to make original researches, by offering suitable rewards for memoirs containing new truth"; to diffuse knowledge, he proposed to publish the memoirs, along with other reports on the progress of the different branches of knowledge, and to give them wide circulation. "In this country," Henry elaborated,

though many excel in the application of science to the practical arts of life, few devote themselves to the continued labor and patient thought necessary to the discovery and development of new truths. The principal cause of this want of attention to original research, is the want, not of proper means, but of proper encouragement. The publication of original memoirs and periodical reports, as contemplated by the programme, will act as a powerful stimulus on the latent talent of our country, by placing in bold relief the real laborers in the field of original research, while it will afford the best materials for the use of those engaged in the diffusion of knowledge.

From its earliest days, then, the Institution committed itself to serious scholarly research on a wide range of topics in the sciences and humanities, and, in the process, it taught that the advancement of learning would be inseparable from its diffusion if the Republic was to thrive and prosper.[46]

V

Ralph Waldo Emerson first lectured at the Smithsonian in the winter of 1861–62, though the occasion is less memorable for the address he gave on the justice of emancipation than for the fact that he had the opportunity to meet Abraham Lincoln, of whom he noted in his journal: "The President impressed me more favorably than I had hoped. A frank, sincere, well-meaning man, with a lawyer's habit of mind, good clear statement of his fact; correct enough, not vulgar, as described, but with a sort of boyish cheerfulness, or that kind of sincerity and jolly good meaning that our class meetings on commencement days show, in telling our old stories over."[47]

46. Rhees, ed., *Smithsonian Institution* (1879), p. 945.
47. *Journals of Ralph Waldo Emerson,* edited by Edward Waldo Emerson and Waldo Emerson Forbes (10 vols.; Boston: Houghton Mifflin Company, 1909–14), IX, 375. Whether or not Lincoln actually attended the lecture is a matter of some debate.

In all probability, Emerson also met Joseph Henry for the first time on that occasion, though there is no testimony to that fact in the journal. The two men could not have been more different in character and intellectual style. Henry, at the peak of his career as a scientist-administrator, had transformed the Smithsonian from a polyglot vision into a flourishing institution, moving in the process into the leadership of organized science in the United States; Emerson, at the peak of his career as a lecturer-essayist, had literally fled the constraints of institutions and for all intents and purposes confined his organizational activities to participation in the Saturday Club in Boston. Henry had the patient, synthesizing mind of the scientist, proceeding from experiment to experiment and from clusters of experiments to the elucidation of more general principles; Emerson, as Oliver Wendell Holmes once remarked, "had neither the patience nor the method of the inductive reasoner; he passed from one thought to another not by logical steps but by airy flights, which left no footprints." But what marked the two in common was that both were self-educated, self-made men, not in the narrow sense of having been unschooled, but rather in that broader Emersonian sense in which genius always educates itself. Indeed, each had literally created the role he played in nineteenth-century American learning.[48]

Born in 1803, the son of the pastor at Boston's First Church, Emerson had his formal education at the Latin School and at Harvard College and then, after a brief period of schoolteaching, at the Harvard Divinity School. He was "approbated to teach" by the Middlesex Association of Ministers in 1826 and, after serving as visiting minister in various pulpits in and around Boston, associated himself with Boston's Second Church, initially as junior pastor to the Reverend Henry Ware, Jr., and soon after as pastor. He performed his duties with more success than satisfaction, however, with the result that he came to feel increasingly constrained in the role; in 1832 he offered his resignation to the congregation, which reluctantly accepted it. Shortly thereafter, he went for a time to Europe, where he traveled through Italy, France, and Great Britain, meeting, among others, Samuel Taylor Coleridge, Thomas Carlyle, William Wordsworth, Walter Savage Landor, and John Stuart Mill. He returned to Boston in 1833, free of regular responsibilities, uncertain about the next phase of his career, and determined to make a contribution in the field of letters.[49]

48. Oliver Wendell Holmes, *Ralph Waldo Emerson, John Lathrop Motley: Two Memoirs*, in *The Works of Oliver Wendell Holmes* (13 vols.; Boston: Houghton, Mifflin and Company, 1892), XI, 283.
49. *Ibid.*, p. 41.

The essential problem Emerson faced, as Henry Nash Smith once observed, was the problem of vocation. Since the earliest days of the Massachusetts colony, it had been assumed that the man who would function as a public teacher—as an intellectual, if one would use a latter-day word—would serve in the ministry or in a professorship (and most professors had been in orders). Emerson himself had been ambivalent about the ministry from the beginning, however; he once remarked that he had decided on the ministry "before he was acquainted with the character of his own mind," and there is evidence from his days as an undergraduate of a profound interest in the crafts of poetry and rhetoric. Had the youthful bachelor of arts been able to obtain a professorship of rhetoric at one of the New England colleges, the problem of vocation might well have been solved. But, having chosen the ministry, Emerson had come up against the constraints of the role. The ostensible reason for his resignation was doctrinal—a concern about the administration of the Lord's Supper—although the deeper reason lay with the ministry as a way of relating to society, with the sense that the ministerial role was fundamentally tradition-bound and therefore increasingly irrelevant to the urban-industrial society that was coming into being. However that may be, having abandoned the ministry, Emerson had no clear alternative vocation to which he could commit himself; he literally had to create one. The role that he eventually did conceive was the role he called "scholar"; and the development that permitted him to perform the role for the remainder of his life was the emergence of the world of lecturing and publishing during the 1830's and 1840's.[50]

As Emerson portrayed the role of scholar in his well-known Phi Beta Kappa address at Harvard in 1837, it had little to do with the "gradgrind" common to the colleges of the time or even with the painstaking investigator exemplified by Joseph Henry. The scholar was rather, in Emerson's words, "Man Thinking." At his best, he was the "delegated intellect" of all men everywhere. All the world, all thought and all experience, constituted his school, and his life was one of continuing education through the influence of nature, books, and action upon his inquiring mind.[51]

50. Henry Nash Smith, "Emerson's Problem of Vocation," *New England Quarterly*, XII (1939), 52–67. The quotation is from a note Emerson wrote in the margins of an essay entitled "Find Your Calling," in Arthur Cushman McGiffert, Jr., ed., *Young Emerson Speaks: Unpublished Discourses on Many Subjects* (Boston: Houghton Mifflin Company, 1938), p. 251.

51. Ralph Waldo Emerson, "The American Scholar" (1837), in *The Complete Works of Ralph Waldo Emerson* (12 vols.; Boston: Houghton, Mifflin and Company, 1903–1904), I, 84.

Of the three, the first great educator in time and importance was nature. The scholar could not afford to know nature secondhand: he beyond all men needed to know it directly, to comprehend its value fully. The scholar's initial sense of nature would come through the examination and classification of objects and phenomena, after the fashion of the scientist; but his goal was not the comprehension of particular laws and generalizations but rather the profound understanding that in the last analysis he and nature proceeded from "one root," that they partook together of the same divinity. To grasp that understanding, in Emerson's view, was the beginning of wisdom.[52]

The second educative influence on the scholar was the mind of the poet, as it flowed through literature, art, and institutions, and especially through books. The scholar needed to consult books, recognizing always that they were created at some particular time in the past by some particular author who had contemplated the world, given it the unique arrangement of his own mind, and then articulated it for others. As such, books were surrogates for direct learning from nature; they embodied truths essentially gleaned by others. Even at their consummate best, as in the works of Shakespeare, for example, they did the fatal disservice of overinfluencing and thus preempting the more difficult process of independent reflection and self-discovery. They were dangerous and they needed to be used with caution; in overvaluing them, the scholar became, not Man Thinking, but a bookworm.

The third educative influence on the scholar was action, the essential, though the subordinate, companion of thought. "Without it," Emerson cautioned, "thought can never ripen into truth. Whilst the world hangs before the eye as a cloud of beauty, we cannot even see its beauty. In action is cowardice, but there can be no scholar without the heroic mind. The preamble of thought, the transition through which it passes from the unconscious to the conscious, is action. Only so much do I know, as I have lived." Like books, action was valuable and necessary in its own right, but it served most fundamentally as a resource: it tested and tempered intellect and completed it in the business of living. "Character is higher than intellect," Emerson counseled. "Thinking is the function. Living is the functionary."[53]

Once educated by nature, books, and action—and that education continued over a lifetime—the scholar's duty was "to cheer, to raise,

52. *Ibid.*
53. *Ibid.*, pp. 94–95, 99.

and to guide men by showing them facts amidst appearances." Like the guardians of Plato's *Republic,* the scholar needed to distinguish between the permanent and the transitory and to teach the permanent as a guide to life. And, to perform that duty, he needed to trust himself with steadfast courage and confidence. "He and only he knows the world," Emerson insisted.

The world of any moment is the merest appearance. Some great decorum, some fetish of a government, some ephemeral trade, or war, or man, is cried up by half mankind and cried down by the other half, as if all depended on this particular up or down. The odds are that the whole question is not worth the poorest thought which the scholar has lost in listening to the controversy. Let him not quit his belief that a popgun is a popgun, though the ancient and honorable of the earth affirm it to be the crack of doom. In silence, in steadiness, in severe abstraction, let him hold by himself; add observation to observation, patient of neglect, patient of reproach, and bide his own time—happy enough if he can satisfy himself alone that this day he has seen something truly.

For Emerson, then, the office of scholar combined the historic roles of philosopher, prophet, poet, critic, and seer. The scholar was the quintessential public teacher, beholden to no individual, group, institution, or government, but responsible to all for the good of all.[54]

The very breadth of the Emersonian idea of learning left ample room for the polarities that were so much a part of Emersonian thought. Edwin Perry Whipple once observed that Emerson was a "Hindoo-Yankee—a cross between Brahma and Poor Richard." He could unite in the same essay—indeed, in the same paragraph—the contemplative and the practical, the sacred and the profane, the altruistic and the selfish. Emerson deeply believed that "no man is able or willing to help any other man," since everyone must learn in his own way, obviously via self-education; yet he talked incessantly of mankind as a whole and of "one mind common to all individual men." In his doctrine of self-reliance and in his lionization of Napoleon as "the agent or attorney of the middle class of modern society; of the throng who fill the markets, shops, counting-houses, manufactories, ships, of the modern world, aiming to be rich," Emerson could sanctify all the values Franklin had celebrated; yet he directed some of his most severe barbs against the materialism, the selfishness, and the cynicism that were coming to the fore during the course of industrialization in England and New England. He could affirm the contribution of technol-

54. *Ibid.,* pp. 100, 102–103.

ogy to the forging of a new national culture in which technology would play a central role; yet he also voiced the common concern of the era that technology would become the master and man the servant. "A man must keep an eye on his servants," Emerson warned, "if he would not have them rule him. Man is a shrewd inventor and is ever taking the hint of a new machine from his own structure, adapting some secret of his anatomy in iron, wood and leather to some required function in the work of the world. But it is found that the machine unmans the user." In the end, it was the user, man, that Emerson deemed preeminent.

A man should not be a silk-worm, nor a nation a tent of caterpillars. . . . The incessant repetition of the same hand-work dwarfs the man, robs him of his strength, wit and versatility, to make a pin-polisher, a buckle-maker, or any other specialty; and presently, in a change of industry, whole towns are sacrificed like ant-hills, when the fashion of shoe-strings supersedes buckles, when cotton takes the place of linen, or railways of turnpikes, or when commons are inclosed by landlords. Then society is admonished of the mischief of the division of labor, and that the best political economy is care and culture of men; for in these crises all are ruined except such as are proper individuals, capable of thought and of new choice and the application of their talent to new labor.[55]

The breadth of Emerson's idea of education also provided leverage for a continuing criticism of the inevitable drift of formal educational institutions toward pedantry. The essay actually entitled "Education," which derived from lectures Emerson had given during the 1830's and 1840's but which was put together by literary representatives for publication in 1876, after Emerson's mental powers had begun to fail, connected closely with the theme of "The American Scholar." The great object of education was moral: "to teach self-trust: to inspire the youthful man with an interest in himself; with a curiosity touching his own nature; to acquaint him with the resources of his mind, and to teach him that there is all his strength, and to inflame him with a piety towards the Grand Mind in which he lives." Thus, young people were urged to read books that inculcated self-trust—"a trust, against all appearances, against all privations" in one's own worth and not in "tricks, plotting, or patronage"; and adults were urged "to respect the child," to discipline a boy's "uproar, fooling and horseplay" and to "arm" his "nature . . . with knowledge in the very direction in which it

55. Edwin Perry Whipple, "Some Recollections of Ralph Waldo Emerson," *Harper's Magazine,* LXV (1882), 579; *Journals of Emerson,* II, 483; Emerson, "History," in *Works,* II, 1; "Napoleon; or, the Man of the World," in *ibid.,* IV, 252; and "Wealth," in *ibid.,* V, 166–167.

points." More than was his wont, Emerson alluded in the essay to the power of particular educational institutions. "Humanly speaking, the school, the college, society make the difference between men. All the fairy tales of Aladdin or the invisible Gyges or the talisman that opens kings' palaces or the enchanted halls underground or in the sea, are only fictions to indicate the one miracle of intellectual enlargement." Having argued thusly, however, Emerson was still mordant in his criticism of contemporary educational institutions. He extolled the "natural" education of the family. "The whole theory of the school is on the nurse's or mother's knee," he observed. "The child is as hot to learn as the mother is to impart. There is mutual delight." And he celebrated the "natural colleges" that had formed throughout history around "natural" teachers—the young men of Athens around Socrates, or of Alexandria around Plotinus, or of Paris around Abelard, or of Germany around Goethe. But he condemned out of hand the effort to organize these "natural" phenomena into mass systems that trained people with military hurry and efficiency. "Our modes of education aim to expedite, to save labor; to do for the masses what cannot be done reverently, one by one: say rather, the whole world is needed for the tuition of each pupil." The only corrective for these "quack" practices, he believed, was "to import into education the wisdom of life. Leave this military hurry and adopt the pace of nature. Her secret is patience."[56]

Now, there was a solvent power in all of this that one associates with the classic critics of academicism—with Erasmus, or Montaigne (who was a favorite of Emerson), or even the young Franklin of the Silence Dogood letters. Emerson himself once observed, "Beware when the great God lets loose a thinker on this planet. Then all things are at risk." As Emerson conceived his self-defined vocation, the task that had always been at the heart of prophecy was of the essence, namely, to focus on human possibility while at the same time criticizing the social structures that constrained that possibility. Yet, like all solvents, which at proper strength dissolve everything at once, Emerson's teachings unmasked the good with the bad and the moderate with the excessive: in the end, they were as withering of academic institutions themselves as of the academicism that can beset them. Emerson attempted to provide correctives for this—balancing the individualism of "The American Scholar" with the civilizing concern of "Culture" and the acquiescence in a beneficent fate of "Circles." Ultimately, however, Emerson's pro-

---

56. Emerson, "Education," in *ibid.*, X, 135, 143, 144, 126, 148, 149, 153–154, 155.

phetic concern was with justice, not with balanced presentations; he believed that men needed unshackling, even from the institutions charged with unshackling them.[57]

In a remarkable way, the individualism of Emerson's thought drew together the contemporary concerns of piety, civility, and learning as they bore on education at the same time as it implicitly criticized them. In his idea of the relation of man to man and nature to the Oversoul, Emerson declared essentially that all men were divine, not the elect alone nor even those alone who had chosen Christ, but all individuals everywhere. Yet he was critical of the contribution of churches of any kind and doubted their educative role in moving men closer to their inborn divinity. Similarly, in his idea of the responsibility of schools and colleges to convey the fundamentals of literature and science, he echoed the contemporary commitment to universal education for general culture; indeed, there are passages in the writings of Emerson and Horace Mann that are all but interchangeable. Moreover, Emerson was not without his own version of a nationalist ardor, seeing America as ideally a nation of heroic men and women, with a great literature created out of their own life, thought, and experience, and ultimately teaching the world "to make the advanced intelligence of mankind in the sufficiency of morals practical." Yet here, too, he was critical of the contribution that schools and colleges might make to truly heroic individuals, at best granting them a propaedeutic function in the larger process of education, and his idea of the breadth of learning was all-encompassing: men learned from nature, books, and action; the "useful arts" contributed to the advance of civilization as well as poetry and painting; and the American scholar needed to consider them all as he searched for the truth to teach the public. In many respects, Emerson's scholar was Calvin's Protestant layman, a priest in his own right who taught and was taught by other priests: Emerson once referred to society as a great school in which "all are teachers and pupils in turn." In other respects, Emerson's scholar was Christian in *The Pilgrim's Progress,* recording his own movement toward sanctification in a journal of reflection and self-scrutiny—in fact, Emerson's journals were eloquent testimony to the vitality of the Puritan and Franklinian traditions of self-education in nineteenth-century America. And, in still other re-

---

57. Emerson, "Circles," in *ibid.,* II, 308. Stephen Whicher makes the point, not merely of the corrective, but of a fundamental shift in Emerson's thought during the 1830's. See *Freedom and Fate: An Inner Life of Ralph Waldo Emerson* (Philadelphia: University of Pennsylvania Press, 1953).

spects, Emerson's scholar was democratic man living in association with other democratic men in a mutually educative society; he liked to refer approvingly to Goethe's tendency to ask of those he met, *"What can you teach me?"*[58]

In a remarkable way, too, the very character and style of Emerson's lectures and writings made them uniquely accessible to the contemporary American public, especially, perhaps, the young. The profusion of aphorisms, the innumerable polarities, the frequent slips into mysticism, and the unequivocal appeal to the new enabled the average American to sense his own deepest aspirations, whatever they happened to be. Emerson noted in *Representative Men* that the heroes he portrayed there were great, not because they were original or unlike the men and women of their time, but precisely because they saw what their contemporaries wanted and shared their desires. As such, it was within the capacity of any person to become great insofar as he could express quintessentially the qualities of his time and place. And, in seeking greatness, he could rely on the stirrings of his own muse or conscience.[59]

Emerson's representative men were also great because they had discovered their divinely appointed tasks, they had followed their respective callings. The heroes among his heroes were Napoleon and Goethe, who best represented, respectively, the external and internal lives of their times. Had he been less modest in his own right, he might have included himself, as the representative teacher of his time, at least with respect to his own country. But the thought probably never crossed his mind. He wrote no autobiography to equal Franklin's; and, though his journals were autobiographical, it is doubtful that he wrote them with a mind to publication in their initial form. Still, by example even more than precept, Emerson taught his ideal of the heroic scholar-teacher sufficiently well for a number of his contemporaries to try to live it, none more self-consciously, perhaps, than Walt Whitman. "I was simmering, simmering, simmering," Whitman once reminisced about his own writing; "Emerson brought me to a boil." When Whitman sent Emerson a copy of the first edition of *Leaves of Grass* in 1855, Emerson wrote him that it was "the most extraordinary piece of wit and wisdom that America has yet contributed." In successive versions, from the pronouncements of the preface to that first edition of *Leaves* to the lengthy explications of *Democratic Vistas* (1870), Whitman described and ex-

---

58. *Journals of Emerson*, X, 144; and Emerson, *Representative Men*, in *Works*, IV, 31, 284.
59. *Ibid.*, pp. 3–35 and *passim*.

emplified the teaching mission he had learned from Emerson, carrying it to its outer limits and producing in the process the bold poetry of the common man that Emerson had envisioned but been unable to write.

I say that democracy can never prove itself beyond cavil, until it founds and luxuriantly grows its own forms of art, poems, schools, theology, displacing all that exists, or that has been produced anywhere in the past, under opposite influences.

It is curious to me that while so many voices, pens, minds, in the press, lecture-rooms, in our Congress, and etc., are discussing intellectual topics, pecuniary dangers, legislative problems, the suffrage, tariff and labor questions, and the various business and benevolent needs of America, with propositions, remedies, often worth deep attention, there is one need, a hiatus the profoundest, that no eye seems to perceive, no voice to state. Our fundamental want today in the United States, with closest, amplest reference to present conditions, and to the future, is of a class, and the clear idea of a class, of native authors, literatures, far different, far higher in grade than any yet known, sacerdotal, modern, fit to cope with our occasions, lands, permeating the whole mass of American mentality, taste, belief, breathing into it a new breath of life, giving it decision, affecting politics far more than the popular superficial suffrage, with results inside and underneath the elections of Presidents or Congresses, radiating, begetting appropriate teachers and schools, manners, costumes, and, as its grandest result, accomplishing, (what neither the schools nor the churches and their clergy have hitherto accomplished, and without which this nation will no more stand, permanently, soundly, than a house will stand without a substratum,) a religious and moral character beneath the political and productive and intellectual bases of the States. For know you not, dear, earnest reader, that the people of our land may all read and write, and may all possess the right to vote—and yet the main things may be entirely lacking?— (and this to supply or suggest them.)

However different in character, style, and mien Whitman might have been—and it is testimony to Emerson's genius as a teacher that he did not permit that basic difference to restrain his encouragement—Whitman was Emerson's American scholar come to life, the god-poet who "announces that which no man foretold," who "stands among partial man for the complete man, and apprises us not of his wealth, but of the commonwealth." [60]

60. John Townsend Trowbridge, *My Own Story with Recollections of Noted Persons* (Boston: Houghton, Mifflin and Company, 1903), p. 367; Ralph Waldo Emerson to Walt Whitman, July 21, 1855, in *Leaves of Grass, The Collected Writings of Walt Whitman*, edited by Gay Wilson Allen and Sculley Bradley (New York: New York University Press, 1965), p. 729; Walt Whitman, *Democratic Vistas* (New York: Smith & McDougal, 1870), pp. 5–6; and Emerson, "The Poet," in *Works*, III, 5.

Chapter 9

THE DILEMMAS OF POPULARIZATION

> The great and immediate functions of exhibitions are to stimulate and educate. They act, not only upon the industrial classes, but upon all classes of men. They increase as well as diffuse knowledge. By bringing together and comparing the results of human effort, new germs of thought are planted, new ideas are awakened, and new inventions are born.
>
> WILLIAM P. BLAKE

The world of public teaching within which Emerson chose to pursue his vocation after leaving the ministry expanded dramatically during the first century of national life. Publishing grew from a minor industry in which individual printers catered to local communities into a major national enterprise. A vigorous lyceum movement, born in the 1820's, brought lecturers on every conceivable topic to hamlets and towns in all parts of the country. And a burgeoning number of libraries, fairs, and museums displayed an astonishing variety of cultural wares to all who would partake of the offering. Every one of these institutions was caught up in the dilemmas of popularization. During an era of intense didacticism, each started out with reasonably well-defined notions of what education would be of most worth; but, in the spirited competition that marked the American cultural economy, they all recognized that to educate one must in the first instance survive. As they reached for clienteles, their notions of educational worth interacted with their interest in survival, and in the process their programs underwent continuing alteration. The Boston Public Library of the 1850's was as different from the subscription libraries of the Revolutionary era as P. T. Barnum's circus was from Charles Willson Peale's museum. And in the changes lay a transformation in the education of the public. Emerson comprehended the transformation, even as he exploited and criticized it, and in so doing he became, by his own criteria, the representative educator of his time.

II

The printer continued as an entrepreneur of education during the early years of the Republic, much in the fashion of Benjamin Franklin. In hamlets and towns throughout the country, enterprising artisans set up shop and served their localities not only as printers but also as authors, editors, bookbinders, booksellers, and librarians. Until well into the nineteenth century, the technology of printing was such that a second-hand press and the several fonts of type necessary to make a beginning could be purchased for as little as $200; and, if the cost of transporting that equipment to some rural byway could be substantial, it was rarely prohibitive. In some instances, the necessary capital seems to have been raised via subscription, in others via patronage, and in still others via borrowing. Whatever the source of the capital, however, the printer was often one of the earliest settlers of a town and therefore one of the most influential. Thus, John Scull and Joseph Hall arrived in Pittsburgh with type and hand press as early as 1786, when the population still numbered fewer than four hundred; while William Maxwell printed the *Laws of the Territory of the United States North-west of the Ohio . . .* , the first book published northwest of the Ohio River, in Cincinnati in 1796, when the town itself was composed mostly of log cabins and a few frame houses and the entire territory had a population of around fifteen thousand.

Like Franklin, whose memory they cherished, the printers of the early national era were enterprising and versatile. Most of them published newspapers, creating much of the copy themselves and borrowing the rest from other printed sources, and a few published magazines. Most also undertook job printing—handbills, tickets, and brochures. From there it was but a short step to sermons, tracts, pamphlets, and books, particularly schoolbooks; and, once there were sermons, tracts, pamphlets, and books, it was but another short step to the establishment of a bookstore with a circulating library. In larger communities, and particularly in cities, the several functions became separate and specialized; in the process the distinctive role of publisher came into being.

The career of Isaiah Thomas, which spanned the Revolutionary and early national periods, furnishes an excellent example. Born in 1749, the son of a Boston ne'er-do-well, Thomas learned the printer's art as an apprentice to Zechariah Fowle and then went on to become Fowle's partner in the establishment of the *Massachusetts Spy.* A supporter of the Revolutionary cause, he fled Boston when it was occupied by the British in 1775 and set up shop in Worcester, where he remained, except for a brief interlude in Salem, for the rest of his life. Building on the income and reputation of the *Spy,* he began during the 1770's to issue magazines, almanacs, and books as well. By the mid-1790's, when his business reached its zenith, he had in his employ at Worcester alone some 150 individuals, and he also maintained partnerships in a number of other cities. Thomas published some of the earliest English dictionaries and Bibles to enjoy widespread circulation in America, as well as the first extensive works of music and the first novel by a native American author. He also published dozens of textbooks, ranging from Nicholas Pike's arithmetic to Sir William Blackstone's *Commentaries on the Laws of England,* along with some of the best English literature of his time, including scores of attractively illustrated children's books.

Now, in the very nature of these diverse activities, Thomas found himself inevitably in the business of educating. For one thing, he quite consciously selected much of what he printed. Franklin had observed many years earlier that printers cheerfully served all writers and paid them well, without regard to which side of any question the writers happened to be on; and, to the extent that printers of the early Republic continued to be entrepreneurs who accepted job printing as it came to them, Franklin's observation remained accurate. But, as was very much the case with Franklin himself, printers also found themselves making independent decisions on their own initiative, supported by their own capital, concerning what might be worthy of issuing or reissuing, and in the making of such decisions standards of quality, desirability, and attractiveness inevitably came into play. It is to Thomas's credit that he recognized the superiority of Noah Webster's speller and grammar, William Perry's dictionary, Nicholas Pike's arithmetic, John Newberry's chapbooks, and such contemporary English stand-bys as *Goody Two-Shoes, Mother Goose,* and *Robinson Crusoe;* but the central fact is that he chose them from among competing alternatives, and probably with as much attention to substance as to salability—in fact, substance and salability were inseparable. Beyond the selections of what to issue, there were the associated activities of dissemination—the stocking and management of the bookstore, the supplying of schoolteachers and their students, and the circulation of printed matter via the mails, which also involved the printer in the business of education.

As printers plied their trade, then, and as they increasingly assumed the role of publishers, they ended up deliberately choosing material for audiences that were already in being (schoolchildren, for instance, or newspaper readers) or that were slowly coming into being (readers of novels, for instance, or subscribers to women's magazines). And, in making these choices, particularly as they went beyond simple decisions to reprint material already extant, they came to serve as mediators between authors aspiring to readership and audiences or publics that were at best ill defined. If one considers, by way of example, the field of magazine publishing, there emerged during the 1820's and 1830's a large number of special periodicals addressed to particular audiences— children, or women, or Baptists, or Democrats, or schoolteachers, or businessmen, or scientists. In some instances, a printer would inaugurate such a periodical and undertake to edit it himself; in others, a printer would engage someone else to perform the editorial function. In either instance, the task of editing was to seek out, commission, attract, and prepare material that would instruct and entertain the perceived audience at the same time as it encouraged that audience to continue to subscribe. In effect, the material was pointedly addressed to the audience at the same time as it actually created or enlarged the audience. In the process, however much crass notions of marketability may have guided the editor, education inevitably took place.

The *Illinois Monthly Magazine* observed editorially in 1831 that the United States was experiencing "a golden age of periodicals." Actually, it was a golden age of publishing in general, with a rapid expansion in book, magazine, and newspaper publication throughout the country, especially in the cities, notably New York, Boston, and Philadelphia. Samuel Griswold Goodrich, who was active in American publishing from 1816 until his death in 1860, included in his autobiography some estimates of book production in the United States between 1820 and 1850, which, though at best approximations, convey a sense of the scope and rapidity of change:

ESTIMATES OF BOOK PRODUCTION
(in dollars)

	1820	1830	1840	1850
Schoolbooks	750,000	1,100,000	2,000,000	5,500,000
Classical books	250,000	350,000	550,000	1,000,000
Theological books	150,000	250,000	300,000	500,000
Law books	200,000	300,000	400,000	700,000
Medical books	150,000	200,000	250,000	400,000
All others	1,000,000	1,300,000	2,000,000	4,400,000
Total	2,500,000	3,500,000	5,500,000	12,500,000

In addition to these raw estimates of dollar volume, at least four additional trends are worthy of note. First, though American publishing was increasingly concentrated in the eastern cities, it remained a comparatively diffuse enterprise, with regional centers in communities like Albany, New York, Cincinnati, Ohio, and Charleston, South Carolina. Second, though book publishing in particular passed increasingly into the hands of a few large firms, the individual entrepreneur who printed, published, edited, bound, and sold pamphlets, almanacs, schoolbooks, and newspapers remained a characteristic player on the American scene through much of the century. Third, though American publishers issued comparatively few original works of belles-lettres during the early decades of the century, preferring to pirate the novels of Scott and Dickens and the essays, biographies, and histories of their European contemporaries, they did send forth a flood of original popular works, ranging from formal textbooks for school use to practical handbooks of self-instruction. And finally, though the reprinting of European works remained a mainstay of American publishing throughout the century, American works did come to dominate the American market by the time of the 1840's.[1]

Goodrich himself remains an excellent example of the single entrepreneur during this period of rapid expansion in American publishing. A native of Connecticut, he had tried several businesses before he entered publishing in partnership with his friend George Sheldon in 1816. When Sheldon died in 1817, Goodrich continued the business on his own. His early issues consisted of such staples as the *Family Bible* and an eight-volume edition of the works of Sir Walter Scott. In 1827 Goodrich began to write his Peter Parley books, a series of textbooks, readers, and anthologies for children presented in the form of tales told by a fictitious old raconteur. In the fashion of many contemporary American authors, including Washington Irving, James Fenimore Cooper, and Walt Whitman, Goodrich issued many of the books under his own imprint. Still later, Goodrich undertook publication of a gift annual called *The Token,* as well as other periodicals addressed to juvenile and adult audiences. In effect, Goodrich was part author, part editor, and part publisher, and his career illustrates the lack of definition in the several roles that persisted until well into the latter part of the century. But it also exemplifies the didactic element that was at the

1. *Illinois Monthly Magazine,* I (1831), 302. The table on book production is a composite of the figures given in S. G. Goodrich, *Recollections of a Lifetime, or Men and Things I Have Seen* (2 vols.; New York: Miller, Orton and Mulligan, 1856), II, 380, 382, 385.

heart of American publishing in the early national period. Goodrich not only prepared books and magazines for children with an explicit didactic concern; he also deliberately undertook to publish American authors, beginning with an edition of the poetry of John Trumbull in 1820 on which he lost a substantial sum of money. Later, in his autobiography, Goodrich noted with special pleasure the shift in American publishing that had taken place during the 1830's and 1840's, from an early preponderance of reprinted English works to a later preponderance of original American writing.

In contrast to Goodrich, the Harper brothers were far more representative of the large eastern publishing houses that came into being during the second and third quarters of the nineteenth century. The Harper firm was organized in 1817 in New York City by James and John Harper, both of whom had recently completed apprenticeships with other printers. Their first book was an edition of an English translation of *Seneca's Morals,* and they followed it with a succession of textbooks, prayer books, hastily produced reprints of Scott novels, and original editions of American works. James and John were soon joined in the business by their brothers, Wesley and Fletcher, and, though the firm continued to print a variety of works for others, principally New York City bookseller-publishers, they found themselves increasingly issuing works under their own imprint. By the end of the 1820's, the firm was widely acknowledged to be the largest book-printing establishment in the United States.

Like Goodrich, the brothers reprinted popular European works and printed original American works, and, like Goodrich, they accepted works proffered to them and commissioned other works as well; unlike Goodrich, they prepared none of their own. In all of this, the element of selection, and with it didacticism, was obviously present. But the brothers went beyond Goodrich in adopting one particular innovation that placed them squarely within the realm of education: as a marketing device, they borrowed the contemporary English practice of issuing series of books labeled "libraries." There were the Family Library (187 titles), the Classical Library (37 titles), the Library of Select Novels (36 titles), the Boy's and Girl's Library (32 titles), the Theological Library (9 titles), the Dramatic Library (5 titles), and the School District Library (in six series comprising 295 titles). What the series did, doubtless for commercial as well as educational purposes, was for all intents and purposes to establish "curricula" for self-study in households, libraries, and churches. No one would argue that the Harpers saw the series explicitly as "curricula"; but, once they had decided on the titles for a series, according to whatever assumptions they might make concerning availability, taste, desire, and marketability, the series *qua* series inevitably functioned as a curriculum, testifying by its very existence that those titles were the most desirable to be read by the designated audience.

Given the circulation of the Family Library over the years, the influence of that particular curriculum must have been prodigious. Including as it did editions of Bacon, Locke, Paley, and Franklin, along with contemporary works by the British reformer Henry Brougham, the Scottish phrenologist George Combe, the German-American economist Francis Lieber, and the American author Richard Henry Dana, the series reflected the essential utilitarianism at the heart of the American idea of prudent learning. That utilitarianism doubtless shaped the Harpers' conception of what would sell, and, once the series was published, that utilitarianism was doubtless strengthened in turn. All the works were essentially popular, with an overwhelming emphasis on history, biography, natural science, and practical wisdom. The theology was abbreviated and nondenominational, as befit a series aimed at a wide audience; while works of native belles-lettres were notable for their scarcity.

A final word should be included about the religious publishers that were contemporary with the Harper firm, since for all the variety of the Harper list and the ingenuity of the Harper marketing effort, the firm managed nowhere near the circulation of the materials proffered by the American Bible Society, the American Tract Society, and the American Sunday-School Union. As has been suggested, those organizations continued to disseminate the Bible and an ancillary devotional literature on a scale unprecedented in history, and it was they, along with the various denominational religious publishers, who provided the preponderant body of reading material for the American public during the first century of national existence.

III

The cost of books and magazines remained quite reasonable during the early decades of the nineteenth century, as a larger reading public combined with technological advance and competition among publishers to keep prices down. Ordinary works of fiction during the 1830's were priced at from $1 to $2, depending on length, and, during periods of cutthroat competition and cost cutting, those prices could tumble to 12½¢ for shorter works and 25¢ for longer ones. The Harper Family Library sold at 45¢ per volume during the years the several volumes were appearing, and after 1845 the complete lot of 187 titles could be had for $80. The subsidized volumes of the American Sunday-School Union went for even less, with the hundred select works of the Sunday-School and Family Library (ranging from 72 to 252 pages in length) selling for $10 in the early 1840's. During the same period, a year's subscription to the *Southern Literary Messenger* cost $5, and to the *Dial* $3, while the publishers of the *Ladies' Wreath*, the "king of the dollar magazines," would ship a club subscription of twenty copies to a single address for $13 annually. Even so, these costs proved prohibitive to many Americans, either because they could not or would not sustain them. The result was that libraries flourished, with many different emphases and clienteles and under many different forms of sponsorship.

The private, individually owned libraries of the provincial era obviously continued—in manses, in physicians' and lawyers' offices, in the studies of amateur scientists and philosophers, and in the homes of ordinary men and women. They provided the basis of a good deal of formal and informal apprenticeship training; and, while few nineteenth-century tales of library experience are as dramatic as Charles Grandison Finney's conversion to Christianity after reading about the Mosaic code in Benjamin Wright's law library, nineteenth-century autobiographies are replete with stories of borrowed books exercising transforming influences. The circulating libraries of the provincial era also continued, principally in the towns and cities, where they were commonly joined to other enterprises—often a printing establishment or a bookstore and sometimes even a millinery shop such as the ones Mary Sprague and Kezia Butler conducted in Boston during the early 1800's.

The cooperative and corporate libraries of the provincial era also continued to flourish. The Harvard College Library remained the largest single collection in the United States during most of the nineteenth century, expanding from 12,000 volumes in 1790 to 154,000 in 1875 (with as many pamphlets in addition), and that exclusive of the numerous other libraries at Harvard maintained by the various professional schools and student societies. The other older college libraries fared variously. The collection of Yale College numbered 78,000 in 1875, again not including the collections of the professional schools and student societies; the collections of the colleges at Columbia and the University of Pennsylvania numbered around 20,000; while the collection of the College of William and Mary numbered only 5,000, having been destroyed by fire in 1859 and again in 1862. Among the newer institutions, such as Bethel in Tennessee or Geneva in Ohio, libraries of under 500 volumes were common.[2]

The several kinds of subscription, association, and proprietary library that had generally passed under the rubric "social library" expanded rapidly during the nineteenth century, the form, like that of the private academy, appearing peculiarly adapted to public effort during the Jacksonian era and after. Every manner of collaborative venture came into being. Subscribers joined together to establish libraries for their own use and often for the use of others as well. Men of high purpose established libraries in which ambitious young apprentices and mechanics might improve themselves vocationally and morally. Merchant clerks established libraries to facilitate their own economic advancement. And the partisans of various social and religious movements founded libraries to promulgate their various social and religious views. As was often the case with academies, both the clientele and the sponsorship of such libraries frequently broadened in the years after their initial establishment, leading in turn to a broadening of their purposes and purviews. Many of them—and they numbered in the hundreds by 1875—came under public support and control in the latter part of the nineteenth century.

The most prevalent kinds of library by far during the 1840's and 1850's were the Sunday school libraries and the district school libraries. Tied as they were to extant popular local institutions—the public school and the church or Sunday school, frequently stocked with collections gathered and approved by distant figures of acknowledged moral and intellectual authority, and easily and cheaply established—these libraries blanketed the country by mid-century, the Sunday school libraries sponsored by the American Sunday-School Union and the district school libraries encouraged first by permissive and then by compulsory legislation enacted in the several states. When William Jones Rhees published his *Manual of Public Libraries* in 1859, he estimated that there were 50,890 libraries in the United States, holding 12,720,686 volumes. Of these, 30,000 libraries, holding 6 million volumes, were

2. U.S., Bureau of Education, *Public Libraries in the United States of America: Special Report* (1876), chap. ii, sec. 2.

Sunday school libraries, and 18,000 libraries, holding 2 million volumes, were district school libraries.[3]

Technically, and particularly in latter-day formulations, the Sunday school libraries would be designated "private" and the district school libraries "public"; but in the minds of the citizenry both were usually seen as public, as indeed were many of the social libraries of the era. As the nineteenth century progressed, however, the term "public" was increasingly reserved for separate local institutions that were publicly supported, publicly controlled, and freely open to all clients on an equal basis. The arguments for public libraries, which began to gain currency after 1850, tended to combine all the assertions in favor of widespread reading—self-culture, moral improvement, and vocational advancement—but their most interesting feature was their similarity to arguments favoring public schools. As the highly influential 1852 report of the trustees of the Boston Public Library stated the case:

If we had no free schools, we should not be a community without education. Large numbers of children would be educated at private schools at the expense of parents able to afford it, and considerable numbers in narrow circumstances would, by the aid of the affluent and liberal, obtain the same advantages. We all feel however that such a state of things would be a poor substitute for our system of public schools, of which it is the best feature that it is a public provision for all; affording equal advantages to poor and rich; furnishing at the public expense an education so good, as to make it an object with all classes to send their children to the public schools.

It needs no argument to prove that, in a republican government, these are features of the system, quite as valuable as the direct benefit of the instruction which it imparts. But it is plain that the same principles apply to the farther progress of education, in which each one must be mainly his own teacher. Why should not this prosperous and liberal city extend some reasonable amount of aid to the foundation and support of a noble public library, to which the young people of both sexes, when they leave the schools, can resort for those works which pertain to general culture, or which are needful for research into any branch of useful knowledge?

Arguments such as these became especially prevalent and persuasive during the third quarter of the century, particularly in New England and the Midwest; and, while one can point to some twenty-five libraries founded before 1850 that might properly be classified as "public" in

3. William J. Rhees, *Manual of Public Libraries, Institutions, and Societies, in the United States and British Provinces of North America* (Philadelphia: J. B. Lippincott, 1859), p. xxviii.

the usage of the Boston Library trustees, 257 such institutions were established in the United States between 1850 and 1875.[4]

As with all educative institutions, the stocking of libraries with books, pamphlets, and periodicals inevitably raised problems of selection. Assuming finite resources, which materials would be made available with what clienteles in mind, and who indeed would make the choices? When Benjamin Franklin and his associates in the junto had organized the Library Company of Philadelphia in 1731, they had started with an annual budget of twenty-five pounds and the assumption that the books purchased would be for the use of the subscribers. Franklin and his friend Thomas Godfrey had selected the initial volumes in consultation with James Logan, and not surprisingly the collection they had chosen was essentially practical, filled with handbooks, histories, atlases, selected classics such as Homer's *Iliad* and Plutarch's *Lives,* and such lively periodicals as the *Tatler,* the *Spectator,* and the *Guardian.*

Later, in the case of other social libraries, the subscribers as a group made the selection, or they designated some representative or representatives to do the actual choosing. As clienteles broadened, however, or as subscribers established libraries expressly designed for clients other than themselves—apprentices, or mechanics, or merchant clerks—there was the inevitable tension between asssumptions concerning what the readers might want and beliefs concerning what would most benefit them. If the fare was unattractive, there would be no readers; if the fare merely catered to popular wants, there would be no uplift. Somewhere in the balance between the two lay the course of education—a course often determined as much by factors of the market and chance as by carefully planned didactic programs. Thus, the book collections of social libraries during the first years of the nineteenth century tended to resemble the content of the periodical press: history, biography, travel, and belles-lettres were the dominant categories, with any drift toward specialization that occurred after 1815 simply reflecting efforts to meet the needs of particular clienteles (juvenile books for children or vocational handbooks for apprentices), much in the way magazines began to cater to special audiences. And the book collections of circulating libraries, which were dependent on per-book rental fees, tended to be even more sensitive to the desires of clients, and therefore

---

4. *Report of the Trustees of the Public Library of the City of Boston, July, 1852* (Boston: J.H. Eastburn, 1852), pp. 7–8; and *Public Libraries in the United States of America,* 781–782.

included an even greater preponderance of fiction, belles-lettres, history, and biography.

As clienteles diversified and as libraries sought to clothe themselves in the mantle of publicness, recommendations appeared in various quarters concerning precisely what the ideally balanced collection ought to include. One of the earliest appeared in 1793 from the pen of Thaddeus Mason Harris, who was serving at the time as Librarian of Harvard. "Surrounded by the largest collection of books in America, and having made it a constant practice to read *all* the English reviews," Harris explained, he was undertaking the responsibility of suggesting books for his less fortunate countrymen—his endeavor being "to form a catalogue for a *small* and *cheap* library, intended to suit the tastes and circumstances of common readers." Harris's list included 276 titles, arranged under three large divisions—memory, reason, and imagination. There was probably more theology in the collection than would have been recommended from other quarters—Harris was, after all, writing from Harvard in New England—and there was probably less in the practical arts and sciences. But a substantial portion of the list did fall within the categories of history, biography, travel, poetry, drama, and fiction, so that even here the taste of that portion of the contemporary reading public who patronized libraries exercised an apparent influence.[5]

Other similarly motivated recommendations appeared from time to time thereafter and doubtless exerted modest influence. But surely the most influential recommendations were those that were actually embodied in published "libraries" of the sort the Harper brothers aggressively marketed. The American Society for the Diffusion of Useful Knowledge was organized in 1836 by a group of eminent men of affairs and announced ambitious plans to publish the American Library for Schools and Families. The society was clearly modeled after the Society for the Diffusion of Useful Knowledge founded by the Scottish reformer Henry Brougham and his associates in London in 1826. But, unlike its more successful antecedent, its plans were never realized. By contrast, those of the American Sunday-School Union were realized, and abundantly so. Under the aggressive leadership of Frederick A. Packard, a Massachusetts attorney who for thirty years served as editorial secretary of the Union, the ASSU prepared several select libraries that

5. Thaddeus Mason Harris, *A Seleced [sic] Catalogue of Some of the Most Esteemed Publications in the English Language* (Boston: L. Thomas and E.T. Andrews, 1793), pp. iv-v.

became the bases of Sunday school, and to a lesser extent, district school libraries throughout the country. Produced cheaply and sold aggressively, the Union's publications dominated American libraries through much of the century, and Packard's tastes exercised a decisive influence in the selection of fare they served to their growing clientele.

During the 1820's, members of the ASSU's Committee on Publications referred to themselves as "dictators to the consciences of thousands of immortal beings," and patently saw themselves as custodians of true values in an exploding world of print that was dominated by the false doctrines of silly fiction. In providing reading matter for millions of ordinary men, women, and children who would patronize local libraries, the committee saw as its preeminent responsibility the selection of material that would lead readers to intellectual and moral improvement. Although the committee was less subtle about its mission than some, and although it clothed its statement of purpose in fewer euphemisms, its position about the responsibility to educate was characteristic of those who selected book collections for the public, whether they were subscribers or proprietors, as was most often the case in the early years of the century, or librarians, as was increasingly the case after 1850.[6]

One final point bears comment. Although the principal thrust of American libraries in the nineteenth century was to popularize their offerings to suit their broadening clienteles, more elitist notions of custodianship also appeared. In institutions such as the Harvard Library, the Boston Athenaeum (founded in 1807), the Astor Library (founded in 1849), the Smithsonian Institution, or the Library of Congress, the notion of custodianship expressed itself in vigorous assertions of the responsibility of cultural preservation. The individuals who led these institutions, men such as William Jones Rhees, Joseph Green Cogswell, Charles A. Cutter, and Ainsworth Rand Spofford, among others, were painfully aware of the superiority of the great European collections, and they led a tireless crusade during the latter half of the century to develop comparable centers of research and scholarship in the United States. Their efforts were in their very nature counter to the more popular trend, but even here a concern for the general good was in evidence as the nation's most articulate and self-conscious librarians urged that republics as well as monarchies needed to be aggressive about their scientific inquiry and aware of their historical traditions, and that well-supplied libraries were crucial elements in the advancement of both enterprises.

6. *American Sunday-School Magazine,* I (1824), 1.

IV

When Franklin recounted the story of the founding of the Library Company of Philadelphia in his *Autobiography*, he alluded to the obvious benefit members of the junto would derive from pooling their books: "By thus clubbing our books to a common library," he observed, "we should . . . have each of us the advantage of using the books of all the other members, which would be nearly as beneficial as if each owned the whole." But he then went on to mention another, equally important advantage that would accrue from having the books easily at hand: collected, arranged, and accessible, they would be "ready to consult in our conferences." Those conferences, of course, were at the very heart of the junto's activities, and it was assumed that reading would invaluably enrich them. Beyond that, reading itself was very much a social act in the eighteenth century. One tended to read aloud and in company, and then to discuss what one had read with others. It remained a social act in the nineteenth century, though in somewhat different ways. Individuals increasingly read silently and in solitude, but it continued to be widely assumed that at some point they would "set" what they had gleaned from their reading through discussion and mutual inquiry. In effect, in the minds of those who thought about the issue, libraries and the self-education they symbolized were inextricably joined to discussions and the mutual education they symbolized. The written word and the spoken word remained inseparable.[7]

The spirit of Franklin's junto—the idea of a club for mutual improvement that united these various functions—continued to hold a central place in the life of the new nation. It was evident in every manner of athenaeum and institute, literary confederation and philosophical academy, and society for the promotion of the sciences, the arts, agriculture, industry, and commerce. Such organizations sprang up by the score during the last decades of the eighteenth century and first decades of the nineteenth, principally in the towns and cities. They frequently displayed extralocal pretensions, and some of them were even chartered by their respective state legislatures; but, in the extent to which they were associated with any particular place, that place tended to be a room or building that joined a library to the opportunity for systematic, sustained discussion among the members. The forms of such discussion

7. *The Autobiography of Benjamin Franklin,* edited by Leonard W. Labaree, Ralph L. Ketcham, Helen C. Boatfield, and Helene H. Fineman (New Haven: Yale University Press, 1964), pp. 130, 142.

were clearly rooted in the Protestant tradition of the study and exegesis of the word, and thus tended to revolve around reading, lecturing, and the formal exchange of ideas. Of these, the lecture has had the most systematic historical scrutiny, and with good reason: the nineteenth century was a great age of lecturing, during which the lecture as a rhetorical, didactic, and literary form surely came into its own. But the less-dramatic enterprise of ordinary men and women exchanging ideas with one another merits equally careful attention, for it bore a crucial kinship, albeit in the cultural realm, to the sort of freewheeling discussion that marked the democratical societies of the 1790's and the Washington Benevolent Societies of the succeeding decade and that subsequently became a hallmark of Jacksonian politics. That sort of discussion educated in cultural affairs quite as effectively as in political affairs; and, for many whose schooling consisted of the year or two necessary to produce minimal literacy, such discussion provided whatever education they were able to obtain beyond their own experience privately considered.

No institution during the first half-century of national life incarnated the educational values of the discussion of cultural affairs quite so well as the American Lyceum. The organization was founded in 1826 by a well-to-do Connecticut farmer turned amateur scientist named Josiah Holbrook. Holbrook had attended Yale during the first decade of the century and had then opened a private school in his native town of Derby. Subsequently, having heard the lectures of the Yale scientist Benjamin Silliman, he had attempted a number of experiments with schools that combined manual training, agricultural education, and formal academic instruction. By the 1820's Holbrook had acquired something of a reputation as a spokesman for the new sciences and a partisan of educational reform. The initial announcement of the Lyceum came in an anonymous letter to William Russell's *American Journal of Education* that, interestingly enough, did not include the term "lyceum." "Sir," it began, "I take the liberty to submit for your consideration, a few articles as regulations for associations for mutual instruction in the sciences, and in useful knowledge generally. . . . It seems to me that if associations . . . could once be started in our villages, and upon a general plan, they would increase with great rapidity, and do more for the general diffusion of knowledge, and for raising the moral and intellectual taste of our countrymen, than any other expedient which can possibly be devised."[8]

8. *American Journal of Education,* I (1826), 594.

Holbrook then went on to state two general objectives for the contemplated associations: first, "to procure for youths an economical and practical education, and to diffuse rational and useful information through the community generally; and, second, "to apply the sciences and the various branches of education to the domestic and useful arts, and to all the common purposes of life." Moreover, he also set forth the means whereby such associations might most effectively be brought into existence: dues would be set at a dollar a year; there would be the usual roster of officers, along with five curators, who would choose any lecturers brought to the association and also oversee whatever books, scientific apparatus, and cabinets of material the association happened to acquire; and there would be a hierarchy of representative county and state "boards of mutual education," capped by a "general board" embracing the entire United States.[9]

A firm believer in his own preachments, Holbrook actually organized the first such association a few weeks after his proposals appeared. Having delivered a course of lectures on the natural sciences at Millbury, in Worcester County, Massachusetts, he succeeded in "inducing thirty or forty of his hearers, farmers and mechanics of the place, to organize themselves into a society for mutual improvement, which at his request was called 'Millbury Lyceum No. 1, Branch of the American Lyceum.'" Within months, sparked by Holbrook's unflagging enthusiasm, a dozen nearby villages had followed Millbury's lead, Worcester County had organized the first county lyceum, and the movement had spread south to Windham County in Connecticut. By 1829 there were lyceums in every region of the country and Holbrook had announced in a widely circulated pamphlet the advantages that would inevitably accrue to any locality that decided to organize such an association: conversation would improve; young people would seek and enjoy a higher level of amusement; the community, having pooled its resources, would enjoy a more economical program of entertainment; local libraries, schools, and academies would benefit from the renewed enthusiasm for education; local teachers would profit from the sustained discussion of educational affairs; and a steady flow of local maps, histories, and surveys would surely eventuate from citizens seeking to exploit their newfound interest in the arts and sciences.

One can point to at least two sources for Holbrook's remarkable set of proposals and the complex of activities they set in motion. Surely one was the record of the British mechanics' institutes and the substantial

9. *Ibid,.* pp. 595, 596.

program of adult education they had managed to mount by the 1820's. The institutes traced their roots to the Andersonian Institution in Glasgow, which had been founded with a bequest from Professor John Anderson, who had willed his museum, his library, and his "philosophical apparatus" to the development of a system of popular education that would be open to all classes and both sexes. In 1800–01, a young professor at the Andersonian named George Birkbeck announced a series of lectures in the field of natural philosophy pointedly directed to artisans and mechanics. Later, after he had moved to London and taken up the practice of medicine there, Birkbeck helped organize the London Institute for the Diffusion of Science, Literature, and the Arts and on several occasions delivered lectures on natural and experimental philosophy to audiences of mechanics and artisans. Also in London, Birkbeck took up with his former classmate at the University of Edinburgh, Henry Brougham, and the two men lent their support to the larger movement of English educational reform. When a group of mechanics who had been involved in the Andersonian's program founded the Glasgow Mechanics' Institution early in 1823, Birkbeck agreed to serve as a patron; and, when a group of London mechanics decided to follow suit later that year and found a mechanics' institute in London, Birkbeck and Brougham were among the sponsors.

In 1824, Brougham wove the threads of what had been happening into a general movement in an address entitled "Practical Observations Upon the Education of the People," which, when it appeared in a published version the following year, went through twenty editions in twelve months. Arguing that the question before the British public was no longer whether the people should be educated but how and how well, Brougham urged the wide development of circulating libraries, conversation clubs, lecture forums, and mechanics' institutes, as typified by the Glasgow and London institutions. And, as if to symbolize the transatlantic exchange of ideas that continued to mark the educational reform movement throughout the nineteenth century, Brougham cited Franklin's *Autobiography* as the most persuasive evidence extant that, given the opportunity, the poor as well as the rich would find that knowledge was indeed power.[10]

The mechanics' institutes and Brougham's account of them were widely reported in the United States, among other places in Russell's *American Journal of Education*. And, though Holbrook made no specif-

10. H. Brougham, *Practical Observations Upon the Education of the People, Addressed to the Working Classes and their Employers* (London: Richard Taylor, 1825).

ic mention of them in 1826, it is likely that he was aware of them. In fact, a decade later, when he outlined a "Universal Lyceum," whereby the benefits of the movement would be made available to the entire world, he proposed Brougham for the presidency of the new organization. However that may be, Holbrook need not have been familiar with contemporary British developments to have come by his own proposals, for the second possible source of his ideas was the American tradition itself. He was doubtless familiar with Franklin's multifarious activities, if not through history and biography, at least through myth. He may well have known of the various public lectureships that graced the Boston and New York cultural scenes throughout the early years of the century. And he may even have known of the Troy (New York) Lyceum, which Amos Eaton, an acquaintance of Holbrook who had also been a student of Silliman, had founded in 1818, and of the Gardiner (Maine) Lyceum, which had been established in 1823 "to give to mechanics and farmers such a scientific education as would enable them to become skillful in their occupations." Absent all these data, he might even have spun his proposals out of whole cloth; the fundamental elements were all around him in a host of institutions thriving in 1826.[11]

Whatever the sources of Holbrook's idea, the Lyceum found fertile soil in the communities of Jacksonian America, flourishing during the late 1820's and early 1830's, probably peaking during the middle and late 1830's, and then slowly waning during the years before the Civil War. It throve best in New England and in the cities of the Middle Atlantic states; it fared less well in the Midwest, owing to sparse population and ineffective transportation; and it worked only sporadically in the South. The National Lyceum convened for the first time in New York City on May 4, 1831, and reconvened annually until 1839. As has already been noted, Holbrook even proposed a "Universal Lyceum" in 1837, but no such organization ever came into being. And, also in 1837, Holbrook established at Berea, Ohio, what he hoped would be the first of a series of Lyceum Villages, the aim being to "engraft" education upon business in such a way as to create models of rational and moral community living; but the Berea enterprise did not last, and although other such ventures were planned no other Lyceum Village ever appeared for any length of time.[12]

In the end, the true vitality of the American Lyceum lay in its local

11. *American Journal of Education*, I, 629–630; and *ibid.*, II (1827), 216.
12. H. O. Sheldon, *A Lecture . . . Upon the Lyceum System of Education, with Some Account of the First Lyceum Village, Berea, Ohio* (Cincinnati: Ephraim Morgan & Co., 1842), p. 4.

branches, which manifested all the diversity of the communities and subcommunities that sponsored them. Some lyceums, like the New Haven Institute, which was founded in August, 1826, as the Apprentices' Literary Association, were essentially workingmen's organizations; others, like the one at Kennebunk, Maine, grew out of reading circles or debating clubs and were thoroughly middle-class in orientation and composition. In cities such as New York, Baltimore, and Chicago, a variety of lyceums came into being to suit a variety of tastes: Chicago in the 1850's boasted a young men's association, a mechanics' institute, a literary union, and a phrenological society, all actively sponsoring lyceum programs and aggressively seeking audiences.

During the early years of the movement, lyceums tended to draw on their own resources for lectures and discussions or at most to reach out to neighboring communities. The most extraordinary instance must surely have been the lyceum at Concord, Massachusetts, which sponsored some 784 lectures, 105 debates, and 14 concerts during its early years, with 301 of the lectures delivered by local residents (98 by Emerson and 19 by Thoreau) and a number of the concerts performed by the local band. The debates traversed a wide range of questions, with the records indicating that over the years the lyceum decided that: (1) imprisonment for debt ought not to be abolished; (2) the immortality of the soul is taught by the light of nature; (3) the multiplicity of books is advantageous to society; (4) the morals of the people have improved; (5) the conferring of literary and scientific degrees upon women would not be desirable; (6) a dense population is more immoral than a scattered one; and (7) copyright ought to be available in the United States to foreign authors.

For all the pretension of some of these conclusions, they afford an important insight into what was probably the most fundamental contribution of the Lyceum of American life. The stated purpose of the organization varied from locality to locality and shifted over time, from Holbrook's initial notion of an agency for the diffusion of practical science that would also ally itself with the common school movement to a much broader institution for cultural and moral uplift, and from Holbrook's initial idea of an informal association for mutual instruction to a much more formal institution for the arrangement of series of lectures. Yet in the end the appeal of the Lyceum lay in the secular vision of the good life it proffered. Emerson liked to refer to the Lyceum as his "pulpit," and in so doing he symbolized the shift in the character of public teaching that was implicit in his own desertion of the Unitarian ministry for a career of lecturing and writing. Emerson's search for vocation corresponded with the rise of a new form of public education outside the church that he and others who trod the lyceum circuit helped to pioneer. It was popular in the same way the evangelical church was popular, in that it began with traditional material in traditional forms that then had to be cast in forms that new audiences coming into being would accept and respond to. As with the books that the Harper brothers published and the social libraries circulated, the substance tended to derive, not from theology, but rather from history, biography, science, and travel. Correspondingly, the goal of the learner was, not salvation, but rather some combination of entertainment and personal improvement. The challenge to the new public teachers was immense, for not only was there no captive audience, as with the established church, there was no traditional audience. "Here is a pulpit," Emerson wrote in his journal, "that makes other pulpits tame and ineffectual—with their cold mechanical preparation for a delivery the most decorous—fine things, pretty things, wise things, but no arrows, no axes, no nectar, no growling, no transpiercing, no loving, no enchantment. Here he must lay himself out utterly, large, enormous, prodigal, on the subject of the hour. Here he may hope for ecstasy and eloquence." [13]

The American Lyceum was itself significant in the cultural and educational life of the nation; but in a very real sense it was simply the largest and best organized of a more significant genre of educative institution that came into its own during the first half of the nineteenth century. There were societies, associations, and institutes of every sort, at which members of particular occupational groups sought improvement through systematic programs of lectures and discussions—farmers' institutes, mechanics' institutes, and teachers' institutes. There were also professional institutes, organized for the upgrading and mutual education of lawyers, physicians, and engineers and often tied to the more general forms of self-organization that marked the emergence of a spirit of professionalism. In addition, the institutes frequently spawned libraries, schools, and serial publications. Thus, the General Society of Mechanics and Tradesmen in New York organized the Mercantile Library there, the Franklin Institute in Philadelphia established a high school, and the Union Agricultural Society in Chicago published the *Prairie Farmer*. In the case of bar associations and medical societies, a

13. *Journals of Ralph Waldo Emerson*, edited by Edward Waldo Emerson and Waldo Emerson Forbes (10 vols.; Boston: Houghton Mifflin Company, 1909-1914), V, 281.

library, a training school, and a professional publication were often among the first activities undertaken. The tradition of voluntary association Tocqueville noted in the society at large was exceptionally strong in the realm of education: that tradition not only proved educative in its own right, it also spawned a host of other educative institutions. That they derived from voluntary effort was a hallmark of their character from the beginning, and indeed the same voluntary associations that organized them often undertook their supervision in the years after their initial creation, thus confirming their responsiveness to the publics that had brought them into being and that continued to provide their clienteles.

V

For all the breadth of the American Lyceum, as Holbrook initially conceived it and as it passed through its various incarnations, there was one theme that sounded fairly consistently through its activities over the several decades of its existence, namely, the effort to develop cabinets of plants, minerals, and other "natural or artificial productions" intended to explicate the wonders of science to the people at large. The theme represented more than yet another instance of Holbrook relentlessly purveying his own enthusiasms, in this instance, a collection of materials he had begun to manufacture in the 1820's known as the Holbrook School Apparatus. For the Holbrook School Apparatus was itself indicative of a far more fundamental element in the popular culture of the early national era—the stuff of Nature conceived as the handiwork of God. In a world that accepted as gospel the precepts of "Lord Bacon, the incomparable Mr. Newton, and the great Mr. Locke," the written and the oral word required as their complement the study of the Book of Nature. It should come as no surprise, therefore—indeed, it was absolutely symbolic—that, once Franklin's junto had actually established its library and stocked it with the books that would inform the junto's "conferences," the collection was soon expanded to include a fascinating range of scientific apparatus, fossils, and other curiosities, so that it became in effect a museum as well as a library and thereby a more complete instrument for the storing and diffusing of knowledge.[14]

The Philadelphia Library Company was not only symbolic in this respect, it was to a degree representative, since many personal and in-

14. [Josiah Holbrook], "The American Lyceum . . . ," *Old South Leaflets*, no. 139 (Boston: T. R. Marvin, 1829), p. 1; and *Autobiography*, 142.

stitutional libraries during the latter years of the eighteenth century deliberately supplemented their books with natural curiosa, usually of diverse origin and almost always of varying authenticity. In the process, some outstanding collections came into being. The Philadelphia botanist John Bartram preserved a vast number of shells, birds, insects, fish, and turtles alongside his books on natural history, and the resultant collection, along with the carefully planned botanical garden in which it was located, doubtless served as the scholarly basis of his own and his son William's scientific careers. The Philadelphia physician Caspar Wistar developed an admirable assemblage of specimens in the course of his work as a professor of anatomy, which subsequently became the basis of the anatomical museum at the University of Pennsylvania. And the New York botanist-physician David Hosack put together a remarkable cabinet of minerals, which he later presented to the College of New Jersey. During the 1750's, Harvard College began to develop the Repository of Curiosities that a century later became the basis of the University Museum in Cambridge. And in 1773 the Library Society of Charleston, taking into their consideration "the many advantages and great credit that would result," decided to collect materials for a full and accurate natural history of South Carolina, and established in the process the first institution in the American provinces actually open to the public as a museum.[15]

The Charleston museum did not flourish, and neither did those affiliated with the several colleges. They all lacked what seems to have held the key to successful museum development during the last years of the eighteenth century and first years of the nineteenth, an energetic entrepreneur with a passion for collecting and a flair for publicity. Three men did display those qualities to a remarkable degree, however, though in different balances and with different outcomes: Pierre Eugène Du Simitière, Charles Willson Peale, and Phineas Taylor Barnum. And the institutions they created tell us much about the character of the American museum during the early national era and the role it played in the larger education of the public.

Du Simitière's genius, however briefly it flared before his untimely death in 1784, consisted in his profound sense of the significance of the events through which he had lived in Revolutionary America, and in his determination to assemble the materials for a "natural and civil history" of his adopted country. A Swiss who came to America via the

15. *South Carolina Gazette and Country Journal,* March 30, 1773.

West Indies—he had arrived in New York in 1763 at the age of twenty-five—Du Simitière early displayed a penchant for collecting flora, fauna, and historical memorabilia and for supplementing them with his own paintings and engravings. Frustrated in an effort to win appointment as "Historiographer to the Congress of the United States"—a device to achieve the patronage he vainly sought all his life—he channeled his energies into creating an "American Museum" in his home on Arch Street in Philadelphia. The collection included everything from fossils, shells, snakes, and Indian relics to coins, catalogues, and broadsides illustrating the history of the recent Revolution, all supplemented by his own water color sketches of birds, plants, and other scenes of nature and engraved portraits of the new nation's dignitaries. It was, in effect, an effort to make natural and civil history live truthfully through their artifacts. Du Simitière opened the museum to the public in May, 1782, on the "encouragement of friends" and in the hope of turning a modest profit. Stimulated by word of mouth as well as tasteful newspaper items and broadsides, the museum flourished for a time, but for all intents and purposes died with its owner.[16]

Peale's effort was more formidable and more enduring. A native of Maryland who had studied portraiture with the English painter Benjamin West, Peale served in the Revolution as a military officer and in various civilian capacities; and it was in the course of his service, in 1777, that he began to paint miniature portraits of the colonial leaders—Washington, Nathanael Greene, the Marquis de Lafayette, and others. It soon occurred to Peale that he might someday create a gallery of portraits and thereby commemorate the war and its heroes, and in 1782 he constructed an exhibition room adjoining his home on Lombard Street in Philadelphia, which he opened "for the reception and entertainment of all lovers of the fine arts, being ornamented with the portraits of a great number of worthy personages." It was the gallery of portraits, enlarged, that became Peale's Museum, or, as he preferred it to be known, the Philadelphia Museum.[17]

In the summer of 1784, Peale was invited to make some drawings of a few mammoth bones, for transmission to a German scholar who had expressed interest in them; and while the relics were in his possession he put them on display in the gallery and discovered that they

16. Pierre Eugène Du Simitière to Thomas Wharton, August 18, 1777, in *Pennsylvania Archives*, 2d ser., III (1875), 121; and Du Simitière to Governor Clinton, November 27, 1782 (Letterbook, Du Simitière mss., Manuscript Division, Library of Congress, Washington, D.C.)

17. *Independent Gazetteer*, November 16, 1782.

were immensely attractive to visitors. The discovery marked a turning point in his conception of his exhibition. Henceforth, it would go beyond a memorializing of the late Revolution to become a world in miniature, a systematic, logical exposition of the entire order of nature. In the process, the "gallery" would become a "museum." The transformation came in two phases. Between 1784 and 1786, Peale devoted himself to developing a new technique of "moving pictures," which combined transparencies painted on glass with sound and lighting effects in such a way as to represent nature undergoing various changes. The scenes varied from a view of Market Street in Philadelphia at the dawn of a new day to a portrayal of the battle between the Bonhomme Richard and the Serapis. After 1786, the "moving pictures" receded into the background—they were reserved for private parties of twenty or more arranged in advance—and Peale resolved not only to enlarge the collection but to classify it according to a modified Linnaean system. His goal now combined rational amusement and systematic instruction, with the instruction focusing on natural forms in their natural contexts, all scientifically ordered. "Can the imagination conceive anything more interesting than such a museum?" he once observed. "Or can there be a more agreeable spectacle to an admirer of the divine Wisdom? Where, within a magnificent pile, every art and every science should be taught, by plans, pictures, real subjects and lectures. To this central magazine of knowledge, all the learned and indigenous would flock, as well as to gain, as to communicate, information."[18]

Once Peale had announced his aim of creating a world in miniature, contributions poured in from near and far, from strangers and friends—birds, snakes, fish, fossils, insects, beasts, minerals, and putrifactions. His exhibits soon burst out of the quarters he had constructed adjoining his home; but, as a member of the American Philosophical Society—he was elected in 1786—and as a curator of its collections, he was invited to move the exhibits to the newly completed Philosophical Hall in 1794. Eight years later, when the Pennsylvania capital was moved from Philadelphia to Lancaster, he obtained the right to display his exhibits in the vacated State House, which, along with the adjoining State House Yard, provided yet additional space. Meanwhile, the collections continued to burgeon, now including a menagerie of bears, monkeys, parrots, and an ancient eagle (whose likeness would later grace the flags and seals of the War Department), all of which roamed

18. Charles Willson Peale, *Discourse Introductory to a Course of Lectures on the Science of Nature* (Philadelphia: Zachariah Poulson, 1800), pp. 34–35.

the yard at will; a collection of machines demonstrating a variety of recent inventions and discoveries, especially the phenomenon of electricity; a standing skeleton of a mastadon, which Peale himself had constructed from bones he and others had unearthed in a dig near Newburgh, New York; numerous portraits of American worthies and assorted curiosities ranging from George Washington's sash to Oliver Cromwell's saltcellar. The sign over the main entrance proclaimed, "MUSEUM: GREAT SCHOOL OF NATURE"; while the sign seen from the yard read, "SCHOOL OF WISDOM: The book of nature open—explore the wondrous work, an institute of laws eternal."[19]

For a while Peale hoped for a public subsidy for his museum, but nothing of the sort was ever forthcoming beyond the space made available in the State House. From the time he opened the museum to the public in 1782 to the time he retired in favor of his sons in 1810, he was essentially a single entrepreneur. He advertised tastefully and well, continually expressing the hope that the "judgment of the candid public" would be favorable, and over the years his museum earned him a comfortable living. But in the delicate balance of instruction vis-à-vis entertainment, of teaching substance he considered valuable versus catering to the whims of his audience, Peale was ever the teacher. He published a catalogue, lectured incessantly (along with the members of his family), collected a library, labeled the specimens, and inscribed suitable quotations from Scripture on the walls; but it was the exhibits themselves that taught. For all their inevitable miscellany, they combined art, science, and history into a grand exposition of nature, in which the paintings represented landscapes, documented events, and portrayed people that were quite as "natural" as the bones, the artifacts, and the stuffed birds. Together, they exhibited the great harmony of life, the ordered law of man and things.[20]

Peale's Museum was widely known and much imitated during his own lifetime and after. In New York the American Museum, under the energetic direction of the amateur scientist Gardiner Baker, was founded in 1791 by the newly organized Tammany Society for "the sole purpose of collecting and preserving whatsoever may relate to the history of our country." It included a library, a menagerie, a waxworks, and a variety of "American curiosities," including a two-headed lamb from Brunswick, New Jersey, and a six-inch horn that was supposed to have

19. Charles Colman Sellers, *Charles Willson Peale* (2 vols.; Philadelphia: American Philosophical Society, 1947), II, 229.

20. *Pennsylvania Packet*, May 19, 1785.

grown out of a woman's head. By 1795 Tammany decided to forsake culture for politics, and the American Museum thereafter passed through the hands of a succession of owners, all of them more or less committed to some combination of natural history and public entertainment. By the 1830's, however, the Museum was at best a languishing institution, and no amount of ballyhoo on the part of the Scudder family, which controlled it at the time, seemed able to restore its fortunes.[21]

Meanwhile, Peale's own son Rembrandt established a museum on the Philadelphia model in Baltimore in 1814, and though it did not prosper financially it did thrive culturally. When one of Rembrandt's paintings, entitled *The Court of Death,* achieved a modest *succès d'estime* in 1822, however, he decided to return to his initial vocation as an artist and lease the Baltimore enterprise to his brother Rubens. Rubens enlarged the collection of natural history, but also added a gallery of paintings; a menagerie of wolves, elks, owls, and alligators; and a program of entertainment that featured performers like Signore Hellenne, who managed to play five different musical instruments at the same time, and Mr. Tilly, who specialized in blowing ornamental glass. In 1825, when the American Museum in New York appeared to be having a particularly bad year, Rubens moved to Manhattan and opened Peale's New York Museum as a direct challenge to the older institution. Rather than finish off the American Museum, however, Peale momentarily energized it, and the two competitors fought bitterly until Peale's Museum failed during the depression of 1837 and passed into receivership.

It was into this New York situation—of an American Museum that was languishing and a Peale's Museum in receivership—that the incomparable promoter Phineas Taylor Barnum moved in 1841. He had been born in Bethel, Connecticut, in 1810, to a family of modest means, and had engaged in a variety of pursuits intended, as he put it, to substitute headwork for handwork in the earning of a living. He had clerked in a store, owned his own business, sold lottery tickets, edited a newspaper, exhibited curiosities, among them an elderly black woman who claimed to be 161 years old and a former nurse to George Washington, and managed entertainment troupes—all of which had taught him much about the daily world of petty commerce and the mercurial character of public taste. Having relocated to New York in 1841, determined never again to be "an itinerant showman," he managed through

21. *New York Journal, & Patriotic Register,* May 25, 1791.

a series of shrewd financial maneuvers to acquire control of the American Museum and Peale's New York Museum. Within months, he had transformed them as The American Museum into the bustling institution that would propel him to world renown. The key would still be a passion for collecting combined with a flair for publicity; but the nature of the collecting, the character of the publicity, and the balance between the two would change dramatically.[22]

Barnum continued the permanent collection of specimens, machines, and paintings; they remained the core of the Museum and his continuing justification of its admission fee. But he vastly expanded and diversified what he called the "transient attractions" to include educated dogs, industrious fleas, jugglers, ventriloquists, gypsies, albinos, giants, dwarfs, rope dancers, singers, musicians, dioramas, panoramas, dissolving views, triumphs of the mechanic arts, and Indians who performed exotic war dances and religious ceremonies. And if on occasion he also exhibited a fake mermaid or a doctored transparency, they would provide, as he put it, a little "clap-trap" to offset "a wilderness of wonderful, instructive, and amusing realities."[23]

Having passionately collected this dazzling array of curiosities, Barnum spared no effort in keeping them relentlessly before the public. "It was my monomania," he later observed, "to make the Museum the town wonder and the town talk." Beyond the usual posters, broadsides, and advertisements, Barnum lavishly employed the staged events, the planted news stories, and the engineered controversies that excited public interest and sent people flocking to the Museum. In the process, of course, the conception of "curiosities" had changed, from labeled, classified, authenticated specimens of the rare and exotic to contrived efforts to titillate and astonish (Barnum himself labeled them "humbug"); publicity was delivered by a recently popularized press attempting to serve a newly won newspaper audience; and a fresh ingredient called "showmanship" had shifted the balance of the two from instruction with a modicum of entertainment to entertainment justified by a modicum of instruction. All the time-honored prejudice against the theatre could now be laid aside as the public flocked to a museum for its music and its dance. Later, in the 1870's, when Barnum created the circus with even less by way of specimens, machines, and paintings, it

22. *The Life of P. T. Barnum, Written by Himself* (London: Sampson Low, Son & Co., 1855), p. 193.
23. *Ibid.*, pp. 202, 203.

was considered the vehicle par excellence for the instruction and entertainment of the young.[24]

If Barnum's particular popularization of the Peale model was one development of the museum during the first half of the nineteenth century, the other was a significant differentiation in the interest of greater specialization. Peale, after all, had founded his collection on a conception of natural history as embracing all of art, history, and science. Others, by contrast, had decided to focus their efforts on more specific interests. Thus, the Reverend Jeremy Belknap and his associates founded the Massachusetts Historical Society in 1791 in order "to *seek* and *find,* to *preserve* and *communicate* literary intelligence, especially in the historical way"; while Belknap's friend John Pintard, who also had helped establish the Tammany-sponsored American Museum in 1791, took the lead in founding the New York Historical Society in 1804, dedicated to similar purposes. Meanwhile, the American Academy of Fine Arts was established in New York in 1802 to collect copies of European sculpture, architecture, and painting, in order, on the one hand, to perfect the genius of American artists and, on the other hand, to leaven the taste of the American public; Pennsylvania followed suit with a similar academy in 1805. And the Academy of Natural Sciences was founded in Philadelphia in 1812, with an initial collection of two thousand mineral specimens purchased for $750 and stored in the home of one of the members. Such institutions multiplied throughout the country during the early decades of the century, waxing and waning in their individual fortunes as patrons and small groups of subscribers paid them greater or lesser heed. Indeed, it was the fact of patronage that principally determined their special educative role, for they were less subject to the market as a decisive element in the shaping of their "curriculum" than to the taste of their patrons or subscribers. As in the contrast between private and subscription libraries, on the one hand, and circulating libraries, on the other, the balance between the taste of the sponsors and the taste of the clientele in determining the cultural fare proffered was different.[25]

As wealth became more available for patronage during the latter half of the century, as notions of public responsibility for the sponsor-

24. *Struggles and Triumphs or, Sixty Years' Recollections of P. T. Barnum* (Buffalo: The Courier Company, 1889), p. 57; and *Life of P. T. Barnum,* p. 203.

25. Jeremy Belknap to Ebenezer Hazard, February 19, 1791, in "Correspondence Between Jeremy Belknap and Ebenezer Hazard, Part II," Massachusetts Historical Society, *Collections,* 5th ser., III (1877), 245.

ship of art, history, and science engaged the wealthy, and as those notions of public responsibility were suffused with aspirations to national eminence, museums of another order and character became possible, symbolized by the virtually simultaneous establishment of three highly significant institutions: the American Museum of Natural History, the Metropolitan Museum of Art, and the Boston Museum of Fine Arts. Their real stories belong to a later era, but the conditions of their founding attest to the new conditions of the post-Civil War era. In the balance between the instruction of the public and its entertainment, they were created decisively to instruct—and indeed, where possible, to extend knowledge as well. In the balance between private patronage and public support, they were established with a mixture of philanthropic contributions and tax moneys that delivered them from the financial immediacies of the market. And in the balance between curricula determined by the tastes of their sponsors and curricula determined by the tastes of their clienteles, it was the tastes of the sponsors that prevailed, though, as Neil Harris has pointed out, the sponsors were far more mediators between a vernacular tradition in the arts and a genteel tradition than they were imposers of a genteel tradition.[26]

Emerson once defined the problem of a democratic civilization as that of providing "culture and inspiration for the citizen." The problem that he saw less clearly, because he was himself in the process of solving it, was the problem of what constitutes a masterpiece in a democracy. Peale, Barnum, and the trustees of the New York and Boston museums in the post-Civil War era proposed varying solutions to Emerson's problem, each involving a different definition of popularization. All would continue to compete for public favor into the twentieth century.[27]

VI

Museums were assumed to have some degree of permanence, though many of those that were actually established flourished for a time and then disappeared. Fairs and exhibitions were assumed in their very nature to be impermanent. They were associated with different aspects of the European tradition, the fair having had religious and commercial origins that dated from the Roman Empire, the exhibition having be-

26. Neil Harris, "The Gilded Age Revisited: Boston and the Museum Movement," *American Quarterly,* XIV (1962), 545–566.
27. Ralph Waldo Emerson, "Wealth," in *The Complete Works of Ralph Waldo Emerson* (12 vols.; Boston: Houghton, Mifflin and Company, 1903–1904), VI, 99.

gun in the displays of artistic works and manufactured products in early modern Italy and France. By the nineteenth century, however, fairs and exhibitions had come to resemble one another in certain aspects that made them important agencies in the education of the public. As collections of exhibits, they imparted information by calling on a variety of the senses. As competitive displays, they encouraged comparison according to standards of judgment that were frequently explicit. As celebrations of accomplishment, they encouraged self-confidence at the same time as they stimulated further aspiration. And, as special events, they interrupted routines, bringing not only recreation but frequently reflection as well. In a manner of speaking, fairs and exhibitions were temporary museums, offering similar appeal and based on similar didactic principles; and, in fact, when New York's Crystal Palace Exhibition closed in 1853, having sustained considerable financial losses owing to inadequate planning and gross mismanagement, none other than P. T. Barnum was called in to revive it (his reluctant conclusion was that "the dead could not be raised").[28]

The earliest fairs on the North American Continent had been colonial market fairs, intended primarily to facilitate commerce but also to make possible amusements such as horseracing, competitive sports, and entertainment by troupes of traveling performers. These market fairs had all but vanished by the time of the Revolution, owing largely to the improvement of communication and transportation in the provincial era. In their place, there appeared during the first decades of independence a series of fairs sponsored by the gentlemen's agricultural societies that sprang up along the eastern seaboard from Kennebec, Maine, to Charleston, South Carolina. Modeled after the societies established by the eighteenth-century English gentry to improve agriculture through the encouragement of experiment and the dissemination of scientific information, these organizations were composed of an elite of well-educated gentlemen farmers interested in "scientific" farming. As one of their varied activities, they sponsored fairs from time to time, at which premiums were offered for everything from first-quality livestock to first-quality homespun and at which the prize-winning animals and products might then be sold. These fairs were marked by the usual gaiety and amusement, but they also came to involve a spirited patriotism, since the improvement of domestic manufacture, especially of cloth, was a prime plank in the nationalist platform.

28. *Barnum's Own Story: The Autobiography of P. T. Barnum,* edited by Waldo R. Browne (New York: Viking Press, 1927), p. 262.

The gentlemen's agricultural societies and the fairs they sponsored attracted the attention of a wide variety of merchants, lawyers, ministers, and physicians, and even a few presidents of the Republic, all of whom professed interest in the improvement of agriculture. But they attracted very few dirt farmers. It was only after both the societies and the fairs were reconceived by Elkanah Watson during the early 1800's that they became more popular instruments of agricultural education. A talented and energetic businessman who had made and lost several fortunes by the time he was fifty, Watson decided in 1807 to seek the satisfactions of "rural felicity." He purchased a substantial farm near Pittsfield, Massachusetts, and resolved to run it according to the best principles of English scientific agriculture. As a beginning, he acquired a pair of Merino sheep, prized for the quality of their wool, and set about persuading his neighbors of the wisdom of doing likewise. In what was surely a promotional effort, he decided one day to display the sheep in the public square at Pittsfield. As he recounted the event, "Many farmers, and even women, were excited by curiosity to attend this first novel, and humble exhibition. It was by this lucky accident, I reasoned thus,—If two animals are capable of exciting so much attention, what would be the effect on a larger scale, with larger animals? The farmers present responded to my remarks with approbation." Thus was born, at least in the recollection of its creator, the idea of the modern agricultural fair.[29]

Three years later, having tirelessly urged the superiority of scientific breeding in general and Merino sheep in particular, Watson joined with twenty-six of his neighbors to announce the Berkshire Cattle Show, which quickly became an annual event; the following year, in 1811, he and his associates organized the Berkshire Agricultural Society, which immediately assumed the sponsorship of the Cattle Show. Thereafter, the show, which was subsequently relabeled an agricultural fair, grew by accretion, becoming in the process the chief activity of the Society. The displays were broadened to include other agricultural products and domestic manufactures as well. The premiums were increased in size and extended to other categories. Patriotic and religious oratory was added to lend dignity to the affair, while marches, processions, and dances were added to lend festivity. Correspondingly, mem-

---

29. Elkanah Watson, *History of the Rise, Progress, and Existing Conditions of the Western Canals in the State of New-York . . . , Together with the Rise, Progress, and Existing State of Modern Agricultural Societies on the Berkshire System, from 1807, to . . . 1820* (Albany: D. Steele, 1820), pp. 115, 116.

bership in the Society was made as attractive as possible to working farmers, and attendance at its fair was made as attractive as possible to all their kin, female and male, young and old. In the end, however, everything remained instrumental to Watson's central purpose, namely, to educate farmers to the need for agricultural improvement through the application of scientific principles. Entertainment might enhance the experience, but it was the exhibits that gave it meaning; it was the exhibits that would teach the farmer to change his ways.

Characteristically, Watson became the indefatigable proponent of agricultural societies organized on the "Berkshire plan": he wrote letters and pamphlets, traveled widely, and gave innumerable addresses, seeking to stimulate the organization of new societies and the transformation of older ones. Under his incessant prodding and with a modicum of state support, a movement flourished for a time, peaked during the early 1820's, and then waned, remaining dormant until the availability of additional state aid brought a flurry of new activity during the 1840's and 1850's. But the agricultural fair in the form that Watson created it became a permanent feature of American life, playing a critical role not only in the continuing education of the American farmer but also in the successive transformations of American agriculture in which education also played a significant part.

The fair, then, was a distinctively rural institution in nineteenth-century America, centrally concerned with the improvement of local agriculture. The exhibition, by contrast, was characteristically urban; and, while it concerned itself with the fine arts from time to time, it came increasingly in the popular mind to be associated with the industrial arts and, more generally, with the spirited competition among nations for industrial preeminence. Industrial exhibitions were fairly common occurrences in the cities of early nineteenth-century Europe, although they tended to be local or at most national in scope. But, in 1851, with the mounting of the great London Exhibition of the Industry of All the Civilized Nations of the World, or the Crystal Palace Exhibition, as it was popularly referred to, there was an important change in the nature of the phenomenon. That exhibit was a truly remarkable enterprise, developed under the sponsorship of Prince Albert and a distinguished royal commission, actively supported in Parliament, and conducted on a scale unprecedented in history; it was, quite literally, the biggest show the world had ever seen. It was housed in a huge rectangular building of glass hung on an iron frame—whence the name Crystal Palace—that provided 800,000 square feet of floor space; it presented an unprecedented number of exhibits—almost 14,000, of which almost half were non-British; and by the time it closed its doors in the autumn of 1851, over 6 million people had visited the pavilion. On top of all these superlatives, it even managed to turn a financial profit.

Americans were not pleased with their country's participation in the London Exhibition. Despite an early hope that the display of American industrial products there would afford Europeans "a juster appreciation and a more perfect knowledge of what this Republic is, than could be attained in any other way," Congress would not appropriate money in support of the venture, leaving American participation to private enterprise. In the end there were 560 American exhibits, ranging from artificial legs to chewing tobacco and including a McCormick reaper, a Prouty and Mears draft plow, a Singer sewing machine, a Morse telegraph, and a Colt revolver, all of which worked admirably. The general utility and mass appeal of these products, often referred to as "American 'notions'," was readily noticed by the British, who concluded that the fruits of American industry could no longer be ignored. "Great Britain has received more useful ideas, and more ingenious inventions, from the United States, through the exhibition, than from all other sources," the London Times duly observed.[30]

If the British learned much from the Crystal Palace Exhibition about American ingenuity, the Americans learned much about the educational value of exhibitions. A group of promoters in New York promptly set about creating an American Crystal Palace Exhibition that would "make a more just and equally sustained exposition of our resources, industry, and arts" than the one recently proffered at London and at the same time "give the masses in America an opportunity to see and compare the manifold productions and applications of the arts of design from abroad." Acting as a joint stock company, they obtained a state charter as an "Association for the Exhibition of the Industry of All Nations" and a city lease for the use of Reservoir Square at 42nd Street and Fifth Avenue (the current site of the New York Public Library), and proceeded to solicit the support of foreign governments. The response was encouraging, but from the beginning the venture was dogged with difficulty. The building was poorly constructed

---

30. *Journal of the Great Exhibition of 1851: Its Origin, History, and Progress* (London: J. Crockford, 1851), p. 141; and *Report of Benj. P. Johnson, Agent for the State of New-York, Appointed to Attend the Exhibition of the Industry of All Nations, Held in London, 1851* (Albany: C. Van Benthuysen, 1852), p. 15.

and not completed on schedule, delaying the opening of the exhibition from May until July. The collecting of exhibits was badly organized. And the finances were mismanaged, leading to considerable losses on the part of the sponsors and many of the participants. Yet, granted these failures, the exhibition provided an incomparable experience for Americans. There were some five thousand exhibits, ranging from surgical instruments to naval ordnance, of which about half were contributed by twenty-three foreign countries. And about a million and a quarter people visited the displays, while a flood of illustrated promotion and reporting carried the "lessons" of the displays to countless others who could not attend personally.[31]

For all its inadequacies, the memory of the New York exhibition lingered on; and, when the time came to develop a suitable means of marking the centennial of the Declaration of Independence in 1876, an international exhibition seemed appropriate. It would nurture international understanding, it would stimulate trade and commerce, it would reunite the nation after a brutal civil war, and it would generally advance the cause of peace. But, most important of all, it would teach the world about the United States—the strength of its people, the character of its ingenuity, and the durability of its institutions. "The great and immediate functions of exhibitions are to stimulate and educate," observed William P. Blake in an address to the Centennial Commission in 1872.

They act, not only upon the industrial classes, but upon all classes of men. They increase as well as diffuse knowledge. By bringing together and comparing the results of human effort, new germs of thought are planted, new ideas are awakened, and new inventions are born. They mark eras in industrial art, and give opportunities to compare the relative progress of nations. In their full scope and meaning they are by no means confined to the exhibition of natural and manufactured products, machines, and processes; but they include all that illustrates the relations of men to each other and to the world in which we live, all products of human thought and activity in all the arts and all the sciences.[32]

Given the New York experience, planning for the centennial exhibition was begun early and well. Congress created a national commission representing all the states and territories to manage the enterprise, and Philadelphia's Fairmount Park was chosen as the site. President

31. William P. Blake, *Great International Expositions: Their Objects, Purposes, Organization, and Results* (Philadelphia: E. C. Markley & Son, 1872), p. 4.

32. *Ibid.*, p. 3.

Grant issued a proclamation setting the precise time the exhibition would be held (April 19 to October 19, 1876), and formal invitations to foreign governments to participate were issued by the secretary of state (thirty-five eventually accepted). In place of the single massive structure made popular by the London Exhibition of 1851, there were 167 buildings on the 236-acre site, which housed some 30,000 exhibits. In the end, more than 8 million people attended, breaking all previous records for international exhibitions.

There is no describing the kaleidoscope of sounds, images, and impressions that greeted visitors to the Centennial, as it came to be known. The buildings themselves must surely have been the strangest collection ever assembled in America, with minarets standing by Gothic towers and Swiss chalets. The Main Building housed the principal exhibits of manufactured products and of educational and scientific activity, together with a large number of displays portraying life in foreign countries. In Machinery Hall, the huge Corliss engine offered a breathtaking vision of power and efficiency. "It rises loftily in the centre of the huge structure," William Dean Howells wrote in the *Atlantic Monthly*, "an athlete of steel and iron with not a superfluous ounce of metal on it; the mighty walking-beams plunge their pistons downward, the enormous fly-wheel revolves with a hoarded power that makes all tremble, the hundred life-like details do their office with unerring intelligence." Agricultural Hall housed sugar-cured hams, plug tobacco, dried fruit, and cases of California silkworms at work, alongside plows, drills, reapers, and threshing machines—Howells thought it "the most exclusively American." Horticulture Hall included a conservatory full of rare tropical trees, forcing houses featuring exotic ferns and shrubs, rooms full of greenhouse equipment, and an outside ornamental garden. Memorial Hall presented admirable collections of sculpture, painting, engraving, photography, and crafts by foreign and American artists. And the United States Government Building housed displays illustrating the work of the various federal agencies, an impressive assortment of military hardware, and the working post office of the exhibition. Beyond these principal structures, there was the Woman's Building, "devoted exclusively to the exhibition of the results of woman's labor"; there were the several structures representing foreign and state governments; and there were the numerous special institutions— the Brewer's Hall, the Butter and Cheese Factory, the Singer Sewing Machine Cottage, the Campbell Printing Press Building, and the like.

And, beyond the standing exhibitions, one might encounter on any given day concerts, dances, regattas, livestock shows, state celebrations, fireworks displays, and athletic tournaments.[33]

If the kaleidoscope of impressions is difficult to conjure, the range of effects is even more so. "The culture obtained by the millions of our people who have found in the fair a mine of information and suggestion, must have a beneficial effect upon the national character," wrote James D. McCabe in his illustrated history of the Centennial.

A tour through the halls and grounds was like a journey around the world, giving an insight into the life and thought of all manner of men, and lifting the visitor above the narrow limits of his surroundings, so that his horizon stretched out to embrace the whole human race. . . . Apart from this general and cosmopolitan culture in which all participated, each found valuable fruits of knowledge adapted to his own need. The farmer saw new machines, seeds, and processes; the mechanic, ingenious inventions and tools, and products of the finest workmanship; the teacher, the educational aids and systems of the world; the man of science, the wonders of nature and the results of the investigations of the best brains of all lands. Thus each returned to his home with a store of information available in his own special trade or profession."[34]

McCabe's rhetoric had a substantial touch of the ceremonial, but it also conveyed a kernel of truth. In the extent to which visitors came prepared to see, the exhibition demonstrated. Moreover, it frequently demonstrated actively rather than passively. The Corliss engine was running, and the kindergarten in the Women's Schoolhouse was in operation three days a week. One could actually taste the Turkish coffee and the German wine, and one could even send a telegram. In addition, there were often lecturers to explain what was going on: Alexander Graham Bell personally demonstrated his electric telephone, as did Thomas A. Edison his American Automatic Telegraph. And, beyond the lectures, there were the prizes and the premiums with their messages concerning standards of judgment; they, too, were often systematically explained by the judges. Finally, beyond the exhibits, the activities, and the prizes, there were the visitors themselves on display to one another—villagers experiencing urbanites, Californians experiencing New Yorkers, Americans experiencing foreigners, and vice versa. That

33. William Dean Howells, "A Sennight of the Centennial," *Atlantic Monthly*, XXXVIII (1876), 96; and James D. McCabe, *The Illustrated History of the Centennial Exhibition* (Philadelphia: Jones Brothers & Co., 1876), p. 589.
34. McCabe, *Illustrated History*, pp. 852–853.

experience later remembered and pondered must surely have been as educative in its own right as the experience of the exhibits themselves.

One last point bears comment. However extensive its audience and its appeal, the Centennial also popularized in the very way it defined its displays. It was first and foremost an exhibition of the applied arts. Memorial Hall quite appropriately displayed the fine arts of painting, sculpture, and engraving; but the remaining 166 buildings and the spaces between them celebrated the arts of everyday life in an industrializing society. In the presentation of this vernacular, the gaucherie of a huge ceramic portraying America astride a bison was juxtaposed with the functional beauty of the Corliss engine. But that very juxtaposing transformed the curriculum of public education, the universe of things and ideas worth knowing, judging, and appreciating.

Chapter 10

LEARNING AND LIVING

It is esteemed a figure of rhetoric to say that a man is educated by his trade or calling, but a more solid or agreeable fact we cannot find.

RALPH WALDO EMERSON

Throughout the first century of its existence, the United States remained a nation of farmers, although the percentage of Americans actually engaged in farming and the character of farm life and work changed dramatically. During the 1780's and 1790's, the vast majority of Americans lived on family farms that were relatively self-sufficient, in that each family produced essentially what it needed to live—food, clothing, furniture, soap, candles, and even farm implements. True, there were cash crops of grain in the Connecticut Valley and the Middle Atlantic states, and of tobacco in the South, but even in those regions the relatively self-sufficient farm predominated. True, too, there were significant numbers of people engaged in fishing, milling, tanning, lumbering, iron making, and shipbuilding, but even some of those carried on their labors in connection with some kind of farm. By the 1860's and 1870's, the percentage of the labor force engaged in agricultural pursuits had declined to just over a half, as growing numbers of Americans had moved into manufacturing and construction, trade and transportation, mining, education, and other services. Moreover, farming itself had been transformed, and, although the rhetoric of the self-sufficient family farm as the bedrock of American freedom persisted, the reality of the mechanized farm producing a cash crop for the market was more and more the rule. In effect, the Centennial Exhibition of 1876 taught Americans about themselves as much as it taught foreigners about America. The reapers and threshers and steam engines and

335

knitting machines announced a transformation that was well under way and that had already profoundly altered American life and education.

II

During the early years of the Republic, most of what a boy or a girl needed to know to share in the maintenance of a farm continued to be learned via the informal processes of apprenticeship within the family. The essential pedagogy was the oldest in the world—a combination of exemplification, demonstration, explanation, oversight, criticism, and suggestion on the part of the more experienced, and of imitation, observation, trial, assistance, practice, inquiry, and listening on the part of the neophyte. Boys helped their fathers (or older brothers) and girls helped their mothers (or older sisters), in order both to contribute to the family's subsistence and to learn the knowledge and skills they would need to sustain themselves as adults. Gender-related job distinctions differed from one ethnic group to another and from region to region, though men tended to do the plowing and women the cooking. The division of labor was neither sacred nor inflexible, however, and when all hands were needed to complete a planting or a harvesting in the face of oncoming rain, every able-bodied individual planted or harvested. On occasion, boys or girls might also serve their apprenticeships in the households of more distant kin or of non-kin, possibly for some minimal wage; but they did so without formal legal arrangement, the imported English institution of apprenticeship to husbandry having fallen into disuse during the provincial era, when chronic shortages of labor made such arrangements unenforceable.

The knowledge and skills transmitted under this system of informal apprenticeship were considerable. A competent farmer needed to know about the management of crops, the care of livestock, the control of pests, the storage of grain, the butchering of animals, the repair of agricultural implements, and the maintenance of houses and barns. A competent farm woman needed to know about the care and cultivation of a vegetable garden, the management of a chicken coop and beehives, the preparation and preservation of foods, and the manufacture of cloth and clothing. Given the extent of crossover in vocational roles and tasks, each had to know much about the work of the other; and together they shared the rearing of children, the care of the sick, and the burial of the dead. To be sure, there were books that codified and systematized much of this knowledge—one thinks immediately of the two-volume anony-

mous work, *American Husbandry,* that appeared in London in 1775—
and there were usually neighbors with whom to compare ideas. But the
extent to which the processes of informal education for competent life
on a farm went on within the household was prodigious.

For all the information and skill that were transmitted from one
generation to the next, American farming was far from efficient during
the latter years of the eighteenth century, a fact commonly noted by
thoughtful observers. The economist Tench Coxe, in a commentary
published in 1794, remarked the inattention to proper fertilization; the
indifference to the quality of seed grain; the poor condition of barns,
stables, and fences; the neglect of orchards; and the general exhaustion
of farmlands in the Middle Atlantic states. A decade later John Taylor
of Caroline wrote poignantly of whole Virginia counties that had once
produced vast quantities of tobacco but that had become so impoverished in the process as to yield nothing of value, not even the wheat
that had been substituted for tobacco. And President Timothy Dwight
of Yale, ever partisan to New England, noted with sadness the general
inferiority of the region's farms: "The principal defects in our husbandry, so far as I am able to judge, are a deficiency in the quantity of labor, necessary to prepare the ground for seed, insufficient manuring,
the want of a good rotation of crops, and slovenliness in cleaning the
ground. The soil is not sufficiently pulverized, nor sufficiently ma-
nured. We are generally ignorant of what crops will best succeed each
other, and our fields are covered with a rank growth of weeds."[1]

It was this sense of scientific and technological backwardness—or at
least thoughtlessness—that led to the organization of the first so-called
gentlemen's agricultural societies that sought to publicize British scientific techniques among American farmers and secure their adoption.
The gentlemen spoke enthusiastically and scientifically, but largely to
one another, with the result that little was accomplished by way of reform. The problem of American agriculture remained one in which an
informal apprenticeship system worked rather efficiently to transmit an
inefficient agricultural technology from one generation to the next.
What changed matters markedly during the early years of the nineteenth century and created the need for a different kind of education

---

1. Tench Coxe, *A View of the United States of America* (Philadelphia: William Hall, and
Wrigley & Berriman, 1794), pp. 358–359; John Taylor, *Arator; Being a Series of Agricultural Essays, Practical & Political* (2d ed.; Georgetown, D. C.: J. M. Carter, 1814), pp. 11–15; and Timothy Dwight, *Travels in New England and New York* (1821–22), edited by Barbara Miller Solomon (3 vols.; Cambridge, Mass.: Harvard University Press, 1969), I, 76.

was the fundamental shift in the farmer's economic situation. The development of overseas markets in Europe and of domestic markets in the burgeoning cities of the East began to hasten the movement from subsistence to commercial agriculture and with it the motivation for more efficient farming. American farmers suddenly wanted knowledge that had been available for a half-century. What became necessary was a supplementary educational system that would substitute new principles and new technologies for some of those being conveyed by traditional informal apprenticeship.

Elkanah Watson's Berkshire societies, with their emphasis on the annual fair as a combination of education and entertainment, were one element in the new system. Watson boasted that his societies were more democratic than the gentlemen's societies and that his broadened sponsorship, coupled with the more effective pedagogy of the fair, provided the basis of their success. But there were two additional elements in their success, both of them economic in character. First, membership in the societies increased and broadened because small subsistence farmers, given the prospect of good returns for cash crops, had new incentive to participate: they had incentive to support the education of the fair and to pay heed to that education when it was proffered. Second, state governments supported the program once it became apparent that large numbers of farmers might be interested and large-scale economic returns to agriculture might be in the offing for modest investments in education. Elkanah Watson's pedagogy was quite as novel and effective as he claimed it to be, but one aspect of its effectiveness was the rise of incentive for his clients.

If Elkanah Watson's societies provided one element of the new educational system, the agricultural press provided another. Watson himself was actually quite skeptical concerning printed materials as instruments for the education of the farmer, contending that they were in their very nature elitist and hence ineffectual. He thought the immediacy of a fair was what the farmer really wanted and needed. Others, however, were more sanguine about print, believing that materials addressed directly to the farmer and his problems could serve as important teachers. One such individual was the Reverend David Wiley, a Presbyterian minister who served as principal of the Columbian Academy at Georgetown, D.C. An alumnus of the College of New Jersey, who enjoyed supplementing his teaching with activities as postmaster, surveyor, miller, merchant, and scientist, Wiley was secretary of the Columbian Agricultural Society for the Promotion of Rural and Domestic Economy; and it was in connection with his efforts on behalf of the Society that he founded the *Agricultural Museum* in the summer of 1810. The semimonthly periodical was scientifically sound and up to date, but somewhat formal and technical in character. It never enjoyed a wide circulation among farmers or anyone else, and, so far as can be determined, it ceased to appear in 1812; but it did herald a genre that would significantly increase farmers' access to specialized yet practical knowledge.

The first continuing scientific periodical addressed to the farmer that actually reached larger numbers of farmers was the *American Farmer,* founded by John Stuart Skinner as an eight-page weekly in 1819 at a subscription rate of four dollars per year. A Marylander, expert in the law, who served as postmaster of Baltimore from 1816 to 1837, Skinner became aware of the exhausted condition of the state's soil and established his journal for the express purpose of developing a scientifically based agriculture. "The great aim, and the chief pride, of the *'American Farmer,'* " he announced, "will be, to collect information from every source, on every branch of husbandry, thus to enable the reader to study the various systems which experience has proved to be the best, under given circumstances; and in short, to put him in possession of that knowledge and skill in the exercise of his means, without which the best farm and the most ample materials, will remain but as so much *dead capital* in the hands of the proprietor." For eleven years, until he sold the magazine for twenty thousand dollars in 1830, Skinner published first-class material on field crop cultivation, horticulture, the uses of fertilizer, soil chemistry, and agricultural machinery. He carried writings by Thomas Jefferson, James Madison, John Taylor, Timothy Pickering, and John C. Calhoun. He conducted a vigorous correspondence that made his editorial office a clearinghouse for the latest theories and practices, and he shared the results with his readers in a lively question and answer column. He reported new inventions and labor-saving devices and kept his readers up to date on rural sports, internal improvements, and domestic economy. And he encouraged informative advertising, printed occasional jokes and poems, and started a "Ladies Department" in an attempt to attract whole familes of readers. Such efforts clearly proved fruitful, as evidenced by the fact that the journal had fifteen hundred subscriptions by its third year and doubtless many times that number by its eleventh, given the substantial sum that Skinner received for it.[2]

Skinner's was the first of scores of similar periodicals. Solomon

2. *American Farmer,* I (1819), 6.

Southwick founded the *Plough Boy* in Albany, New York, two months after the first issue of the *American Farmer* was published; Thomas Green Fessenden founded the *New England Farmer* in Boston in 1822; and Edmund Ruffin founded the *Farmer's Register* in Shellbanks, Virginia, in 1833. By the time of the Civil War, at least four hundred had been established, of which some fifty to sixty were still active, with a combined circulation in the neighborhood of a quarter million. As with all contemporary periodicals, they tended to reflect the interests and personalities of their editors. They were openly didactic, advising their readers on everything from how to rear children to how to vote on impending legislation. And they were unabashedly personal: the *American Farmer* described Skinner's travels through the country; the *New England Farmer* manifested Fessenden's abiding interest in horticulture (in fact, the Massachusetts Horticultural Society originated from a discussion in his office); the *Cultivator* conveyed Jesse Buel's unshakable faith in agricultural schools; and the *American Agriculturist* revealed the Allen brothers' abiding distaste for "rank humbugs." Yet these very qualities contributed to their popularity. They reached hundreds of thousands of farm families on a regular basis; and, though they doubtless purveyed a good deal of misinformation and folk nonsense, they contributed significantly to the diffusion of new knowledge and new techniques among American farmers. As Ruffin observed in a widely quoted lecture in 1851, "Notwithstanding all the existing obstacles and difficulties, American agriculture has made greater progress in the last thirty years, than in all previous time. This greater progress is mainly due to the diffusion of agricultural papers. In the actual absence of all other means, these publications, almost alone, have rendered good service in making known discoveries in the science, and spreading knowledge of improvements in the art of agriculture." Ruffin, of course, was not a disinterested commentator, having himself edited a distinguished agricultural journal for years, and his observation partook of the same partiality as Watson's concerning agricultural societies; but he had indeed captured an essential truth about the role of the press in popularizing the new scientific agriculture. Moreover, beyond the information they conveyed, the farm journals persistently advised their readers to seek additional means of continuing their education, recommending books, pamphlets, and almanacs; urging the formation of reading clubs and experimenting societies; and encouraging attendance at lectures, lyceums, and fairs.[3]

3. *American Agriculturist*, IV (1845), 335; and *Cultivator*, new ser., VIII (1851), 91–92.

The third element in the new educational system consisted of formal instruction in agriculture given in schools, academies, institutes, and colleges. This form of instruction reached those few with more systematic and reliable knowledge and was likely to lead to additional experiment and inquiry, to the adaptation of tested knowledge to specific situations, and to the development of new knowledge. The Gardiner Lyceum, established in Maine in 1821, offered instruction in a variety of subjects "to practical men however employed" (especially farmers and mechanics), the goal being to make them "skillful in their occupations." The Rensselaer Institute, founded in New York in 1824, offered instruction in chemistry, botany, and zoology and sponsored teaching demonstrations of agricultural techniques and the use of fertilizer in the cultivation of vegetables. And Michigan Agricultural College was founded in 1855 via legislation directing that the chief purpose and design of the institution be to improve and teach the science and practice of agriculture. Meanwhile, agricultural professorships, agricultural programs, and agricultural courses appeared in countless academies, colleges, and universities, on a more or less permanent basis; and, though it would be a half-century before the substance of the study of agriculture would be systematized and codified, the combination of formal courses with work on a demonstration farm was clearly in evidence by the 1850's. When the Morrill Act was passed in 1862, making available the wherewithal for a college of agriculture in every state, it merely nationalized the trend toward some combination of formal schoolwork directed to the advancement of a scientifically based agriculture that had been developing over forty years. Later, under the aegis of the Morrill institutions, the fair, the press, and the college would be joined to form an organized system of education with the express purpose of continually improving American agriculture. But that linking would itself require as much imagination and ingenuity as the initial creation of the several discrete elements.[4]

A final point bears comment. The new agricultural education affected farming most profoundly in the North and the West, and in those parts of the pre-Civil War South where family farms and free labor prevailed. It was less influential in the region dominated by the large slave plantation. However interested the owners may have been in a more scientific and rational agriculture, any aspirations they might have harbored in that direction ultimately had to contend with the stubborn realities of the slave system. Early in the century John Taylor of

4. *American Journal of Education*, II (1827), 216.

Caroline described slavery as "a misfortune to agriculture incapable of removal, and only within the reach of palliation"; and, however much the slaveowners tried to ignore or transcend the misfortune, they were generally aware of it. It tied the region to a one-crop system of commercial staples that would provide maximum returns to cultivation by large numbers of unskilled human beings. The one-crop system in turn prevented a desirable rotation of crops, necessitating reclamation of the land by costly fertilizers, for which funds were never available, owing to the cost of feeding the unskilled laborers. And the unskilled laborers proved unadept in any case at applying fertilizer or using machines or introducing any of the dozens of other fundamental reforms from improved tillage to more effective drainage that were at the heart of the new agriculture.[5]

But adeptness in the last analysis was not really the issue. The plantation owners were committed to the slave system; and, while they were willing to sell a few slaves from time to time to obtain the capital to buy much-needed fertilizer, their commitment to maintaining the system sharply limited their options. They were unwilling on the one hand to dispose of their slaves and unwilling on the other hand to permit them sufficient education to make them economically efficient in the face of northern and western competition. And the slaves, in turn, were scarcely inspired to learn. Neither the owners nor the slaves had the economic incentive that fueled the new agricultural education in the North and West. The owners were more committed to a way of life than to rational agricultural production, and so indeed were the slaves, who, in maintaining their own pace and resisting efforts toward rationalization, merely demonstrated their own commitment to values and concepts of dignity that were not in the control of the masters. In this realm as in others, the slaves were proffered one curriculum but learned another, which they themselves valued, constructed, and taught.

III

The agricultural economy of the 1780's and 1790's included a household-handicraft-mill complex that accounted for most of the manufacturing of the early Republic. Within this complex, household manufacture was far and away the leading source of production: the farm family made an astonishing portion of the goods it needed, from soap to candles to clothing to furniture to hoes and rakes and scythes. It was

5. Taylor, *Arator*, p. 57.

production for use rather than sale, it drew upon raw materials produced on the farm, and it rested for its perpetuation from one generation to the next on the same system of informal apprenticeship that pertained in the more general realm of agricultural production.

Alongside household manufacture was the production of craftsmen
and mills. In smaller and newer communities, blacksmiths, cobblers,
coopers, and tailors would join a farm household from time to time, in
the fashion of traditional journeymen, and practice their arts with materials produced by the family. In larger and older communities, such
artisans would set up shop, either in concert with a farm they themselves managed, or independently. The burden of their effort went into
"bespoke" work, specially ordered by individual customers, although in
their free time they might also manufacture products for future sale. In
addition, there was the production associated with gristmills, sawmills,
papermills, breweries, tanneries, brickyards, and ironworks, usually
run by merchant or artisan entrepreneurs, occasionally, once again, as
supplements to farms or shops. Such establishments were ordinarily
small in size and local in operation. They tended to draw upon neighborhood sources for their raw materials and to serve neighborhood
markets with their finished products. There were exceptions, to be
sure: the distilleries of New England and the tar kilns of the Carolinas
served national and even international markets, but they were very
much departures from the rule.

The arts and mysteries practiced in these shops, mills, and "manufactories" were perpetuated through a more formal system of apprenticeship that had developed during the colonial era. It involved a formal
contract between a youngster (most often a boy, occasionally a girl), a
master craftsman or tradesman, and the youngster's parent(s) or guardian. The most important elements in the contract were the youngster's
promise to serve the master in all lawful commands and capacities over
a stipulated period of time and the master's promise in turn to teach
the youngster the arts and mysteries associated with a particular craft
or trade. Other elements that were often embodied in the contract included some sort of payment in cash or kind during the period of the
apprenticeship or at the time of its conclusion and sundry agreements
on the part of the master to provide food, clothing, schooling, or other
appurtenances to the youngster during the course of the apprenticeship.
Whereas such contracts had been registered with the town or county
authorities during the early part of the eighteenth century, that formality had tended to disappear by the time of the Revolution.

The sustained embargos of the early nineteenth century, followed as they were by the War of 1812, put a premium on household manufacture. It rose dramatically for a time, peaking around 1815. Thereafter, it fell off fairly rapidly in the Northeast, with the decline becoming more general during the 1840's and 1850's (it survived longest on the frontier, where the absence of transportation threw settlers onto their own resources of skill and material, and on large southern slave plantations, where owners tried to exploit their oversupply of labor as fully as possible). Simultaneously, there was an enlargement of shop production, an extension for a time of domestic or putting-out arrangements, and the beginning of the factory system. All these developments had prodigious consequences for apprenticeship, and more generally for the ways in which Americans prepared themselves and were prepared to enter upon the work that would gain them their livelihood.

Insofar as shops expanded in size but persisted in character, apprenticeship remained the most common form of craft training. The printshop provides a useful example. Milton W. Hamilton's study of the country printer in New York State between 1785 and 1830 reveals that the traditional chapel, or local unit of the ancient printers' guild, continued vigorously in its teaching of the customs and rules of the craft as well as in the support it lent to established modes of vocational entrance and instruction. Boys aspiring to become printers generally entered upon their apprenticeship at the age of fourteen or fifteen (though the age varied from seven to eighteen at the extremes) via a formal contract signed by the boy, the master printer, and the parent or guardian. During the nineteenth century, it became customary to provide a modest compensation to the boy—twenty-five to forty dollars seems to have been the rule by the 1840's. The traditional term of apprenticeship was seven years, but most contracts specified five or six and many boys served fewer; the same shortage of labor and prevalence of opportunity that made long apprenticeships difficult to enforce in the provincial era persisted into the national era. The ordinary duties of an apprentice ranged from the household chores that the printer's natural children might perform to the running of errands and the delivery of newspapers, the preparation of sheepskins for the inking of the press (a dirty job that was doubtless the source of the appellation "printer's devil"), and the actual business of typesetting and presswork. Some masters shared a fund of practical wisdom during the course of the apprenticeship, others assumed hard work was itself the best teacher. Some sent the apprentice to school, others relied on apprentices' libraries or gave the matter no thought. It was a taxing, frequently grinding, regimen, but those who completed it had a skill for which there was a substantial market throughout the nineteenth century, and those who could put together the few hundred dollars required for the purchase of a press and some type had ready access to a single entrepreneurship.[6]

Most country printshops were run by owner-masters and a small number of journeymen or apprentices or both. The development of large urban newspapers and book publishers, however, and the combining of steam power with improved mechanical presses during the 1840's and 1850's, fundamentally changed the character of the printing industry in the East. The owner-printer like Horace Greeley, who had served the same apprenticeship as the journeymen printers who worked for him, gave way to the full-time editor and the merchant publisher, neither of whom had ever been a printer. The skilled pressman, who could run off several hundred sheets per hour on a traditional Ramage press, found himself feeding paper into a Hoe "lightning press" in the 1840's, thereby helping to run off eight thousand sheets per hour but at the same time displacing a large number of his brother printers. And printers in general were forced to compete for wages with reporters, editors, and advertising salesmen. In response to this situation, printers organized some of the earliest craft unions in the country, on the local level as early as 1794 and on the national level with the establishment of the National Typographical Union in 1852. Beyond their obvious concern with bread-and-butter issues, these organizations gave particular attention to the enforcement of a genuinely educative apprenticeship and to resisting the employment of half-trained journeymen; and, while they were less than wholly successful, they did manage to retain a pattern of minimal training that made of apprenticeship more than simply a job classification calling for no skills and low pay. Even so, Greeley remarked as early as 1845 that the "golden age" of printing was passing away, and urged those who were still young to go West, "where independence and plenty may be found."[7]

The printers were able to retain their sense of craft, however much they were diminished in status, in the new publishing industry that came into being in the 1840's and 1850's, and they were also able to retain a measure of control over the character of apprenticeship. The development of the shoe industry during the same period led to a very different situation for the shoemakers, or cordwainers, as they were called

6. Milton W. Hamilton, *The Country Printer: New York, 1785–1830* (New York: Columbia University Press, 1936), chap. ii.

7. *New York Tribune*, September 15, 1845.

during the later eighteenth century. Most shoes in the colonial period were the products of household manufacture: they were made of leather produced and tanned on the farm or in a community tanning pit, either by the farmer himself or by an itinerant cobbler (possibly a neighboring farmer) who came for a time and worked the homemade raw materials into boots or brogans. But from the earliest times there were also craftsmen who specialized in shoemaking and who took orders for "bespoke" work. Located principally in the larger market towns like Philadelphia, New York, and Boston, they bought their leather from neighboring farmers or from merchants or sea captains who imported it, and they made the entire shoe, using a kit of tools that had not changed appreciably since the medieval period. In the process, they hired journeymen and took on apprentices, using contracts for the latter that embodied the usual quid pro quo of instruction in the art and mystery of the trade in return for faithful and loyal service over a stipulated period of time.

Given its failure to develop as either a port (because of the inadequacy of its harbor) or as a farming center (because of the poor quality of its soil), the town of Lynn, Massachusetts, had become something of a center for shoe production during the 1750's and 1760's, supplying not only its own needs but the needs of neighboring communities as well. When the Revolution cut off the traditional supply of imported English shoes, Lynn's local industry boomed; sales not only increased in nearby markets but along the entire eastern seaboard. When the cessation of hostilities permitted the return of English imports, Lynn's shoemakers continued to compete for those domestic markets. In the process, a transformation was wrought in the shoe industry that radically changed the nature of apprenticeship.

The transformation proceeded through three phases. In the initial phase, beginning around 1790, merchants from Boston and Salem, noting the existence of an expanding market for Lynn's shoes, undertook first to supply the leather and other materials that the shoemakers would need to manufacture the shoes and then to sell the final products after they had been manufactured. The immediate consequence was not so much to change the conditions of manufacture as to separate the shoemaker from his customers; but the longer-range consequence was that the system proved immensely lucrative, with the result that pressure for increased production mounted and maximum efficiency tended to replace maximum quality as a goal to be achieved.

This led to the second phase of the transformation, beginning around 1810, in which a significant division of labor occurred. The master (assisted by his journeymen) no longer made shoes in their entirety but devoted a larger and larger share of his own time to cutting leather into usable parts in what was called a "central shop," leaving it to women working at home to "bind" (stitch) the pieces that formed the upper part of the shoe, and to journeymen working in what was called a "ten-footer" (a building used exclusively as a shop) actually to "make" the shoe, that is, to fit the upper part that had been stitched by the women to the last and to attach it to the inner and outer soles. The women brought into the manufacturing process at this stage were initially the wives and daughters of the journeymen, but as time passed and as production goals increased they simply became any women willing to apply their knowledge of stitchery to the process of binding. There were still apprentices who worked with the journeymen, but they no longer saw or participated in the entire process of shoemaking. Interestingly, the Philadelphia shoemakers railed against these developments, complaining that untrained labor in Massachusetts was producing inferior shoes at cut-rate prices. However that may have been, the fact was that the customs of the craft were no longer as vigorously pursued in Lynn as they were in Philadelphia, in part at least because Philadelphia shoemakers continued to manufacture custom-made products for particular customers and to maintain the traditions of apprenticeship, while Lynn shoemakers were manufacturing standard products for anonymous customers and were therefore not able to perpetuate the arts and dignity of their craft.

In the third phase of the transformation, which began around 1855, steam power and various sorts of labor-saving machinery were added to the productive process, climaxing with the introduction of the Blake-McKay machine for stitching bottoms during the later 1860's. Thereafter, it became more economical to gather workers together in a single factory than to supply them with pieces for finishing in several different establishments. Thereafter, too, both the binding and the making processes could be accomplished via machines operated by individuals who had not gone through an extensive period of training but who had learned one element in the productive process well, usually through some sort of understudy arrangement that combined the necessary minimum by way of explanation, imitation, correction, and practice. For all intents and purposes, apprenticeship died out as a lengthy training process in craftsmanship and became instead a category of beginning employment signifying no skills and low pay. A national association called the Knights of St. Crispin was organized in 1867, one of the avowed purposes of which was to keep "green hands" out of the shoe industry, and there were vigorous lodges in Lynn that mounted substantial campaigns to prevent the importation of unskilled Chinese labor from California into the shoe factories of Lynn. But, whatever their success in resisting the Chinese, they failed in their effort to resist unskilled labor; and as early as 1872 the International Grand Scribe of the organization advised a meeting of the Boston Lodge that the Crispins would do better to fight against the wage reductions that were surely in the offing than to try to regain control over the entry of new recruits to the trade. The depression of 1873 bore out his prediction and did much to hasten the early demise of the organization.[8]

The printers, then, managed to maintain the tradition of formal apprenticeship as systematic training for a trade; the shoemakers, on the other hand, at least in Lynn, did not. A third pattern is best exemplified, perhaps, by the cotton industry of New England, where the informal apprenticeship that prepared boys and girls for household production was transferred to the factory, though at a far less complex level of skill. The familiar story begins with the establishment of Samuel Slater's mill at Pawtucket, Rhode Island, in 1790, in association with the merchants William Almy and Smith Brown, for the spinning of cotton yarn. Like all other elements in the making of cloth, the spinning of cotton yarn had traditionally been carried on in households by women and girls using manually operated spinning wheels (indeed, the term "spinster" derived from that function). The yarn was then bleached and woven in the household, and subsequently made into clothing and other wares for household use. What was new about the Slater mill was that it brought together under one roof the spinning jenny invented by the Englishman James Hargreaves in 1764 and the water frame invented by the Englishman Richard Arkwright in 1769 and joined them to the power of a local waterfall. Slater had memorized the designs of the jenny and the frame as an apprentice in a Derbyshire cotton mill during the 1780's and had then, in violation of English law, immigrated to the United States with the express purpose of reproducing them. What was also new about the Slater mill was that, in an effort to keep expenses to a minimum, the machines were operated by local children hired for wages.

The decision to use children was not extraordinary. It was common for youngsters of eight, nine, and ten to carry heavy burdens in farm

8. Blanche Evans Hazard, *The Organization of the Boot and Shoe Industry in Massachusetts Before 1875* (Cambridge, Mass.: Harvard University Press, 1921), pp. 153–155.

households of the 1790's, and it was not uncommon for youngsters of those ages to be apprenticed to other households or to shops. Moreover, the tasks to be performed in the mill were even less complicated than the task of spinning with a spinning wheel. The cotton was spread on the carding machines, which combed their fibers until they lay parallel. Another machine took the carded cotton and formed it into rovings, loose soft rolls of parallel fibers. And the spinning machine then twisted the fibers into yarn. The machines were so simple to operate that the only adult expertise required was by way of supervision and the occasional repair of the machines.

Slater himself taught and oversaw the youngsters during the early months, showing each one his or her tasks, drawing up rules to be followed, and generally keeping order. When the firm built a larger mill in 1793, however, his management problems multiplied: there were larger numbers of children to supervise and more frequent encounters with parents over wages, hours, and attendance, problems aggravated by the inefficiency of Almy and Brown. As a consequence, when Slater in 1800 formed a new partnership and built an even larger mill on the other side of the river (retaining his managerial role at the mill built in 1793), he began to recruit whole families rather than individual children. The new arrangement relieved Slater and his partners of the responsibilities of oversight in the factories: the parents themselves supervised the children at work and in the process not only maintained social discipline but provided substantial legitimatization for the employment of young children.

Slater continued to use the new arrangement in his own mill, his records indicating that in 1816 his labor force comprised one family with eight members working, one family with seven, two families with five, four families with four, and five families with three, along with eight single men and four single women. Moreover, the so-called family system became fairly common in the smaller cotton mills of Rhode Island, Connecticut, and southern Massachusetts. With the organization of the Boston Manufacturing Company of Waltham in 1813, however, an important alternative to the family system emerged, namely, the recruitment of a large labor force of young women between the ages of approximately eighteen and twenty-two who would live in well-supervised boardinghouses maintained by the company. The young women were recruited from the New England countryside by paid agents of the firm, who held out the prospect of interesting work in a different environment for a few years under quasi-familial conditions, during which money could be earned for a dowry or for other personal or familial purposes. Since the Boston Manufacturing Company included power looms in its factories along with the yarn-making machinery, the work was slightly more complicated than the work in the Slater mill, but only slightly, and by all reports the young women learned the tasks that were assigned to them fairly rapidly via the same understudy methods as the workers in the Lynn shoe factory.

Now, the term "apprentice" was used from time to time to refer to both the children in the Slater mills and the young women in the Boston Manufacturing Company mills; but, from the earliest instances of the 1790's, the term was devoid of any connotation of formal systematic instruction. It merely referred to a beginning worker who would tend the machines. At no point was it assumed or implied that the employers would teach the apprentices the arts and mysteries of a craft, though admittedly the boardinghouse scheme involved the employer in quasi-familial nurture and surveillance (the family system obviously relieved the employer of this responsibility with respect to the children). In essence, then, apprenticeship in the cotton industry from the beginning signified a status in the labor force rather than an arrangement involving systematic training or instruction.

It must not be assumed that the transformation of manufacturing followed any standard or linear pattern of development during the nineteenth century, or even that the character of apprenticeship within the same craft or trade changed in the same ways in all regions of the country. As has been indicated, formal apprenticeships in the printing craft proved much more durable in country towns than in large cities. Similarly, long after ready-made New England shoes had become widely and cheaply available in the South, shoemaking remained a household industry on many slave plantations, and shoemakers (free blacks as well as whites) who had learned their craft via apprenticeship continued to ply their trade in most southern cities. On the other hand, there were water-powered factories in Georgia where unfree blacks and free whites worked side by side as spinners and weavers, tending machines in patterns of activity that were indistinguishable from those in New England.

Yet there was one educational problem that proved ubiquitous wherever factories did appear, and that was the problem of nurturing and maintaining industrial discipline. The rhythms of the household-handicraft-mill complex of the late eighteenth century were essentially based on agricultural time. People followed a work calendar largely governed by the seasons, though modified for holidays, and by a work day based on some compromise between external demand and personal preference. It was common for households to manufacture clothing and agricultural implements during the winter and for journeymen to absent themselves from their shops on occasional Saturdays and Mondays and even longer periods around the usual election day festivities. Factories, with their dependence of machines on people and of each element in the productive process on all the others, could not be made to work efficiently on such a schedule. They required a shift from agricultural time to the much more precise categories of industrial time, with its sharply delineated and periodized work day. Moreover, along with this shift in timing and rhythm, the factory demanded concomitant shifts in habits of attention and behavior, under which workers could no longer act according to whim or preference but were required instead to adjust to the needs of the productive process and the other workers involved in it.

The values and attitudes associated with industrial discipline were those of Poor Richard—inner discipline, hard work, punctuality, frugality, sobriety, orderliness, and prudence—and they had been taught to the American people via almanacs and other genres of popular literature since the middle of the eighteenth century. With the development of the factory in the nineteenth century, however, they were taught with renewed vigor and growing intensity, not merely by a burgeoning popular literature, but also by churches, schools, and voluntary organizations, as well as by the factories themselves. The evangelical movement of the 1820's, 1830's, and 1840's was persistent in its delivery of messages concerning the virtue of personal self-discipline, while the schools taught, not only through textbook preachments, but also through the very character of their organization—the grouping, periodizing, and objective impersonality were not unlike those of the factory. In similar manner, a spate of voluntary associations came into being dedicated to the advancement of temperance, the elimination of idleness, and the enforcement of a self-denying morality. And the factories published long and detailed lists of rules, rewarding observance (and the resultant productivity) with premiums and punishing infractions with fines and dismissal. Beyond that, they vigorously proclaimed the moral influence of manufacturing itself, in keeping people from idleness, in creating prosperity, and in advancing the national interest.

The values of industrial discipline were taught with heightened intensity, then, by a growing number of institutions, but they were not unfailingly learned; for, if the factory owners saw themselves in common cause with their employees in the acceptance and advancement of these values, the employees did not uniformly share the values. Some did, to be sure: there is evidence of workers in the shoe factories of Lynn and in the boardinghouses of the Boston Manufacturing Company of Waltham who took pleasure in their work and harbored no sense of grievance against their employers or alienation from them. But others resented both the industrial discipline itself and the assertions of common cause that they saw as rationalizations for vicious exploitation; and they sought through their unions and their benevolent societies alternative patterns of living and working, as well as alternative educational arrangements that might help bring them into being.

Granted this, it would be anachronistic to see any sharply defined and fully developed class conflict during the period before the 1870's. Particularly in the newly industrialized towns and cities, there was a growing separation of experience between those who owned and operated the new factories and those who worked in them, a separation that was frequently compounded by ethnic, religious,. and racial factors; and that separation did provide the basis for an increasingly articulate class consciousness during the 1850's and 1860's, a consciousness that was both heightened and taught by the emerging labor movement. Nevertheless, for every Nathan Appleton, an exemplar of socially responsible elitism and a founder of the Boston Manufacturing Company, whose apprenticeship had been as a clerk to his brother and whose only experience with cotton weaving before he invested five-thousand dollars in Francis Lowell's Waltham power mill had been as an interested observer, there was also a Horace Greeley, who ran a large urban newspaper establishment but who had himself come up through a standard printer's apprenticeship. And, more representative than either, perhaps, were the shoe manufacturers at Lynn on the eve of the Civil War. A majority had had experience as shoemakers, and some had been the sons of shoemakers. They had been drawn from the upper reaches of the trade, to be sure, and they had had unusually good access to capital and to management expertise. But they had shared a measure of experience in common with their workers; and, although as they reflected upon that experience they saw it differently, the fact of the sharing remained an important element of continuity in their lives.

IV

The formal apprenticeship system of the 1780's and 1790's trained not only craftsmen and tradesmen in the arts and mysteries of their vocations but physicians, lawyers, and ministers as well. The traditional English modes of preparing such professionals in the universities, Inns of Court, and hospitals had not taken root in the colonies, and there had been a gradual devolution of professional training from the more theoretical and systematic instruction associated with institutions of higher learning to the more practical and informal education associated with apprenticeship. By the time of Independence the range of competence in the various professions had become enormous, from physicians familiar with the latest European science to empirics who knew only herbal medicine, from attorneys steeped in the common law to pleaders who knew only the arts of persuasion, from Congregational ministers thoroughly grounded in the literature of theology to Methodist preachers who knew only the word itself. A few professorships of medicine, law, and divinity had been established at the College of Philadelphia, King's College, the College of William and Mary, and Harvard, and there were vigorous proponents in every state of higher standards of education and certification; but the tension between high standards and easy accessibility was already ubiquitous and would mark the debates over professional training until well after the Civil War.

In medicine, the character of apprenticeship training had become fairly standard by the early years of the nineteenth century. The aspiring physician, usually a youngster around eighteen years of age (though some apprentices were as young as fifteen and some as old as twenty-five) who had completed several years of schooling (some of which might even have been classical) would apprentice himself to a practicing physician (called a "preceptor"), with the usual promised exchange of services and obligations: the preceptor agreed to furnish instruction in the science and art of medicine and also to provide whatever books and equipment might be needed during the course of training; the apprentice agreed to serve the preceptor in all reasonable requests and also to pay a fee that was ordinarily set at one-hundred dollars a year. The apprenticeship commonly ran three years in length and was divided into two phases. During the first phase, the apprentice would "read medicine," systematically perusing textbooks in the fields of chemistry, botany, anatomy, physiology, materia medica, pharmacy, and clinical medicine. Dissections on animal and human cadavers were often undertaken during this first phase, and the apprentice also performed simple duties around the physician's office and household. During the second phase, the apprentice would accompany the physician on his calls, assisting him in the usual tasks of bloodletting, blistering, mixing and administering drugs, dressing wounds, delivering babies, and performing surgery. At the conclusion of the stipulated term, the preceptor would award the apprentice a certificate testifying to his excellent training, his loyal service, and his patent qualification to practice medicine.

The assets of this system of training were considerable. The apprentice studied under a preceptor who was actively practicing the arts and sciences he was purporting to teach; and, after the apprentice had immersed himself for a time in textbook knowledge, he was offered the chance to learn by doing, proceeding as an understudy from the simple to the complex tasks involved in the occupation. Yet, that said, the shortcomings of the system were legion. Quite apart from the ability and previous preparation of the apprentice, the quality of the entire enterprise depended upon the knowledge and concern of the preceptor. If he was well versed in medical knowledge and techniques and cared deeply about teaching them, the apprenticeship could be invaluable; if he was a hack carrying on a routine practice and cared only about the fees and assistance associated with apprenticeship, it could prove worthless. Moreover, even when the preceptor was competent and caring, he suffered all the limitations of a single individual with a given set of textbooks carrying on a particular practice in one community, often in isolation from other physicians and if not in isolation almost always in competition with them.

It was the recognition of these limitations by both the preceptors and the apprentices that led to the most significant developments in medical education during the nineteenth century. One of these was the movement toward licensing. As physicians formed local and state medical societies during the late eighteenth and early nineteenth centuries and sought to control entry into practice via licensing, they quickly came to appreciate the advantage that would flow from having a testimony to competence by a single preceptor-physician converted into a license to practice granted by the state on recommendation by a medical society; and for a time physicians pressed for that arrangement, though they did not always have their way in the several state legislatures.

More importantly, physicians began to acknowledge the advantage of organizing medical schools to undertake some of the more systematic instruction of the apprenticeship, with the result that the first three quarters of the nineteenth century witnessed a dramatic proliferation of such institutions under the aegis and proprietorship of the practitioners themselves. They came into being in various ways. In communities where a college was already in existence, the physicians would seek an opportunity to add medical courses to the curriculum or even to develop a full-scale medical program or medical school. In communities where there wasn't a college, the physicians would seek a charter authorizing them to create a medical school *de novo,* or, having created one without legislative authority, they would seek an affiliation with some extant institution nearby. In 1783 there were two medical schools in the United States, and by 1876 there were seventy-eight that were formally reported by the Bureau of Education and doubtless others operating on an informal basis. They varied tremendously in size and character, but they did share certain features in common. As a rule, the course of instruction consisted of two four-month terms that were seen as complementary to two years and two summers of apprenticeship with a preceptor. The curriculum covered three basic fields, not dissimilar to the fields comprised by the "reading" phase of the traditional apprenticeship: the basic sciences (chemistry, anatomy, physiology, and possibly botany, physics, and zoology), the theory and diagnosis of disease, and the treatment of disease, including materia medica, surgery, and midwifery. The lecture method was the dominant pedagogical form, with some clinical dissection, usually carried out in a remote corner of the building, and some demonstration of medical or surgical techniques, usually under conditions where observation was difficult or even impossible. Upon completion of a three-year course, consisting of two terms of schooling and twenty-eight months of apprenticeship, the student was awarded the M.D. degree. The financial, professional, and personal connections between physicians as practitioners, preceptors, and professors were numerous and close, with the result that medical schools were both convenient and profitable to those fortunate enough to control them. Given that convenience and profitability, and given the rise of medical sectarianism during the 1830's and 1840's (the growth of radically differing theories of treatment), the schools competed vigorously for students, and one outcome was that standards of entrance and requirements of graduation steadily deteriorated during the decades before the Civil War.[9]

9. U.S., Bureau of Education, *Report of the Commissioner of Education for the Year 1876,* pp. 752–755.

No school conveys the flavor of this era in American medical education more authentically than the medical college at Castleton, Vermont, a proprietary institution founded in 1818 by three local physicians as a convenience for their apprentices and a source of additional income for themselves. Though the founders had been trained via apprenticeship, they were able to recruit to the faculty graduates of the medical schools of Harvard, Dartmouth, Bowdoin, the University of Pennsylvania, and even the Royal College of Physicians of Edinburgh, Scotland. The college had six regular professors teaching the usual fields of botany, chemistry, anatomy, physiology, clinical practice, materia medica, theory and practice of medicine, and medical jurisprudence; and it had in addition a varying cohort of visiting professors, most of whom were practicing physicians who taught part time at Castleton, bringing with them their own apprentices. During the forty-three years of its existence, Castleton affiliated with Middlebury College for a time (1820–1837), suspended operation for a time (1838–1840), and frequently reorganized; but it managed to teach some 2,700 students and to graduate 1,422, a larger number than any other contemporary New England medical school. Like most schools of the era, it maintained no admission requirements and offered little by way of clinical instruction; but the academic fare it did provide was clearly superior to what most aspiring physicians could gain from a single preceptor, and that superiority, however marginal, was the key to Castleton's success.

As the number of medical schools increased, the supply of physicians burgeoned, and a clamor arose within the profession for heightened admission and graduation requirements. While many of the arguments advanced were predictable—self-serving professors arguing for open admissions versus self-serving practitioners arguing for restriction—there was at least one rather remarkable exchange between Martyn Paine of the New York University Medical School and Nathan Smith Davis of the Broome County (New York) Medical Society, who would later play a key role in the organization of the American Medical Association. In two widely circulated addresses during the mid-1840's, Paine maintained that sharply increased standards of medical education would "turn from our medical schools most of their aspirants," particularly those from the poor and middling classes, ruin any number of flourishing medical schools, and in the end dramatically reduce the general standard of medical care by loosing increased quackery upon the world. Let the best schools train an elite, Paine argued, but let there be other schools to provide sound medical education to poorer students at moderate cost. So far as Davis was concerned, the issue was solely one of standards. The only true questions, he wrote, "are, whether our system contains important defects; and if so, whether they admit of being remedied." The issue was never joined solely in educational terms, since the question of restriction was ever lurking in the background. Nevertheless, the issue was one that bedeviled every form of professional education throughout the nineteenth century.[10]

Paine and Davis may have argued over how much and what kind of medical schooling ought to be available to aspiring physicians, but the value of schooling was not brought into question. By the 1840's the medical profession had clearly opted for schooling as a desirable complement to apprenticeship, and indeed the number of young physicians who annually won the right to practice via the M.D. degree far exceeded the number who won it via licensure by a medical society. Developments in the field of law went in much the same direction but far less rapidly. Legal education was also carried on via apprenticeship, and law schools also came into being in significant numbers during the early years of the nineteenth century; but they did not multiply at the same pace as medical schools, and they did not train the same proportion of new recruits to the profession.

The character of apprenticeship to the law was far less structured and standardized during the early years of the nineteenth century than the character of apprenticeship to medicine. The aspiring lawyer entered a law office for a clerkship that was usually ill defined and casually conducted. He "read" law, as the medical student "read" medicine, commonly out of *Coke upon Littleton* (1628), the first volume of Sir Edward Coke's four-volume commentaries on the common law; Blackstone's *Commentaries* (1765-1769), the popular four-volume exposition of the common law delivered by Sir William Blackstone in 1758 as the first Vinerian Professor of Law at Oxford; and contemporary statute books. He also copied legal documents by hand, served process, and generally assisted his preceptor. Since he had to be admitted to the bar by a court, usually some court of local jurisdiction, it was frequently the length of time served rather than the character of the substance conveyed that was certified by the preceptor. When, as part of the more general movement to open up access to positions of political influence, requirements for admission to the bar were reduced or abolished during

10. Martyn Paine, "Medical Education in the United States," *Boston Medical and Surgical Journal*, XXIX (1843), 302; and Nathan Smith Davis, "Medical Reform," *New York Journal of Medicine*, IX (1847), 402.

the 1840's and 1850's, even that limited form of certification frequently went by the board.

As in medicine, some preceptors were well grounded in the substance of the law and assiduous about their teaching responsibilities. Thus, Lemuel Shaw of Boston, who was in the habit of taking large numbers of apprentices into his office during the 1820's, drew up the following rules to govern their conduct:

1. Students, on their entrance who have previously been at a law school, or in any other office as students, will be expected to state particularly what books they have read, the progress they have made in each branch of the law.

2. Students are requested to report to me each Monday in the forenoon the course of their reading the preceding week, and receive such advice and direction as to the pursuits of the current week as the case may require. In case of the absence or engagement of either party on Monday forenoon, such conference to be had as soon thereafter as circumstances will permit.

3. At any and all other times students are invited to call me and enter into free conversation upon subjects connected with their studies, and especially in reference to those changes and alterations of the general law which may have been effected by the Statutes of the Commonwealth and by local usage, and in respect to which therefore little can be found in books.

4. As one of the main objects of the attendance of students in the office of an attorney and counsellor is practice, they will be employed in conveyancing, pleading, copying, and other writing as the business of the office may require.

5. As order, diligence, and industry are essential to success in so laborious a profession, students will accordingly be expected to attend in the office, unless some other arrangement is made in particular cases, during those hours which are usually appropriated to business, and to apply themselves to the appropriate studies and business in the office.

6. If a student proposes to take a journey or to be absent for any considerable time he will be expected to give notice of the fact and the probable length of his absence, and if he is confined by sickness or other necessary cause he will be expected to give notice of the fact.

Other preceptors were less detailed and careful about their oversight, and the haphazard enforcement of requirements for admission to the bar in many localities simply confirmed in many instances a haphazard process of apprenticeship.[11]

The earliest teaching of the law at the colleges came into being with

11. The rules are reproduced in Frederic Hathaway Chase, *Lemuel Shaw, Chief Justice of the Supreme Court of Massachusetts, 1830–1860* (Boston: Houghton Mifflin Company, 1918), pp. 120–121.

the appointment of George Wythe as professor of law and police at the College of William and Mary in 1779, of James Wilson as professor of law at the University of Pennsylvania in 1789, and of James Kent as professor of law at Columbia College in 1794. As in medicine, however, the most significant early law schools developed under the aegis and proprietorship of individual practitioners or groups of practitioners seeking a more economical and systematic way of teaching their apprentices. Some of these institutions affiliated with extant colleges or universities; others thrived under private auspices, sometimes with a formal charter, more frequently without one. In fact, the most influential of all the early schools, the one established at Litchfield, Connecticut, by Tapping Reeve, neither had a charter nor was affiliated with a college or university.

Reeve, the son of a Presbyterian minister, had attended the College of New Jersey and served as a grammar school master and a college tutor before deciding to study law under Jesse Root of Hartford, Connecticut. Upon being admitted to the bar in 1772, Reeve settled in Litchfield, the fourth largest town in Connecticut, some twenty-five miles west of Hartford, and began to practice law. Like many contemporary practitioners, he decided two years later to supplement his income by accepting apprentices, and he did so well at it that in 1784, when his wife's health demanded that the teaching activities be removed from the household, he was able to erect a small edifice in his back yard to be devoted wholly to the instruction. When Reeve was appointed to the Superior Court in 1798, he solicited the help of a former student, James Gould, and the two men ran the school together until 1820. Thereafter Gould conducted it with two assistants until 1833, when the development of competing law schools at Yale, Harvard, and Columbia and the general relaxation of requirements for admission to the bar occasioned the demise of the institution.

From the beginning, the Litchfield Law School was an outstanding success, largely as a result of Reeve's systematic and comprehensive lectures. In all, he delivered 139 of them, covering domestic relations, executors and administrators, contracts, equity, torts, pleading, evidence, mercantile law, and real property. Later, when Gould joined him, debt collection, procedure, and criminal law were added. The lectures were not published, but students who left with a complete set of notes and sources had in their possession an incomparable reservoir of legal lore, principle, and wisdom, all directly relevant to practice. In addition, they had had the opportunity to join in moot courts, debating societies, informal review sessions, and regular examinations. During a single year's residence, a student could obtain as thorough and comprehensive a review of the common law as a system of connected rational principles as could be acquired anywhere in the United States.

During the fifty-nine years of its existence, the Litchfield Law School produced an extraordinary number of lawyers who went on to distinguished careers of public service—two vice-presidents of the United States, three Supreme Court justices, six cabinet officers, forty judges of higher state courts, and well over a hundred governors, senators, and congressmen. But its more significant function was to serve during its time as a paradigmatic alternative to the more customary and less systematic "reading" of law in a lawyer's office. There were various contemporary enterprises more or less like Litchfield, including several established by its graduates; and, during the 1830's and 1840's, university-based law schools developed even more systematic and comprehensive curricula, taught by professors who published their commentaries as textbooks for serious study, including self-study. By 1876 there were forty-two such institutions, supplemented by an indeterminate number of private proprietary ventures. But the point to bear in mind is that they proffered curricular models of uncertain influence, since a majority of those aspiring to the law still proceeded solely via apprenticeship, and admission to the bar remained a less than formidable hurdle. Whereas the debate over medical education during the middle years of the nineteenth century was addressed to the kind and extent of schooling that would be most appropriate for American physicians, the debate over legal education still focused on the value of schooling in the first place.[12]

In the field of theological education, the range of variation in character and quality was even greater than in medical and legal education, owing partly to regional factors and differences in supply and demand but even more significantly to profound ideological differences among the sects and denominations coupled with the fact that each sect licensed and ordained its own clergymen. In addition, there was a much greater degree of overlap between the substance of liberal education as taught in schools and colleges and the particular professional training seen as appropriate to a minister than was the case in medicine and

12. *Report of the Commissioner of Education . . . 1876*, pp. 750–751.

law. The result was that by the 1830's and 1840's some ministers had undergone a longer and more rigorous academic preparation for their work than any American-trained physician or lawyer, while others had undergone as little training as the worst-trained physician or lawyer and perhaps even less.

Ministerial education among the Congregationalists, the Episcopalians, and the Presbyterians at the time of Independence consisted of training in the liberal arts at one or another of several dozen academies and colleges followed by special training in the field of divinity. Since there were no theological seminaries as such before the establishment of the New Brunswick Theological Seminary in 1784, postgraduate training was obtained either by remaining at the academy or college for further systematic study or via an apprenticeship with a practicing minister. Perhaps even more than in medicine or law, the apprenticeship involved systematic reading and study in several fairly well defined fields, including Bible study (coupled with the Biblical languages, especially Greek and Hebrew), Judeo-Christian history, systematic theology, and a smattering of homiletics and liturgics; though, like apprenticeships in medicine and law, theological training also included assisting the preceptor in his round of pastoral duties. Joseph Bellamy of Bethlehem, Connecticut, began taking students in 1742 and continued the practice until his death in 1790; indeed, it may well have been his work that gave Tapping Reeve the initial idea for the effort that became the Litchfield Law School. Bellamy's methods were described in some detail by one of his more prominent students:

It was his custom to furnish his pupils with a set of questions covering the whole field of theology, and then to give them a list of books, corresponding to the several subjects which they were to investigate; and in the progress of their inquiries he was accustomed almost daily to examine them, to meet whatever difficulties they might have found, and to put himself in the attitude of an objector, with a view at once to extend their knowledge and increase their intellectual acumen. When they had gone through the prescribed course of reading, he required them to write dissertations on the several subjects which had occupied their attention; and, afterwards, sermons on the points of doctrine which he deemed most important, and finally sermons on such experimental and practical topics as they might choose to select. He was particularly earnest in inculcating the importance of a high tone of spiritual feeling as an element of ministerial character and success.

Once a young man had studied with Bellamy for a year or two, he could present himself for examination before an appropriate ministerial body, doubtless aided by testimonials from Bellamy, and seek ordination and a license to preach. Once ordained, he could himself seek students; there was nothing to prevent him from doing so beyond the stubborn realities of the market.[13]

By contrast, ministerial education among the Methodists and Baptists at the time of Independence was neither as sustained nor as systematic. In those denominations, the important qualification was that the aspiring minister be truly moved by the love of God to preach. If one gave persuasive evidence of that call to the bishop (among the Methodists) or the congregation (among the Baptists), formal learning in matters other than Scripture, doctrine, and prayer were not only unnecessary but possibly even distracting in that they might well lead preachers away from the experience of ordinary people. When this doctrinal proclivity was compounded by the pressing need for clergymen occasioned by the rapid increase in communicants, it led to a very different conception of ministerial training from that of the Congregationalists, Episcopalians, and Presbyterians. From time to time, a Methodist bishop would appoint a junior preacher to ride a circuit with a more experienced colleague, but in days of rapid expansion even that form of understudy gave way to the pedagogy of plunging in and learning by doing.

One can point to the founding of seminaries for the training of clergymen by virtually all the denominations and sects during the first half-century of national life—by the Dutch Reformed in 1784, the Roman Catholics in 1791, the Moravians in 1807, the Congregationalists in 1808, the Presbyterians in 1812, the Lutherans in 1815, the Episcopalians in 1819, the Baptists in 1820, the German Reformed in 1825, and the Methodists in 1839. In addition, most denominations and sects joined in the sponsorship of colleges, many of which sent a significant proportion of their graduates into ministerial careers. But the salient fact of ministerial education during the pre-Civil War era was not the founding of these seminaries; since, if one recognizes that the Methodists and Baptists by 1850 had more than twice as many churches between them as all the other denominations and sects combined, one realizes that the majority of ministers were trained by some sort of self-study. The central fact is rather the persistence and indeed the

13. William B. Sprague, *Annals of the American Pulpit* (9 vols.; New York: Robert Carter & Brothers, 1866–1869), I, 405–406.

widening of the gap between what different groups defined as appropriate preparation for a clergyman.[14]

At one end of the spectrum, for example, there was the Andover Theological Seminary, established in 1808 by conservative elements in the Congregational Church, after the Hollis Professorship of Divinity at Harvard had been lost to a Unitarian, the Reverend Henry Ware. The seminary required a baccalaureate degree from a liberal arts college or equivalent preparation for admission (candidates were personally examined in Latin, Greek, and Hebrew by the faculty), and it asked all entrants to contract to remain for the entire three-year course. During the 1830's and 1840's, the curriculum, taught by a distinguished faculty, covered the fields of sacred literature (Moses Stuart and Edward Robinson), sacred rhetoric (Thomas H. Skinner), ecclesiastical history (Ralph Emerson), theology (Leonard Woods), homiletics (Ebenezer Porter), and pastoral duties (Ralph Emerson). Most of the students came from Amherst, Williams, Middlebury, and Dartmouth—Harvard and Yale, after all, had their own divinity courses—and most went out to Congregational pulpits in the New England region or to missions in the West or even abroad.

The contrast between the training offered at Andover and that demanded of contemporary Methodist preachers could not have been more stark. Once candidates had satisfied their bishops or presiding elders with respect to their piety, diligence, and depth of commitment, they were asked to embark upon a course of reading and study prescribed by the bishops and overseen by the presiding elders. During the early years of the century, it was assumed that the work would take about two years; later, it was extended to four. The list of readings published in the *Discipline* of 1852 included the Bible, the *Discipline,* and such works as Wesley's sermons and Watson's life of Wesley. Taken in its totality, the list was slender in size and limited in scope, and there is every indication that it was enforced by examinations that were less than stringent. Doubtless, there were well-schooled Methodist preachers who completed the work at such institutions as Randolph Macon in Virginia, Wesleyan in Connecticut, or McKendree in Illinois and then went on to lifetimes of fruitful self-study; and, doubtless, there were intellectual drones who completed the work at Amherst and at Andover. But the character of American theological education through-

14. The dates given for the founding of theological seminaries vary significantly within the literature, owing to differences in the meaning assigned to the words "founding" and "seminary."

out much of the nineteenth century remained extremely variegated, with marked differences in the educational arrangements maintained and enforced by the several denominations and sects.[15]

Beyond the three traditional learned professions, several other occupations moved toward professionalization with varying degress of rapidity and success during the nineteenth century. With the building of canals and railroads and the development of manufacturing industries, civil and mechanical engineering came into their own; and, though apprenticeship continued to be the leading form of engineering education before the Civil War, institutions such as the military academy at West Point, Rensselaer Institute, and the various university-based schools of applied science began to provide alternative academic routes to engineering careers, and movement in that direction was accelerated by the colleges of mechanic arts founded under the Morrill Act grants after 1862. Also, with the popularization of schooling, there was considerable pressure for the professionalization of teaching, and indeed several state-sponsored normal schools came into being during the 1830's and 1840's and men like J. Orville Taylor and Henry Barnard set out to define the intellectual substance of a science of pedagogy. Nevertheless, the overwhelming majority of teachers continued to prepare for their work (if they purposefully prepared for it at all) in the schools themselves, and what they learned about the so-called art and science of teaching came via informal (and usually unknowing) apprenticeship to the teachers under whom they themselves had studied, supplemented from time to time by a textbook or two or even attendance at a teachers' institute (following the example of agriculture, the school reformers of the 1830's and 1840's saw a combination of normal schools, teacher associations, and teachers' institutes as a new education that would update what had been learned under the informal apprenticeship of early schooling). Similar efforts toward professionalization via advanced academic training went forward in dentistry, pharmacy, business, and veterinary medicine, though with only modest results before the Civil War; apprenticeship remained the principal route to all those occupations.

However much these various occupations differed in the combinations of academic and apprentice training that were required for entry into practice, they shared a number of educational problems during the

15. *The Doctrines and Discipline of the Methodist Episcopal Church* (New York: Carlton & Phillips, 1852), pp. 227–232.

first part of the nineteenth century. For one thing, they all experienced the conflict between "shop culture" and "school culture" in the development of their educational arrangements, that is, continuing argument between those who extolled the advantages of systematic on-the-job training in genuine work situations under the tutelage of experienced practitioners and those who proclaimed the superior efficiency, effectiveness, and modernity of schooling. Since most practitioners in all the professions had been trained via "shop culture" during the early decades of the century, the exceptions being college professors and clergymen of certain denominations, the proponents of schooling faced a consistent war against custom and habit. The conflicts were sharp and not easily reconciled, and they continued within professional schools even after such schools had been established.[16]

Not surprisingly, proponents of schooling usually encountered the initial opposition of professional societies, given the domination of these societies by apprentice-trained practitioners. These organizations first came into being on the local and state levels as voluntary associations of like-minded individuals. They invariably professed educational purposes and indeed were often important mediating agencies for the introduction of new knowledge and skills into the work of practitioners. Equally important, however, they carried on regulatory functions, involving themselves centrally in the determination of standards, licensure, the formulation of educational programs, and, more generally, the articulation of professional interests (often stated in the rhetoric of public interest). In connection with these activities, they also nurtured a form of professional consciousness, a culture of professionalism oriented to knowledge, technical skill, efficient organization, peer evaluation, and public service, that both incorporated and reinforced certain central middle-class values.

It should also be recalled that neither the substance nor the level of professional education was sharply distinguishable from much that was included in the contemporary collegiate curriculum. Medical school chemistry was not very different from college chemistry, and engineering mathematics was not very different from college mathematics. Consequently, college attendance frequently served to reduce the amount of time required for professional preparation and certification, not only for the ministry, but also for medicine, law, and the other professions.

16. Monte A. Calvert, *The Mechanical Engineer in America, 1830–1910: Professional Cultures in Conflict* (Baltimore: The Johns Hopkins University Press, 1967).

Finally, the various professions were fairly uniform in their discrimination against women and blacks. For all intents and purposes, there were no female or black physicians or lawyers before the Civil War, Elizabeth Blackwell and numerous black folk healers to the contrary notwithstanding; and there were relatively few female or black preachers, primarily the handful of women serving Quaker meetings and of blacks serving Methodist and Baptist organizations. Teaching was the only one of the professionalizing occupations genuinely open to women at this time—it shifted from a largely male to a largely female occupation during the second third of the nineteenth century—but teaching continued to be male dominated. In general, women and blacks were excluded from apprenticeships and professional schools, not by explicit rules and regulation, but by the pervasive assumption that professional roles were white male roles. As opportunites for schooling increasingly opened up to women and blacks, access to the professions broadened, but that was largely a post-Civil War phenomenon, and when it did happen it happened slowly and sporadically.

Part IV

AN AMERICAN EDUCATION

As a nation, we are educated more by contact with each other, by business, by newspapers, magazines, and circulating libraries, by public
meetings and conventions, by lyceums, by speeches in Congress, in the
state legislatures, and at political gatherings, and in various other ways,
than by direct instructions imparted in the school room. And if so
much general intelligence, as now unquestionably characterizes us as a
people, is the result of the present state of things, what might we not
anticipate if to all these influences were superadded the advantages of a
well organized and comprehensive system of primary education?

ENOCH COBB WINES

INTRODUCTION

The Revolutionary generation was direct and explicit about the need to create a new American education, cleansed of the corruption of European monarchial forms and rooted in the purified immediacies of American life, literature, and culture. And, to that end, they spun endless plans for complicated systems of schools, universities, and institutes that would ensure to the young Republic an informed and sober citizenry who would follow a wise and virtuous leadership. None of the plans succeeded—not Jefferson's or Rush's or Webster's, or even Samuel Knox's or Samuel Harrison Smith's, both of which shared honors in the American Philosophical Society's contest of 1795. But the ideas they embodied remained in circulation, to test and be tested by the institutions Americans brought into being as they wrestled with the age-old problems of how to educate themselves and their children.

A half-century later, the outlines of a distinctive American educational system could be dimly perceived, one that resembled parts of all the earlier plans but followed none in its entirety. It was a system much commented upon by the growing number of European visitors who crossed the Atlantic to observe and assess the "great experiment" in self-government. Thus, the English author Thomas Hamilton praised the ready availability of public schooling, the multiplicity of colleges, and the prevalence of voluntary churches, while lamenting what he deemed to be the crass utilitarianism of American intellectual life and the bitter disputatiousness of American religious affairs. By contrast, the German diplomat Francis Grund, seeking to rebut Hamilton's somewhat jaundiced view, pointed to the salutary effects of churches and benevolent societies, schools and colleges, and newspapers and libraries on the American democratic character. And a few years later the Scottish journalist Alexander Mackay and the Polish revolutionary

Adam G. de Gurowski presented warmly favorable accounts of American education in works that applauded the efforts of Americans to extend liberty and equality at the same time as they called Americans sharply to task for countenancing slavery.[1]

There were Americans, too, who were able to see their emerging system in the large. The New Jersey schoolmaster Enoch Cobb Wines, for example, in an extraordinary tract called *Hints on a System of Popular Education,* observed in 1838: "As a nation, we are educated more by contact with each other, by business, by newspapers, magazines, and circulating libraries, by public meetings and conventions, by lyceums, by speeches in Congress, in the state legislatures, and at political gatherings, and in various other ways, than by direct instructions imparted in the school room." If so much "general intelligence" had already been achieved through those means, Wines continued, what might not be anticipated from the addition of a well-organized and comprehensive system of primary schooling? Unlike Wines, however, most Americans focused their attention on the local and the immediate. They were aware of the general structures that were becoming ever more prevalent during the antebellum period; but such national phenomena as the united evangelical front, or the movement for public schooling, or the demand for an expanded college curriculum, or the explosion of penny journalism were more likely to appear locally as the itinerations of a harried preacher riding on muleback from congregation to congregation, or the struggles of a newly appointed schoolteacher to keep from being thrown out of her classroom by the larger youngsters, or the trials of an overextended college president attempting to keep his institution financially afloat, or the efforts of an enterprising printer to develop a sufficient number of profitable sidelines to permit him to publish a newspaper at a loss. The matter-of-factness of such ventures rendered them no less valuable to the clients they served—indeed, the matter-of-factness was itself an aspect of the popularization of American education; but it did tend to focus the attention of Americans on the concrete (if not the purified) immediacies of education rather than on the larger system of which they were part.[2]

1. Thomas Hamilton, *Men and Manners in America* (1833; reprint ed.; 2 vols.; New York: Augustus M. Kelley, Publishers, 1968); Francis J. Grund, *The Americans in Their Moral, Social, and Political Relations* (1837; reprint ed.; New York: Johnson Reprint Corporation, 1968); Alexander Mackay, *The Western World; or, Travels in the United States in 1846–47* (1849; reprint ed.; 3 vols.; New York: Negro Universities Press, 1968); and Adam G. de Gurowski, *America and Europe* (New York: D. Appleton and Company, 1857).

2. E. C. Wines, *Hints on a System of Popular Education* (Philadelphia: Hogan and Thompson, 1838), p. 158.

Chapter 11

INSTITUTIONS

"Come in, Johnny," says the father.
"I won't."
"I tell you, come in directly, sir,—do you hear?"
"I won't," replies the urchin, taking to his heels.
"A sturdy republican, sir," says his father to me, smiling at the boy's resolute disobedience.

FREDERICK MARRYAT

The household remained the fundamental institution of social organization in early national America and, for the vast majority of Americans, the central agency of deliberate cultural transmission. In newly settled frontier regions, it frequently educated much as it had during the early stages of development in the middle and southern colonies, taking unto itself functions ordinarily performed by church and school. In the older regions, however, it found itself increasingly sharing its educative functions with church, school, and other community agencies.

The average size of the American household declined significantly between 1790 and 1870, from 5.79 individuals to 5.09 individuals, reflecting on the one hand a falling birth rate and on the other hand the tendency of fewer households to include two or more nuclear families or single nuclear families living with additional kin or boarders. Yet there were important variations from region to region and as between urban and rural areas, with both fertility rates and household sizes being smaller in New England than in other regions and in urban as contrasted with rural districts within the same region. In addition, the American population as a whole tended to be younger than contemporary European populations, with 70 percent of Americans at midcen-

371

tury reported as under the age of thirty, as compared with 63 percent of Englishmen and 52 percent of Frenchmen.[1]

Certain overall changes characterized the American household during the early national era, though, once again, it is always hazardous to generalize. Most important, perhaps, was the shift of various kinds of work from the household to the shop, the factory, and the market—a shift that dramatically altered the character of apprenticeship and the educative role of parents vis-à-vis those of other adults. The shift occurred first in the cities and factory towns of the East, but it augured changes that became increasingly widespread during the later years of the century. Of a different order, perhaps, though significant in that it served as a countervailing influence to those set in motion by the relocation of work, was the development of an ethic of domesticity. Taught insistently to an emerging middle class by every manner of treatise, self-instruction manual, and women's magazine, the notion of domesticity sharpened the boundaries between household and community, rendered them more impenetrable, and designated more stringently than before who had the right and responsibility to teach (the mother beyond all others) and who needed to be counteracted (a broadly undefined "them," including employers, self-interested corrupters of youth, and strangers in general). Finally, there was the effect of what George W. Pierson has called the "M-factor" in American history—the business of incessant geographic movement—on the relationship of household and kin. We know that in the settlement of new regions kinship ties often determined who actually came, especially in the second and third waves. But we also know that, as early as 1850, roughly a fifth of the native population was living in states other than those in which they had been born. To the extent that the American household was embedded in a network of kin, those kin were more likely to be geographically distant rather than close by. Furthermore, the psychological relationship to those kin was transformed, as the orientation within families shifted from the family into which one was born to the family one created by marrying, as the cement binding the family together was increasingly defined as love rather than obligation, and as individualism

1. U.S., Bureau of the Census, *Historical Statistics of the United States, Colonial Times to 1970* (2 vols.; Washington, D.C.: Government Printing Office, 1975), I, 41; and J. Potter, "The Growth of Population in America, 1700-1860," in D.V. Glass and D.E.C. Eversley, eds., *Population in History: Essays in Historical Demography* (Chicago: Aldine Publishing, 1965), p. 688. The average size of the American household for 1790 is computed for the free white population only; the figure for 1870 is for the aggregate population.

within the family itself profoundly altered the roles of adults with respect to their children and to one another.[2]

Paralleling the contrapuntal influences acting upon the household itself was the proliferation of new institutions to assume functions formerly carried on by the household, namely, the almshouse, the asylum, the reformatory, and the penitentiary. All were organized as custodial institutions, and all, with the possible exception of the almshouse, professed rehabilitative, or educative, aspirations, though the tension between such aspirations and the realities of custodianship was manifest from the beginning. Their development stemmed from the demographic conditions of nineteenth-century America coupled with a heightened concern for finding institutional means for maintaining social order; and they all had precedents of one sort or another in England and on the Continent. But what was significant about these institutions was the extent to which they were explicitly seen, on the one hand, as surrogates for families—the metaphors of the household abounded in the literature of custodial institutions—and, on the other hand, as complements to families in the building and maintenance of the virtuous society.

As it had since time immemorial, the household carried on much of its education through the processes of imitation and explanation, with adults and older siblings modeling attitudes and behavior and youngsters purposely or inadvertantly absorbing them. The entire enterprise was made more self-conscious by the demands of domesticity, which assigned the family in general and the mother in particular responsibility for the early formation of character. To be sure, domesticity was accepted in different degrees by different social classes, with well-to-do, genteel families tending to subscribe to its tenets more fully and more easily than poorer families. Yet domesticity was a pervasive notion, and as it spread beyond the middle class it lent new urgency to the tasks of household education.

In some realms at least, families tended to be quite deliberate about their teaching. One such realm was discipline and the whole complex of attitudes and behaviors associated with it, which in their very nature called to the fore the parents' most deeply held convictions concerning the definition of virtue and the ways in which human nature might be dealt with in order to achieve it. Obviously, given the multiplicity of

2. George W. Pierson, *The Moving American* (New York: Alfred A. Knopf, 1973), p. 29 and *passim;* J. D. B. De Bow, ed., *Statistical View of the United States, . . . Being a Compendium of the Seventh Census* (Washington, D.C.: A. O. P. Nicholson, 1854), p. 61.

traditions and beliefs concerning piety and civility in early national America, a considerable variety of parental pedagogical styles was in evidence, ranging from the ready infliction of violent punishment, as recommended by the Reverend John S. C. Abbott, to the affectionate nurturance of innate goodness, as recommended by A. Bronson Alcott. The drift in practice was away from harshness and toward leniency, as testified to by any number of foreign travelers who noted the comparative indulgence of American parents and the resultant impudence of their children. Thus, the English author Frederick Marryat recounted the following exchange in his *Diary in America* (1839):

> "Johnny, my dear, come here," says his mama.
> "I won't," cries Johnny.
> "You must, my love, you are all wet, and you'll catch cold."
> "I won't," replies Johnny.
> "Come, my sweet, and I've something for you."
> "I won't."
> "Oh! Mr. _____, do, pray make Johnny come in."
> "Come in, Johnny," says the father.
> "I won't."
> "I tell you, come in directly, sir,—do you hear?"
> "I won't," replies the urchin, taking to his heels.
> "A sturdy republican, sir," says his father to me, smiling at the boy's resolute disobedience.

Of course, Marryat's description cannot be taken at face value and should not be read as a capsule generalization; but it does represent a not-atypical English perception of American childrearing. However that may be, in most families the process of disciplining the young was doubtless more complex and often inconsistent, with alternations between an affectionate indulgence and periodical efforts to break down what was seen as stubborn juvenile willfulness.[3]

Another realm in which families undertook systematic instruction was in the transmission of information and skills. Families of Missouri Synod Lutherans taught their children German; families of Sephardic Jews taught their children Hebrew. Fathers taught their sons to shoot, hunt, and trap; mothers taught their daughters to garden, cook, and

---

3. Jacob S. C. Abbott, *The Mother at Home: or, the Principles of Maternal Duty Familiarly Illustrated,* revised and corrected by Daniel Walton (London: John Mason, 1834), chaps. ii and iii; and Frederick Marryat, *A Diary in America* (3 vols.; London: Longman, Orme, Brown, Green and Longmans, 1839), III, 284–285. See also Francis Wayland's suggestions regarding child discipline in *The Elements of Moral Science* (rev. ed.; Boston: Gould, Kendall, and Lincoln, 1841), pp. 314–325.

sew. Parents taught their children to till the soil, look after animals, manufacture candles, and repair clothing. Siblings taught their brothers and sisters to play games and manage the social intricacies of church and school. Reading tended to be taught somewhat later than in colonial times and more often than not in school, though it was commonly encountered for the first time at home, since it was generally carried on aloud and in groups rather than silently and alone as in later times. As for apprenticeship, it persisted into the nineteenth century (though less formally than in colonial times), particularly in the arts, crafts, and trades; and, although the rise of shops and factories removed much of such training from the household, to the extent that artisanship and retailing remained household occupations, apprenticeship remained a household phenomenon.

Finally, there was the realm of values, traditionally of preeminent concern to the family. Here, teaching went forward in a variety of forms, from the quite systematic participation in family worship that was common in Methodist and Baptist households, to the subtle but equally systematic instruction in gender roles that went on in all households as boys and girls were taught what was deemed appropriate and inappropriate, to the special consciousness of class that was nurtured as well-to-do youngsters were taught the obligations of gentility and impoverished youngsters were made aware of their vulnerability to exploitation. Here, too, more than in other realms, families joined together to reinforce their teaching, via church groups, benevolent societies, and fraternal organizations.

However much one may generalize about household education in early national America, there was a certain inescapable particularity about the phenomenon as it proceeded within different religious, ethnic, and racial groups that imparted a characteristically variegated quality to American education in the large. The Mormons, for example, created their special version of the polygamous family, in intimate relationship with their special version of a Hebraic-Christian church, that in its very nature occasioned variant balances of paternal and maternal teaching responsibilities as well as unusually complex patterns of sibling relationships. On a much smaller scale, but illustrative of the opportunity for variation in the open spaces of the American continent, the socialists of the Nashoba community and the perfectionists of the Oneida community created their special versions of the communal family, again in intimate relationship with other religiously or ideologically rationalized communal institutions.

Beyond all else, however, diversity was occasioned by continuing immigration. The substantial German influx of the 1830's and 1840's and particularly the 1850's brought a cohesive family structure marked by stability of settlement, parental and grandparental collaboration in the process of childrearing, arranged marriages, and an extensive network of active and enduring kin relationships. The great Irish migration of the 1840's and 1850's was more complex, involving a movement not only from Ireland to America but also from country to town. Moreover, whereas earlier Irish immigrants, like the Germans, had tended to migrate in family groups, those who came after the Great Famine of the later 1840's tended to come in familial stages, with fathers or older male children arriving first as a kind of advance guard and remaining family members arriving later. An impoverished rural peasantry driven from the land by economic disaster, the Irish flocked to the eastern cities, where they established their particular variant of the stem family closely tied to a special ethnic version of the Roman Catholic church. Patriarchalism was regnant: women, once married, rarely worked outside the home; and children, seen as economic assets, were expected to obtain jobs at an early age. Yet the stem family in Ireland had been rooted in an essential relationship with the land that was wholly lacking in America, with the result that Irish households suffered an unusual degree of strain during their early years in the new environment. Finally, the great Chinese migration of the 1860's and 1870's brought the Chinese extended family to the cities and mining towns of the Far West, with its network of kin extending five thousand miles across the Pacific and sustained by various versions of Confucianism. But it was essentially a promontory of that extended family, composed overwhelmingly of male sojourners who had every intention of returning to China once they had been able to save a sufficient sum of money—usually several hundred dollars—to enable them to live out their lives in comfort at home.

One can maintain, then, that the household taught, but there was a world of difference between the education of middle-class German children nurtured by the modified extended families of Milwaukee, of lower-class Irish children sent to work at the earliest possible age in the mills of Fall River, and of lower-class Chinese men panning for gold in the hills of California but instructed via letter by elders in the vicinity of Canton. And, beyond these primordial differences, there was the relentless process of Americanization and the tension created by the inescapable fact of a discordant education. The household, almost always in association with an ethnic church and a related configuration of benevolent and fraternal organizations, taught one language and culture; the educative institutions of the host society taught another. Yet here, too, there were differences from group to group. The Irish, less impeded by language differences, were often segregated and indeed segregated themselves as Roman Catholics; the Germans, more impeded by language differences, were less often reviled and segregated on the basis of religion and class. In both instances, mothers who had worked as domestics before marriage and, in the German case, who continued to work as domestics after marriage, were frequently able to teach the characteristic American dress, mannerisms, and attitudes they had learned in the homes of their employers. The Chinese, by contrast, actively segregated themselves. As sojourners, condemned by the dominant society and having no interest in joining it, they concentrated on surviving while earning the nest egg that would enable them to return to their homeland. Only later, when the thought of remaining occurred to some, did they change from sojourners to immigrants, to face all the problems of a discordant education in a particularly virulent form.

Finally, there were the households that were subject to the dynamics of racial segregation. As has already been indicated, blacks, both slave and free, lived overwhelmingly in nuclear households embedded in networks of kin. On smaller southern farms where one or two black families shared the work with a single white family, black families educated their young much as white families did, and indeed black and white children mixed easily in quasi-sibling relationships during their early years. Black parents systematically transmitted information, skills, and values, and probably disciplined their children in a fashion similar to neighboring whites, though the added dimension of the limits set by racial segregation was ever present in the definition of appropriate attitudes, behaviors, and relationships. On larger southern plantations, the quarter community was founded on a complex of nuclear households, though fictive parents and grandparents often served as surrogates for blood-related parents and grandparents. Mothers carried substantial responsibilities for teaching children the essentials of food preparation, household manufacture, religious belief, and the modes and means of relating to whites, including contending with white abuse. Fathers taught the skills of hunting, fishing, and food preservation, and particular arts and crafts where they were capable. They also carried responsibility for transmitting stories incorporating the threads of family history and the more general lore of the quarter community, including themes of black dignity and ultimate freedom—tasks, incidentally, that they frequently shared with community elders, including natural and fictive grandparents. In the northern cities, black households behaved much like lower-class white households, once again with the added dimension of racial segregation in the definition of attitudes, behaviors, and relationships. In all of this, black households worked in association with networks of segregated black social and benevolent organizations, and especially black churches. And in all of this, too, blacks encountered the harshest form of a discordant education, with sharp disjunctions between household teaching concerning black dignity and the teaching of the dominant white society concerning black inferiority.

Among the various Indian tribes and peoples, there was an extraordinary variety of marital and familial forms, though the differing structures and institutions shared a number of elements in common. For one thing, marriages tended to be arranged by adults, according to the customs of the tribe. Some tribes practiced polygamy; others, like the Iroquois, practiced monogamy. But all embedded the family unit, however defined, within an extensive and well-defined network of kin. Equally importantly, every tribe followed long-established customs concerning who precisely was responsible for teaching what to whom. Corporal punishment was rare, and mild and ritually circumscribed when practiced, with the result that praise and ridicule were widely used as prime pedagogical instruments. Fathers and mothers were assigned well-defined teaching roles, but religious societies claiming supernatural sanction also carried on much essential instruction, especially in the realm of values. Finally, there were formal *rites de passage* that provided additional instruction at the same time as they marked the transition point from childhood to adulthood. Among the Indians, too, there was the constant impingement of a discordant education, as the dominant white society vacillated among the policies of incorporation, protective segregation, and extinction—an impingement, as carried out by earnest schoolteachers, missionaries, Indian agents, and military units, that was probably more aggressively pursued than with any other subgroup of the society.

II

The educative influence of the church continued powerfully during the early national era, even more so than during the eighteenth century. The actual number of churches rose steadily from 1783 to 1876, as did the number of different sects and denominations represented. More important, perhaps, the increase in the number of churches was larger proportionately than the increase in population, with the ratio declining for a time, from one church to roughly 1,000 individuals in 1780 to one church to 1,100 individuals in 1800, and then rising from one church to 609 individuals in 1850 to one church to 532 individuals in 1870.[4]

TABLE VI*
CHURCHES IN THE UNITED STATES

Denominations	1850 Churches	1860 Churches	1870 Churches
All Denominations	38,061	54,009	72,459
Baptist (regular)	9,376	11,221	14,474
Baptist (other)	187	929	1,355
Christian	875	2,068	3,578
Congregational	1,725	2,234	2,887
Episcopal (Protestant)	1,459	2,145	2,835
Evangelical Association	39		815
Friends	726	726	692
Jewish	36	77	189
Lutheran	1,231	2,128	3,032
Methodist	13,302	19,883	25,278
Miscellaneous	122	2	27
Moravian (Unitas Fratrum)	344	49	72
Mormon	16	24	189
New Jerusalem (Swedenborgian)	21	58	90
Presbyterian (regular)	4,826	5,061	6,262
Presbyterian (other)	32	1,345	1,562
Reformed Church in America (late Dutch Reformed)	335	440	471
Reformed Church in the United States (late German Reformed)	341	676	1,256
Roman Catholic	1,222	2,550	4,127
Second Advent	25	70	225
Shaker	11	12	18
Spiritualist		17	95
Unitarian	245	264	331
United Brethren in Christ	14		1,445
Universalist	530	664	719
Unknown (local missions)	22		26
Unknown (union)	999	1,366	409

*The data for the table are drawn from Francis A. Walker, ed., *A Compendium of the Ninth Census* (Washington, D.C.: Government Printing Office, 1872), pp. 514–515.

4. The figures for 1780 and 1800 are from Edwin Scott Gaustad, *Historical Atlas of Religion in America* (New York: Harper & Row, 1962), pp. 4 and 162 respectively; the figures for 1850 are from *A Compendium of the Seventh Census*, p. 138; and those for 1870 are from Francis A. Walker, ed., *A Compendium of the Ninth Census* (Washington, D.C.: Government Printing Office, 1872), p. 514.

One fascinating factor in the increase of church influence—a phenomenon noted by many contemporary observers—was that it occurred at precisely the time when state legislatures and constitutional conventions were acting to eliminate traditional compulsions in the realm of religion. By 1783 the number of states without legal establishments of religion had grown to seven; in the remaining six (New Hampshire, Massachusetts, Connecticut, Maryland, Virginia, and South Carolina), establishment was usually maintained via arrangements that mandated or permitted the collection of taxes for the support of "public teachers" of the Christian religion. In an increasingly heterogeneous society, however, the determination of which public teachers of which denominations would enjoy such support raised thorny questions, and the political attack on establishment was unrelenting. Those favoring the arrangement sought to preserve it by constantly broadening the groups included within its embrace; but, almost in the nature of things, statutes could not be made broad enough to please everyone, with the result that the direction of change was clearly toward disestablishment. Virginia enacted Jefferson's Bill for Religious Freedom in 1786. The federal Constitution was amended in 1791 to include the provision that "Congress shall make no law respecting an establishment of religion, or prohibiting the free exercise thereof. . . ." And the remaining states disestablished religion via legislation or constitutional provision over the next four decades, with Massachusetts being the last to act in 1833. The net result of all this, however, was not to inhibit religion but rather to stimulate it. As the irrepressible Lyman Beecher noted in his diary concerning Connecticut's action of 1818, disestablishment was "the best thing that ever happened to the State of Connecticut. It cut the churches loose from dependence on state support. It threw them wholly on their own resources and on God." And as Alexis de Tocqueville remarked in 1835,

Religion in America takes no direct part in the government of society, but it must be regarded as the first of their political institutions; for if it does not impart a taste for freedom, it facilitates the use of it. Indeed, it is in this same point of view that the inhabitants of the United States themselves look upon religious belief. I do not know whether all Americans have a sincere faith in their religion—for who can search the human heart?—but I am certain that they hold it to be indispensable to the maintenance of republican institutions. This opinion is not peculiar to a class of citizens or to a party, but it belongs to the whole nation and to every rank of society.[5]

Given the context of religious freedom that resulted from disestablishment, the phenomenon of denominationalism, already emergent during the eighteenth-century awakenings, came to full fruition. The American churches became voluntary churches, each viewing itself and in turn viewed by others as incarnating a particular version of the general truth of Christianity. As voluntary churches, they were forced to seek continuing renewal from within, hence their commitment to revivals, and continuing replenishment from without, hence their commitment to missions. And both revivals and missions depended, in the last analysis, on persuasion or, alternatively, on the substance and pedagogy of evangelical teaching. Given a heterogeneous population on the one hand and a multiplicity of religious options on the other, the American situation came increasingly to be marked by doctrinal pluralism, organizational aggressiveness, and the constant pursuit of communicants. Obversely, a spirit of live-and-let-live, with frequent collaborative efforts in matters penultimate, prevailed.

Nowhere in the educational apparatus of the church was the impact of voluntarism more pronounced than in the realm of preaching. From the beginning, American churches had tended to be prophetic rather than sacramental, with the preaching function at the very heart of public worship. The awakenings of the eighteenth century had strengthened that tendency, placing a premium on that special kind of vivid evangelical preaching that awesomely portrayed the terrors of hell in the effort to stimulate the rebirth that would lead ultimately to salvation. There had been bitter controversies, to be sure, over questions of style and substance, and the result had often been separatism and fragmentation within the church. But there could be no mistaking the tendency toward evangelical preaching, and even the Old Lights, who opposed it, were not impervious to its influence.

5. The Massachusetts Constitution of 1780, in *The Federal and State Constitutions, Colonial Charters, and Other Organic Laws,* edited by Francis Newton Thorpe (7 vols.; Washington, D.C.: Government Printing Office, 1909), III, 1890; The Constitution of the United States, in Henry Steele Commager, ed., *Documents of American History* (9th ed.; 2 vols.; New York: Appleton-Century-Crofts, 1973), I, 146; *The Autobiography of Lyman Beecher,* edited by Barbara M. Cross (2 vols.; Cambridge, Mass.: Harvard University Press, 1961), I, 151; and Alexis de Tocqueville, *Democracy in America,* edited by Phillips Bradley (2 vols.; New York: Alfred A. Knopf, 1945), I, 305. With respect to Beecher's comment, it is interesting to note that he had actively resisted disestablishment before it had been legislated.

During the nineteenth century, particularly after the complex of revivals associated with the so-called second awakening, the variation in preaching styles became even greater, ranging from the carefully written but dryly read sermons of well-schooled Episcopal, Congregational, and Presbyterian divines to the rousing impromptu messages delivered by untutored Methodist or Baptist laymen. But there were certain characteristic features of American preaching in general that were already clearly discernible by the 1830's and 1840's. As the Presbyterian clergyman Robert Baird delineated them in his descriptive treatise *Religion in the United States of America* (1844), American preaching tended to be simple in design, earnest in tone, doctrinal in substance, and direct, immediate, and practical in its aim and intended effect. Moreover, though Baird's generalizations were clearly drawn from the Protestant churches, it is important to note that the sermon also assumed a greater importance in the public worship of Jews and Roman Catholics.[6]

Interestingly, since he himself had attended Washington and Jefferson Colleges and the Princeton Theological Seminary, Baird was unstinting in his defense of popular preaching by unlettered ministers. Their plain style, he noted, "is often far more likely to benefit their usual hearers, than would that of a learned doctor of divinity issuing from some great university. Their language, though not refined, is intelligible to those to whom it is addressed. Their illustrations may not be classical, but they will probably be drawn from the Bible or from scenes amid which their hearers move, and the events with which they are familiar...." Beyond that, and in this respect Baird's argument was especially revealing, the substance of their preaching was essentially stabilizing. "To them the country owes much of its conservative character," he noted, "for no men have inculcated more effectively those doctrines which promote obedience to law, respect for magistracy, and the maintenance of civil government...." This conservative bent of American preaching, not only on the part of unlettered ministers but on the part of learned ministers as well, was widely noted. Although American clergymen could be found on both sides of every major political conflict in pre-Civil War America and indeed on both sides of the "irrepressible conflict" itself, the more general patriotism, traditionalism, and proclivity for the status quo that characterized most American

6. Robert Baird, *Religion in the United States of America* (Glasgow: Blackie and Son, 1844), pp. 434–441.

clergymen was undeniable. There were radical accompaniments of that traditionalism, not least the zealous transnationalism that marked missionary efforts abroad, but its essential thrust was to affirm the legitimacy of the standing order. Patriotism and Protestantism suffused one another, as the churches developed a Protestant *paideia* that was widely taught as an American *paideia*. In fact, the churches did everything possible to render the two indistinguishable and therefore interchangeable. Moreover, many synagogues and non-Protestant churches drifted in similar directions, though the ideological contradictions implicit in the drift were not lost upon them.[7]

As in colonial times, the churches continued to serve as centers of formal and informal education. Ministers systematically instructed various age groups in correct doctrine and appropriate liturgy. They visited the households of their parishioners, comforting the sick and counseling the well (always in the context of the rich complex of meaning provided by sound doctrine). Depending on their denominational affiliations, they itinerated from time to time to serve as missionaries to the unconverted in neighborhoods near and far. And they maintained a vigorous interest in various quasi-official capacities in the public affairs of their communities. In different but related fashion, the families that constituted the congregation carried on their own mutual education, ranging from formal discussions of Scripture and its bearing on everyday life, to lively debates on political issues dividing the community, to informal exchanges on everything from cooking recipes to clothing styles to appropriate ways of carrying on a courtship. In newly settled regions of the country, the churches often served as meeting houses, courts, schools, and post offices, alternating public secular functions with private sacred functions in a way that inevitably mixed the two and thereby, willy-nilly, broadened the purview of church teaching. In the older regions, churches played a more traditional and clearly defined role, though again, given their quasi-public character even after disestablishment, it was a role that frequently intermixed sacred and secular functions.

As has already been indicated, one of the most interesting developments of the early national era was the proliferation of ancillary institutions specially designed to assist the church in carrying out its educative obligations. Sunday schools, young people's study groups, men's and women's organizations, Bible and tract societies, schools, acade-

7. *Ibid.*, pp. 433 and 434.

mies, and colleges of various sorts, camp meetings, and mission enterprises—all provided opportunities for formal study and instruction, in combination with different degrees of sociability, entertainment, and recreation. They immeasurably enhanced both the scope and the intensity of church teaching, providing organized contexts within which those who desired it (and probably some who didn't) could live a good part of their lives under the stimulus and discipline of religious teaching. In fact, the differences between a family partaking of the full range of activities of a Congregational church and its affiliated institutions in an Indiana town during the 1850's and a family in a loosely organized utopian community in the same state at the same time were more ones of degree than of kind.

As with the household, the church played a crucial mediative function in the Americanization of immigrants. In many immigrant communities, language, ethnicity, and religious observance combined to form the core of a tradition that was aggressively purveyed by a configuration of household, church, school, newspaper, and benevolent organization, with the church as intellectual leader and organizational center. Such was the case with the several Roman Catholic subcommunities of New York City, where Irish Catholics, German Catholics, and Italian Catholics sought to maintain not only their own characteristic language and culture but also their own special versions of Roman Catholic worship—an effort, incidentally, that frequently foundered on the predominance of Irish priests in the city. Such was also the case with the German Lutherans and Roman Catholics in Milwaukee, though the dynamics were somewhat different, owing to the proliferation there of ethnic organizations whose membership crossed religious lines. And, since the differences among these communities suggest the varying roles of the church within different immigrant communities and different configurations of education, they are especially instructive. Where ethnic churches were vigorous in the development of parochial schools, as was the case with New York's Irish Catholic community and Milwaukee's German Catholic and German Lutheran communities, the potential Americanizing influence of the local public schools was lessened. Where ethnic churches were less vigorous, as was the case with New York's German Catholic community—largely, incidentally, because the Germans were able to obtain bilingual instruction in the local ward schools—the Americanizing influence of the public schools was heightened. Many factors were at play as the churches became involved in the tensions and dynamics of a discordant education, and none was more important than a particular church's responsiveness to the phenomenon of Americanization. More often than not, the nature of a church's response to the American scene depended on the social class and ethnic background of its communicants as well as on its internal cohesiveness. But within most denominations conflicts and splits did emerge: the Lutheran churches split over the role of the German language, the Jewish community over the role of the Hebrew language in the liturgy, and the Roman Catholic church over a wide variety of issues, ranging from whether Irish families would hold their wakes at home or at church to whether ethnic background would play a role in clerical assignments. Yet, whatever the balance between new and old, in the end Americanization was a two-way exchange. As Kathleen Neils Conzen has argued about Milwaukee, the city became Germanized as the Germans became Americanized, with the churches among the organizations at the heart of that process of mutual education.[8]

Within the black community, organized religion was frequently associated with two very different pedagogies. In the South, white and black preachers associated with the Baptist and Methodist churches and sponsored by the slaveowners sought to instruct blacks in the doctrines of white supremacy, black inferiority, and the legitimacy of slavery at the same time that clandestine black congregations under the leadership of indigenous religious leaders sought to nurture and inspire the contrary doctrines of black equality and ultimate freedom. In the North, black churches functioned in a manner highly similar to white churches, though within a community walled off by a combination of de jure and de facto segregation. The Reverend Amos G. Beman's African Congregational Church in New Haven during the 1850's furnishes an excellent example. It was a center of religious instruction, devotion, and ceremony, but it served also as a meeting house, a community center, and, not surprisingly, a refuge for fugitive slaves. It spawned its own network of benevolent associations, library clubs, adult forums, and temperance societies; it housed a Sunday school; and it served as a source of news and literature on black affairs in general and on abolitionist activity in particular. The dynamics of a discordant education evident there were not different from the ones evident in the South, with members of the congregation subjected to both the explicit teachings of surrounding white institutions and the implicit teaching of enforced segregation. But, under Beman's vigorous leadership, the combination of households that formed the congregation and the complex of

8. Kathleen Neils Conzen, *Immigrant Milwaukee, 1836–1860: Accommodation and Community in a Frontier City* (Cambridge, Mass.: Harvard University Press, 1976), pp. 225–228.

ancillary educative institutions associated with the church provided an unusually influential countereducation to that teaching, and doubtless contributed much to the vitality, stability, and pride of New Haven's black community.

In the case of the Indians, the question was one of organized Christian churches as represented by missionaries actually at cultural war with the religious institutions that were part and parcel of tribal social structures. The missionary and the medicine man taught their respective curricula, the missionary's representing the promontory of a larger social and cultural system he wished the Indian to adopt, the medicine man's representing a complex of ideas and practices that sustained and gave meaning to the social and cultural world in which the Indian lived. It was a discordant education with even less overlap than that of new European immigrants, who had at least known churches in the Old World, though not fundamentally different from that encountered by newly arrived Afro-Americans. That it proved destructive of individual identities and entire tribal societies should not be surprising, for the change required by acceptance of the missionary's teaching was more profound and sweeping than any faced by European immigrants of any ethnic background.

It is difficult to generalize about the ministerial career during the early national era, owing to profound differences from denomination to denomination and from region to region. Among Congregationalists and Presbyterians, especially in New England, there was a decided shift from an older pattern under which a minister would settle in a particular community and remain there for the rest of his life, to a newer pattern under which it was assumed that he would be "called" to a series of congregations during the course of a lifetime; Lyman Beecher's moves from East Hampton, Long Island, to Litchfield, Connecticut, to the Hanover Street Church in Boston are illustrative. Among Methodists and Baptists, by contrast, the tradition of unschooled preachers "called to the service of the Lord" led to more informal arrangements between ministers and congregations, with Methodist and Baptist preachers often pursuing more than one occupation simultaneously. The Methodist clergyman Lorenzo Dow, for example, peddled "Dow's Family Medicine" while preaching in Connecticut during the 1820's and the Baptist clergyman Billington McCarter Sanders conducted Mercer Institute (which later became Mercer College) while preaching in Georgia during the 1830's. Beecher, incidentally, went to the Hanover Street Church at an annual salary of two thousand dollars; Methodist preachers during the 1820's tended to earn between one hundred and three hundred dollars a year, depending on the size of their households, while many a Baptist preacher during that decade ministered to his congregation gratis.

Assuming, then, that diversity was the rule, two careers can be useful in illustrating the range and extent of educational activity in which evangelical clergymen tended to become involved during the course of an active life in the service of the Lord. Asa Turner was born and reared in Massachusetts, attended Yale, and won ordination in 1830. While at Yale he joined an "association" of seven theology students, known as the "Yale Band," who pledged to collaborate in launching an institution of learning in Illinois, some "to engage as instructors in the seminary," others "to occupy—as preachers—important stations in the surrounding country." Turner proceeded to establish a church in Quincy, Illinois, in 1830 and became a founding trustee of Illinois College; and for the next eight years he was indefatigable in educational causes, taking the lead in establishing a school in Quincy, soliciting funds for the college, organizing camp meetings in the westernmost part of the state, and assisting in the formation of new congregations. In 1838 he removed to Denmark, Iowa, where he established another church (the first Congregational church west of the Mississippi), obtained a charter for a new institution called Denmark Academy, assisted an "Iowa Band" that had earlier gathered at the Andover Theological Seminary in the founding of Iowa College (which later merged with Grinnell), and campaigned for a public school system.[9]

John Mason Peck pursued a similar career under Baptist auspices. Born and reared in Connecticut, Peck attended the common schools there, farmed for a number of years, and then felt the call to preach in the Baptist church. He became interested in mission work and went West in 1817, working in St. Louis for a time and then relocating in 1822 to Rock Spring, Illinois, which he made the headquarters for unending itinerations over the next forty years through Illinois, Indiana, and Missouri. In the course of his labors, he founded countless Bible societies, tract societies, and Sunday schools, established Rock Spring Seminary (later Shurtleff College) to train teachers and ministers, edited a variety of religious periodicals, and served as agent for the Western Baptist Publication Society, all while preaching to innumerable white and black congregations, partaking of revivals, counseling new preachers, and meeting with associations of clergymen and laymen. In effect, Turner and Peck lived the crusade to civilize the West that

9. Theron Baldwin *et al.*, Certificate of Association, February 21, 1829 (Illinois College mss., Illinois College Library, Jacksonville).

Beecher preached, and in so doing they incarnated the educational thrust of nondenominational evangelical Protestantism during the pre-Civil War period.

III

Schooling came into its own during the early national era, as part of a more general phenomenon throughout western Europe and North America in which the United States was an acknowledged leader. The increase in the number of schools and the extent of schooling that had already been apparent during the latter years of the eighteenth century persisted into the nineteenth, to the point where schooling had become widely available in the older, more settled regions by the 1820's and 1830's. But the diversity of schooling also persisted, so that what was available came in many modes, from the semiformal classes that met in farmhouse kitchens and frontier churches, to the charity schools of New York and Philadelphia, to the town-sponsored ventures of New England, to the various church-supported systems maintained by the Quakers, the Presbyterians, and the Episcopalians, to the quasi-public academies that sprang up in every region of the country. The support of these institutions was as varied as their form, ranging from fees paid directly to the teacher, to subscriptions contributed by parents and friends, to tithes collected from parishioners and congregations, to interest yielded by public and private endowment funds, to taxes levied on real property, to every conceivable combination of these devices. The public school movement of the 1840's and 1850's built on this foundation, extending schooling to those regions where it had been sparse, regularizing schooling in those regions where it had been intermittent, systematizing schooling in those regions where it had become prevalent, and generally shifting the support of schooling to the relatively certain foundation of tax funds.

The three basic types of colonial school also persisted into the early national era. The English school stressed reading, spelling, writing, and arithmetic, with the common addition of geography and history. It was almost always a single unit in a single building during the eighteenth century, frequently enrolling youngsters from two or three to fourteen years of age, and it remained a single unit during much of the nineteenth, at least in the rural districts and smaller townships that made up most of the United States. In the more populous regions, however, the English school evolved organizationally into a variety of differentiated units variously named and catering to differing age groups. A primary school might accept students at the age of five or six and hold them for some two or three years, sending them on to some sort of English grammar school or intermediate school, the particular names and forms evolving through improvisation, depending on the character of the student population, the availability of buildings, and the particular notions of schooling abroad in the locality at any given time. The Latin grammar school continued to flourish, but principally in the cities and larger towns of the East. It accepted boys at the age of nine or ten, assuming that they could read and write English and had some knowledge of English grammar, and then led them through a four- or five-year curriculum that focused on Latin and Greek, with varying additional studies in history, geography, and mathematics (usually geometry, algebra, and trigonometry). Finally, the academy, which reached the height of its development during the nineteenth century, became a characteristically American catchall school that enrolled such students as it could attract and taught them such subjects of the English or Latin-grammar curriculum as seemed appropriate. It was frequently a boarding school, but it almost always accepted day students as well.

Three new types of institution also emerged during the nineteenth century. The first was the infant school, which was borrowed from Great Britain, where it seems to have originated as part of Robert Owen's experiment at New Lanark. Growing up initially in the eastern cities, it was designed for children between the ages of two and seven and was obviously created to place the very young in a quasi-domestic environment under the supervision of a quasi-maternal female teacher (an environment quite different from the common roughhouse atmosphere of the district school, which tended in the early decades of the century to be under tough male control). The innovation flourished for a time and then died out, as the age deemed appropriate for school entry increased to five or six and as female teachers began to move into the primary schools. Later, in the 1850's, the infant school was revived as the kindergarten, developed by the disciples of the German pedagogical theorist Friedrich Froebel.

A second emergent type of institution was the high school, which originated in Boston as an alternative to the Latin grammar school for those who wished to continue with the work of the English curriculum, although it quickly developed into a public institution offering the option of an English or a classical curriculum as it was copied in smaller communities. For all intents and purposes, the high school reproduced under public auspices the upper reaches of the academy, making available to day students at modest cost or gratis what had formerly been available to boarding students at more substantial cost. Where a local high school developed as a continuation of the primary or grammar or intermediate school, it constituted an additional rung on what was increasingly perceived as an American educational ladder, or unitary school system, in contradistinction to the dual school systems of England, France, and Prussia, where the institutions that prepared the vast majority of young people for life were structurally separated from those that prepared a small minority of young people for further education in the university.

A final residual category might be labeled, in Henry Barnard's phrase, "supplementary schools," or schools that supplied "deficiencies" in the education of individuals whose school attendance had been "prematurely abridged, or from any cause interfered with." Such schools grew up during the early national era under private, quasi-public, and public auspices for special groups of students having special educational needs that the community thought would best be met in separate educational institutions, including handicapped youngsters, particularly the blind, the deaf, and the feeble-minded; youngsters judged incorrigible or delinquent; and black and Indian youngsters deemed unacceptable in regular classrooms. In a number of instances, the right of communities to conduct such institutions was challenged legally, as, for example, in *Ex Parte Crouse* (1838), where the father of a Philadelphia youngster named Mary Ann Crouse sought unsuccessfully on Sixth Amendment grounds to overturn her commitment to the House of Refuge there (the court held that natural parents, when unequal to the task of education or unworthy of it, might be superseded by "the *parens patriae,* or common guardian of the community") or in *Roberts* v. *City of Boston* (1849), where the father of a Boston youngster named Sarah Roberts sought, again unsuccessfully, on the basis of the guarantees in the Massachusetts constitution to enroll her in a white primary school nearer her home than the black primary school to which she had been assigned (the court held that the City of Boston had the right to maintain "separate but equal" facilities for blacks). But throughout the period the right to conduct such schools was generally assumed by state legislatures and upheld by the courts.[10]

Textbooks became more numerous during the early national era, extending the variety of options available within any given classroom; and, while there can be no ready assumption that what was in the text-

---

10. *Journal of the Rhode Island Institute of Instruction,* I (1845–46), 60; *Ex Parte Crouse,* 4 Wharton (Pa.), 9 (1838); and *Roberts* v. *City of Boston,* 59 Mass. 198, 200 (1849).

books was necessarily taught, much less learned, textbooks were seen by parents, teachers, and students alike as providing whatever structure and order or, in contemporary terms, "system" there would be in the various subjects of the curriculum. In the teaching of reading, the hornbooks and primers of colonial days gave way to a profusion of spellers and readers that vied for the attention of schoolteachers, school board members, and parents. Among the spellers, Noah Webster's and Lyman Cobb's were the leaders during the early decades of the nineteenth century, among the readers, Noah Webster's, Caleb Bingham's, Lindley Murray's, and then, after the 1840's, the series of graded texts put together by William Holmes and Alexander Hamilton McGuffey. Spellers concentrated on lists of words arranged in order of length, complexity, and difficulty, but initially tended to include some reading matter and occasionally some elementary arithmetic as well. Readers brought together stories, verse, expositions, historical accounts, essays, speeches, and excerpts from belles-lettres, also arranged in order of length, complexity, and difficulty, and usually supplemented these with lists of words to be mastered. And a number of texts, especially primers for beginners, sought to combine exercises in both spelling and reading. By and large, the spellers and readers continued to lead the student from the alphabet through a syllabarium to lists of syllabified words and selections of reading matter that incorporated them. The earliest exception was the textbook of Samuel Worcester (1828), who attempted to substitute the whole-word method of teaching reading (originated by the German educator Friedrich Gedike and the French educator Jean Joseph Jacotot) for the alphabet-syllable method. Later exceptions, developed after the Civil War, attempted to substitute a phonic method, whereby words were taught through their phonetic elements rather than their alphabetic sounds and syllables.[11]

11. Noah Webster, *A Grammatical Institute, of the English Language, Comprising, an Easy, Concise, and Systematic Method of Education, Designed for the Use of English Schools in America;* Part I (Hartford: Hudson & Goodwin, [1793]); Lyman Cobb, *Cobb's New Primary Spelling Book, in Four Parts* (New York: Collins & Brother, 1847); Noah Webster, *A Grammatical Institute, of the English Language,* Part III (Hartford: Barlow & Babcock, 1785); Caleb Bingham, *The American Preceptor, Being a New Selection of Lessons for Reading and Speaking* (2d ed.; Boston: I. Thomas and E. T. Andrews, 1795); Lindley Murray, *The English Reader* (New York: Isaac Collins, 1799); [William Holmes McGuffey], *Eclectic First Reader* (Cincinnati: Truman and Smith, 1836), *The Eclectic Second Reader* (Cincinnati: Truman and Smith, 1836), *Eclectic Third Reader* (Cincinnati: Truman and Smith, 1837), and *Eclectic Fourth Reader* (Cincinnati: Truman and Smith, 1837); [Alexander Hamilton McGuffey], *McGuffey's Rhetorical Guide or Fifth Reader* (Cincinnati: W. B. Smith, 1844), and *McGuffey's New Sixth Eclectic Reader* (Cincinnati: W. B. Smith and Company, 1857); and Samuel Worcester, *A Primer of the English Language* (Boston: Hillard, Gray, Little, and Wilkins, 1828).

Among the more interesting features of the readers was the shift after 1783 in the character of the material included, from an overwhelming emphasis on religious prose and poetry to a more diverse fare of stories about animals, birds, and children, frequently with a message to be conveyed or a moral to be drawn. Increasingly, too, orations from Revolutionary days, biographies of Revolutionary heroes, and other patriotic material found its way into the readers; and, particularly in the McGuffey series, there were substantial selections from such English authors as Shakespeare, Milton, Addison, Scott, and Dickens, and such American authors as Longfellow, Hawthorne, and Bryant. Over the years, readers also began to be much more richly illustrated with pictures of youngsters doing chores and at play. Finally, and the point is especially relevant to a society that emphasized persuasive oratory in its politics, many readers included material on pronunciation and elocution.

Writing continued to be taught through the imitation of models of Italian cursive script. A major pedagogical innovation came, however, with the publication in 1791 of John Jenkins's *The Art of Writing*. Jenkins analyzed the various letters of cursive script into their component elements, discovering that a half-dozen interchangeable strokes could constitute virtually all the letters of the alphabet. Jenkins's textbook taught, seriatim, the strokes, then the letters, then entire words, and then whole sentences, maintaining, on the one hand, that any student could learn the Jenkins system without the assistance of a tutor and, on the other hand, that once the system had been mastered any student could teach it without an apprenticeship. Jenkins's method was widely imitated, notably by Henry Dean in *The Analytic Guide to the Art of Penmanship* (1804), which went through several editions and quickly overshadowed Jenkins's own textbooks; but the method in one version or another dominated American penmanship instruction until the 1860's and 1870's, when the rapid diffusion of steel pens made the ornate slanted script of Platt Rogers Spencer a more appropriate model for students to imitate.[12]

English grammar entered the primary school curriculum during the early national era as a subject ancillary to reading and writing, with writing seen not merely as penmanship but as the beginning of composition. As embodied in the leading textbooks of the time, including the

12. John Jenkins, *The Art of Writing, Reduced to a Plain and Easy System* (Boston: I. Thomas and E. T. Andrews, 1791); and Henry Dean, *The Analytic Guide to the Art of Penmanship* (Salem, Mass.: Joshua Cushing, 1804).

English import by Lindley Murray (who had himself been born and educated in America) and later the books by Noah Webster, Goold Brown, and Peter Bullions, English grammar included orthography, etymology, syntax, and prosody. It was taught principally by the memorization of definitions, rules, and models, and, though it doubtless did lead to the writing of compositions in some instances, the gap between the memorization and the composing was prodigious.[13]

Arithmetic became far more significant in the primary school curriculum after 1783, though with that increased significance came fundamental shifts in its content and character. As embodied in the textbooks of Nicholas Pike, Warren Colburn, and especially Joseph Ray, it included fewer topics like foreign exchange and compound denominationate numbers (3 yards, 2 feet, 5 inches) and emphasized instead mental manipulations of whole numbers and common fractions. Pike's textbook was a veritable mathematical reference book that took the student from simple arithmetic through logarithms, geometry, trigonometry, and algebra, using the traditional method of rules followed by model problems. Colburn's textbook was the first to use the inductive method, with the rule being drawn from numerous examples rather than stated as explicit precept. Typically the first exercise was, "How many thumbs have you on your right hand? How many on your left? How many on both together?" Ray's textbooks also employed the inductive method but went beyond Colburn to form a graded series, much like the McGuffey series, with which they were contemporary.[14]

Geography and history were relatively new areas within the primary school curriculum. They had appeared sporadically (and at more advanced levels) during the last decades of the eighteenth and first decades of the nineteenth centuries but became more common as the nineteenth century progressed. As embodied in Jedidiah Morse's *Geography Made Easy* (1784), the geography of the United States was presented state by state, with attention to political subdivisions, climate, topography, people, institutions, and products. Samuel G. Goodrich's geographies, which began to appear in the 1830's, tended to be more

13. Lindley Murray, *English Grammar* (York, England: Wilson, Spence, and Mawman, 1795); Noah Webster, *A Grammatical Institute, of the English Language,* Part II; Goold Brown,, *Institutes of English Grammar* (New York: published by the author, 1823); and Peter Bullions, *Analytic and Practical Grammar of the English Language* (New York: Pratt, Woodford & Co., 1849).

14. Nicholas Pike, *A New and Complete System of Arithmetic* (Newburyport, Mass.: John Mycall, 1788); Warren Colburn, *First Lessons in Arithmetic on the Plan of Pestalozzi* (2d ed.; Boston: Cummings and Hilliard, 1821); and Joseph Ray, *Ray's Eclectic Arithmetic on the Inductive and Analytic Methods of Instruction* (Cincinnati: Truman & Smith, 1837). The quote is from Colburn, *First Lessons in Arithmetic,* p. 1.

readable and more attractively illustrated, and, like the McGuffey readers and the Ray arithmetics, more effectively graded in difficulty. The first United States history textbooks for the lower schools were compiled by a Philadelphia printer named John M'Culloch during the 1780's and 1790's, and, though they were cut-and-paste products taken from other sources, they did present an ordered account of American history from "aboriginal" times to the Revolution. Later, Samuel G. Goodrich, again during the 1830's, entered the field with an attractively illustrated series of graded texts that quickly captured a considerable share of the market. Like the readers, geography and history textbooks engaged in a considerable amount of moralizing at the same time that they purveyed information, teaching quite directly the superiority of Americans and American institutions, the inferiority of colored peoples, the truth of the Protestant Christian religion, and, in the case of the vast majority of books, which were produced in the Northeast, the evils of slavery.[15]

Latin and Greek grammar and literature continued to be taught at more advanced levels and in fairly traditional style, though teachers of classical languages during the early national era could increasingly assume, as their colonial predecessors could not, that their students had systematically studied English spelling, reading, and grammar. The shift made a considerable difference; for, when students first encountered grammar, they were not merely older but also somewhat more familiar with the systematic study of language and somewhat more habituated to the pedagogy by which languages were taught.

A host of other subjects appeared in school curricula: sewing and French for girls, bookkeeping and science for boys, and elocution, physiology, drawing, and music for both sexes. But spelling, reading, writing, grammar, arithmetic, geography, and history were the staples that by the 1840's and 1850's had become readily available in most settled regions. One additional subject that was universally mandated, either explicitly or implicitly, was the teaching of virtue or good behavior. The Massachusetts school law of 1789 phrased the requirement in representative language when it enjoined all teachers to exert "their best endeavors, to impress on the minds of children and youth committed to their care and instruction, the principles of piety, justice and a sacred regard to truth, love to their country, humanity and universal benevolence, sobriety, industry and frugality, chastity, moderation and

15. Jedidiah Morse, *Geography Made Easy* (New Haven: Meigs, Bowen & Dana, 1784); and Samuel G. Goodrich, *A Geographical View of the United States* (New York: W.W. Reed, 1829).

temperance, and those other virtues which are the ornament of human society, and the basis upon which the republican Constitution is structured." The injunction was taken to mean the systematic teaching of nondenominational Christianity, conveyed by prayers of the sort that Isaac Watts had composed for children in the eighteenth century and that the American Sunday-School Union included in its publications during the nineteenth, by readings from the Bible (in the King James Version), by stories in which virtue was rewarded (or served as its own reward) and vice punished, and by systematic enforcement of a stern code of behavior that was deemed exemplary of Christian living. Given the evangelical effort to identify nondenominational Protestantism with righteous republicanism, the teaching of virtue went hand in hand with the teaching of patriotism, with the result that God, country, and temperance were often inseparably intertwined in the preachments of teachers and textbooks. There were variant versions of this substance in Roman Catholic schools, Jewish schools, and more assertively denominational Protestant schools, a substance occasionally compounded by particular strains of ethnicity; but the schools were more alike than different in the extent to which they explicitly taught some value system that combined piety, patriotism, and good behavior.[16]

The one-room district school that placed a single teacher in daily contact with between forty and sixty boys and girls of varying ages over a two- or three-month period during the winter or during the summer remained the rule in most parts of the United States. Through an informal method of grouping different children for different subjects at different levels, the teacher attempted to keep the youngsters at work on various tasks. Sometimes the entire student group would go through a sing-song drill together, spelling a group of words, reciting a multiplication table, or listing the capitals of the states; sometimes groups of three or four students would recite together; and sometimes individual students would take turns going through a question-and-answer drill with the teacher. In the interstices of the process, there was doubtless a good deal of room for sibling- and peer-mediated instruction. But it was on the whole a relatively inefficient process, especially, as was usually the case, in the hands of an inexperienced teacher. Moreover, the associated disciplinary problems were often quite serious. The tradition of "turning out the teacher," immortalized in quaint works of nineteenth-century fiction, had a basis in reality, and it was often the job of

16. Massachusetts, *Laws of the Commonwealth of Massachusetts* (1789), chap. xix.

the new teacher to test his or her strength against that of the "big boys" before the class could get down to a term of serious work.

One response to pedagogical inefficiency and the problems associated with it, as well as to the steady rise of school populations and school costs, was the monitorial system. As developed by English educators contending with similar problems, notably a London teacher named Joseph Lancaster, the system was based on two sets of pedagogical innovations, first, a carefully sequenced arrangement of the subject matter to be taught and an elaborate system of directives for teaching it, and, second, the use of older children as monitors to teach the younger children. As the system was actually practiced in the United States—at its peak during the early 1820's there were more than 150 Lancasterian schools in the country—it yielded initial economies in the resources needed to deal with large numbers of primary school children; but the quasi-military organization implicit in the system proved odious to both parents and school board members, and the system was gradually abandoned during the 1830's. By that time, however, the organization of graded classes based on some combination of age and academic achievement was providing an alternative means of coping with pedagogical inefficiency, particularly in urban areas where the Lancasterian system had been most widely applied. The grouping of children thereby made possible permitted a concentration of effort and an economy of time, while also solving the problems inherent in the continued mixing of old and young children. As grading developed in particular localities, it yielded varying school units with varying combinations of grades; yet, by the time of the Civil War, one could already discern alongside the more traditional district school system, with its preponderance of one-room schoolhouses, an urban system in which a youngster could proceed from a primary school though some kind of intermediate or grammar school to a high school or academy. Moreover, following the example of the academies, which included both courses preparing for college entrance and courses preparing for "life," most public schools offered advanced study in the staple subjects supplemented by a choice of college-preparatory or vocational training—bookkeeping, or surveying, or mercantile mathematics—and it was this that lent a special unitary character to the American school system that was significantly different from its Western European counterparts and widely perceived as a peculiarly American innovation.[17]

17. The number of Lancasterian schools is from an estimate given in the *Fourteenth Report of the British and Foreign School Society* (1819), p. 61.

Given the centrality of the textbook and the copybook in the work of the school, the pedagogy of the teachers inevitably involved some consistent stance toward the material. As Barbara Finkelstein has pointed out, some teachers placed the burden of learning almost entirely on the students, serving as intellectual overseers of the process of study. Others were essentially taskmasters, moving groups of students in concert through the material. And still others, in smaller numbers, attempted to embellish, elaborate, or even explain the material in the textbooks, serving in effect as interpreters. Whatever pedagogical stance the teacher maintained, however, there was the ever-present problem of discipline. The methods of this realm ranged from sheer physical coercion enforced by corporal punishment, to more subtle forms of chastisement and humiliation, to the systematic use of competition, rivalry, and symbolic and material incentives, to the more kindly and nurturant methods that marked a few avant-garde Pestalozzian schools.[18]

Two additional points bear comment. First, there was varying opportunity for schooling among different social groups, and varying utilization as well. Schooling was far less available to blacks and Indians than to whites—recall that it was actually illegal in many of the southern states to teach slaves to read and write. Schooling was both less available and less utilized by first-generation immigrants than by second-generation immigrants or native-born whites. And, among first- and second-generation immigrants, it was less used by working-class Irish families in New York and New England than by middle-class German families in the Midwest. Finally, schooling was available in far greater variety and over far larger time spans to males than to females: comparatively few women went to academies and colleges before the Civil War, and the options available to them in those academies and colleges were more constrained and constricted. Beyond that, even in coeducational situations, there were physical and psychological barriers in everything from classrooms and schoolyards to the subjects of the curriculum in which females were supposed to display interest, ability, and achievement.

Second, with the popularization of schooling, there was a decided change in the character and composition of the teaching profession. There was in the first place a definite feminization of the teaching

18. Barbara Joan Finkelstein, "Governing the Young, Teacher Behavior in American Primary Schools, 1820–1880: A Documentary History" (doctoral thesis, Teachers College, Columbia University, 1970). Henry Barnard was one commentator who emphasized the centrality of student learning. See Jean and Robert McClintock, eds., *Henry Barnard's School Architecture* (New York: Teachers College Press, 1970), pp. 25–26.

force, particularly in the primary and intermediate grades, where the enrollment gains were the greatest. There were many reasons for the shift, some explicitly proffered, some implicitly recognized. Women, it was maintained, were far more suited by temperament, disposition, and purity of morals to work with younger children and better able to bring the best qualities of the "domestic circle" to the enterprise of the school. They were also willing to work for half the pay of men (sometimes even a third), and the men who held supervisory positions in the schools or on school committees found them more amenable to suggestion. Along with feminization, there was a decided move to professionalize teaching, to make of it a sacred calling second only to the ministry in its importance to the society. Particularly among male high school and academy teachers and the leaders of newly developing state and city education departments, raising the sights of teachers and providing training for their efforts became a matter of first concern. Interestingly, however, the lists of those participating in organizations like the American Institute of Instruction and the Western Literary Institute and College of Professional Teachers suggest that the concept of a teaching profession was largely reserved for the males who were considered the leaders of popular schooling and for whom professional training was deemed necessary and appropriate. Whether or not it was intended, professionalization served to create an almost exclusively male elite and thereby assured continuing male control of an increasingly female occupation.

Given the range of institutions called schools, the variation in the length and character of teaching careers was enormous: Asa Turner, having attended the district schools of Templeton, Massachusetts, as a boy, taught a few winter sessions in the same schools before deciding to become a minister; Moses Waddel, having attended Hampden-Sydney College, spent over a quarter-century in teaching, first as head of an academy at Willington, South Carolina, between 1804 and 1819, and then as president of the University of Georgia between 1819 and 1829. Yet the decisive fact of the era was the movement of women into teaching in unprecedented numbers. The careers of two such women exemplify what was often the transitory character of such careers.

Zilpah Polly Grant was born in Norfolk, Connecticut, in 1794 and began teaching in nearby schools at the age of fifteen in order to help support her family (her father had died when she was two). In 1820, after her mother had remarried, she became both a student and a teacher at the Reverend Joseph Emerson's female seminary at Byfield, Massachusetts; she moved on from there to teach at a school at Winsted,

Connecticut; then, in 1823, she returned to Emerson's seminary, which had moved to Saugus, Massachusetts; in the following year, she took over the newly founded Adams Female Academy at Londonderry, New Hampshire; and in 1828, after a quarrel with the trustees over religious and curricular matters, she went on to Ipswich, Massachusetts, where she conducted the Ipswich Female Seminary in collaboration with Mary Lyon, a friend from Emerson's school, who later founded Mount Holyoke Seminary. Grant left Ipswich in 1839, in poor health, and never returned to teaching, marrying William Bostwick Bannister, a prominent Dedham, Massachusetts, lawyer, in 1841.

Unlike Grant, Alice Money taught for only a few years, though, as with Grant, those years were marked by constant movement from position to position. A native of England who had come to the United States in 1848 at the age of two, Money had moved to Iowa as a teenager with her father and stepmother (her mother had died soon after their arrival in America). Eager to escape from her role as seamstress, nursemaid, and general aid to the family, Money decided to prepare herself for teaching at Albion Academy in Marshalltown. Studying while working to earn her tuition (she took the place of a hired sheepherder on the family farm), she managed in a single semester to qualify for a teaching certificate in the common branches, but could not "get a school." Following additional work at Albion, she did obtain a position in Grundy County, some sixteen miles from her home. She taught twelve students (five of whom left at harvest time), she was paid twenty-five dollars a month, she boarded with a family in the neighborhood, and she reported that she liked "the teaching part but not the discipline." During the summer of 1868, she moved to a school nearer home, where she taught some forty pupils; and then in the summer of 1869 she moved again, to a school at which the older students had turned out several previous teachers. Money survived, but at the end of that summer she gave up teaching to marry Dr. Elmer Y. Lawrence, a local physician, and did not again work outside her household.

Whereas Zilpah Grant had taught a fairly rigorous curriculum at Ipswich, Alice Money was often a few lessons ahead of her students; but both women taught for a limited period of time in their lives and in a constant succession of jobs. As one contemporary observed in a letter to a friend, "Teachers are migratory characters."[19]

19. Floy Lawrence Emhoff, "A Pioneer School Teacher in Central Iowa," *Iowa Journal of History and Politics*, XXXIII (1935), 381, 385; and Ira Moore to Edward Wellington, November 20, 1851, quoted in Geraldine Jonçich Clifford, "Home and School in 19th Century America: Some Personal-History Reports from the United States," *History of Education Quarterly*, XVIII (1978), 19.

I V

Colleges, universities, and other so-called seminaries of learning were founded in droves during the first century of the Republic, and there is really no way of counting them accurately, partly because of the looseness of definition and partly because they were not only founded in large numbers but they expired in significant numbers, too. There were at least 13 collegiate-level institutions with charters empowering them to grant degrees in 1783, and, if one were to add the academies that offered what was clearly collegiate-level instruction, the number of institutions of higher learning would more appropriately be set at 20 or 25. By 1831 the *American Almanac* listed 46 colleges, along with 22 theological seminaries, 16 medical schools, and 7 law schools. By 1850 the Census could report 119 colleges, along with 44 theological seminaries, 36 medical schools, and 16 law schools. And by 1876 the United States Bureau of Education could report 356 colleges and universities, 124 theological seminaries, 78 medical schools, and 42 law schools. Many of these institutions remained loosely defined for years: the theological schools taught general as well as professional subjects, and the medical and dental schools taught popular science.[20]

The colleges were especially interesting, having come into being for every conceivable purpose, from religious enthusiasm to community boosterism. The military academy at West Point was established in 1802 to train officers for the armed services, and ended up training most of the pre–Civil War engineers in the United States who did not come solely via the route of apprenticeship. It was not formally a college and granted no degrees; but it functioned as a college and was more influential than most. The Free Academy, which later became the College of the City of New York, was created in 1847 to train youngsters who could not afford to pay for higher education. Michigan Agricultural College was founded in 1855 to train farmers. Vassar College was founded in 1861 to train women. And Howard University was founded in 1867 to train blacks. Many an institution that originated in a burst of community aspiration was later saved by denominational

---

20. *The American Almanac and Repository of Useful Knowledge for the Year 1831* (2d ed.; Boston: Gray and Bowen, no date), pp. 166–167, 169; De Bow, ed., *Compendium of the Seventh Census,* p. 145; and U.S., Bureau of Education, *Report of the Commissioner of Education for the Year 1876,* pp. 698–707, 738–742, 748–749, 752–754. The report also noted 25 colleges not included among the 356 from which no information had been received (see p. 728).

support, while others that originated in bursts of religious enthusiasm were later saved by community support. Institutions established for Roman Catholics attracted Protestants; institutions established to prepare teachers ended up preparing journalists as well. The sponsorship, clientele, and curriculum of American higher education were diverse, shifting, at best vaguely defined, and, more than anywhere else in the world, relentlessly popular. As the Reverend Absalom Peters, one of the early leaders of the American Home Missionary Society, remarked in 1851 concerning the "advantages" of higher education:

It was never intelligently proposed to concentrate these advantages in a single university, 'cum privilegio,' nor to confine them to a few colleges, at great distances from each other. The wide extent of the country, the prospective increase of population, the form of government, the independence of the states, and above all the Protestant principle of universal education, have forbidden such a design; and the colleges have adapted themselves to their appropriate spheres, in accordance with this state of things. They have thus trained the public mind to feel, that a college, in each district of convenient extent, is a great blessing to the people. It is therefore placed beyond all doubt, that our country, in the whole extent of it, is to be a land of colleges.[21]

A number of factors combined to make the United States a "land of colleges" during the nineteenth century. For one thing, the early land policy of the federal government, as set forth by the Ordinances of 1785 and 1787 and as continued in the enabling laws that brought new states into the Union, set aside the income from certain specified lands for the support not only of schools but also of "seminaries of learning." And, while in some states the funds were grossly mismanaged and in others it took years to establish such seminaries, most had used the funds by 1876 to set up some sort of public institutions of higher learning. Later, in 1862, the funds granted by the federal government under the Morrill Act, to establish colleges of agriculture and the mechanic arts, provided further stimulus to the founding of new institutions and the expansion of older ones. Another source of interest and support lay in denominational and interdenominational organizations. To the extent that the evangelical movement was an organizing movement, it organized colleges as well as churches, and for kindred purposes: colleges were widely seen, by particular denominations and by organizations like the American Education Society and the American Home Missionary Soci-

21. Absalom Peters, *College Religious Institutions: A Discourse, . . . Before the Society for the Promotion of Collegiate and Theological Education at the West* (New York: John F. Trow, 1851), p. 13.

ety, as centers of religious leadership and sources of public piety, and therefore as ancillary to the church in the preservation of a free society.

Yet, even beyond these more formal institutional sources, the colleges were sponsored and supported by the communities that patronized and sustained them. They were essentially local institutions, nurtured by local leaders, articulately appreciated by local citizenries, and, like the churches and schools of the time, seen primarily as community— and in that sense public—institutions. Much has been made in this respect of the Dartmouth College Case, which came before the United States Supreme Court in 1819. The issue arose in 1815 out of a conflict between President John Wheelock of Dartmouth College and his board of trustees over who would control the affairs of the institution. Wheelock had gone to the legislature and asked for an investigation of the board, and the trustees, not surprisingly, had responded by dismissing Wheelock and electing a successor named Francis Brown. The conflict quickly became politicized as one of the issues in the election of 1816, and, when the Democrats won that election, they moved, under the leadership of Governor William Plumer, to amend Dartmouth's charter to transform the college into Dartmouth University with an enlarged board of trustees. The old trustees did not accept the legislation; the new trustees met, dismissed Brown, and reelected Wheelock to the presidency; and the stage was thereby set for a battle in the courts, in which the old trustees challenged the right of the legislature to amend the charter. The New Hampshire Supreme Court, in a unanimous opinion delivered by Chief Justice William M. Richardson in 1817, sustained the right of the legislature to do so. On appeal, the United States Supreme Court, in a five-to-one decision delivered by Chief Justice John Marshall, ruled that Dartmouth was a private eleemosynary corporation, that its charter was a contract under the terms of the United States Constitution, and that the New Hampshire legislation of 1816 had infringed that contract and was therefore unconstitutional. The college was thereby returned to the hands of the old board.

For many who have studied the decision, it represented a clear victory for private over public interests, and thereby encouraged the founding of innumerable private colleges in the succeeding decades. But, as John S. Whitehead has pointed out, one of the first actions of the old board after it had won the case was to petition the legislature for additional public support; and the legislature in turn sought continually during the 1820's to make the college more responsive to public interest. The quarrel was not over whether the college had public responsibility in the large sense, it was rather over how that responsibility would be supported, overseen, and discharged. Moreover, since Marshall's decision was not widely commented upon in its own time, it is unlikely that it had any significant effect one way or another upon the image of colleges as community institutions in the public mind.[22]

In looking at the curriculum of the colleges, it is important to view them in the context of both preparatory and coordinate institutions. While a unitary system of schooling—embracing primary school, then intermediate school, then high school, grammar school, or academy, and then college (or theological seminary, medical school, or law school)— had begun to emerge by the 1850's and 1860's, the precise place of the college in that system and indeed the precise character of the system itself were neither well defined nor universally understood. Thus, Baynard Rush Hall, the first professor at the "seminary" that became Indiana University, in describing the confusion at the opening of classes in 1824, inadvertently portrayed the unclarities characteristic of the larger situation. Boys of varying preparation arrived at the "seminary" to study curricula of varying emphases ("Daddy says he doesn't see no sort a use in the high larn'd things—and he wants me to larn Inglish only, and bookkeepin, and surveyin, so as to tend store and run a line"), and some had to be sent away as either inadequately prepared or desirous of curricula that were not available. Hall's account was a good-humored caricature, to be sure; yet most of the newer seminaries of learning faced exactly the same problem, and, while some youngsters were sent away, others were accommodated in hastily established preparatory departments or in newly constructed collegiate programs that departed substantially from traditional offerings. When such new programs did appear, they were not very different from those developed at special-purpose institutions for particular clienteles. Thus, the military academy at West Point and later the Rensselaer Institute pioneered in the development of advanced mathematics, chemistry, physics, and engineering, as well as laboratory instruction in the natural sciences. Later, when these sciences entered the curriculum of the liberal arts colleges, the substance and methods developed at West Point and Rensselaer became the models. Similarly, painting and music appeared in the early female seminaries alongside the more traditional work in languages, mathematics, history, and the sciences; and, when women were accept-

22. John S. Whitehead, *The Separation of College and State: Columbia, Dartmouth, Harvard, and Yale, 1776–1876* (New Haven: Yale University Press, 1973).

ed in growing numbers into the midwestern universities, these subjects appeared in similar form. Interestingly, French was taught both at West Point and at the female seminaries, but at West Point it was intended to afford the cadets access to French military science while at the female seminaries it was intended to afford the young women access to belles-lettres. Similarly, drawing was taught at both Rensselaer and the female seminaries, but again the subject was intended to serve significantly different purposes. Later, when French and drawing entered the curricula at coeducational institutions, these differences tended to persist. Finally, it is important to recognize that throughout the nineteenth century chemistry was taught in medical schools as well as colleges, ethics was taught in theological seminaries as well as colleges, and physics was taught in engineering schools as well as colleges. Thus, to look only at the colleges for evidence of instruction in the arts and sciences would be to miss important phases of American higher education.[23]

Granted the importance of context, the colleges did maintain a fairly consistent core of subjects that were considered to be at the heart of a liberal education. To a great extent, the Yale Report of 1828 both reflected and strengthened the academic consensus with respect to that core, and it is therefore interesting to examine the undergraduate curriculum at Yale during the later 1820's as indicative of that consensus if not entirely representative of colleges at large. Candidates for admission to Yale were expected to stand examination in Cicero's orations, Virgil's *Aeneid*, Sallust's histories, and Latin grammar and prosody; in the Greek Testament and Greek grammar; and in English grammar, arithmetic, and geography. The course leading to the Bachelor of Arts degree was four years in length and was taught by a faculty consisting of the president, five professors—one in chemistry, mineralogy, and geology; one in the Hebrew, Greek, and Latin languages; one in mathematics, natural philosophy, and astronomy; one in divinity; and one in rhetoric and oratory—and seven tutors. The freshman class read Latin out of Livy and Horace and Greek out of Homer, Hesiod, Sophocles, and Euripides, and also studied arithmetic, algebra, and geometry (out of Euclid). The sophomore class read Latin out of Horace and Cicero and Greek out of Xenophon, Plato, and Aristotle; continued with geometry and went on to trigonometry, logarithms, and navigation (mostly out of President Jeremiah Day's textbooks); and also undertook rhe-

23. Robert Carlton [Baynard Rush Hall], *The New Purchase or, Seven and a Half Years in the Far West* (Princeton, N.J.: Princeton University Press, 1916), p. 324.

toric (out of Alexander Jamieson's text). The junior class studied Cicero, Tacitus, physics and astronomy (out of William Enfield's text), calculus (out of Samuel Vince's text), logic (out of Levi Hedge's text), history (out of A. F. Tytler's text), and, as an elective, Hebrew, French, or Spanish. And the senior class continued in Greek and Latin, also studied rhetoric (out of Hugh Blair's text), natural theology and moral philosophy (mostly out of William Paley's texts), and political economy (out of Jean Baptiste Say's text), and received a smattering of chemistry, mineralogy, geology, and physics.[24]

Most courses were taught by recitation. The four classes were divided into divisions, each under the leadership of a tutor, who saw it as his chief responsibility to examine the individual students daily in the substance of the textbook. The work in science consisted largely of lectures interspersed with laboratory demonstrations. The work in mathematics involved the memorization of rules and the effort to apply the rules to individual problems. In addition there was some writing of compositions on the part of the students studying rhetoric; there were disputations by juniors and seniors in connection with the work in logic and moral philosophy; and the president lectured to the senior class on matters of morals, ethics, and divinity. Public examinations were conducted twice a year, in May and in September, over a period of roughly a week in duration, and there were additional examinations for graduating seniors at the end of the four years of study.

Yale was the largest American college in the latter 1820's and could boast the most geographically diverse student body. It may well have been the most influential American college as well. But those facts granted, it is important to note that during the half-century following the Yale Report of 1828, the curriculum of American colleges diversified relentlessly. Even in 1828, Harvard had already begun its movement toward departmentalization, the University of Virginia already permitted students to choose among eight schools, and Union College offered a parallel scientific course leading, not to an alternative bachelor's degree, but to the Bachelor of Arts degree. And there were other colleges that were forced by the lack of preparation of their students to feature in their undergraduate program, not the work Yale required for graduation, but rather the work Yale required for admission. During

---

24. *Catalogue of the Officers and Students in Yale College, 1828-9* (New Haven: C. Adams, [1828]), pp. 24–25. The contemporary Harvard curriculum was strikingly similar to Yale's. See *A Catalogue of the Officers and Students of the University of Cambridge, September, 1826* (Cambridge, Mass.: University Press–Hillard and Metcalf, 1825), p. 3.

the 1830's, 1840's, and 1850's, the drift of most colleges was toward more options, more modern languages in place of classical languages, more scientific studies, more utilitarian emphases, and more direct experience (as symbolized best, perhaps, by the manual-labor colleges)—a drift that culminated in the policies set in motion by the Morrill Act of 1862. While the precise nature of a college of agriculture or of mechanic arts was not really defined until the 1880's, the legislation of 1862 was pivotal in forcing the definition; and that definition in turn helped to accelerate the movement toward utilitarianism in the liberal arts curriculum.

What Cotton Mather had referred to in the eighteenth century as "the collegiate way of life" also persisted during the nineteenth. Thus, the college curriculum included along with formal courses of study the numerous activities undertaken by the faculty for the students—chapel services, common residential and dining arrangements, and religious revivals—and by the students for one another—literary societies, fraternity activities, athletics, and, again, religious revivals. Particularly in the more traditional institutions, where the curriculum remained somewhat more inflexible, the literary societies became central vehicles for intellectual activities that went beyond the bounds of the required studies. Indeed, Frederick A. P. Barnard once remarked of his undergraduate years between 1824 and 1828, "No part of my training at Yale College seems to me to have been more beneficial than that which I derived from the practice of speaking and debating in the literary society to which I belonged." And Barnard, it should be remembered, ended up as an academic. On the other side, the recreation provided by a range of activities from religious revivals to athletic activities provided an important antidote to the often grinding and increasingly competitive realm of formal academic instruction. And all of this so-called extracurricular activity became especially significant and influential as a result of the American propensity for locating colleges in isolated rural regions in order to protect the students from the moral depredations of urban life.[25]

The colleges of the 1780's and 1790's tended to be conducted by a strong president who was almost always a clergyman, assisted by one or two professorial colleagues who were also almost always clergymen and

25. Cotton Mather, Magnalia Christi Americana; or, The Ecclesiastical History of New-England (1702), edited by Thomas Robbins (2 vols.; Hartford, Conn.: Silus Andrus and Sons, 1853–1855), II, 10; and Anson Phelps Stokes, Memorials of Eminent Yale Men (2 vols.; New Haven: Yale University Press, 1914), I, 249.

a somewhat larger number of tutors who were generally recent graduates of the institution. The president and professors were commonly trained in the classics and divinity—the exceptions were the few professors of the natural sciences—and saw themselves as generalists rather than specialists and as pedagogues rather than scholars. In many of the newer and smaller colleges of the 1830's, 1840's, and 1850's, the faculty was of similar character. A professor assisted by a few tutors would carry on the instruction of some forty to fifty students in the entire range of the curriculum from the classics to moral philosophy. In older and larger colleges, however, there was a slow but significant transformation in the background and training of those appointed to presidencies and professorships. Increasingly, they tended to be laymen, specialists, and scholars, and were therefore able to displace the tutors in the regular business of instruction. Particularly as German university ideals began to have an effect during the 1840's and 1850's, the instructional level in a few colleges rose dramatically in terms of substantive and pedagogical quality. Well-trained scholars began to depart from a mere slavishness to textbooks and to use the lecture and the laboratory to impart vitality to scholarly material. But the movement was slow, uneven, and far from universal. As late as the 1870's James McCosh, newly appointed as president at Princeton, could shock the older faculty by proposing that new courses be established alongside the traditional work in classics, mathematics, and philosophy, and that the college acquire the library and laboratory resources necessary to attract first-rate scholars to teach these courses. And Nicholas Murray Butler could find at Columbia a small old-fashioned college with a faculty that carried on "dry-as-dust" drill and a library that was open only a few hours a day and locked the rest of the time. Yet even Butler, who was fond of contrasting the old-time college with the university he had such an important hand in building, did not end up wholly condemnatory. The college did its work well, he concluded, and the young men who attended it in the 1870's "carried away a discipline, a range of information and interest and a love for the college itself that have never since been equalled, no matter what or how many improvements in the life and work of the college have been effected."[26]

There were professors of international repute at the nineteenth-century colleges and universities whose lives would exemplify the upper

26. Nicholas Murray Butler, *Across the Busy Years: Recollections and Reflections* (2 vols.; New York: Charles Scribner's Sons, 1939), I, 65, 63.

reaches of the higher learning in America: George Ticknor, Benjamin Peirce, Jared Sparks, Louis Agassiz, and Asa Gray at Harvard; Benjamin Silliman and Josiah Willard Gibbs at Yale; Francis Lieber at Columbia; Henry Wadsworth Longfellow at Bowdoin; Joseph Henry at Princeton; Francis Wayland at Brown. But the more typical professor of the era was less specialized, less scholarly, and less well known outside his local community. Elisha Mitchell was one such professor. Born in Connecticut in 1793, he attended Yale and then taught for a time, first at Dr. Eigenbrodt's school in Jamaica, Long Island, then at a girl's school in New London, Connecticut, and then back at Yale. In 1817, he was called to a professorship of mathematics and natural philosophy at the University of North Carolina at a salary of one thousand dollars a year. On receiving the call, he decided to study at Andover Theological Seminary for a brief period and qualified there for a license to preach. He then proceeded to Chapel Hill in January, 1818, and stayed there for the remaining thirty-nine years of his life, teaching, in addition to mathematics and natural philosophy, chemistry, botany, zoology, geology, and mineralogy. He conducted scientific studies of the natural history and geology of North Carolina; he contributed to Silliman's *American Journal of Science* and also wrote for local agricultural publications; and he participated fully in the life of the university, taking an active role in curriculum development (he actually toured the northern universities and reported on their curricula), arbitrating student discipline cases, seeking to expand library holdings and museum collections, and serving as acting president at one time and as bursar at another. For four decades, until his accidental death during a research expedition in 1857, Mitchell incarnated the spirit of the higher learning in North Carolina.

In a somewhat different way, Julian Momson Sturtevant incarnated the spirit of the higher learning in Illinois. Sturtevant was born in Warren, Connecticut, in 1805. He attended school there and in Ohio and then studied at Yale, completing his undergraduate work in 1826, teaching school for a session in New Canaan, Connecticut, and then returning to Yale for studies in divinity. He associated himself with the "Yale Band" in 1829 and, after his ordination as a Congregational minister that year, moved to Jacksonville, Illinois, where he became one of the founding members of the Illinois College faculty. From 1830, when the college opened with nine students, until 1885, a year before he died, Sturtevant served variously as professor of mathematics, natural philosophy, and astronomy, professor of mental and moral philosophy, and president. He participated vigorously in the religious, political, and educational affairs of the new state; he resisted efforts, both from within and without the college, to exert a narrow sectarian control over academic programs; and he worked hard as president to maintain the college's fiscal solvency. After his death, an alumnus who had studied with Sturtevant during the 1830's wrote of him: "Dr. Sturtevant taught his pupils to think for themselves. Almost every professor tells his pupils, in words, to do their own thinking. But very few manifest real pleasure in freedom of thought on the part of their pupils when it reveals itself in the earnest questioning of their own expressed opinions. But it often seemed to me that Dr. Sturtevant enjoyed the respectful boldness of a student who dared to controvert his declared views, and gave plausible reasons for his dissent." It was no small tribute to a clerical professor who had taught controversial subject matter during an era of intense sectarian conflict.[27]

V

College attendance numbered in the thousands on the eve of the Civil War; newspaper readership numbered in the millions. The character and quality of the educative experience involved was, of course, profoundly different. College life for the student enrolled in an institution away from home was ordinarily an intense, sustained, and often total experience: the undergraduate lived as one of an isolated company of young men or women, instructed or supervised by a faculty consisting of one or more professors helped by a few tutors only slightly older than the undergraduates. The isolated community became a surrogate family and a surrogate church, and fulfilled many of the functions of both during a crucial stage of the life-cycle. A newspaper, by contrast, provided its readers with far less intense and far more ephemeral experience. But it did arrive daily or weekly, from the same source and in the same format, and thereby provided a sustained source of information, instruction, and entertainment from the same person or persons. Moreover, given common interpretations of what constituted the news and the events to be reported, there was an increasing measure of similarity between one newspaper and another: newspapers tended to support and confirm one another's views of the world. Most interesting, perhaps, more than a few newspaper editors fancied themselves latter-

27. R. W. Patterson, "Dr. Julian M. Sturtevant," *Advance,* March 18, 1886.

day surrogates for the church and the school, with the high responsibility of ministering to and instructing the emerging newspaper public.

As one looks at the substance of the education purveyed by nineteenth-century newspapers, it consisted of several elements. The first was information about commercial matters. The newspapers were filled with paid advertisements for goods and services, patent medicines and foods of various kinds, shipping information and transportation schedules. These, alongside commercial intelligence carried as a public service by the editor, gave readers, particularly in the cities and larger towns, a sense of the market that was nowhere else available. Newspapers had expanded during the eighteenth century to give precisely that sort of information as quickly and as accurately as possible; they elaborated that information during the nineteenth century, as a service both to their general readers and to various specialized commercial audiences.

A second element in the substance conveyed by the newspapers was public information about public affairs. One of the great shifts in the instruction newspapers provided during the nineteenth century was from an emphasis on European political and economic affairs to an emphasis on American political and economic affairs, particularly at the national level. For a society of localities, this was an exceedingly important public teaching role, one that newspapers had begun to play on a significant scale during the later provincial era and one that they continued to play on an ever larger scale after Independence. By reporting presidential speeches, congressional debates, and Supreme Court decisions, diplomatic and military ventures of every kind, and other political events occurring in Washington, the newspapers defined the realm of public affairs; and, even though particular editors and readers took different positions on different issues, there was growing agreement, furthered by the incessant plagiarism of newspapers from one another, as to what the issues were. Later, when the telegraph and the cable enabled the sharing of information to go forward at a more rapid pace and in far more timely fashion, the newspapers were able to influence the formation of public opinion even more directly and thereby to affect the development of public policy. Put otherwise, the newspapers educated by creating a realm of discourse within which individuals and groups debated various positions.

A third element in the substance conveyed by the newspapers was public information about public personalities. In seeking to attract and cater to ever larger audiences by publishing sensational news and sentimental stories about other human beings, the newspapers created yet another realm of discourse, this one about celebrities of one sort or another. One's view on the Robinson-Jewett murder trial of 1836 in New York; or on the Millerite prophecy concerning the end of the world on October 21, 1844; or on the talents of Jenny Lind, who arrived to P. T. Barnum's massive fanfare in 1850; or on the Heenan-Morrissey prize fight of 1858 was important in the informal conversation of church, tavern, or workplace. There was, in effect, a new reality created by the press that was different from the diurnal reality of the world, and to be au courant one needed to have an opinion on that new reality.

Finally, the newspapers printed literature, humor, advice, poetry, and formal instruction in history, geography, and the sciences; in fact, they printed adult versions of the entire curriculum of the schools. And hence it is no wonder that books of advice for young men who wished to get ahead in the world urged their readers to subscribe to a responsible newspaper. Beyond the substance they conveyed that defined public affairs and created new worlds of reality, the newspapers carried forward instruction in precisely the same realm as the schools. And here, too, they served their readers as continuing sources of teaching and entertainment.

In all of this, newspapers were rarely read in isolation or apart from particular social contexts. Their instruction was almost always mediated by and refracted within other educative institutions. Thus, for example, most newspapers by the 1830's and the 1840's were probably read within the household, with the result that on the one hand they began to include sections first for women and later for children and on the other hand their messages were commonly interpreted by discussions among family members. What one thought of Heenan versus Morrissey was in some respects dependent upon what the other members of the household thought concerning the respective merits of the two prize fighters. Beyond that, households tended to choose newspapers that reflected the ethnic, religious, and political bias of the adults, with the result that the newspaper selected tended to confirm the view of the world held by the household and to interpret public affairs from the perspective of the household. In so doing, it not only conveyed its substance within a particular social construction of reality but also helped create a larger reality within which all other education undertaken by members of the household went forward. Its influence was subtle and pervasive but increasingly inescapable as the press became popularized during the middle decades of the nineteenth century.

James Gordon Bennett and Horace Greeley may have set the trends in pre-Civil War journalism, and indeed their lives signaled a new editorial role that was coming into being in the burgeoning cities of the East. But it is important to bear in mind that they were in many respects atypical. The ordinary newspaper read by the ordinary American was put together, not by a hard-driving editor aided by a staff of enterprising reporters, but rather by an entrepreneurial printer who, with the assistance of an apprentice or two, prepared the material (writing it on his own or copying it from elsewhere), set it in type, ran it though the press, and delivered it or put it into the mails. Joseph Charless and William Williams were entrepreneurial printers of this kind. Charless was born in Ireland in 1772 and came to the United States in 1795. He probably learned the printing trade in Ireland, since the first evidences of him in the United States place him in Lewistown, Pennsylvania, and in Philadelphia, where he was already active in the affairs of printing. Charless went to Lexington, Kentucky, in 1803 and there, in collaboration with Francis Peniston, launched the *Independent Gazette*. Four years later, he moved to Louisville, where he launched the *Louisville Gazette*. And the following year he moved to St Louis, where he launched the *Missouri Gazette,* with the imposing prospectus: "It is self evident that in every country where the rays of the press is [*sic*] not clouded by despotic power, that the people have arrived to the highest grade of civilization, there science holds her head erect, and bids her sons to call into action those talents which lie in a good soil inviting cultivation. The inviolation of the press is co-existent with the liberties of the people, they live or die together, it is the vestal fire upon the preservation of which, the fate of nations depends; and the most pure hands officiating for the whole community, should be incessantly employed in keeping it alive." Charless changed the name of the paper several times over the next several years, but he continued to publish it until he retired in 1820, with brief interruptions during the War of 1812 when the printshop ran out of paper or ink. Moreover, during the time he published the *Gazette,* he also printed and sold books, maintained a part interest in an apothecary, and ran a boardinghouse. Interestingly, in 1822 Edward Charless, who had served as a journeyman printer in his father's shop, assumed publication of the *Missouri Gazette,* changing its name to the *Missouri Republican* and issuing it until 1837.[28]

28. David Kaser, *Joseph Charless: Printer in the Western Country* (Philadelphia: University of Pennsylvania Press, 1963), p. 61.

William Williams's career was in many ways similar. He was born in Framingham, Massachusetts, in 1787 and moved with his family to Utica, New York, in 1790. He served an apprenticeship to printing there between 1800 and 1807 and then entered into a partnership with his former master, Asahel Seward, that lasted seventeen years, after which he struck out on his own. During the period between 1814 and 1834, Williams published no less than seven newspapers—the *Utica Club,* the *Utica Patrol,* the *Utica Patriot and Patrol,* the *Utica Sentinel,* the *Utica Christian Repository,* the *Utica Elucidator,* and the *Utica American Citizen.* In addition, he printed and published a steady flow of religious materials and schoolbooks, ran a thriving bookstore; served as an elder of the First Presbyterian Church, a director of the local library, and a village trustee; and taught Bible classes and a Sunday school. Despite his entrepreneurial vigor, however, he suffered financial instability, and a sheriff's sale in 1834 began a long decline that led eventually to the closing of his business in 1840. For all his ingenuity and versatility, Williams had been unable to make the publishing of newspapers financially feasible.

Chapter 12

CONFIGURATIONS

The great experiment of Lowell is an experiment of another kind: it is
an experiment whether we can preserve here a pure and virtuous population. . . . There have been laid for us here the foundations of a great
success—a method of business well devised, and carefully adjusted part
to part, a system of public instruction planned on a broad and generous
scale, churches, Sunday schools, libraries, charities, numberless institutions to enlighten, guide, and bless this growing city.

HENRY A. MILES

The family, the church, the school, the college, and the newspaper remained primary educative institutions during the first century of national life. The way in which they patterned themselves into configurations of education, however, changed in a number of ways. First, the
basic configuration increasingly involved at least three significant components: institutions of organized work external to the household, principally the mill and the factory but also the mine, the shop, the office,
the retail establishment, and the government bureau; custodial institutions like the house of refuge, the orphan asylum, the penitentiary; and
institutions for the diffusion of special kinds of knowledge, such as libraries, lyceums, fairs, and museums. Second, there was a shift in the
relative power of the several elements of the educational configuration,
partly because there were now more educational institutions and partly
because the society shifted the foci of its economic and spiritual investments in education. Thus, the educative influence of the school and the
newspaper probably grew in relation to that of the household and the
church, and the educative influence of the external place of work increasingly mediated the influence of all other education during the
years of active adult employment—it simply loomed larger as a selective

414

shaper of aspiration, taste, and outlook, though obviously it shaped in interaction with household and church. That said, a third generalization should immediately be added, namely, that there was the continuously revitalized influence of the evangelical church working in concert with households, Sunday schools, common schools, colleges, Bible and tract societies, missionary organizations, and authorized publishing houses. As has been indicated, the relationships among these agencies were political, pedagogical, and personal: they were controlled, supported, and managed by the same kinds and classes of people; they used methods and materials that reflected a common subscription to evangelical values and a pervasive evangelical exhortative style; and they embraced the same sorts of people, teachers as well as learners. Finally, a familiar caveat must be added: the slave plantation, the Indian reservation, and voluntary and involuntary ghettos created by utopian striving and systematic segregation all persisted, as alternative educational configurations more or less isolated from the mainstream.

Like generalizations regarding the colonial era, however, generalizations regarding the nineteenth century apply variously in different communities. By way of example, therefore, Lowell, Massachusetts; Sumter District, South Carolina; Macoupin County, Illinois; and New York City may be useful to consider. The reasons for the choices are obvious. Lowell offers insight into the impact of the factory, though the so-called Waltham system of cotton manufacture that prevailed there represented only one among several patterns of early industrial development. Sumter District provides instances of large plantations with substantial black quarter communities comprising a hundred or more slaves, though such plantations were the exception rather than the rule, not only in Sumter but throughout the pre-Civil War South. Macoupin County reveals the dynamics of community building on the frontier, though a county in the Texas cattle country or on the Minnesota iron range would obviously present different pictures. And New York City reveals the dynamics of urbanization and metropolitanization, though, once again, the city was also unique in its role as the principal port of entry for thousands of immigrants and as the cultural and economic capital of the nation at large.

II

Lowell originated as part of the town of Chelmsford, situated at the confluence of the Merrimack and Concord rivers in northeastern Massachusetts, some twenty-five miles from Boston. In 1820 it had a population of seven hundred; when it was incorporated as a town in 1826, the population had grown to twenty-five hundred; by the time it was incorporated as a city in 1836, it had grown to eighteen thousand; and by 1846 it stood at thirty thousand. There had been earlier manufacturing of cloth, bootstraps, glass, and gunpowder, but the great divide in the early history of the community came in 1823, when the Waltham system of cotton manufacture was established in Lowell. The Waltham system involved three central elements: first, corporate ownership; second, the combining of yarn and cloth production under a single roof; and, third, the recruitment as workers of young, unmarried women from the surrounding rural region, who lived in company-owned boardinghouses under quasi-familial supervision by company overseers. The system was first established in Lowell by the Merrimack Manufacturing Company, an offshoot of the Boston Manufacturing Company of Waltham. Subsequently, the Hamilton Corporation (incorporated in 1825), the Appleton and Lowell Corporations (1828), and the Suffolk, Tremont, and Lawrence Corporations (1831) constructed plants incorporating similar arrangements, so that by 1836, the city could boast an investment of over $6 million in textile factories that employed over six thousand operatives.

Obviously, Lowell was first and foremost a factory town, a "city of spindles," and the mills and their varied activities played an important role in the lives of the people who lived there; but Lowell was also in many respects a characteristic New England community. It was, in the first place, a community of households, overwhelmingly white (there were never more than a few score blacks), Protestant, native-born, and of English origin, though inclusive from the beginning of growing numbers of foreign-born immigrants, initially Irish and Scots (the Irish were brought in to build the canals that crisscrossed through the community and to lay the foundations of the mills, while the Scots worked as weavers in the carpet factories), and later, after the Civil War, French Canadians. These households reared their children and governed their lives according to the characteristic patterns of their ethnicity and religion, the native-born tending to relate to the Congregational churches, the Irish affiliating with the Roman Catholic church and its associated complex of religious and benevolent organizations, the Scots taking the lead in founding a Presbyterian church, and the French not only affiliating with the Roman Catholic church but also forging a variety of new organizations to assist them in maintaining their distinctive language and culture.[1]

Lowell was also a community of churches, which patently reflected the variegated character of the population. There were Congregational churches from the time of original settlement, which proliferated with the increase in communicants via birth and immigration. Other churches developed out of informal gatherings that then laid the bases for more formal institutional life: the Episcopal church grew out of a series of religious meetings organized by the Merrimack Company for its employees and their children; the first Baptist church grew out of prayer sessions held at the home of the postmaster; the first Methodist church grew out of classes and sermons conducted at the "Old Red School-House"; and the first Roman Catholic church grew out of activities organized around the monthly visits of a priest who traveled the twenty-five miles from Salem to hold services for communicants in Lowell. By 1845 the city could boast twenty-three separate churches housed in nineteen buildings, with two more in construction, representing Congregationalist, Baptist, Universalist, Methodist, Christian, Roman Catholic, Episcopalian, and Unitarian affiliations. All these institutions carried on the usual range of educational activities, both on their own and through affiliated societies; and, beyond those, the Protestant churches organized the Lowell Sabbath School Union in 1836, which became the vehicle for the formal instruction of between four and five thousand students annually during the next few decades.[2]

Lowell was also a community committed to schooling. At the time of its incorporation in 1826, Lowell already comprised five school districts, and at the first town meeting after incorporation a general superintending school committee was established to oversee school affairs. By 1840 the city had built what must have been one of the most complete systems of public schooling of any community of its size in the nation. The Lowell School Committee that year reported 21 primary schools (including one in the almshouse), 6 grammar schools, and one high school, with an overall daily attendance of 1,932 out of a total of 4,015 children between the ages of four and sixteen. By 1850, there were 46 primary schools, 9 grammar schools, and one high school, with an overall daily attendance of 4,283 out of a total of 5,432 children between

1. The phrase "city of spindles" is from the *Voice of Industry*, November 7, 1845.
2. Henry A. Miles, *Lowell, As It Was, and As It Is* (Lowell, Mass.: Power and Bagley, 1845), p. 97.

the ages of four and sixteen. Among these were a number of publicly supported parochial schools established for the youngsters of the Irish community under a local political arrangement widely referred to as "the Lowell plan"; and, although these so-called Irish schools were consistently more crowded than their Yankee counterparts, the presence of significant numbers in the Irish grammar schools bespoke the willingness of Irish parents to use the schools to extend their children's social and economic opportunities (on the other hand, only a small number of Irish youngsters went on to the high school). Beyond the public schools, there were several academies located conveniently nearby, including the Central Village Academy at Dracut and the Westford Academy at Westford, where those who sought a more selective company in which to pursue secondary education could obtain it; and of course there was Harvard College located approximately twenty miles to the southeast.[3]

Lowell also boasted a number of newspapers of varying character. The *Lowell Journal* was the oldest, having begun as the *Chelmsford Courier* in 1824. Issued as a weekly, it concerned itself with politics, literature, and local intelligence, conducted a column called "communications," and devoted as much space to announcements of marriages and deaths as it did to editorials and political commentary. It became more politically focused during the late 1820's, sharply criticizing Jackson for his devotion to the "spoils system"; but the same editorial column that leveled an attack on the president could describe the American Temperance Society and note the presence of a certain "mechanical genius" in Boston. In 1835, the *Lowell Courier* was established as a triweekly in conection with the *Journal*. In addition, for varying periods of a few months to a few years, Lowell was also the source of political papers (the *Lowell Advertiser*, Democrat; the *Massachusetts Era*, Free Soil; the *Lowell Daily Citizen*, Republican), labor papers (the *Lowell Offering*, the *Voice of Industry*), religious papers (the *Star of Bethlehem*, Universalist; the *Christian Era*, Baptist), temperance papers (the *Magara*), antislavery papers (the *Middlesex Standard*, edited by the poet John Greenleaf Whittier), and a foreign language paper (*L'Echo du Canada*). Also, given the fact that Boston was only twenty-five miles away and connected by rail as well as by an inexpensive postal system, Lowell was able to draw upon an even wider spectrum of newspaper

3. *Annual Report of the School Committee of the City of Lowell* (1840), p. 2; and *Twenty-Fifth Annual Report of the School Committee of the City of Lowell* (1850), pp. 4–8.

substance and opinion than was produced within it own confines.[4]

Finally, Lowell was a community suffused with the New England ethos of self-improvement, and indeed it is this ethos that explains much of the educative experience of the first generation of mill operatives. For example, it illuminates the decisions of young farm women to leave their own households in distant communities in order to come to Lowell to work in the factories. Whatever else the factories promised, they promised better wages than the two other occupations open to young unmarried women during the years before the teaching force was feminized, namely, domestic work and piece sewing. Many young women came with the explicit goal of earning sufficient funds to salvage a family farm or accumulate a dowry or trousseau; others came to earn enough to send some poor but aspiring brother through an academy or college. Still others came for less specific or idealistic reasons. The high literacy rate of young Massachusetts females, combined with rapid improvement in the means of communication between Boston and the New England interior, led many to dread the prospect of life on isolated farmsteads and to dream instead of varying employments, easy access to printed materials, continuing association with young people of similar age, the ready availability of urban recreation, and perhaps even the possibility of marriage to a wealthy and cultured businessman. Whatever the motives in individual instances, the existence of Lowell did hold out the option of a new life-style, one rendered the more appealing by the knowledge, which separated the native-born from later immigrant workers, that there was always home to return to and marriage to anticipate.

Once the young women entered the mills, several kinds of education proceeded simultaneously. First, there was the education they underwent in work skills and routines, which was overseen by the owners and the managers. The process was one of informal apprenticeship, in which the newcomer worked initially as a spare hand in collaboration with a more experienced partner, gradually "learning by doing," later spelling either the partner or some absentee for a brief period of time, and eventually taking on a regular job. As one operative described it, "I went into the mill, and was put to learn with a very patient girl. . . . They set me setting shuttles, and tying weaver's knots, and such things, and now I have improved so that I can take care of one loom. I could take care of two if only I had eyes in the back part of my head." Once

4. *Lowell Journal,* March 3, 1830, and January 5, 1831.

an operative moved into a regular job, there was still a good deal of working in pairs, which provided continuing opportunity not only for mutual assistance but also for mutual training in the skills associated with the work.[5]

Second, there was the education of the dormitories, overseen, to be sure, by the owners and their employed housekeepers but simultaneously teaching group norms and standards enforced by peer pressures revolving around acceptance and shunning. The romantic literature on Lowell celebrated the uplifting thrust of these pressures in enforcing high standards of moral conduct; but, as Thomas Dublin has pointed out, it was these same pressures that helped weld the young women into a cohesive group of strikers during the labor unrest of 1834 and 1836 and into an articulate group of petitioners during the campaign for a ten-hour day in the 1840's. In addition, the young women engaged in frequent informal discussions on such contemporary issues as antislavery, phrenology, hydropathy, and, with growing militancy, the rights of labor; they read voraciously, a habit fed by their willingness to share books and to sustain subscription libraries; and they indulged in the delightful practice of pasting interesting newspaper and magazine articles on factory walls for perusal or of hiding them under chairs for consultation between work assignments (before the speedups and technological advances of the 1840's, there were frequent interruptions of the work routine).[6]

For many of the young women involved in such activities, the years in Lowell proved to be, and indeed were perceived to be, profoundly educational. One derives a clear sense of that perception from such well-known works as Lucy Larcom's *An Idyl [sic] of Work* and Harriet Robinson's *Loom and Spindle*. Interestingly, the same theme was explicitly articulated in the reminiscences of one of the young men who worked in the mills during the 1830's, the Reverend Varnum Lincoln. Lincoln, the eldest in a family of seven children, had been forced to leave Lowell High School and enter the mills after his father had died. As he himself related it:

Now, although a cotton mill cannot be called, technically, a school, yet this new position was to me, in an important sense, a theatre of mental development. It brought me in contact with new minds and new ideas. At that time Lowell had reason to be proud of its operatives. . . . Some of them had been

5. *Lowell Offering*, IV (1844), 170.
6. Thomas Dublin, *Women at Work: The Transformation of Work and Community in Lowell, Massachusetts, 1826–1860* (New York: Columbia University Press, 1979).

schoolteachers, and there were others who came to earn money in order to prepare themselves for that profession. All had brought with them from their homes by the hillside and valley their church-going habits, love of reading, and generally a strong desire for larger intellectual culture. They read and talked on the important questions of the day. And many of the questions then agitated were profoundly exciting and radical. There seemed to be a general awakening in the public mind to new thoughts and measures in the political and moral world. Abolitionism, Transcendentalism, Fourierism, Temperance, Grahamism, and other kindred topics relating to human welfare, filled the air and entered the workshops and mills of Lowell. And many were the sharp debates and comparison of notes that were held over the loom and spinning frame on those themes. This was to me a new kind of education, but it opened to me a larger world, stimulated thought, encouraged reading, and proved in the end intellectually profitable.

Shortly after entering the cotton mill, Lincoln "graduated" from the mills to the large machine shop of the Lowell Locks and Canals Company, where Irish workers had predominated from the beginning. Nevertheless, his informal education continued apace. Once again, as he himself related it:

Fortunately, this change also proved a school favorable to the acquisition of knowledge and mental development. It brought me into the society of a class of intelligent young men, who, while they toiled over the engine or the lathe, had high aims and employed their leisure hours in securing that which would make their lives more useful to themselves and their fellow-beings. As one of the means of self-improvement that these young men had established was a debating society, that met weekly in a Lowell room on the right as you enter the Mechanics Building. This society was for many years one of the institutions of Lowell. It was largely attended. And its exercises consisting of discussions, mock trials, readings, and declamations, proved a most valuable school to those who availed themselves of its privileges.[7]

Lincoln's account points to a third element in the education of the young millhands, namely, the education that went forward through agencies outside the factory. Many of the operatives remained in close touch with their familial households; in fact, relationships of kith and kin were often central in determining patterns of recruitment to and departure from the mills. Beyond that, the operatives had access to a variety of educative institutions in Lowell itself, some of which were specifically intended to bring the factory hands into regular contact with

7. Varnum Lincoln, "My Schools and Teachers in Lowell Sixty Years Ago," in *Contributions of the Old Residents' Historical Association*, Lowell, Mass., V (1894), 135–136, 138.

other townsfolk. Churches were obviously such centers. Even more important were Sunday schools, which millworkers attended regularly and in which, interestingly, they often taught. Free evening schools for adults, which emerged during the 1840's under the auspices of the city's remarkable minister-at-large, Horatio Wood, also brought together operatives and other townsfolk of varying social strata, as did a variety of private evening schools that taught subjects like geography, penmanship, and foreign languages.

In addition to the Young Men's Debating Society described by Lincoln, Lowell boasted other educative agencies specifically geared to factory operatives, male as well as female. The City School Library, opened in 1844, contained over eight-thousand volumes by 1853, and operated as a remarkably ambitious government-sponsored subscription library, offering lending privileges at fifty cents a year. A lyceum also functioned regularly from the mid-1840's on, featuring such speakers as Horace Greeley, Orestes Brownson, Theodore Parker, and Benjamin Silliman, along with numerous residents of Lowell.

Finally, the factory operatives read newspapers, not only their own, initially the *Lowell Offering* and later the *Voice of Industry,* but also local papers like the *Lowell Journal* and the *Lowell Courier* and Boston papers like the *Evening Transcript.* In this connection, it is interesting to note that the *Offering* originated in the "improvement circles" organized by two Universalist ministers for the operatives during the 1830's. One of the two, the Reverend Abel C. Thomas, had encouraged the young women to write original pieces for their mutual edification, and by 1840 he had become sufficiently impressed with the quality of the material to gather the best of it into a pamphlet. The pamphlet was successful in attracting public attention, and it was this that prompted Harriet Curtis and Harriet Farley to initiate serial publication a year later. One can exaggerate the significance of the *Offering:* the fact is that few of the operatives wrote for it. But the manner of its founding via a denomination that was not only isolated from but actually frowned upon by Lowell's manufacturers reveals the extent to which self-motivated workers, in a diverse urban setting, could move beyond the bounds of paternalistic control.

Now, there were tensions in all this that are important to recognize. The explicitly articulated and strictly enforced rules and routines of the mills and their attached boardinghouses contributed much to the creation of a disciplined work force for Lowell's factories. The owners who imposed the rules and routines justified them in the rhetoric of "moral protection" for the young workers during their period of residence in Lowell, and indeed the owners saw themselves as standing *in loco parentis*; yet the effect of the rules and regulations was to substitute the more stringent demands of industrial time for the looser rhythms of agricultural time that the young workers had learned as children in their rural households. That said, however, it should also be noted that the mills and dormitories were never "total institutions," in the sense in which Erving Goffman has used that phrase. They housed communities that developed their own norms and values, quite beyond those imposed by the owners, and those communities served as mediating agencies for the operatives' external education during the period of their membership in the work force. For those who chose to participate in the cultural activities proffered by Lowell, despite the demands of a seventy-hour work week, the sojourn in Lowell could be as liberating in some respects as it was constraining in others.[8]

Both Lowell and the mills changed appreciably during the later 1840's and the 1850's. The city's population continued to grow, reaching 33,382 in 1850, 36,827 in 1860, and 40,928 in 1870, and it continued to diversify: by 1870 some 35 percent of the residents were foreign-born, most of them (over three-quarters) Irish and most of them poor. Not surprisingly, St. Patrick's and St. Peter's churches expanded their activities, though they were always crowded and chronically constrained by insufficient funds (additional churches were not organized until the 1880's). The various pastors of St. Patrick's and St. Peter's played a vigorous role in the affairs of organizations like the Lowell Benevolent Society, the Catholic Temperance Society, the St. Patrick's Charity Society, and the Sodality of the Immaculate Conception, as well as in interdenominational groups like the Lowell Fuel Society, which carried on a considerable program of charitable work among the poor. And they took a special interest in the schooling of Irish children. For a time, it appeared as if "the Lowell Plan," under which Irish children attended publicly supported parochial schools that were part of the public school system, would continue to suffice; but during the early 1850's that system came under attack from two sources: the school board expressed concern over the rapid expansion of the school population and the Irish clergy expressed concern over what they perceived to be sharpening Protestant prejudice.[9]

In 1852 the Reverend John O'Brien, the pastor of St. Patrick's,

8. Miles, *Lowell*, p. 131; and Erving Goffman, *Asylums: Essays on the Social Situation of Mental Patients and Other Inmates* (Garden City, N.Y.: Anchor Books, 1961).

9. U.S., Bureau of the Census, *The Statistics of the Population of the United States, . . . Compiled from the Original Returns of the Ninth Census* (1870), pp. 166, 390.

persuaded the Sisters of Notre Dame to establish an academy and free school for girls in Lowell, and the launching of that enterprise marked the beginning of a shift to church-sponsored parochial schooling on the part of the Irish community. Most of the Irish children who went to school during the 1850's and 1860's, however, continued to attend public institutions. The school authorities on their side manifested growing anxiety about discipline and truancy; and, when the Massachusetts legislature in 1850 authorized cities and towns "to make all needful provisions and arrangements concerning habitual truants and children not attending school, without any regular and lawful occupation, between the ages of six and fifteen," the Lowell board moved promptly to have the City Council pass a law imposing a twenty-dollar fine and possible imprisonment on any child between the ages of six and fifteen who was neither in school nor at work, to establish a local reform school (Lowell was the only city in the state other than Boston to do so), and to employ a full-time truant officer. Like most reformatories, the Lowell facility was intended to exercise symbolic deterrence at the same time as it attempted to rehabilitate recalcitrant youth, and in the end it housed only a small number of youngsters—fewer than two dozen a year. But the truant officer was as vigorous as he was symbolic, arresting several hundred boys and girls a year, most of them Irish. Taken together, the establishment of the new facility and the employment of the new official represented a significant development in the history of the Lowell school system, for it marked a considerable enlargement of activity designed to take account of growing public concern over the baneful effects of "idleness," "vice," and "internal commotions."[10]

As for the mills, the 1840's and 1850's witnessed profound changes in the character of their educational activities. For one thing, a growing number of Irish immigrants entered the work force: at one of Lowell's largest mills, for example, the proportion of foreign-born operatives (most of whom were Irish) rose from 8 percent in 1845 to 60 percent in 1860. The new millhands were less likely to have had several years of schooling and therefore less likely to be literate, though they were by no means generally illiterate, the literacy rate in contemporary Ireland running somewhere between 50 and 70 percent. They were also less likely to be motivated by the traditional New England drive toward self-improvement and more likely to be the victims of ethnic and reli-

10. Massachusetts, *Acts and Resolves Passed by the General Court of Massachusetts* (1850), pp. 468–469; *Twenty-Second Annual Report of the School Committee of the City of Lowell* (1847), p. 33; and *Twentieth Annual Report of the School Committee of the City of Lowell* (1846), p. 18.

gious prejudice, with the result that they were less likely to avail themselves of the general run of Lowell's libraries, lyceums, and cultural facilities. Rather, the Irish tended to restrict themselves to a more limited round of activities associated with their households, their churches, and their ethnic community, with its taverns, its complex of benevolent associations, and its periodical publications like the *Boston Pilot,* and in so doing to develop both a distinctive Irish-American working-class culture and a distinctive Irish-American configuration of education. Further, a growing proportion of males entered the work force, who were more likely to have family responsibilities and to use their spare time for political and social activities and, not least, activities on behalf of the nascent trade union movement. In addition, the Irish in general were less likely to leave the mills after four or five years, having at their disposal fewer alternatives than their native-born predecessors of the 1830's. Finally, the Irish chose more to reside with their kin or as boarders in private establishments. Worker families, most or all of whom labored in the mills, lived increasingly in their own households in working-class neighborhoods rather than in company-owned dormitories, a pattern more closely resembling that of other manufacturing communities in Massachusetts and elsewhere. The effect of this, of course, was to reduce the immediate educative influence of the factory in favor of that of the neighborhood, though at the same time it eliminated the cultural opportunities the boardinghouses had provided—such as they had been.[11]

III

Sumter District, South Carolina, presents a quite different set of educational configurations. The district, situated in the fertile plains of the upper pine belt some forty miles east of the city of Columbia, was created by the state legislature on January 1, 1800. The principal dynamic of its economic life during the first half of the nineteenth century was the boom in cotton cultivation following the invention of the cotton gin and the subsequent development of cotton as a staple money crop. But there were other industries as well. A "gentlemen of great mechanical knowledge" built a water-powered cotton factory near the town of Stateburg in 1790 at about the same time as Samuel Slater built his

11. Dublin, *Women at Work,* p. 147; Oliver MacDonagh, "The Irish Famine Emigration to the United States," *Perspectives in American History,* X (1976), 380; and Carlo M. Cipolla, *Literacy in the Development of the West* (Baltimore: Penguin Books, 1969), p. 114.

factory in Pawtucket and following essentially the same principles; and, although the Stateburg venture failed financially, there were similar enterprises in Sumter during the early nineteenth century. In addition, there were grain mills of various sorts, nail-making and agricultural implement shops, and retail establishments to service the large number of travelers who passed through Sumter on the way to Alabama, Mississippi, and Louisiana. Yet the district remained essentially agricultural during much of the nineteenth century, with cotton as the principal product.[12]

Since Sumter's geographic boundaries changed over time, it is difficult to obtain demographic statistics that are comparable. The best estimates place the population at 13,103 in 1800, 28,277 in 1830, 23,859 in 1860 (the decline owing to the creation of Clarendon County in 1855, part of which was taken from Sumter District), and 25,268 in 1870. The black population increased both absolutely and proportionally during this period, from 6,864, or 52 percent, in 1800 to 17,002, or 71 percent, in 1860, with the overwhelming majority of the blacks being of unfree status. As was true throughout the South, most white families in Sumter did not own slaves, and most of those white families that did own slaves owned ten or fewer. Only 2 percent of the Sumter slaveholders in 1850 actually owned a hundred or more slaves, but their plantations accounted for a significant fraction of the total slave population of the district, perhaps as high as 25 percent.[13]

Prior to the Revolution, there were three churches in Sumter: St. Mark's Church (Anglican), Black River Church (Presbyterian), and High Hills Church (Baptist). Between the Revolution and the Civil War, additional churches were established in several ways. Some, like the Bethel Baptist Church of Claremont, split off from already functioning institutions, in that instance the High Hills Baptist Church. Some developed in the wake of Methodist circuit riders, such as Francis Asbury, who first visited the region in 1785, and James Jenkins, who began riding what was called the Santee Circuit in 1795. And a few grew up in connection with some specific ethnic group, for example, the Roman Catholic church in Sumterville, organized to serve the town's Irish population. A map of the district drawn in the early 1820's indicates at least twenty-six separate church buildings, but the number of congregations was probably higher, since there were almost surely

12. *American Museum*, VIII (1790), Appendix IV, 11.
13. *Statistics of Population, . . . Ninth Census*, pp. 60–61. The data on slaveholding are drawn from the manuscript returns of the 1850 census.

congregations without permanent quarters. A half-century later, the Census of 1870 reported some forty congregations, including nineteen Methodist, nine Baptist, eight Presbyterian, three Episcopalian, and one Roman Catholic. By that time, too, there were numerous auxiliary agencies, such as the Sumter Bible Society, the YMCA, and a variety of libraries and Sunday schools that had developed in connection with the several churches. Also, Sumter District as early as 1802 began to serve as the scene of an annual Methodist camp meeting usually held in the vicinity of Sumterville or nearby Lynchburg, often lasting some five or six days, and always catering to an interdenominational clientele. Families would come from miles around, and, indeed, as the affair became a well-established aspect of Sumter's religious life, particular families would occupy the same tents or cottages year after year, with the result that the camp meeting served the purposes not only of religious revival but also of information exchange, business transaction, and social intercourse.[14]

The first schools in Sumter emerged in connection with the churches. Even before the Revolution, the ministers of the Black River Church and St. Mark's Church conducted regular classes, and there is evidence of "old-field schools" that convened in abandoned log cabins. From an early date there were also academies, such as the Claremont Academy in Stateburg, which opened in 1786, closed in 1788, and then reopened in 1819. Like Claremont, most of the academies enjoyed brief or intermittent lives, and it is virtually impossible to determine how many of them actually existed at any given time. Some of the academies were teacher-owned, some were organized by parents, and some were incorporated by societies of one sort or another. Some were supported by tuition, some by lotteries and tuition, and some by endowments and tuition. Some were boarding schools, some day schools. Some were opened to all comers; others, like the Claremont Orphan Academy, catered to special clienteles. Since academy curricula usually depended in part on the particular students who happened to be enrolled, it is also difficult to generalize about what subjects were offered, though it is likely that most of the institutions provided opportunities to go beyond the three R's. A family might send its son to the Sumter Military, Gymnastic, and Classical School to obtain a combination of "academical learning" and the "manly arts," or it might send its daughter to Mrs. Campbell's School for Young Ladies to study geography, astron-

14. The map is reproduced in Janie Revill, *Sumter District* (no place: State Printing Co., 1968). *Statistics of Population, . . . Ninth Census,* p. 553.

omy, embroidery, needlework, and the social graces. The central fact is that academies, in varied forms, provided a substantial measure of the schooling that was available to children of the district during the antebellum period.

With the exception of a few elite institutions that managed to attract statewide clienteles, however, Sumter's academies did not cater to either the highest or the lowest classes of white society, and certainly not to any portion of black society. Wealthier parents tended to have their children tutored at home, while poorer parents desirous of schooling for their youngsters sent them to the public schools organized under the Free School Law of 1811. By 1826 Sumter District had forty-three such public schools enrolling 289 youngsters; by 1853, with a much larger white population, there were sixty-five public schools enrolling 442 youngsters; and by 1860 there were seventy-four public schools enrolling 844 youngsters. Given the provision in the law of 1811 that, in localities where more children applied for public schooling than could be accommodated, first preference would go to the poor and orphaned, there was a continuing stigma attached to attendance at public schools, and they were never on a par with the academies in prestige or quality. In general there was less school-going among white children in Sumter District than in contemporary northern or midwestern communities, though not as much less as historians of education have traditionally inferred by looking solely at the records of public school attendance.[15]

Sumter District also offered a number of opportunities for systematic self-education. By 1809 both Stateburg and Sumterville had circulating libraries, and by 1855 Sumterville also boasted its own bookstore. There were numerous agricultural fairs organized by the Sumter Agricultural Association and a variety of traveling medical shows, circuses, and concert troupes. There were also several fraternal societies, such as the Masons, the Odd Fellows, and the Sumterville Mechanics' Association, and there were clubs and debating societies organized for literary and social purposes.

Finally, there were the local newspapers, initially the *Claremont Gazette,* which flourished in the post-Revolutionary decade as a booster organ urging Stateburg as the state capital, and, forty years after, the *Sumter Gazette,* which flourished in the 1830's as a voice favoring nul-

15. South Carolina, *Acts and Resolutions of the General Assembly of South Carolina* (1826), p. 49; South Carolina, *Reports and Resolutions of the General Assembly of South Carolina* (1853), p. 259; and South Carolina, *Reports and Resolutions of the General Assembly of South Carolina* (1860), pp. 402–403.

lification. Later, in 1846, the *Sumter Banner* appeared as a local paper dedicated to Democratic politics and the economic development of Sumterville via a rail connection to Charleston; and, in 1850, the *Black River Watchman*, as a competitor dedicated to the same causes (the two papers merged in 1857, as the *Sumter Watchman*). The *Banner* and the *Watchman* carried the debate during the 1850's between the "submissionists" (to Congress), the "secessionists" (who believed South Carolina should secede alone), and the "cooperationists" (who believed South Carolina should secede only if other southern states would collaborate in leaving the Union), and not surprisingly the *Watchman* after 1857 uncompromisingly supported the Confederacy. Not surprisingly, too, when the Union army occupied Sumterville in April, 1865, soldier-printers took over the press and issued a single pro-Union issue of a new paper called the *Banner of Freedom*, which reported the latest Union victories and warned the inhabitants that they had been defeated and would do well to conduct themselves accordingly.

All these opportunities were available either exclusively or principally for whites. Even for free blacks—and from 1800 on there were always a few hundred free blacks in Sumter District—the chance to participate in church activities was at best restricted, and access to formal schooling, virtually nil. The fact is neither the state nor the locality took kindly to free blacks, and during the 1820's they came increasingly under suspicion and subject to sharp restrictions on their activities and pursuits (one law actually required that every free black male over the age of fifteen have a white freeholder as a court-sanctioned guardian). As a result, their social and educational relationships were limited to those that involved other blacks or the very few whites with whom they maintained either formal or habitual association. Yet, a few did make their way in the world, taking advantage of the opportunities available to them. At least one, a remarkable man named William Ellison, having served a regular apprenticeship as a ginwright in the community of Wynnsboro, some fifty miles to the northwest of Sumter, established himself in that craft in Stateburg, initially earning enough money to purchase his freedom and subsequently gathering together a small fortune in holdings, including a substantial cotton plantation, forty or fifty slaves, and a number of properties in Stateburg itself. But Ellison was the exception. Most free blacks led lives of ever-narrowing constraint, increasingly punctuated by regulation and harassment from the white community.

For the slaves, the differences were even more drastic. In small slaveowning households, black youngsters might spend their earliest years in close and continuing association with their white agemates; but sometime between the ages of seven and ten their paths would diverge, with the black youngsters' education thereafter limited to whatever might come from marginal participation in the church or from apprenticeship to some adult artisan. A few did learn to read and write, but informally, alongside their white agemates. Otherwise, what they learned came via informal education in the ordinary business of living. The farm of Jonathan Weston, located about five miles north of Sumterville during the period after 1811, provides an excellent example. It was an establishment small enough to be worked by Weston, his wife and children, and a few slaves, yet it was large enough to provide virtually everything those residing on the farm required. In addition to the separate living quarters for the whites and the blacks, the farmstead included a field, an orchard, a vegetable garden, and a pasture; stables, a barn, a cattleshed and fowlhouse, and a tanning vat; a smokehouse, a cider mill, a corn crib, a wheathouse, beehives, a blacksmith shop, a more general workshop, and a loom room. The Westons and their slaves doubtless worked side by side, with Weston, who had learned farming as a boy in North Carolina, and his wife teaching most of what needed to be taught to whites and blacks alike. The living derived from the farm was sufficient, but the regimen was severe, as testified to by the fact that two of the Weston sons ran away before reaching the age of twenty-one. What is more significant, however, is that the education of blacks and whites continued to overlap in important respects, despite the social and psychological walls that separated the two groups and despite the drastic differences in the opportunities available to them.

In the larger slaveowning households, there was an even wider segregation along racial lines. In many ways, these establishments were merely larger and more complex versions of the Weston plantation, including extensive fields of cotton cultivated and harvested by gangs of slaves under the supervision of black drivers and white overseers, and even greater numbers of specialized functions: the plantation of Matthew Singleton, for example, which boasted several hundred slaves, invested substantial energy and resources in the breeding and racing of thoroughbred horses, as well as in a large and diversified household staff, supervised by the wife of the owner and a small number of trusted blacks. The white youngsters on such plantations would be tutored at home, the males in preparation for one of the elite academies in the state, for example, the Mount Zion Society School at Winnsboro, or Beaufort College or the College of South Carolina or the College of Charleston, the females perhaps in preparation for a school such as the Bradford Springs Female Institute or the Harmony Female College, both located in Sumter. The education provided at such institutions, coupled with the education of the household, nurtured a special sense of racial and class superiority, social obligation, regional loyalty, and the particular male-female roles associated with southern chivalry that became the special hallmark of large plantation owners throughout the South during the decades preceding the Civil War.

The slave youngsters would grow up in the quarter community—on the Singleton plantation, essentially a collection of two-family shacks, generally populated by nuclear groups of father, mother, and natural offspring, though, since kin relationships were extensive and titles like "uncle," "aunt," "grandmother," and "grandfather" were used generationally rather than specifically, there were networks of kin that transcended the boundaries not only of the shacks but of the plantation itself. Children lived during much of the year with their parents, and were taught the customs and values of the plantation at large and of the quarter community in particular by their parents and other adult slaves. During the hot and uncomfortable summers, the slave children were removed to a special place away from the plantation proper and left to play and frolic under the tutelage of several older female slaves. But even in the midst of that relatively carefree existence there were special behaviors to be learned, as, for example, when the master and mistress would visit and the children were taught appropriate modes of submissive bowing and curtsying. Because children spent time with their parents, they were able to watch them at work and in that way began to learn skills and attitudes via imitation: Jacob Stroyer, who grew up on the Singleton plantation, recalled spending his early years with his father around the barnyard animals, with which his father worked as a hostler. Sometime after reaching the age of seven, the youngsters would be assigned to work on the plantation, the task selected reflecting the work that needed to be done, the talents and abilities of the youngster, and even, from time to time, the youngster's expression of preference. From that time forward, the learning of work roles came via more or less formal apprenticeship arrangements, with unrelenting, violent, and often irrational punishment intermixed with the usual pedagogical processes of imitation, explanation, correction, reward, and criticism. The owners, overseers, and slaves of some planta-

tions worshipped together in nearby churches or residential establishments, with slaves grouped in special pews in the rear; elsewhere,
segregated services for blacks were conducted by local or itinerant
Methodist or Baptist preachers. As a rule, these services taught the values and attitudes of the owners—white superiority, black inferiority,
and black submissiveness. But, beyond these more formal Christian observances, there were the clandestine activities of indigenous black congregations, which transmitted an eclectic culture of black folklore, a
version of Christianity, and the remembered experience of accommodation and protest. And, beyond those activities, it is clear that quarter
communities on various plantations maintained communication with
one another and even with blacks outside the state and in the West
Indies. In effect, then, there were separate but overlapping configurations of education for whites and blacks, which almost always sought to
nurture conflicting values and loyalties in youngsters and adults alike,
obviously with varying results.

IV

Macoupin County, Illinois, provides yet another story. Located roughly
sixty miles northeast of St. Louis, between Madison County, which
borders on Missouri, and Sangamon County, which includes Springfield, Macoupin furnishes a particular version of the educational configurations of the nineteenth-century frontier. The first settlers came to
Macoupin in the 1810's but as late as 1817 the region could boast only
five families. During the next decade immigration increased steadily
though slowly, with most of the settlers coming from the southern
states, especially Kentucky, the Carolinas, Tennessee, Virginia, and
Georgia. The county was officially organized in 1829, interestingly
enough, over the objections of the Methodist preacher Peter Cartwright, who insisted that "God had set apart this region as a reservation for the geese and ducks." While the geese and ducks lost out, the
county soon acquired the uncomplimentary nickname of the Frog Pond
Kingdom. The new county's population stood at approximately two
thousand in 1830, slightly over twelve thousand in 1850, and almost
thirty-three thousand in 1870. There were small numbers of free blacks
from 1830 on: Illinois outlawed slavery in 1824, but white Illinoisians
were generally hostile to blacks and in many localities excluded them
from the polls, juries, the militia, and the public schools. After 1800
there was also a substantial influx of European immigrants, with the

proportion of foreign-born individuals rising from 6 percent in that year, most having come from England, to 15 percent in 1870, the greatest numbers having come from Germany and Ireland. While the proportion itself does not seem significant, it is important to note that for every foreign-born resident of the county in 1870, there were two who had been nurtured in immigrant households. Stated otherwise, despite the overwhelmingly native-born and southern cast of the county's population at mid-century, twenty years later nearly one out of three residents had been reared in an immigrant household.[16]

Throughout the nineteenth century the chief industry of Macoupin County was agriculture. Its rich prairie lands produced large annual crops of Indian corn, as well as smaller crops of wheat, oats, vegetables, fruits, and hay. In addition, there was the kindred pursuit of stock raising, with its associated wool- and meat-producing industries. Beyond those, particularly at the county seat of Carlinville, there were mills, agricultural implement shops, carriage and wagon manufacturers, blacksmith shops, breweries, banking and retail establishments, and, from the 1860's on, a number of coal mines. Also, the Alton and Springfield railroad, built between 1849 and 1852, cut directly across the county and eventually connected it with St. Louis and Chicago, thereby bringing the inhabitants of Macoupin both physically and intellectually within the reach of the two primary urban centers of the region. Even so, most of the work pursued in Macoupin represented household industry or agriculture, taught and learned via the pedagogy of formal and informal apprenticeship.

What is known of Macoupin's churches tends to support the traditional view that religion tamed the frontier, though it is difficult to obtain precise figures on the number of people who actually took part in church activities. The Methodists and the Baptists were the first to arrive: they could boast seven churches each in 1850, thirteen and seventeen, respectively, in 1860, and twenty-five and twenty in 1870. The Presbyterians were right behind, with two churches in 1850, eleven in 1860, and ten in 1870. And there were also small numbers of Congregational, Lutheran, and Roman Catholic churches. Relative to the total population, Macoupin had one church for every six hundred people in 1850, one for every five hundred in 1860, and one for every four hun-

16. Francis A. Walker, ed., *A Compendium of the Ninth Census* (Washington, D.C.: Government Printing Office, 1872), pp. 38, 408; and J. D. B. De Bow, ed., *Statistical View of the United States, . . . Being a Compendium of the Seventh Census* (Washington, D.C.: A. O. P. Nicholson, 1854), p. 219.

dred in 1870; though it is probable that at no time did more than a quarter of the population have any formal church connections, and it is difficult in any case to determine the nature, intensity, and effects of those connections on the part of those who maintained them. Certainly one indication of change over time was that the leading religious issue of the 1830's was irreligion, the leading religious issue of the 1850's was doctrinal orthodoxy, and the leading religious issue of the 1870's was institution building, especially parochial schools. In any case, the churches themselves maintained vigorous and varied programs of education. Many ministers functioned simultaneously as preachers, schoolmasters, and Sunday-school leaders, teaching parents and children to read and interpret the Scriptures, nurturing Christian piety, enforcing standards of behavior via church discipline, and creating networks of associated voluntary organizations that in their very nature taught participation at the same time as they furthered such causes as temperance.[17]

There is early evidence of a school at the county seat of Carlinville, where the Methodist circuit rider Stith Otwell and his wife Mary lived when they first arrived in 1831. And from a reminiscence Mrs. Otwell left in 1870 under the name Mrs. Mary Byram Wright, it is also clear that schooling in Carlinville was offered not only in the schoolhouse but in every manner of public and private building; conversely, the house the Otwells later built for themselves served not only as their residence but also as the county surveyor's office, the post office, and a dry-goods store (interestingly, church services were not ordinarily held there, since all the denominations used the county courthouse for that purpose during the 1830's). Thus, the doubling up or tripling up of functions that had manifested itself in seventeenth-century Virginia appears to have been a continuing phenomenon of frontier development. Buildings served multiple purposes and people played multiple roles. In any case, the school statistics for 1850 and 1870 indicate that schooling, of some indeterminate kind and duration, was well-nigh universal from the earliest years of midwestern development. Thus, the Census of 1850 reported the existence of 72 public schools in Macoupin County taught by 73 teachers and enrolling 1,958 pupils. Moreover, the same census reported 3,356 youngsters as attending school. Now, the discrepancy

17. U.S., Bureau of the Census, *The Seventh Census of the United States* (1850), pp. 738–746; U.S., Bureau of the Census, *Statistics of the United States, . . . Compiled from the Original Returns and Being the Final Exhibit of the Eighth Census* (1860), pp. 374–375; and *Statistics of Population, . . . Ninth Census*, p. 535.

between the figures for public school enrollment and school attendance was common in the Census of 1850, and in Macoupin County as in many other places the larger figure doubtless included youngsters attending private schools, Sunday schools, and quasi-schools of every sort and variety. What is important about mid-century Macoupin is that roughly 90 percent of a total population of 3,715 between the ages of five and fourteen was spending some time in some kind of school, and this fully five years before the Illinois legislature established a state-wide, tax-supported public school system. By 1870 the school attendance figure was 8,201, of a total population of 10,954 between the ages of five and eighteen; but by that time public schooling accounted for most of the number. Academies of the sort that were common in Lowell and in Sumter District were never as prevalent in Macoupin County; and, after the passage of the Illinois school law of 1855, they were few in number and insignificant in influence—an interesting phenomenon in a community initially settled by large numbers of southerners. Obversely, public schooling was far more inclusive of the white population than was the case in contemporary Sumter.[18]

Macoupin also had its own institution of higher learning, Blackburn University. Characteristically for the era and the region, it arose from a combination of boosterism and religiosity, originating under the sponsorship of a Presbyterian minister-entrepreneur named Gideon Blackburn. Born in Kentucky in 1772 to a family of Scots-Irish descent, Blackburn had spent some twenty-nine years as a teacher and missionary before accepting the pastorate of the Louisville Presbyterian Church in 1823 and then the presidency of Centre College of Kentucky in 1827. Upon moving to Macoupin County six years later, he became immediately convinced that an institution of higher learning would be vital to the social and economic development of the region; and, in a typical whirlwind fund-raising trip through the cities of the Northeast, he managed to raise enough money to buy sixteen thousand acres of local Illinois land. In 1837 he conveyed the holdings to a number of distinguished citizens whom he designated as trustees, with the requirement that they use their influence to obtain a charter for an institution of learning to be located at Carlinville, the object of which would be "to promote the general interests of education, and to prepare young men for the gospel-ministry." Blackburn died soon thereafter, and, for var-

18. Mrs. Mary Byram Wright, "Personal Recollections of the Early Settlement of Carlinville, Illinois," *Journal of the Illinois State Historical Society*, XVIII (1925–26), 668–685; *Seventh Census*, pp. 696–699, 722, 725; and *Statistics of Population,... Ninth Census*, pp. 408, 626.

ious reasons having to do mainly with the competition of localities for colleges and universities, the charter was not obtained for twenty years. But it was ultimately granted, and the trustees were able to inaugurate classes at the preparatory level in 1850 and to add programs at the post-secondary level during the later 1860's. By 1870 Blackburn University could claim not only a preparatory department but full collegiate and theological departments as well. The first college class was graduated that year, with seven students receiving A.B.'s.[19]

Finally, there were the Macoupin County newspapers, which developed rather later than was the case in other contemporary communities. Before 1852 the inhabitants were dependent upon the St. Louis and Alton papers for their news, a situation that was not particularly painful, given the presence of the railroad. In that year, however, the *Macoupin Statesman* was established as a Whig paper by Jefferson L. Dugger, who maintained it for three years and then sold it to George H. Holliday, who changed its name to the *Spectator* and its politics to Democratic. Thereafter, the paper went through a series of shifts in ownership, reorganizations, and reincarnations, emerging in the 1870's as the *Macoupin Times*. In 1856 the *Free Democrat* was established in Carlinville by W. C. Phillips as a Republican counterpart of the *Spectator,* and it continued into the 1870's. Beyond those, there were local papers like the *Girard Enterprise* and the *Virden Record,* literary papers like the *Blackburn Gazette,* and foreign papers like the *Volksblatt;* and, as the rail network connecting the Alton and Springfield Railroad to other lines developed, newspapers from outside the county also found their way into homes in increasing numbers. The papers assumed various forms, emphasized various topics, and employed various pedagogical styles. The most interesting in this respect was the *Carlinville Free Democrat.* It was for all intents and purposes a carbon copy of Horace Greeley's *Tribune,* differing only in size and geographical focus. It used all of Greeley's pedagogical devices, from the featuring of editorials to the personification of issues (Polk's war, Douglas's bill, Taney's decision); and, like many a newspaper of the time, it virtually ignored local news.

The configuration suggested here, of household, church, school, and newspaper, teaching in concert a common curriculum of the English language, Protestantism, patriotism, social participation and social discipline, along with whatever particulars there might have been of class,

19. Thomas Rinaker, "Gideon Blackburn, The Founder of Blackburn University, Carlinville, Illinois," *Journal of the Illinois State Historical Society,* XVII (1924), 404.

denomination, ethnicity, political persuasion, and work, pertained to most of the boys and girls who grew up in Macoupin County during the 1850's and 1860's. But there were dissenters on ethnic and religious grounds who chose to develop their own special configurations, separate from but overlapping with those of the dominant native-born Protestant majority. For example, most German settlers in and around Carlinville were members of the Evangelical Lutheran Church. Dependent for ministers upon the Missouri-Ohio Synod, they found their opportunity for formal congregational worship irregular at best. Furthermore, such sermons as they did hear apparently gave them little satisfaction. They sorely missed "the historic Lutheran emphasis on Scripture alone—faith alone—grace alone." In 1856 eighteen German families gathered to fulfill their "sacred Christian duty" by issuing a call to a promising young seminarian at the Fort Wayne Seminary in Indiana, Edmund Multanowski. The call emphasized educational as well as ministerial duties, asking Multanowski "always to preach the word of God to us pure and unadulterated according to the clear Lutheran Confessions and diligently to instruct our children therein; to administer the holy Sacraments, and by a pious life and conduct to set us a shining example." Unlike the Congregationalists and the Presbyterians, the German Lutherans were as concerned with preserving a language and way of life as with inculcating a set of religious beliefs, and so they took strong action to preserve both in the face of the undenominational evangelical challenge.[20]

Carlinville's Lutherans supported Multanowski entirely out of periodic subscriptions, offering him a rent-free house, firewood, a regular salary of twelve dollars per month, and additional fees for baptisms and marriages—a better arrangement, incidentally, than that enjoyed by most Methodist and Baptist pastors. Multanowski held services first in the local courthouse and then in a rundown facility owned by the Presbyterians, for which the Lutherans paid heating and cleaning costs. The arrangement was that the Lutherans would begin their services after the Presbyterians were through, usually around 1:00 P.M., after which they would hold their *Christenlehre,* a German analogue to the Sunday school. By 1859 the Lutherans had erected their own meeting place, and were thereby enabled to hold services in the morning and to keep afternoons free for the instruction of youth of postconfirmation age (formal Sunday-school services for younger children were not arranged until much later).

20. *A Century with Christ, 1856–1956* (Carlinville, Ill.: no publisher, 1956), pp. 8, 7.

Multanowski's duties were as much academic as they were religious. He ran what was, in effect, a moving school for members of his congregation, six hours a day, nearly eleven months a year. On two days of each week he conducted school in Carlinville, and then on two other days he moved through the surrounding countryside. For those who were not members of the Lutheran church—doubtless German families who wished to inculcate the German language and German customs but who were not of the evangelical Lutheran persuasion—a fee of twenty-five cents per day was charged. In addition, parents in the hinterland were expected to provide for the pastor's conveyance out and back. Multanowski also gave singing lessons in his home on Wednesday evenings, since he had made the hymnal a central feature of church services.

Multanowski's church was never very large, its membership perhaps totaling some thirty-eight families at its peak. But the size was seriously diminished in 1859 after a serious doctrinal controversy, reported by a partisan church historian as follows: "In the beginning almost all Germans attended the service. But when the Lutheran doctrine rang clear and Christian conduct according to God's word was insisted on, some turned their backs on the services." The upshot was a schism that led to the formation of a new evangelical Lutheran church, leaving the original church with only fourteen families; not surprisingly, Multanowski departed for Sheboygan, Wisconsin, in 1860. In May of that year the original Lutheran congregation extended an invitation to Pastor Carl Ludwig Geyer of Lebanon, Wisconsin, offering him an arrangement far superior to the one Multanowski had enjoyed. As "preacher, pastor, and schoolteacher" Geyer would receive two hundred dollars annually, the use of a parsonage and garden adjoining the church, and forty cents per month for instructing children whose parents were not members of the congregation. Geyer accepted and within a year had done much to rebuild the earlier strength of the church. In addition to running a day school for children, he conducted adult Bible study classes every Wednesday evening, at which members met to discuss the Scriptures and the learned commentaries. By 1863 the day school had grown to the point where, in view of Geyer's poor health, it was necessary to employ a separate teacher. A student from Addison Teachers' Seminary was hired temporarily for $100 a year plus board and laundry, and then, two years later, another teacher was hired permanently at $150 per year. Significantly, a precondition of the appointment of the second teacher was that he be proficient in English, a stipulation that suggests that previous teachers had manifested insufficient command of the language and that parents in the Carlinville area were increasingly feeling the necessity of providing formal instruction in English so that their children could participate in the wider Macoupin community at the same time that they remained faithful to their religious and cultural heritage. The dissenting evangelical Lutheran church did less well. Pastors came and went at frequent intervals and the congregation refused to affiliate with any synod until 1868, when it joined the Evangelical Synod and obtained the Reverend C. Witte as permanent pastor. The following year an attempt was made to enrich the church's educational offerings by hiring John F. Hemje as an instructor for the parochial school. But periodic doctrinal crises and the renaissance of the original Lutheran congregation created continuing difficulties for the dissenting group, who were unable to put their parochial school on a full-time basis until 1878.[21]

The effort of Carlinville's German Lutherans to build a separate configuration of household, church, school, and, after 1870, German-language newspaper suggests both the possibilities and difficulties of maintaining cultural identity on the central Illinois frontier. The call in the mid-1860's for a teacher proficient in English reveals a growing awareness after more than a decade of experience in America that it would no longer suffice to instruct children solely in the ways of the old country. It may also have indicated that the Germans were having difficulty keeping their fellow countrymen in the fold and the children of their fellow countrymen under the influence of parochial tutelage. To bring English into the curriculum, as either the language or the object of instruction, was to offer parents who could afford private tuition a flexible alternative to the public school. Yet, despite difficulties, the German Lutherans did survive as a distinct subcommunity. To be sure, they did not have the political power of their countrymen in nearby St. Louis, who, as Selwyn Troen has pointed out, were able to have the German language and elements of German culture taught in the public schools; Carlinville's Germans constituted a substantial but not a politically significant subcommunity within a primarily native-born population accustomed to exercising leadership. While they undoubtedly were subjected to a certain degree of harassment for choosing to keep their children out of the public schools, they were able to coexist with the native-born community because neither had cause to be unduly intolerant

21. *Ibid.*, pp. 8, 11.

of the other. Both communities saw population growth as a prime pre-requisite of economic progress, and the booster spirit, if nothing else, provided a palliative for whatever ethnic prejudices either might have felt.[22]

Much the same situation doubtless prevailed with respect to the Roman Catholic population of Carlinville, though the information on this group is more ephemeral. What is known is that fifteen Irish families started St. Mary's Catholic Church in 1856, and that parochial classes were instituted at about the same time, though a school was not formally established until several years later. Furthermore, it is also known that in 1868 some thirty-five German families split off from the Irish Catholic congregation to found St. Joseph's. Whether or not it was religious differences that separated the two groups is not clear, but the fact that the Germans held services in both German and English suggests that the main element of contention was cultural. Both Irish and German Catholics also set up separate configurations of education that overlapped only partially with the dominant configuration. Thus, a youngster might grow up in one of Carlinville's German households where the language of the old country was spoken by parents and grandparents, receive his or her education in a German church and a German parochial school, but at the same time maintain increasingly significant cultural associations with members of other ethnic groups, particularly in connection with work activities. On the other hand, it was quite possible to live one's life largely within the cultural and educational confines of a particular subcommunity and voluntarily to restrict one's activities essentially to that subcommunity.

V

New York underwent a remarkable development during the first century of nationhood. The population not only increased phenomenally, from 23,610 in 1786 to 942,292 in 1870, it diversified as well, so that whereas the city was largely Anglo-American in the 1780's, with small subcommunities of Dutch, German, Irish, French, and African descent, it had become overwhelmingly cosmopolitan by the 1850's, with fully half the inhabitants reporting themselves as foreign-born. Furthermore, with allowance for cyclical variation, the economy boomed, owing partly to the transatlantic trade and immigration made possible by the

22. Selwyn K. Troen, *The Public and the Schools: Shaping the St. Louis System, 1838–1920* (Columbia: University of Missouri Press, 1975).

greatest natural harbor in the Western hemisphere and partly to the internal trade and migration made possible by the Erie Canal. By mid-century the city had achieved preeminence in the commercial and manufacturing affairs of the country.[23]

Predictably, household education was extremely diverse in the city, with respect to everything from the language of communication and the cultural substance conveyed to the customary pattern of relationships with kin and neighbors. At one end of the social spectrum were the families of "established" New Yorkers, many of whom, like Philip Hone, employed the services of resident tutors to supplement a fairly intense and directed familial education in piety and civility. At the other end were the families of newly arrived immigrants, living under crowded conditions (in the seven wards below Canal Street, the population density rose from 94.5 persons per acre in 1820 to 163.5 in 1850) in quarters bereft of water, light, or fresh air (29,000 individuals were reported in 1850 to be living in cellars) and often as uncertain of their traditional ways as they were ignorant of the new ways that surrounded them. Clustering in ethnic neighborhoods like the Five Points (Irish), *Kleindeutschland* (German), or the Seventh Ward (Scandinavian), such families often split generationally, with the old seeking to preserve the traditions they had brought, while the young, more quickly Americanized via the streets and occasionally the schools, became in effect the purveyors of the new culture. As for the "middling sort," they eagerly pursued the city's myriad opportunities, sending their children to the schools that were increasingly available after the 1820's and 1830's and attempting to place them in promising apprenticeships thereafter. Variations notwithstanding, the households of New York City functioned within an ambience of incessant movement, geographically, as kin moved back and forth across the Atlantic and as households sought to improve their circumstances through relocation within the city, socially, as families scrambled up or slipped down the ladder of economic opportunity, and spiritually, as individuals tried to find their way in a culturally alien world.[24]

As was the case everywhere in the United States, work was carried on in substantial measure as an extension of household life. A port city with excellent connections to the hinterland, New York had a thriving

23. Ira Rosenwaike, *Population History of New York City* (Syracuse, N.Y.: Syracuse University Press, 1972), pp. 18, 63, 42.
24. Thomas Adams, *et al., Population, Land Values and Government* (New York: Regional Plan Committee of New York and Its Environs, 1929), p. 54; and *Twentieth Annual Report of the New York Association for Improving the Condition of the Poor* (1863), p. 38.

commerce in foreign goods: the city's merchants, for example, had a near monopoly on woolen and cotton goods from England, on linens from Ireland and Germany, and on silks and laces from France. Being a port city, New York could also boast shipyards, railyards, and other facilities for the construction and servicing of transportation. But New York was not merely a port, it was a manufacturing center that had every kind of industry: it boasted iron and steel foundries, sugar refineries, clothing factories, and breweries; it served as a national center for the manufacture of furniture and pianos and as a regional center for the manufacture of garments; and it had every manner of specialized craft and trade. In addition, it was a center of retailing, with every sort of hotel, restaurant, shop, and service. While some of this trade and manufacture proceeded in large establishments, for example, ironworks and piano plants, employing well over a hundred workers, most of it went on in small shops and stores that were extensions of the owners' households. The city's garment industry was essentially a network of immigrant seamstresses who sewed at home, while the influx of cobblers from Germany and Ireland during the later 1840's actually slowed the shift to factory production in the city's boot and shoe industry.

One important element in the recruitment of workers was the concentration of different ethnic and racial groups in various occupations. The merchant houses tended to be owned and controlled by families of New England background who used a combination of household and apprenticeship education to transmit the skills of management from one generation to the next. The shipyards along Corlear's Hook tended to attract native-born craftsmen. The Germans dominated the woodworking trades, the manufacture of pianos, and the production of household and farm implements. The Jews worked as tailors and as peddlers. The Irish were disproportionately represented in unskilled construction work and household service. The blacks found themselves confined to unskilled labor or to jobs as barbers, waiters, or coachmen. Since recruitment to occupations operated largely via word of mouth passed along informal networks of kin and kith, these concentrations tended to persist over the generations. Moreover, since the influx of newcomers was itself an important factor in the continued economic growth of the city, there was always work for the able-bodied but unskilled—a phenomenon that not only led many immigrant families to settle in New York but that also occasionally disturbed familial relationships after settlement, as when the daughter of an Irish family found work as a domestic and through that achieved a degree of independence that would have been impossible in the old country.

There were 22 places of worship in New York in 1794, reflecting the largely Anglo-American character of the late eighteenth-century city—4 Presbyterian churches, 3 Dutch Reformed, 3 Episcopal, 2 German Lutheran, 2 Quaker, 2 Baptist, 2 Methodist, 1 French Protestant, 1 Moravian, 1 Roman Catholic, and 1 Jewish synagogue. The number grew to 55 in 1811, to 99 in 1825, to 252 in 1855, and to 450 in 1870, including not only the full range of Protestant denominations along with 40 Roman Catholic churches and 27 Jewish synagogues, but numerous special congregations organized along particular ethnic or racial lines—German Episcopal, for example, or Irish Catholic, Scotch Presbyterian, Greek Orthodox, Spanish-Portuguese Jewish, or African Methodist. Not surprisingly, in addition to the formal instruction they offered in religious substance, values, and liturgy, these institutions became centers for the various subcommunities that dominated their congregations, spawning in the process a considerable variety of ethnoreligious schools, clubs, benevolent societies, cultural organizations, newspapers, and magazines that were inspirited with the general values of the sponsoring church or synagogue but then went far beyond.[25]

Furthermore, the churches, united across demoninational lines in the evangelical movement, took the lead in creating new institutions explicitly intended to alleviate the effects of poverty via a broad program of public education and individual rehabilitation. The Orphan Asylum Society, founded in 1807, created a shelter to provide instruction in reading, writing, arithmetic, and domestic affairs, along with a sound moral education in a homelike atmosphere presided over by a "pious and respectable man and his wife." The New York Society for the Prevention of Pauperism, organized in 1816, set out determinedly to discover, isolate, and eliminate the causes of poverty in the city. The Society began by collecting and disseminating information on the general problem of vagrancy but quickly settled on the development of a "reformatory," to be known as the House of Refuge, as its chief project. Initially conceived as a residential facility that would serve as both a school of moral rehabilitation and a training center for mechanical skills, the institution was opened in 1825 and soon became designated the official state agency in New York City for the rehabilitation of ju-

25. Rosenwaike, *Population History of New York City*, pp. 24–30, 52–54; J. F. Richmond, *New York and Its Institutions, 1609–1872* (New York: E. B. Treat, 1872), pp. 144–156; and *Statistics of Population, . . . Ninth Census*, p. 549.

venile delinquents. The New York City Tract Society, organized in 1827, dedicated itself to education against intemperance, swearing, and Sabbath breaking among all classes of society, but soon found itself concentrating predominantly on prayer meetings, Bible classes, and charitable activities for the city's unchurched poor; and as a result in 1843 it helped to create the New York Association for Improving the Condition of the Poor for the express purpose of carrying on mission work among the impoverished, via religious services, prayer meetings, industrial classes, employment referral services, and libraries. The New York Female Moral Reform Society, founded in 1834, undertook a two-sided program intended, on the one hand, to advance moral perfection among all people, largely through publications, and, on the other hand, to rehabilitate prostitutes, mainly through the maintenance of a household that began as a refuge for wayward girls but eventually evolved into what was for all intents and purposes an employment bureau for unskilled women. And the Children's Aid Society, founded in 1853, set about combining charitable assistance, self-help, and moral education in a program that began with industrial classes and a "lodging house for newsboys" (a girls' lodging house was added in 1862) and quickly expanded to include reading rooms, Sunday meetings, and eventually a placement system under which slum children were sent to reside with farm families in order that they might enjoy the uplifting influence of rural life and escape the degrading influence of urban life. So it was also with scores of other mission organizations, each of which sought in its own way to wed the moral fervor of benevolence to more or less pragmatic programs of education, rehabilitation, and assistance.[26]

With respect to schooling, New York was subject to the same general influences that pressed for popularization across the country. By the 1790's there was a fairly large network of common pay schools in the city, which youngsters of either sex could attend at modest cost (the charge was between sixteen and twenty-four shillings per quarter), supplemented by a small number of charity schools conducted by various religious organizations and a variety of specialized entrepreneurial schools. In 1805, on the initiative of the Quaker philanthropist Thomas Eddy, the Free School Society was organized, "for the education of such poor children as do not belong to or are not provided for by any

26. Mrs. Jonathan Odell, et al., eds., Origin and History of the Orphan Asylum Society in the City of New York, 1806–1896 (2 vols.; New York: Bonnel, Siler & Co., 1899), I, 9; Thomas Eddy to William Allen, June 7, 1818, in Samuel L. Knapp, The Life of Thomas Eddy (New York: Conner & Cooke, 1834), p. 277; and First Annual Report of the Children's Aid Society (1854), p. 10.

religious society." Committed to the Lancasterian system of monitorial instruction, the Society enlarged its activities quite rapidly, to a point where by 1820 it was reaching over two thousand children a year.[27]

The legislature, cognizant of the fact that the city's poorest children were receiving their schooling primarily in institutions maintained by missionary organizations such as the Free School Society, the Orphan Asylum Society, and the Manumission Society (which ran the African Free Schools), apportioned most of the public money the city was due from the state common school fund to the support of these groups. Thereby were the grounds laid for the political conflict that began during the 1820's. As will be recalled, the various churches that conducted schools wanted a share of the funds at the same time as the Free School Society (renamed the Public School Society in 1826) wanted to monopolize them; and to complicate the political situation even further the leaders of the Roman Catholic church became increasingly assertive during the 1830's concerning their inability to use the schools of the Public School Society because of their decided Protestant bias. The controversy peaked in 1842, when the legislature enacted a law establishing a board of education for the city and placing the schools of the Society and all other eleemosynary institutions enjoying state support under the jurisdiction of the board. The Society went out of existence in 1853; but the result of the legislation setting up the board was the development of two school systems in the city, the public system created in 1842 and the alternative system that the Roman Catholic authorities decided to create with their own money when they lost in the legislature. Politics aside, schooling was widely available in New York City by 1860, though varied in quality and differentially used. Of a total population of 813,669 that year, 153,000 were enrolled in the public schools; but the average daily attendance was only 58,000, reflecting an unusual degree of illness, truancy, and poor record keeping. In addition, 14,000 youngsters were enrolled in the Roman Catholic school system, and several thousand more were enrolled in independent schools and in schools managed by charitable organizations like the Children's Aid Society.[28]

The higher learning also expanded in size, scope, and diversity during the nineteenth century. King's College, rechartered as Columbia

27. Act of Incorporation, Free School Society of New York, in William Oland Bourne, *History of the Public School Society of the City of New York* (New York: Wm. Wood & Co., 1870), p. 4.

28. Diane S. Ravitch, *The Great School Wars: New York City, 1805–1973* (New York: Basic Books, 1974), appendix.

College in 1784, increased its enrollment and enlarged its offering, but it remained in essence a small, elite institution until its transformation under Frederick A. P. Barnard, Seth Low, and Nicholas Murray Butler, beginning in the 1880's. Studies in law were conducted intermittently from 1794, when James Kent delivered his first lectures, until 1857, when the Faculty of Jurisprudence was formally organized. Studies in medicine were transferred to the College of Physicians and Surgeons in 1813, but then reestablished, de jure, when that college and Columbia formed an alliance in 1860. And studies in engineering were introduced with the founding of the School of Mines in 1863. In addition to Columbia, the city could boast the University of the City of New York (which became New York University), founded in 1831; St. John's College (which became Fordham), founded in 1841; St. Francis Xavier College (which awarded its degrees via St. John's until its own chartering in 1861), founded in 1847; the Free Academy (which became the College of the City of New York), also founded in 1847; and Rutgers Female College, founded in 1867. There were also numerous preparatory institutions, some of them connected with the colleges, all of them private or quasi-public (New York had no free public high school until 1897); and there were independent professional schools of law, medicine, theology, pharmacy, veterinary science, and dentistry. Most interesting of all these institutions, perhaps, was the Peter Cooper Union for the Advancement of Science and Art, incorporated in 1857 as both an academy and a college; for, beyond the formal courses it offered in the arts and sciences, it featured an evening school for young ladies, mechanics, and apprentices (in effect, all those least able to find higher education elsewhere); lectures in languages, literature, oratory, telegraphy, design, and engraving; a reading room open to the public; an art gallery; and a museum of rare inventions.

The city also boasted a plethora of institutions for the advancement, preservation, diffusion, and sharing of culture. In addition to the New York Society Library, which dated from the provincial era and which by the 1830's had become the third largest in the nation, there was the Astor Library, founded in 1849 as a free noncirculating reference library, the Mercantile Library, the Apprentices' Library, the Printers' Free Library, the Women's Library, the New York Catholic Library, and the Maimonides Library. There was also the Athenaeum, modeled on the ones in Boston and Philadelphia, which included a reference library, a reading room containing periodicals, a museum, a laboratory for scientific experiments, and a lecture department; the Lyceum of

Natural History; the Historical Society; the Literary and Philosophical Society; the Academy of Fine Arts; and, of course, Barnum's Museum. And beyond those there were the theatres, the opera houses, and the music halls that made the city a cultural as well as a commercial and manufacturing center, and there were the clubs (Union League, Century, Travellers, Welch, Young Cambrians, Société Lyrique Française, Vereine), the benevolent and fraternal associations (New England Society in the City of New York, St. Nicholas Society, Hibernian Universal Benevolent Society), and, more generally, the taverns and ale houses where diurnal social relations—and with them mutual education—proceeded apace.

Finally, New York City was a center of printing and publishing, with the result that books, pamphlets, tracts, and magazines of every sort and variety issued from its presses by the thousands. And it was the leader in the popularization of the newspaper. Not only did penny dailies such as the *Sun,* the *Herald,* and the *Transcript* circulate briskly among people of all classes (newspapers were still passed from hand to hand in the nineteenth century, so that readership was always considerably larger than circulation), but there was also a unique range of specialized journals like the *Commercial Advertiser* (mercantile), the *Evening Post* (Democratic), the *Tribune* (Republican), the *Christian Advocate* (Methodist), the *Observer* (Presbyterian), the *Freeman's Journal* (Roman Catholic), the *Jewish Messenger,* the *Truth Teller* (Irish), the *New Yorker Staats-Zeitung* (German), the *Freedom's Journal* (Afro-American), and many more. Beyond their general significance as purveyors of news, the foreign-language papers in particular served as vital agencies for the mediation of the new culture to the immigrant community; indeed, for many adults they became the single most important systematic educative influence in the new environment.

Several points bear comment concerning the rich and variegated educational environment that was New York City in the nineteenth century. At the very least, the point of multitudinousness needs to be made. Every interest, every occupation, every ethnic, religious, racial, and social role had its exemplars, its zealots, and its opportunities for formal or informal study. The journalist James Henri Browne remarked in 1869 that "almost every game, and pleasure, and circle of artists and literary men, has its nucleus and focus in the form of a club, and club life of some sort is growing more and more in favor and fashion." He was alluding, of course, to clubs like the Century or the Eclectic, but his assertion was equally apt in a broader sense. In nineteenth-century New York City, one had the opportunity to seek and undergo a greater range and diversity of experience than anywhere else in the country. True, the opportunity needed to be recognized, desired, and actually accessible to be utilized, and the recognition, the desire, and the accessibility were neither equal nor universal throughout the city. But it is undeniable that extensive and varied opportunities were both socially present and widely used.

Second, given the social, economic, ethnic, religious, and racial diversity of the population, the number of alternative configurations of education became as remarkable as the sheer breadth of the available opportunity. With the increase in size of the population, the culturally homogeneous residential neighborhood became more and more the rule throughout the nineteenth century. One could grow up in a well-to-do household of English background, study with a resident tutor, participate in the activities (and later the affairs) of Trinity Church, attend Columbia College, work in a merchant house or a law firm, read the *New York Times* and *Harper's Monthly Magazine,* and play an active role in the Union League Club, without having much, or indeed any, contact with a contemporary who grew up in an impoverished Irish immigrant household, participated in the activities of the local Roman Catholic parish church, attended the parish school for a year or two, worked as a driver for a brewery, read the *Irish American,* took an active role in St. Patrick's Friendly Society, and spent a good deal of time at a favorite tavern. There were parallel configurations of Swedish-Lutheran education, German-Reformed education, Afro-American-Methodist education, and many other ethnoreligious combinations. For all the educational opportunity that the city held out to its inhabitants and visitors, the world of any given individual was almost always bounded by one or another particular configuration of education. And the educational experience of any particular person was inevitably caught up in the tension between the two.

Finally, the city was pivotal in the continuing educational exchange between Europe and the United States, on the one hand, and between New York and the nation, on the other. As the nineteenth century progressed, the American image of Europe was increasingly refracted through the cultural apparatus of the New York press and publishing houses; of New York's theaters, concert halls, opera houses, and museums; and of New York's manufacturing establishments. Conversely, what Europe knew of the United States was increasingly refracted through the same apparatus. In short, New York during the nineteenth

century became a mediator of both national and international education. The substance taught did not always originate in New York, for
the city was a magnet that attracted New England evangelists like Lyman Beecher, upstate editors like Horace Greeley, and immigrant piano manufacturers like the Steinways. But the substance and the styles
and the values of such people were, once again, transmitted near and
far via New York's pedagogical machinery. By the 1870's the city was
serving the classic function of the metropolis teaching its hinterland;
and in the process its cultural values and institutions intruded, more or
less, into local and regional configurations of education throughout the
country.

Chapter 13

LIVES

> I never attended school but three quarters, and then I believe I got turned out once or twice. Yes, sir, I got turned out, for what the schoolmasters in their benighted stupidity termed "bad conduct," but which subsequent events have satisfactorily proven to have been merely a striking and precocious manifestation of genius.
>
> MICHAEL WALSH

The educational opportunities available within different communities varied significantly throughout the nineteenth century, and so, too, did the uses different individuals made of those opportunities. Lucy Larcom and Harriet Hanson Robinson were contemporaries in Lowell: both grew up amid old New England families in small New England towns; both worshiped as children in the Congregational church; both received the typical schooling of the 1820's and 1830's; and both worked in the Lowell mills. Yet the two became very different women, each in her own way reflecting the unique combination of temperament, aspiration, learning, and fortune that inevitably goes into the formation of human character. To study the educational biography of a Larcom or a Robinson is to particularize even further any generalizations about the patterns of American education that came into being between 1783 and 1876.

To that end, it is worth considering the education of seven nineteenth-century Americans: Larcom; Jacob Stroyer and Irving E. Lowery, who came to manhood as slaves in Sumter District; John McAuley Palmer and James Henry Magee, who received important segments of their education in Macoupin County; and William Earl Dodge and Michael Walsh, who had most of their education in New York City. Their experience cannot typify the ways in which other peo-

450

ple moved through the educational configurations of Lowell, Sumter, Macoupin, or New York, but their educational life histories do suggest some of the characteristic features of American education during the first century of national existence. Beyond that, their experience illustrates both the extraordinary variegation of nineteenth-century American education and the striking range of human character that always issues, to greater or lesser extent, from any particular set of educational arrangements, whatever the time or the place in human history.

II

Lucy Larcom is probably the best known of the early operatives to work in the Lowell factories, owing largely to the enduring interest in her autobiography, *A New England Girlhood,* as a document of American social history. Born in Beverly, Massachusetts, in 1824 into the large family of a merchant sea captain named Benjamin Larcom, she grew up in a pleasant ambience bounded by household, church, school, and local community. "We understand ourselves best and are best understood by others," she remarked in her later years, "through the persons who come nearest to us in our earliest years." At least retrospectively, Larcom was aware of the educational significance of a number of the early figures in her life: her maternal grandfather, who had been a soldier in the Revolutionary War ("the greatest distinction we could imagine"); her "studious" and reserved father, who was frequently absorbed in books; her "chatty and social" mother, who obviously lavished affection on her ten children; her elder sister Emilie, who early shaped Lucy's literary tastes, filled her with fairy tales and a love of Romantic poetry, and also served as a more general teacher and exemplar; her brother John, who first set her to writing poetry; and her numerous aunts, natural and adopted, who taught her everything from family lore to sewing and the other arts of domesticity.[1]

Larcom claimed that she learned to read at the age of two, from her father and her Aunt Lucy; and, in a household where books were valued, she quickly became an omnivorous reader, beginning with Mother Goose, the hymns of Isaac Watts, the stories of Maria Edgeworth, *The Pilgrim's Progress,* and, *mirabile dictu,* the poetry of Lord Byron, and soon proceeding to belles-lettres in general and novels in particular, the

---

1. Lucy Larcom, *A New England Girlhood* (1889; reprint ed.; New York: Corinth Books, 1961), p. 27.

latter borrowed surreptitiously by her sisters from a local circulating library. Like the other children of the neighborhood, Larcom began school at the age of two. "The mothers of those large families," she later recalled, "had to resort to some means of keeping their little ones out of mischief, while they attended to their domestic duties. Not much more than that sort of temporary guardianship was expected from the good dame who had us in charge." The "good dame" was a woman known to all as Aunt Hannah, who held class in her kitchen and sitting room above Captain Larcom's shop, and who taught Lucy, not only how to read ("I learned my letters in a few days, standing at Aunt Hannah's knee while she pointed them out in the spelling-book with a pin, skipping over the 'a b abs' into words of one and two syllables, thence taking a flying leap into the New Testament, in which there is concurrent family testimony that I was reading at the age of two years and a half"), but also how to spin yarn. Years later, when Larcom decided to become a teacher, she traced her first aspirations toward the vocation from her days under Aunt Hannah's tutelage.[2]

As a child, Larcom also enjoyed the round of activities that went forward under the auspices of the local Congregational church. She began to attend meetings at a very young age and clearly remembered the hymns, the sermons, the Scripture readings, and the ceremonies in which the entire family participated. In addition, she also recalled local community festivals—the training days, election days, independence days, and thanksgiving days during which the spirit of republicanism was kept "fresh and wide-awake." All this constituted a profoundly influential education: for Lucy Larcom the various components of the configuration that was early nineteenth-century Beverly proved complementary and mutually reinforcing, and they decisively shaped her character and her aspirations.[3]

Captain Larcom died when Lucy was seven. Soon thereafter Lucy's mother moved the family to Lowell, where she took a job as a housekeeper in one of the factory-connected boardinghouses, while Lucy and her younger sister attended one of Lowell's grammar schools and the older girls went to work in the factory. Newly built of red brick, the house was quickly filled with "a large feminine family" of approximately twenty to thirty that included several of Lucy's cousins. Most of the boarders came from New Hampshire and Vermont, and, as Larcom

2. *Ibid.*, p. 44.
3. *Ibid.*, p. 98.

put it, "there was a fresh, breezy sociability about them." They slept several to a room, waking before dawn to hurry to the mills before the gates closed at five. They ate lunch and supper in a large dining room, which doubled as a sitting room in the evenings, when the girls gathered around the tables to sew, talk, or read. Often, newsboys, shoe dealers, booksellers, and the like interrupted their leisure hours. Remembering one such evening, Larcom later wrote:

> A pedlar came in while they stayed, whose wares
> The girls sat cheapening. A phrenologist
> Displaced the pedlar, and the tide of mirth
> Flowed in around the tables, as he read
> The cranial character of each to each.

In addition to receiving informal education from peddlers and phrenologists, the young women attended lyceum lectures, where they heard such speakers as Edward Everett, Ralph Waldo Emerson, and John Quincy Adams; they participated in Sunday-school activities, as pupils and as teachers; they entered into dozens of discussion and study groups, both inside and outside the dormitories; and they studied everything from German to Chaucer to botany in night classes, often with the assistance of one or another "literary lady."[4]

Emilie, now become "a strong, earnest-hearted woman," continued to serve as teacher and exemplar to her younger kin—in Lucy's words, "our model, and the ideal of our heroine-worship." Emilie looked after Lucy and her agemates, insisting that they take cold baths every morning, urging them to keep edifying reading ever at hand (Emilie herself began with "Watts on the Improvement of the Mind" and proceeded to "Locke on the Understanding"), cautioning them against being "mentally defrauded" by the circumstances that had forced them to enter paid employment so early, and assisting them in the preparation and issuance of a little literary publication called "The Diving Bell." Later, it was Emilie who put Lucy in touch with the group of "bright girls" that had formed the "Improvement Circle" from which the *Lowell Offering* would issue. Beyond Emilie, Lucy met others destined to be significant in her education, including a Congregationalist minister, who taught her and other young women from the factories ethics out of

4. *Ibid.*, pp. 152, 242; and Lucy Larcom, *An Idyl [sic] of Work* (Boston: James R. Osgood and Company, 1875), p. 96.

Francis Wayland's *Elements of Moral Science,* and the abolitionist poet and journalist John Greenleaf Whittier, with whom she formed a life-long friendship.[5]

At the age of eleven, circumstances forced Lucy to drop out of grammar school to enter upon full-time work in the mills. She began as a doffer, who, together with a half-dozen other youngsters, was charged with changing the bobbins on the spinning-frame every forty-five minutes or so. The task was relatively undemanding, and Lucy could remember frolicking among the spinning frames and exploring the mysteries of the carding room, the dressing room, and the weaving room. Later, she became a spinner, and recalled the sense of pleasant companionship she shared with the young women she worked with at the spinning frames, in a room brightened by house plants and decorated at window work stations with cuttings of poems, stories, and newspaper articles (the mill regulations prohibited books [including Bibles, which were apparently confiscated by the overseers in substantial numbers], so that printed material used as decoration was in effect an imaginative subterfuge). After that she worked in the cloth room, alongside her sister Emilie in the sort of kin association that was quite common during the early years of the mills. There she was able to pursue her program of systematic reading and study with the full acquiescence of the supervisor. She also contributed verse to the *Operatives' Magazine,* initially published by the Congregationalist Improvement Association, with which she and her sister had affiliated, and then to the *Lowell Offering* when it merged with the *Operatives' Magazine.* The verse was characteristically romantic in style—the sort Emilie had taught her to love—and doubtless reflected an attitude toward life that deflected her attention from some of the social and economic conflicts that divided the operatives in their attitudes toward the mills and their owners.

Like many of her contemporaries, Larcom dreamed of a career beyond the mills. When her sister Emilie married and then decided in 1846 to move to Illinois with her husband and their infant son, Lucy accepted their invitation to relocate with them. She taught in a district school for a time but eventually enrolled in the Monticello Female Seminary at Godfrey, Illinois, where she supported her studies by teaching in the preparatory department. Monticello's principal, Philena Fobes, quickly became a new exemplar. Described by Larcom as a strong "guiding angel" sent to meet her on her "life-road" at precisely

5. Larcom, *A New England Girlhood,* pp. 167, 168, 170, 174.

the time she was most needed, Fobes played a crucial role in Larcom's education. Emilie's marriage had doubtless affected their relationship, probably lessening the closeness of the years in Lowell and apparently leaving Lucy in "need" of guidance and nurture. Not surprisingly, therefore, she looked back on her work in the Lowell mill and the Illinois district school as the best part of her early education, but claimed that the seminary course had been the capstone of her later development. She even wrote that it had taught her "what education really is: the penetrating deeper and rising higher into life, as well as making continually wider explorations; the rounding of the whole human being out of its nebulous elements into form, as planets and suns are rounded, until they give out safe and steady light. This makes the process an infinite one, not possible to be completed at any school."[6]

Upon completing the course at Monticello, Larcom returned to Massachusetts, where she taught for a number of years, first at Wheaton, and then at Bradford Seminary. But writing remained her first interest, and as a mature woman Larcom became a poet, an editor of magazines for young people (*Our Young Folks* and *St. Nicholas*), an anthologist, and an autobiographer. Toward the end of her life, in the final act of her continuing self-education, she decided, through the good offices of the Reverend Phillips Brooks, to enter the Episcopal church. She died in Boston in 1893.

Larcom's biography furnishes an instructive example of the crucial role of same-sex friendships in the education of nineteenth-century American women. And it also suggests the wisdom of caution in generalizing about the impact of the factory experience. The mills and their boardinghouses were influential in Larcom's education, but the experience she brought to all that she encountered in the mills inevitably shaped both the manner in which she underwent and responded to that experience and the nature of the experience that followed. Like all life histories, Larcom's was unique; but at least in this respect her experience was entirely representative. Put otherwise, Larcom's life was simply different from that of Harriet Hanson Robinson, who also came from an old New England family and whose widowed mother also boarded operatives for a Lowell factory, but who early manifested a greater militance than Larcom and whose marriage to an ardent young Free Soil journalist in 1848 led her to a position of leadership in the women's suffrage movement. And it was different again from that of

6. *Ibid.*, pp. 268, 269.

Sarah G. Bagley, who was initially as content as Larcom with the life of the mill but who decided in the 1840's that the operatives needed to organize in protest against exploitative conditions and who ended up a full-time labor organizer for the Female Labor Reform Association. What is more, Larcom's life bore little resemblance to that of Margaret Baxter, an Irish immigrant who went to work in the mills in 1848 and advanced rather quickly because she had learned to read, or to that of Catherine Matthews, also an Irish immigrant, who went to work in the mills in 1849 but who began as a sweeper and remained a sweeper for more than a decade, owing partly to the fact that she was illiterate. In effect, the education of the factory mediated other educative influences, but it neither replaced them nor rendered them ineffectual, and one must therefore scrutinize the entire education of an individual or a group of individuals before seeking to determine the particular effects of the factory on their lives and characters.

III

We are fortunate in having two extant slave narratives describing life in Sumter District, one by Jacob Stroyer and one by Irving E. Lowery. The two men were born on plantations less than twenty miles apart, Stroyer in 1849 and Lowery in 1850. After emancipation, they both became ministers in the Methodist Episcopal church, which identifies them, incidentally, as anything but ordinary; yet their reminiscences tell us much about the educational dynamics of plantation slavery.

Jacob Stroyer grew up on one of the several Singleton family plantations in the southwest corner of Sumter District, some twenty-eight miles from Columbia. His master, Matthew R. Singleton, was the second son of Colonel Richard Singleton, who had originally amassed the lands and the fortune they represented. While the chief crop was cotton, one gleans from the narrative the remarkable range of agricultural, manufacturing, and recreational activities that took place on the plantation—including horse racing, in which Stroyer became involved as a jockey. In all, there were some four hundred slaves on Matthew Singleton's establishment, who formed the substantial quarter community within which Stroyer came of age.

Four educational themes emerge from Stroyer's autobiography: his own growing personal strength and self-respect; the capricious but inexorable cruelty of thè white world; the vitality of the quarter community, and particularly of Stroyer's immediate family; and the opportunities for self-education via the church, especially after emancipation. Stroyer's narrative begins, "My father was born in Sierra Leone, Africa." The sentence is a fitting introduction, for Stroyer admired his father, deliberately modeled himself after him, and was able clearly to distinguish between the man, whom he loved, and the slave role that the man had been forced to assume. Stroyer's father had a name of his own, which he was prohibited from using, the master preferring that he be known as William Singleton; and beyond his name he had clear recollections of his African heritage, which he doubtless passed on to his children in the story-telling times that were part of the diurnal routine in the Stroyer household. Stroyer's mother had come from a family of carpenters, blacksmiths, house servants, and drivers, and, though she herself served as a field hand, there is evidence that she had grown up in the Singleton household, probably as a playmate of the young Matthew. She may even have learned to read in that capacity, sitting in on the lessons of her white agemates and mimicking them as they mastered the exercises in their primers.[7]

Before he learned to ride, Stroyer's life was centered in the quarter community. He spent summers at the Sand Hill (the Singletons' "summer seat," four miles from the main plantation) with the other slave children who were too young to work. The food was unpalatable but the discipline was lax; three or four older black women cared for the 80 to 150 youngsters who roamed freely in the woods, being interrupted only occasionally to be scrubbed for some forthcoming visit of the master and mistress. Winters were spent on the plantation proper, though Stroyer tells little of the daily life there. What does emerge clearly from the narrative, however, is that the relative integrity of his daily family life, as evidenced by strict rules about going to bed early, prohibitions against joining in adult conversation, and requirements concerning nightly family prayer, along with the embedment of that family life in a cohesive community, gave Stroyer a sense of personal security that was strong enough to endure the harsh lessons administered by the white community.[8]

Stroyer's family was apparently large and closely knit. His father had a first wife, who bore him seven children, and a second wife, who bore him eight; Jacob was the third son of the second wife. Stroyer's parents, though prohibited from legal marriage, maintained a lasting

7. Jacob Stroyer, *My Life in the South* (4th ed.; Salem, Mass.: Newcomb & Gauss, 1898), p. 7.
8. *Ibid.*, p. 8.

relationship, and the narrative attests to the care, affection, and concern they lavished upon their youngsters. Jacob's story about his family's re-action to a series of vicious beatings by the white trainer Boney Young is indicative. Having reached the limits of his endurance, Jacob had re-solved to fight Young at the next opportunity. His father counseled against such a course, maintaining that resistance would only bring the trainer's ire down on the entire family. His mother offered to intercede with the master, but, again, his father responded that the trainer would only seek vengeance on the family through his friend the overseer. The family talked far into the night about the matter, and, before retiring, the elder Stroyer voiced a prayer for freedom: "Lord, hasten the time when these children shall be their own free men and women." Clearly, though the members of Stroyer's family were limited in their ability to provide actual assistance, they could and did endure suffering together, which helped to impose meaning on their situation and thereby to miti-gate the damage it inflicted.

The larger community in which the Stroyers lived had its own rules of equity and justice that were clearly sanctioned by a special version of Christianity and stringently enforced from within. And this, too, was a source of strength for Jacob. Thus, when an older boy named Gilbert took to whipping the younger children at the Sand Hill one summer, Jacob exposed him to some adult slaves working nearby, who in due course examined the evidence, brought Gilbert to trial, had him whipped, and forced him to apologize to the youngsters he had abused. When considered, incidents such as this were a vital source for the dig-nity and agency evidenced in a life such as Stroyer's.[9]

Jacob's father looked after the hogs and cows and, in later years, the horses and mules. While still a young boy, Jacob began to help his father at this "occupation of hostler," and it was in the course of his as-sistance that he formed the desire to be a jockey. The decision brought him into direct personal contact with the harsh realities of the slave sys-tem. From the time he began to ride, while still too small to do so, to the time he gave it up because he had become too heavy, Stroyer was subjected to unending physical cruelty. He was whipped when he climbed onto a horse, he was whipped when he fell off a horse, and he was whipped for no reason at all; and, when he was badly hurt by a horse that stepped on his cheek, he was not even given the day off. Al-though he came only slowly and haltingly to the realization that his

9. *Ibid.*, p. 22.

"dear father and mother" and the rest of his "fellow Negroes" were utterly defenseless in the face of harsh mistreatment, he derived comfort from his father's continued faith in his children's ultimate liberation and from his parents' pride in his skill as a jockey. Indeed, his decision to become a skilled jockey, aided and abetted by the confidence and encouragement of his parents, was an important element in the development of his own aspirations for education.[10]

The decision to become a jockey was frustrated, however, when Matthew Singleton died suddenly and the racehorses had to be sold to pay the family's debts. Hence, Stroyer decided instead to become a "famous carpenter" and pursued the requisite training with a remarkable perseverance. Indeed, his story of that quest represents something of a turning point in the autobiography. With the racehorses gone, he told Mrs. Singleton that her late husband had promised him that when he became too heavy to ride horses he would be given an opportunity to learn carpentry. Mrs. Singleton consented, but a new overseer named William Turner protested, cautioning her, "That is the worst thing you can do, madam, to allow a Negro to have his choice about what he shall do." Against the overseer's advice, Mrs. Singleton held to her decision and arranged for Stroyer to learn the trade from one of the carpenters in the quarter community. The overseer in turn responded during periods when she was away by ordering Jacob to work as a field hand. But Stroyer persevered in his aspiration through whippings and beatings, and eventually learned the art.

By the time he reached his teens, Stroyer had also learned to read (the probability is that his mother had taught him); he had realized his ambition to learn a trade; he had manifested an ability to decide when to submit to and when to resist white authority; and he had even demonstrated the capability of sabotaging the plans of his supervisors. Not surprisingly, William Turner had clearly identified young Stroyer as a dangerous influence, and, had the Civil War not intervened, he would most likely have become an increasingly troublesome slave. But the very qualities that made him troublesome were the integrity, the determination, and the striving that provided the motive force for further education. Stroyer had made choices and he had acted upon them; even before emancipation, he was gaining his freedom.[11]

During the war, Stroyer spent a year working on the fortifications

10. *Ibid.*, pp. 17, 18.
11. *Ibid.*, pp. 11, 30.

at Sullivan's Island, near Charleston, and was wounded by gunfire at Fort Sumter. Although he was still enslaved and living among other untutored blacks, he was free enough from constant surveillance to pursue his education openly; indeed, he even claimed to have studied his spelling book while under bombardment from northern guns. Obviously, his early experience had given him sufficient self-respect to reach through the smallest cracks in the wall of oppression that stood between him and the freedom that he (and his father) craved. After emancipation, Stroyer made his way north to New England, where he studied for a time in the evening schools of Worcester, Massachusetts, and obtained a license as a local preacher in the African Methodist Episcopal church. At the time he published his autobiography in 1879, he was seeking funds for the continuation of his theological studies at Talladega College in Alabama; and, while the narrative is decidedly colored by that purpose, its value and authenticity remain considerable. Stroyer's life points to the singular importance of individual initiative in the use made of educational opportunity in the nineteenth century, and especially in those extraordinary instances in which individuals managed to transcend the constraints imposed by slavery. And it suggests, too, the crucial importance of the family and the church in enabling blacks to develop that initiative in the face of relentless efforts to deny it to them at the outset and to frustrate its realization once it had appeared.

The stark brutalities that pepper the Stroyer narrative are virtually absent from the account of his contemporary, Irving E. Lowery. Lowery pointedly wrote his reminiscences as a "record of the better life of those days," as an effort to balance accounts (like Stroyer's) that focused on the "evil side." Although it is possible that the slaves on John Frierson's plantation in the southeastern part of Sumter District were consistently better treated than those on the Singleton plantations—for one thing, there were only forty-five of them in the Frierson establishment, which surely made a difference, and, for another, Frierson had been educated for the ministry, though he had not in the end followed that calling, and was widely considered the best educated man in the district—Lowery's account indicates that it may have been his own close and continuing personal association with the Frierson family that encouraged him to write about the less harsh realities of what he called "life on the old plantation."[12]

12. I. E. Lowery, *Life on the Old Plantation in Ante-Bellum Days* (Columbia, S.C.: The State Company, 1911), p. 10.

There is little about Lowery's parents in the narrative. It states that they were mulattoes, that they felt close to the Friersons, and that his father had managed to purchase his own freedom and that of his mother, Lowery's grandmother, before the war, and was in the process of purchasing his wife's freedom when emancipation was proclaimed. The narrative also indicates that his mother was a deeply pious woman, who made the Lowery household a lively center for training in the Christian life and who prayed that God would call one of her sons to be a preacher (which, as Lowery pointed out, meant to be an exhorter or class leader on the old plantation and not a fully ordained minister). Lowery alluded to her hope at two points in his story. Thus, apart from the literary style of the set-piece slave narrative, the hope was probably significant in his own educational career, although, given Lowery's silence concerning his family, the point must be tentatively advanced.

At an early age, Lowery became Mr. Frierson's waiting boy and moved into the plantation house itself, away from his kin. He took his meals in the big house, slept on a little pallet at the foot of the Friersons' bed, accompanied Frierson on his business and social calls, and even prayed with the Friersons at the family altar. He did play with the other slave boys and at times was required to work in the fields; but, as Lowery readily admitted, he was "something of a privileged character." Obviously cut off from the culture of the quarter community and obviously the recipient of consistently kind and special treatment, Lowery experienced an education that was dominated by the instruction of the white household.[13]

Virtually all of Lowery's anecdotes recount aspects of the white pedagogy that he accepted without reservation. Frierson was a pillar of the Shiloh Methodist Church, and he took his slaves to services and Sunday school there at least once a month. In addition, he also employed a black preacher to instruct them on the plantation. He did so, according to Lowery, "to keep the slaves—and especially the younger ones—out of mischief," to ensure their spiritual and moral uplift, and to keep them from desecrating God's holy day. The preachers Frierson employed made a "deep impression," if not on the entire assemblage, at least on Lowery himself—he was actually able to recall verbatim a sermon he had heard as a boy on the theme that running away was a sin that could not be hidden from God.[14]

---

13. *Ibid.*, p. 103.
14. *Ibid.*, pp. 70, 80.

Lowery's account of "life on the old plantation" was doubtless a good deal rosier than the actuality, even assuming that Frierson was a model slaveowner. But there is no reason to discount his narrative completely as mere exaggeration. Lowery was only too aware that Frierson was not a typical master and that he himself was not a typical slave, and indeed that, despite Frierson's continuing efforts, others among the slaves stole, ran away, and even murdered. The narrative simply attests to the power of white pedagogy when it was not undermined, either by anomalous white cruelty or by contradictory black teaching. In fact, it is a poignant irony that shortly after emancipation Lowery was actually beaten by Frierson's son for becoming too "frolicsome" during the course of some work in the fields, with the result that Lowery left the plantation in a rage to work with his father on a rented farm nearby. It was then, at the age of sixteen, that he began the academic odyssey that led to an influential career in the Methodist Episcopal church.[15]

Interestingly, when Lowery first made known to his father his desire to obtain some schooling, his father promptly enrolled him in a new school that had just been opened in Sumter District through the generosity of a New England philanthropic organization. The father thought that schooling would be a fine adjunct to work on the farm, but that "work should be first in importance." The son, starting from the beginning with the alphabet but finding the experience exhilarating, found that doctrine "very distasteful" and promptly ran away and obtained a job with the railroad. The father waited until the end of the month and then claimed the son's wages, as his parent. The son soon returned home. But the father, rather than proceeding to break his will, acquiesced in his aspirations and resolved to assist him in his efforts.[16]

Meanwhile, a seminary named Baker's Institute had been established in Charleston in 1865 with the express purpose of training young men for the ministry. One of the first to enter was a resident of Sumter District named Joseph Wofford White. White in turn converted Lowery, helped him to obtain a license to exhort in 1868, and then facilitated his entry into Baker's Institute. Now sponsored by the South Carolina Conference, Lowery subsequently attended the Wesleyan Academy in Massachusetts, taught school for a time in Sumter, won ordination, married, and then proceeded through a series of pulpits of increasing regional significance, from Summerville (near Charleston), to

15. *Ibid.*, p. 105.
16. *Ibid.*, p. 19.

Greenville (in the northwest part of the state), to Charleston, to Aiken. He contributed to the columns of the *Witness,* a church publication; he received a master's degree from Claflin University; and he became an acknowledged leader of the church in South Carolina.

Lowery had experienced a profoundly different education from Stroyer's; yet each had emerged from the slave experience with a sufficient sense of personal integrity and aspiration to make effective use of educational opportunities that became available after emancipation. Others among their contemporaries, some of whom appear ephemerally on the margins of their accounts, were less fortunate: Josh, the jokester who stole from his fellow slaves; Aunt Betty and Granny the cook, who were devoted house servants; Monday and Jim, who were able field hands; Cyrus and Stepney, who resisted an overseer and were lynched summarily when the overseer died mysteriously a few days later. The education of such individuals cannot be detailed and indeed will never really be known; but for that very reason it ought not to be described in overly simple generalizations. Slave education was a complex phenomenon involving different combinations of white and black pedagogy, transmitted via different configurations of household, church, and school; and its impact on the life and character of any given individual must be ascertained in its fullest possible particularity, given the data at hand.

IV

John McAuley Palmer was born in Kentucky on September 13, 1817, to a family of British background and Baptist persuasion. He recalled his father as an omnivorous reader who "made himself familiar with the meager political literature of the day and became an admirer and devoted adherent of Mr. Jefferson." He recalled his mother as a woman "of the old type," who reared the children, cared for the household, and produced the food and clothing for a family of ten. At the time of John's birth, his father was a cabinetmaker; but in 1819 he succumbed to the lure of cheap fertile land in the so-called Green River Country of Kentucky and purchased a farm there, so that the family spent the next decade producing substantial crops of corn and tobacco. The elder Palmer took an active part in local and state politics, keeping abreast of affairs via meetings and newspapers and playing a vigorous role in Andrew Jackson's campaign for the presidency—John even remembered him carrying a hickory bush to the polls on election day in 1828 as a "sign of his faith." John's father was also a man of considerable courage and independence of spirit. In a region where whiskey was not only ubiquitous but the symbol of good hospitality, the elder Palmer took the pledge of temperance after perusing a volume of discourses by Lyman Beecher. And in a region where slavery was not only customary but an important element in the agricultural economy, he resisted the efforts of a patrol to search his premises during a time of considerable agitation over the possibility of a "rising." However courageous, his action brought suspicion upon the family, and in 1831 the decision was made to depart for the free soil of neighboring Illinois. In the spring of that year, the elder Palmer purchased a farm in Madison County, directly to the east of the burgeoning city of St. Louis, and shortly thereafter the family made the move.[17]

John Palmer was fourteen when he arrived in Illinois. He had attended the district schools of Christian County, Kentucky, which had proffered "the essential branches of education as they were then understood—reading, writing, and arithmetic as far as the 'Rule of Three,'" and he could scarcely remember a time when he could not read. But his most significant early education had come from the household, as the farm had been worked, the necessaries of life produced and procured, and the political questions that agitated the locality discussed and decided upon. By his own reports (and a cursory biographical study bears them out), his father's independence of mind and spirit proved exemplary: throughout his life John Palmer would go his own way, frequently in the face of sharp and sustained criticism and occasionally at considerable personal and political cost.[18]

Once settled in Illinois, John helped with the farm—his responsibilities doubtless increased since his mother died shortly after the move—and worked at odd jobs in and around the neighborhood. Sometime around the age of sixteen, his father offered him "his time," that is, release from the customary condition of service within the household until the age of twenty-one, and John decided to obtain additional schooling at Shurtleff College, the manual labor school that had been founded at Upper Alton, Illinois, by the Reverend John Mason Peck. There followed a five-year period in which young Palmer alternated between work, school (Shurtleff College), and school-*cum*-work. The skills necessary for his various jobs, which ranged from mixing mortar,

17. *Personal Recollections of John M. Palmer: The Story of an Earnest Life* (Cincinnati: The Robert Clarke Company, 1901), pp. 2, 14, 8.
18. *Ibid.*, p. 4.

to building roads, to selling clocks, to teaching school, were learned via informal apprenticeship. But the educational importance of the period was surely elsewhere; for it was during these years that Palmer bought himself a copy of Blackstone, formed an initial resolve to become a lawyer, and met Stephen A. Douglas in a boardinghouse while on the road selling clocks. Douglas was running for Congress at the time, and the two men formed a friendship that was to prove valuable and enduring. But the relationship was educationally significant because Douglas furnished a "brilliant example" that "changed the current of Palmer's life, and gave him fresh courage, impetus and determination to become a lawyer."[19]

Interestingly, the process of becoming a lawyer involved Palmer in three significant educative relationships. The first was with his older brother, Elihu, with whom John had initially gone to Shurtleff College and who had subsequently entered the ministry as a Baptist preacher. Palmer described him as a remarkable man, bright, industrious, athletic, and musical, and possessed of a natural mechanical skill and a great flair for languages. Elihu had married, established a household, and built a congregation in Carlinville, and, once John had resolved seriously to study law, he accepted his brother's invitation to reside in his household while he served his apprenticeship in the law office of one of his brother's friends. Residence with Elihu was surely influential in strengthening John's intellectual independence: he recalled Elihu as "profoundly sincere in his opinions upon all subjects," earnest in his doctrinal beliefs, and opposed to slavery and all forms of human oppression "with an intensity that almost amounted to fanaticism." The lively interest in politics that had suffused the Palmer household in Kentucky continued to suffuse the Palmer household in Carlinville.[20]

The second educative relationship was with Elihu's friend John S. Greathouse, a Carlinville attorney who took John into his office as an apprentice. Palmer described Greathouse as a "well-read lawyer," who gave him Blackstone's *Commentaries* to read, along with Coke on Littleton (with the notes of Francis Hargrave and Charles Butler) and a one-volume edition of the Illinois Supreme Court reports. In addition, Greathouse opened his library to the young apprentice and thereby made available, not only Blackstone and Coke, but also Lord Raymond's reports of cases in the courts of King's Bench and Common

19. *Ibid.*, p. 15; and *History of Macoupin County, Illinois . . . and Biographical Sketches of Some of Its Prominent Men and Pioneers* (Philadelphia: Brink, McDonough & Co., 1879), p. 90.
20. Palmer, *Recollections*, p. 18.

Pleas, Sir Francis Buller's introduction to the law related to trials at *nisi prius,* Thomas Starkie's and Leonard McNally's treatises on evidence, and Joseph Chitty's treatise on pleading. Finally, Greathouse encouraged Palmer to earn a few dollars by preparing deeds, examining land titles, and appearing at the bar as counsel for the defense in an assault case, which he won, incidentally, despite a good deal of evidence in support of the plaintiff's case.[21]

The third educative relationship was with Douglas, who was in Springfield when Palmer went there in December, 1838, to obtain a license to practice law and who not only sponsored the young candidate before the bar but also served as one of his examiners. Douglas was extraordinarily kind to Palmer at this time, or so at least Palmer remembered, and impressed him as well by delivering a vigorous comment about the need for lawyers to collect their fees while examining him for the bar. Because the relationship was more intermittent than the one with Greathouse, one cannot argue that Douglas was a mentor, but his interest in Palmer, as well as his example, doubtless helped the aspiring young lawyer to recognize his own potential. During his visit to Springfield, perhaps through the good offices of Douglas, Palmer also met a young attorney by the name of Abraham Lincoln. And this "tall, long, bony man," who entertained his audiences with a speech "that was full of logic, anecdote and common sense," became a lifelong friend as well as his colleague at the Illinois bar.[22]

Palmer had enjoyed the advantage of a number of terms of schooling, first in the district schools of Christian County, Kentucky, and then at Shurtleff College; but the essence of his education was self-instruction. Even his own description of his study in Greathouse's office suggests this:

I read carefully, with a glossary of law terms, and made full notes. I did not in my notes, as a rule, merely quote the language of the authors I read, but my effort was to grasp the subject and state it in my own language; my conception of the meaning of what I read was often inaccurate, but I think on the whole the method I adopted was preferable to any other. It promoted brevity and terseness, and aided systematizing the knowledge acquired; and I think my experience justified me in saying that knowledge of the law, acquired by this method, is much longer retained and more easily and intelligently applied to practical use, than it can be when the student merely masters words of his author or instructor. I may add here . . . that it is essential to a successful study of

21. *Ibid.,* p. 27.
22. *History of Macoupin,* p. 90.

the law that the student should master the history of the people with whom laws originate. Laws are but expressions of the feelings, habits and necessities of mankind, and can only be understood by a thorough familiarity with their history, and of their applications and uses. I read English history and Reeves' History of the English Law with great profit.

Palmer's self-instruction was not limited to the law, however. Initially a poor public speaker, owing to a stammer which he had suffered from boyhood, he was able to overcome the handicap through a systematic program of self-study, self-training, and self-discipline.[23]

Finally, given the fact that Palmer sought and succeeded in a career in politics, the learning that derived from observation must be noted in considering his continuing education. The only school of politics on the nineteenth-century frontier was the school of experience. Palmer lost his first election in a campaign for a county clerkship in 1838, but he won his second in a campaign for a probate judgeship in 1843. Thereafter, he went on to the state senate, became an influential member of the Illinois Democratic Party and then of the newly founded Republican Party, was subsequently elected to the governorship of Illinois and then to the United States Senate, and in 1896 even ran for the presidency on the ticket of the Gold Democrats (he attracted only 130,000 votes). He also mounted a military career during the same period, raising a company during the Mexican War and serving as its captain, and then raising a regiment during the Civil War and serving as its colonel (he subsequently rose to the rank of major general). At a time when American military arrangements were rooted essentially in the militia system, technical competence in military affairs took second place to the political competence associated with leadership, so that in Palmer's military as well as his political career a continuing self-education in the arts of organization and persuasion was vital to success. Sadly, however, in both careers the stubborn and courageous independence Palmer had learned in his father's and his brother's households set a ceiling on his success. His biographer called him a "conscientious turncoat," indicating the shifts of opinion and allegiance he found himself constantly forced to undergo in the interest of principle. It was a style that he had learned early and practiced constantly and that in the end was seen by those close to him as the most authentic and enduring mark of his character.[24]

23. Palmer, *Recollections*, pp. 27–28.
24. George Thomas Palmer, *A Conscientious Turncoat: The Story of John M. Palmer, 1817–1900* (New Haven: Yale University Press, 1941).

What we know of James Henry Magee comes largely from an autobiography entitled *The Night of Affliction and Morning of Recovery,* published in 1873. The work is a potpourri of reminiscence, reflection, documentation, and preachment, with the central theme being the triumph over adversity that the author managed to achieve with the continuing assistance of God. Magee was apparently deliberately poisoned as a boy by a disaffected friend of the Magee family who had been refused a loan by Magee's father. The result had been a dreadful degenerative disease that had incapacitated Magee for sustained periods of time but that he had transcended with the help of faith, family, and friends. By his mid-thirties, when the autobiography was written, he had come out of the long "night of affliction" and was enjoying the first glow of the "morning of recovery."

Magee was born on June 23, 1839, in Madison County, the same county where the Palmers had purchased their farm after deciding to leave Kentucky in 1831. His parents were natives of Kentucky. His father, a pork-packer by trade, had been born free; his mother had been born into slavery and had been purchased from her master by her husband-to-be before their marriage. The young couple had then moved to Illinois, where they had been able to rent a farm in Madison County and start a family. Young J. H. Magee (called Henry by his parents) spent his first years on that farm and helped work it with the other members of his family. Later, around 1845, when his brother Samuel married and purchased a farm in Macoupin County (near the town of Shipman), Henry went with several of his brothers to serve as "prairie breakers" in readying the land for cultivation. Eventually, the entire family resettled on that homestead. The warmth and camaraderie of the Magees shine through the early pages of the autobiographical account, as do the diurnal tragedies of life on the frontier, particularly the sudden death of his brother Lazarus when the wind blew over an oak tree under which his mother had placed him while she worked and the lingering death of his sister Elizabeth, who had been "a constant sufferer both in body and mind." Equally important, the autobiography speaks directly of the care and nurturance of Magee's mother, whose devotion seems to have sustained him through his long periods of illness following the poisoning.[25]

25. J. H. Magee, *The Night of Affliction and Morning of Recovery: An Autobiography* (Cincinnati: published by the author, 1873), pp. 16, 20.

Magee began his schooling with his brother Alfred in a district school after his father had gone personally to the teacher, a Mrs. Tunsil, to make the arrangements. Then, along with the other children, he attended a "colored school" on the east side of Samuel Magee's farm. And then, "for some considerable time," he was sent to the nearby "Brooklyn district school." After a while, however, some of the white parents complained to the school trustees about their children having to attend school with blacks, and the trustees concluded that it would be best, "for peace sake," as Magee put it, if the Magees withdrew their youngster. Almost as soon as he was withdrawn from the Brooklyn school, a new school was established by a white woman with a special interest in teaching black children, and Henry went there for a half-year, after which he was "detained at home to attend to duties connected with the farm." With the exception of the particular problem of race encountered at the Brooklyn school, it was a typical frontier experience of irregular, intermittent schooling, involving a variety of teachers at a succession of different institutions.[26]

Henry was fourteen when he was poisoned, and the months immediately thereafter were a nightmare of physical pain, despairing treatment by a succession of physicians, and near brushes with death. Nevertheless, Magee slowly regained his strength under the constant ministrations of his mother, and in 1855 he was sufficiently strong to undergo conversion and join the Piasa Baptist Church and then to go with his brothers Alfred and Samuel—Samuel and his wife had visited there earlier—to Racine, Wisconsin, where they were welcomed to the intermediate department of the local high school as the only blacks among three hundred scholars in attendance. They studied English, mathematics, and mental and moral philosophy under teachers who took a special interest in them; they attended the Sunday school of the First Baptist Church; and they joined in the social activities of the Benevolent Society of Racine. After remaining some six months, the brothers (and Samuel's wife) returned to the family homestead in Macoupin.

Up to this time, Henry had lived all his life within the supportive ambience of the Magee household or with siblings. It was only after the sojourn in Racine that he began to venture forth on his own. He took a job as a schoolmaster in the town of Jerseyville, some ten miles from Shipman, where an uncle named P. S. Breeden had established resi-

26. *Ibid.*, pp. 17–18.

dence; but while there he chose to live in a boardinghouse rather than with his uncle's family and, in his own words, made it his business to add to his stock of knowledge by studying what he had not previously known. Later, he taught at a district school in Ridge Prairie, which was somewhat nearer to the Magee homestead and, under the tutelage of a man named Davis, learned the rudiments of Latin. During this time in Ridge Prairie, Magee also experienced the call to preach and resolved to enter the ministry. He was ordained at the Piasa Baptist Church in the spring of 1863, and in September of that year he was called to the pulpit of the Salem Church in Wood River, near Alton. A year and a half later, he moved to the pastorship of the Baptist Church in Toronto. By then, the unquenchable thirst for further formal education that he had come to feel was an absolute necessity for the proper performance of his ministerial duties was clearly in evidence. During the first months of his stay in Toronto he employed a tutor to assist him in his studies of the Latin language and literature, and later, over a two-year period, he attended the Toronto Grammar School. The progress he was able to make there equipped him for the culminating stage of his formal education, attendance at a theological seminary.

"When I first began to preach," Magee recalled in his autobiography, "I had an unsatisfying [sic] desire to see Spurgeon, the great London Baptist Minister. And I have often sat down at home with my dear mother, and read portions from Spurgeon's sermons, and said, 'Mother, I do wish I could see and hear Mr. Spurgeon.' My mother was always hopeful and never discouraged her children in any thing that was right and commendable. She would say, 'Henry, the Lord may open a way for you to go to England after a while.'" That way opened in 1867. Magee came upon a pamphlet by Spurgeon, indicating that Spurgeon was president of an institution called the Pastor's College, specifically dedicated to the training of young preachers "for the responsible work of more efficiently preaching the gospel." Magee therefore wrote to Spurgeon, only to learn that the institution had more applications than it could possibly handle. Undaunted, he and a friend named John Graves persisted. And, when Graves simply went to England and managed to gain admission to the college, Magee was sufficiently heartened by his friend's example to follow suit. Through Graves, he obtained an interview with Spurgeon and on the basis of the interview was accepted for study. There followed a fascinating year in which Magee pursued work in English, mathematics, ancient and modern history, geography, the sciences, Greek, Latin, and Hebrew, as well as theology. The course was tailor-made for each student, and Magee derived a profound sense of fulfillment from it. What is more, since the students were encouraged to preach to the poor and unchurched of London during the course of their studies, Magee found ample opportunity to make direct and immediate use of what he learned. And with the delights of London thrown into the mix—its art, its history, its science, and its culture—the experience was memorable indeed.[27]

Magee returned to North America during the summer of 1868, bearing a library of invaluable theological works given him by Spurgeon. He was greeted on his arrival by word that his beloved mother was dying. He rushed home, and, as if symbolically, she died on the morning of his arrival. It proved, in his words, his greatest loss in the world. That same year he married and established his own family and moved to the principalship of the Baptist College at Nashville. The next year he moved to Alton, as teacher of the black public school there and then as pastor of the Baptist Church. And he was called the following year to the pulpit of the Union Baptist Church in Cincinnati. From that base, he enjoyed growing influence, in politics, as editor of a black newspaper, in entrepreneurship and benevolent activity, and as founder of the Illinois Colored Historical Society.

Though there were crucial differences, the similarities in the educational biographies of Palmer and Magee are particularly worthy of note. They transcend the confines of race or ethnicity and they patently illustrate that individuals made their own way, irregularly, intermittently, and indeterminately, through the educational configurations of the nineteenth-century frontier, going back and forth across the permeable boundaries of household, church, school, and apprenticeship, largely self-motivated and largely self-directed. Within institutions and without, they encountered others who became significant educationally, through nurturance, or through exemplarity, or through facilitation; and, at all points, initiative, stamina, and persistence made profound differences.

V

William Earl Dodge was the fourth child and second son of David Low and Sarah Cleveland Dodge. Both parents were old New Englanders of strong Protestant background. Married in 1798, David and Sarah

27. *Ibid.*, p. 92.

Dodge moved back and forth between New England and New York
City during the years when William was growing up. As a result, William did not become a permanent resident of New York until he was
twenty. But he was in and out of the city as a child, he held his first
clerkship there, and he learned a great deal about the vagaries of commerce from the financial considerations that necessitated his family's
moves.

David Dodge was a dry goods merchant and cotton manufacturer,
having early abandoned a career as a schoolteacher. Originally a clerk
in a Norwich, Connecticut, store, Dodge moved to Hartford in 1802,
where William was born three years later. In 1806 a partnership with
the Boston firm of S. & H. Higginson led the Dodges to New York
City, where David established the Higginsons' New York office. In
1813, after the Higginson firm went bankrupt, David Dodge became
the general agent for the Bozrah Manufacturing Company and moved
his family to Bozrahville, near Norwich. In 1815 the family returned to
New York, in 1819 they went back to Bozrahville, and in 1825 they returned to New York yet again. Two years later, David Dodge retired
and devoted his remaining twenty-five years to religious and literary
activities. Like so many of the families that formed the elite of nineteenth-century New York, the Dodges were migrants from New England; and the networks of kin and friendship they maintained, despite
their migratory status, were as important in their son's career as they
were more generally in the formation of the city's business community.

At best, David Dodge must have been a difficult individual to live
with. One of his daughters wrote of him that he was a man "of highly
nervous organization . . . excitable in temperament—in temper even fiery . . . An autocrat in his household, he was nevertheless tender in his
affections—a devoted husband and father, though oversevere in parental authority. He had all the elements of popularity; was a remarkable
conversationalist, and a profitable, as well as delightful companion, so
that as a man he was widely and enthusiastically beloved. Yet, his severity in family government, and his ever-living sense of man's superiority over woman . . . made him more feared than loved in his family."[28]

From birth, William was an alert and energetic child. He played
with his siblings, delighted in animals, especially horses, and remem-

28. Laura Stedman and George M. Gould, *Life and Letters of Edmund Clarence Stedman* (2 vols.; New York: Moffat, Yard and Company, 1910), I, 6.

bered celebrating the end of the War of 1812 with other boys by writing "Peace! Peace!" across the walls of New York City. He learned to read and write with ease and appeared "singularly responsive to religious impressions." As one of William's sisters later put it, "There was no effeminacy, no unnatural soberness or sentimentality." Clearly, William Dodge had the potential of following in his father's footsteps.[29]

If the strong model provided by David Dodge coupled with the innate ability manifested by William explains a good deal about the early development of William's personality, so, too, does the "sound judgment and remarkably good common sense" of Sarah Dodge, who was above all a faithful and pious Christian. William was close to his mother, who provided the warmth, affection, and stability that his father was unable to give. Most likely, therefore, it was from his mother that William derived the optimism, the friendliness, and the good nature that made him popular as both a child and an adult.[30]

Schooling as such was relatively unimportant in William Dodge's education. His mother taught him to read at home and he attended at least three different schools, one in New York City, one in Norwich, and one in Mendham, New Jersey, the last presided over by his maternal uncle, the Reverend Samuel Hansen Cox. He also attended church with his family and took an active part in the continuing round of prayers and religious meetings that were so central in his parents' lives. But it was the attitudes and values that William acquired through modeling that were the most important elements in his education. It was these that laid the groundwork for the subsequent training that became part and parcel of his entrance into the mercantile community of New York City.

When William was thirteen and in his first year at his uncle's school at Mendham, the Merritt brothers, Quaker friends of David Dodge, opened a dry goods store on Pearl Street in New York City. Soon thereafter they asked David Dodge to make good a promise he had made to let them have William as a clerk. Interestingly, Dodge chose to leave the decision to his son. The "autocrat," who usually decided family matters without so much as a nod to consultation, wrote to his son, giving him permission to accept the Merritts' offer if he so chose. William took the clerkship and thereby made a definite vocational choice, for, as Allan Horlick has pointed out, such a clerkship was

29. D. Stuart Dodge, ed., *Memorials of William E. Dodge* (New York: Anson D. F. Randolph and Company, 1887), p. 10.
    30. *Ibid.*, p. 279.

the first step on the road to a career as merchant in nineteenth-century New York. In fact, time as a clerk was to an aspiring merchant what attendance at college was to an aspiring minister.[31]

William worked with the Merritts for only a year. His duties were menial: he swept the store, made the fire, and trimmed the lamps; as he himself wrote in 1880, he "did the work now done by the porters." He was also responsible for collecting and transporting the goods bought at auction and for making the necessary inventories. Whatever the task, however, Dodge performed it with enthusiasm and verve, and managed also to find time to socialize with his fellow clerks, engaging in shoving contests at the post office and helping to set traps in which strangers sank up to their knees in the slush of Pearl Street. By the end of the year, the Merritts were sufficiently pleased with William's work to present him with a "massive, old-fashioned, double cased bracket [silver] time piece," which he wore proudly for years.[32]

William left the Merritt concern in 1819. His father was suffering financial problems and he thought it would be helpful if he returned to Bozrahville to clerk in the country store adjacent to his father's cotton mill. Once in Bozrahville, he performed duties similar to those he had carried out for the Merritts, although in Bozrahville he had more direct experience with customers than had been the case in New York. Indeed, he became such a popular salesman, especially with women, that many of the farmers' wives who visited the store would not dismount until William was free to help them. By the time he was eighteen, William's knowledge of business had become sufficiently broad so that he was trusted with going to New York City to buy the complete stock.

It was also during this period that William underwent religious conversion. Both of his parents were deeply pious, and his father was an active evangelist. In fact, the Bozrahville mill and store were the scenes of constant revivals. Given this context, it would have been difficult to remain outside the fold. In any case, the conversion itself represented a turning point in William's life. By temperament an energetic person who set exacting standards for himself, Dodge apparently became more self-assured and self-accepting. The routines of his life remained vigorous, but the demands inherent in those routines seem to have become less harsh because they were increasingly internalized.

31. Allan Stanley Horlick, *Country Boys and Merchant Princes: The Social Control of Young Men in New York* (Lewisburg, Pa.: Bucknell University Press, 1975).

32. Carlos Martyn, *William E. Dodge: The Christian Merchant* (New York: Funk & Wagnalls Company, 1890), p. 35; and Dodge, ed., *Memorials of William E. Dodge*, p. 23.

William was no longer a boy attempting to play the merchant role; he was a young man becoming a merchant.

Once William had joined the church—he was seventeen when he did so—his life took on a new economy of purpose. He married Melissa Phelps, the daughter of old family friends, and with his father's assistance went into the dry goods business on his own. Eleven years later, he dissolved his firm to join his father-in-law in what became Phelps, Dodge & Company. He had already had the best training a merchant could have—experience at every level of business and the responsibility of running his own firm—and he was ready for the wider scope that the international metals trade provided. Dodge's rise was not from rags to riches, nor was it accomplished solely on his own initiative. Pushing ahead was not countenanced in the nineteenth-century mercantile community, while hard work and personal sponsorship were, and Dodge's initiation into business conformed to the expectations of his time.

Dodge flourished in the role for which he had been educated. Despite the cyclical depressions of the era, the business of Phelps, Dodge increased and diversified. Dodge's share in the partnership expanded with his responsibilities. And so, too, did his all-important Christian duties. Dodge was a founding member of the New York Young Men's Bible Society and the New York City Mission and Tract Society. Although all these activities proved mutually reinforcing and enhanced his continued personal development, a trip to the South that Dodge made when he was thirty-five precipitated a period of searching self-doubt. He had gone South to settle the firm's relationship with a New Orleans commission house, and his travels provided his first direct acquaintance with the plantation system. The loneliness and discomfort of the trip combined with the exposure to a way of life that seemed largely alien heightened his abhorrence of "the curse of slavery." More importantly, perhaps, the trip afforded an opportunity to reflect on the direction of his life. In the future, he wrote to his wife, his duties to God, family, the church, and the world would not be disregarded. "While I have no idea of slighting business," he concluded, "I will not hereafter undertake more than I can attend to without neglecting other and more important things,—and of this, by the assistance of God, I intend to be my own judge."[33]

Dodge returned to New York with a renewed sense of calling. As a

33. Dodge, ed., *Memorials of William E. Dodge*, pp. 28, 34.

businessman he became more of a mercantile capitalist than the merchant-manager he had been. He was an early and large investor in railroads and often lent his capital to smaller, struggling businesses in which he had an interest. As a politician and philanthropist, he also increasingly served as a spokesman for the New York mercantile community. His colleagues sent him to Congress in 1864 and elected him president of the Chamber of Commerce for eight consecutive years. And his work for the Board of Indian Commissioners, the American Board of Commissioners for Foreign Missions, the General Assembly of the Presbyterian Church, the Evangelical Alliance, and the temperance movement simply represented an extension of his responsibilities as a "Christian merchant." To the end of his long life, he worked energetically to fulfill his messianic dreams.[34]

If Dodge's life was a study in coherence and integrity, the life of his contemporary Michael Walsh was a study in anomaly. Walsh served three terms in the New York State Assembly and a term in Congress as well; but he also served two terms as a prisoner on Blackwell's Island. He was a sincere champion of the common man, but he was also an egotistical demagogue. He was an outspoken opponent of backroom politics, but he organized a political gang into a genuine challenge to the power of Tammany Hall. Yet the anomalous elements in the character of this radical democrat who fancied himself a latter-day Napoleon should not obscure the more consistent qualities of the man—his flair for the dramatic, his drive toward independence, his fascination with power, and his chronic inability to sustain commitments. To a degree, Walsh was characteristically American; in fact, the early stages of his education call to mind the education of Benjamin Franklin. But if Franklin's education exemplifies the distance genius can travel on its own, Walsh's illustrates the limitations of such an odyssey for lesser men.

The facts of Walsh's early life are unclear. Some accounts give the date of his birth as 1810, others as 1815. All agree that he was born in Ireland, though the exact place of his birth has not been established. Even the age at which he came to New York City remains uncertain. All that can be said with confidence is that Michael Walsh was born in Ireland during the second decade of the nineteenth century and soon thereafter came to New York City with his mother, Ellen Keefe, to join his father, Mike Welsh [sic], who had settled there sometime earlier

34. Martyn, *William E. Dodge: The Christian Merchant.*

and become the proprietor of a mahogany yard and a furniture store.

The outline of Walsh's early education is equally sketchy. He grew up in a large family—there were probably five brothers and sisters—and attended St. Peter's, the city's oldest Roman Catholic school. Sometime between the ages of ten and sixteen, he was apprenticed to a lithographer, though he quickly broke his indenture and ran away to Philadelphia. He subsequently returned to New York to resume his training but soon made off again, this time for the South. In Florida he apparently took part in a brief military campaign against the Indians; and in New Orleans he supported himself (and contributed to the support of his family) through various kinds of manual labor, including work as a cabin boy, deck hand, and fireman on a variety of Mississippi river boats. In 1839, Walsh returned to New York City, to become a printer, a newspaper reporter and editor, and, above all, a politician.

Walsh's later writings and speeches permit one to add some flesh to this skeletal account. He announced one day in Congress, for example, that he had left St. Peter's School, not because he was sent to work, as were so many Irish youngsters, but rather because "I got turned out." Similarly, he proudly explained in an article he published in the *Aurora* that he had abandoned his job as a lithographer's apprentice because "then I was a boy—a small, poor, devil-may-care kind of runaway boy, whose very soul recoiled at restraint—who preferred leaving a good home, and sleeping in outhouses at lumberyards, half starved to being bound out as an apprentice." Walsh was apparently a rebellious youngster of independent spirit, who could learn more in a shop than in a classroom and more again in the world at large. At the lithographer's establishment he had been able to find Charley Soran, "the poet," who became his "sincere friend" and probably his tutor in prose as well as poetry. In the course of his travels, he had been able to discover what he called "the knowledge . . . of human nature." Indeed, "the blackguard" (policeman) who had "insolently driven" him from the steps of the Bank of the United States in Philadelphia provided Mike with his first lesson in politics. The incident was to "prey upon" him for many years, he later wrote, and it was to this one incident that he always returned when asked to explain his opposition to the Bank and to all that it represented in terms of privilege, monopoly, and wealth.[35]

35. U.S., Congress, House, *Congressional Globe,* 33d Cong., 1st sess., 1854, XXVII, pt. 2, 1231; and *Sketches of the Speeches and Writings of Michael Walsh Including His Poems and Correspondence Compiled by a Committee of the Spartan Association* (New York: Thomas McSpedon, 1843), pp. 82, 86, 56, 83.

Mike Walsh's education, then, even as a child, came primarily from his own observations of the world around him, as well as from what he could learn by way of skills and knowledge from the men he counted as his "sincere friends." As a congressman, he argued that "a man can be a man without being drilled through college. It is far better to know the men among whom one lives, than to know of men who have been dead three thousand years," and he also stated that he "would not barter away all the practical knowledge I have received in lumber and ship-yards for all the Latin that was ever spoken in ancient Rome." His education did not nurture intellect, but it bred an acute and worldly in-telligence, deriving from a remarkable ability to learn from observation and reflection.[36]

One is not born independent, one learns the quality; and, during the early years of his education, Mike Walsh's father was very much his model and his guide. A veteran of the Irish rebellion of 1789 who, it has been claimed, was rather eccentric in his political opinions, Welsh [sic] was the major source of his son's early education. The stories young Mike heard at his "father's fireside" were more than likely the initial stimulus for his extraordinary powers of imagination and may also have influenced his unusually apt and colorful use of language. Be-yond that, Mike Walsh lived his independence—he would not, for ex-ample, apply for American citizenship because he thought the govern-ment was insufficiently republican—and his son sought to follow his example.[37]

When Mike Walsh returned to New York in 1839, he achieved his maturity. In that year he married Catherine Wiley (Riley?), thus cross-ing the traditional divide within Irish society between youth and adult-hood. In the following year, he organized "The Spartan Association," an anti-Tammany club of radical young democrats, thereby giving no-tice that he was ultimately a politician, even if a journalist and printer by trade. And in 1842 he founded a short-lived newspaper, *The Knick-erbocker,* thereby creating a vehicle through which he could express himself fully and freely on the causes that stirred his ire. During the next few years, Walsh was in and out of public office (1846, 1847, 1852–1854), as he was in and out of jail (1843, 1846) on charges of as-sault, battery, and libel. He occasionally edited his own newspapers— the *Subterranean,* which ran intermittently in the 1840's, was the most

36. U.S., Congress, House, *Congressional Globe,* 33d Cong., 1st sess., 1854, XXVIII, pt. 2, 1231.

37. *Sketches,* p. 55.

important of the journals he issued—and he occasionally wrote for other papers.

In the early years of his political career, those during which he became "intimately acquainted with every hole and corner from the Battery to Dry Dock, and from Washington Market to Harlem," because his "beat" was all of Manhattan, Walsh was able to understand, to articulate, and to organize the wide-ranging resentments of a significant segment of New York's workingmen and mechanics. The Spartan Association, which was originally formed at The Comet, a Mott Street public house, although Dunn's Sixth Street Hotel later became its headquarters, never put forward a coherent program. But Walsh's statements of the Spartans' accomplishments, however inflated, illustrate how shrewd he could be in identifying the local issues that were important to his constituency.[38]

Walsh was drawn to the bars and saloons of New York because it was there that he and his "boys" felt at home; and it was for essentially the same reason that he was also drawn to the city's printshops and editorial offices. His geniality and facility with language allowed him to move easily between those two nerve centers of the city's political life. In fact, one of the more important reforms he suggested, the establishment of a government printing office to publish authorized copies of congressional speeches, testified to his appreciation of the degree to which newspapers influenced what the public knew and thought, as well as his sense of the advantages, at least for the outsider, that would accrue from having information with which to challenge the reporting of men like Horace Greeley, one of his favorite bêtes noires.

Walsh's effort to use newspapers to gain power was surely educative for him, whatever its effects on his readers. To report the news, he had to investigate; to persuade his readers, he had to sharpen his rhetorical skills. And, beyond these technical advances, his work also forced him to extend his "beat" beyond Manhattan. It was as the *Aurora's* correspondent that Walsh visited newspaper editors all along the route from New York to Washington; and it was as the partner of George Henry Evans, a leading mid-century agrarian reformer who for a time merged his paper, the *Working Man's Advocate,* with Walsh's *Subterranean,* that Walsh attended a workingmen's convention in Boston, traveled to Lowell to speak to the factory women and agitate for labor organization, and visited Brook Farm. What Walsh learned from

38. *Subterranean,* February 28, 1846.

all this is not clear. At the least, he probably garnered tidbits of information for his stock of knowledge; at the worst, he confirmed his increasingly self-destructive sense of personal importance. However that may be, over time, though the balance was always precarious, Walsh became less interested in the problems of the workingmen and more interested in himself. At the outset, though scarcely above securing a speaker's platform by physical force, Walsh had tended to seek attention and power by discussing issues. As the years passed, however, he sought it more and more by posturing. He was furious with his followers, for example, when in 1846, after he had been sentenced to a six-month term in the penitentiary, they persuaded the governor to have him released four months early, in June. He had wanted to serve his full sentence, so that his martyr-like return to New York could be made in the autumn, on the eve of the November election. Similarly, his attempted resignation from the New York State Assembly in 1847 made no sense whatever. Since it had not been tendered in writing and therefore could not be accepted, the action was apparently nothing more than a crass bid for public notice. Ousted from political life in 1854, when it was revealed that he had never become an American citizen, Walsh simply disintegrated. When George Steers, a wealthy shipbuilder, commissioned him to go to Russia to obtain contracts to construct vessels for the Russian navy, Walsh cavorted through Europe, returning to New York as a penniless steerage passenger, without ever having reached his appointed destination. And, when he was found dead in an alley on March 17, 1859, he had last been seen leaving a bar at 2:00 A.M., more than a little drunk.

Michael Walsh was a gifted autodidact, who made a genuine contribution to the political life of New York City. As one historian has argued, the years that followed his death, ushering in an era of Tammany corruption and boss rule, could well have used more such men to "lift the lid from the city's political stench-pots and let the fresh air in." Unfortunately, however, Walsh did not learn to use power effectively or in the long-run interest of the people who gave him their allegiance and their votes. Beyond his inclination to drink himself into incoherence, he seems to have gone astray because the drive, the imagination, and the independence that served him so well at the outset of his career were never disciplined and channeled in the service of some worthy cause. They mastered him rather than vice versa, so that the very qualities that led him to Congress led him to Blackwell's Island as well.[39]

39. Frank C. Rogers, Jr., "Mike Walsh: A Voice of Protest" (masters thesis, Columbia University, 1950), p. 122.

Chapter 14

CHARACTERISTICS

The benefits which thus result from a liberal system of education and a
cheap press to the working classes of the United States can hardly be
overestimated in a national point of view; but it is to the cooperation of
both that they must undoubtedly be ascribed.

JOSEPH WHITWORTH

Tocqueville, with his characteristic incisiveness, caught much of the
spirit of American education in the remarkable first volume of the *Democracy*. How was it, he asked, that a democratic republic had come to
exist in the United States? He proposed three "principal causes": first,
the peculiar and accidental situation in which Providence had placed
the Americans (the fact that the nation had no powerful neighbors, no
central metropolis, and the riches of a boundless continent to exploit);
second, the laws that created a unique political system, to wit, a federal
form of polity, which combined "the power of a great republic with the
security of a small one," strong local institutions, which limited "the
despotism of the majority" and at the same time imparted "a taste for
freedom and the art of being free," and a vigorous judiciary, which re-
pressed "the excesses of democracy"; and third, the customs and manners of the people—the entire panoply of moral and intellectual habits
and ideas "which constitute their character of mind." Of the three,
Tocqueville concluded, the laws contributed more to the maintenance of
a democratic republic than physical circumstances, and the customs and
manners of the people even more than the laws. In the end, it was custom that he judged the "peculiar cause" that enabled the Americans to
sustain their democratic republic.[1]

1. Alexis de Tocqueville, *Democracy in America*, edited by Phillips Bradley (2 vols.; New
York: Alfred A. Knopf, 1945), I, chap. xvii.

What, then, were the sources of American custom? In Tocqueville's analysis, the American character derived from the special combination of formal instruction, informal nurture, and individual self-reflection that constituted the essential education of the American citizenry. As Tocqueville explicated it, the American family provided a relatively weak education, in comparison with the great aristocratic families of Europe. American marriages were more freely entered into as partnerships between equals; and laws abolishing primogeniture had reduced the influence of parents on children and strengthened the influence of siblings and agemates on one another. Parental authority ended earlier and more decisively, with the result that each generation was left free to become a new society. And, in place of its traditional role as the preeminent shaper of values, aspirations, and character, the family had become a refuge from the tensions of the political and social world.

Closely related to these changes, and indeed partly in consequence of them, the public instruction given by churches, schools, and other institutions for the diffusion of knowledge and values took on greater importance. The churches, however plural the particular doctrines they taught, nurtured certain universal beliefs and values that provided a solid foundation for the operation of democratic institutions and procedures. The schools, however different their quality from North to South, conveyed not only literacy but certain elemental notions of human knowledge, the doctrines and evidences of Christianity, and the principles of constitutional government. And the press, however varied its issue, created and strengthened the voluntary associations—or publics—that stood between anarchic individualism on the one hand and despotic majoritarianism on the other.

Beyond these, there was the larger education that derived from political participation. "The citizen of the United States does not acquire his practical science and his positive notions from books," Tocqueville observed; "the instruction he has acquired may have prepared him for receiving those ideas, but it did not furnish them. The American learns to know the laws by participating in the act of legislation; and he takes a lesson in the forms of government by governing. The great work of society is ever going on before his eyes and, as it were, under his hands." In the United States, Tocqueville concluded, the aim of education was politics; in Europe, its principal object was to fit men for private life. Thus did education sustain custom among the Americans, via a continuing process of cultural recreation as fundamental to a democratic republic as the breaking up of family fortunes and the distribution of political power.[2]

For all his incisiveness, Tocqueville had his blind spots, about education as about much else. He generalized about the family from the more genteel segments of the middle class, with whom he spent most of his time, and without reference to the gentry of the South or the immigrants of the North. He generalized about political participation from a traditional New England township model, which early and decisively impressed itself upon his mind as paradigmatically American, but he gave little attention to the impact of industrialization on New England town life in general or on political participation in particular. And he drew his generalizations about Americans as individuals from white males, whatever the disclaimers—and the conflicting evidence—in his chapters on women, blacks, and Indians. Finally, as has often been pointed out, Tocqueville continually confused a democratic ideal that he saw coming into being with an American reality that he insisted he was observing. Yet, all such qualifications notwithstanding, the young Frenchman did capture the central tendencies of American education. Others may have presented the details more fully and more accurately; Tocqueville, more than any contemporary, grasped the whole.[3]

I I

Popularization and multitudinousness, in tandem, were the distinguishing features of American education during the nineteenth century. They manifested themselves, first, in the general prevalence of churches, schools, colleges, and newspapers; second, in the unprecedented development and multiplication of new educative forms; third, in the transformation of curricula evident in all educative agencies; and, fourth, in the community-based character of the institutions that emerged.

2. *Ibid.*, I, 318.
3. Given Tocqueville's penchant for theorizing, it is well to point out that all of the principal phenomena he perceived with respect to American education were also noted by other foreign commentators: by the German diplomat Francis J. Grund in *The Americans, in Their Moral, Social, and Political Relations* (Boston: Marsh, Capen & Lyon, 1837); by the Scottish journalist Alexander Mackay in *The Western World, or Travels in the United States in 1846 and 1847* (3 vols.; London: Richard Bentley, 1849); by the English geologist Sir Charles Lyell in *A Second Visit to the United States of North America* (2 vols.; New York: Harper & Brothers, 1849); and by the Polish revolutionary Adam G. de Gurowski in *America and Europe* (New York: D. Appleton and Company, 1859). It is also interesting to note the reception given *Democracy in America* by Tocqueville's European contemporaries, particularly, in light of his emerging role as a bellwether of British liberalism, by John Stuart Mill in the *London Review*, II (1835-1836), 85-129, and the *Edinburgh Review*, CXLV (1840-1841), 1-47.

In the most elemental terms, churches, schools, colleges, and newspapers simply became more accessible during the first century of national life. In every instance, the number of such institutions increased at a rate faster than the population; and, in every instance, the length, depth, and intensity of the educative experiences they proffered also increased. The expansion was not wholly linear: there were declines for particular regions at particular times, for example, in the ratio of school enrollment to the total population of young people in communities that received large numbers of immigrants during the 1850's, or in the availability of churches, schools, and colleges in regions devastated by military actions during the 1860's. On the whole, however, the tendency was toward a greater popularization of education with respect to numbers, insofar as educative institutions were more generally available and more generally used.

The development and multiplication of new institutional forms further expanded the availability of education by making opportunities for teaching and learning more diverse in method, substance, and timing. Publishers, partaking of the characteristic commitment to didacticism that marked the era (didacticism, after all, was good business as well as good citizenship), printed materials in a variety of formats that allowed the autodidact to pursue instruction according to his or her own fancy and at his or her own pace. An individual who had been taught something systematically at an earlier age could carry the effort forward at a later age, while an individual who had missed the opportunity at an earlier age could initiate it via self-study at a later age. Moreover, as how-to-do-it materials diversified in substance and approach, from the informal advice columns of newspapers to formal textbooks systematically explicating various subjects, a widening range of learning styles could be served and satisfied.

What was true of publishers in these respects was true as well of libraries, lyceums, museums, fairs, institutes, and expositions. The opportunity for education broadened, as what might have been missed at school could be obtained at a lyceum, or as what might have been conveyed in the family could be superseded by what was taught at an institute. The sheer extent and variety of educational opportunity increased exponentially, as more institutions offered more experiences in more realms to more people. Once again, popularization with respect to numbers was enhanced.

Availability, of course, is not synonymous with use. Educative agencies reached out to ever larger and more varied clienteles with ever greater success. And the success of one institution enhanced the success of another; indeed, the relationship was one factor in the complementarity that marked contemporary configurations of education. Churches and schools conveyed literacy, thereby creating a clientele for publishers and libraries; publishers printed more, and more varied, materials; and libraries made the materials freely or cheaply available, thereby encouraging the churches and schools in their efforts to extend literacy. Lyceums reached out for participants whose curiosity about matters cultural had been piqued by the schools; lyceums in turn sent their audiences on to the exhibits of museums, fairs, and expositions. The forces of popularization in various institutions were mutually reinforcing, as each enlarged the potential clientele of all the others. Yet, granted the upward spiraling of numbers, there were groups that did not or could not partake. Some were isolated from the process by geographic distance: they lived far from schools, libraries, lyceums, and fairs; they were illiterate or semiliterate; and they were able to live satisfactorily according to their own values without participating in the expanding world of education. Others were isolated from the process by what one might call psychic distance. They may have been within walking distance of schools, libraries, lyceums, and fairs, but such institutions were not part of the world as they perceived it. They were either not moved to participate, or they felt they ought not to participate because the institutions were for one reason or another not for them, or they believed that the price of participation in terms of violence to their own values was not worth the conflict. Some were removed from the process by force—slaves or Indians, who were prohibited from learning to read, for example. Some were removed from the process by tradition—women, for example, who were taught that higher education was unnecessary and inappropriate. And some removed themselves from the process out of principle—Mennonites, for example, who took seriously the Old Testament dictum that "in much wisdom is much grief." In the end, then, along with the increasing availability of educative institutions, there was increasing variety in the use made of these institutions, among different ethnic, religious, racial, geographic, and social groups, and between the sexes.

Granted differential use by various segments of the population, the larger and more diverse clienteles of educative institutions during the first century of nationhood transformed the curricula of those institutions. The churches proffered a more diverse fare, offering under the conditions of denominational pluralism a liturgy to suit every taste; and, even beyond that, they tended to move toward a more embracing and more beneficent theology capable of attracting as broad a spectrum of the population as possible. In like fashion, the schools and colleges proffered a more extensive, more practical, and less intellectually restrictive curriculum, for all intents and purposes providing something of intellectual value to all who came. And publishers, libraries, lyceums, museums, fairs, institutes, and expositions proffered materials, lectures, displays, and events designed to entertain while they edified. In the process, the knowledge, attitudes, values, skills, and sensibilities that were the very substance of education were also popularized, pointedly attracting larger and more diverse clienteles, which in turn demanded ever broader and more diverse curricula. Groups that could not obtain what they desired from extant institutions founded new ones to provide what they wanted; and both the extant institutions and the new ones ended up broadening their appeal to attract larger clienteles. Once again, however, the trend was neither universal nor unilinear. Traditional institutions coexisted with new ones, and indeed on occasion became more traditional in the effort to maintain distinctive roles. The old and the tried were not necessarily left behind by popularization, since the multiplication and diversification of the whole number of institutions were as significant an aspect of the phenomenon as the broadening of particular institutions.

Finally, whether public or private in the particulars of their support and control, nineteenth-century institutions of education tended to present themselves and in turn to be perceived as community institutions; indeed, in the view of their leaders, the very fact that they were educative institutions made them community institutions. Particular churches were seen as private institutions, but churches in general were regarded as community institutions. Similarly, schools, academies, and colleges were variously supported by tax funds, public endowments, subscriptions, and tuition, and variously controlled by school committees or boards of trustees; but they were also regarded as community institutions. And the same can be said for libraries, lyceums, museums, fairs, institutes, and expositions. Even publishers, particularly newspaper publishers, cloaked themselves in the mantle of community service. Horace Greeley and P. T. Barnum, no less than Lyman Beecher, Horace Mann, and Francis Wayland, saw themselves and presented themselves to the citizenry at large as public-spirited community servants. With respect to support, the posture was at the least good business: it broadened the potential financial base. With respect to control, however, it had a curiously ambivalent political effect. On the one hand, it tended to lift education "above the fray." Beecher sought to enlist all (Protestant) denominations in the campaign to save the West; Mann spoke of successive generations of men as constituting "one great Commonwealth" and of the property of the Commonwealth as "pledged for the education of all its youth"; Wayland, like every other college president of the era, attempted to build an inclusive interdenominational foundation for the development of Brown; and Greeley and Barnum sought to address the largest possible clientele as self-appointed spokesmen for that clientele. On the other hand, it also plunged it into the midst of the fray, and indeed some of the sharpest conflicts of the era were fought over educational issues. Beecher was embroiled in continuing theological and political controversy during his presidency of Lane Theological Seminary, as was Mann during his secretaryship of the Massachusetts Board of Education. Given its popular character, education was ever vulnerable to direct confrontations over financing and support and intense conflicts over the substance of the curriculum; beyond that, it was an important symbolic issue, like temperance, on which communities could bitterly divide precisely because the stakes were highest in the realm of principle. It was Aristotle who once remarked that when people set out to educate, they invariably have in mind some vision of the good life, and, since visions of the good life will surely differ, education is inescapably caught up in politics. Americans of the early national era were aware of this; in fact, as often as not, they defined what they were and what they hoped to be in conflicts over the ends and means of education.[4]

Given the general tendency toward popularization, where did the United States stand with respect to other nations? The Census of 1850 undertook some comparisons with respect to schooling (using as an index the ratio of students to the total population) and came up with the following results:[5]

4. *Tenth Annual Report of the Board of Education, Together with the Tenth Annual Report of the Secretary of the Board* (1846), p. 127.

5. J. D. B. De Bow, ed., *Statistical View of the United States, . . . Being a Compendium of the Seventh Census* (Washington, D.C.: A. O. P. Nicholson, 1854), pp. 148, 133, 137; and [Horace Mann], *Census of Great Britain, 1851: Religious Worship, England and Wales* (London: George E. Eyre and William Spottiswoode, 1853), p. clxxviii.

RATIO OF SCHOLARS AT SCHOOLS
TO THE WHOLE POPULATION (1850)

Country	Ratio of Students to Total Population
Maine	32%
Denmark	21
U. S. (excluding slaves)	20
U. S. (including slaves)	18
Sweden	18
Saxony	17
Prussia	16
Norway	14
Belgium	12
Great Britain (on the books)	12
Great Britain (in attendance March 3, 1851)	14
France	10
Austria	7
Holland	7
Ireland	7
Greece	6
Russia	2
Portugal	1

That census also included the following comparative data on numbers of churches:

NUMBER OF CHURCHES IN THE UNITED STATES (Population: 23,192,000)		NUMBER OF CHURCHES IN GREAT BRITAIN (Population: 20,817,000)		NUMBER OF CHURCHES IN GREAT BRITAIN IN PARLIAMENTARY CENSUS OF 1851	
Baptist	9,360	Baptist	2,489		
Congregational	1,716	Congregational	3,244	Baptist	2,485
Episcopal	1,461	Anglican	14,078	Congregational	2,960
Lutheran	1,221	Methodist	11,807	Anglican	13,854
Methodist	13,338	Roman Catholic	570	Methodist	9,742
Presbyterian	4,863	Other	610	Roman Catholic	566
Roman Catholic	1,227	Total	32,798	Other	1,352
Other	4,997			Total	30,959
Total	38,183				

Thirty years later, in 1880, Michael G. Mulhall undertook a variety of such comparisons in his statistical study, *The Progress of the World*. With respect to schooling, again comparing the number of schoolchildren to the total population, the results were as follows:[6]

	1830	1878
Germany	17%	17%
United States	15	19
Scandinavia	14	14
Switzerland	13	15
Low Countries	12	16
United Kingdom	9	15
France	7	13
British Colonies	6	21
Austria	5	9
Spain	4	8
Italy	3	7
Spanish America	2	4
Turkey	2	2
Russia	–	2

With respect to newspapers, the results were as follows:[7]

	No. in 1840	No. in 1880	Tons Paper	Circulation in 1880	Population in 1880
United Kingdom	493	1,836	168,000	2,000,000	26,000,000
United States	830	6,432	525,000	4,000,000	50,000,000
France	776	1,280	134,000		
Germany	305	2,350	244,000		
Austria	132	876	92,000		
Russia	204	318	72,000		
Low Countries	75	376	40,000		
Scandinavia	104	120	30,000		
Italy	210	1,124	38,000		
Spain and Portugal	92	150	10,000		
Switzerland	54	230	17,000		
Spanish America	98	850	20,000	6,000,000	
Canada	88	340	20,000		
West Indies	37	50	5,000		
Australia	43	220	15,000		
Turkey	8	72			
Persia	2	–			
India	63	644			
China	4	–	30,000		
Africa	14	40			
Sandwich Islands	1	6			
Japan	–	34			
	3,633	17,348	1,470,000		

6. Michael G. Mulhall, *The Progress of the World in Arts, Agriculture, Commerce, Manufactures, Instruction, Railways, and Public Wealth Since the Beginning of the Nineteenth Century* (London: Edward Stanford, 1880), p. 89.
7. *Ibid.*, p. 91.

With respect to book publication, the results were as follows:[8]

ANNUAL AVERAGE OF NEW WORKS

	1826 to 1832	1866 to 1869
Great Britain	1,060	3,220
United States	1,013	2,165
Germany	5,530	9,095
France	4,640	7,350
	12,243	21,830

And with respect to free libraries, the results were as follows:[9]

	Number of Free Libraries (1880)	Number of Volumes (1880)
United Kingdom	153	2,500,000
Italy	210	4,250,000
France	350	7,000,000
Switzerland	1,654	
United States	164,815	45,500,000

Mulhall's estimates were gross judgments, with later (and sounder) statistics indicating that they were sometimes off by as much as 20 percent. Yet Mulhall's calculations were essentially sound in the gross relative positions they assigned to various nations. And from those relative positions it is clear that, at least on the basis of accessibility and use, the popularization of American education had advanced markedly during the nineteenth century, with the result that the United States by the 1870's could (and did) boast of having developed what was in many respects the most popular system of education in the world.

III

Among the significant direct outcomes of the popularization of education was not only a continuing spread of literacy but a change in the character of literacy. Literacy statistics were first gathered in the Census of 1840. During that census, as well as the Censuses of 1850 and 1860, the marshals were asked to enumerate the number of persons over twenty years of age unable to read and write. Many of the data used were self-reported and obviously subject to the errors usually associated with such

8. *Ibid.*, p. 92.
9. *Ibid.*, p. 93.

reports of literacy. After all, how likely were people to admit that they were unable to read and write? But, as reported, the percentage of illiterates in the white population over the age of twenty rose from 9 percent in 1840 to 11 percent in 1850 and then declined to 9 percent in 1860. The data for 1840 made no distinctions with respect to sex, race, and nativity. When these distinctions were introduced in 1850 and 1860, it was discovered, not surprisingly, that the rates of illiteracy were generally higher among women than among men, among blacks than among whites (though the slaves were carried as illiterate by definition, and that was by no means the case; literacy may have run as high as 5 percent in the slave community), and among foreign-born than among native-born. In all three censuses, illiteracy was lowest in New England and highest in the South. The Census of 1870 changed the basis of reporting illiteracy: the marshals were asked to enumerate in separate categories the number of persons ten years of age and upwards who were unable to read and unable to write, with writing (the more stringent criterion) the necessary skill in determining literacy. With blacks actually canvassed rather than arbitrarily defined in large numbers as illiterate, the percentage of illiterates over nine years of age was 20 percent, with the figure ranging from 7 percent in New England to 46 percent in the South Atlantic region. The percentage of female illiterates remained slightly higher than the percentage of male illiterates (21.9 percent as compared with 18.3 percent). The percentage of white illiterates was 11.5 percent while the percentage of black illiterates was 81.4 percent.[10]

Mulhall included the following data on adult literacy in Europe in his 1880 survey:

PERCENTAGE OF ADULTS
ABLE TO READ AND WRITE

	1830	1878
Scotland	80%	85%
Germany	79	88
England	56	77
France	36	70
Ireland	48	66
Italy	25	45
Average	53	70

10. De Bow, ed., *Compendium of the Seventh Census,* p. 152; and Francis A. Walker, ed., *A Compendium of the Ninth Census* (Washington, D.C.: Government Printing Office, 1872), pp. 456–459.

Clearly, the white population of the United States would compare quite favorably with the countries Mulhall studied in both 1830 and 1870. The general population would also compare favorably, but less so. Once again, Mulhall's estimates were gross, but more recent data support his suggestion that the American population was quantitatively among the most literate in the world during the first three-quarters of the nineteenth century.[11]

At the minimum, literacy implies the technical ability to read and write. But, once that minimum ability has been established, there are ancillary questions: What sort of reading and writing, and to what purpose? Certainly, a person who simply reads passages from the Scriptures and the liturgy year in and year out but senses little need to read anything beyond is literate in a different way from one who regularly reads a newspaper in order to keep up with public affairs. And, certainly, a person who simply affixes his or her name to some formal document (as often as not prepared by someone else) on two or three occasions during a lifetime is literate in a different way from one who engages in correspondence, keeps a diary, or publishes a point of view on matters of public debate. If literacy is seen, not merely as a technical skill, but rather as an interaction between an individual with a technical skill and a particular literary environment, one can discern shifts in the character as well as the quantity of literacy from one era to another.

By the end of the provincial period, American literacy was clearly shifting, from a more traditional inert literacy in which people read the Bible and a few other works of devotion and instruction but not much else, to a more liberating literacy in which they reached out to an expanding world of print for information and guidance on private and public affairs. Not all Americans participated in the process (blacks and Indians were kept from literacy, and women were assumed not to need it), but more and more did as a growing number of readers (who had learned to read in households, churches, and schools, and via self-instruction) stimulated an expanding press, which in turn stimulated the motivation to read. That shift continued into the national era as a general trend, though different segments of the population participated in different ways and some did not participate at all.

Now, the mere fact of liberating literacy connects with a number

11. Mulhall, *Progress of the World*, p. 88.

of related phenomena. First, in its very nature, access to printed materials—particularly those emanating from a variety of sources in a relatively permissive atmosphere—can open people's minds to change, to new ideas and influences, to new goals and aspirations. Choices and opportunities are depicted and detailed that simply would not have occurred to kith and kin in the immediacies of oral interchange. Of course, literacy cannot confer agency, in and of itself; but literacy does hold the makings of agency, insofar as it helps people to see beyond the boundaries of household, parish, and neighborhood. Since literacy simultaneously systematizes and individualizes experience, it makes possible new technologies of organization—well symbolized, perhaps, by merchant's accounts—at the same time as it facilitates the self-conscious individualization of belief and behavior—consider, alternatively, the private handwritten letter. To the extent that literacy rationalizes experience, it can and often does strengthen the power of extant educative institutions; to the extent that literacy individualizes experience, it can and does become a tool for reflecting upon extant educative institutions and criticizing their efforts. Third, in an expanding literary environment, literacy tends to create a demand for more literacy, both within the same generation and into the next: the newly literate are likely to desire more literacy for themselves, for their contemporaries, and for their children.

All these phenomena, already manifest in provincial America, persisted and expanded in national America. Not only did rates of technical literacy increase; the opportunity and impetus to use literacy also increased. To be sure, some groups used literacy calculatedly to constrain—the occasional slaveowners, for example, who taught their slaves to read so that they could learn their place more effectively via white interpretations of Scripture, or those factory owners who supported schools for the poor because they believed a schooled population would be a more docile and more efficient wage-earning population. Even in such instances, however, the constraints were difficult to maintain: literate slaves sooner or later came upon the writings of the abolitionists and literate working people sooner or later came upon the writings of union organizers. However that may be, the point remains that the literary environment as a whole expanded impressively during the nineteenth century, and with it the opportunity to use literacy for liberation. Mulhall sensed this when he compared a number of societies according to the criterion of the circulation of letters per inhabitant, with the following results:

NUMBER OF LETTERS PER INHABITANT

	1867	1877		1867	1877
United Kingdom	27	35	Austria-Hungary	6	8
Switzerland	24	30	Canada	6	8
United States	15	19	Spain and Portugal	4	5
Australia	13	18	Italy	3	4
Germany	9	15	Spanish America	1.5	2
Low Countries	9	14	Greece	1.5	2
France	10	10	Russia	.75	1
Scandinavia	7	9	Japan	–	1

Mulhall then went on to perform an intriguing mathematical computation. "If letters and newspapers be taken as a measure of enlightenment," he wrote, "it will be found that Great Britain and the United States stand for half the world," the daily circulation being as follows:

	Letters	Newspapers	Total
United Kingdom	3,000,000	2,000,000	5,000,000
United States	2,000,000	4,000,000	6,000,000
Other countries	5,000,000	6,000,000	11,000,000
	10,000,000	12,000,000	22,000,000

However meaningless the sums, in and of themselves, and however ethnocentric the definition of "the world," Mulhall's point about the character of literacy in the United Kingdom and the United States was essentially sound.[12]

Undoubtedly, the trend toward liberating literacy was the most fundamental outcome of the American system of popular education during the first century of national life, but it was an outcome that was closely connected to several others. Tocqueville observed that the object of education in the United States was to fit men for politics, or public life, and, at least so far as the white "middling" elements of American society were concerned, his observation was well founded. The American family increasingly limited its authority by limiting the force, purview, and extent of its education: it reduced its traditional prerogative in selecting occupations, marriage partners, and life-styles; it created an authority structure that demanded less deference of child to adult, in more circumscribed realms and over shorter periods of time; and it shared

12. *Ibid.*, pp. 94–95.

more and more of the education of the young with churches, schools, and colleges. All these other educators, acting in relation to the family, taught, among other things, the attitudes and skills of agency and participation. The churches taught not only that all could be saved but that all held it within their own powers to achieve salvation. The schools taught a correlative version of patriotism, namely, that all (white) men and women had roles to play in the life of the Republic and that all owed it to the polity to fulfill those roles. And the colleges taught an equally correlative version of responsible and virtuous leadership. Indeed, it was widely held that the churches, the schools, and the colleges needed to nurture the necessary altruism and convey the necessary information for the republican experiment to escape the dangers of crass individual self-interest. Further, it was maintained that the experience offered within the churches, schools, and colleges—all, in a sense, perfected communities—would train young people for the arts of orderly public participation and for the variety of interchanges beyond the family that were at the heart of community life. And in that respect it is well to note that the very essence of the common-school ideology, as preached by Charles Fenton Mercer in Virginia, Horace Mann in Massachusetts, John Pierce in Michigan, and the other "friends of education" in other states, held that in the common school all would meet as "children" of a "common mother," namely, the commonwealth, irrespective of differences in social, religious, ethnic, and class background. All did not, of course, but enough did to make the ideology meaningful to a broad spectrum of Americans.[13]

In the political sphere the attitudes and skills of agency and participation, articulated by newspapers and exercised in voluntary associations, including political parties, created a "can-do" mentality that stimulated such related phenomena as the commitment to reform, the idea of a responsive leadership, and the principle of distributive justice. In the economic sphere, particularly as family agriculture gave way to industrialism in agriculture as well as in manufacturing, the attitudes and skills of agency and participation led to technological invention and innovation as the rational augmentation of human efficacy: the phenomenon can be seen in the invention of the steel-tipped plow that made the Great Plains arable as well as in the functional organization of the American factory so widely commented upon by Europeans in

13. Tocqueville, *Democracy in America*, I, 318; and Charles Fenton Mercer, *A Discourse on Popular Education* (Princeton, N.J.: D. A. Borrenstein, 1826), p. 76.

the 1850's. And, in the social sphere, the attitudes and skills of agency and participation led to both the ideology and the reality of mobility, as men and women moved geographically and occupationally with a freedom and facility unprecedented in earlier eras; in the Lowells and the Sumtervilles as well as in the Carlinvilles, it was what one knew as well as whom one knew and what one owned that conferred a place in the stratum widely and vaguely defined as "middle-class."

In all of this, intellect itself was transformed into intelligence. Agency and participation encouraged and reinforced the utilitarian tendency in American life and thought. And, as that utilitarian thrust manifested itself in education, it focused attention on the role of ideas in the betterment of everyday life. Education was pursued less often for its own sake and increasingly as an instrument for personal advancement and social improvement. In consequence, as more people were educated in more functional ways, science, art, and literature were transformed, along with intellect. For some, these transformations meant devaluation. Thus, the Reverend Sydney Smith, in a much-quoted article in the *Edinburgh Review,* sharply questioned the cultural creativity and worth of the new society:

> During the thirty or forty years of their independence, they have done absolutely nothing for the sciences, for the arts, for literature, or even for the statesmen-like studies of politics or political economy. . . . In the four quarters of the globe, who reads an American book? or goes to an American play? or looks at an American picture or statue? What does the world yet owe to American physicians or surgeons? What new substances have their chemists discovered? or what old ones have they analyzed? What new constellations have they discovered by the telescopes of Americans?—what have they done in mathematics? . . . Finally, under which of the tyrannical governments of Europe is every sixth man a slave whom his fellow creatures may buy and sell and torture? When these questions are fairly and favorably answered, their laudatory epithets may be allowed.

And even Tocqueville, who was disposed to praise everything American, observed that

> America has hitherto produced very few writers of distinction, it possesses no great historians and not a single eminent poet. The inhabitants of that country look upon literature properly so-called with a kind of disapprobation, and there are towns of second-rate importance in Europe in which more literary works are annually published than in the twenty-four states of the Union put together. The spirit of the American is adverse to general ideas: it does not seek theoretical discoveries. Neither politics nor manufactures direct them to

such speculations, and although new laws are perpetually enacted in the United States, no great writers there have hitherto inquired into the general principles of legislation. The Americans have lawyers and commentators, but no jurists; and they furnish examples rather than lessons to the world.

Yet the question, recognized by few contemporaries, was whether the domain of creativity had merely shifted, along with the yardsticks for judging it. Were not the intellect and the culture of the new society better represented by the highly original essays of Emerson and the sparely functional design of clipper ships than by the blatantly imitative novels of William Gilmore Simms or the decidedly stylized landscapes of Thomas Cole? Few American critics were aware of the shift—Horatio Greenough and William Dunlap recognized it more than most—but the shift was inextricably involved in the popularization of American education.[14]

The attitudes, skills, and sensibilities associated with literacy, agency, participation, and intelligence were mutually reinforcing and of a piece, and their thrust in American life was, on balance, in the direction of increasing diversity and choice. The important phrase, of course, is "on balance"; for there is abundant evidence that families, churches, schools, and colleges continued to try to form youngsters along particular lines, and that newspapers and voluntary associations continued to propound particular ideologies. But one need not deny the fact that groups used education for their own purposes, which could be demeaning and coercive as well as enhancing and altruistic, to affirm the equally important fact that the multitude of groups doing so, and the greater availability of diverse options that resulted from their efforts, extended the range of choice for individuals. If nothing else, the near-universal ability to read, write, and interact with individuals who were not kin that was fostered by the churches and the schools afforded people the possibility of release from geographical and social place, and in so doing augmented personal liberty. The caveat needs reiteration: education did not necessarily augment liberty for slaves or for Indians or for the voluntarily and involuntarily segregated, or for those who failed to perceive the opportunities or who were prevented from taking advantage of them; but these omissions must not obscure the extension of opportunity for others beyond what they might have enjoyed earlier or elsewhere.

By advancing liberty, popular education also advanced equality, at

14. *Edinburgh Review,* XXXIII (1820), 79-80; and Tocqueville, *Democracy in America,* I, 315.

least in the sense in which that term was used during the nineteenth century. It afforded more varied and extensive opportunities to many who had previously enjoyed rather limited opportunities, and thereby broadened access to life chances that had formerly been confined to the few. One need not argue that Blackburn University was the equal of Harvard College to grant that the United States of 1876 with 356 colleges had moved considerably beyond the America of 1776 with 9 colleges or the England of 1870 with 4 universities. And one need not deny the continuing influence of ability, wealth, status, and luck to affirm the role of education in facilitating access to positions of prestige, influence, and personal fulfillment: Lucy Larcom's career in teaching and letters, John McAuley Palmer's in law and politics (and even Michael Walsh's in politics), William Earl Dodge's in business, and Jacob Stroyer's, Irving E. Lowery's, and James Henry Magee's in the ministry are all cases in point. Indeed, the very existence of such a variety of career patterns was inextricably tied to the expansion of education: not only were increasing numbers of occupations coming to have formal educational requirements for initial entry and advancement, but education was itself helping to create a greater number and range of vocational options.

Finally, popular education proffered a sense of comity, community, and common aspiration to a people who were increasing in number, diversifying in origin, and insistently mobile. In short, it helped to define an American *paideia*. Granted that the *paideia* that emerged was never static and that it varied significantly from place to place, it still may be fairly characterized as a Christian *paideia* that united the symbols of Protestantism, the values of the Old and New Testaments, *Poor Richard's Almanack*, and the *Federalist* papers, and the aspirations asserted on the Great Seal. It was also a national *paideia*, however much it had its roots in New England; and, though it did not transcend the social, political, and intellectual differences that culminated in the Civil War, it did come to the fore again during the great centennial celebration of 1876. In the end, the role of popular education in defining that *paideia* and in teaching it to a polyglot population spread across a continent may have been the most significant educational achievement of the century. The Revolutionary generation had called for the creation of a new republican citizenry of virtuous character, abiding patriotism, and prudent wisdom, fit to develop a favored nation whose Seal proclaimed to the world Virgil's aphorism, *Novus ordo seclorum* (A new order of the ages has begun). However imperfect the outcome, American education had taken the nurture of such individuals to be its highest order of obligation.

Nowhere is the impact of the American *paideia* on the American character so clearly seen (and symbolized) as in the interaction between the real and the mythic education of Abraham Lincoln. The real education is well enough known: childhood nurture in the constricted and near-illiterate household of Thomas and Nancy Hanks Lincoln (and later Sarah Johnston Lincoln), first in Kentucky and then in Indiana; the brief and intermittent periods of formal schooling, the aggregate of which "did not amount to one year"; the efforts toward self-improvement through systematic perusal of a few important works (the Bible, *Robinson Crusoe, The Pilgrim's Progress,* the *Autobiography* of Benjamin Franklin, Weems's *Life of Washington,* Paine's *Age of Reason,* and Volney's *Ruins*); the systematic avoidance of church membership and camp-meeting revivalism and indeed the superb mimicry of revivalist preaching on Monday mornings; the fondness for story-telling that was turned, through calculated study of orators and audiences, into the gift of rhetoric; the move to Illinois and with it the expanding sense of the world that came through visits to New Orleans, active (and successful) participation in politics, and the study and practice of the law; and, finally, the rise from local political effort to the national statesmanship that brought with it the presidency. It was a characteristic frontier education for its time, not very different from John Palmer's, and it bestowed upon Lincoln the qualities of decency, patriotism, and pragmatism that marked his extraordinary performance as president. In effect, Lincoln *was* the new republican individual of virtuous character, abiding patriotism, and prudent wisdom.[15]

The legend that came into being after his assassination created a folk hero and invested him with these qualities in hyperbole; the folk hero, in turn, proceeded to teach by example. And, as David Donald has observed, the Lincoln of folklore had a significance even beyond the Lincoln of actuality. For the Lincoln of folklore embodied what ordinary inarticulate Americans cherished as ideals. Put otherwise, if the Lincoln of actuality imbibed the American *paideia,* the Lincoln of folklore personified it and, in reflecting it back on education writ large, helped transmit it to successive generations of Americans.[16]

15. Abraham Lincoln, "Autobiography Written for John L. Scripps [June, 1860]," in *The Collected Works of Abraham Lincoln,* edited by Roy B. Basler (8 vols.; New Brunswick, N.J.: Rutgers University Press, 1953), IV, 62.

16. David Donald, *Lincoln Reconsidered: Essays on the Civil War Era* (2d ed., enlarged; New York: Random House, 1961), chap. viii.

IV

From the beginning, there had been a millennial strain in the American *paideia* that reached beyond the confines of the North American continent to the world at large. The Puritans had envisioned their city upon a hill, with the eyes of all people upon them; and the Revolutionary generation had conceived of themselves as acting "for all mankind." Amidst the excitement of the early nineteenth-century revivals, American education was seized with a newly buoyant millennialism that preached the conversion of the world in a single generation. "How can we better testify our appreciation of . . . free institutions," the Reverend A. J. Codman sermonized in 1836, "than by laboring to plant them in other lands?" As part of the "new order of the ages," it would be the responsibility of American education to proffer the American *paideia* to peoples everywhere. And, since God favored the undertaking, there was never any doubt as to the outcome. Even the dour Samuel Miller, who had warned his countrymen about the sin of pride implicit in most educational philosophies, agreed that the millennium would come, "before a long lapse of time."[17]

One way of proffering the American *paideia* to the peoples of the world was through a variety of church missions. Many such missions were launched and sustained by the American Board of Commissioners for Foreign Missions, one of the earliest of the interdenominational organizations that formed the evangelical united front. Beginning in 1812, the Board dispatched missionaries to India, Ceylon, Hawaii, Greece, Turkey, Syria, China, Japan, and Africa. Typically New Yorkers and New Englanders of great piety who had first heard the call at colleges such as Amherst or Williams or at the Andover Theological Seminary, or, somewhat later, at Mount Holyoke, these men and women established churches, schools, and presses, published Bibles and tracts, newspapers and magazines, and dictionaries and textbooks, and generally engaged in the business of teaching all who would listen. As was the case with missions to the Indians in North America, they often had difficulty in determining where Christianity ended and Americanism began. However much they adapted to local custom, shift-

17. John Codman, *The Duty of American Christians to Send the Gospel to the Heathen* (Boston: Crocker & Brewster, 1836), p. 15; and Samuel Miller, *A Sermon Delivered in the Middle Church, New Haven, Connecticut* (Boston: Crocker & Brewster, 1822), p. 28.

ing from English to the native language in one place and from language instruction to the liturgy in another, they invariably taught a version of the American *paideia*; and, however much they sought to avoid direct involvement in politics—European missionaries marveled at the Americans' success in eschewing politics—they invariably ended up in roles that were at least ancillary to politics. Indeed, John Quincy Adams noted as a member of a congressional committee on foreign relations in 1843 that American missionaries in Hawaii had given the American people more abiding ties with that island than any other, "by a virtual right of conquest, not over the freedom of their brother man by the brutal arm of physical power, but over the mind and heart by the celestial panoply of the gospel of peace and love." There was not always harmony between American diplomatic officials, American merchants, and American missionaries—in fact, merchants often lamented the coming of missionaries because their preaching about money being the root of evil seemed to make commerce more difficult—but all exemplified versions of American culture wherever they went, and the missionaries added systematic teaching to that exemplification.[18]

Missionary efforts fared more or less well in different regions, depending on the character and receptivity of the host society, the nature of the competition (English missionaries did not always welcome American missionaries), and the skill of the missionaries themselves. In the Middle East and in China, American Board missionaries made few converts at any time; on the other hand, the Mormon missions to England during the 1840's converted well over twenty thousand individuals, of whom almost ten thousand eventually immigrated to the United States. Perhaps the most interesting such venture was the one that became Liberia, where the missionaries were part of a larger community of free American blacks settled in Africa under the aegis of the American Colonization Society. There, a version of the American *paideia* became the basis for a stratified black society rather closely resembling the planter society of the South during the antebellum period. And the black churchmen of that society ministered, not only to Liberians, but also to African blacks in the community surrounding the settlement. In the end, whether in the Middle East, China, England, Liberia, or elsewhere, the most significant educational influence of the early missions may have been on the missionaries themselves. Some, to be sure, with-

18. U.S., Congress, House Reports, 27th Cong., 3d sess., 1843, 426, 93, 2.

drew into enclaves and learned little of the language and culture of the people they hoped to convert; others steeped themselves in that language and culture and, having done so, became important channels for conveying them to their fellow Americans. The world may not have been converted in a generation, but it did become somewhat better known to Americans.

If the efforts of missionaries systematically to transmit a special version of the American *paideia* to other people represented one side of the transnational influence of American education, the efforts of other peoples systematically to adopt versions of the American *paideia* represented the other. These latter efforts went forward in a variety of fields, from politics to manufacturing to industrial design, but most significantly in the realm of education, where American ideas and institutions were early recognized as among the more original inventions of the new society. As is well known, the popularization of education was a general Western, not a uniquely American, phenomenon, and the principal figures in the movement were acquainted with one another and in continuing communication. Thus, for example, Methodist, Owenite, and Lancasterian ideas and strategies deeply affected American education during the first half of the nineteenth century, while the American experience was itself known and variously interpreted by contemporary Englishmen. Or, to take another example, the development of rehabilitative and custodial institutions such as the asylum, the reformatory, and the penitentiary was a transatlantic phenomenon in which Europeans and Americans exchanged both ideas and models. The movement may have found fertile soil in Jacksonian America, but it was neither uniquely Jacksonian nor uniquely American. What was different about the nineteenth century was the shift in the balance of exchange, from American dependence during the colonial era to a more symmetrical give-and-take relationship. Americans continued to borrow in many realms, from the substance of French mathematics to the organization of German universities; but Americans also began to teach by example, particularly to those disposed by intellectual or political predilection to learn. Frances Trollope's report on the domestic manners of the Americans, Philip Schaff's report on the churches of America, P. A. Siljestrom's report on the schools of America, and Gustave de Beaumont and Alexis de Tocqueville's report on the prisons of America were avidly read in many quarters of Europe, and there was a good deal of style setting eastward that was of a different order from the seventeenth-century romanticizing of the noble savages or the eighteenth-century lionizing of Franklin in his fur cap.[19]

The English case is especially interesting. Given the similarities of language and culture and the special historical relationship, Englishmen throughout the nineteenth century manifested an ambivalence with respect to the Americans, who were seen, on the one hand, as a cultural colony with much to learn and, on the other hand, as a cultural avantgarde with much to teach. Depending upon where one stood on the political spectrum, one praised or damned the Americans. Thus, English radicals of the 1830's sharply attacked the Anglican establishment and praised American voluntarism for the protection it afforded all denominations without provision for the maintenance of any. The English conservatives replied that the American experience was fraught with danger, since social disintegration and "pagan darkness" were already following in the wake of disestablishment. Similarly, the radicals campaigned for a free and open press delivered from "taxes on knowledge," and for a free and nonsectarian public school built on the American model; while the conservatives pointed to the popular cults and fanaticisms that had followed in the wake of popular schooling divorced from the saving power of established piety. It was but a short step for the radicals to generalize concerning the superiority of all things American. Thus, the *English Chartist Circular* exclaimed in 1841: "American is not only a phenomenon in the history of nations, but an *example* worthy of *emulation* of all who invoke the sacred name of liberty,—who long to see her blessings diffused, and her cause triumphant over the dark fiends of despotism, vice, and wretchedness." And Richard Cobden and John Bright were so effusive on the glorious example of the American Republic in the House of Commons during the 1850's that they became widely known as "the two members for the United States."[20]

What happened in England was more or less repeated in other

19. Frances Trollope, *Domestic Manners of the Americans* (1832; reprint ed.; New York: Dodd, Mead & Company, 1927); Philip Schaff, *America: A Sketch of the Political, Social, and Religious Character of the United States of North America* (New York: C. Scribner, 1855); P. A. Siljestrom, *Educational Institutions of the United States, Their Character and Organizations,* translated by Frederica Rowan (London: John Chapman, 1853); Gustave de Beaumont and Alexis de Tocqueville, *On the Penitentiary System of the United States, and Its Application in France,* translated by Francis Liebner (Philadelphia: Carey, Lea & Blanchard, 1833).

20. *English Chartist Circular, and Temperance Record for England and Wales,* I (1841), 1; and *Speeches on Questions of Public Policy by Richard Cobden,* edited by John Bright and James E. Thorold Rogers (2 vols.; London: Macmillan and Company, 1870), II, 253.

Western countries. The German scholar Christophe Daniel Ebeling devoted his lifetime to writing a seven-volume *North American Geography and History* as a monument to the "happy state" of American society. The Decembrist leader Kondratii Ryleyev, who was hanged for treason in 1826, was known to believe that there were no good governments except in America. And the Argentine educator Domingo Faustino Sarmiento, who rose to the presidency of his native country, sought to redesign the Argentine political and social system along American lines. However prideful their assumption, Americans who believed they were acting "for all mankind" had their admirers abroad who shared the belief.[21]

If the systematic study of the American example became a noticeable element of European politics during the nineteenth century, the sudden recognition of the import of that example came principally through exposure to American technology. Here, too, the English case is especially interesting. During the late eighteenth and early nineteenth centuries, the flow of technical knowledge in the industrial arts had been decidedly westward, from England to the United States: Samuel Slater's reproduction from memory of the textile machinery of James Hargreaves and Richard Arkwright is merely the best-known instance among many. Then, at the Crystal Palace Exposition of 1851, the beginning of a reversal occurred. The American exhibit, known as the "prairie ground," was in the early months of the exposition the object of considerable European derision. Located between superb displays of Russian, Austrian, and French art, it was at first glance a random collection of objects—railroad switches, ice-making machines, a McCormick reaper, a selection of artificial limbs, and the like—all poorly organized, wholly lacking in contemporary aesthetic value, and utilitarian in the extreme. Yet, when the yacht *America* outraced its British competitors and the McCormick reaper outperformed its British counterparts, the Europeans took a second look, and derision turned to fascination, not merely with the performance of the American objects but with their manufacture. What the Europeans suddenly realized was the extraordinary advances the Americans had made in combining utilitarian design with the innovation of interchangeable parts.

Two years later, when the Americans organized their own exposi-

21. Christophe Daniel Ebeling to Mr. President [Ezra] Stiles, June 26, 1784, in Charles I. Landis, "Charles [Christophe] Daniel Ebeling, Who from 1793 to 1816 Published in Germany a Geography and History of the United States in Seven Volumes," *Proceedings of the Pennsylvania German Society*, XXXVI (1925), 21.

tion in New York, the British government included among its delegates Joseph Whitworth, an imaginative manufacturer of machine tools, and George Wallis, head of the Government School of Art and Design in Birmingham. Since the New York exposition was delayed in opening, Whitworth and Wallis decided to use the time available to visit a number of American manufacturing centers and observe firsthand the production of the objects that would be displayed at the exposition. Their reports to the House of Commons in 1854 and 1855 were a revelation. Concentrating on the production of arms in the United States, where the use of interchangeable parts had been carried to a fine art, but including as well the entire range of production, from textiles to railroad equipment, Whitworth and Wallis for all intents and purposes explicated "the American system of manufacture" for their British countrymen. And their report was sufficiently persuasive to initiate widespread efforts toward reform in English industry, beginning with the work of the Enfield Armoury. The movement was not uniformly successful, for handicraft methods long in use proved remarkably durable. But the American example remained in the forefront of the British effort for a generation.[22]

Interestingly, when Whitworth and Wallis reflected on the sources of American innovativeness in manufacturing, they ended up, in the fashion of Tocqueville, pointing to American education. American workers were surely as knowledgeable about combinations to resist innovation as their English counterparts, the two commissioners maintained, so that the absence of such resistance in the United States could not be explained by an ignorance of unionism. Rather, it had to be explained by education. As Whitworth put it:

In every state in the Union, and particularly in the North, education is, by means of the common schools, placed within the reach of each individual, and all classes avail themselves of the opportunities afforded. The desire of knowledge so early implanted is greatly increased, while the facilities for diffusing it are amply provided through the instrumentality of an almost universal press. No taxation of any kind has been suffered to interfere with the free development of this powerful agent for promoting the intelligence of the people, and the consequence is, that where the humblest laborer can indulge in the luxury of his daily paper, everybody reads, and thought and intelligence penetrate through the lowest grades of society. The benefits which thus result from a lib-

22. Nathan Rosenberg, ed., *The American System of Manufactures: The Report of the Committee on the Machinery of the United States 1855 and The Special Reports of George Wallis and Joseph Whitworth 1854* (Edinburgh: Edinburgh University Press, 1969).

eral system of education and a cheap press to the working classes of the United States can hardly be overestimated in a national point of view; but it is to the cooperation of both that they must undoubtedly be ascribed. For if, selecting a proof from among the European states, the condition of Prussia be considered, it will be found that the people of that country, as a body, have not made that progress which, from the great attention paid to the education of all classes, might have been anticipated; and this must certainly be ascribed to the restrictions laid upon the press, which have so materially impeded the general advancement of the people. Wherever education and an unrestricted press are allowed full scope to exercise their united influence, progress and improvement are the certain results, and among the many benefits which arise from their joint cooperation may be ranked most prominently the value which they teach men to place upon intelligent contrivance; the readiness with which they cause new improvements to be received, and the impulse which they thus unavoidably give to that inventive spirit which is gradually emancipating man from the rude forms of labor, and making what were regarded as the luxuries of one age to be looked upon in the next as the ordinary and necessary conditions of human existence.

As was the case with Tocqueville's affirmation of the educational bases of American democracy, quite apart from the objective accuracy of Whitworth's assertion that education was ultimately responsible for American technological innovativeness, the *fact* of his assertion was of crucial importance; for it focused British attention, and, via Britain, European attention, on American education as the source of what was admirable in American life. Furthermore, in focusing European attention on the issue, it ultimately strengthened the belief of Americans themselves in the special saving grace of their educative institutions.[23]

Charles Dickens once remarked that Americans would be better off "if they loved the real less and ideal somewhat more." Yet, when the world sought to study and learn from America, it studied the real and proceeded to invest it with ideal qualities. As Goethe put it, America, unconstrained by "useless remembering and unrewarding strife," was the hope of all who found themselves restricted in their present circumstances. Yet the very investing of the real with ideal qualities rendered those Europeans who chose to make the investment more susceptible to American teaching, which itself tended to suffuse the actualities of American life with the force of American aspirations.[24]

23. *Ibid.*, p. 389.
24. Charles Dickens, *American Notes, and Reprinted Pieces* (London: Chapman and Hall, [1868]), p. 147; and Johann Wolfgang von Goethe, "To America," translated by Stephen Spender, in Thomas Mann, ed., *The Permanent Goethe* (New York: The Dial Press, 1948), p. 655.

EPILOGUE

It is the faith of Americans that they will be able to accomplish all that any other civilization can do, besides adding thereto a culture in free individuality to an extent hitherto unattained. A civilization wherein all can partake in the subjugation of the elements, and possess a competence at such easy terms as to leave the greater part of life for higher culture, is the goal to which every American confidently looks.

WILLIAM T. HARRIS

The signal achievement of popular education during the first century of the Republic was to help define an American *paideia* and teach it to a polyglot population spread across a continent. Yet that *paideia* was variously perceived and applied by different segments of the population in different regions of the country. The *paideia* celebrated the values of the Old and New Testaments; but to the Reverend Charles Grandison Finney in Oberlin, Ohio, those values precluded human slavery, while to the Reverend Frederick A. Ross in Huntsville, Alabama, those values not only permitted slavery but actually ordained it. The *paideia* celebrated the values of the Constitution; but to Daniel Webster those values made the legitimate enactments of the federal government binding upon the states, while to John C. Calhoun those values reserved to the states the ultimate power to accept those federal enactments deemed legitimate and to nullify those deemed illegitimate.

During the first decades of the nineteenth century, such differences were not strictly regional. The Virginia Presbyterian John Holt Rice inveighed against the cancer of slavery in the columns of the *Christian Monitor,* which he edited between 1815 and 1817, while Francis Wayland declared in 1838 that God had placed no injunction on man with respect to slavery and indeed that the Constitution had enjoined citizens to let the issue alone. Similarly, the *Sumter Gazette* supported the principle of nullification during the early 1830's, but the *Southern Whig,* also published in Sumterville, supported the Unionist view. The differences became more regional, however, during the 1840's and 1850's. Thus, Rice's opposition to slavery became increasingly muted as the years passed, and by the time of his death in 1831 he had concluded

507

that churchmen had best avoid such temporal questions and leave them entirely to the state. Wayland, on the other hand, moved increasingly into the antislavery camp, and by the 1850's he was excoriating slavery as a sinful practice whose extension into the Kansas-Nebraska Territory would be a double offense against the moral law. As for the people of Sumter, they had access to a one-party press during the later 1840's and 1850's, uncompromisingly committed to the states' rights position. Newspapers espousing the Unionist view had to be imported from elsewhere.

Education played a significant role in the emergence of these regional versions of the American *paideia*; and, indeed, particularly as education interacted with politics to create a context within which events and actions might be interpreted, it played a role in the coming of the Civil War. The churches, the colleges, and the press were particularly involved. As is well known, the churches were torn by the controversy over slavery. The Old School-New School split of 1837 among the Presbyterians was not expressly over slavery, but it was a North-South division that eventually led to conflicting preaching concerning the issue in the two regions. The Methodist Episcopal Church split three ways, with perfectionist groups espousing abolitionism seceding in the North and with strongly episcopal-minded southern groups organizing the Methodist Episcopal Church, South, in 1845. There were similar splits among the Baptists, with abolitionists defecting in the North and the organization of the Southern Baptist Convention in the South, also in 1845. In the end, the splits not only permitted the teaching of drastically different views concerning slavery, but profoundly differing views of the American *paideia* that became the heart of a growing regional consciousness.

Much the same thing happened with the colleges. Abolitionism made considerable headway among faculty and student bodies in the North and the Midwest. There were active abolitionist movements on many campuses: the University of Michigan housed a secret society dedicated to smuggling runaway slaves into Canada; and Oberlin College, Franklin College (Ohio), Illinois College, and New York College actually became known as abolitionist seminaries. At the same time, abolitionism was increasingly suppressed and rooted out in the colleges of the South. South Carolina College was a center of political and religious heterodoxy under the free-thinking Thomas Cooper during the 1820's; it became a center of conservative proslavery apologetics under James H. Thornwell during the 1850's. Professors like Thomas Dew at the College of William and Mary and A. T. Bledsoe at the University of Virginia helped systematize and rationalize the proslavery argument. And Episcopal Bishop Leonidas Polk, a graduate of West Point, led in the founding of the University of the South at Sewanee, Tennessee, where sons of southern planters could be taught a sound southern *paideia,* with the proslavery argument at its core. Particularly as it became fashionable during the 1850's to warn against the corrupting influences of a northern education, the southern colleges led in the nurturance of a special sense of regional consciousness and pride among the southern elite.

Finally, and perhaps most importantly, the press was relentless in its educative efforts in both the North and the South. The northern antislavery movement poured a steady stream of printed matter into every region of the country. In 1836 the American Anti-Slavery Society reported that it had published 5,000 bound volumes, 8,500 pamphlets, and 36,800 circulars, and 5,000 prints during the previous year. Its quarterly *Anti-Slavery Magazine* had an annual circulation of 5,500, and its four monthly journals (*Human Rights,* the *Anti-Slavery Record,* the *Emancipator,* and the *Slave's Friend*) had a combined annual circulation of 1,040,000. More general newspapers sympathetic to antislavery like Greeley's *Tribune,* with its huge national circulation, hammered away at the issue year in and year out. During the 1840's and 1850's the South attempted to stem the flow and to counter it with its own journals and newspapers, but the material could not be interdicted, even among blacks, much less whites.[1]

Perhaps the most extraordinary educational phenomenon in this respect was Harriet Beecher Stowe's *Uncle Tom's Cabin.* After serialization in the *National Era* during 1851–52, the book was published on March, 1852, in a two-volume edition by Jewett & Company in Boston. Within eight weeks, it had sold 50,000 copies (100,000 volumes)—a phenomenon "without precedent in the history of this country," announced *Norton's Literary Gazette.* By November sales had reached 120,000 in the Western hemisphere and there had been nineteen editions in England, one of which sold 180,000. By the end of the year, the book had been translated into Italian, Spanish, Danish, Swedish, Dutch, Flemish, German, French, Polish, and Magyar, and by March, 1853, sales in the United States had reached 300,000 copies. Given a

1. *Third Annual Report of the American Anti-Slavery Society* (1836), p. 35. In fact, most of annual budget of approximately $18.5 million went for publications (p. 31).

population of around 26 million people and assuming that sales statistics were low since they did not take into account pirated editions, the sheer penetration of the work was striking: there was a copy in circulation for every eighty individuals. No book other than the Bible had ever had a comparable numerical impact.[2]

Stowe's vivid and gripping presentation of the problems of slavery in human terms, using all the contemporary devices of the sentimental novel, created a sensation. In the North the work was read and discussed everywhere, obviously fanning the fires of popular interest in the slavery issue. A few days after its appearance, William Lloyd Garrison's *Liberator* announced that the "remarkable and thrilling" work was "selling with great rapidity"; and several months later the *Literary World* noted that "the Uncle Tom epidemic still rages with unabated virulence." In the South the work evoked interest, anger, and rebuttal: it was widely read, despite efforts to ban its sale and circulation; Stowe was pilloried in the press as a hypocrite and moral scavenger; and a plethora of equally didactic proslavery novels appeared under such titles as *Aunt Phillis's Cabin; or, Southern Life As It Is*; *Uncle Robin in His Cabin in Virginia and Tom Without One in Boston*; *Buckingham's Hall*; and *The Master's House*. In both regions stage plays, children's books, and magazine articles based on the novel itself and the novels written to rebut it reached large popular audiences of all ages.[3]

Mrs. Stowe herself once outlined what she believed the effects of *Uncle Tom's Cabin* had been: first, to moderate the bitterness of extreme abolitionists; second, to convert to the abolitionist cause many whom this bitterness had repelled; third, to inspire among free blacks throughout the country self-respect, hope, and confidence; and, finally, to inspire throughout the entire American population a kinder feeling toward all blacks. She had really intended the book to be read principally by southern Americans. Not surprisingly, the controversies caused her intense dismay. In the end, Lincoln himself expressed the view of many Americans when he greeted her on a visit to the White House as "the little woman who wrote the book that made this big war."[4]

2. Harriet Beecher Stowe, *Uncle Tom's Cabin; or, Life Among the Lowly,* edited by Kenneth L. Lynn (Cambridge, Mass.: Harvard University Press, 1962), XXVI; and *Norton's Literary Gazette*, II (1853), 108. See also J. C. Furnas, *Goodbye to Uncle Tom* (New York: William Sloane Associates, 1956).

3. *Liberator*, April 2, 1852: and *Literary World*, XI (1852), 355.

4. Charles Edward Stowe, *Life of Harriet Beecher Stowe Compiled from Her Letters and Journals* (Boston: Houghton, Mifflin and Company, 1889), p. 169; Mrs. Stowe's recollection of Lincoln's comment is given in Carl Sandburg, *Abraham Lincoln: The War Years* (5 vols.; New York: Harcourt, Brace & Co., 1936), II, 201.

One could argue endlessly over whether *Uncle Tom's Cabin* had really made the big war, but no one would deny that it had contributed to the consciousness of separatism that ultimately led to war. And, in this sense, the pivotal character of Stowe's didactic effort exemplifies the interaction between education and politics that helped precipitate the war. Stowe's book obviously came into a prepared environment in which events in education had been transforming a common American *paideia* with variant regional interpretations into two increasingly different—and opposing—American *paideias*. The Fugitive Slave Law of 1850 and the Compromise of 1850 had occasioned sharp political controversy, which had itself heightened the consciousness of difference between North and South—a consciousness growing out of conflicting political interest and the articulation of opinion associated with conflicting political interest. In addition, the American public had become habituated to the sentimental novel as a literary form during the first half of the nineteenth century. Stowe's substance was of considerable public interest, therefore, and the literary form she used was generally familiar. Whatever effect her didactic message had on readers, it patently enhanced the consciousness of difference between North and South, which in turn became the context for the even sharper political controversy surrounding the Kansas-Nebraska Act of 1854. In the interaction of education and politics, both the differences and the consciousness of those differences grew, and they did so at the expense of what remained of a common American *paideia*. Yet it is important to note that the common *paideia* never disappeared entirely. Even when the point of no return had been crossed and hostilities erupted, both parties justified their stands in the terms of that common *paideia*. And when the issue was settled at Appomattox Court House, that common *paideia* remained as a basis for subsequent relationships.

II

Like the Revolution, the Civil War disrupted and destroyed, in education as in other domains. Schools and churches in the zones of battle, commonly located at crossroads and other nodes of the transportation network and commonly viewed as public buildings, were frequently commandeered by the military as lookout stations, fortified positions, and barracks; once commandeered, they were all too often misused by their occupants or destroyed by the enemy. Colleges in the South were converted into hospitals (Wake Forest College), barracks (University of

Richmond), stables (Maryville College), quartermaster stores (University of Georgia), and military training centers (University of Alabama). In the process, particularly as such facilities changed hands from time to time, fences were torn up for firewood, buildings were looted, libraries were scattered, and laboratories were smashed. So it was also with printing presses, which, even when they managed to survive the direct effects of hostilities, were often closed down for lack of paper. The fate of the printshop of Allan A. Gilbert and H. L. Darr in Sumter was typical. As has been indicated, when Union troops passed through the town during the second week of April, 1865 (actually after Lee had surrendered), they used the press from which the *Sumter Watchman* had appeared to publish a single issue of a newspaper called the *Banner of Freedom*, in which they announced their victory. That done, they wrecked the press and scrambled the type.

Though the conversion and destruction of property were serious, the disruption and scattering of teachers and students were even more deleterious. Ministers on both sides became chaplains, leaving congregations decimated by enlistments. Schoolmasters and college professors enlisted or moved into war-related industries, frequently taking students with them. At the University of Michigan, President Henry Philip Tappan organized a rally on the Monday following the surrender of Fort Sumter and began a process whereby the university sent several companies of alumni and students into the Union army. And, at Oberlin College, James Monroe, the professor of rhetoric and belles-lettres, called for enlistments at a meeting the following week and helped organize a company of students, which was appropriately named the Monroe Rifles in his honor (Giles W. Shurtleff, one of the Latin tutors, was elected captain). Similarly, at Stewart College in Tennessee, Professor W. A. Forbes organized a drill company in 1860, and, after the surrender of Fort Sumter, every able-bodied student at the college with the exception of two northerners volunteered for the Army of Tennessee. Thereafter, the college simply closed. Essentially the same thing happened at the College of Charleston, where a group of students under the leadership of two faculty members actually participated in the bombardment of Fort Sumter. Even in those institutions where the faculty tried to dissuade the students from immediate military service, students enlisted on their own; and, although the percentage of faculty members, recent alumni, and students who served the Confederacy was probably greater than the percentage who served the Union, colleges, and to some extent secondary schools, were profoundly affected in the North as well. For those who did not go off to war, there were drills, rallies, patriotic observances, and a curriculum considerably constricted, on the one hand, by a general fear of disloyalty (loyalty oaths were widely applied during the war years) and, on the other hand, by the general scattering of expertise.

However much churches, schools, and colleges, particularly in the South, may have been disrupted and destroyed by the war, there was a larger process of education that continued and indeed quickened. For the soldiers of both armies, the war meant hardship, and, if one survived, a testing of one's mettle. It also meant exposure to other people and other places, which, coming at a time of extreme stress, often prompted reflection and comparison. From Florida, for example, Frederick Fleet, the eldest son of a Virginia plantation family, wrote to his father, "How different is Florida, the land of flowers, from what I had imagined it! Instead of being a vast garden, with wild flowers of brilliant hue and delicious fragrance growing all over the woods, and the climate as mild and delightful as one could desire, I have seen only vast forests of pine, in a great many cases, with water from four to twelve inches deep, standing for acres and acres, and only in the gardens, flowers bloom." And from Columbus, Kentucky, Chauncey Cooke, a Wisconsin farm boy, wrote to his parents:

We are really in the "Sunny South." The slaves, contrabands, we call them, are flocking into Columbus by the hundred. General Thomas of the regular army is here enlisting them for war. All the old buildings on the edge of the town are more than full. You never meet one but he jerks his hat off and bows and shows the whitest teeth. I never saw a bunch of them together, but I could pick out an Uncle Tom, a Quimbo, a Sambo, a Chloe, an Eliza, or any other character in *Uncle Tom's Cabin*. The women take in a lot of dimes washing for the soldiers, and the men around picking up odd jobs. I like to talk with them. They are funny enough, and the stories they tell of slave life are stories never to be forgotten.[5]

For noncombatants, the dislocations occasioned by the war sometimes proved immensely educative. In the North, as men entered the service, many women were forced rapidly to learn new skills. Some moved into industrial jobs; others became farmers; and still others trav-

5. Betsy Fleet and John D. P. Fuller, eds., *Green Mount: A Virginia Plantation Family During the Civil War: Being the Journal of Benjamin Robert Fleet and Letters of His Family* (Lexington: University of Kentucky Press, 1962), p. 319; Chauncey Cooke's letter is given in Henry Steele Commager, ed., *The Blue and the Gray; The Story of the Civil War as Told by Participants* (2 vols.; Indianapolis: The Bobbs-Merrill Company, 1950), I, 469.

eled to distant places for the first time and faced the agonizing experiences of the war alongside the men. Louisa May Alcott's well-known sojourn as a nurse in Washington, D.C., had become a fairly common experience among New England girls of middle-class background by the end of hostilities. For men and women alike, the demands and dislocations of the war required the learning of new behaviors, new attitudes, and new knowledge, which in turn became the basis for fundamentally different life-styles in the postwar period. In the South, as Anne Firor Scott has pointed out, the conflict marked the great divide between "the antebellum lady" and "the new woman"—the woman who pursued formal schooling and paid employment and who, years later, having gained the franchise, would look back on the war as the cataclysmic event that had ushered in the new order. With respect to the energies and occupations of intellectuals, the war was also a great watershed. Thus, upon leaving the army, Frederick Fleet, the soldier who so disliked the pine forests of Florida, was able to complete his formal education at the University of Virginia. That he ultimately chose to become the first superintendent of the Culver Military Academy suggests the enduring effect of his military experience as well as the transformations that the war had wrought in the planter class; the Fleet plantation itself had become the setting for the Green Mount Home School for Young Ladies, presided over by Fleet's mother and three sisters. And, in the North, the war had a lasting effect on individuals as different as the jurist Oliver Wendell Holmes, Jr., and the philanthropic organizer Louisa Lee Schuyler.[6]

Beyond the immediate experience of expanded horizons and necessitated change, the Civil War put a generation into contact with the realities of large-scale organization. For one thing, there was the organization of the armed forces themselves. Granted the informality and localism of the American citizen army, those who served in it and those who led it were alike immersed in the experience of carrying forward activities on a scale with few precedents in civilian life. There were simply no counterparts of a division moving from encampment to encampment or of a campaign in which several hundred thousand men played hundreds of different roles under some form of coordinated leadership. For another, there was the organization of the numerous services ancillary to the armies themselves: the large arsenals on both sides

6. Anne Firor Scott, *The Southern Lady: From Pedestal to Politics, 1830–1930* (Chicago: University of Chicago Press, 1970).

for the manufacture of military equipment; the intricate networks of supply to deliver food, clothing, and matériel to the troops; and the federations of missions, organizations, and societies that formed the Christian Commission and the Sanitary Commission and their counterparts on the Confederate side. Finally, there was the novel experience of conscription on both sides, of the organization of government to exact and enforce the obligation of military service and the discipline and training associated with it upon individual citizens. In many ways, conscription may have been the most significant and portentous educational development to be associated with the war; for it brought citizens into an educational relationship with government that was new and untried, however much it appeared continuous with earlier conceptions of responsibilities to the militia.

This experience in large-scale organization that the war advanced in both the military and the civilian spheres influenced education in at least three important domains. First, it affected the religious instruction of the troops by corps of chaplains in both armies, who not only solicited the divine favor for one side or the other but who sermonized continually, baptized new converts, reclaimed backsliders, and generally kept the fires of revivalism burning, particularly among the Confederates. The diary of a Southern Methodist chaplain, the Reverend John B. McFerrin, affords a vivid picture of this instruction:

> The Federals occupied Chattanooga, and for weeks the two armies were in full view of each other. All along the foot of Missionary Ridge we preached almost every night to crowded assemblies, and many precious souls were brought to God. After the battle of Missionary Ridge the Confederate army retreated and went into Winter quarters at Dalton, Ga. During these many months the chaplains and missionaries were at work—preaching, visiting the sick, and distributing Bibles, tracts, and religious newspapers. There was preaching in Dalton every night but four, for four months; and in the camps all around the city, preaching and prayer meetings occurred every night. The soldiers erected stands, improvised seats, and even built log churches, where they worshipped God in spirit and in truth. The result was that thousands were happily converted and were prepared for the future that awaited them. Officers and men alike were brought under religious influence. In all my life, perhaps, I never witnessed more displays of God's power in the awakening and conversion of sinners than in these protracted meetings during the winter and spring of 1863–64.[7]

7. The quote is given in Gross Alexander, *History of the Methodist Episcopal Church, South* (New York: The Christian Literature Co., 1894), p. 72.

Second, organization affected the education of blacks. As the northern armies moved deeper and deeper into the South, blacks flocked to the army camps, presenting the Union generals not only with immediate supply problems of food and clothing but also with long-range educational problems, initially under the supervision of the Union army, and later under the auspices of the Freedmen's Bureau, which was established in 1865. Hundreds of northern teachers were brought South to teach thousands of black children and adults. Like the army in which it began, the effort to teach the freedmen was organized on a vast scale, however inefficient the particulars may have been at any given time and place; and, beyond its immediate effect in advancing literacy, it set in motion a number of significant movements. It brought the federal government into the direct work of education on a much larger scale than had previously been the case with the Indians. It laid the basis for institutions of black higher education that would stand alongside the denominational colleges that came into being during the 1860's and 1870's. And it energized the northern concern for the education of southerners that was to prove both a boon and a bane for succeeding generations: on the one side, it brought northern expertise into the work of black education at a time when southern white expertise was unwilling and southern black expertise was largely—though not wholly—unavailable; on the other side, in the very act of doing so it surrounded popular instruction, particularly of blacks, with an aura of northern imperialism and paternalism that created tremendous resistance to the movement among more regionally conscious southerners.

Third, organization affected higher education throughout the country through the Morrill Act of 1862. Granted that the legislation had originated in the 1850's for educational reasons, it was enacted as a wartime measure and as part of a comprehensive Republican legislative program to unite the North and the West that included the Morrill Tariff of 1861, the Homestead Act of 1862, and the National Banking Act of 1863. It joined a policy for disposing of public lands to a policy of developing expertise in agriculture and the mechanic arts on a national scale; and, though the states organized the land grant colleges in very different ways, the colleges provided the beginning of a national network of educational research and development institutions that the federal government would subsequently use for a variety of enterprises, from the training of reserve officers for the armed forces, to the reform of agricultural production, to the renovation of rural community life.

Finally, organization affected the press as a public educator. Given the particular character of the war as a civil conflict and given the extent of popular involvement in the war effort on both the military and the civilian sides, there was a hunger for information that slowly transformed the substance of newspapers. For one thing, whereas the antebellum period had been the heyday of the editor, the war period moved the reporter into prominence: readers increasingly demanded news separated from comment. By 1866 James Parton could observe in the columns of the *North American Review,* "The power of the editorial lessens as the intelligence of the people increases. The prestige of the editorial is gone . . . the news is the point of rivalry; it is that for which nineteen twentieths of the people buy newspapers." In the effort to obtain news promptly, publishers had to muster the resources to maintain reporters in the field. The larger urban newspapers were able to build a substantial lead over the smaller, one-man operations that served most localities, and an organization like the New York Associated Press, an alliance of the larger newspapers that had been founded in 1848, was able to combine pooled resources with the skillful use of telegraph services to dominate the field. That domination of the New York press, once established, was never broken; and the gradual separation of news from editorial comment served to strengthen both: canons of reporting developed that made the news columns increasingly informative, and vigorous editorializing played a significant role in molding public opinion with respect to the aims and conduct of the war. In the end, leaders on both sides had to heed the press in a way that had not previously been the case in any such conflict.[8]

III

All these changes persisted beyond the Civil War and into Reconstruction, with the qualification, of course, that the Confederate army disbanded and the Union army became for a time, under the first Reconstruction Act, an army of occupation. Armies of occupation educate, however crassly and cruelly; and during the decade of rule by the generals the South was subjected to a relentless barrage of northern teaching, preaching, and discipline. Indeed, much of Reconstruction policy was essentially educational, based on the generally held northern assumption that the best way ultimately to regenerate the South would be

8. *North American Review,* CII (1866), 375–376.

through the wide dissemination of the northern version of the American *paideia*. This was deemed particularly relevant to the freedmen, for whom the very act of emancipation had carried "the sacred promise *to educate*."[9]

The same organizational effort, therefore, that had managed the widespread education of blacks, that had provided the wherewithal for the development of the land grant colleges, and that had transformed the American press, persisted with added vigor during the years of Reconstruction. There was an attempt to reunite the churches that had split during the antebellum period (following the Presbyterians, the Methodists, and the Baptists, the Episcopalians had split in 1861), but the crass attempt of the northern branches to absorb their southern counterparts with the southern ministers left out proved a poor basis for reconciliation; with the exception of the Episcopalians, those denominations that had been torn by schism continued to go their separate ways. There was a concerted effort to build public school systems along New England lines throughout the South, which waxed for a time amid heated debates over the question of racially mixed schools and then receded in the face of scarce resources and white resistance. And, in this connection, no phenomenon appeared more forcefully or universally than the eagerness of southern blacks to obtain an education. Booker T. Washington described it years later as a "veritable fever."

I can recall vividly the picture not only of children, but of men and women, some of whom had reached the age of sixty or seventy, tramping along the country roads with a spelling-book or a Bible in their hands. It did not seem to occur to any one that age was any obstacle to learning in books. With weak and unaccustomed eyes, old men and old women would struggle along month after month in their effort to master the primer in order to get, if possible, a little knowledge of the Bible. Some of them succeeded; many of them failed. To these latter the thought of passing from earth without being able to read the Bible was a source of deep sorrow.

The places for holding school were anywhere and everywhere; the freedmen could not wait for schoolhouses to be built or for teachers to be provided. They got up before day and studied in their cabins by the light of pine knots. They sat up until late at night, drooping over their books, trying to master the secrets they contained. More than once, I have seen a fire in the woods at night with a dozen or more people of both sexes and of all ages sitting about with book in hands studying their lessons. Sometimes they would fasten their primers between the ploughshares, so that they could read as they ploughed.

9. *Proceedings of the Sixth Annual Meeting of the National Teachers Association* (1865), p. 242.

Beyond their determination to learn, blacks manifested a widespread willingness to pay for their education, via taxes, tithes, and tuition—an attitude the more remarkable, since it was far from universally shared by southern whites. There was also a drive to rebuild colleges and universities and to add new facilities for the higher education of blacks; the latter movement drew substantial support from northern church organizations like the American Missionary Association, the Freedmen's Aid Society of the Methodist Episcopal Church, and the missionary arms of the Presbyterian Church, North, the Baptist Church of the Northern States, the Protestant Episcopal Church, and the Society of Friends, and led to the founding, among others, of Fisk, Atlanta, Biddle, Straight, Tougaloo, and Claflin universities. And there was a comparable effort to revivify the independence of the southern press, though the effort was complicated by the tendency of Radical state governments to follow the traditional practice of letting public printing contracts to sympathetic publishers.[10]

Two aspects of the educational efforts of these years bear special attention. First, with the failure of the Baptist, Methodist, and Presbyterian denominations to reunite, the southern branches of those denominations were left to continue teaching their own versions of the American *paideia,* with the result that their particular form of conservative revivalist preaching became a regional variant that persisted in substance and style long after its northern counterpart had been transformed by the conditions and requirements of industrialism. Even more importantly, perhaps, the southern churches released their black congregations to go their own way, with the result that the black churches became critically significant nurseries for the development of black values, black interpretations of the national *paideia,* and an indigenous black leadership. Second, there was a drift in educational policy toward ever greater reliance on the schools and colleges as institutions of social reform and uplift. The American Missionary Association and its associated denominational organizations did not concentrate on evangelization via the churches, they concentrated on instruction via the schools; in fact, the first report of the Freedmen's Aid Society of the Methodist Episcopal church explicitly stated, not only that the evangelization of the freedmen of the South was more important than the evangelization of the distant heathen, but also that schools and colleges would be more effective vehicles of evangelization than missions. Unlike the antebellum

10. Booker T. Washington, *The Story of the Negro: The Rise of the Race from Slavery* (2 vols.; New York: Doubleday, Page & Company, 1909), II, 141, 137–138.

campaign of the 1830's for the salvation of the West, the campaign of the 1870's for the salvation of the South was carried forward almost entirely by schools and colleges.

Of course, this concentration on schooling merely reflected an emerging national consensus, for Horace Mann's generation had already persuaded the American people to shift the burden of their educational investment to the schools. And in the two great educational thrusts of the 1870's, to reconstruct the South and to reunite the nation, the counsel of Mann and his contemporaries prevailed. A new generation of educational leaders, nurtured by the teaching and the example of Mann and trained up in the increasingly organized and systematized school systems of the North and the West, had moved to the forefront of educational affairs—men like Albert P. Marble of Worcester, John D. Philbrick of Boston, James P. Wickersham of Harrisburg, Andrew Dickson White of Ithaca, James B. Angell of Ann Arbor, and, preeminent among them, William T. Harris of St. Louis. They were as aware as any previous generation that families, churches, libraries, and indeed the entire apparatus of civic institutions, educate; but, unlike previous generations, they were willing to stake the nation's future primarily on its schools and colleges. Harris, only forty-one years of age in 1876 but already one of the nation's foremost philosophers, articulated their view. Families, churches, and civic institutions *train,* he maintained, and the outcomes of their education are unconscious habit and ungrounded inclination, taught ceaselessly over the years via oral interchange. The schools and colleges, on the other hand, *instruct*; they convey the techniques of study via the printed word and thereby enable the student to develop self-activity, and, through self-activity, individuality. As Harris continued:

It will be readily granted that textbook education begins earlier and forms a more important feature in this country than elsewhere.

The justification for this I find in the development of our national idea. It is founded on no new principle, but fundamentally it is the same as that agreed upon all the world over. Education should excite in the most ready way the powers of the pupil to self-activity. Not what the teacher does for him, but what he is made to do for himself, is of value. Although this lies at the bottom of other national ideas, it is not so explicitly recognized as in our own. It is in an embryonic state in those; in ours it has unfolded and realized itself so that we are everywhere and always impelled by it to throw responsibility on the individual. Hence, our theory is: The sooner we can make the youth able to pursue his course of culture for himself, the sooner may we graduate him from the school. To give him the tools of thought is our province. When we have initiated him into the technique of learning, he may be trusted to pursue his course for himself. . . .

It is the faith of Americans that they will be able to accomplish all that any other civilization can do, besides adding thereto a culture in free individuality to an extent hitherto unattained. A civilization wherein all can partake in the subjugation of the elements, and possess a competence at such easy terms as to leave the greater part of life for higher culture, is the goal to which every American confidently looks.

The common man shall be rich in conquests over the material world of time and space, and not only this but over the world of mind, the heritage of culture, the realized intelligence of all mankind.[11]

For Harris and his contemporaries, considering the nation's promise on the occasion of its centennial, a "new order of the ages" had become truly possible for the first time. The nation had been tested in the crucible of civil war and had endured. The dream of the founding fathers was now capable of realization, on a sound rational basis; and, as the founding fathers had themselves understood, a new order of education would be at the heart of the achievement.

11. William T. Harris, *The Theory of Education* (Syracuse, N.Y.: C. W. Bardeen, 1898), pp. 32–35.

BIBLIOGRAPHICAL ESSAY

Every prudent man dealeth with knowledge.

PROVERBS

The present volume continues in the historiographical mode of *American Education: The Colonial Experience, 1607–1783* (New York: Harper & Row, 1970). The historiographical position it reflects is explicated in the bibliographical essay in *American Education: The Colonial Experience,* in my earlier monograph *The Wonderful World of Ellwood Patterson Cubberley: An Essay on the Historiography of American Education* (New York: Bureau of Publications, Teachers College, Columbia University, 1965), and in the note on problematics and sources appended to my 1976 Merle Curti Lectures, *Traditions of American Education* (New York: Basic Books, 1977). The present volume is also substantively continuous with *American Education: The Colonial Experience*; and, although I shall not repeatedly allude to that work, it does provide background for the entire volume.

Given the way in which I approach the study of education, certain standard works in social and intellectual history have proved consistently valuable, among them Howard Mumford Jones, *O Strange New World: American Culture: The Formative Years* (New York: The Viking Press, 1964); Russel Blaine Nye, *The Cultural Life of the New Nation, 1776–1830* (New York: Harper & Brothers, 1960) and *Society and Culture in America, 1830–1860* (New York: Harper & Row, 1974); Merle Curti, *The Growth of American Thought* (3d ed.; New York: Harper & Row, 1964); Herbert W. Schneider, *A History of American Philosophy* (2d ed.; New York: Columbia University Press, 1963); Elizabeth Flower and Murray G. Murphy, *A History of Philosophy in America* (2 vols.; New York: Capricorn Books, 1977); Vernon Louis Parrington, *Main Currents in American Thought: The Romantic Revolution,* 1800–1860 (New York: Harcourt, Brace, and Company, 1927); Robert E. Spiller *et al.,* eds., *Literary History of the United States* (4th ed.; 2 vols.; New York: The Macmillan Company, 1974); Richard M. Dorson, *America in Legend: Folklore from the Colonial Period to the Present* (New York: Pantheon Books, 1973); Oliver W. Larkin, *Art and Life in America* (rev. ed.; New York: Holt, Rinehart and Winston, 1960); Marshall B. Davidson, *Life*

523

in America (2 vols.; Boston: Houghton Mifflin Company, 1951); Perry Miller, *The Life of the Mind in America from the Revolution to the Civil War* (New York; Harcourt, Brace & World, 1965); Sydney E. Ahlstrom, *A Religious History of the American People* (New Haven: Yale University Press, 1972); Robert T. Handy, *A History of the Churches in the United States and Canada* (New York: Oxford University Press, 1977); Frank Luther Mott, *American Journalism: A History, 1690–1960* (3d ed.; New York: The Macmillan Company, 1962) and *A History of American Magazines* (5 vols.; Cambridge, Mass.: Harvard University Press, 1930–1968); Daniel J. Boorstin, *The Americans: The National Experience* (New York: Random House, 1965); and those superb older works, John Bach McMaster, *A History of the People of the United States from the Revolution to the Civil War* (8 vols.; New York: D. Appleton and Company, 1883–1913); Henry Adams, *History of the United States of America During the Administrations of Jefferson and Madison* (9 vols.; New York: Charles Scribner's Sons, 1889–1898); and Edward Channing, *A History of the United States* (6 vols.; New York: The Macmillan Company, 1905–1925).

Also valuable were such reference works as Frank Friedel, ed., *Harvard Guide to American History* (rev. ed.; 2 vols.; Cambridge, Mass.: Harvard University Press, 1974); Charles O. Paullin, *Atlas of the Historical Geography of the United States*, edited by John K. Wright (Washington, D.C.: Carnegie Institution of Washington, 1932); U.S., Bureau of the Census, *Historical Statistics of the United States, Colonial Times to 1970* (2 vols.; Washington, D.C.: Government Printing Office, 1975); Jurgen Herbst, *The History of American Education* (Northbrook, Del.: AHM Publishing Corporation, 1973); Nelson R. Burr et al., *A Critical Bibliography of Religion in America* (2 vols.; Princeton, N.J.: Princeton University Press, 1961); William B. Sprague, *Annals of the American Pulpit* (9 vols.; New York: Robert Carter & Brothers, 1866–1869); Edwin Scott Gaustad, *Historical Atlas of Religion in America* (New York: Harper & Row, 1962); Allen Johnson et al., eds., *Dictionary of American Biography* (24+ vols.; New York: Charles Scribner's Sons, 1928–   ); *The International Library of Negro Life and History* (7 vols.; New York: Publishers Company, 1967–1968); and Edward T. James et al., *Notable American Women, 1607–1950: A Biographical Dictionary* (3 vols.; Cambridge, Mass.: Harvard University Press, 1971). And, like everyone who has studied the early national era, I found immensely useful Charles Evans, ed., *American Bibliography* (12 vols., with a 13th edited by Clifford K. Shipton; imprint varies, 1903–1955) and Joseph Sabin and Wilberforce Eames, eds., *Bibliotheca Americana* (29 vols.; New York: publisher varies, 1868–1936), along with the Early American Imprints series based upon them, issued by the American Antiquarian Society under the editorship of Clifford K. Shipton.

Several standard collections of documents have proved helpful, including Henry Steele Commager, ed., *Documents of American History* (9th ed.; 2 vols.; New York: Appleton-Century-Crofts, 1973); John R. Commons et al., *A Documentary History of American Industrial Society* (11 vols.; Cleveland: The Arthur H. Clark Company, 1910–1911); Edgar W. Knight, ed., *A Documentary History of Education in the South Before 1860* (5 vols.; Chapel Hill: University of North Carolina Press, 1949–1953); H. Shelton Smith, Robert T. Handy, and Lefferts A. Loetscher, eds., *American Christianity: An Historical Interpretation with Representative Documents* (2 vols.; New York: Charles Scribner's Sons, 1960); William Warren Sweet, ed., *Religion on the American Frontier* (reprint ed.; 4 vols.; New York: Cooper Square Publishers, 1964); Richard Hofstadter and Wilson Smith, eds., *American Higher Education: A Documentary His-*

tory (2 vols.; Chicago: University of Chicago Press, 1961); Sol Cohen, ed., *Education in the United States: A Documentary History* (5 vols.; New York: Random House, 1974); Robert H. Bremner, ed., *Children and Youth in America: A Documentary History* (3 vols.; Cambridge, Mass.; Harvard University Press, 1970–1974); Wilcomb E. Washburn, ed., *The American Indian and the United States: A Documentary History* (4 vols.; New York: Random House, 1975); and George P. Rawick, ed., *The American Slave: A Composite Autobiography* (19 vols.; Westport, Conn.: Greenwood Publishing Co., 1972–1974).

INTRODUCTION

The international context of the American Revolution is developed in R. R. Palmer, *The Age of the Democratic Revolution: A Political History of Europe and America, 1760–1800* (2 vols.; Princeton, N.J.: Princeton University Press, 1959–1964). The best introductions to Richard Price as a pivotal figure in Anglo-American political thought and activities are D. O. Thomas, *The Honest Mind: The Thought and Work of Richard Price* (Oxford: Clarendon Press, 1977); Carl B. Cone, *Torchbearer of Freedom: The Influence of Richard Price on Eighteenth-Century Thought* (Lexington: University of Kentucky Press, 1952); Henri Laboucheix, *Richard Price: Théoricien de la Révolution Américaine, Le Philosophe et Le Sociologue, Le Pamphlétaire et L'Orateur* (Paris: Didier, 1970); and Bernard Peach, ed., *Richard Price and the Ethical Foundations of the American Revolution* (Durham, N.C.: Duke University Press, 1979). The Peach volume includes a reprint of the second edition (1785) of Price's *Observations on the Importance of the American Revolution and the Means of Making It a Benefit to the World.* The attitudes of the Revolutionary generation toward education are discussed in Frederick Rudolph, ed., *Essays on Education in the Early Republic* (Cambridge, Mass.: Harvard University Press, 1965); Eva T. H. Brann, *Paradoxes of Education in a Republic* (Chicago: University of Chicago Press, 1979); David Tyack, "Forming the National Character: Paradox in the Educational Thought of the Revolutionary Generation," *Harvard Educational Review,* XXXVI (1966), 29–41; Jonathan Messerli, "The Columbian Complex: The Impulse to National Consolidation," *History of Education Quarterly,* VII (1967), 417–431; Linda K. Kerber, "Daughters of Columbia: Educating Women for the Republic, 1787–1805," in Stanley Elkins and Eric McKitrick, eds., *The Hofstadter Aegis: A Memorial* (New York: Alfred A. Knopf, 1974), pp. 36–59; Victor Daniel Brooks, Jr., "Education and Politics in the New Nation—A Study of the Educational Policies of the Federalists" (doctoral thesis, University of Pennsylvania, 1974); Daniel J. Boorstin, *The Lost World of Thomas Jefferson* (New York: Henry Holt and Company, 1948); and Allen O. Hansen, *Liberalism and American Education in the Eighteenth Century* (New York: The Macmillan Company, 1926).

The more general political thought of the Revolutionary generation is explicated in a considerable literature, which is incisively reviewed in Robert E. Shalhope, "Toward a Republican Synthesis: The Emergence of an Understanding of Republicanism in American Historiography," *William and Mary Quarterly,* 3d ser., XXIX (1972), 49–80; the most useful sources for the immediate post-Revolutionary years are Gordon S. Wood, *The Creation of the American Republic, 1776–1787* (Chapel Hill: University of North Carolina Press, 1969) and Gerald Stourzh, *Alexander Hamilton and the Idea of Republican Government* (Stanford, Calif.: Stanford University Press, 1970). The broader context of American Enlightenment thought is developed in Henry F. May, *The Enlightenment in America* (New York: Oxford University Press, 1976) and in the several essays constituting the Summer, 1976, issue of *American Quarterly* (XXVIII [1976], 147–293). The millennial strain in the thought of the Revolutionary generation is dealt with in Ernest Lee Tuveson, *Redeemer Nation: The Idea of America's Millennial Role* (Chicago: University of Chicago Press, 1968); Christopher M. Beam, "Millennialism and American Nationalism, 1740–1800," *Journal of Presbyterian History*, LIV (1976), 182–199; Russel B. Nye, *This Almost Chosen People: Essays in the History of American Ideas* (East Lansing: Michigan State University Press, 1966); Rutherford E. Dalmage, "The American Idea of Progress, 1750–1800," *Proceedings of the American Philosophical Society*, XCI (1947), 307–314; and Edward McNall Burns, *The American Idea of Mission: Concepts of National Purpose and Destiny* (New Brunswick, N.J.: Rutgers University Press, 1957).

The changing character of the American population during the first century of national existence is discussed in Warren S. Thompson and P. K. Whelpton, *Population Trends in the United States* (New York: McGraw-Hill Book Company, 1933) and Donald J. Bogue, *The Population of the United States* (Glencoe, Ill.: The Free Press of Glencoe, 1959), though details must be drawn from such sources as J. Potter, "The Growth of Population in America, 1700–1860," in D. V. Glass and D. E. C. Eversley, eds., *Population in History: Essays in Historical Demography* (Chicago: Aldine Publishing Company, 1965); *A Century of Population Growth from the First Census of the United States to the Twelfth, 1790–1900* (Washington, D.C.: Government Printing Office, 1909); U.S., Bureau of the Census, *Historical Statistics of the United States, Colonial Times to 1970* (2 vols.; Washington, D.C.: Government Printing Office, 1975); Maldwyn Allen Jones, *American Immigration* (Chicago: University of Chicago Press, 1960); Charlotte Erickson, *Invisible Immigrants: The Adaptation of English and Scottish Immigrants in Nineteenth-Century America* (Coral Gables, Fla.: University of Miami Press, 1972); Gunther Barth, *Bitter Strength: A History of the Chinese in the United States* (Cambridge, Mass.: Harvard University Press, 1964); Oliver MacDonagh, "The Irish Famine Emigration to the United States," *Perspectives in American History*, X (1976), 357–446, John Hope Franklin, *From Slavery to Freedom: A History of Negro Americans* (4th ed.; New York: Alfred A. Knopf, 1974); and Wilcomb E. Washburn, *The Indian in America* (New York: Harper & Row, 1975). The notion of America as refuge is discussed in Cecil D. Eby, "America as 'Asylum': A Dual Image," *American Quarterly*, XIV (1962), 483–489.

There is a surprising dearth of historical scholarship on the problem of who constituted the citizenry of the Republic at different times in its history. F. G. Franklin, "The Legislative History of Naturalization in the United States, 1776–1795," *Annual Report of the American Historical Association for the Year 1901* (2 vols.; Washington, D.C.: Government Printing Office, 1902), I, 301–317, and Sidney Kansas, *Citizenship in the United States of America* (New York: Washington Publishing Company, 1936) are older works; James H. Kettner, *The Development of American Citizenship, 1608–1870* (Chapel Hill: University of North Carolina Press, 1978) is more recent and more comprehensive. None deals satisfactorily with the problem of citizenship for women. The best work in that regard is Richard B. Morris, *Studies in the History of American Law, with Special Reference to the Seventeenth and Eighteenth Centuries* (New York: Columbia University Press, 1930), although the complexities involved in the civil status of women are not Morris's special problem.

The notion of America as empire is developed in Richard W. Van Alstyne, *The Rising American Empire* (New York: Oxford University Press, 1960) and *Genesis of American Nationalism* (Waltham, Mass.: Blaisdell Publishing Company, 1970). The best sources on early efforts to work out a public land policy are Merrill Jensen, *The New Nation: A History of the United States During the Confederation, 1781–1789* (New York: Alfred A. Knopf, 1950); Roy M. Robbins, *Our Landed Heritage: The Public Domain, 1776–1970* (2d rev. ed.; Lincoln: University of Nebraska Press, 1976); Benjamin Horace Hibbard, *A History of the Public Land Policies* (New York: The Macmillan Company, 1924); and Payson Jackson Treat, *The National Land System* (New York: E. B. Treat & Company, 1910). The best works on the early federal land ordinances and their bearing on education are George W. Knight, *History and Management of Land Grants for Education in the Northwest Territory* (New York: G. P. Putnam's Sons, 1885) and Howard Cromwell Taylor, *The Educational Significance of the Early Federal Land Ordinances* (New York: Bureau of Publications, Teachers College, Columbia University, 1922). Jensen obviously disagrees with Knight concerning the effect of Jefferson's proposals of 1784 on the Ordinance of 1785; my own reading of the documents concurs with Jensen's. George Dargo, *Jefferson's Louisiana: Politics and the Clash of Legal Traditions* (Cambridge, Mass.: Harvard University Press, 1975) is an incisive study of the problems of incorporating Lower Louisiana into the Union.

My notion of an American vernacular in education draws upon the discussion of a vernacular in the arts in Constance Rourke, *The Roots of American Culture and Other Essays,* edited by Van Wyck Brooks (New York: Harcourt, Brace, and Company, 1942); John A. Kouwenhoven, *Made in America: The Arts in Modern Civilization* (Garden City, N.Y.: Doubleday and Company, 1948) and *The Beer Can by the Highway: Essays on What Is "American" About America* (Garden City, N.Y.: Doubleday and Company, 1961). It joins the idea of popularization to an element of conscious creation and design (*an* element, for the vernacular evolved quite spontaneously at the same time as individuals tried consciously to shape it), though it does not insist to the extent that the art historians have insisted upon indigenousness. As I argued in *American Education: The Colonial Experience,* American education has always combined the borrowed with the indigenous, in different proportions at different times.

INTRODUCTION TO PART I: THE KINGDOM OF GOD

The role of the clergy in attempting to define an American *paideia* and the categories of religious thought within which the effort was carried forward are the substance of a considerable literature, which derives in its modern form from H. Richard Niebuhr's pathbreaking work, *The Kingdom of God in America* (New York: Harper & Brothers, 1937). Among the more recent writings that have elucidated the theme are Sidney E. Mead, *The Lively Experiment: The Shaping of Christianity in America* (New York: Harper & Row, 1963); Perry Miller, *The Life of the Mind in America from the Revolution to the Civil War* (New York: Harcourt, Brace & World, 1965); William A. Clebsch, *From Sacred to Profane America: The Role of Religion in American History* (New York: Harper & Row, 1968); Robert T. Handy, *A Christian America: Protestant Hopes and Historical Realities* (New York: Oxford University Press, 1971); and the several essays in Elwyn A. Smith, ed., *The Religion of the Republic* (Philadelphia: Fortress Press, 1971). The millennial strain that runs throughout the effort has been the subject of a literature in its own right. That literature is discriminatingly reviewed in

David E. Smith, "Millenarian Scholarship in America," *American Quarterly*, XVII (1965), 535–549, and Hillel Schwartz, "The End of the Beginning: Millenarian Studies, 1969–1975," *Religious Studies Review*, II (July, 1976), 1–15. The most interesting recent contributions are Ernest Lee Tuveson, *Redeemer Nation: The Idea of America's Millennial Role* (Chicago: University of Chicago Press, 1968); J. F. Maclear, "The Republic and the Millennium," in Smith, ed., *Religion of the Republic*, pp. 183–216; Ernest R. Sandeen, *The Roots of Fundamentalism: British and American Millenarianism, 1800–1930* (Chicago: University of Chicago Press, 1970); Christopher Merriman Beam, "Millennialism in American Thought" (doctoral thesis, University of Illinois, 1976); and J. F. C. Harrison, *The Second Coming: Popular Millenarianism, 1780–1850* (New Brunswick, N.J.: Rutgers University Press, 1979). Following Tuveson's suggestion in *Redeemer Nation*, I am using "millenarian" to signify the belief in a dramatic second coming of Christ and "millennial" to signify a gradual triumph of Christian principles in the world.

The origin of the design for the Great Seal of the United States is discussed in *The Papers of Thomas Jefferson*, edited by Julian P. Boyd (19+ vols.; Princeton, N.J.: Princeton University Press, 1950–   ), I, 474–497, and Richard S. Patterson and Richardson Dougall, *The Eagle and the Shield: A History of the Great Seal of the United States* (Washington, D.C.: Department of State, 1976).

CHAPTER 1: BENEVOLENT PIETIES

At least five biographies of Thomas Paine appeared during the 1970's: Audrey Williamson, *Thomas Paine: His Life, Work and Times* (London: George Allen & Unwin, 1973); Samuel Edwards, *Rebel! A Biography of Tom Paine* (New York: Praeger, 1974); David Freeman Hawke, *Paine* (New York: Harper & Row, 1974); Eric Foner, *Tom Paine and Revolutionary America* (New York: Oxford University Press, 1976); and Jerome D. Wilson and William F. Ricketson, *Thomas Paine* (Boston: Twayne Publishers, 1978). Of the five, the Hawke and Foner volumes are the most useful to scholars. Harry Hayden Clark's introduction to *Thomas Paine: Representative Selections, with Introduction, Bibliography, and Notes* (New York: American Book Company, 1944) remains the best general discussion of Paine's thought. Clark's "An Historical Interpretation of Thomas Paine's Religion," *University of California Chronicle*, XXXV (1933), 56–87; "Thomas Paine's Relation to Voltaire and Rousseau," *Revue Anglo-Américaine*, IX (1932), 305–318, 393–405; and "Thomas Paine's Theories of Rhetoric," *Transactions of the Wisconsin Academy of Sciences, Arts and Letters*, XXVIII (1933), 307–339, are similarly illuminating. The standard collections of Paine's works are *The Writings of Thomas Paine*, edited by Moncure Daniel Conway (4 vols.; New York: G. P. Putnam's Sons, 1894–1896), and *The Complete Writings of Thomas Paine*, edited by Philip S. Foner (2 vols.; Secaucus, N.J.: The Citadel Press, 1945). The international context of Paine's thought is developed in R. R. Palmer, *The Age of the Democratic Revolution: A Political History of Europe and America, 1760–1800* (2 vols.; Princeton, N.J.: Princeton University Press, 1959–1964); Carl B. Cone, *The English Jacobins: Reformers in Late 18th Century England* (New York: Charles Scribner's Sons, 1968); and Albert Goodwin, *The Friends of Liberty: The English Democratic Movement in the Age of the French Revolution* (Cambridge, Mass.: Harvard University Press, 1979). American deism and Paine's role in the deist movement are dealt with in G. Adolf Koch, *Republican Religion: The American Revolution and the Cult of Reason* (New York: Henry Holt and Company, 1933) and Herbert M. Morais, *Deism in Eighteenth Century America* (New York: Columbia University Press, 1934). The continued vitality of Paine's ideas in nineteenth-century America is documented in Albert Post, *Popular Freethought in America, 1825–1850* (New York: Columbia University Press, 1943). The role of education in the deist utopia *Equality— A Political Romance* is discussed in Charles Orville Burgess, "The Educational State in America: Selected Views on Learning as the Key to Utopia, 1800–1924" (doctoral thesis, University of Wisconsin, 1962). The work itself was republished as *Equality; or, A History of Lithconia* (Philadelphia: The Liberal Union, 1837).

The most incisive recent discussion of the life, work, and thought of Samuel Stanhope Smith is Douglas Sloan, *The Scottish Enlightenment and the American College Ideal* (New York: Teachers College Press, 1971). Sloan includes a discriminating review of the literature on Smith in the bibliography of that volume. Other useful writings on Smith include Samuel Holt Monk, "Samuel Stanhope Smith: Friend of Rational Liberty," in Willard Thorp, ed., *The Lives of Eighteen from Princeton* (Princeton, N.J.: Princeton University Press, 1946); William H. Hudnut III, "Samuel Stanhope Smith: Enlightened Conservative," *Journal of the History of Ideas*, XVII (1956), 540–552; Winthrop D. Jordan's introduction to the John Harvard Library edition of the 1810 printing of Smith's *An Essay on the Causes of the Variety of Complexion and Figure in the Human Species* (Cambridge, Mass.: Harvard University Press, 1965); and the substantial sections on Smith in John Maclean's older but eminently illuminating *History of the College of New Jersey, from Its Origin in 1746 to the Commencement of 1854* (2 vols.; Philadelphia: J. B. Lippincott & Company, 1877). The standard editions of Smith's works are *The Lectures, Corrected and Improved, Which Have Been Delivered for a Series of Years, in the College of New Jersey; on the Subjects of Moral and Political Philosophy* (2 vols.; Trenton: Daniel Fenton, 1812) and *Sermons of Samuel Stanhope Smith* (2 vols.; Philadelphia: S. Potter, 1821). The largest collection of Smith papers is in the Princeton University Library.

Gladys Bryson, *Man and Society: The Scottish Inquiry of the Eighteenth Century* (Princeton, N.J.: Princeton University Press, 1945) remains an indispensable guide to the social thought of the leading Scottish philosophers. Sloan, *The Scottish Enlightenment and the American College Ideal;* Sydney E. Ahlstrom, "The Scottish Philosophy and American Theology," *Church History*, XXIV (1955), 257–272; Andrew Dunnett Hook, "Literary and Cultural Relations Between Scotland and America, 1763–1830" (doctoral thesis, Princeton University, 1960); Richard J. Petersen, "Scottish Common Sense in America, 1768–1850: An Evaluation of Its Influence" (doctoral thesis, The American University, 1963); Wilson Smith, *Professors & Public Ethics: Studies of Northern Moral Philosophers Before the Civil War* (Ithaca, N.Y.: Cornell University Press, 1956); D. H. Meyer, *The Instructed Conscience: The Shaping of the American National Mind* (Philadelphia: University of Pennsylvania Press, 1972); and Elizabeth Flower and Murray G. Murphy, *A History of Philosophy in America* (2 vols.; New York: Capricorn Books, 1977) are helpful in estimating the influence of the Scottish philosophy on American thought and education. D. L. LeMathieu, *The Mind of William Paley: A Philosopher and His Age* (Lincoln: University of Nebraska Press, 1976) is an incisive analysis of Paley's philosophy and theology.

The best sources for the life and thought of William Ellery Channing are Robert L. Patterson, *The Philosophy of William Ellery Channing* (New York: Bookman Associates, 1952); David P. Edgell, *William Ellery Channing: An Intellectual Portrait*

(Boston: Beacon Press, 1955); Arthur W. Brown, *Always Young for Liberty: A Biography of William Ellery Channing* (Syracuse, N.Y.: Syracuse University Press, 1956); and Madeleine H. Rice, *Federal Street Pastor: The Life of William Ellery Channing* (New Haven: College and University Press, 1961). Conrad Wright's introduction to *Three Prophets of Religious Liberalism: Channing, Emerson, Parker* (Boston: Beacon Press, 1961) and his essay on Channing in *The Liberal Christians: Essays on American Unitarian History* (Boston: Beacon Press, 1970) are incisive in relating Channing to Unitarianism. Wright's *The Beginnings of Unitarianism in America* (Boston: Starr King Press, 1955) remains the definitive study of the origins of Unitarian thought. The earliest edition of Channing's collected writings is *The Works of William E. Channing* (6 vols.; Boston: J. Munroe and Company, 1841–1845); I used the more convenient one-volume edition published as *The Works of William E. Channing* (new ed.; Boston: American Unitarian Association, 1886). On Channing and Transcendentalism, see Harold Clarke Goddard, *Studies in New England Transcendentalism* (New York: Columbia University Press, 1908), which concludes that Channing was a Transcendentalist; Arthur I. Ladu, "Channing and Transcendentalism," *American Literature,* XI (1939), 129–137, which concludes that he was not a Transcendentalist; and Arthur W. Brown, *William Ellery Channing* (New Haven: College and University Press, 1961), which concludes that he maintained a warm but critical relationship with Transcendentalism. For the incorporation of Channing's values and attitudes into some of the more influential belles-lettres of the nineteenth century, see Vernon Louis Parrington, *Main Currents in American Thought: The Romantic Revolution, 1800–1860* (New York: Harcourt, Brace and Company, 1927) and Van Wyck Brooks, *The Flowering of New England, 1815–1865* (New York: E. P. Dutton & Co., 1936). For the special version of Channing's values and attitudes that appeared as Harvard moral philosophy, see Daniel Walker Howe, *The Unitarian Conscience: Harvard Moral Philosophy, 1805–1861* (Cambridge, Mass.: Harvard University Press, 1970).

James Walter Fraser, "Pedagogue for God's Kingdom: Lyman Beecher and the Second Great Awakening" (doctoral thesis, Teachers College, Columbia University, 1975) is an incisive and comprehensive study of Beecher's educational ideas and activities, with a discriminating annotated bibliography of primary and secondary sources. Vincent Harding, "Lyman Beecher and the Transformation of American Protestantism, 1775–1863" (doctoral thesis, University of Chicago, 1965); Raymond Lee Wood, "Lyman Beecher, 1775–1863: A Biographical Study" (doctoral thesis, Yale University, 1970); and Stuart C. Henry, *Unvanquished Puritan: A Portrait of Lyman Beecher* (Grand Rapids, Mich.: William B. Eerdmans Publishing Company, 1973) are useful biographical accounts. I have always regarded Constance Rourke's more popular portrait in *Trumpets of Jubilee* (New York: Harcourt, Brace and Company, 1927) as a pioneering effort. *The Autobiography of Lyman Beecher,* edited by Barbara M. Cross (2 vols.; Cambridge, Mass.: Harvard University Press, 1961) is the John Harvard Library edition of the 1864 version edited by Charles Beecher; it is a treasure trove of information about Beecher's views and perceptions of the world. The standard edition of Beecher's writings is *Beecher's Works* (3 vols.; Boston: John P. Jewett, 1852–53). *A Plea for the West* (2d ed.; Cincinnati: Truman & Smith, 1835) and *A Plea for Colleges* (2d ed.; Cincinnati: Truman & Smith, 1836) are essential for an understanding of Beecher's views on education; *The Memory of Our Fathers* (Boston: T. R. Marvin, 1828) is essential for an understanding, not only of Beecher's millennialism, but also of the millennialism that suffused the discussion of educational affairs during the first century of national life. Sidney E. Mead, "Lyman Beecher and Connecticut Orthodoxy's Campaign Against the Unitarians, 1819–1826," *Church History*, IX (1940), 218–234, documents Beecher's role in the attack on the "Unitarian heresy."

The best systematic biography of Charles Grandison Finney is James E. Johnson, "The Life of Charles Grandison Finney" (doctoral thesis, Syracuse University, 1959). The best sources for Finney's ideas are William G. McLoughlin, Jr., *Modern Revivalism: Charles Grandison Finney to Billy Graham* (New York: The Ronald Press Company, 1959); William Lester McClelland, "Church and Ministry in the Life and Thought of Charles G. Finney" (doctoral thesis, Princeton Theological Seminary, 1967); James E. Johnson, "Charles G. Finney and Oberlin Perfectionism," *Journal of Presbyterian History*, XLVI (1968), 42–57, 128–138, and "Charles G. Finney and a Theology of Revivalism," *Church History*, XXXVIII (1968), 338–358; and J. Stanley Mattson, "Charles Grandison Finney and the Emerging Tradition of 'New Measure' Revivalism" (doctoral thesis, University of North Carolina, 1970). Finney's contributions at Oberlin are depicted in James William Lee, "The Development of Theology at Oberlin" (doctoral thesis, Drew University, 1952) and Robert Samuel Fletcher, *A History of Oberlin College from Its Foundation Through the Civil War* (2 vols.; Oberlin, Ohio: Oberlin College, 1943). Finney's preaching and views on preaching are discussed by William G. McLoughlin in his introduction to the John Harvard Library edition of Finney's *Lectures on Revivals of Religion* (Cambridge, Mass.: Harvard University Press, 1960), as well as in Roy Alan Cheesebro, "The Preaching of Charles G. Finney" (doctoral thesis, Yale University, 1948). There is no standard edition of Finney's writings. In addition to the *Lectures on Revivals of Religion*, there are two volumes of *Lectures on Systematic Theology* (Oberlin, Ohio: James M. Fitch, 1846–47) and *Memoirs of Rev. Charles G. Finney, Written by Himself* (New York: A. S. Barnes & Company, 1876). There are comprehensive bibliographies of the writings of Finney in the Cheesebro and McClelland theses. The principal collection of Finney papers is in the Oberlin College Library.

Charles Robert Foster, "Horace Bushnell on Education" (doctoral thesis, Teachers College, Columbia University, 1971) is a thoughtful study of Bushnell's educational ideas, with a useful critical bibliography. Barbara M. Cross, *Horace Bushnell: Minister to a Changing America* (Chicago: University of Chicago Press, 1958) and Howard A. Barnes, "Horace Bushnell: An American Christian Gentleman" (doctoral thesis, University of Iowa, 1970) are discerning biographies, though Barnes is highly critical of Cross's portrayal of Bushnell as a person. The Barnes thesis also includes an excellent critical bibliography. The best study on Bushnell's chief work, *Christian Nurture*, is Rachel Henderlite, "The Theological Basis of Horace Bushnell's *Christian Nurture*" (doctoral thesis, Yale University, 1947); David Stanley Steward, "Horace Bushnell and Contemporary Christian Education: A Study of Revelation and Nurture" (doctoral thesis, Yale University, 1966) is also useful. Frank Hugh Foster, *A Genetic History of the New England Theology* (Chicago: University of Chicago Press, 1907) develops the intellectual context for Bushnell's thought. Louise Weeks, "Horace Bushnell on Black America," *Religious Education*, LXVIII (1973), 28–41, points incisively to the blindness on Bushnell's part to the spiritual and educational needs of blacks, a blindness widely shared by Bushnell's clerical contemporaries. The best source of material on Bushnell's life is his daughter's work *Life and Letters of Horace Bushnell*, edited by Mary Bushnell Cheney (New York: Harper & Brothers, 1880). There is no standard edition of Bushnell's writings, though a complete list of his published works is given in

Horace Bushnell, *The Spirit in Man* (New York: Charles Scribner's Sons, 1903). H. Shelton Smith, ed., *Horace Bushnell* (New York: Oxford University Press, 1965) presents an admirable selection of Bushnell's writings, with an incisive introduction. Horace Bushnell, *Christian Nurture,* with an introduction by Luther A. Weigle (New Haven: Yale University Press, 1966) is a convenient edition of Bushnell's best-known treatise.

CHAPTER 2: THE EVANGELICAL CRUSADE

An immense body of scholarship over the past quarter-century has conclusively established the evangelical Protestant tradition as the decisive religious tradition of nineteenth-century America. Put in educational terms, this is to say that the American *paideia* as defined by Lyman Beecher, Charles Grandison Finney, Horace Bushnell, and kindred intellectuals came to predominate in all parts of the country. It was by no means the sole definition, for a kind of existential pluralism prevailed in the open spaces of early national America that left room for variant versions of the American *paideia;* but the evangelical Protestant version did triumph, affecting nonevangelicals and non-Protestants, if only in forcing them to define and inculcate alternative *paideias.*

The best general work is Sydney E. Ahlstrom, *A Religious History of the American People* (New Haven: Yale University Press, 1972). The earlier works of William Warren Sweet, including *Revivalism in America: Its Origins, Growth and Decline* (New York: Charles Scribner's Sons, 1944), *Religion in the Development of American Culture, 1765–1840* (New York: Charles Scribner's Sons, 1952), and *Religion on the American Frontier* (reprint ed.; New York: Cooper Square Publishers, 1964), remain highly useful. Also valuable are Charles Roy Keller, *The Second Great Awakening in Connecticut* (New Haven: Yale University Press, 1942); Charles E. Cunningham, *Timothy Dwight, 1752–1817: A Biography* (New York: The Macmillan Company, 1942); Whitney R. Cross, *The Burned-Over District: The Social and Intellectual History of Enthusiastic Religion in Western New York, 1800–1850* (Ithaca, N.Y.: Cornell University Press, 1950); Timothy L. Smith, *Revivalism and Social Reform in Mid-Nineteenth-Century America* (New York: Abingdon Press, 1957); Sidney E. Mead, *The Lively Experiment: The Shaping of Christianity in America* (New York: Harper & Row, 1963), *Nathaniel William Tayler, 1786–1858: A Connecticut Liberal* (Chicago: University of Chicago Press, 1942), and "The Rise of the Evangelical Conception of the Ministry in America (1607–1850)," in H. Richard Niebuhr and Daniel D. Williams, *The Ministry in Historical Perspectives* (New York: Harper & Brothers, 1956), chap. viii; William G. McLoughlin, Jr., *Modern Revivalism: Charles Grandison Finney to Billy Graham* (New York: The Ronald Press Company, 1959); Perry Miller, "From the Covenant to the Revival," in James Ward Smith and A. Leland Jamison, eds., *The Shaping of American Religion* (Princeton, N.J.: Princeton University Press, 1961), pp. 322–368, and *The Life of the Mind in America from the Revolution to the Civil War* (New York: Harcourt, Brace & World, 1965); Walter Brownlow Posey, *Frontier Mission: A History of Religion West of the Southern Appalachians to 1861* (Lexington: University of Kentucky Press, 1966); John Opie, Jr., "James McGready: Theologian of Frontier Revivalism," *Church History,* XXXIV (1965), 445–456; Martin E. Marty, *Righteous Empire: The Protestant Experience in America* (New York: The Dial Press, 1970); Lois Wendland Banner, "The Protestant Crusade: Religious Missions, Benevolence, and Reform in the United States, 1790–1840" (doctoral thesis,

Columbia University, 1970); Ernest Trice Thompson, *Presbyterians in the South* (3 vols.; Richmond, Va.: John Knox Press, 1963-1973); John B. Boles, *The Great Revival, 1787-1805: The Origins of the Southern Evangelical Mind* (Lexington: The University Press of Kentucky, 1972); Milton C. Sernett, *Black Religion and American Evangelicalism: White Protestants, Plantation Missions, and the Flowering of Negro Christianity, 1787-1865* (Metuchen, N.J.: Scarecrow Press, 1975); Donald G. Mathews, *Religion in the Old South* (Chicago: University of Chicago Press, 1977); and E. Brooks Holifield, *The Gentlemen Theologians: American Theology in Southern Culture, 1795-1860* (Durham, N.C.: Duke University Press, 1978).

The camp meeting as a religious and social phenomenon is portrayed in Charles A. Johnson, *The Frontier Camp Meeting: Religion's Harvest Time* (Dallas: Southern Methodist University Press, 1955); Bernard A. Weisberger, *They Gathered at the River: The Story of the Great Revivalists and Their Impact upon Religion in America* (Boston: Little, Brown and Company, 1958); Dickson D. Bruce, *And They All Sang Hallelujah: Plain-Folk Camp-Meeting Religion, 1800-1845* (Knoxville: University of Tennessee Press, 1974); John B. Boles, *The Great Revival, 1787-1805;* and Whitney R. Cross, *The Burned-Over District.* The urban side of the evangelical movement is discussed in Charles I. Foster, "The Urban Missionary Movement, 1814-1837," *Pennsylvania Magazine of History and Biography,* LXXV (1951), 47-65; Richard Carwardine, "The Second Great Awakening in the Urban Centers: An Examination of Methodism and the 'New Measures,'" *Journal of American History,* LIX (1972-73), 327-340; Carroll Smith Rosenberg, *Religion and the Rise of the American City: The New York City Mission Movement 1812-1870* (Ithaca, N.Y.: Cornell University Press, 1971); Paul Boyer, *Urban Masses and Moral Order in America, 1820-1920* (Cambridge, Mass.: Harvard University Press, 1978); and, interestingly, Jay P. Dolan, *Catholic Revivalism: The American Experience, 1830-1900* (Notre Dame, Ind.: University of Notre Dame Press, 1978). The transatlantic character of the movement is discussed in Frank Thistlethwaite, *The Anglo-American Connection in the Early Nineteenth Century* (Philadelphia: University of Pennsylvania Press, 1959); Charles I. Foster, *An Errand of Mercy: The Evangelical United Front, 1790-1837* . (Chapel Hill: University of North Carolina Press, 1960); and Richard Carwardine, *Transatlantic Revivalism: Popular Evangelicalism in Britain and America, 1790-1865* (Westport, Conn.: Greenwood Press, 1978). With respect to the British side, Maurice J. Quinlan, *Victorian Prelude: A History of English Manners, 1700-1830* (New York: Columbia University Press, 1941); Ford K. Brown, *Fathers of the Victorians: The Age of Wilberforce* (Cambridge: Cambridge University Press, 1961); Paul Sangster, *Pity My Simplicity: The Evangelical Revival and the Religious Education of Children, 1738-1800* (London: The Epworth Press, 1963); John McLeisch, *Evangelical Religion and Popular Education: A Modern Interpretation* (London: Methuen & Co., 1969); J. M. Goldstrom, *The Social Content of Education, 1808-1870: A Study of the Working Class School Reader in England and Ireland* (Shannon: Irish University Press, 1972); and Thomas Walter Laqueur, *Religion and Respectability: Sunday Schools and Working Class Culture, 1780-1850* (New Haven: Yale University Press, 1976) are especially helpful.

The thought of the clergy on social issues is explicated in John R. Bodo, *The Protestant Clergy and Public Issues, 1812-1848* (Princeton, N.J.: Princeton University Press, 1954); Charles C. Cole, Jr., *The Social Ideas of the Northern Evangelists, 1826-1860* (New York: Columbia University Press, 1954); Walter Brownlow Posey, *Frontier Mission,* John Lee Eighmy, *Churches in Cultural Captivity: A History of the Social At-*

titudes of Southern Baptists (Knoxville: University of Tennessee Press, 1972), Conrad James Engelder, "The Churches and Slavery: A Study of the Attitudes Toward Slavery of the Major Protestant Denominations" (doctoral thesis, University of Michigan, 1964); Donald G. Mathews, *Slavery and Methodism: A Chapter in American Morality, 1780-1845* (Princeton, N.J.: Princeton University Press, 1965) and *Religion in the Old South;* and James H. Moorhead, *American Apocalypse: Yankee Protestants and the Civil War, 1860-1869* (New Haven: Yale University Press, 1978). The structure of denominationalism associated with evangelical Protestantism is discussed in Sidney Mead, *The Lively Experiment,* chap. vii; Martin Marty, *Righteous Empire,* chap. vii; Timothy L. Smith, "Congregation, State, and Denomination: The Forming of the American Religious Structure," *William and Mary Quarterly,* 3d ser., XXV (1968), 155-176; and Samuel C. Pearson, Jr., "From Church to Denomination: American Congregationalism in the Nineteenth Century," *Church History,* XXXVIII (1969), 67-87.

Emory Stevens Buckle, ed., *The History of American Methodism* (3 vols.; New York: Abingdon Press, 1964) is the standard work. It is usefully supplemented on the domestic side by John L. Peters, *Christian Perfection and American Methodism* (New York: Abingdon Press, 1956); Walter Brownlow Posey, *The Development of Methodism in the Old Southwest, 1783-1824* (Tuscaloosa, Ala.: Weatherford Printing Company, 1933); Wade C. Barclay *et al., History of Methodist Missions* (4+ vols.; New York: Board of Missions and Church Extension of the Methodist Church, 1949–), I; and Donald G. Mathews, "The Methodist Mission to the Slaves, 1829-1844," *Journal of American History,* LI (1964-65), 615-31; and on the transatlantic side by Robert F. Wearmouth, *Methodism and the Working-Class Movements of England, 1800-1850* (London: The Epworth Press, 1937) and *Methodism and the Common People of the Eighteenth Century* (London: The Epworth Press, 1945) and Bernard Semmel, *The Methodist Revolution* (New York: Basic Books, 1973). H. K. Carroll, *Francis Asbury in the Making of American Methodism* (New York: Methodist Book Concern, 1923); La Vere C. Rudolph, *Francis Asbury* (New York: Abingdon Press, 1966) and *The Journal and Letters of Francis Asbury,* edited by Elmer T. Clark *et al.* (3 vols.; Nashville, Tenn.: Abingdon Press, 1958) are the principal sources for Asbury's life and thought.

I found Donald G. Mathews, "The Second Great Awakening as an Organizing Process, 1780-1830: An Hypothesis," *American Quarterly,* XXI (1969), 23-43; drawing as it does upon T. Scott Miyakawa, *Protestants and Pioneers: Individualism and Conformity on the American Frontier* (Chicago: University of Chicago Press, 1964), a seminal work of synthesis. Edwin Scott Gaustad, *Historical Atlas of Religion in America* (New York: Harper & Row, 1962) and Nelson R. Burr *et al., A Critical Bibliography of Religion in America* (2 vols.; Princeton, N.J.: Princeton University Press, 1961) remain the standard reference sources.

The rise of interdenominational—or paradenominational—organizations is depicted in Charles I. Foster, *An Errand of Mercy* and Clifford S. Griffin, *Their Brothers' Keepers: Moral Stewardship in the United States, 1800-1865* (New Brunswick, N.J.: Rutgers University Press, 1960). The theological underpinnings of the organizational movement in the doctrine of "disinterested benevolence" are explicated by Oliver Wendell Elsbree, "Samuel Hopkins and His Doctrine of Benevolence," *New England Quarterly,* VIII (1935), 534-550; the theological underpinnings in a reformulated relationship between church and state are explicated in James Fulton Maclear, " 'The

True American Union' of Church and State: The Reconstruction of the Theocratic Tradition," *Church History*, XXVIII (1959), 41–62; the theological underpinnings in a conception of Christian unity are explicated in Lefferts A. Loetscher, "The Problem of Christian Unity in Early Nineteenth-Century America," *Church History*, XXXII (1963), 3–16. Griffin takes issue with the notions of disinterestedness and benevolence in "Religious Benevolence as Social Control, 1815–1860," *Mississippi Valley Historical Review*, XLVI (1957–58), 423–444; Lois W. Banner in turn takes issue with Griffin in "Religious Benevolence as Social Control: A Critique of an Interpretation," *Journal of American History*, LX (1973–74), 23–41. Foster includes a fairly comprehensive list of the societies on pp. 275–280 of his book.

Clifton Jackson Phillips, *Protestant America and the Pagan World: The First Half Century of the American Board of Commissioners for Foreign Missions, 1810–1860* (Cambridge, Mass.: Harvard University Press, 1969) is the standard history. The papers of the Board are at the Houghton Library at Harvard University and at the Congregational Library in Boston. Natalie Ann Naylor, "Raising a Learned Ministry: The American Education Society, 1815–1860" (doctoral thesis, Teachers College, Columbia University, 1971) is the standard history. David F. Allmendinger, Jr., *Paupers and Scholars: The Transformation of Student Life in Nineteenth-Century New England* (New York: St. Martin's Press, 1975) includes a substantial section on the American Education Society. The papers of the Society are at the Congregational Library in Boston. Henry Otis Dwight, *The Centennial History of the American Bible Society* (New York: The Macmillan Company, 1916) and John M. Gibson, *Soldiers of the Word: The Story of the American Bible Society* (New York: Philosophical Library, 1958) are celebratory accounts, with no scholarly apparatus, but they remain the fullest chronicles of events. The papers of the Society are at the Society's headquarters in New York City. Edwin Wilbur Rice, *The Sunday-School Movement and the American Sunday-School Union, 1780–1917* (Philadelphia: American Sunday-School Union, 1917) is uncritical but reliably informative. Anne Mary Boylan, " 'The Nursery of the Church': Evangelical Protestant Sunday Schools, 1820–1880" (doctoral thesis, University of Wisconsin, 1973) is a substantial scholarly study that includes a good deal on the ASSU. William Bean Kennedy, *The Shaping of Protestant Education: An Interpretation of the Sunday School and the Development of Protestant Educational Strategy in the United States, 1789–1860* (New York: Association Press, 1966) and Robert W. Lynn and Elliott Wright, *The Big Little School: Sunday Child of American Protestantism* (New York: Harper & Row, 1971) are brief interpretive studies of the movement, with the ASSU in the background. The papers of the Union are at the Presbyterian Historical Society in Philadelphia. Harvey George Neufeldt, "The American Tract Society, 1825–1865: An Examination of Its Religious, Economic, Social, and Political Ideas" (doctoral thesis, Michigan State University, 1971) is a substantial scholarly study. Most of the papers of the ATS were destroyed by fire years ago; those that remain are at the headquarters of the American Bible Society in New York City. Colin Brummitt Goodykoontz, *Home Missions on the American Frontier with Particular Reference to the American Home Missionary Society* (Caldwell, Idaho: The Caxton Printers, 1939) is uncritical but, again, informative. The papers of the AHMS are at the Chicago Theological Seminary Library. The English Dudley system for organizing and canvassing a rural region or urban neighborhood and its importation into the United States are discussed in Charles I. Foster, *An Errand of Mercy*. Foster also includes a description of the "great campaign" to "civilize" the West and save it from barbarism (and Catholicism), as do Ray Allen Billington, *The Protestant Crusade, 1800–1860: A Study of the Origins of American Nativism* (New York: The Macmillan Company, 1938); Richard Lyle Power, "A Crusade to Extend Yankee Culture, 1820–1865," *New England Quarterly*, XIII (1940), 638–653; and Malcolm Lyle Warford, "Piety Politics, and Pedagogy: An Evangelical Protestant Tradition in Higher Education at Lane, Oberlin, and Berea, 1834–1904 (doctoral thesis, Teachers College, Columbia University, 1973).

The evangelical thrust via the new childrearing literature is discussed in Anne L. Kuhn, *The Mother's Role in Childhood Education: New England Concepts, 1830–1860* (New Haven: Yale University Press, 1947); Robert Sunley, "Early Nineteenth-Century American Literature on Child Rearing," in Margaret Mead and Martha Wolfenstein, eds., *Childhood in Contemporary Cultures* (Chicago: University of Chicago Press, 1955), chap. ix; Bernard Wishy, *The Child and the Republic: The Dawn of Modern Child Nurture* (Philadelphia: University of Pennsylvania Press, 1968); Peter Gregg Slater, "Views of Children and of Child Rearing During the Early National Period: A Study in the New England Intellect" (doctoral thesis, University of California, Berkeley, 1970); Mary Patricia Ryan, "American Society and the Cult of Domesticity" (doctoral thesis, University of California, Santa Barbara, 1971); and Philip Greven, *The Protestant Temperament: Patterns of Child-Rearing, Religious Experience, and the Self in Early America* (New York: Alfred A. Knopf, 1977).

The evangelical thrust via the Sunday school is depicted in Anne Mary Boylan, "'The Nursery of the Church': Evangelical Protestant Sunday Schools, 1820–1880"; William Bean Kennedy, *The Shaping of Protestant Education;* and Robert W. Lynn and Elliott Wright, *The Big Little School.* The close interrelationship between Sunday schools and public schools is developed in David Marion McCord, "Sunday School and Public School: An Exploration of Their Relationship with Special Reference to Indiana, 1790–1860" (doctoral thesis, Purdue University, 1976).

Curiously, the public schools have been traditionally portrayed as less related to the evangelical Protestant movement than they actually were, while the colleges have been traditionally portrayed as more exclusively related to the evangelical Protestant movement than they actually were. A traditional view of the public schools is presented in my own work, *The American Common School: An Historic Conception* (New York: Bureau of Publications, Teachers College, Columbia University, 1951); the sense of separation between the public school movement and nondenominational Protestantism conveyed there doubtless derives from a tendency to read twentieth-century distinctions between the public and the private back into the nineteenth, a tendency supported by the overgeneralization of Horace Mann's wars with the Protestant clergy in Massachusetts to the rest of the country. A traditional view of the colleges is presented in Donald G. Tewksbury, *The Founding of American Colleges and Universities Before the Civil War* (New York: Bureau of Publications, Teachers College, Columbia University, 1932); the sense of close relationship between the denominations and the colleges conveyed there probably derives from a similar tendency to read twentieth-century distinctions between the public and the private back into the nineteenth. The corrective to the traditional view of public schooling is provided in Timothy L. Smith, "Protestant Schooling and American Nationality, 1800–1850," *Journal of American History*, LIII (1966–67), 679–795, and David Tyack, "The Kingdom of God and the Common

School," *Harvard Educational Review,* XXXVI (1966), 447–469; while the corrective to the traditional view of the colleges is provided in David B. Potts, "American Colleges in the Nineteenth Century: From Localism to Denominationalism," *History of Education Quarterly,* XI (1971), 363–380, and "'College Enthusiasm!' as Public Response, 1800–1860," *Harvard Educational Review,* XLVII (1977), 28–42. In both instances, of course, the intellectual thrust of the correctives derives from a fuller understanding of nineteenth-century nondenominational Protestantism and its relation to the public life of the nation.

For the founding of the YMCA, see Charles Howard Hopkins, *History of the Y.M.C.A. in North America* (New York: Association Press, 1951) and Paul Boyer, *Urban Masses and Moral Order in America, 1820–1920.* Evangelicism was also a significant factor in the founding of rehabilitative and custodial institutions, which are discussed in W. David Lewis, *From Newgate to Dannemora: The Rise of the Penitentiary in New York, 1796–1838* (Ithaca, N.Y.: Cornell University Press, 1965); Robert S. Pickett, *House of Refuge: Origins of Juvenile Reform in New York State, 1815–1857* (Syracuse, N.Y.: Syracuse University Press, 1969); David J. Rothman, *The Discovery of the Asylum: Social Order and Disorder in the New Republic* (Boston: Little, Brown and Company, 1971); Joseph M. Hawes, *Children in Urban Society: Juvenile Delinquency in Nineteenth-Century America* (New York: Oxford University Press, 1971); Gerald N. Grob, *Mental Institutions in America: Social Policy to 1875* (New York: The Free Press, 1973); Robert M. Mennel, *Thorns & Thistles: Juvenile Delinquents in the United States, 1825–1940* (Hanover, N.H.: The University Press of New England, 1973); and Steven L. Schlossman, *Love and the American Delinquent: The Theory and Practice of "Progressive" Juvenile Justice, 1825–1920* (Chicago: University of Chicago Press, 1977). For the notion of spiritualizing the factory, see Thomas Bender, *Toward an Urban Vision: Ideas and Institutions in Nineteenth-Century America* (Lexington: The University Press of Kentucky, 1975).

The similarities and overlaps in the materials used in the Sunday schools and public schools and circulated by the American Tract Society are best discerned, of course, by perusing the materials themselves, which are widely available in the original. The values expounded by the materials prepared by the American Sunday-School Union are set forth in Edwin Wilbur Rice, *The Sunday-School Movement and the American Sunday-School Union, 1780–1917.* It should be borne in mind, however, as noted in David Marion McCord, "Sunday School and Public School: An Exploration of Their Relationship with Special Reference to Indiana, 1790–1860," that the full range of materials or even part of it was not always available to individual Sunday schools. The way in which the materials were taught, with emphasis on the stimulation of conversion, is discussed in Anne Mary Boylan, "'The Nursery of the Church': Evangelical Protestant Sunday Schools, 1820–1880." The British origins of the Sunday-school literature are illuminated by Paul Sangster, *Pity My Simplicity: The Evangelical Revival and the Religious Education of Children, 1738–1800.* The values conveyed by the materials prepared by the American Tract Society are set forth in Harvey George Neufeldt, "The American Tract Society, 1825–1865: An Examination of Its Religious, Economic, Social, and Political Ideas."

There is a considerable literature on the McGuffeys and the McGuffey readers. William Holmes McGuffey compiled the first four readers; his brother Alexander Hamilton McGuffey compiled the fifth and sixth. James Arnold Scully, "A Biography of William Holmes McGuffey" (doctoral thesis, University of Cincinnati, 1967) is a scholarly work; Alice McGuffey Ruggles, *The Story of the McGuffeys* (New York: American Book Company, 1950) is more popular. Harvey C. Minnich, *William Holmes McGuffey and His Readers* (New York: American Book Company, 1936); Richard D. Mosier, *Making the American Mind: Social and Moral Ideas in the McGuffey Readers* (New York: King's Crown Press, 1947); Robert Wood Lynn, "Civil Catechetics in Mid-Victorian America: Some Notes About American Civil Religion, Past and Present," *Religious Education*, LXVIII (1973), 5–27; and John H. Westerhoff III, *McGuffey and His Readers: Piety, Morality, and Education in Nineteenth-Century America* (Nashville: Abingdon, 1978) are analyses of the substance of the readers. The Westerhoff study includes a systematic content analysis of the first four readers and is the most effective of the four in locating the readers within the evangelical tradition. The Mosier study, given its title, elicited a sharp critique by Philip D. Jordan in the *American Historical Review*, LIII (1947–48), 569, of the so-called McGuffey myth, propagated above all by Mark Sullivan in the second volume of *Our Times: The United States, 1900–1925* (6 vols.; New York: Charles Scribner's Sons, 1926–1935), to the effect that the readers had shaped the American mind and character. It was rather the other way around, Jordan averred: the American mind had shaped the readers. The debate, of course, raised the perennial chicken-egg question. The readers alone did not shape the American mind; nor, however, were they uninfluential, particularly insofar as, in concert with similar materials circulated by other institutions, they nurtured and sustained the values and outlooks of the dominant American *paideia* of their time. Put otherwise, Jordan's argument and Mosier's have been incorporated into my own. Stanley W. Lindberg, *The Annotated McGuffey: Selections from the McGuffey Eclectic Readers, 1836–1920* (New York: Van Nostrand Reinhold Company, 1976) explores the changing content of the readers over the years and traces the origins of many of the commonplaces that were included. The best collection of McGuffeyiana is at Miami University, Oxford, Ohio, where there is also a McGuffey museum.

For the more general context of nineteenth-century children's literature, Rosalie V. Halsey, *Forgotten Books of the American Nursery: A History of the Development of the American Storybook* (Boston: Goodspeed, 1911); A. S. W. Rosenbach, *Early American Children's Books* (1933; reprint ed.; New York: Kraus Reprint Corporation, 1966); Monica Kiefer, *American Children Through Their Books, 1700–1835* (Philadelphia: University of Pennsylvania Press, 1948); John Nietz, *Old Textbooks* (Pittsburgh: University of Pittsburgh Press, 1961); Charles Carpenter, *History of American Schoolbooks* (Philadelphia: University of Pennsylvania Press, 1963); Ruth Miller Elson, *Guardians of Tradition: American Schoolbooks of the Nineteenth Century* (Lincoln: University of Nebraska Press, 1964); and F. J. Harvey Darton, *Children's Books in England: Five Centuries of Social Life* (Cambridge: Cambridge University Press, 1966) are useful sources.

CHAPTER 3: MODES OF SECTARIANISM

The best scholarly review of the various communitarian experiments of the first two-thirds of the nineteenth century remains Alice Felt Tyler, *Freedom's Ferment: Phases of American Social History to 1860* (Minneapolis: University of Minnesota Press,

1944). Characteristically for the era during which she wrote, Tyler divided her section on "Cults and Utopias" into a first part, on religious communities, and a second part, on socialist communities. The more recent reinterpretation of communitarian striving arising from studies of millennialism reveals the distinction to be artificial; hence, my grouping of New Harmony, Fruitlands, and the Great Basin Kingdom in a single chapter as "modes of sectarianism." Arthur Eugene Bestor, Jr., *Backwoods Utopias: The Sectarian and Owenite Phases of Communitarian Socialism in America, 1663–1829* (Philadelphia: University of Pennsylvania Press, 1950) and "Patent-Office Models of the Good Society: Some Relationships Between Social Reform and Westward Expansion," *American Historical Review*, LVIII (1952–53), 505–526, are illuminating, as are a succession of more popular works from John Humphrey Noyes, *History of American Socialisms* (1870; reprint ed.; New York: Hillary House, 1961) to Everett Webber, *Escape to Utopia: The Communal Movement in America* (New York: Hastings House Publishers, 1959). Frank E. Manuel, ed., *Utopias and Utopian Thought* (Boston: Houghton Mifflin Company, 1966) is a useful collection of essays.

The best work on the Owenite movement as a transatlantic phenomenon is J. F. C. Harrison, *Quest for the New Moral World: Robert Owen and the Owenites in Britain and America* (New York: Charles Scribner's Sons, 1969), which includes a comprehensive scholarly bibliography. Archibald Muir Black, "The Educational Work of Robert Owen" (doctoral thesis, St. Andrews University, 1949); Arthur Eugene Bestor, Jr., *Backwoods Utopias;* and Harold Silver, *The Concept of Popular Education: A Study of Ideas and Social Movements in the Early Nineteenth Century* (London: Macgibbon & Kee, 1965) discuss Owen's views and the experiments at New Lanark. Frank Podmore, *Robert Owen: A Biography* (2 vols.; London: Hutchinson, 1906); G. D. H. Cole, *Robert Owen* (Boston: Little, Brown and Company, 1925); Roland Hill Harvey, *Robert Owen: Social Idealist* (Berkeley: University of California Press, 1949); and Margaret Cole, *Robert Owen of New Lanark, 1771–1858* (London: Batchworth Press, 1953) are useful biographies. *The Life of Robert Owen, Written by Himself* (2 vols.; London: Effingham, Wilson, 1857–1858) is an autobiography, with an appendix reprinting Owen's publications to 1820. Robert Owen, *A New View of Society and Other Writings,* edited by G. D. H. Cole (London: J. M. Dent & Sons, 1927); John F. C. Harrison, ed., *Utopianism and Education: Robert Owen and the Owenites* (New York: Teachers College Press, 1968); and Harold Silver, *Robert Owen on Education* (Cambridge: Cambridge University Press, 1969) are convenient selections of Owen's writings. Kate Silber, *Pestalozzi: The Man and His Work* (London: Routledge and Kegan Paul, 1960) and Hugh M. Pollard, *Pioneers of Popular Education, 1760–1850* (Cambridge, Mass.: Harvard University Press, 1957) explicate the work at Hofwyl that made such a profound impression on Owen. Donald E. Pitzer, ed., *Robert Owen's American Legacy* (Indianapolis: Indiana Historical Society, 1972), the published proceedings of the Robert Owen Bicentennial Conference, held in 1971 at New Harmony in celebration of the two hundredth anniversary of Owen's birth, is a first-class collection of historical assessments.

Beyond Harrison's *Quest for a New Moral World* and Bestor's *Backwoods Utopias,* the best sources for the New Harmony experiment are George G. Lockwood, *The New Harmony Movement* (1905; reprint ed.; New York: Dover Publications, 1971) and William E. Wilson, *The Angel and the Serpent: The Story of New Harmony* (Bloomington: Indiana University Press, 1964). Karl J. R. Arndt, *George Rapp's Harmony*

Society, 1785–1847 (Philadelphia: University of Pennsylvania Press, 1965) is a scholarly account of the Rappites, from whom Owen purchased New Harmony. Richard William Leopold, *Robert Dale Owen* (Cambridge, Mass.: Harvard University Press, 1940) and Keith Heathcote Thompson, "The Educational Work of Robert Dale Owen" (doctoral thesis, University of California, Berkeley, 1948) are the best sources for the life and work of Owen's eldest son. Robert Dale Owen, *Threading My Way: Twenty-Seven Years of Autobiography* (New York: G. W. Carleton, 1874) is illuminating not only for Owen but also for New Harmony. There is an excellent collection of documents relating to the New Harmony experiment, including the *New-Harmony Gazette*, the *New-Harmony and Nashoba Gazette*, and the *Disseminator of Useful Knowledge*, and a substantial collection of Robert Dale Owen papers, at the Workingmen's Institute at New Harmony. Other collections of Robert Dale Owen papers are at the Indiana Historical Society and the Purdue University Library.

Harvey L. Carter, "William Maclure," *Indiana Magazine of History*, XXXI (1935), 83–91; J. Percy Moore, "William Maclure—Scientist and Humanitarian," *Proceedings of the American Philosophical Society*, XLI (1947), 234–249; W. H. G. Armytage, "William Maclure, 1763–1840: A British Interpretation," *Indiana Magazine of History*, XLVII (1951), 1–20; and William Frank Kipnis, "Propagating the Pestalozzian: The Story of William Maclure's Involvement in Efforts to Affect Educational and Social Reforms in the Early Nineteenth Century" (doctoral thesis, Loyola University of Chicago, 1972) are informative on Maclure, as is Arthur Eugene Bestor, Jr., ed., "Education and Reform at New Harmony: Correspondence of William Maclure and Marie Duclos Fretageot, 1820–1833," *Indiana Historical Society Publications*, XV (1948), 283–417. William Maclure, *Opinions on Various Subjects, Dedicated to the Industrious Producers* (3 vols.; New Harmony, Ind.: printed at the school press, 1831–1838) is an edition of Maclure's writings, taken largely from the *Disseminator of Useful Knowledge*. The work of Maclure and of Joseph Neef at New Harmony is discussed in Charles Orville Burgess, "The Educational State in America: Selected Views on Learning as the Key to Utopia, 1800–1924" (doctoral thesis, University of Wisconsin, 1962); Thomas A. Barlow, "Channels of Pestalozzianism into the United States" (doctoral thesis, University of Kansas, 1963); and Gerald Lee Gutek, *Joseph Neef: The Americanization of Pestalozzianism* (Tuscaloosa: The University of Alabama Press, 1978).

The subsequent history of Robert Dale Owen's ideas during the late 1820's and the 1830's and 1840's can be found in Richard William Leopold, *Robert Dale Owen;* Keith Heathcote Thompson, "The Educational Work of Robert Dale Owen"; Lawrence A. Cremin, *The American Common School: An Historic Conception* (New York: Bureau of Publications, Teachers College, Columbia University, 1951); and Rush Welter, *Popular Education and Democratic Thought in America* (New York: Columbia University Press, 1962).

The definitive biography of Amos Bronson Alcott is Odell Shepard, *Pedlar's Progress: The Life of Bronson Alcott* (Boston: Little, Brown and Company, 1937). Alcott's educational ideas are set forth in George E. Haefner, *A Critical Estimate of the Educational Theories and Practices of A. Bronson Alcott* (New York: Columbia University Press, 1937); Dorothy McCuskey, *Bronson Alcott, Teacher* (New York: The Macmillan Company, 1940); and David B. Ripley, "The Educational Ideas, Implementations and Influences of A. Bronson Alcott" (doctoral thesis, University of Iowa, 1971). Alcott's child-rearing practices, including his remarkable journals of the development of his elder daughters, Anna and Louisa May, are depicted in Charles Strickland, "A Transcendentalist Father: The Child Rearing Practices of Bronson Alcott," *Perspectives in American History*, III (1969), 5–73. His work at the Temple School during the 1830's is described in [Elizabeth Peabody], *Record of a School: Exemplifying the General Principles of Spiritual Culture* (2d ed.; Boston: Russell, Shattuck & Company, 1836) and his own *Conversations with Children on the Gospels* (2 vols.; Boston: James Munroe, 1836–1837). And his efforts as superintendent of the Concord, Massachusetts, public schools between 1859 and 1865 (at an annual salary of $100) are documented in his reports reprinted in Amos Bronson Alcott, *Essays on Education (1830–1862)*, edited by Walter Harding (Gainesville, Fla.: Scholar's Facsimiles & Reprints, 1960). Odell Shepard, ed., *The Journal of Bronson Alcott* (Boston: Little, Brown and Company, 1938) and Richard Herrnstadt, ed., *The Letters of A. Bronson Alcott* (2 vols.; Ames: Iowa State University Press, 1969) present selections from Alcott's voluminous papers; the papers themselves are at the Houghton Library at Harvard University.

Alcott's critically important friendship with Ralph Waldo Emerson is described in Hubert Hoeltje, *Sheltering Tree: A Story of the Friendship of Ralph Waldo Emerson and Amos Bronson Alcott* (Durham, N.C.: Duke University Press, 1943) and H. Burnell Pannill, "Bronson Alcott: Emerson's 'Tedious Archangel,' " in Stuart C. Henry, ed., *A Miscellany of American Christianity: Essays in Honor of H. Shelton Smith* (Durham, N.C.: Duke University Press, 1963), pp. 225–247. Alcott's place in the Transcendentalist movement is discussed in Octavius Brooks Frothingham, *Transcendentalism in New England* [1876] (reprint ed.; New York: Harper & Brothers, 1959); F. O. Matthiessen, *American Renaissance: Art and Expression in the Age of Emerson and Whitman* (London: Oxford University Press, 1941); Perry Miller, ed., *The Transcendentalists: An Anthology* (Cambridge, Mass.: Harvard University Press, 1950); Frederick I. Carpenter, *American Literature and the Dream* (New York: Philosophical Library, 1955); William R. Hutchinson, *The Transcendentalist Ministers: Church Reform in the New England Renaissance* (New Haven: Yale University Press, 1959); Herbert W. Schneider, *A History of American Philosophy* (2d ed.; New York: Columbia University Press, 1963); Lawrence Buell, *Literary Transcendentalism: Style and Vision in the American Renaissance* (Ithaca, N.Y.: Cornell University Press, 1973); and Elizabeth Flower and Murray G. Murphy, *A History of Philosophy in America* (2 vols.; New York: Capricorn Books, 1977). The experiment at Fruitlands is dealt with in Franklin B. Sanborn, *Bronson Alcott at Alcott House, England and Fruitlands, New England (1842–1844)* (Cedar Rapids, Iowa: Torch Press, 1908) and Clara Endicott Sears, ed., *Bronson Alcott's Fruitlands* (Boston: Houghton Mifflin and Company, 1915). For Louisa May Alcott, see Martha Saxton, *Louisa May: A Modern Biography of Louisa May Alcott* (Boston: Houghton Mifflin Company, 1977).

The classic history of the Mormons is B. H. Roberts, *Comprehensive History of the Church of Jesus Christ of Latter-day Saints* (6 vols.: Salt Lake City, Utah: published by the Church, 1930). It is celebratory but rich in reliable information and detail. Davis Britton, "B. H. Roberts as Historian," *Dialogue: A Journal of Mormon Thought* (1968), 25–44, is a sympathetic but critical review. During the half-century since Roberts published his work, and particularly during the last twenty-five years, there has been an impressive flow of revisionist historical scholarship, originating from both within the fold and without. Marvin S. Hill, "The Historiography of Mormonism," *Church History* (1959), 418–426; Leonard J. Arrington, "Scholarly Studies of Mormonism in the Twentieth Century," *Dialogue*, I (1966), 15–32; "Reappraisals of Mormon History," *ibid.*, vol. I, no. 3 (Autumn, 1966), pp. 23–134; and the continuing reviews of the literature in *Dialogue* are helpful guides to the new material.

Among the works that have been most valuable for my own studies are Ephraim Edward Ericksen, *The Psychological and Ethical Aspects of Mormon Group Life* (Chicago: University of Chicago Press, 1922); Lowry Nelson, "The Mormon Village: A Study in Social Origins," *Proceedings of the Utah Academy of Sciences*, VII (1930), 11–37; William J. McNiff, *Heaven on Earth: A Planned Mormon Society* (Oxford, Ohio: The Mississippi Valley Press, 1940); Fawn M. Brodie, *No Man Knows My History: The Life of Joseph Smith* (2d ed., rev.; New York: Alfred A. Knopf, 1971); David Brion Davis, "The New England Origins of Mormonism," *The New England Quarterly*, XXVI (1953), 147–168, Kimball Young, *Isn't One Wife Enough?* (New York: Henry Holt and Company, 1954); Stanley S. Ivins, "Notes on Mormon Polygamy," *Western Humanities Review*, X (1956), 229–239; Thomas F. O'Dea, *The Mormons* (Chicago: University of Chicago Press, 1957); Leonard J. Arrington, *Great Basin Kingdom: An Economic History of the Latter-day Saints, 1830–1900* (Cambridge, Mass.: Harvard University Press, 1958); Sterling M. McMurrin, *The Theological Foundations of the Mormon Religion* (Salt Lake City: University of Utah Press, 1965); Robert Bruce Flanders, *Nauvoo: Kingdom on the Mississippi* (Urbana: University of Illinois Press, 1965); Klaus J. Hansen, *Quest for Empire: The Political Kingdom of God and the Council of Fifty in Mormon History* (Lansing: Michigan State University Press, 1967); Leonard J. Arrington, Feramorz Y. Fox, and Dean L. May, *Building the City of God: Community & Cooperation among the Mormons* (Salt Lake City, Utah: Deseret Book Company, 1976); and J. F. C. Harrison, *The Second Coming: Popular Millenarianism, 1780–1850* (New Brunswick, N. J.; Rutgers University Press, 1979).

The fullest printed collection of documents relating to the early Mormons is *The History of the Church of Jesus Christ of Latter-day Saints: Period I, History of Joseph Smith, by himself,* with an introduction and notes by B. H. Roberts (6 vols., Salt Lake City, Utah: published by the Church, 1902). William Mulder and A. Russell Mortenson, eds., *Among the Mormons: Historic Accounts by Contemporary Observers* (New York: Alfred A. Knopf, 1958) is a convenient modern collection of primary sources. Marvin S. Hill and James B. Allen, eds., *Mormonism and American Culture* (New York: Harper & Row, 1972) is an excellent collection of interpretive articles. The principal collection of papers relating to the early history of the Mormons is at the Church Archives of The Church of Jesus Christ of Latter-day Saints in Salt Lake City, Utah.

INTRODUCTION TO PART II: THE VIRTUOUS REPUBLIC

As mentioned above, the commonplaces of republican argument with respect to education are discussed in Frederick Rudolph, ed., *Essays on Education in the Early Republic* (Cambridge, Mass.: Harvard University Press, 1965); Eva T. H. Brann, *Paradoxes of Education in a Republic* (Chicago: University of Chicago Press, 1979); David Tyack, "Forming the National Character: Paradox in the Educational Thought of the Revolutionary Generation," *Harvard Educational Review*, XXXVI (1966), 29–41; Jonathan Messerli, "The Columbian Complex: The Impulse to National Consolidation," *History of Education Quarterly*, VII (1967), 417–431; Linda K. Kerber, "Daughters of Columbia: Educating Women for the Republic, 1787–1805," in Stanley Elkins and Eric

McKitrick, eds., *The Hofstadter Aegis: A Memorial* (New York: Alfred A. Knopf, 1974); Victor Daniel Brooks, Jr., "Education and Politics in the New Nation—A Study of the Educational Policies of the Federalists" (doctoral thesis, University of Pennsylvania, 1974); Daniel J. Boorstin, *The Lost World of Thomas Jefferson* (New York: Henry Holt and Company, 1948); and Allen O. Hansen, *Liberalism and American Education in the Eighteenth Century* (New York: The Macmillan Company, 1926). A convenient summary is given in Russel Blaine Nye, *The Cultural Life of the New Nation, 1776–1830* (New York: Harper & Brothers, 1960). The best sources for the more general political thought of the Revolutionary generation are Gordon S. Wood, *The Creation of the American Republic, 1776–1787* (Chapel Hill: University of North Carolina Press, 1969) and Gerald Stourzh, *Alexander Hamilton and the Idea of Republican Government* (Stanford, Calif.: Stanford University Press, 1970); both, interestingly, pay only slight attention to education, which loomed large in the political theory of the Revolutionary generation. The best source for the millennial strain in the political thought of the Revolutionary generation is Ernest Lee Tuveson, *Redeemer Nation: The Life of America's Millennial Role* (Chicago: University of Chicago Press, 1968).

CHAPTER 4: REPUBLICAN CIVILITIES

The definitive biography of Thomas Jefferson is Dumas Malone, *Jefferson and His Time* (5+ vols.; Boston: Little, Brown and Company, 1948–   ); Merrill D. Peterson, *Thomas Jefferson & the New Nation: A Biography* (New York: Oxford University Press, 1970) is the best one-volume life. *Autobiography of Thomas Jefferson,* with an introduction by Dumas Malone (New York: Capricorn Books, 1959) is a convenient edition. *The Papers of Thomas Jefferson,* edited by Julian Boyd et al. (19+ vols.; Princeton, N.J.: Princeton University Press, 1950–   ) promises to be the standard edition. Meanwhile, these remain useful: *The Writings of Thomas Jefferson,* edited by Paul Leicester Ford (10 vols.; New York: G. P. Putnam's Sons, 1892–1899); *The Writings of Thomas Jefferson,* edited by Andrew A. Lipscomb and Albert Ellery Bergh (20 vols.; Washington, D.C.: Thomas Jefferson Memorial Association, 1903–1904); Saul K. Padover, ed., *The Complete Jefferson* (New York: Tudor Publishing Company, 1943); and Philip S. Foner, ed., *Basic Writings of Thomas Jefferson* (New York: Willey Book Company, 1944). *Correspondence Between Thomas Jefferson and Pierre Samuel Du Pont de Nemours, 1798–1817,* edited by Dumas Malone (Boston: Houghton Mifflin Company, 1930) and *The Adams-Jefferson Letters: The Complete Correspondence Between Thomas Jefferson and Abigail and John Adams,* edited by Lester J. Cappon (2 vols.; Chapel Hill: University of North Carolina Press, 1959) are important, more limited collections. Gilbert Chinard, *Jefferson et les Ideologues d'après Sa Correspondence Inedité avec Destutt de Tracy, Cabanis, J.-B. Say, et Auguste Comte,* The Johns Hopkins Studies in Literatures and Languages, extra vol. I (Baltimore: The Johns Hopkins University Press, 1925) is excellent for the French motif in Jefferson's thought. Adrienne Koch, *The Philosophy of Thomas Jefferson* (New York: Columbia University Press, 1943) deals incisively with Jefferson's thought, devoting appropriate attention to the French influence; and, given that influence, Emmet Kennedy, *A Philosopher in the Age of Revolution: Destutt de Tracy and the Origins of "Ideology"* (Philadelphia: American Philosophical Society, 1978) is especially relevant.

Roy J. Honeywell, *The Educational Work of Thomas Jefferson* (Cambridge,

Mass.: Harvard University Press, 1931); James B. Conant, *Thomas Jefferson and the Development of American Public Education* (Berkeley: University of California Press, 1962), and Robert D. Heslep, *Thomas Jefferson & Education* (New York: Random House, 1969) are useful studies of Jefferson's thought and activities with respect to the schools and the University of Virginia. *Early History of the University of Virginia as Contained in the Letters of Thomas Jefferson and Joseph C. Cabell* (Richmond.: T. W. Randolph, 1856) is especially illuminating with respect to the university. R. Freeman Butts, *The American Tradition in Religion and Education* (Boston: Beacon Press, 1951) is useful on Jefferson's thought and activities with respect to the establishment of religion. And Frank Luther Mott, *Jefferson and the Press* (Baton Rouge: Louisiana State University Press, 1943) is useful on Jefferson's thought and activities with respect to the press. It is interesting to contrast Conant's interpretation with that of Rush Welter in *Popular Education and Democratic Thought in America* (New York: Columbia University Press, 1962) on the question of Jefferson's elitism. Gordon C. Lee, ed., *Crusade Against Ignorance: Thomas Jefferson on Education* (New York: Teachers College Press, 1961) is a convenient collection of documents.

Bernard W. Sheehan, *Seeds of Extinction: Jeffersonian Philanthropy and the American Indian* (Chapel Hill: University of North Carolina Press, 1973); William Cohen, "Thomas Jefferson and the Problem of Slavery," *Journal of American History*, LVI (1969-70), 503-526; and Frederick M. Binder, *The Color Problem in Early National America as Viewed by John Adams, Jefferson, and Jackson* (The Hague: Mouton, 1968) discuss Jefferson's attitudes toward the education of Indians and blacks. Charles Maurice Wiltse, *The Jeffersonian Tradition in American Democracy* (Chapel Hill: University of North Carolina Press, 1935) and Merrill D. Peterson, *The Jeffersonian Image in the American Mind* (New York: Oxford University Press, 1960) trace the continuing relevance of Jeffersonian ideas and American perceptions of that relevance. The chief collections of Jefferson papers are at the Library of Congress, the University of Virginia, and the Massachusetts Historical Society.

The best biography of Benjamin Rush remains Nathan G. Goodman, *Benjamin Rush: Physician and Citizen, 1746-1813* (Philadelphia: University of Pennsylvania Press, 1934). Among the more recent works, Carl Binger, *Revolutionary Doctor: Benjamin Rush, 1746-1813* (New York: W. W. Norton & Company, 1966) stresses Rush's role as a physician; David Freeman Hawke, *Benjamin Rush: Revolutionary Gadfly* (Indianapolis: The Bobbs Merrill Company, 1971) stresses his role in the politics of the Revolutionary era; and Donald J. D'Elia, *Benjamin Rush: Philosopher of the American Revolution* (Philadelphia: The American Philosophical Society, 1974) stresses the development of his thought. *The Autobiography of Benjamin Rush,* edited by George W. Corner (Princeton, N.J.: Princeton University Press, 1948) brings together his "Travels Through Life" and his commonplace book. *Letters of Benjamin Rush,* edited by L. H. Butterfield (2 vols.; Princeton, N.J.: Princeton University Press, 1951) brings together his correspondence; and John A. Schutz and Douglass Adair, eds., *The Spur of Fame: Dialogues of John Adams and Benjamin Rush, 1805-1813* (San Marino, Calif.: The Huntington Library, 1966) brings together the appropriate letters from the Butterfield collection with Adams's replies.

James A. Bonar, "Benjamin Rush and the Theory and Practice of Republican Education in Pennsylvania" (doctoral thesis, The Johns Hopkins University, 1965) is the best introduction to Rush's efforts in education, though it concentrates heavily on his role in the founding of Dickinson College. L. H. Butterfield, "Benjamin Rush and the Beginnings of 'John and Mary's College' over Susquehanna," in *Bulwark of Liberty: Early Years at Dickinson: The Boyd Lee Spahr Lectures in Americana* (New York: Fleming H. Revell Company, 1950), I, (1947–1950), 29–53, and "Benjamin Rush as a Promoter of Useful Knowledge," *Proceedings of the American Philosophical Society*, XCII (1948), 26–36; Donald J. D'Elia, "Benjamin Rush, America's Philosopher of Revolutionary Education," in *The Boyd Lee Spahr Lectures in Americana* (York, Pa.: York Composition Company, 1970), IV (1962–1969), 57–82, "The Republican Theology of Benjamin Rush," *Pennsylvania History*, XXX (1966), 187–203, and "Jefferson, Rush, and the Limits of Philosophical Friendship," *Proceedings of the American Philosophical Society*, CXVII (1973), 333–343; and Hyman Kuritz, "Benjamin Rush: His Theory of Republican Education," *History of Education Quarterly*, VII (1967), 432–451, are also helpful. Harry G. Good, *Benjamin Rush and His Services to American Education* (Berne, Ind.: Witness Press, 1918) and Dagobert D. Runes, ed., *The Selected Writings of Benjamin Rush* (New York: Philosophical Library, 1947) are convenient selections of writings. The Rush papers are at the Historical Society of Pennsylvania.

For many years, the standard reference on the early plans for a national system of education was Allen Oscar Hansen, *Liberalism and American Education in the Eighteenth Century* (New York: The Macmillan Company, 1926), which includes a substantial section on the activities of the American Philosophical Society on behalf of a national system. The work presents a simplistic view of American republicanism, however, and confines its attention with respect to the Society's contest of 1795 to the winning plans of Samuel Knox and Samuel Harrison Smith. More recently, Frederick Rudolph included the Knox and Smith plans in *Essays on Education in the Early Republic* (Cambridge, Mass.: Harvard University Press, 1965), along with the roughly contemporary plans of Benjamin Rush, Noah Webster, Robert Coram, Simeon Doggett, and Amable-Louis-Rose de Lafitte du Corteil; but, again, he chose to give no attention to the other plans that were submitted in the Society's contest.

The development of the Society during the eighteenth century is recounted in Brooke Hindle, *The Pursuit of Science in Revolutionary America, 1735–1789* (Chapel Hill: University of North Carolina Press, 1956) and "The Rise of the American Philosophical Society, 1776–1787" (doctoral thesis, University of Pennsylvania, 1949); Gilbert Chinard, "The American Philosophical Society and the World of Science (1768–1800)," *Proceedings of the American Philosophical Society*, LXXXVI (1942–43), 91–102; Carl Van Doren, "The Beginnings of the American Philosophical Society," *ibid.*, 277–289; and Linda K. Kerber, *Federalists in Dissent: Imagery and Ideology in Jeffersonian America* (Ithaca, N.Y.: Cornell University Press, 1970). The plans submitted in response to the contest of 1795 are in the library of the American Philosophical Society. Merle M. Odgers discusses the several plans, along with the educational ideas of Jefferson, Du Pont de Nemours, Rush, Coram, and Lafitte du Corteil in "Education and the American Philosophical Society," *Proceedings of the American Philosophical Society*, LXXXVII (1943–44), 12–24; David Madsen discusses the contemporary proposals for a national university in *The National University: Enduring Dream of the USA* (Detroit: Wayne State University Press, 1966). Ashley Foster, "The Educational Views of Samuel Knox" (doctoral thesis, New York University, 1951) and Seymour Brostoff, "The Social and Political Views of Samuel Harrison Smith" (doctoral thesis, New York University, 1951) are informative studies of the two winners. Pierre Samuel Du Pont de Nemours's plan is printed as Du Pont de Nemours, *National Education in the United States of America,* translated by B. G. Du Pont (Newark, Del.: University of Delaware Press, 1923). Ambrose Saricks, *Pierre Samuel Du Pont de Nemours* (Lawrence: University of Kansas Press, 1965) is a recent biography. My arguments with respect to a republican style in education also draw upon the data and conclusions in Daniel Jules Booth, "Popular Educational Thought of the Early National Period in America, 1776-1830: A Survey and Analysis of Published Essays and Addresses" (doctoral thesis, University of Colorado, 1974).

The standard biography of Adam Smith remains John Rae, *Life of Adam Smith* (1895), with an introduction by Jacob Viner (New York: Augustus M. Kelley, 1965). C. R. Fay, *Adam Smith and the Scotland of His Day* (Cambridge: Cambridge University Press, 1956) and E. G. West, *Adam Smith* (New Rochelle, N.Y.: Arlington House, 1969) are also useful. J. Ralph Lindgren, *The Social Philosophy of Adam Smith* (The Hague: Martinus Nyhoff, 1973); Samuel Hollander, *The Economics of Adam Smith* (Toronto: University of Toronto Press, 1973); D. A. Riesman, *Adam Smith's Sociological Economics* (London: Croom Helm, 1976); and Charles Flinn Arrowood, *The Theory of Education in the Political Philosophy of Adam Smith* (Austin, Tex.: privately printed, 1945) discuss Smith's social and educational theories. The essays in Fred R. Glahe, ed., *Adam Smith and the Wealth of Nations, 1776-1976* (Boulder: Colorado Associated University Press, 1976) undertake a bicentennial appraisal. Adam Smith, *An Inquiry into the Nature and Causes of the Wealth of Nations,* edited by Edwin Cannan (New York: Random House, 1937) is a convenient edition. For Bernard Mandeville's ideas and their influence on British educational thought and practice, see Bernard Mandeville, *The Fable of the Bees, or Private Vices, Publick Benefits,* edited by K. F. B. Kaye (2 vols.: Oxford: Clarendon Press, 1924) and M. G. Jones, *The Charity School Movement: A Study of Eighteenth Century Puritanism in Action* (1938; reprint ed.; Hamden, Conn.: Archon Books, 1958). For Jean Baptiste Say as an explicator of Smith's ideas, Ernest Teilhac, *L'Oeuvre Économique de Jean Baptiste Say* (Paris: F. Alcan, 1927) remains the most illuminating discussion.

Joseph Dorfman's magisterial *The Economic Mind in American Civilization* (5 vols.; New York: The Viking Press, 1946-1959) is the most comprehensive account of the development of American economic thought. Ernest Teilhac, *Pioneers of American Economic Thought in the Nineteenth Century,* translated by E. A. J. Johnson (New York: The Macmillan Company, 1936), and Drew Randall McCoy, "The Republican Revolution: Political Economy in Jeffersonian America, 1776-1817" (doctoral thesis, University of Virginia, 1976) concentrate on the early national era. Michael Joseph Lalor O'Connor, *Origins of Academic Economics in the United States* (New York: Columbia University Press, 1944) focuses on the economics taught in the colleges and schools. In addition, Charles Patrick Neill, *Daniel Raymond: An Early Chapter in the History of Economic Theory in the United States* (Baltimore: The Johns Hopkins University Press, 1897) is useful for Raymond; Edward Pessen, "The Ideology of Stephen Simpson, Upper Class Champion of the Early Philadelphia Workingmen's Movement," *Pennsylvania History,* XXII (1965), 328-340, is useful for Simpson; and Theodore Rawson Crane, "Francis Wayland and Brown University, 1796-1841" (doctoral thesis, Harvard University, 1959) is useful for Wayland. Roscoe Dale LeCount, Jr., "The Politics of Public Education: New York State, 1795-1841" (doctoral thesis,

Teachers College, Columbia University, 1971) stresses the arguments deriving from political economy in the development of public education in New York State, as does E. G. West, "The Political Economy of American Public School Legislation," *Journal of Law and Economics,* X (1967), 101-128, which should be read along with West's *Education and the State: A Study in Political Economy* (London: The Institute of Economic Affairs, 1965) and *Education and the Industrial Revolution* (New York: Barnes & Noble, 1975).

Jonathan Messerli, *Horace Mann: A Biography* (New York: Alfred A. Knopf, 1972) is the best portrayal. It replaces a succession of filiopietistic accounts running from Mary Peabody Mann, *Life of Horace Mann, By His Wife,* first published in 1867 and subsequently republished as the first volume of *Life and Works of Horace Mann* (5 vols.; Boston: Lee and Shepard, 1891), to E. I. F. Williams, *Horace Mann* (New York: The Macmillan Company, 1937). Raymond B. Culver, *Horace Mann and Religion in the Massachusetts Public Schools* (New Haven: Yale University Press, 1929); Merle Curti, *The Social Ideas of American Educators* (New York: Charles Scribner's Sons, 1935); Robert L. Straker, *The Unseen Harvest: Horace Mann and Antioch College* (Yellow Springs, Ohio: Antioch College, 1955); Neil Gerard McCluskey, *Public Schools and Moral Education: The Influence of Horace Mann, William Torrey Harris, and John Dewey* (New York: Columbia University Press, 1958); Jonathan C. Messerli, "Horace Mann and Teacher Education," in George Z. F. Bereday and Joseph A. Lawerys, eds., *The Education and Training of Teachers: The Year Book of Education, 1963* (New York: Harcourt, Brace & World, 1963), pp. 70-84; Kathleen Edgerton Kendell, "Education as 'the Balance Wheel of Social Machinery': Horace Mann's Arguments and Proofs," *Quarterly Journal of Speech and Education,* LIV (1968), 13-21; and Maris A. Vinovskis, "Horace Mann on the Economic Productivity of Education," *New England Quarterly,* XLIII (1970), 550-571, are useful discussions of Mann's social and educational ideas. John D. Davies, *Phrenology, Fad and Science: A 19th-Century Crusade* (New Haven: Yale University Press, 1955) provides the background for Mann's commitment to phrenology. Lawrence A. Cremin, *The American Common School: An Historic Conception* (New York: Bureau of Publications, Teachers College, Columbia University, 1951) deals with the political context of Mann's work as secretary of the Massachusetts Board of Education. *Life and Works of Horace Mann* reprints his lectures and annual reports to the Massachusetts Board of Education. Lawrence A. Cremin, ed., *The Republic and the School: Horace Mann on the Education of Free Men* (New York: Bureau of Publications, Teachers College, Columbia University, 1957) presents excerpts from Mann's annual reports; Louis Filler, ed., *Horace Mann on the Crisis in Education* (Yellow Springs, Ohio: The Antioch Press, 1965) is a more general anthology of Mann's writings. Clyde S. King, *Horace Mann, 1796-1859: A Bibliography* (Dobbs Ferry, N.Y.: Oceana Publications, 1966) is a comprehensive bibliography. The principal collections of Mann papers are at the Massachusetts Historical Society and at Antioch College.

Kathryn Kish Sklar, *Catharine Beecher: A Study in Domesticity* (New Haven: Yale University Press, 1973) is the definitive biography. Joan N. Burstyn, "Catharine Beecher and the Education of American Women," *New England Quarterly,* XLVII (1974), 386-403, and Mae Elizabeth Harveson, *Catharine Esther Beecher: Pioneer Educator* (Philadelphia: University of Pennsylvania, 1932) are thoughtful introductions to Beecher's educational ideas. Eleanor Flexner, *Mary Wollstonecraft* (New York:

Coward, McCann & Geohegan, 1972) and Claire Tomalin, *The Life and Death of Mary Wollstonecraft* (New York: Harcourt Brace Jovanovich, 1974) are excellent sources for Wollstonecraft's influence. Thomas Woody, *A History of Women's Education in the United States* (1929; reprint ed.; 2 vols.; New York: Octagon Books, 1966) and Willystine Goodsell, ed., *Pioneers of Women's Education in the United States* (New York: McGraw-Hill Book Company, 1931) remain the most informative sources on the issue of women's schooling in nineteenth-century America. Barbara M. Cross, ed., *The Educated Woman in America: Selected Writings of Catharine Beecher, Margaret Fuller, and M. Carey Thomas* (New York: Teachers College Press, 1965); Mary Patricia Ryan, "American Society and the Cult of Domesticity" (doctoral thesis, University of California, Santa Barbara, 1971); Carroll Smith-Rosenberg, "The Female World of Love and Ritual: Relations Between Women in Nineteenth-Century America," *Signs: Journal of Women in Culture and Society,* I (1975), 1–29; Eleanor Flexner, *Century of Struggle: The Woman's Rights Movement in the United States* (rev. ed.; Cambridge, Mass.: Harvard University Press, 1975); Nancy F. Cott, *The Bonds of Womanhood: "Woman's Sphere" in New England, 1780–1835* (New Haven: Yale University Press, 1977); Anne Firor Scott, "What, Then, Is the American: This New Woman?" *Journal of American History,* LXV (1978–79), 679–703; and Maris A. Vinovskis and Richard M. Bernard, "Beyond Catharine Beecher: Female Education in the Antebellum Period," *Signs: Journal of Women in Culture and Society,* III (1978), 865–869, provide a useful context for Beecher's arguments. The principal collections of Beecher papers are at the Schlesinger Library at Radcliffe College, the Yale University Library, and the Stowe-Day Foundation in Hartford, Connecticut.

CHAPTER 5: SYSTEMS OF SCHOOLING

I reviewed the literature on nineteenth-century American schooling in *The Wonderful World of Ellwood Patterson Cubberley: An Essay on the Historiography of American Education* (New York: Bureau of Publications, Teachers College, Columbia University, 1965). My argument there was that the traditional chronicles of American education had been narrowly institutional, full of anachronism, and painfully moralistic. A decade and a half later, the field is still bedeviled by similar problems. The most significant change in the better literature that has appeared since 1965 has been the development of a far greater degree of precision in the data presented and in the inferences drawn and a far greater richness in the relationships explored between educational and social phenomena. But problems of anachronism have been at the heart of the major historiographical disagreements since 1965, as scholars have read the problems of the 1960's and 1970's back into the nineteenth century. The results have been mixed: on the one hand, there has been a greater political sophistication and skepticism among historians of education, which is all to the good; on the other hand, there has been a tendency to overdraw judgments of the extent to which schooling has liberated or constrained students. As I have argued elsewhere, schooling, and indeed all educational efforts, invariably do both, but in different combinations and balances at different times for different individuals *(Public Education* [New York: Basic Books, 1976], pp. 27–53, and *Traditions of American Education* [New York: Basic Books, 1977], pp. 34–38, 85–87, 127–128). One can always find evidence of liberating and constraining elements in any educational program: the question is in what balance and with what effect upon which individuals. The question is admittedly fraught with difficulty, but at least it saves one from simplistic answers.

The more imaginative of the recent studies of nineteenth-century American school systems have dealt with city rather than state systems, for example, David Tyack, "Bureaucracy and the Common School: The Example of Portland, Oregon, 1851-1913," *American Quarterly*, XIX (1967), 475-498, and *The One Best System: A History of American Urban Education* (Cambridge, Mass.: Harvard University Press, 1974); Julia Agnes Duffy, "The Proper Objects of a Gratuitous Education: The Free-School Society of the City of New York, 1805-1826" (doctoral thesis, Teachers College, Columbia University, 1968); William Worcester Cutler III, "Philosophy, Philanthropy, and Public Education: A Social History of the New York Public School Society, 1805-1852" (doctoral thesis, Cornell University, 1968) and "Status, Values, and the Education of the Poor: The Trustees of the New York Public School Society, 1805-1853," *American Quarterly*, XXIV (1972), 69-85; Michael B. Katz, "The Emergence of Bureaucracy in Urban Education: The Boston Case, 1850-1884," *History of Education Quarterly*, VIII (1968), 155-158, 319-357; Sharon Ordman Geltner, "The Common Schools of Los Angeles, 1850-1900" (doctoral thesis, University of California, Los Angeles, 1972); Carl F. Kaestle, *The Evolution of an Urban School System: New York City, 1750-1850* (Cambridge, Mass.: Harvard University Press, 1973); Stanley K. Schultz, *The Culture Factory: Boston Public Schools, 1789-1860* (New York: Oxford University Press, 1973); Diane Ravitch, *The Great School Wars: New York City, 1805-1973. A History of the Public Schools as Battlefield of Social Change* (New York: Basic Books, 1974); and Selwyn K. Troen, *The Public and the Schools: Shaping the St. Louis System, 1836-1929* (Columbia: University of Missouri Press, 1975). But there have been interesting studies of state systems as well, among them Alan Frederick Quick, "The History and Development of Common School Education in Oregon, 1849-1872" (doctoral thesis, University of Oregon, 1963); Hendrik D. Gideonse, "Common School Reform: Connecticut, 1838-1854" (doctoral thesis, Harvard University, 1963); Samuel James Matheson, "A History of Public Schools in Colorado: 1859-1880" (doctoral thesis, University of Denver, 1963); Forrest David Mathews, "The Politics of Education in the Deep South: Georgia and Alabama, 1830-1860" (doctoral thesis, Teachers College, Columbia University, 1965); John Donald Pulliam, "A History of the Struggle for a Free Common School System in Illinois from 1818 to the Civil War" (doctoral thesis, University of Illinois, 1965); Lloyd P. Jorgenson, *The Founding of Public Education in Wisconsin* (Madison: State Historical Society of Wisconsin, 1966); Roscoe Dale LeCount, Jr., "The Politics of Public Education: New York State, 1795-1851" (doctoral thesis, Teachers College, Columbia University, 1971); and Howard Kane Macauley, Jr., "A Social and Intellectual History of Elementary Education in Pennsylvania to 1860" (doctoral thesis, University of Pennsylvania, 1972).

Charles E. Bidwell, "The Moral Significance of the Common School: A Sociological Study of Local Patterns of School Control and Moral Education in Massachusetts and New York, 1837-1840," *History of Education Quarterly*, VI (1966), 50-91, is a careful analysis of the politics of moral and religious education in the communities of those states during a critical period. Michael B. Katz, *The Irony of Early School Reform: Educational Innovation in Mid-Nineteenth Century Massachusetts* (Cambridge, Mass.: Harvard University Press, 1968) deals with similar issues in one state, suggesting, first, that the school system was imposed on the working class by the middle and upper classes; second, that one element in the imposition was a new pedagogy that sought to internalize restraint; and third, that another element of the imposition was the incorporation of a reform school into the system to rehabilitate youngsters judged delinquent. Further, in "From Voluntarism to Bureaucracy in American Education," *Sociology of Education,* XLIV (1971), 297–332, Katz maintains that four models of organization (system) prevailed in nineteenth century schooling: paternal voluntarism, democratic localism, corporate voluntarism, and incipient bureaucracy. He sees the first model, as exemplified by the Public School Society in New York City, as preindustrial; the second, as exemplified by rural school districts, and the third, as exemplified by incorporated academies, as rural phenomena; and the last, as exemplified by the Boston public schools at midcentury, as an urban phenomenon. My own interpretation suggests that Katz overgeneralizes from specific findings. By and large, public schooling was not imposed during the first century of national life, except on the Indians and the defeated South, though it was not universally preferred either; it came to prevail via the ordinary political processes of the time. Moreover, pedagogies seeking to nurture social restraints in the young were scarcely the invention of nineteenth-century Americans; they have been in use in one form or another since the time of the ancient Hebrews, in free as well as unfree societies, so that, once again, the question is one of the balance at any given time between restraint and empowerment and of what different students learn in any case. As for the four models, they did indeed coexist and continued to do so throughout the century; but, in the overwhelming number of communities where public schooling prevailed, the organization that Katz labels "democratic localism" prevailed, even in cities like New York. In the matter of the reform school, Katz made a durably original contribution by showing the extent to which public school systems after midcentury increasingly included rehabilitative and custodial components for youngsters judged to be unruly. Katz's work is criticized, along with that of several other historians, in Diane Ravitch, *The Revisionists Revised: A Critique of the Radical Attack on the Schools* (New York: Basic Books, 1978). Katz responds in "An Apology for American Educational History," *Harvard Educational Review,* XLIX (1979), 225–266. A much more complex—and precise—picture of schooling in Massachusetts is given in Carl F. Kaestle and Maris A. Vinovskis, *Education and Social Change in Nineteenth-Century Massachusetts* (Cambridge: Cambridge University Press, 1980), which started out as a comparison of rural and urban education but ended up as a much broader and more comprehensive study.

The development of state public school systems is discussed in Lawrence A. Cremin, *The American Common School: An Historic Conception* (New York: Bureau of Publications, Teachers College, Columbia University, 1951). Early compulsory schooling legislation and its effects are dealt with in William M. Landes and Lewis C. Solmon, "Compulsory Schooling Legislation: An Economic Analysis of Law and Social Change in the Nineteenth Century," *Journal of Economic History,* XXXII (1972), 54–91. The development of colleges and universities in relation to state public school systems can be gleaned from John S. Brubacher and Willis Rudy, *Higher Education in Transition: A History of American Colleges and Universities, 1636–1976* (3d ed.; New York: Harper & Row, 1976) and Richard Hofstadter and Wilson Smith, eds., *American Higher Education: A Documentary History* (2 vols.; Chicago: University of Chicago Press, 1961). The Morrill Act is discussed in Edward Danforth Eddy, *Colleges for Our Land and Time: The Land-Grant Idea in American Education* (New York: Harper & Brothers, 1957); Allan Nevins, *The State Universities and Democracy* (Urbana: University of Illinois Press, 1972); Gordon C. Lee, "The Morrill Act and Education," *British Journal of Educational Studies,* XII (1963-64), 19-40; and Paul W. Gates, *Agriculture and the Civil War* (New York: Alfred A. Knopf, 1965).

For New York, the data in those works can be usefully supplemented by Thomas E. Finegan, ed., *Free Schools: A Documentary History of the Free School Movement in New York State* (Albany: University of the State of New York, 1921); Franklin B. Hough, *Historical and Statistical Record of the University of the State of New York During the Century from 1784 to 1884* (Albany: Weed, Parsons & Company, 1885); Sidney Sherwood, *The University of the State of New York: History of Higher Education in the State of New York* (Washington, D.C.: Government Printing Office, 1900); and Frank C. Abbott, *Government Policy and Higher Education: A Study of the University of the State of New York, 1784-1949* (Ithaca, N.Y.: Cornell University Press, 1968). For Massachusetts, George H. Martin's classic *The Evolution of the Massachusetts Public School System: A Historical Sketch* (New York: D. Appleton and Company, 1908) remains an admirable source of information. For Virginia, William A. Maddox, *The Free School Idea in Virginia Before the Civil War* (New York: Bureau of Publications, Teachers College, Columbia University, 1918); A. J. Morrison, *The Beginnings of Public Education in Virginia, 1776-1860* (Richmond, State Board of Education, 1917); and Philip Alexander Bruce, *History of the University of Virginia, 1819-1919* (5 vols.; New York: The Macmillan Company, 1920-1922) are helpful. Similarly useful for Michigan are John D. Pierce, "Origin and Progress of the Michigan School System," *Michigan Pioneer Collections,* I (1877), 37-45; Harold B. Brooks, "Founding of the Michigan Public School System," *Michigan History,* XXXIII (1949), 291-306; Archie P. Nevins, "The Kalamazoo Case," *ibid.,* XLIV (1960), 91-100; Frank B. Woodford, *Mr. Jefferson's Disciple: A Life of Justice Woodward* (East Lansing: Michigan State College Press, 1953); *Records of the University of Michigan, 1817-1837* (Ann Arbor: published by the University, 1935); Howard H. Peckham, *The Making of the University of Michigan, 1817-1967* (Ann Arbor: University of Michigan Press, 1967); and William C. Ringenberg, "Church Colleges vs. State University," *Michigan History,* LV (1975), 305-320.

For the problem of shifting definitions of the public and the private in education during the early nineteenth century, see Bernard Bailyn, "Education as a Discipline: Some Historical Notes," in John Walton and James L. Kuethe, eds., *The Discipline of Education* (Madison: University of Wisconsin Press, 1963); John Walter Gifford, *Historical Development of the New York State High School System* (Albany: J. B. Lyon, 1922); Lawrence A. Cremin, *The American Common School;* Theodore R. Sizer, ed., *The Age of the Academies* (New York: Bureau of Publications, Teachers College, Columbia University, 1964); Robert D. Cross, "Origins of the Catholic Parochial Schools in America," *American Benedictine Review,* XVI (1965), 194-209; Julia Agnes Duffy, "The Proper Objects of a Gratuitous Education"; William Worcester Cutler III, "Philosophy, Philanthropy, and Public Education"; and John S. Whitehead, *The Separation of a College and State: Columbia, Dartmouth, Harvard, and Yale, 1776-1876* (New Haven: Yale University Press, 1973). For the development of the Roman Catholic school system, see Vincent P. Lannie, *Public Money and Parochial Education: Bishop Hughes, Governor Seward, and the New York School Controversy* (Cleveland: The Press of Case Western Reserve University, 1968); John Webb Pratt, *Religion, Politics, and Diversity: The Church-State Theme in New York History* (Ithaca, N.Y.: Cornell University Press, 1967); Jerome Edward Diffley, "Catholic Reaction to American Public Education" (doctoral thesis, Notre Dame University, 1959); and Glen E. Gabert, Jr., "A History of the Roman Catholic Parochial School System in the United States: A Documentary Interpretation" (doctoral thesis, Loyola University of Chicago, 1971). For the effort to develop a Presbyterian parochial school system, see Lewis Joseph Sherrill, *Presbyterian Parochial Schools: 1846–1870* (New Haven: Yale University Press, 1932) and John Edwards Trowbridge, "Presbyterian Interest in Elementary Education in New Jersey, 1816–1866" (doctoral thesis, Rutgers University, 1957). For the development of Lutheran parochial schools, see John Silber Damm, "The Growth and Decline of Lutheran Parochial Schools in the United States, 1638–1962" (doctoral thesis, Teachers College, Columbia University, 1963). Lloyd P. Gartner, ed., *Jewish Education in the United States: A Documentary History* (New York: Teachers College Press, 1969) and "Temples of Liberty Unpolluted: American Jews and the Public Schools, 1840–1875" in Bertram Wallace Korn, ed., *A Bicentennial Festschrift for Jacob Rader Marcus* (New York: Ktav Publishing House, 1976); and Judah Pilch, ed., *A History of Jewish Education in the United States* (New York: The American Association for Jewish Education, 1969) document nineteenth-century Jewish ambivalence on the question of public versus Jewish schools.

The politics of education is the leading motif of virtually all the works already cited in connection with this chapter. To those already mentioned should be added Sidney L. Jackson, *America's Struggle for Free Schools: Social Tension and Education in New England and New York, 1827–42* (1941; reprint ed.; New York: Russell & Russell, 1965); Rush Welter, *Popular Education and Democratic Thought in America* (New York: Columbia University Press, 1962); Jay Pawa, "The Attitude of Labor Organizations in New York State Toward Public Education, 1829–1890" (doctoral thesis, Teachers College, Columbia University, 1964); Mary McDougall Gordon, "Union with the Virtuous Past: The Development of School Reform in Massachusetts, 1789–1837" (doctoral thesis, University of Pittsburgh, 1974); Samuel Bowles and Herbert Gintis, *Schooling in Capitalist America: Education Reform and the Contradictions of Economic Life* (New York: Basic Books, 1976); and Alexander James Field, "Educational Reform and Manufacturing Development in Mid-Nineteenth Century Massachusetts" (doctoral thesis, University of California, Berkeley, 1976) and "Educational Expansion in Mid-Nineteenth-Century Massachusetts: Human-Capital Formation or Structural Reinforcement?" *Harvard Educational Review*, XLVI (1976), 521–552.

With respect to the "friends of education" specifically mentioned in Part IV of the chapter, all are the subjects of biographies in the *Dictionary of American Biography*, with the exception of J. Orville Taylor, who is discussed in Paul D. Travers, "John Orville Taylor: A Forgotten Educator," *History of Education Quarterly*, IX (1969), 57–63. Many of those mentioned, as well as others who might also have been mentioned, are portrayed in Henry Barnard, *Memoirs of Teachers, Educators, and Promoters and Benefactors of Education, Literature, and Science* (2d ed.; New York: F. C. Brownell, 1861). A number have also been the subjects of recent scholarly biographies, for example, Jonathan Messerli, *Horace Mann: A Biography;* Vincent P. Lannie, ed., *Henry Barnard: American Educator* (New York: Teachers College Press, 1974); Robert B. Downs, *Henry Barnard* (Boston: Twayne Publishers, 1977); Samuel S. Britt, Jr., "Henry Ruffner, 19th Century Educator" (doctoral thesis, University of Arizona,

1962); Andrew A. Sherockman, "Caleb Mills: Pioneer Educator in Indiana" (doctoral thesis, University of Pittsburgh, 1955); John Stanley Harker, "The Life and Contributions of Calvin Ellis Stowe" (doctoral thesis, University of Pittsburgh, 1951); Kathryn Kish Sklar, *Catharine Beecher: A Study in American Domesticity* (New Haven: Yale University Press, 1973); and Helen Louise Jennings, "John Mason Peck and the Impact of New England on the Old Northwest" (doctoral thesis, University of Southern California, 1961).

The educational periodicals of the era are listed by Barnard in the *American Journal of Education*, XV (1865), 383–384. They are discussed in Sheldon Emmor Davis, *Educational Periodicals of the Nineteenth Century* (Washington, D.C.: United States Bureau of Education, 1919); Richard Emmons Thursfield, *Henry Barnard's American Journal of Education* (Baltimore: The Johns Hopkins University Press, 1945); and Sally Harris Wertheim, "Educational Periodicals: Propaganda Sheets for the Ohio Common Schools" (doctoral thesis, Case Western Reserve University, 1970). The organizational activities of the "friends of education," which frequently combined political and professional agenda, are portrayed in Paul H. Mattingly, *The Classless Profession: American Schoolmen in the Nineteenth Century* (New York: New York University Press, 1975) and Roman Joseph Schweikert, "The Western Literary Institute and College of Professional Teachers: An Instrument in the Creation of a Profession" (doctoral thesis, University of Cincinnati, 1971). For examples of communications among the "friends of education," see the selections from the Barnard-Mann correspondence (at the New York University Library) in Vincent P. Lannie, ed., *Henry Barnard*, and Edgar W. Knight, "More Evidence of Horace Mann's Influence in the South," *Educational Forum*, XII (1948), 167–184, and "Some Evidence of Henry Barnard's Influence in the South," *ibid.*, XIII (1949), 301–312. For the early informational role of the United States Bureau of Education, see Lawrence A. Cremin, *The Wonderful World of Ellwood Patterson Cubberley* and Donald R. Warren, *To Enforce Education: A History of the Founding Years of the United States Office of Education* (Detroit: Wayne State University Press, 1974). For an interpretation of the politics of public schooling similar to my own, see David B. Tyack, "The Spread of Public Schooling in Victorian America: In Search of a Reinterpretation," *History of Education*, VII (1978), 173–182.

The statistics in Part V of the chapter are derived from the reports of the United States Census. The best recent demographic analyses of pre-Civil War schooling are Albert Fishlow, "The American Common School Revival: Fact or Fancy?" in Henry Rosovsky, ed., *Industrialization in Two Systems: Essays in Honor of Alexander Gerschenkron* (New York: John Wiley & Sons, 1966), pp. 40–67, and "Levels of Nineteenth-Century American Investment in Education," *Journal of Economic History*, XXVI (1966), 418–436; and Lee Soltow and Edward Stevens, "Economic Aspects of School Participation in Mid-Nineteenth-Century United States," *Journal of Interdisciplinary History*, VIII (1977), 221–243. Carl F. Kaestle and Maris A. Vinovskis, *Education and Social Change in Nineteenth-Century Massachusetts*, and Vinovskis, "Trends in Massachusetts Education, 1826–1860," *History of Education Quarterly*, XII (1972), 501–529, present a sophisticated statistical analysis of schooling in a single state; while Maris A. Vinovskis and Richard M. Bernard, "Beyond Catharine Beecher: Female Education in the Antebellum Period," *Signs: Journal of Women in Culture and Society*, III (1978), 856–869, presents a similarly sophisticated statistical analysis of schooling among women. Herman G. Richey, "Reappraisal of the State School Systems

554   BIBLIOGRAPHICAL ESSAY

of the Pre-Civil-War Period," *Elementary School Journal,* XLI (1940-41), 118-29, and "The Persistence of Educational Progress During the Decade of the Civil War," *ibid.,* XLII (1941-42), 358-366, 456-463; and Sterling G. Brinkley, "Growth of School Attendance and Literacy in the United States Since 1840," *Journal of Experimental Education,* XXVI (1957-58), 51-66, are older studies that remain useful.

The literature on the outcomes of nineteenth-century schooling is sparse and largely inferential, as it must be, given that schooling is only one among many influences on students and also that individual students come to schools with different purposes and past experiences and hence learn different things in different ways. Frank E. Coburn, "The Educational Level of the Jacksonians," *History of Education Quarterly,* VII (1967), 515-520, is a study of the formal education of American leaders, using 968 biographies of national and state officials from the time of the First Continental Congress of 1774 to the time of the Thirty-Sixth Congress terminating in 1861. Michael B. Katz, *Class, Bureaucracy, and Schools: The Illusion of Educational Change in America* (New York: Praeger Publishers, 1971) relies heavily on the theory of bureaucracy to infer the outcomes of schooling, while Samuel Bowles and Herbert Gintis, *Schooling in Capitalist America: Educational Reform and the Contradictions of Economic Life* (New York: Basic Books, 1976) relies in a similar fashion on the Marxian theory of structural correspondence between the social relations of education and the social relations of production. My own sense of such inference, which I explicate in *Public Education* (New York: Basic Books, 1976), is that, given the particularities of educational interactions, they should be used by historians as indicators of possible sources of data, but they should not be used as substitutes for data. Hence, the note of caution in my assertions about the outcomes of schooling.

Granted the caveat, the assertions I have advanced concerning the outcomes of schooling are based essentially on the observations and reminiscences of contemporaries, for example, the sources collected in Barbara Joan Finkelstein, "Governing the Young, Teacher Behavior in American Primary Schools, 1820-1880: A Documentary History" (doctoral thesis, Teachers College, Columbia University, 1970) and listed in Barbara J. Finkelstein, "Schooling and Schoolteachers: Selected Bibliography of Autobiographies in the Nineteenth Century," *History of Education Quarterly,* XIV (1974), 293-300; the reminiscences collected in Thomas R. Garth, ed., *Old School Days: Being Reminiscences of a Passing Generation* (Ann Arbor, Mich.: Edwards Brothers, 1925), a copy of which I came upon in the Cubberley Library at Stanford University; the reminiscences gathered in The *"How I Was Educated"* Papers from the Forum Magazine (New York: D. Appleton and Company, 1896), which includes educational autobiographies by Edward E. Hale, Thomas Wentworth Higginson, Frederick A. P. Barnard, John H. Vincent, William T. Harris, S. C. Bartlett, J. R. Kendrick, Timothy Dwight, E. G. Robinson, James B. Angell, and Andrew D. White; the commentaries of foreign visitors, including the ones mentioned on pp. 577-578 *infra,* the unpublished documents synthesized in Geraldine Jonçich Clifford, "Home and School in 19th Century America: Some Personal-History Reports from the United States," *History of Education Quarterly,* XVIII (1978), 3-34; the firsthand accounts reported in state historical journals, an excellent bibliography of which is Lloyd P. Jorgenson, "Materials on the History of Education in State Historical Journals," *History of Education Quarterly,* VII (1967), 234-254, 369-389, VIII (1968), 510-527, and IX (1969), 73-87; and a host of individual ephemera like Mrs. M. L. T. Hartman, *Schools in Wyoming Valley Seven-*

ty-Five Years Ago (Wilkes-Barre, Pa.: reprinted from the *Wilkes-Barre Record,* 1893) or Marshall A. Barber, *The Schoolhouse at Prairie View* (Lawrence: University of Kansas Press, 1953).

With respect to Tables II and III, the best sources for statistical data on schooling before 1876 are the reports of the United States Census and of the several state departments of education as they developed. Albert Fishlow compares the reliability of the two types of reports in the Appendix to "The Common School Revival: Fact or Fancy," in Rosovsky, ed., *Industrialization in Two Systems,* pp. 40–67. Beginning in 1840, the Bureau of the Census collected data on the extent of schooling from two sources, school officials and families. Obviously there were discrepancies in the resulting returns, owing not only to varying degrees of accuracy but also to differing definitions of schooling. For an analysis of the discrepancy in Macoupin County, Illinois, in 1850 and in 1870, see pp. 434–435 *supra.* The data for Tables II and III are drawn from the reports of school officials. *The American Almanac* is also a useful source of statistical data on schooling, though it should be borne in mind that the *Almanac*'s data are almost always taken from some other source; thus, the data on college enrollments during the pre-Civil War era are generally taken from the reports of the American Education Society. With the establishment of the United States Bureau of Education in 1867 and the appointment of Henry Barnard as the first United States Commissioner of Education, the reports of the commissioner became an excellent source of data on schooling, though, given different modes and times of data collection, its statistics almost always differed from those of the Bureau of the Census.

CHAPTER 6: EDUCATION BY COLLISION

There is a long-standing dearth of good scholarly materials on the history of American newspapers. Frank Luther Mott's *American Journalism: A History, 1690–1960* (3d ed.; The Macmillian Company, 1962) has dominated the field since its initial appearance in 1941; and, while it is an admirable piece of work, it is written from the perspective of a professional journalist. Thus, Mott deplores the "party press" of the early national era and hails the emergence of "professional" journalism during the mid-nineteenth century. The heritage of the press from the American Revolution is discussed in Arthur M. Schlesinger, *Prelude to Independence: The Newspaper War on Britain, 1764–1776* (New York: Alfred A. Knopf, 1958); Edmund S. and Helen M. Morgan, *The Stamp Act Crisis: Prologue to Revolution* (rev. ed.; New York: Collier Books, 1963); Bernard Bailyn, *The Ideological Origins of the American Revolution* (Cambridge, Mass.: Harvard University Press, 1967); and Philip Davidson, *Propaganda and the American Revolution* (Chapel Hill: University of North Carolina Press, 1941). The press during the first years of the Republic is portrayed in David Hackett Fischer, *The Revolution of Conservatism: The Federalist Party in the Era of Jeffersonian Democracy* (New York: Harper & Row, 1965) and Donald H. Stewart, *The Opposition Press of the Federalist Period* (Albany: State University of New York Press, 1969). The Alien and Sedition Acts are dealt with in Frank Maloy Anderson, "The Enforcement of the Alien and Sedition Laws," *Annual Report of the American Historical Association, 1912* (Washington, D.C.: American Historical Association, 1914); John C. Miller, *Crisis in Freedom: The Alien and Sedition Acts* (Boston: Little, Brown and Company, 1952); and James Morton Smith, *Freedom's Fetters: The Alien and Sedition Laws and Ameri-*

can *Civil Liberties* (Ithaca, N.Y.: Cornell University Press, 1956). Frank H. O'Brien, *The Story of the Sun* (1918; new ed.; New York: D. Appleton and Co., 1928); Allan Nevins, *The Evening Post: A Century of Journalism* (New York: Boni and Liveright, 1922); J. Cutler Andrews, *Pittsburgh's Post-Gazette: First Newspaper West of the Alleghenies* (Boston: Chapman & Grimes, 1936); Oliver Carlson, *The Man Who Made the News: James Gordon Bennett* (New York: Duell, Sloan and Pearce, 1942); James Eugene Smith, *One Hundred Years of Hartford's Courant, from Colonial Times Through the Civil War* (New Haven: Yale University Press, 1949); Francis Brown, *Raymond of the Times* (New York: W. W. Norton & Company, 1951); Stanley Nelson Worton, "William Leggett, Political Journalist: A Study in Democratic Thought" (doctoral thesis, Columbia University, 1954); Calder M. Pickett, "Six New York Newspapers and Their Response to Technology in the Nineteenth Century" (doctoral thesis, University of Minnesota, 1959); Bernard A. Weisberger, *The American Newspaperman* (Chicago: University of Chicago Press, 1961); Dwight Nikkelson, *"The Kentucky Gazette:* The Herald of a Noisy World" (doctoral thesis, University of Kentucky, 1963); Albert McLean, Jr., *William Cullen Bryant* (Boston: Twayne Publishers, 1964); and Michael Schudson, *Discovering the News: A Social History of American Newspapers* (New York: Basic Books, 1978) are helpful for the period after the War of 1812. The histories of printers and printing are also valuable, for example, Milton W. Hamilton, *The Country Printer: New York State, 1785–1830* (New York: Columbia University Press, 1936); John Clyde Oswald, *Printing in the Americas* (New York: The Gregg Publishing Company, 1937); Rollo G. Silver, *The American Printer, 1787–1825* (Charlottesville: The University Press of Virginia, 1967); and David Kaser, *Joseph Charless: Printer in the Western Country* (Philadelphia: University of Pennsylvania Press, 1963), as are the sections on printers and newspapers in regional and local histories—Guion Griffis Johnson, *Ante-Bellum North Carolina: A Social History* (Chapel Hill: University of North Carolina Press, 1937), chap. xxv; R. Carlyle Buley, *The Old Northwest: Pioneer Period, 1815–1840* (2 vols.; Bloomington: Indiana University Press, 1950), II, chap. xv; and Allan Nevins, "The Newspapers of New York State, 1783–1900," in Alexander C. Flick, ed., *History of the State of New York* (10 vols.; New York: Columbia University Press, 1933–1937), IX, 267–305, are splendid illustrations. I have also profited from the studies of my student Gary Gaffield, which he generously shared with me and which will appear in his forthcoming doctoral thesis, "The Editor as Educator: Democratic Journalism in America, 1815–1845." All these sources draw heavily on the newspapers themselves, to which Clarence S. Brigham, *History and Bibliography of American Newspapers, 1690–1820* (2 vols.; Worcester, Mass.: American Antiquarian Society, 1947) and Winifred Gregory, ed., *American Newspapers, 1820–1936: A Union List of Files Available in the United States and Canada* (New York: The H. W. Wilson Company, 1937) remain indispensable guides. Given the significance of the postal system as a circulator of newspapers and the explicit governmental policy of encouraging the circulation and exchange of ideas via low postal rates, Wesley Everett Rich, *The History of the United States Post Office to the Year 1829* (Cambridge, Mass.: Harvard University Press, 1924) and Wayne E. Fuller, *The American Mail: Enlarger of the Common Life* (Chicago: University of Chicago Press, 1972) are additionally relevant. My source for William Manning is *The Key of Libberty,* edited by Samuel Eliot Morison (Billerica, Mass.: The Manning Association, 1922).

Glyndon G. Van Deusen, *Horace Greeley: Nineteenth-Century Crusader* (Philadelphia: University of Pennsylvania Press, 1964) is the definitive biography. Earle D. Ross, "Horace Greeley and the Beginnings of the New Agriculture," *Agricultural History*, VII (1933), 3–17; Ralph Ray Fahrney, *Horace Greeley and the Tribune in the Civil War* (Cedar Rapids, Iowa: The Torch Press, 1936); Henry Luther Stoddard, *Horace Greeley: Printer, Editor, Crusader* (New York: G. P. Putnam's Sons, 1946); and William Harlan Hale, *Horace Greeley: Voice of the People* (New York: Harper & Brothers, 1950) are also useful, as are Greeley's own published books, *Hints Toward Reform, in Lectures, Addresses, and Other Writings* (New York: Harper & Brothers, 1850) and *Recollections of a Busy Life* (New York: J. B. Ford & Co., 1868). Eric Foner, *Free Soil, Free Labor, Free Men: The Ideology of the Republican Party Before the Civil War* (New York: Oxford University Press, 1970) provides an excellent context for the substance of Greeley's political thought.

Eugene Perry Link, *Democratic-Republican Societies, 1790–1800* (New York: Columbia University Press, 1942) provides the principal entree into the world of the democratic societies. William Miller, "The Democratic Societies and the Whiskey Insurrection," *Pennsylvania Magazine of History and Biography*, LXII (1938), 324–349, and "First Fruits of Republican Organization: Political Aspects of the Congressional Election of 1794," *ibid.*, LXIII (1939), 118–143, are illuminating with respect to the political activities of the societies. Charles Downer Hazen, *Contemporary American Opinion of the French Revolution* (Baltimore: The Johns Hopkins University Press, 1897); R. R. Palmer, *The Age of the Democratic Revolution: A Political History of Europe and America, 1760–1800* (2 vols.; Princeton, N.J.: Princeton University Press, 1959–1964); Carl B. Cone, *The English Jacobins: Reformers in Late 18th Century England* (New York: Charles Scribner's Sons, 1968); and Albert Goodwin, *The Friends of Liberty: The English Democratic Movement in the Age of the French Revolution* (Cambridge, Mass.: Harvard University Press, 1979) are valuable with respect to the international context. David Hackett Fischer, *The Revolution of American Conservatism* is the best source for the Federalist societies that emerged by way of response.

Richard Hofstadter, *The Idea of a Party System: The Rise of a Legitimate Opposition in the United States, 1780–1840* (Berkeley: University of California Press, 1970) is an engaging discussion of the development of the party system and, with it, the idea of a legitimate opposition. Joseph Charles, *The Origins of the American Party System: Three Essays* (Williamsburg, Va.: The Institute of Early American History and Culture, 1956); Noble E. Cunningham, Jr., *The Jeffersonian Republicans* (Chapel Hill: University of North Carolina Press, 1957) and *The Jeffersonian Republicans in Power: Party Operations, 1801–1809* (Chapel Hill: University of North Carolina Press, 1963); Marshall Smelser, "The Federalist Period as an Age of Passion," *American Quarterly*, X (1958), 391–419; John C. Miller, *The Federalist Era, 1789–1801* (New York: Harper & Bros., 1960); William Nisbet Chambers, *Political Parties in a New Nation: An American Experience, 1776–1809* (New York: Oxford University Press, 1963); David Hackett Fischer, *The Revolution of American Conservatism;* Roy F. Nichols, *The Invention of the American Political System* (New York: The Macmillan Company, 1967); James M. Banner, *To the Hartford Convention: The Federalists and the Origins of Party Politics in Massachusetts, 1789–1815* (New York: Alfred A. Knopf, 1970); Linda K. Kerber, *Federalists in Dissent: Imagery and Ideology in Jeffersonian America* (Ithaca, N.Y.: Cornell University Press, 1970); Richard Buel, Jr., *Securing the Revolution:*

558   BIBLIOGRAPHICAL ESSAY

Ideology in American Politics, 1789–1815 (Ithaca, N.Y.: Cornell University Press, 1972); and Lance Banning, *The Jeffersonian Persuasion: Evolution of a Party Ideology* (Ithaca, N.Y.: Cornell University Press, 1978) are also useful on the political life of the new nation.

The role of voluntarism in the religious life of the society is a phenomenon that has been noted by American church historians from Robert Baird, *Religion in the United States of America* (Glasgow: Blackie and Son, 1844) through Sidney E. Mead, *The Shaping of Christianity in America* (New York: Harper & Row, 1963) and Sidney E. Ahlstrom, *A Religious History of the American People* (New Haven: Yale University Press, 1972), and by a host of foreign observers, whose commentaries are gathered together in Milton B. Powell, ed., *The Voluntary Church: American Religious Life, 1740–1860, Seen Through the Eyes of European Visitors* (New York: The Macmillan Company, 1967). Voluntary association in the life of the society at large is discussed in Noel P. Gist, *Secret Societies: A Cultural Study of Fraternalism in the United States* (Columbia: University of Missouri Press, 1940); Frank Warren Crow, "The Age of Reason: Societies for Social and Economic Improvement in the United States, 1783–1815" (doctoral thesis, University of Wisconsin, 1952); Rowland Berthoff, *An Unsettled People: Social Order and Disorder in American History* (New York: Harper & Row, 1971); Walter S. Glazer, "Participation and Power: Voluntary Association and the Functional Organization of Cincinnati in 1840," *Historical Methods Newsletter,* V (1972), 151–68; Richard D. Brown, "The Emergence of Voluntary Associations in Massachusetts, 1760–1830," *Journal of Voluntary Action Research,* II (1973), 64–73, and "The Emergence of Urban Society in Rural Massachusetts, 1760–1820," *Journal of American History,* LXI (1974–75), 29–51; Gregory H. Singleton, "Protestant Voluntary Organizations and the Shaping of Victorian America," *American Quarterly,* XXVII (1975), 549–560; Dorothy Ann Lipson, *Freemasonry in Connecticut* (Princeton, N.J.: Princeton University Press, 1977); and Don Harrison Doyle, *The Social Order of a Frontier Community: Jacksonville, Illinois, 1825–70* (Urbana: University of Illinois Press, 1978). The more general effects of widespread participation in voluntary associations and, through voluntary associations, in community and community-building affairs is discussed in Stanley Elkins and Eric McKitrick, "A Meaning for Turner's Frontier," *Political Science Quarterly,* LXIX (1954), 321–353, 565–602. The effects of participation in voluntary societies on the part of women, given their exclusion from the suffrage, is noted in Keith Melder, "Ladies Bountiful: Organized Women's Benevolence in Early 19th-Century America," *New York History,* XLVIII (1967), 231–254; Lois Wendland Banner, "The Protestant Crusade: Religious Missions, Benevolence, and Reform in the United States, 1790–1840" (doctoral thesis, Columbia University, 1970); Nancy F. Cott, *The Bonds of Womanhood: "Woman's Sphere" in New England, 1780–1835* (New Haven: Yale University Press, 1977); Barbara J. Berg, *The Remembered Gate: Origins of American Feminism: The Woman and the City, 1800–1860* (New York: Oxford University Press, 1978); and Anne M. Boylan, "Evangelical Womanhood in the Nineteenth Century: The Role of Women in Sunday Schools," *Feminist Studies,* IV (October, 1978), 62–80.

Alexis de Tocqueville's *Democracy in America,* edited by Phillips Bradley (2 vols.; Alfred A. Knopf, 1945) was widely read by American contemporaries, some of whom doubtless found confirmation for their own observations about the role of newspapers and voluntary associations in the society, others of whom doubtless made Tocqueville's observations their own. However that may be, the phenomena Tocqueville describes were sufficiently widely noted and commented upon, by foreign and domestic observers alike, to establish their validity conclusively. Frederick Grimke read and admired *Democracy in America* and alluded to it and to Tocqueville's *The Old Régime and the French Revolution* (1856), translated by Stuart Gilbert (Garden City, N.Y.: Doubleday and Company, 1955) at several points in *The Nature and Tendency of Free Institutions*, edited by John William Ward (Cambridge, Mass.: Harvard University Press, 1968). Nevertheless, Grimke's discussion of the *Democracy* is sufficiently critical in tone and substance to convey Grimke's absolute independence of mind, as indeed does the overall quality of his treatise; Ward refers to it as "the single best book written by an American in the nineteenth century on the meaning of our political way of life" (*ibid.*, p. 3). Interestingly, John Stuart Mill noted in his lengthy review of the *Democracy* (*Edinburgh Review*, LXXI [1840–41], 1–47) that the phenomena Tocqueville saw as embodying the spirit of democracy, among them, a host of newspapers and voluntary associations, were as manifest in aristocratic England as they were in democratic America, and probably a result of the commercial spirit abroad in both countries rather than the democratic spirit—a view that would support those who see modernization as the chief synthesizing theme in nineteenth-century American life, for example, Richard D. Brown in *Modernization: The Transformation of American Life, 1600–1865* (New York: Hill and Wang, 1976). For the circulation of information during the nineteenth century and its contribution to notions of American community, see Allan R. Pred's remarkable study *Urban Growth and the Circulation of Information: The United States of Cities, 1790–1840* (Cambridge, Mass.: Harvard University Press, 1973).

Chapter 7: Outcasts

Thomas E. Gossett, *Race: The History of an Idea in America* (Dallas: Southern Methodist University Press, 1963); William Stanton, *The Leopard's Spots: Scientific Attitudes Toward Race in America, 1815–1859* (Chicago: University of Chicago Press, 1960); and George M. Fredrickson, *The Black Image in the White Mind: The Debate on Afro-American Character and Destiny, 1817–1914* (New York: Harper & Row, 1971) explicate the racial attitudes of nineteenth-century Americans. David Brion Davis, *The Problem of Slavery in Western Culture* (Ithaca, N.Y.: Cornell University Press, 1966) and *The Problem of Slavery in an Age of Revolution: 1770–1823* (Ithaca, N.Y.: Cornell University Press, 1975) and Winthrop D. Jordan, *White over Black: American Attitudes Toward the Negro, 1550–1812* (Chapel Hill: University of North Carolina Press, 1968) place the problem of slavery in historical and comparative perspective. Frederick M. Binder, *The Color Problem in Early National America as Viewed by John Adams, Jefferson, and Jackson* (The Hague: Mouton, 1968) and Donald L. Robinson, *Slavery in the Structure of American Politics, 1765–1820* (New York: Harcourt Brace Jovanovich, 1971) trace the role of slavery in the politics of the new nation. William Sumner Jenkins, *Pro-Slavery Thought in the Old South* (Chapel Hill: University of North Carolina Press, 1935); H. Shelton Smith, *In His Image, But . . . : Racism in Southern Religion, 1780–1910* (Durham: Duke University Press, 1972); and Larry E. Tise, "Proslavery Ideology: A Social and Intellectual History of the Defense of Slavery in America, 1790–1840" (doctoral thesis, University of North Carolina, 1974) are the best analyses of the proslavery argument. George Fitzhugh, *Cannibals*

560 BIBLIOGRAPHICAL ESSAY

All! Or, Slaves Without Masters, edited by C. Vann Woodward (Cambridge, Mass.: Harvard University Press, 1960); *The Pro-Slavery Argument; as Maintained by the Most Distinguished Writers of the Southern States, Containing the Several Essays, on the Subject, of Chancellor Harper, Governor Hammond, Dr. Simms, and Professor Dew* (Charleston, S.C.: Walker, Richards & Co., 1852); and E. N. Elliott, ed., *Cotton Is King, and Pro-Slavery Arguments: Comprising the Writings of Hammond, Harper, Christy, Stringfellow, Hodge, Bledsoe, and Cartwright, on This Important Subject* (Augusta, Ga.: Pritchard, Abbott & Loomis, 1860) are contemporary proslavery writings. Eric L. McKitrick, ed., *Slavery Defended: The Views of the Old South* (Englewood Cliffs, N.J.: Prentice-Hall, 1963) is a convenient anthology of proslavery literature. Louis Filler, *The Crusade Against Slavery, 1830-1860* (New York: Harper & Row, 1960) and Dwight Lowell Dumond, *Antislavery: The Crusade for Freedom in America* (Ann Arbor: University of Michigan Press, 1961) are comprehensive accounts of the abolitionist movement. Martin Duberman, ed., *The Antislavery Vanguard: New Essays on the Abolitionists* (Princeton, N.J.: Princeton University Press, 1965) presents varying interpretations of the abolitionists. John L. Thomas, ed., *Slavery Attacked: The Abolitionist Crusade* (Englewood Cliffs, N.J.: Prentice-Hall, 1965) and William H. Pease and Jane H. Pease, eds., *The Antislavery Argument* (Indianapolis: Bobbs-Merrill, 1965) are convenient collections of abolitionist writings. John Hope Franklin, *From Slavery to Freedom: A History of Negro Americans* (4th ed.; New York: Alfred A. Knopf, 1974) is the best comprehensive history of American blacks.

Kenneth M. Stampp, *The Peculiar Institution: Slavery in the Ante-Bellum South* (New York: Alfred A. Knopf, 1961); Eugene D. Genovese, *The World the Slaveholders Made: Two Essays in Interpretation* (New York: Pantheon Books, 1969) and *Roll, Jordan, Roll: The World the Slaves Made* (New York: Pantheon Books, 1974); and Elinor Miller and Eugene D. Genovese, eds., *Plantation, Town, and County: Essays on the Local History of American Slave Society* (Urbana: University of Illinois Press, 1974) depict the slave plantation as an institution. Vera Rubin and Arthur Tuden, eds., *Comparative Perspectives on Slavery in New World Plantation Societies* (New York: The New York Academy of Sciences, 1977) affords a comparative perspective on the American experience. Richard C. Wade, *Slavery in the Cities: The South, 1820-1860* (New York: Oxford University Press, 1964) focuses on the urban experience; Robert S. Starobin, *Industrial Society in the Old South* (New York: Oxford University Press, 1970) focuses on the industrial experience. Stanley M. Elkins, *Slavery: A Problem in American Institutional and Intellectual Life* (Chicago: University of Chicago Press, 1959) and John W. Blassingame, *The Slave Community: Plantation Life in the Ante-Bellum South* (New York: Oxford University Press, 1972) are two much-discussed studies that draw upon social-science concepts in illuminating the slave experience. The debates and discussions concerning their validity are collected, respectively, in Ann J. Lane, ed., *The Debate over Slavery: Stanley Elkins and His Critics* (Urbana: University of Illinois Press, 1971) and Al-Tony Gilmore, ed., *Revisiting Blassingame's The Slave Community: The Scholars Respond* (Westport, Conn.: Greenwood Press, 1978).

The best work on the discordant pedagogies of the slave plantation is Thomas L. Webber, *Deep Like the Rivers: Education in the Slave Quarter Community, 1831-1865* (New York: W. W. Norton & Company, 1978). Webber's discussion of the pedagogy of the white community is usefully supplemented by Kenneth M. Stampp, *The Peculiar Institution;* John Spencer Bassett, *The Southern Plantation Overseer, as Revealed in*

His Letters (Northampton, Mass.: Smith College, 1925); William K. Scarborough, *The Overseer: Plantation Management in the Old South* (Baton Rouge: Louisiana State University Press, 1966); and Charles C. Jones, *The Religious Instruction of Negroes, in the United States* (1842; reprint ed.; New York: Negro Universities Press, 1969). Webber's discussion of the pedagogy of the black community is usefully supplemented by Mason Crum, *Gullah: Negro Life in the Carolina Sea Islands* (Durham, N.C.: Duke University Press, 1940); Stanley Feldstein, *Once a Slave: The Slaves' View of Slavery* (New York: William Morrow and Company, 1971); Eugene D. Genovese, *Roll, Jordan, Roll;* Herbert G. Gutman, *The Black Family in Slavery and Freedom, 1750-1925* (New York: Pantheon Books, 1976); Nathan Irvin Huggins, *Black Odyssey: The Afro-American Ordeal in Slavery* (New York: Pantheon Books, 1977); Albert J. Raboteau, *Slave Religion: The "Invisible Institution" in the Antebellum South* (New York: Oxford University Press, 1978); and Lawrence W. Levine, *Black Culture and Black Consciousness: Afro-American Folk Thought from Slavery to Freedom* (New York: Oxford University Press, 1978). William Francis Allen, Charles Pickard, and Lucy McKim Garrison, eds., *Slave Songs in the United States* (New York: A. Simpson & Co., 1867) is the classic contemporary collection.

Leon F. Litwack, *North of Slavery: The Negro in the Free States, 1790-1860* (Chicago: University of Chicago Press, 1961) and Ira Berlin, *Slaves Without Masters: The Free Negro in the Antebellum South* (New York: Pantheon Books, 1974) provide the best entree into the life of the free blacks; both include excellent commentaries on the previous literature. Carter G. Woodson, *The Education of the Negro Prior to 1861: A History of the Education of the Colored People of the United States from the Beginning of Slavery to the Civil War* (Washington, D.C.: The Associated Publishers, 1919) and *The History of the Negro Church* (Washington, D.C.: The Associated Publishers, 1921); Carol V. R. George, *Segregated Sabbaths: Richard Allen and the Rise of Independent Black Churches, 1760-1840* (New York: Oxford University Press, 1973); David Martin Ment, "Racial Segregation in the Public Schools of New England and New York, 1840-1940" (doctoral thesis, Teachers College, Columbia University, 1975); and Claudia Christie Foster, "Motives, Means, and Ends in Gradual Abolitionist Education, 1785 to 1830" (doctoral thesis, Teachers College, Columbia University, 1977) are useful for the education of free blacks.

Elizabeth W. Miller and Mary L. Fisher, *The Negro in America: A Bibliography* (2d ed.; Cambridge, Mass.: Harvard University Press, 1970); Dorothy B. Porter, *The Negro in the United States: A Selected Bibliography* (Washington, D.C.: Library of Congress, 1970); and Russell C. Brignano, *Black Americans in Autobiography: An Annotated Bibliography of Autobiographies and Autobiographical Books Written Since the Civil War* (Durham, N.C.: Duke University Press, 1974) are the best general bibliographies. George P. Rawick, ed., *The American Slave: A Composite Autobiography* (19 vols.; Westport, Conn.: Greenwood Publishing Co., 1972-1974) is a superb collection of slave narratives, with an interpretive volume by Rawick entitled *From Sundown to Sunup: The Making of the Black Community.*

Roy Harvey Pearce, *The Savages of America: A Study of the Indian and the Idea of Civilization* (rev. ed.; Baltimore: The Johns Hopkins University Press, 1965); Francis Paul Prucha, "The Image of the Indian in Pre-Civil War America," in Prucha *et al.*, *Indiana Historical Society Lectures, 1970-71* (Indianapolis: Indiana Historical Society, 1971); and Brian William Dippie, "The Vanishing American: Popular Attitudes and

American Policy in the Nineteenth Century (doctoral thesis, University of Texas, 1970) explicate the attitudes of white Americans toward the Indians. William Stanton, *The Leopard's Spots* and Thomas F. Gossett, *Race* include sections on the Indians in their more general discussions. The best scholarly history of the Indians is Wilcomb E. Washburn, *The Indian in America* (New York: Harper & Row, 1975). William T. Hagen, *American Indians* (Chicago: University of Chicago Press, 1961); Alice Marriott and Carol K. Rachlin, *American Epic: The Story of the American Indian* (New York: G. P. Putnam's Sons, 1969); and Angie Debo, *A History of the Indians of the United States* (Norman: University of Oklahoma Press, 1970) are also useful general accounts. Wilcomb E. Washburn, ed., *The Indian and the White Man* (Garden City, N.Y.: Doubleday and Company, 1964) and Edward H. Spicer, ed., *A Short History of the Indians of the United States* (New York: Van Nostrand Reinhold Company, 1969) are convenient selections of documents.

Francis Paul Prucha, *American Indian Policy in the Formative Years: The Indian Trade and Intercourse Acts, 1790-1834* (Lincoln: University of Nebraska Press, 1962); Frederick M. Binder, *The Color Problem in Early National America;* Reginald Horsman, *Expansion and American Indian Policy, 1783-1812* (East Lansing: Michigan State University Press, 1967); Bernard W. Sheehan, *Seeds of Extinction: Jeffersonian Philanthropy and the American Indian* (Chapel Hill: University of North Carolina Press, 1973); and Herman J. Viola, *Thomas L. McKenney: Architect of America's Early Indian Policy, 1816-1830* (Chicago: Sage Books, 1974) deal with policies toward the Indians during the first half-century of national life. Grant Foreman, *Advancing the Frontier, 1830-1860* (Norman: University of Oklahoma Press, 1933); Ronald N. Satz, *American Indian Policy in the Jacksonian Era* (Lincoln: University of Nebraska Press, 1975); and Francis Paul Prucha, "Andrew Jackson's Indian Policy: A Reassessment," *Journal of American History*, LVI (1969-70), 527-539; and "American Indian Policy in the 1840's: Visions of Reform," in John G. Clark, ed., *The Frontier Challenge: Responses to the Trans-Mississippi West* (Lawrence: University Press of Kansas, 1971), pp. 81-110, deal with policies during the Jacksonian era. Robert A. Trennert, Jr., *Alternative to Extinction: Federal Indian Policy and the Beginnings of the Reservation System, 1846-51* (Philadelphia: Temple University Press, 1975) and William T. Hagen, "Indian Policy after the Civil War: The Reservation Experience," in Francis Paul Prucha et al., *Indiana Historical Society Lectures, 1970-71*, pp. 21-36, deal with the emergence of the commitment to reservations during the later 1840's and the 1850's.

Grant Foreman, *The Five Civilized Tribes* (Norman: University of Oklahoma Press, 1934) and *Indian Removal: The Emigration of the Five Civilized Tribes* (Norman: University of Oklahoma Press, 1953) discuss the lives of the Cherokees, Chickasaws, Choctaws, Creeks, and Seminoles, the development of the policy of removal with respect to them, and the tragic affair of their removal. Foreman's work is usefully supplemented by Marion L. Starkey, *The Cherokee Nation* (New York: Alfred A. Knopf, 1946); R. S. Cotterill, *The Southern Indians: The Story of the Civilized Tribes Before Removal* (Norman: University of Oklahoma Press, 1954); and Angie Debo, *The Rise and Fall of the Choctaw Republic* (2d ed.; Norman: University of Oklahoma Press, 1961). Robert H. Skelton, "A History of the Educational System of the Cherokee Nation, 1801-1910" (doctoral thesis, University of Arkansas, 1970) is the fullest scholarly treatment of the extraordinary response of the Cherokees to the proffer of "civilization." Grant Foreman, *Sequoyah* (Norman: University of Oklahoma Press, 1938) and

Ralph Henry Gabriel, *Elias Boudinot, Cherokee, and His America* (Norman: University of Oklahoma Press, 1941) are relevant biographies.

The best book on the discordant pedagogies encountered by the Indians is Robert E. Berkhofer, Jr., *Salvation and the Savage: An Analysis of Protestant Missions and American Indian Response, 1787–1862* (Lexington: University of Kentucky Press, 1965). Sherburne F. Cook, *The Conflict Between the California Indian and White Civilization, 1940–43* (Berkeley: University of California Press, 1943) and Edward H. Spicer, *Cycles of Conquest: The Impact of Spain, Mexico, and the United States on the Indians of the Southwest, 1533–1960* (Tucson: University of Arizona Press, 1962) also illuminate the problem. Berkhofer's discussion of the pedagogy of the white community is usefully supplemented by Ruth A. Gallagher, "The Indian Agent in the United States before 1850," *Iowa Journal of History and Politics,* XIV (1916), 3–56, and "The Indian Agent in the United States since 1850," *ibid.,* 173–238; Evelyn C. Adams, *American Indian Education: Government Schools and Economic Progress* (New York: King's Crown Press, 1946); Harold S. Faust, "The Presbyterian Mission to the American Indian During the Period of Indian Removal (1838–1893)" (doctoral thesis, Temple University, 1943); William W. Graves, *The First Protestant Osage Missions, 1820–1837* (Oswego, Kans.: The Carpenter Press, 1949); Robert F. Berkhofer, Jr., "Model Zions for the American Indian," *American Quarterly,* XV (1963), 176–190; R. Pierce Beaver, *Church, State, and the American Indians: Two and a Half Centuries of Partnership in Missions Between Protestant Churches and Government* (St. Louis: Concordia Publishing House, 1966); Clifton Jackson Phillips, *Protestant America and the Pagan World: The First Half Century of the American Board of Commissioners for Foreign Missions, 1810–1860* (Cambridge, Mass.: Harvard University Press, 1969); and Francis Paul Prucha, *Broadax and Bayonet: The Role of the United States Army in the Development of the Northwest, 1815–1869* (Lincoln: University of Nebraska Press, 1967). Berkhofer's discussion of the pedagogy of the Indian community is usefully supplemented by such contemporary works as Henry R. Schoolcraft, *Information Respecting the History, Conditions and Prospects of the Indian Tribes of the United States* (5 vols.; Philadelphia: Lippincott, Grambo & Co., 1853–1856) and George Catlin, *Illustrations of the Manners, Customs, and Condition of the North American Indians with Letters and Notes* (2 vols.; 10th ed.; London: Henry G. Bohn, 1866) and such later ethnographic accounts as Stith Thompson, ed., *Tales of the North American Indians* (Cambridge, Mass.: Harvard University Press, 1929); George A. Pettitt, *Primitive Education in North America* (Berkeley: University of California Press, 1946); and Harold E. Driver, *Indians of North America* (Chicago: University of Chicago Press, 1961), though the later accounts need to be used with caution, since they tend to be synchronic rather than diachronic in character and to assume the persistence of beliefs and customs over long periods of time.

Henry F. Dobyns, "Estimating Aboriginal American Population: An Appraisal of Techniques with a New Hemispheric Estimate," *Current Anthropology,* VII (1966), 229–449, is a model demographic analysis. The bibliographies in William N. Fenton *et al., American Indian and White Relations to 1830: Needs and Opportunities for Study* (Chapel Hill: University of North Carolina Press, 1957); William T. Hagen, *American Indians;* Robert F. Berkhofer, Jr., *Salvation and the Savage;* Ronald A. Satz, *American Indian Policy in the Jacksonian Era;* and Wilcomb E. Washburn, *The Indian in America* are especially helpful. Wilcomb E. Washburn, *The American Indian and the Unit-*

ed States (4 vols.; New York: Random House, 1973) is a useful collection of government documents.

I discuss the tensions implicit in the processes of Americanization in "Americanization: A Perspective," *UCLA Educator*, X (December, 1976), 5–10. The tensions within and among white Americans concerning education for blacks and Indians are poignantly symbolized by the closing down of two Connecticut schools during the 1820's and 1830's, Prudence Crandall's school for black girls at Canterbury and the ABCFM school for Indian boys at Cornwall. For the first controversy, see Edmund Fuller, *Prudence Crandall: An Incident of Racism in Nineteenth-Century Connecticut* (Middletown, Conn.: Wesleyan University Press, 1971). For the second, see John Andrew, "Educating the Heathen: the Foreign Mission School Controversy and American Ideals," *Journal of American Studies*, XII (1978), 331–342.

INTRODUCTION TO PART III: THE PRUDENT SOCIETY

The utilitarian strain in the educational thought of the Revolutionary generation is documented in Daniel J. Boorstin, *The Lost World of Thomas Jefferson* (New York: Henry Holt and Company, 1948); Frederick Rudolph, ed., *Essays on Education in the Early Republic* (Cambridge, Mass.: Harvard University Press, 1963); Daniel Jules Booth, "Popular Educational Thought of the Early National Period in America, 1776–1830: A Survey and Analysis of Published Essays and Addresses" (doctoral thesis, University of Colorado, 1974); and Eva T. H. Brann, *Paradoxes of Education in a Republic* (Chicago: University of Chicago Press, 1979). The disagreements over detail run through the pages of Linda K. Kerber, *Federalists in Dissent: Imagery and Ideology in Jeffersonian America* (Ithaca, N.Y.: Cornell University Press, 1970). The persistence of the strain and of the disagreements connected with it are dealt with in a considerable literature, including, *inter alia*, Merle Curti, *The Social Ideas of American Educators* (New York: Charles Scribner's Sons, 1935), *American Paradox: The Conflict of Thought and Action* (New Brunswick, N.J.: Rutgers University Press, 1956), and *The Growth of American Thought* (3d ed.; New York: Harper & Row, 1964); R. Freeman Butts, *The College Charts Its Course: Historical Conceptions and Current Proposals* (New York: McGraw-Hill Book Company, 1939); Carl Bode, *The Anatomy of American Popular Culture, 1840–1861* (Berkeley: University of California Press, 1959); Richard Hofstadter, *Anti-intellectualism in American Life* (New York: Alfred A. Knopf, 1963); Russel B. Nye, *The Unembarrassed Muse: The Popular Arts in America* (New York: The Dial Press, 1970); and George H. Daniels, *Science in American Society* (New York: Alfred A. Knopf, 1971).

CHAPTER 8: PRUDENT LEARNING

The best biography of Benjamin Franklin is Carl Van Doren, *Benjamin Franklin* (New York: The Viking Press, 1938). *The Autobiography of Benjamin Franklin*, edited by Leonard W. Labaree, Ralph L. Ketcham, Helen B. Boatfield, and Helene H. Fineman (New Haven: Yale University Press, 1964) is the most informative edition of that work. *The Papers of Benjamin Franklin*, edited by Leonard W. Labaree *et al.* (18+ vols.; New Haven: Yale University Press, 1959–   ) is the most recent and authoritative collection of Franklin's writings. *The Writings of Benjamin Franklin*, edited by Albert Henry Smyth (10 vols.; New York: The Macmillan Company, 1904–1907), remains a highly useful edition. David Levin, "The Autobiography of Benjamin Franklin: The Puritan Experimenter in Life and Art," *Yale Review,* LIII (1963–64), 258–275; John William Ward, "Who Was Benjamin Franklin?" *American Scholar,* XXXII (1963), 541–553; and Robert F. Sayre, *The Examined Self: Benjamin Franklin, Henry Adams, Henry James* (Princeton, N.J.: Princeton University Press, 1964) are incisive explorations of Franklin's character and of the *Autobiography* in refracting that character for subsequent generations, as are some of the older essays collected in Charles I. Sanford, ed., *Benjamin Franklin and the American Character* (Boston: D. C. Heath and Company, 1955).

For the projection of Franklinian ideals into the nineteenth century, Richard D. Mosier, *Making the American Mind: Social and Moral Ideas in the McGuffey Readers* (New York: King's Crown Press, 1947); Irvin G. Wyllie, *The Self-Made Man in America: The Myth of Rags to Riches* (New Brunswick, N.J.: Rutgers University Press, 1954); Ruth Miller Elson, *Guardians of Tradition: American Schoolbooks of the Nineteenth Century* (Lincoln: University of Nebraska Press, 1964); John G. Cawelti, *Apostles of the Self-Made Man: Changing Concepts of Success in America* (Chicago: University of Chicago Press, 1965) and Richard Weiss, *The American Myth of Success: From Horatio Alger to Norman Vincent Peale* (New York: Basic Books, 1969) are helpful analyses. J. F. C. Harrison, *Learning and Living, 1790–1960: A Study in the History of the English Adult Education Movement* (London: Routledge and Kegan Paul, 1961) includes an incisive analysis of the English self-help movement. The literature on Channing is discussed on pp. 529–530 *supra.* The self-help literature, of which Alcott's guides are quintessential examples, is portrayed from quite different perspectives by Carl Bode, *The Anatomy of American Popular Culture, 1840–1861* (Berkeley: University of California Press, 1959) and Allen Stanley Horlick, *Country Boys and Merchant Princes: The Social Control of Young Men in New York* (Lewisburg, Pa.: Bucknell University Press, 1975). There is an article on William Andrus Alcott in the *Dictionary of American Biography,* and there is an autobiography entitled *Confessions of a Schoolmaster* (rev. ed.; Reading, Pa.: H. A. Lantz, 1856). The literature on Horatio Alger, Jr., is replete with legend and even some fraudulent biography based on a nonexistent diary. Edwin P. Hoyt, *Horatio's Boys: The Life and Works of Horatio Alger, Jr.* (Radnor, Pa.: Chilton Book Company, 1974) appears to be authoritative. The values in the Alger novels are analyzed by Rychard Fink in his introduction to Horatio Alger, Jr., *Ragged Dick and Mark, the Match Boy* (New York: Collier Books, 1962); Richard Wohl, "The 'Rags to Riches Story': An Episode of Secular Idealism," in Reinhard Bendix and Seymour Martin Lipset, eds., *Class, Status and Power: A Reader in Social Stratification* (Glencoe, Ill.: The Free Press, 1953), pp. 388–395; and Michael Zuckerman, "The Nursery Tales of Horatio Alger," *American Quarterly,* XXIV (1972), 191–209.

Harry R. Warfel, *Noah Webster: Schoolmaster to America* (New York: The Macmillan Company, 1936) is the standard biography. Dennis Patrick Rusche, "An Empire of Reason: A Study of the Writings of Noah Webster" (doctoral thesis, University of Iowa, 1975) and Richard Meryl Rollins, "The Long Journey of Noah Webster" (doctoral thesis, Michigan State University, 1976) are recent studies of Webster's thought. Ervin C. Shoemaker, *Noah Webster: Pioneer of Learning* (New York: Columbia University Press, 1936) deals with Webster's work as an educator. In the introductory essay to the edition he edited of Noah Webster's *American Spelling Book* (New York: Bureau of Publications, Teachers College, Columbia University, 1962), Henry Steele Commager views Webster's lexicographical efforts as an important nationalizing influence in American culture; Richard M. Rollins, "Words as Social Control: Noah Webster and the Creation of the American Dictionary," *American Quarterly*, XXVIII (1976), 415–430, sees those efforts as a constraining evangelical influence. Emily Ellsworth Ford Skeel and Edwin H. Carpenter, Jr., *A Bibliography of the Writings of Noah Webster* (New York: New York Public Library, 1958) is a splendid critical bibliography. Emily Ellsworth Fowler Ford and Emily Ellsworth Ford Skeel, eds., *Notes on the Life of Noah Webster* (2 vols.: New York: privately printed, 1912) is an invaluable compilation of the diary and letters; Harry R. Warfel, ed., *Letters of Noah Webster* (New York: Library Publishers, 1953) is the standard edition of the correspondence. Noah Webster, *On Being American: Selected Writings, 1783–1828*, edited by Homer D. Babbage, Jr. (New York: Frederick A. Praeger, Publishers, 1967) is a convenient anthology. H. L. Mencken, *The American Language: An Inquiry into the Development of English in the United States, Together with Supplements I and II* (3 vols.; New York: Alfred A. Knopf, 1936–1948) provides an excellent context within which to consider Webster's linguistic contribution.

The debates over the college curriculum after the War of 1812 are discussed in George P. Schmidt, "Intellectual Crosscurrents in American Colleges, 1825–1855," *American Historical Review*, XLII (1936–37), 46–57; R. Freeman Butts, *The College Charts Its Course: Historical Conceptions and Current Proposals* (New York: McGraw-Hill Book Company, 1939); Douglas Sloan, "Harmony, Chaos, and Consensus: The American College Curriculum," *Teachers College Record*, LXXIII (1971–1972), 221–251; and Frederick Rudolph, *Curriculum: A History of the Undergraduate Course of Study Since 1636* (San Francisco: Jossey-Bass Publishers, 1977). For the developments at Amherst, see Claude Moore Fuess, *Amherst: The Story of a New England College* (Boston: Little, Brown and Company, 1935). For developments at the University of Virginia, see Philip Alexander Bruce, *History of the University of Virginia, 1819–1919* (5 vols.; New York: The Macmillan Company, 1920–1922), I. For Ticknor's efforts at Harvard, see David B. Tyack, *George Ticknor and the Boston Brahmins* (Cambridge, Mass.: Harvard University Press, 1967). O. W. Long, *Thomas Jefferson and George Ticknor: A Chapter in American Scholarship* (Williamstown, Mass.: The McClelland Press, 1933) is a fascinating study of the Jefferson-Ticknor correspondence on the reform of the higher learning. For Nott's efforts at Union, see Codman Hislop, *Eliphalet Nott* (Middletown, Conn.: Wesleyan University Press, 1971). For Marsh's efforts at Vermont, see *The Remains of the Rev. James Marsh*, compiled by Joseph Torrey (1843; reprint ed.; Port Washington, N.Y.: Kennikat Press, 1971) and Julian I. Lindsay, *Tradition Looks Forward: The University of Vermont, a History, 1791–1904* (Burlington: University of Vermont Press, 1954). Richard Hofstadter and Wilson Smith, eds., *American Higher Education: A Documentary History* (2 vols.; Chicago: University of Chicago Press, 1961) is an admirable collection of documents.

The Yale Report of 1828 has been variously interpreted. R. Freeman Butts, *The College Charts Its Course;* Frederick Rudolph, *The American College and University: A History* (New York: Alfred A. Knopf, 1962); and Melvin I. Urofsky, "Reforms and Response: The Yale Report of 1828," *History of Education Quarterly*, V (1965), 53–

67, portray the document as aristocratic and reactionary. Ralph Henry Gabriel, *Religion and Learning at Yale: The Church of Christ in the College and University, 1757–1957* (New Haven: Yale University Press, 1958) and Brooks Mather Kelley, *Yale: A History.* (New Haven: Yale University Press, 1975) are more sympathetic. Douglas Sloan transforms the problem by viewing the document in context, as stipulating a role for the college in relation to graduate and professional education, within the university and without.

The best works on Wayland as an educator are Theodore Rawson Crane, "Francis Wayland and Brown University, 1796–1841" (doctoral thesis, Harvard University, 1959) and *Francis Wayland: Political Economist as Educator* (Providence: Brown University Press, 1962). William G. Roelker, *Francis Wayland: A Neglected Pioneer of Higher Education* (Worcester, Mass.: American Antiquarian Society, 1944) remains useful. For Brown, see Walter C. Bronson, *The History of Brown University, 1764–1914* (Providence: published by the University, 1914) and Donald Fleming, *Science and Technology in Providence, 1760–1914: An Essay in the History of Brown University in the Metropolitan Community* (Providence: Brown University, 1952). Wayland's best-known writings on education are *Thoughts on the Present Collegiate System in the United States* (Boston: Gould, Kendall, & Lincoln, 1842), *Report to the Corporation of Brown University, on Changes in the System of Collegiate Education, Read March 28, 1850* (Providence: George H. Whitney, 1850), and *The Education Demanded by the People of the United States* (Boston: Phillips, Sampson, and Company, 1855), though the educational ideas, both explicit and implicit, in *The Elements of Political Economy* (New York: Leavitt, Lord & Company, 1837) and *The Elements of Moral Science,* edited by Joseph Blau (Cambridge, Mass.: Harvard University Press, 1973), should not be ignored. The principal collection of Wayland papers is at the John Hay Library at Brown University. For Lindsley, see *The Works of Philip Lindsley,* edited by Le Roy J. Halsey (3 vols.; Philadelphia: J. B. Lippincott & Co., 1859–1866), which includes a biographical sketch by Halsey as a supplement to Volume III. For Tappan, see Charles M. Perry, *Henry Philip Tappan: Philosopher and University President* (Ann Arbor: University of Michigan Press, 1933).

There is no adequate history of the Smithsonian Institution. The best scholarly discussions of its early years are Madge E. Pickard, "Government and Science in the United States: Historical Backgrounds," *Journal of the History of Medicine and Allied Sciences,* I (1946), 446–481; A. Hunter Dupree, *Science in the Federal Government* (Cambridge, Mass.: Harvard University Press, 1957); and Wilcomb E. Washburn, "Joseph Henry's Conception of the Purpose of the Smithsonian Institution," in Whitfield J. Bell, Jr., *et al., A Cabinet of Curiosities: Five Episodes in the Evaluation of American Museums* (Charlottesville: The University Press of Virginia, 1967), pp. 106–166. George Brown Goode, ed., *The Smithsonian Institution, 1846–1896: The History of Its First Half-Century* (Washington, D.C.: The Smithsonian Institution, 1897) is also valuable. William J. Rhees, ed., *The Smithsonian Institution: Documents Relating to Its Origin and History* (Washington, D.C.: The Smithsonian Institution, 1879) and *The Smithsonian Institution: Documents Relative to Its Origins and History, 1835–1899* (2 vols.; Washington, D.C.: Government Printing Office, 1901) present the debates surrounding the creation of the Smithsonian, in which the range of nineteenth-century American attitudes concerning the role of science in human affairs is brilliantly illuminated. Dirk J. Struik, *Yankee Science in the Making* (Boston: Little, Brown and

Company, 1948); Charles E. Rosenberg, "Science and American Thought," in David D. Van Tassel and Michael G. Hall, eds., *Science and Society in the United States* (Homewood, Ill.: The Dorsey Press, 1966), pp. 135–189; and George H. Daniels, *American Science in the Age of Jackson* (New York: Columbia University Press, 1968) and *Science in American Society* (New York: Alfred A. Knopf, 1971) are useful contextual materials, as is Edwin Layton, "Mirror-Image Twins: The Communities of Science and Technology in 19th Century America," *Technology and Culture,* XII (1971), 561–580, which discusses the critical relationships between the cultures of the scientific and the technological communities—in this respect, Jacob Bigelow, *Elements of Technology* (Boston: Hilliard, Gray, Little, and Wilkins, 1829) and *An Address on the Limits of Education* (Boston: E. P. Dutton & Company, 1865) and Timothy Walker, "Defence of Mechanical Philosophy," *North American Review,* XXXIII (1831), 122–136, bear perusal. Thomas Coulson, *Joseph Henry: His Life and Work* (Princeton, N.J.: Princeton University Press, 1950) is the standard biography. *The Papers of Joseph Henry,* edited by Nathan Reingold (3+ vols.; Washington, D.C.: Smithsonian Institution Press, 1972–   ) promises to be the definitive edition of Henry's writings.

Ralph L. Rusk, *The Life of Ralph Waldo Emerson* (New York: Charles Scribner's Sons, 1949) is the definitive biography. *The Letters of Ralph Waldo Emerson,* edited by Ralph L. Rusk (6 vols.; Columbia University Press, 1939) is the standard edition of the correspondence. Ralph Waldo Emerson, *Early Lectures,* edited by Stephen E. Whicher *et al.* (3 vols.; Cambridge, Mass.: Harvard University Press, 1959–1964), and *Journals and Miscellaneous Notebooks,* edited by William H. Gilman *et al.* (14+ vols.; Cambridge, Mass.: Harvard University Press, 1960–) also promise to be definitive. George Willis, ed., *A Bibliography of Ralph Waldo Emerson* (Boston: Houghton Mifflin and Company, 1908) is an excellent guide to the various editions of Emerson's publications. *The Complete Works of Ralph Waldo Emerson,* edited by Edward Waldo Emerson (12 vols.; Boston: Houghton Mifflin and Company, 1903–1904) has long been standard. The principal collection of Emerson papers is at the Houghton Library at Harvard University.

Of the voluminous literature on Emerson, the following have proved most illuminating for my analysis: Henry Nash Smith, "Emerson's Problem of Vocation–A Note on 'The American Scholar,'" *New England Quarterly,* XII (1939), 52–67; F. O. Matthiessen, *American Renaissance: Art and Expression in the Age of Emerson and Whitman* (New York: Oxford University Press, 1941); Daniel Aaron, *Men of Good Hope: The Study of American Progressives* (New York: Oxford University Press, 1951); Sherman Paul, *Emerson's Angle of Vision* (Cambridge, Mass.: Harvard University Press, 1952); Stephen E. Whicher, *Freedom and Fate: An Inner Life of Ralph Waldo Emerson* (Philadelphia: University of Pennsylvania Press, 1953); Perry Miller, *Errand into the Wilderness* (Cambridge, Mass.: Harvard University Press, 1956); and Quentin Anderson, *The Imperial Self: An Essay in American Literary and Cultural History* (New York: Alfred A. Knopf, 1971). John F. Kasson, *Civilizing the Machine: Technology and Republican Values in America, 1776–1900* (New York: Grossman Publishers, 1976) deals incisively with Emerson's ambivalence toward technology. Marshall H. Cowan, *City of the West: Emerson, America, and Urban Metaphor* (New Haven: Yale University Press, 1967) deals imaginatively with Emerson's ambivalence toward cities. Albert E. Lewis, "The Contribution of Ralph Waldo Emerson to American Education" (doctoral thesis, Stanford University, 1943) and Maxine Greene, *The*

Public School and the Private Vision (New York: Random House, 1965) deal sensitively with Emerson's ideas on education. Howard Mumford Jones, ed., *Emerson on Education* (New York: Teachers College Press, 1966) is a convenient anthology with an informed introduction.

Gay Wilson Allen, *The Solitary Singer: A Critical Biography of Walt Whitman* (rev. ed.; New York: New York University Press, 1967) is the definitive biography. The intellectual relationship between Emerson and Whitman is incisively explicated in F. O. Matthiessen, *American Renaissance*. The correspondence of Emerson and Whitman concerning *Leaves of Grass* is carried in the critical apparatus of Walt Whitman, *Leaves of Grass,* edited by Harold W. Blodgett and Sculley Bradley (New York: New York University Press, 1965).

CHAPTER 9: THE DILEMMAS OF POPULARIZATION

E. Douglas Branch, *The Sentimental Years, 1836–1860* (New York: D. Appleton-Century Company, 1934) and Robert E. Riegel, *Young America, 1830–1840* (Norman: University of Oklahoma Press, 1949) are older histories that deal with many of the issues and institutions raised in this chapter. They tend to be uncritical, but they are filled with useful information and bear close rereading. In a somewhat different way, despite the earnest didacticism that attended many of the ventures described in this chapter, Foster Rhea Dulles, *America Learns to Play* (New York: D. Appleton-Century Company, 1940) is a valuable contextual source throughout.

Hellmut Lehmann-Haupt *et al., The Book in America: A History of the Making and Selling of Books in the United States* (2d ed.; New York: R. R. Bowker Company, 1951) and the first volume of John Tebbel, *A History of Book Publishing in the United States* (3+ vols.; New York: R. R. Bowker, 1972–) are the best works on American publishing during the early national era. Given the lack of differentiation between printing and publishing throughout much of the United States during most of the nineteenth century, the sources on printers and printing cited on pp. 555–557 *supra* are relevant here. Madeleine B. Stern, *Imprints on History: Book Publishers and American Frontiers* (Bloomington: Indiana University Press, 1956); J. H. Powell, *The Books of a New Nation: United States Government Publications, 1774–1814* (Philadelphia: University of Pennsylvania Press, 1957); Walter Sutton, *The Western Book Trade: Cincinnati as a Nineteenth-Century Publishing and Book-Trade Center* (Columbus: Ohio State University Press, 1961); and Charles A. Madison, *Book Publishing in America* (New York: McGraw-Hill Book Company, 1966) are also useful, as are most of the essays in David Kaser, ed., *Books in America's Past: Essays Honoring Rudolph H. Gjelsness* (Charlottesville: The University Press of Virginia, 1966). Clifford K. Shipton, *Isaiah Thomas: Printer, Patriot and Philanthropist, 1749–1832* (Rochester, N.Y.: Printing House of Leo Hart, 1948) is the authoritative biography of the foremost early national printer-publisher. S. G. Goodrich, *Recollections of a Lifetime, or Men and Things I Have Seen* (2 vols.; New York: Miller, Orton and Mulligan, 1856) is a treasure trove of information on nineteenth-century publishing; Daniel Roselle, *Samuel Griswold Goodrich, Creator of Peter Parley: A Study of His Life and Work* (Albany: State University of New York Press, 1968) is a recent biography. Eugene Exman, *The Brothers Harper: A Unique Publishing Partnership and Its Impact upon the Cultural Life of America from 1817 to 1853* (New York: Harper & Row, 1965) is an authoritative account; Morely Acklon, "The Rise of the House of Dutton," in *Seventy-Five Years of Publishing* (New York: E. P. Dutton & Company, 1927) and Ellen B. Ballou, *The Building of the House: Houghton Mifflin's Formative Years* (Boston: Houghton Mifflin Company, 1970) depict contemporary ventures. The literature that emanated from nineteenth-century publishers is discussed in William Charvat, *Literary Publishing in America, 1790–1850* (Philadelphia: University of Pennsylvania Press, 1959); Robert E. Spiller *et al.*, eds., *Literary History of the United States* (4th ed.; rev.; 2 vols.; New York: The Macmillan Company, 1974); and Russel B. Nye, *The Unembarrassed Muse: The Popular Arts in America* (New York: The Dial Press, 1970).

Jesse H. Shera, *Foundations of the Public Library* (Chicago: University of Chicago Press, 1949) and Sidney Ditzion, "Social Reform, Education, and the Library, 1850–1900," *Library Quarterly*, IX (1939), 156–184, "Mechanics' and Mercantile Libraries," *ibid.*, X (1940), 192–219, "The District-School Library, 1835–55," *ibid.*, 545–577, and *Arsenals of a Democratic Culture: A Social History of the American Public Library Movement in New England and the Middle States from 1850 to 1900* (Chicago: American Library Association, 1947) are the best general writings on the development of nineteenth-century libraries. Letha Pearl McGuire, "A Study of the Public Library Movement in Iowa," *Iowa Journal of History and Politics*, XXXV (1937), 22–72; Frank L. Tolman, "Libraries and Lyceums," in Alexander C. Flick, ed., *History of the State of New York* (9 vols.; New York: Columbia University Press, 1933–1937), IX, 47–91; and Frederic D. Aldrich, *The School Library in Ohio, with Special Emphasis on Its Legislative History* (New York: The Scarecrow Press, 1959) are useful state studies. Walter Muir Whitehill, *Boston Public Library: A Centennial History* (Cambridge, Mass.: Harvard University Press, 1956) is an account of the most influential nineteenth-century public library. Ronald Story, "Class and Culture in Boston: The Athenaeum, 1807–1860," *American Quarterly*, XXVII (1975), 178–199, discusses the role of the Boston elite in the founding of the Athenaeum. William Dawson Johnston, *History of the Library of Congress* (Washington, D.C.: Government Printing Office, 1904) and Phyllis Dain, *The New York Public Library: A History of Its Founding and Early Years* (New York: New York Public Library, 1972) are histories of important research collections. Frank Keller Walter, "A Poor but Respectable Relation—The Sunday School Library," *Library Quarterly*, XII (1942), 731–739, is a brief but informative essay, which is usefully supplemented by Edwin Wilbur Rice, *The Sunday-School Movement and the American Sunday-School Union, 1780–1917* (Philadelphia: The American Sunday-School Union, 1917). Michael Harris, "The Purpose of the American Public Library: A Revisionist Interpretation of History," *Library Journal*, XCVIII (1973), 2509–2514, takes issue with the assertion of the traditional historiography that the public library derived from democratic aspirations; it is usefully complemented by Phyllis Dain, "Ambivalence and Paradox: The Social Bonds of the Public Library," *Library Journal*, C (1975), 261–266. William J. Rhees, *Manual of Public Libraries, Institutions, and Societies, in the United States and British Provinces of North America* (Philadelphia: J. B. Lippincott, 1859) and U.S., Bureau of Education, *Public Libraries in the United States of America: Special Report* (Washington, D.C.: Government Printing Office, 1876) are gold mines of statistical and other data.

Milton Rubincam, "History of Benjamin Franklin's Junto Club," *Junto Selections: Essays on the History of Pennsylvania* (Washington, D.C.: Pennsylvania Historica: Junto, 1946) and Dorothy Fear Grimm, "A History of the Library Company of

Philadelphia, 1731-1835" (doctoral thesis, University of Pennsylvania, 1955) are the best sources, apart from Franklin's *Autobiography* itself, for the development of the Junto and its associated library. The references discussed on pp. 557-558 *supra* explicate the development of associations in the realms of art, agriculture, industry, commerce, politics, religion, and culture during the first century of national life. Carl Bode, *The American Lyceum: Town Meeting of the Mind* (New York: Oxford University Press, 1956) is the best cultural history. Cecil B. Hayes, *The American Lyceum: Its History and Contribution to Education* (Washington, D.C.: Government Printing Office, 1932); Paul Stoddard, "The American Lyceum" (doctoral thesis, Yale University, 1947); and James Kelso, "The American Lyceum: An American Institution" (doctoral thesis, Harvard University, 1952) are also useful. J. F. C. Harrison, *Learning and Living, 1790-1960: A History of the English Adult Education Movement* (London: Routledge and Kegan Paul, 1961); Frances Hawes, *Henry Brougham* (New York: St. Martin's Press, 1956); and Elaine Anne Storella, "'O, What a World of Profit and Delight': The Society for the Diffusion of Useful Knowledge" (doctoral thesis, Brandeis University, 1969) illuminate the British context.

There is no adequate history of American museums. The charming scholarly essays collected in Whitfield J. Bell, Jr., *A Cabinet of Curiosities: Five Episodes in the Evolution of American Museums* (Charlottesville: The University Press of Virginia, 1967) are the closest thing there is to a beginning. Paul G. Sifton, "Pierre Eugène Du Simitière (1737-1784): Collector in Revolutionary America" (doctoral thesis, University of Pennsylvania, 1960) and "A Disordered Life: The American Career of Pierre Eugène Du Simitière," *Manuscripts,* XXV (1973), 235-253, are the best works on the Revolutionary portraitist, engraver, historiographer, and collector. Charles Coleman Sellers, *Charles Willson Peale* (2 vols.; Philadelphia: American Philosophical Society, 1947) is a splendid biography. Robert M. and Gale S. McClung, "Tammany's Remarkable Gardiner Baker: New York's First Museum Proprietor, Menagerie Keeper, and Promoter Extraordinary," *New York Historical Society Quarterly,* XLII (1957), 143-169, and Lloyd Haberly, "The American Museum from Baker to Barnum," *ibid.,* XLIII (1959), 273-287, present helpful information on New York City museums before the entry of P. T. Barnum upon the scene. Neil Harris, *Humbug: The Art of P. T. Barnum* (Boston: Little, Brown and Company, 1973) is a splendid biography of Barnum that is especially incisive on the cultural context of the era. Barnum left an autobiography in several versions, which were assembled in a single annotated edition in George S. Bryan, ed., *Struggles and Triumphs; or, The Life of P. T. Barnum, Written by Himself* (2 vols.; New York: Alfred A. Knopf, 1927).

Walter Muir Whitehill, *Independent Historical Societies: An Enquiry into Their Research and Publication Functions and Their Financial Future* (Boston: The Boston Athenaeum, 1962) is replete with valuable historical data. Oliver W. Larkin, *Samuel F. B. Morse and American Democratic Art* (Boston: Little, Brown, and Company, 1954); Lillian B. Miller, *Patrons and Patriotism: The Encouragement of the Fine Arts in the United States, 1790-1860* (Chicago: University of Chicago Press, 1966); and Nathaniel Burt, *Palaces for the People: A Social History of the American Art Museum* (Boston: Little, Brown and Company, 1977) deal with the rise of the art museum in America. John Michael Kennedy, "Philanthropy and Science in New York City: The American Museum of Natural History, 1868-1968" (doctoral thesis, Yale University, 1968); Calvin Tomkins, *Merchants and Masterpieces: The Story of the Metropolitan*

Museum of Art (New York: E. P. Dutton & Co., 1970); Walter Muir Whitehill, *Museum of Fine Arts, Boston: A Centennial History* (2 vols.; Cambridge, Mass.: Harvard University Press, 1970); Neil Harris, "The Gilded Age Revisited: Boston and the Museum Movement," *American Quarterly*, XIV (1962), 545–566; and Douglas Sloan, "Science in New York City, 1867–1907," *Isis*, LXXI (1980), 35–76, deal with the origins of the three great museums.

In considering the development of the museum as an educational institution, it is well to bear in mind André Malraux's fascinating observation at the opening of *The Voices of Silence*, translated by Stuart Gilbert (Garden City, N.Y.: Doubleday & Company, 1953) to the effect that the museum in its very nature imposes upon the spectator a new attitude toward the works on display. The imposition, I would judge, is as significant with respect to works of nature and technology as it is to works of art.

Wayne C. Neely, *The Agricultural Fair* (New York: Columbia University Press, 1935) is the best scholarly work on the development of the fair. It includes substantial material on the early English and American societies for agricultural improvement and on the pioneering of Elkanah Watson. Alfred Charles True, *A History of Agricultural Education in the United States, 1785–1925* (Washington, D.C.: Government Printing Office, 1929) and Percy Wells Bidwell and John I. Falconer, *History of Agriculture in the Northern United States, 1620–1860* (Washington, D.C.: Carnegie Institution of Washington, 1925) also include substantial discussions. Christopher Hobhouse, *1851 and the Crystal Palace* (London: John Murray, 1950); Patrick Beaver, *The Crystal Palace, 1851–1936: A Portrait in Victorian Enterprise* (London: Hugh Evelyn, 1970); and Richard D. Altick, *The Shows of London: A Panoramic History of Exhibitions, 1600–1862* (Cambridge, Mass.: Harvard University Press, 1978) are vivid portrayals of the London exposition of 1851. *The Crystal Palace Exhibition Illustrated Catalogue, London, 1851: An Unabridged Republication of The Art-Journal Special Issue* (New York: Dover Publications, 1970) presents detailed information and illustrations. Charles Hirschfeld, "America on Exhibition: The New York Crystal Palace," *American Quarterly*, IX (1957), 101–116, and *Art and Industry: As Represented in the Exhibition at the Crystal Palace*, edited by Horace Greeley (New York: Redfield, 1853), depict the New York effort. Christine Hunter Davidson, "The Centennial of 1876: The Exposition and Culture for America" (doctoral thesis, Yale University, 1948) is the best scholarly work on the Philadelphia centennial exhibition; Lillian B. Miller, "Engines, Marbles, and Canvases: The Centennial Exposition of 1876," in Lillian B. Miller *et al.*, *Indiana Historical Society Lectures, 1972–73* (Indianapolis: Indiana Historical Society, 1973) advances incisive judgments concerning the art displayed at the exposition; James D. McCabe, *The Illustrated History of the Centennial Exhibition* (Philadelphia: Jones Brothers & Co., 1876) and John S. Ingram, *The Centennial Exhibition Described and Illustrated* (Philadelphia: Hubbard, 1887) are detailed contemporary descriptions. Merle Curti, "America at the World Fairs, 1851–1893," in *Probing Our Past* (New York: Harper & Brothers, 1955), chap. x; Halvdan Koht, *The American Spirit in Europe: A Survey of Transatlantic Influences* (Philadelphia: University of Pennsylvania Press, 1949), chap. vi; and John G. Cawelti, "America on Display: The World's Fairs of 1876, 1893, 1933," in Frederick Cople Jaher, ed., *The Age of Industrialism in America* (New York: Free Press, 1963), pp. 317–363, are general discussions of cross-national teaching and learning via international expositions.

CHAPTER 10: LEARNING AND LIVING

Douglass C. North, *The Economic Growth of the United States, 1790–1860* (Englewood Cliffs, N.J.: Prentice-Hall, 1961); Curtis P. Nettles, *The Emergence of a National Economy, 1775–1815* (New York: Holt, Rinehart and Winston, 1962); Paul W. Gates, *The Farmer's Age: Agriculture, 1815–1860* (New York: Holt, Rinehart and Winston, 1960); and George Rogers Taylor, *The Transportation Revolution, 1815–1860* (New York: Rinehart and Company, 1951) are comprehensive scholarly treatments of the economic development of the new nation. Percy Wells Bidwell and John Falconer, *History of Agriculture in the Northern United States, 1620–1860* (Washington, D.C.: Carnegie Institution of Washington, 1925); Percy Wells Bidwell, "The Agricultural Revolution in New England," *American Historical Review*, XXVI (1920–21), 683–702; and Lewis C. Gray, *History of Agriculture in the Southern United States to 1860* (2 vols.; Washington, D.C.: Carnegie Institution of Washington, 1933) remain the fundamental studies of agriculture. Douglas Bowers, *A List of References for the History of Agriculture in the United States, 1790–1840* (Davis: Agricultural History Center, University of California, 1969) is a comprehensive annotated bibliography, with a substantial section on agricultural societies and agricultural journals. Wayne C. Neeley, *The Agricultural Fair* (New York: Columbia University Press, 1935) is the best source on the agricultural societies as educational agencies for the improvement of agricultural methods. Albert Lowther Demaree, *The American Agricultural Press, 1819–1860* (New York: Columbia University Press, 1941) is the best source on the agricultural press as an educative agency. Richard Bardolph, *Agricultural Literature and the Early Illinois Farmer* (Urbana: University of Illinois Press, 1948) is a useful specialized study. William E. Ogilvie, *Pioneer Agricultural Journalists: Brief Biographical Sketches of Some of the Early Editors in the Field of Agricultural Journalism* (Chicago: Arthur G. Leonard, 1927); Avery O. Craven, *Edmund Ruffin, Southerner: A Study in Secession* (New York: D. Appleton and Co., 1932); Harry J. Carman, *Jesse Buel, Agricultural Reformer: Selections from His Writings* (New York: Columbia University Press, 1947); and Harold A. Bierck, Jr., "Spoils, Soils, and Skinner," *Maryland Historical Magazine*, XLIX (1954), 21–40, 143–155, portray some of the better known editor-reformers. Alfred Charles True, *A History of Agricultural Education in the United States, 1785–1925* (Washington, D.C.: Government Printing Office, 1929) deals with the societies and the journals as educators but concentrates on varieties of formal schooling. The interaction of the availability of education and the development of commercial agriculture in the North and West is incisively portrayed by Paul W. Gates in *The Farmer's Age*. The contrasting predicament of the southern plantation owners is depicted in Eugene D. Genovese, *The Political Economy of Slavery: Studies in the Economic & Society of the Slave South* (New York: Random House, 1967).

Victor S. Clark, *History of Manufactures in the United States* (3 vols.; Washington, D.C.: Carnegie Institution of Washington, 1929); Balthasar Henry Meyer *et al.*, *History of Transportation in the United States before 1860* (Washington, D.C.: Carnegie Institution of Washington, 1917); and John R. Commons *et al.*, *History of Labour in the United States* (4 vols.; New York: The Macmillan Company, 1918) remain the fundamental sources for the development of manufacturing in the United States. Rolla Mil-

574 BIBLIOGRAPHICAL ESSAY

ton Tryon, *Household Manufactures in the United States, 1640–1860: A Study in Industrial History* (Chicago: University of Chicago Press, 1917) is the standard work on household manufacture in early America. Robert H. Bremner, ed., *Children and Youth in America: A Documentary History* (3 vols.; Cambridge, Mass.: Harvard University Press, 1970–1974), I, includes substantial material on early apprenticeship practices. Paul H. Douglas, *American Apprenticeship and Industrial Education* (New York: privately printed, 1921) and Marcus Wilson Jernegan, *Laboring and Dependent Classes in Colonial America, 1607–1783* (Chicago: University of Chicago Press, 1931) are older but still useful studies.

Apprenticeship in the early nineteenth-century printing industry is depicted in Milton W. Hamilton, *The Country Printer: New York, 1785–1830* (New York: Columbia University Press, 1936) and Rollo G. Silver, *The American Printer, 1787–1825* (Charlottesville: The University Press of Virginia, 1967). The role of the early printers' unions in attempting to enforce apprenticeship standards is dealt with in Silver, *The American Printer;* in John R. Commons *et al., History of Labour in the United States,* I; and in Norman Ware, *The Industrial Worker, 1840–1860: The Reaction of American Industrial Society to the Advance of the Industrial Revolution* (Boston: Houghton Mifflin Company, 1924). Blanche Evans Hazard, *The Organization of the Boot and Shoe Industry in Massachusetts Before 1875* (Cambridge, Mass.: Harvard University Press, 1921), Paul Gustaf Faler, "Workingmen, Mechanics and Social Change: Lynn, Massachusetts 1800–1860" (doctoral thesis, University of Wisconsin, 1971) and "Cultural Aspects of the Industrial Revolution: Lynn, Massachusetts, Shoemakers and Industrial Morality, 1826–1860," *Labor History,* XV (1974), 367–397, and Alan Dawley, *Class and Community: The Industrial Revolution in Lynn* (Cambridge, Mass.: Harvard University Press, 1976) trace the evolution of boot and shoe manufacture in Lynn. Brendan Francis Gilbane, "A Social History of Samuel Slater's Pawtucket, 1790–1830" (doctoral thesis, Boston University, 1969) is an authoritative account of the development and organization of Slater's enterprise; *Memoir of Samuel Slater, The Father of American Manufactures* (2d ed.; Philadelphia: no publisher, 1836) is an invaluable contemporary source. Caroline F. Ware, *The Early New England Cotton Manufacture* (Boston: Houghton Mifflin Company, 1931); Ernest McPherson Lander, Jr., *The Textile Industry in Antebellum South Carolina* (Baton Rouge: Louisiana State University Press, 1969); and Anthony F. C. Wallace, *Rockdale: The Growth of an American Village in the Early Industrial Revolution* (New York: Alfred A. Knopf, 1978) depict contemporary textile manufacturing elsewhere; Wallace's anthropologically trained eye adds a rich concreteness of detail not present in previous studies.

Sidney Pollard, "Factory Discipline in the Industrial Revolution," *Economic History Review,* 2d ser., XVI (1963–64), 254–271, and E. P. Thompson, "Time, Work-Discipline, and Industrial Capitalism," *Past & Present,* no. 38 (December, 1967), 56–97, are two informed discussions of the problem of industrial discipline. Brendan Francis Gilbane, "A Social History of Samuel Slater's Pawtucket, 1790–1830" and Paul Faler, "Cultural Aspects of the Industrial Revolution" discuss the problem with specific reference to Pawtucket and Lynn. Bruce Gordon Laurie, "The Working People of Philadelphia, 1828–1853" (doctoral thesis, University of Pittsburgh, 1971) and "'Nothing on Compulsion': Life Styles of Philadelphia Artisans, 1820–1850," *Labor History,* XV (1974), 337–366; Herbert G. Gutman, *Work, Culture, and Society in In-*

dustrializing America (New York: Alfred A. Knopf, 1976); Daniel T. Rodgers, *The Work Ethic in Industrial America, 1850–1920* (Chicago: University of Chicago Press, 1978); and Paul Boyer, *Urban Masses and Moral Order in America, 1820–1920* (Cambridge, Mass.: Harvard University Press, 1978) discuss the problem more generally.

Francis W. Gregory, *Nathan Appleton: Merchant and Entrepreneur, 1779–1861* (Charlottesville: The University Press of Virginia, 1975) is the best biography of Appleton. Glyndon G. Van Deusen, *Horace Greeley: Nineteenth Century Crusader* (Philadelphia: University of Pennsylvania Press, 1953) is the best biography of Greeley. Alan Dawley, *Class and Community* portrays the shoe manufacturers of Lynn.

Daniel H. Calhoun, *Professional Lives in America: Structure and Aspiration, 1750–1850* (Cambridge, Mass.: Harvard University Press, 1965) is the best general discussion of professionals and their formal and informal education in early national America. Francis R. Packard, *History of Medicine in the United States* (2 vols.; New York: P. B. Hoeber, 1931); Richard Harrison Shryock, *Medicine and Society in America, 1660–1860* (New York: New York University Press, 1960) and *Medicine in America: Historical Essays* (Baltimore: The Johns Hopkins University Press, 1966); and William G. Rothstein, *American Physicians in the Nineteenth Century: From Sects to Science* (Baltimore: The Johns Hopkins University Press, 1972) deal broadly with the development of medicine and the medical profession in relation to American society. Richard Harrison Shryock, *Medical Licensing in America, 1650–1965* (Baltimore: The Johns Hopkins University Press, 1967) traces the development of licensing practices; Joseph F. Kett, *The Formation of the American Medical Profession: The Role of Institutions, 1780–1860* (New Haven: Yale University Press, 1968) traces the emergence of the profession *qua* profession in the United States. Gert H. Brieger, ed., *Medical America in the Nineteenth Century* (Baltimore: The Johns Hopkins University Press, 1972) is an informative collection of documents. William Frederick Norwood, *Medical Education in the United States Before the Civil War* (Philadelphia: University of Pennsylvania Press, 1944) and Martin Kaufman, *American Medical Education: The Formative Years, 1765–1910* (Westport, Conn.: Greenwood Press, 1976) discuss the development of medical education. For the medical college at Castleton, Vermont, see Frederick Waite, "Birth of the First Proprietory Medical School in New England, at Castleton, Vermont, in 1818," *Annals of Medical History,* new ser., VII (1935), 242–252, and *The First Medical College in Vermont: Castleton, 1818–1862* (Montpelier, Vt.: Vermont Historical Society, 1949). The Paine-Davis debate is discussed in Martin Kaufman, *American Medical Education;* see also Otto F. Kampmeier, "Nathan Smith Davis, 1817–1904: A Biographical Essay," *Journal of Medical Education,* XXXIV (1958–59), 496–508.

J. Willard Hurst, *Law and the Conditions of Freedom in the Nineteenth-Century United States* (Madison: University of Wisconsin Press, 1956) and *Law and Social Order in the United States* (Ithaca, N.Y.: Cornell University Press, 1977) and Morton J. Horwitz, *The Transformation of American Law, 1780–1860* (Cambridge, Mass.: Harvard University Press, 1977) deal broadly with the development of the law in early national America. Anton-Hermann Chroust, *The Rise of the Legal Profession in America* (2 vols.; Norman: University of Oklahoma Press, 1965) deals with the development of the legal profession. Alfred Zantzinger Reed, *Training for the Public Profession of the Law* (New York: Carnegie Foundation for the Advancement of Teaching, 1921) remains the most informative comprehensive treatment of nineteenth-century legal education in the United States; Anton-Hermann Chroust, *The Rise of the Legal Profession in America* and William R. Johnson, *Schooled Lawyers: A Study in the Class of Professional Cultures* (New York: New York University Press, 1978) are also useful discussions. Samuel H. Fisher, *The Litchfield Law School, 1775–1833* (New Haven: Yale University Press, 1933) and *The Litchfield Law School, 1774–1833: Biographical Catalogue of Students* (New Haven: Yale University Press, 1946) are the best sources for the Reeve-Gould enterprise. Manuscript notes of Reeve's and Gould's lectures, probably for 1817, are in the Columbia University Law Library.

Sydney E. Ahlstrom, *A Religious History of the American People* (New Haven: Yale University Press, 1972) deals broadly with the development of American religion. Donald M. Scott, *From Office to Profession: The New England Ministry, 1750–1850* (Philadelphia: University of Pennsylvania Press, 1978) discusses the transformation of the ministry of the older churches in the older, more settled regions. William O. Shewmaker, "The Training of the Protestant Ministry in the United States of America Before the Establishment of Theological Seminaries," *Papers of the American Society of Church History*, 2d ser., VI (1921), 73–202; Mary Latimer Gambrell, *Ministerial Training in Eighteenth Century New England* (New York: Columbia University Press, 1937); B. Sadtler, "The Education of Ministers by Private Tutors, Before the Establishment of Theological Seminaries," *Lutheran Church Review*, XIII (1894), 167–183; and Roland H. Bainton, *Yale and the Ministry: A History of Education for the Christian Ministry at Yale from the Founding in 1701* (New York: Harper & Brothers, 1957) discuss the preparation of ministers before the development of theological seminaries. Frank Dixon McCloy, "The Founding of Protestant Theological Seminaries in the United States of America, 1784–1840" (doctoral thesis, Harvard University, 1959) and Natalie A. Naylor, "The Theological Seminary in the Configuration of American Higher Education: The Ante-Bellum Years," *History of Education Quarterly*, XVII (1977), 17–30, are the best comprehensive studies of the development of theological seminaries; Naylor, "Raising an Educated Ministry: The American Education Society, 1815–1860" (doctoral thesis, Teachers College, Columbia University, 1971) is also valuable. Leonard Woods, *History of the Andover Theological Seminary* (Boston: J. R. Osgood and Company, 1884) and Henry K. Rowe, *History of Andover Theological Seminary* (Newton, Mass.: no publisher, 1933) are the standard accounts; for the training of Methodist ministers, see Emory Stevens Bucke, ed., *The History of American Methodism* (3 vols.; New York: Abingdon Press, 1964), I.

Daniel H. Calhoun, *The American Civil Engineer* (Cambridge, Mass.: The M.I.T. Press, 1960); Monte A. Calvert, *The Mechanical Engineer in America, 1830–1910: Professional Cultures in Conflict* (Baltimore: The Johns Hopkins University Press, 1967); and Raymond H. Merritt, *Engineering in American Society, 1850–1875* (Lexington: The University Press of Kentucky, 1969) are the best books on the development of engineering and the education of engineers during the nineteenth century. Sidney Forman, *West Point: A History of the United States Military Academy* (New York: Columbia University Press, 1950) and Palmer C. Ricketts, *History of Rensselaer Polytechnic Institute, 1824–1934* (3d ed.; New York: J. Wiley & Sons, 1934) are useful studies of early technical education. Willard Elsbree, *The American Teacher: Evolution of a Profession in a Democracy* (New York: American Book Company, 1939) remains the best work on schoolteaching in the nineteenth century. Roman Joseph Schweikert, "The Western Literary Institute and College of Professional Teachers: An Instrument in the Creation of a Profession" (doctoral thesis, University of Cincinnati, 1971) and Paul H. Mattingly, *The Classless Profession: American Schoolmen in the Nineteenth Century* (New York: New York University Press, 1975) depict the emergence of an elite, professionally oriented leadership within the teaching profession. Richard Emmons Thursfield, *Henry Barnard's American Journal of Education* (Baltimore: The Johns Hopkins University Press, 1945) documents Barnard's aspirations to professionalism via a new scholarship of education. Merle L. Borrowman, *The Liberal and Technical in Teacher Education: A Historical Survey of American Thought* (New York: Bureau of Publications, Teachers College, Columbia University, 1956) deals with the ideas and assumptions of the early normal school educators; Arthur O. Norton, *The First State Normal School: The Journals of Cyrus Pierce and Mary Swift* (Cambridge, Mass.: Harvard University Press, 1926) is a revealing collection of documents. Monte A. Calvert, *The Mechanical Engineer in America, 1830–1910* and William R. Johnson, *Schooled Lawyers* document the conflict between "shop culture" and "school culture" within two professions.

INTRODUCTION TO PART IV: AN AMERICAN EDUCATION

The observations and impressions of foreign visitors who came to the United States during the nineteenth century furnish an exceedingly important resource for the historian, but they must be used critically; the same perspective from a foreign culture that often led to profound and arresting insights could also lead to partiality and misapprehension. Granted the caveat, many of those who visited the United States during the nineteenth century went out of their way to study and remark upon American education, and the remarks bear close scrutiny. Henry T. Tuckerman, *America and Her Commentators* (1864; reprint ed.; New York: Antiquarian Press, 1961) is a contemporary discussion of the commentaries by an American apologist; Marc Machter and Frances Wein, eds., *Abroad in America: Visitors to the New Nation, 1776–1914* (Reading, Mass.: Addison Wesley Publishing Company, 1976) is a more balanced series of essays. Among the travel accounts that pay substantial attention to American education are Sándor Bölöni Farkas, *Journey to North America, 1831,* edited by Arpad Kadarkay (Santa Barbara, Calif.: American Bibliographical Center, 1978); Thomas Hamilton, *Men and Manners in America* (1833; reprint ed.; New York: Augustus M. Kelley, Publishers, 1968); Alexis de Tocqueville, *Democracy in America,* edited by Phillips Bradley (2 vols.; New York: Alfred A. Knopf, 1945); Francis J. Grund, *The Americans in Their Moral, Social, and Political Relations* (1837; reprint ed.; New York: Johnson Reprint Corporation, 1968); Michael Aaron Rockland, ed., *Sarmiento's Travels in the United States in 1847* (Princeton, N.J.: Princeton University Press, 1970); Alexander Mackay, *The Western World; or, Travels in the United States in 1846–47* (1849; reprint ed.; 3 vols.; New York: Negro Universities Press, 1949); Charles Lyell, *A Second Visit to the United States of North America* (2 vols.; New York: Harper & Brothers, 1849); P. A. Siljestrom, *The Educational Institutions of the United States: Their Character and Organization,* translated by Frederica Rowan (London: John Chapman, 1853); Philip Schaff, *America: A Sketch of Its Political, Social, and Religious Character,* edited by Perry Miller (Cambridge, Mass.: Harvard University Press, 1961); Adam G. de Gurowski, *America and Europe* (New York: D. Appleton and Company, 1857); James Fraser, *Report to the Commissioners Appointed by Her Majesty to Inquire into the Education Given in Schools in England Not Comprised Within Her Majesty's Two Recent Commissions* (London: Her Majesty's Stationery Office, 1866); and Francis Adams, *The Free School System of the United States* (London: Chapman and Hall, 1875).

Enoch Cobb Wines is better known for his work as a prison reformer, and particularly for the report he did with Theodore William Dwight, *Report in the Prisons and Reformatories of the United States and Canada, Made to the Legislature of New York, January, 1867* (Albany: Van Benthuysen & Sons, 1867), and his own survey, *The State of Prisons and of Child-Saving Institutions in the Civilized World* (1880; reprint ed.; Montclair, N.J.: Patterson Smith, 1968). But his *Hints on a System of Popular Education* (Philadelphia: Hogan and Thompson, 1838) was an important work on education in its time and bears close perusal. There is an essay on Wines in the *Dictionary of American Biography*.

CHAPTER 11: INSTITUTIONS

I reviewed the literature on the family as educator in "The Family as Educator: Some Comments on the Recent Historiography," in Hope Jensen Leichter, ed., *The Family as Educator* (New York: Teachers College Press, 1974), pp. 76–91, and "Family-Community Linkages in American Education: Some Comments on the Recent Historiography," in Hope Jensen Leichter, ed., *Families and Communities as Educators* (New York: Teachers College Press, 1979), pp. 119–140. The literature on domesticity is discussed on p. 536 *supra,* the literature on the development of extrafamilial rehabilitative and custodial institutions is discussed on p. 537 *supra,* the literature on the black family is discussed on pp. 560–561 *supra,* and the literature on the Indian family is discussed on pp. 562–563 *supra.* Among the more valuable recent writings on the nineteenth-century family as educator are Blaine T. Williams, "The Frontier Family: Demographic Fact and Historical Myth," in Harold M. Hollingworth and Sandra L. Myers, eds., *Essays on the American West* (Austin: University of Texas Press, 1969), pp. 40–65; Carole Teplitz West, "The Informal Education of Southern Children as Revealed in the Literature of the Period 1830–1860" (doctoral thesis, University of North Carolina, 1969); Joseph F. Kett, "Growing Up in Rural New England, 1800–1840," in Tamara K. Hareven, *Anonymous Americans: Explorations in Nineteenth-Century Social History* (Englewood Cliffs, N.J.: Prentice-Hall, 1971), pp. 1–16, and *Rites of Passage: Adolescence in America, 1790 to the Present* (New York: Basic Books, 1977); Bernard Faber, *Guardians of Virtue: Salem Families in 1800* (New York: Basic Books, 1972); Daniel Scott Smith, "Parental Power and Marriage Patterns: An Analysis of Historical Trends in Hingham, Massachusetts," *Journal of Marriage and the Family,* XXXV (1973), 419–428; Barbara Finkelstein, "In Fear of Childhood: Relationships Between Parents and Teachers in Popular Primary Schools in the Nineteenth Century," *History of Childhood Quarterly,* III (1975–76), 321–336; Herbert G. Gutman, *The Black Family in Slavery and Freedom, 1750–1925* (New York: Pantheon Books, 1976); Thomas L. Webber, *Deep Like the Rivers: Education in the Slave Quarter Community, 1831–1865* (New York: W. W. Norton & Company, 1978); Susan E. Hirsch, *Roots of the American Working Class: The Industrialization of Crafts in Newark, 1800–1860* (Philadelphia: University of Pennsylvania Press, 1978); Anthony F. C. Wallace, *Rockdale: The Growth of an American Village in the Early Industrial Revo-*

lution (New York: Alfred A. Knopf, 1978); and Geraldine Jonçich Clifford, "Home and School in 19th Century America: Some Personal-History Reports from the United States," *History of Education Quarterly*, XVIII (1978), 3–34. Many of the essays in John Demos and Sarane Spence Boocock, eds., *Turning Points: Historical and Sociological Essays on the Family* (Chicago: University of Chicago Press, 1978) are also relevant.

Laurence Admiral Glasco, "Ethnicity and Social Structure: Irish, Germans and Native-Born of Buffalo, N.Y., 1850–1860" (doctoral thesis, State University of New York at Buffalo, 1973); Julius Silverman, "Patterns of Working Class Family and Community Life: The Irish in New York City, 1845–1865" (master's thesis, Columbia University, 1973); Robert E. Kennedy, Jr., *The Irish: Emigration, Marriage, and Fertility* (Berkeley: University of California Press, 1973); Oliver MacDonagh, "The Irish Famine Emigration to the United States," *Perspectives in American History*, X (1976), 375–446; Albert Gibbs Mitchell, Jr., "Irish Family Patterns in Nineteenth-Century Ireland and Lowell, Massachusetts" (doctoral thesis, Boston University, 1976); and Lynn H. Lees and John Modell, "The Irish Countryman Urbanized: A Comparative Perspective on the Famine Migration," *Journal of Urban History*, III (1977), 391–408, deal with the Irish family in Ireland and the United States. Mack Walker, *Germany and the Emigration, 1816–1885* (Cambridge, Mass.: Harvard University Press, 1964) and *German Home Towns: Community, State, and General Estate, 1648–1871* (Ithaca N.Y.: Cornell University Press, 1971); Wolfgang Köllmann and Peter Marschalck, "German Emigration to the United States," *Perspectives in American History*, VII (1973), 499–554; and Kathleen Neils Conzen, *Immigrant Milwaukee, 1836–1860: Accommodation and Community in a Frontier City* (Cambridge, Mass.: Harvard University Press, 1976) deal with the German family in Germany and the United States. And Olga Lang, *Chinese Family and Society* (New Haven: Yale University Press, 1946); Ping Chiu, *Chinese Labor in California, 1850–1880: An Economic Study* (Madison: State Historical Society of Wisconsin, 1963); Gunther Barth, *Bitter Strength: A History of the Chinese in the United States, 1850–1870* (Cambridge, Mass.: Harvard University Press, 1964); Maurice Freeman, *Chinese Lineage and Society: Fukien and Kwangtung* (New York: Humanities Press, 1966); and Melford S. Weiss, *Valley City: A Chinese Community in America* (Cambridge, Mass.: Schenkman Publishing Company, 1974) deal with the Chinese family in China and the United States. Timothy L. Smith, "Religion and Ethnicity in America," *American Historical Review*, LXXXIII (1978), 1155–1185, provides a general context within which to consider the culture of immigrant families.

Most of the literature discussed in connection with Chapter 2 is also relevant here. The disestablishment of the churches is dealt with in R. Freeman Butts, *The American Tradition in Religion and Education* (Boston: Beacon Press, 1950) and Leo Pfeffer, *Church, State, and Freedom* (Boston: Beacon Press, 1953). Anson Phelps Stokes, ed., *Church and State in the United States* (3 vols.; New York: Harper & Brothers, 1950) is a valuable collection of documents. Sidney E. Mead, "The Rise of the Evangelical Conception of the Ministry in America (1605–1850)," in H. Richard Niebuhr and Daniel D. Williams, eds., *The Ministry in Historical Perspectives* (New York: Harper & Brothers, 1956), pp. 207–246, deals with the changing role of the ministry. Robert Baird, *Religion in the United States of America* (Glasgow: Blackie and Son, 1844); Dewitte Holland, ed., *Preaching in American History* (Nashville: Abingdon Press,

1969); Henry H. Mitchell, *Black Preaching* (Philadelphia: J. B. Lippincott Company, 1970); Albert J. Raboteau, *Slave Religion: The "Invisible Institution" in the Antebellum South* (New York: Oxford University Press, 1978); Lawrence Buell, "The Unitarian Movement and the Art of Preaching in 19th Century America," *American Quarterly,* XXIV (1972), 166–190; and J. P. Dolan, *Catholic Revivalism: The American Experience, 1830–1900* (Notre Dame, Ind.: University of Notre Dame Press, 1978) discuss the style and substance of nineteenth-century preaching. Jay P. Dolan, *The Immigrant Church: New York's Irish and German Catholics, 1815–1865* (Baltimore: The Johns Hopkins University Press, 1975) discusses the Irish and German Roman Catholic churches in New York, with special attention to the phenomenon of Americanization. Kathleen Neils Conzen, *Immigrant Milwaukee, 1836–1860* deals similarly with the German Lutheran and Roman Catholic churches of Milwaukee. The literature explicating the discordant education proffered by religious institutions in the black and Indian communities is discussed on pp. 560–563 *supra.* William R. Sprague, *Annals of the American Pulpit* (9 vols.; New York: Robert Carter & Brothers, 1866–1869) is an incomparable source for the multifarious activities of the Protestant clergy in the realm of education. It should be supplemented, of course, by works such as Maynard Geiger, *Franciscan Missionaries in Hispanic California, 1769–1848* (San Marino, Calif.: The Huntington Library, 1969); John Tracy Ellis, *American Catholicism* (Chicago: University of Chicago Press, 1956); Jay F. Dolan, *The Immigrant Church;* Leon A. Jick, *The Americanization of the Synagogue, 1820–1870* (Hanover, N.H.: University Press of New England, 1976); and Janis Clavo, "Quaker Women Ministers in Nineteenth Century America," *Quaker History,* LXIII (1974), 75–93. George F. Magoun, *Asa Turner: A Home Missionary Patriarch and His Times* (Boston: Congregational Sunday-School and Publishing Society, 1889) is a useful, if uncritical, biography. Helen Louise Jennings, "John Mason Peck and the Impact of New England on the Old Northwest" (doctoral thesis, University of Southern California, 1961) is an able scholarly biography of Peck; it is usefully supplemented by Paul M. Harrison, ed., *Forty Years of Pioneer Life: Memoir of John Mason Peck, D.D.; Edited from His Journals and Correspondence by Rufus Babcock* (Carbondale: Southern Illinois University Press, 1965).

Most of the literature discussed in connection with Chapter 5 is also relevant here. Beyond that literature, the best sources for the actual life of the schools during the nineteenth century are the state school reports and state common school journals and, especially, Henry Barnard's *American Journal of Education.* Beyond those sources, there are the first-hand observations and reminiscences listed on pp. 554–555 *supra.* For the infant school, see Dean May and Maris A. Vinovskis, "A Ray of Millennial Light: Early Education and Social Reform in the Infant School Movement in Massachusetts, 1826–1840," in Tamara K. Hareven, ed., *Family and Kin in American Urban Communities* (New York: New Viewpoints Press, 1977), pp. 62–99, and Carl F. Kaestle and Maris A. Vinovskis, "From Apron Strings to ABC's: Parents, Children, and Schooling in Nineteenth-Century Massachusetts," in John Demos and Sarane Spence Boocock, eds., *Turning Points,* pp. 39–80. For the high school, see Elmer Ellsworth Brown, *The Making of Our Middle Schools* (London: Longmans, Green and Co., 1902), an older treatise whose information is still reliable. For the monitorial school, see Carl F. Kaestle, ed., *Joseph Lancaster and the Monitorial School Movement* (New York: Teachers College Press, 1973). For "supplementary schools," see, *inter alia,* Robert S. Pickett, *House of Refuge: Origins of Juvenile Reform in New York State, 1815–1857* (Syracuse, N.Y.: Syracuse University Press, 1969); Joseph M. Hawes, *Children in Urban Society: Juvenile Delinquency in Nineteenth-Century America* (New York: Oxford University Press, 1971); Harold Schwartz, *Samuel Gridley Howe, Social Reformer* (Cambridge, Mass.: Harvard University Press, 1956); and Leo Kanner, *A History of the Care and Study of the Mentally Retarded* (Springfield, Ill.: Charles C. Thomas, 1964). For *Ex Parte Crouse,* see Sanford J. Fox, "Juvenile Justice Reform: An Historical Perspective," *Stanford Law Review,* XXII (1970), 1187–1239. For *Roberts v. City of Boston,* see Leonard Levy and Harlan B. Phillips, "The *Roberts* Case: Source of the 'Separate but Equal' Doctrine," *American Historical Review,* LVI (1950–51), 510–518.

John Nietz, *Old Textbooks* (Pittsburgh: University of Pittsburgh Press, 1961) and *The Evolution of American Secondary School Textbooks* (Rutland, Vt.: Charles E. Tuttle Company, 1966) and Charles Carpenter, *History of American Schoolbooks* (Philadelphia: University of Pennsylvania Press, 1962) are authoritative, comprehensive sources. For reading textbooks generally, see Ruth Miller Elson, *Guardians of Tradition: American Schoolbooks of the Nineteenth Century* (Lincoln: University of Nebraska Press, 1964); for conceptions of reading instruction, see Mitford M. Mathews, *Teaching to Read: Historically Considered* (Chicago: University of Chicago Press, 1966). For writing textbooks generally, see Ray Nash, *American Writing Masters and Copybooks: History and Bibliography Through Colonial Times* (Boston: Colonial Society of Massachusetts, 1959) and *American Penmanship, 1800–1850: A History of Writing and a Bibliography of Copybooks from Jenkins to Spencer* (Worcester, Mass.: American Antiquarian Society, 1969). For arithmetic textbooks generally, see Henry Lester Smith, Merrill T. Eaton, and Kathleen Dugdale, *One Hundred Fifty Years of Arithmetic Textbooks* (Bloomington: Bureau of Cooperative Research and Field Services, Indiana University, 1945). And for grammar textbooks generally, see Henry Lester Smith, Kathleen Dugdale, Beulah Faris Steele, and Robert Steward McElhinney, *One Hundred Fifty Years of Grammar Textbooks* (Bloomington: Division of Research and Field Services, Indiana University, 1946). For the teaching of good behavior (for which, read piety and religion), see Robert Michaelsen, *Piety in the Public School: Trends and Issues in the Relationship Between Religion and the Public School in the United States* (New York: The Macmillan Company, 1970) and David B. Tyack, "Onward Christian Soldiers: Religion in the American Common School," in Paul Nash, ed., *History and Education: The Educational Uses of the Past* (New York: Random House, 1970).

For the diurnal experience of schooling, see Barbara Joan Finkelstein, "Governing the Young, Teacher Behavior in American Primary Schools, 1820–1880: A Documentary History" (doctoral thesis, Teachers College, Columbia University, 1970), "The Moral Dimensions of Pedagogy," *American Studies,* XV (1974–75), 79–91, and "Pedagogy as Intrusion: Teaching Values in Popular Primary Schools in the Nineteenth Century," *History of Childhood Quarterly,* II (1974–75), 349–78, as well as the sources cited on pp. 554–555 *supra.* For the schooling of blacks, see C. G. Woodson, *The Education of the Negro Prior to 1861: A History of the Education of the Colored People of the United States from the Beginning of Slavery to the Civil War* (Washington, D.C.: The Associated Publishers, 1919); Henry Allen Bullock, *A History of Negro Education in the South from 1619 to the Present* (Cambridge, Mass.: Harvard University Press, 1967); and the sources cited on pp. 560–561 *supra.* For the schooling of Indians, see Evelyn C. Adams, *American Indian Education: Government Schools and Economic Progress* (New York: King's Crown Press, 1946) and the sources cited on pp. 000–000 *supra*. For the schooling of immigrants, see Carl F. Kaestle, *The Evolution of an Urban School System: New York City, 1750–1850* (Cambridge, Mass.: Harvard University Press, 1973); Stanley K. Schultz, *The Culture Factory: Boston Public Schools, 1789–1860* (New York: Oxford University Press, 1973); Diane Ravitch, *The Great School Wars, New York City, 1805–1973: A History of the Public Schools as Battlefield of Social Change* (New York: Basic Books, 1974); David B. Tyack, *The One Best System: A History of American Urban Education* (Cambridge, Mass.: Harvard University Press, 1974); Kathleen Neils Conzen, *Immigrant Milwaukee;* and James W. Sanders, *The Education of an Urban Minority: Catholics in Chicago, 1833–1965* (New York: Oxford University Press, 1977). And for the schooling of women, see Thomas Woody, *A History of Women's Education in the United States* (1929; reprint ed.; 2 vols.; New York: Octagon Books, 1966) and Maris A. Vinovskis and Richard M. Bernard, "Beyond Catharine Beecher: Female Education in the Antebellum Period," *Signs: Journal of Women in Culture and Society,* III (1978), 856–859.

Schoolteachers and schoolteaching are discussed in Willard Elsbree, *The American Teacher: Evolution of a Profession in a Democracy* (New York: American Book Company, 1939) and Geraldine Jonçich Clifford, "Home and School in 19th Century America." There is an excellent biography of Zilpah Polly Grant by Sydney R. MacLean in *Notable American Women,* along with a useful bibliography. Floy Lawrence Emhoff, "A Pioneer School Teacher in Central Iowa," *Iowa Journal of History and Politics,* XXXIII (1935), 376–395, portrays Alice Money.

The historiography of higher education has been reshaped in recent years by three related lines of inquiry. The first, represented by David F. Allmendinger, Jr., *Paupers and Scholars: The Transformation of Student Life in Nineteenth-Century New England* (New York: St. Martin's Press, 1973); Colin Bradley Burke, "The Quiet Influence: The American Colleges and Their Students, 1800–1860" (doctoral thesis, Washington University, 1973); and Steven J. Novak, *The Rights of Youth: American Colleges and Student Revolt, 1798–1815* (Cambridge, Mass.: Harvard University Press, 1977) has explored the experience of higher education from the vantage point of the student. The second, represented by David B. Potts, "Baptist Colleges in the Development of American Society, 1812–1861" (doctoral thesis, Harvard University, 1967) and "American Colleges in the Nineteenth Century: From Localism to Denominationalism," *History of Education Quarterly,* XI (1971), 363–380; Jurgen Herbst, "The American Revolution and the American University," *Perspectives in American History,* X (1976), 279–354; and Howard Miller, *The Revolutionary College: American Presbyterian Higher Education, 1707–1837* (New York: New York University Press, 1976), has explored the relationship of higher education to the polity, the community, and the several denominations. And the third, represented by Daniel H. Calhoun, *Professional Lives in America: Structure and Aspiration, 1750–1850* (Cambridge, Mass.: Harvard University Press, 1965); Douglas Sloan, "Harmony, Chaos, and Consensus: The American College Curriculum," *Teachers College Record,* LXXIII (1971–72), 221–251; D. H. Meyer, *The Instructed Conscience: The Shaping of the American National Ethic* (Philadelphia: University of Pennsylvania Press, 1972); James McLachlan, "American Colleges and the Transmission of Culture: The Case of the Mugwumps," in Stanley Elkins and Eric

McKitrick, eds., *The Hofstadter Aegis: A Memorial* (New York: Alfred A. Knopf, 1974), pp. 184–206; Stanley M. Guralnick, *Science and the Ante-Bellum American College* (Philadelphia: The American Philosophical Society, 1975); and Natalie A. Naylor, "The Theological Seminary in the Configuration of American Higher Education: The Ante-Bellum Years," *History of Education Quarterly*, XVII (1977), 17–30, has explored the curriculum of higher education, viewing the colleges as one element in a larger configuration of institutions. David B. Potts, " 'College Enthusiasm!' as Public Response, 1800–1860," *Harvard Educational Review*, XLVII (1977), 28–42, and James McLachlan, "The American College in the Nineteenth Century: Toward a Reappraisal," *Teachers College Record*, LXXX (1978–79), 287–306, are useful syntheses. E. Merton Coulter, *College Life in the Old South* (New York: The Macmillan Company, 1928); Richard Hofstadter and Walter P. Metzger, *The Development of Academic Freedom in the United States* (New York: Columbia University Press, 1955); George P. Schmidt, *The Liberal Arts College: A Chapter in American Cultural History* (New Brunswick, N.J.: Rutgers University Press, 1957); Edward J. Power, *A History of Catholic Higher Education in the United States* (Milwaukee: The Bruce Publishing Company, 1958); Frederick Rudolph, *The American College and University: A History* (New York: Alfred A. Knopf, 1962); and John S. Brubacher and Willis Rudy, *Higher Education in Transition: A History of American Colleges and Universities, 1636–1976* (3d ed.; New York: Harper & Row, 1976) are useful general sources, and the last-named includes an excellent bibliography of histories of individual institutions. Richard Hofstadter and Wilson Smith, eds., *American Higher Education: A Documentary History* (2 vols.; Chicago: University of Chicago Press, 1961) is a valuable collection of sources.

Donald G. Tewksbury, *The Founding of American Colleges and Universities Before the Civil War* (New York: Bureau of Publications, Teachers College, Columbia University, 1932) is the classic treatise on the expansion in the number of colleges; Natalie A. Naylor, "The Ante-Bellum College Movement: A Reappraisal of Tewksbury's Founding of American Colleges and Universities," *History of Education Quarterly*, XIII (1973), 261–274, is an incisive critique. For the influence of the Morrill Act on American higher education, see the sources cited on pp. 550–551 *supra*. For the Dartmouth College Case, see John S. Whitehead, *The Separation of College and State: Columbia, Dartmouth, Harvard, and Yale, 1776–1876* (New Haven: Yale University Press, 1973) and Steven J. Novak, "The College in the Dartmouth College Case: A Reinterpretation," *New England Quarterly*, XLVII (1974), 550–563. For the curriculum of the colleges, see Frederick Rudolph, *Curriculum: A History of the Undergraduate Course of Study Since 1636* (San Francisco: Jossey-Bass Publishers, 1977). For the program at Yale, see Brooks Mather Kelley, *Yale: A History* (New Haven: Yale University Press, 1974). For the role of student societies, see Rita Segal Saslaw, "Student Societies: Nineteenth Century Establishment" (doctoral thesis, Case Western Reserve University, 1971); James McLachlan, "The *Choice of Hercules*: American Student Societies in the Early 19th Century," in Lawrence Stone, ed., *The University in Society: Europe, Scotland, and the United States from the 16th to the 20th Century* (2 vols.; Princeton, N.J.: Princeton University Press, 1974), II, 449–494; and Lowell Simpson, "The Little Republics: Undergraduate Literary Societies at Columbia, Dartmouth, Princeton, and Yale, 1753–1865" (doctoral thesis, Teachers College, Columbia University, 1976). For the women's colleges, see Thomas Woody, *A History of Women's Edu-*

cation in the United States; Mabel Newcomer, *A Century of Higher Education for Women* (New York: Harper & Brothers, 1959); and Eleanor Flexner, *Century of Struggle: The Women's Rights Movement in the United States* (rev. ed.; Cambridge, Mass.: Harvard University Press, 1975).

For the transformation of the professoriate, see George P. Schmidt, *The Old Time College President* (New York: Columbia University Press, 1930); M. St. Mel Kennedy, "The Changing Academic Characteristics of the Nineteenth-Century American College Teacher" (doctoral thesis, Saint Louis University, 1961); Mark Brocklebank Beach, "Professors, Presidents and Trustees: A Study of University Governance, 1825-1918" (doctoral thesis, University of Wisconsin, 1966); and Robert A. McCaughey, "The Transformation of American Academic Life: Harvard University, 1821-1892," *Perspectives in American History,* VIII (1974), 239-332. The best source for Elisha Mitchell is Kemp P. Battle, *History of the University of North Carolina from Its Beginning to the Death of President Swain, 1789-1868* (2 vols.; Raleigh, N.C.: Edwards & Broughton Printing Company, 1907-1912); there is also an article on Mitchell in the *Dictionary of American Biography.* The best sources for Julian Momson Sturtevant are *An Autobiography,* edited by J. M. Sturtevant, Jr. (New York: Fleming H. Revell Company, 1896), and Charles Henry Rammelkamp, *Illinois College: A Centennial History, 1829-1929* (New Haven: Yale University Press, 1928).

Nineteenth-century newspapers are depicted in the sources listed on pp. 555-557 *supra.* For Joseph Charless, see David Kaser, *Joseph Charless: Printer in the Western Country* (Philadelphia: University of Pennsylvania Press, 1963). For William Williams, see Milton Hamilton, *The Country Printer: New York State, 1785-1830* (New York: Columbia University Press, 1936) and Madeleine B. Stern, *William Williams: Pioneer Printer of Utica, New York, 1787-1850* (Charlottesville: Bibliographical Society of the University of Virginia, 1951).

CHAPTER 12: CONFIGURATIONS

The conceptual framework for this chapter is set forth in my discussion of the configuration of education as an interrelated complex of educative institutions, in *Public Education* (New York: Basic Books, 1976). The essays by Hope Jensen Leichter and J. W. Getzels in Leichter, ed., *Families and Communities as Educators* (New York: Teachers College Press, 1979) further explicate the theoretical aspects.

The industrial experiment at Lowell, Massachusetts, has been the subject of a considerable literature over the years, in part because of the inherent fascination of the subject and in part because of the wealth of primary source material on which to draw. Thomas Bender, *Toward an Urban Vision: Ideas and Institutions in Nineteenth-Century America* (Lexington: The University Press of Kentucky, 1975), chap. iv, and John F. Kasson, *Civilizing the Machine: Technology and Republican Values in America, 1776-1900* (New York: Grossman Publishers, 1976), chap. ii, are the most interesting recent discussions. John Coolidge, *Mill and Mansion: A Study of Architecture and Society in Lowell, Massachusetts, 1820-1865* (New York: Columbia University Press, 1942) remains the most comprehensive scholarly treatment. Frederick W. Coburn, *History of Lowell and Its People* (3 vols.; New York: Lewis Historical Publishing Company, 1920) is a traditional but highly informative account. D. Hamilton Hurd, ed., *History of Middlesex County, Massachusetts* (3 vols.; Philadelphia: J. W. Lewis & Co.,

1890); *Illustrated History of Lowell and Vicinity* (Lowell, Mass.: Courier-Citizen Company, 1897); and Edwin P. Conklin, *Middlesex County and Its People* (4 vols.; New York: Lewis Historical Publishing Company, 1927) are also useful. Henry A. Miles, *Lowell, As It Was, and As It Is* (Lowell, Mass.: Powers and Bagley, 1845) is a contemporary account by a native enthusiast; William Scoresby, *American Factories and Their Female Operatives* (London: Longman, Brown, Green and Longman, 1845) is a contemporary account by a foreign enthusiast. The *Annual Reports* of the Lowell School Committee are rich sources of statistical data and commentary; the *Contributions of the Old Residents' Historical Association* and the *Contributions of the Lowell Historical Society* include, *inter alia,* useful firsthand reminiscences. The records of the textile companies are at the Baker Library at Harvard University; there are extensive collections of papers at the Lowell University Library.

Robert F. Dalzell, Jr., "The Rise of the Waltham-Lowell System and Some Thoughts on the Political Economy of Modernization in Ante-Bellum Massachusetts," *Perspectives in American History,* IX (1975), 119-168, is an excellent modern account of the rise of the textile industry in Lowell. Paul F. McGouldrick, *New England Textiles in the Nineteenth Century: Profits and Investments* (Cambridge, Mass.: Harvard University Press, 1968); Caroline F. Ware, *The Early New England Cotton Manufacture* (Boston: Houghton Mifflin Company, 1931); and Norman Ware, *The Industrial Worker, 1840-1860: The Reaction of American Industrial Society to the Advance of the Industrial Revolution* (Boston: Houghton Mifflin Company, 1924) are also informative. Thomas Louis Dublin, *Women at Work: The Transformation of Work and Community in Lowell, Massachusetts, 1826-1860* (New York: Columbia University Press, 1979), "Women, Work, and Protest in the Early Lowell Mills: 'The Oppressing Hand of Avarice Would Enslave Us,'" *Labor History,* XVI (1975), 99-116, and "Women, Work, and the Family: Female Operatives in the Lowell Mills, 1830-1860," *Feminist Studies,* III (1975), 30-40, present the most comprehensive and detailed work on the lives of the women operatives. Harriet H. Robinson, *Loom and Spindle; or, Life among the Early Mill Girls* (New York: Thomas Y. Crowell, 1898); Bertha Monica Stearns, "Early Factory Magazines in New England: The Lowell Offering and Its Contemporaries," *Journal of Economic and Business History,* II (1929-30), 684-705; Hannah Josephson, *The Golden Threads: New England's Mill Girls and Magnates* (New York: Duell, Sloan, and Pearce, 1949); Benita Eisler, ed., *The Lowell Offering: Writings by New England Mill Women (1840-1845)* (Philadelphia: J. B. Lippincott Company, 1977); and Barbara Mayer Wertheimer, *We Were There: The Story of Working Women in America* (New York: Pantheon Books, 1977) provide valuable additional data. Oliver MacDonagh, "The Irish Famine Emigration to the United States," *Perspectives in American History,* X (1976), 375-446; George F. O'Dwyer, *Irish Catholic Genesis of Lowell* (Lowell, Mass.: Sullivan Brothers, 1920); H. M. Gitelman, "The Waltham System and the Coming of the Irish," *Labor History,* VIII (1967), 227-263; Albert Gibbs Mitchell, Jr., "Irish Family Patterns in Nineteenth-Century Ireland and Lowell, Massachusetts" (doctoral thesis, Boston University, 1976); and Steven Dubnuff, "The Family and Absence from Work: Irish Workers in a Lowell, Massachusetts Cotton Mill, 1860" (doctoral thesis, Brandeis University, 1976) and "Gender, the Family, and the Problem of Work Motivation in a Transition to Industrial Capitalism," *Journal of Family History,* IV (1979), 121-136, illuminate the special situation of the Irish immigrants. David Isaac Bruck, "The Schools of Lowell, 1824-1861: A Case Study in the Origins of Modern Public Education in America" (bachelor's thesis, Harvard College, 1971) deals specifically with public school policies. The sources cited with reference to Lucy Larcom on p. 588 *infra* are also relevant.

Anne King Gregorie, *History of Sumter County, South Carolina* (Sumter, S. C.: Library Board of Sumter County, 1954) and Janie Revill, *Sumter District* (no place: The State Printing Company, 1968) are the chief secondary works on Sumter County. Susan Markey Fickling, "The Christianization of the Negro in South Carolina, 1830–1860" (master's thesis, University of South Carolina, 1923); J. Perrin Anderson, "Public Education in Ante-Bellum South Carolina," *Proceedings of the South Carolina Historical Association* (1933), 3–11; Rosser H. Taylor, *Ante-Bellum South Carolina: A Social and Cultural History* (Chapel Hill: University of North Carolina Press, 1942); Annie Houghes Mallard, "Religious Work of South Carolina Baptists Among the Slaves from 1781 to 1830" (master's thesis, University of South Carolina, 1946); Thomas McAlpin Stubbs, "The Fourth Estate of Sumter, South Carolina," *South Carolina Historical Magazine*, LIV (1953), 185–200; Ernest McPherson Lander, Jr., *The Textile Industry in Antebellum South Carolina* (Baton Rouge: Louisiana State University Press, 1969); and Chalmers Gaston Davidson, *The Last Foray: The South Carolina Planters of 1860, A Sociological Study* (Columbia: University of South Carolina Press, 1971) contain a good deal of relevant information. There are valuable collections of papers relating to Sumter County at the South Caroliniana Library of the University of South Carolina and at the South Carolina Department of Archives and History in Columbia. The sources cited with reference to Jacob Stroyer and I. E. Lowery on pp. 588–589 *infra* are also relevant.

History of Macoupin County, Illinois (Philadelphia: Brink, McDonough & Co., 1879) is the chief secondary source for Macoupin County. Mrs. Mary Byram Wright, "Personal Recollections of the Early Settlement of Carlinville, Illinois," *Journal of the Illinois State Historical Society*, XVIII (1925–26), 668–685; Everett R. Turnbull, "A Century of Methodism in Carlinville, Illinois," *ibid*, XXIV (1931–32), 243–298; and Thomas Rinaker, "Gideon Blackburn, The Founder of Blackburn University, Carlinville, Illinois," *ibid.*, XVII (1924–25), 398–410, contain useful data on education. There are extensive collections of documents at the Carlinville Public Library. The sources cited with reference to John M. Palmer and James Henry Magee on p. 589 *infra* are also relevant.

There is no good scholarly history of New York City during the nineteenth century. Edward Robb Ellis, *The Epic of New York City* (New York: Coward-McCann, 1966) is a popular narrative. Ira Rosenwaike, *Population History of New York City* (Syracuse: Syracuse University Press, 1972) is an admirable demographic study. Robert Greenhalgh Albion, *The Rise of the New York Port, 1815–1860* (New York: Charles Scribner's Sons, 1939) is a fundamental economic study. Robert Ernst, *Immigrant Life in New York City, 1825–1863* (New York: King's Crown Press, 1949) is a valuable social history, as are Hyman B. Grinstein, *The Rise of the Jewish Community of New York, 1654–1860* (Philadelphia: The Jewish Publication Society of America, 1945) and Jay P. Dolan, *The Immigrant Church: New York's Irish and German Catholics, 1815–1865* (Baltimore: The Johns Hopkins University Press, 1975). William Oland Bourne, *History of the Public School Society of the City of New York* (New York: William Wood & Co., 1870); Julia Agnes Duffy, "The Proper Objects of a Gratuitous Education: The Free-School Society of the City of New York, 1805–1826" (doctoral thesis,

Teachers College, Columbia University, 1968); William Worcester Cutler III, "Philosophy, Philanthropy, and Public Education: A Social History of the New York Public School Society, 1805-1852" (doctoral thesis, Cornell University, 1968) and "Status, Values, and the Education of the Poor: The Trustees of the New York Public School Society, 1805-1853," *American Quarterly*, XXIV (1972), 69-85; Raymond A. Mohl, "Education as Social Control in New York City, 1784-1825," *New York History*, LI (1970), 219-237; Carl F. Kaestle, *The Evolution of an Urban School System: New York City, 1750-1850* (Cambridge, Mass.: Harvard University Press, 1973); Diane Ravitch, *The Great School Wars, New York City, 1805-1973: A History of the Public Schools as Battlefield of Social Change* (New York: Basic Books, 1974); David Martin Ment, "Racial Segregation in the Public Schools of New England and New York, 1840-1940" (doctoral thesis, Teachers College, Columbia University, 1975); and Claudia Christie Foster, "Motives, Means, and Ends in Gradual Abolitionist Education, 1785 to 1830" (doctoral thesis, Teachers College, Columbia University, 1977) treat the development of schooling in the city. Raymond A. Mohl, "Poverty, Public Relief, and Private Charity in New York City, 1784-1805" (doctoral thesis, New York University, 1967) deals with early public welfare efforts; Carroll Smith Rosenberg, *Religion and the Rise of the American City: The New York City Mission Movement, 1812-1870* (Ithaca, N. Y.: Cornell University Press, 1971); Mania Kleinburd Baghdadi, "Protestants, Poverty and Urban Growth: A Study of the Organization of Charity in Boston and New York, 1820-1865" (doctoral thesis, Brown University, 1975); and Paul Boyer, *Urban Masses and Moral Order in America, 1820-1920* (Cambridge, Mass.: Harvard University Press, 1978) deal with the multifarious enterprises of the mission movement; George P. Jacoby, *Catholic Child Care in Nineteenth Century New York* (Washington, D. C.: The Catholic University Press, 1941) deals with Roman Catholic counterparts. Allan Stanley Horlick, *Country Boys and Merchant Princes: The Social Control of Young Men in New York* (Lewisburg, Pa.: Bucknell University Press, 1975) depicts the changing world of apprenticeship to commerce. J. F. Richmond, *New York and Its Institutions, 1609-1872* (New York: E. B. Treat, 1872) is a treasure trove of information about the city's religious, social, and cultural organizations. Allan Nevins, "The Newspapers of New York State, 1783-1900," in Alexander C. Flick, ed., *History of the State of New York* (10 vols.; New York: Columbia University Press, 1933-1937), IX, chap. viii, stresses the city's nationally influential press.

There are numerous histories of individual institutions, for example, Shepherd Knapp, *A History of the Brick Presbyterian Church in the City of New York* (New York: Trustees of the Brick Presbyterian Church, 1909); L. Nelson Nichols, *History of the Broadway Tabernacle of New York City* (New Haven: The Tuttle, Morehouse and Taylor Co., 1940); Theodore Francis Jones, ed., *New York University, 1832-1932* (New York: New York University Press, 1933); Austin Baxter Keep, *History of the New York Society Library* (New York: printed for the trustees, 1908); Mrs. Jonathan Odell *et al.*, eds., *Origins and History of the Orphan Asylum Society in the City of New York, 1806-1896* (2 vols.; New York: Bonnel, Silver & Co., 1899); *The Children's Aid Society of New York: Its History, Plan, and Results* (New York: Waykoop and Hallenbeck, 1893); Miriam Z. Langsam, *Children West: A History of the Placing Out System of the New York Children's Aid Society, 1853-1890* (Madison: State Historical Society of Wisconsin, 1964); Robert S. Pickett, *House of Refuge: Origins of Juvenile Reform in New York State, 1815-1857* (Syracuse, N. Y.: Syracuse University Press, 1969); and

Allan Nevins, *The Evening Post: A Century of Journalism* (New York: Boni and Liveright, 1922). There are also many relevant biographies, for example, Samuel L. Knapp, *The Life of Thomas Eddy* (New York: Conner & Cooke, 1834); Joanna Bethune, *Life of Mrs. Isabella Graham by Her Daughter* (New York: John S. Taylor, 1839); Glyndon G. Van Deusen, *Horace Greeley: Nineteenth-Century Crusader* (Philadelphia: University of Pennsylvania Press, 1953); William Russell Hoyt, "The Religious Thought of Gardiner Spring, with Particular Reference to His Doctrine of Sin and Salvation" (doctoral thesis, Duke University, 1962); and Neil Harris, *Humbug: The Art of P. T. Barnum* (Boston: Little, Brown and Company, 1973). *The Diary of Philip Hone, 1828-1851,* edited by Allan Nevins (New York: Dodd, Mead & Company, 1936), is merely one among many firsthand commentaries. The New York Public Library, the New York Historical Society Library, and the libraries of the city's several universities are replete with collections of relevant documents and papers, as are the archives of organizations as various as the Young Men's Christian Association and the Irish American Historical Society. The sources cited with reference to William E. Dodge and Michael Walsh on p. 589 *infra* are also relevant.

Chapter 13: Lives

The conceptual framework for this chapter is set forth in my discussion of the educational biography as a life history prepared with educational matters uppermost in mind, in *Public Education* (New York: Basic Books, 1976). Hope Jensen Leichter, "Families and Communities as Educators: Some Concepts of Relationship," in Leichter, ed., *Families and Communities as Educators* (New York: Teachers College Press, 1979), pp. 3-94, and Ellen Condliffe Lagemann, *A Generation of Women: Education in the Lives of Progressive Reformers* (Cambridge, Mass.: Harvard University Press, 1979) further explicate the theoretical aspects. One could attempt to develop the similarities and convergences in groups of educational biographies in order to undertake studies of national character, as suggested by the materials discussed in Michael McGiffert, "Selected Writings on American National Character," *American Quarterly,* XV (1963), 270-288. But my own preference is to use educational biographies to indicate both the unique and the common aspects of educational experience.

Lucy Larcom, *A New England Girlhood* (1889; reprint ed.; New York: Corinth Books, 1961) is the basic source for Larcom's life and education. Daniel Dulany Addison, *Lucy Larcom: Life, Letters, and Diary* (Boston: Houghton, Mifflin and Company, 1894) is a substantial biography. There are articles on Larcom, Harriet Hanson Robinson, and Sarah G. Bagley in *Notable American Women*. My information on Margaret Baxter and Catherine Matthews derives from unpublished data generously provided by Thomas Dublin, which were gathered in connection with *Women at Work: The Transformation of Work and Community in Lowell, Massachusetts, 1826-1860* (New York: Columbia University Press, 1979). The sources cited with reference to Lowell, Massachusetts, on pp. 584-586 *supra* are also relevant.

Jacob Stroyer, *My Life in the South* (4th ed.; Salem, Mass.: Newcomb & Gauss, 1898) and I. E. Lowery, *Life on the Old Plantation in Ante-Bellum Days* (Columbia, S.C.: The State Co., 1911) are the basic sources for the lives and education of Stroyer and Lowery. For Stroyer's master, see Virginia Eliza Singleton, *The Singletons of South Carolina* (Columbia, S.C.: no publisher, 1914). In preparing the educational biographies of Stroyer and Lowery, I have profited from the readiness of my student Toni Thalenberg to share with me the research on her forthcoming doctoral thesis, "The Stolen Education," a study of the education of enslaved blacks. The sources cited with reference to Sumter County, South Carolina, on p. 586 *supra* are also relevant.

Personal Recollections of John M. Palmer: The Story of an Earnest Life (Cincinnati: The Robert Clarke Company, 1901) is the basic source for Palmer's life and education. Palmer also prepared a brief autobiographical sketch for the *History of Macoupin County, Illinois* (Philadelphia: Brink, McDonough & Co., 1879), pp. 89-93. George Thomas Palmer, *A Conscientious Turncoat: The Story of John M. Palmer, 1817-1900* (New Haven: Yale University Press, 1941) is the standard biography. J. H. Magee, *The Night of Affliction and Morning of Recovery: An Autobiography* (Cincinnati: published by the author, 1879) is the basic source for the life and education of Magee. The sources cited with reference to Macoupin County, Illinois, on p. 586 *supra* are also relevant.

D. Stuart Dodge, *Memorials of William E. Dodge* (New York: A. D. F. Randolph and Company, 1887) is the basic source for William E. Dodge's life and education. Carlos Martyn, *William E. Dodge: The Christian Merchant* (New York: Funk & Wagnalls Company, 1890) is an older biography filled with quotations from contemporary documents and reminiscences. Richard Lowitt, *A Merchant Prince of the Nineteenth Century: William E. Dodge* (New York: Columbia University Press, 1954) is a modern biography. *Memorial of Mr. David L. Dodge, Consisting of an Autobiography . . . With a Few Selections from His Writing* (Boston: published for the family by S. K. Whipple & Co., 1854) is an autobiography of William E. Dodge's father. Allen Stanley Horlick, *Country Boys and Merchant Princes: The Social Control of Young Men in New York* (Lewisburgh, Pa.: Bucknell University Press, 1975) discusses Dodge at length as an example of education for a merchant's career in nineteenth-century New York. The principal secondary sources for the life and education of Michael Walsh are Frank C. Rogers, Jr., "Mike Walsh: A Voice of Protest" (master's thesis, Columbia University, 1950) and Robert Ernst, "The One and Only Mike Walsh," *New York Historical Society Quarterly*, XXXVI (1952), 43-65. *Sketches of the Speeches and Writings of Michael Walsh Including His Poems and Correspondence Compiled by a Committee of the Spartan Association* (New York: Thomas McSpedon, 1843) brings together a variety of primary sources, including an autobiographical story, "The Adventures of Billy Bisbee." J. Fairfax McLaughlin, *The Life and Times of John Kelley, Tribune of the People* (New York: The American News Co., 1885); M. R. Werner, *Tammany Hall* (Garden City, N.Y.: Doubleday, Doran & Co., 1929); and M. P. Breen, *Thirty Years of New York Politics Up to Date* (New York: published by the author, 1899) contains brief descriptions of Walsh. There are biographies of both Dodge and Walsh in the *Dictionary of American Biography*. The sources cited with reference to New York City on pp. 586-588 *supra* are also relevant.

CHAPTER 14: CHARACTERISTICS

Phillips Bradley discusses at length the reception of Tocqueville's *Democracy* in both Europe and America in his introduction to Alexis de Tocqueville, *Democracy in America* (2 vols.; New York: Alfred A. Knopf, 1945). Given the continuing Anglo-American dialogue during the nineteenth century on the nature of liberal democracy, I have been particularly interested in John Stuart Mill's comments on *Democracy* in the *London Review,* II (1935-36), 85-129, and the *Edinburgh Review,* CXLV (1840-41), 1-47. George W. Pierson, *Tocqueville and Beaumont in America* (New York: Oxford University Press, 1938) traces Tocqueville's travels through the United States. Jack Lively, *The Social and Political Thought of Alexis de Tocqueville* (Oxford: Clarendon Press, 1962); Richard Herr, *Tocqueville and the Old Regime* (Princeton, N.J.: Princeton University Press, 1962); and Marvin Zetterbaum, *Tocqueville and the Problem of Democracy* (Stanford, Calif.: Stanford University Press, 1967) are incisive analyses of Tocqueville's political thought. David Riesman, "Tocqueville as Ethnographer," *American Scholar,* XXX (1961), 174-187, and Cushing Strout, "Tocqueville's Duality: Describing America and Thinking of Europe," *American Quarterly,* XXI (1969), 87-99, discuss Tocqueville as an observer of American institutions.

The comparative data on education in the Census of 1850 are carried in *The Seventh Census of the United States, 1850* (Washington, D.C.: Robert Armstrong, 1853), pp. lv-lxvi, and J. D. B. De Bow, ed., *Statistical View of the United States ... Being a Compendium of the Seventh Census* (Washington, D.C.: A. O. P. Nicholson, 1854), pp. 137, 148, and 160-161. I have supplemented the data there with additional data from Horace Mann's *Census of Great Britain, 1851* (London: G. E. Eyre and W. Spottiswoode, 1853), which was the source De Bow used in any case for his British statistics (the English Horace Mann, incidentally, is not to be confused with the American Horace Mann). Modern comparative data on schooling and the circulation of mail can be obtained from B. R. Mitchell, *European Historical Statistics, 1750-1970* (New York: Columbia University Press, 1975); modern comparative data on the issuance and circulation of newspapers can be obtained from Dewey Eugene Carroll, "Newspaper and Periodical Production in Countries of Europe, 1600-1950: A Quantitative Historical Analysis of Patterns of Growth" (doctoral thesis, University of Illinois, 1966). Modern comparative data on literacy can be obtained from Carlo M. Cipolla, *Literacy and Development in the West* (Baltimore: Penguin Books, 1969). It should be recognized, of course, that many of the modern data derive from precisely the same sources as used by Michael G. Mulhall in preparing *The Progress of the World in Arts, Agriculture, Commerce, Manufactures, Instruction, Railways, and Public Wealth Since the Beginning of the Nineteenth Century* (London: Edward Stanford, 1880). U.S., Bureau of Education, *Public Libraries in the United States of America: Special Report* (Washington, D.C.: Government Printing Office, 1876) and *Report of the Commissioner of Education for the Year 1876* (Washington, D.C.: Government Printing Office, 1878) are incomparable sources of data on libraries, schools, colleges, and universities.

I reviewed the recent literature on literacy in "Reading, Writing, and Literacy," *Review of Education,* I (1975), 516-521. For a contemporary review of the statistics from 1840 to 1870, see Edwin Leigh, "Illiteracy in the United States," *American Journal of Education,* XIX (1870), 801-835. For a more recent review, see Sterling G. Brinkley, "Growth of School Attendance and Literacy in the United States Since 1840," *Journal of Experimental Education,* XXVI (1957-58), 51-66, and, for the period since 1870, Sanford Winston, *Illiteracy in the United States* (Chapel Hill: University of North Carolina Press, 1930). For recent comparative studies, see Carlo M. Cipolla, *Literacy and Development in the West;* Lawrence Stone, "Literacy and Education in England, 1640-1900," *Past & Present,* no. 42 (February, 1969), 69-139; the several essays in Egil Johansson, ed., *Literacy and Society in a Historical Perspec-*

tive: A Conference Report (Umeå, Sweden: University of Umeå, 1973); and R. S. Schofield, "Dimensions of Illiteracy, 1750–1850," *Explorations in Economic History,* X (1972–73), 437–454. For the consequences of literacy, see David Riesman, *The Oral Tradition, the Written Word, and the Screen Image* (Yellow Springs, Ohio: The Antioch Press, 1956) and Jack Goody and Ian Watt, "The Consequences of Literacy," *Comparative Studies in History and Society,* V (1962–63), 304–345.

On the transformation of intellect into intelligence, I am taking issue with my late colleague Richard Hofstadter in *Anti-intellectualism in American Life* (New York: Alfred A. Knopf, 1962) and inclining rather toward the views of Constance Rourke in *The Roots of American Culture and Other Essays,* edited by Van Wyck Brooks (New York: Harcourt, Brace & Company, 1942) and John A. Kouwenhoven in *Made in America: The Arts in Modern Civilization* (Garden City, N.Y.: Doubleday and Company, 1948). It is not that there was no anti-intellectualism in nineteenth-century America—far from it. It is rather that, in defining intellect at the outset in contrast to intelligence, Hofstadter precluded a consideration of the very transformation of intellect into intelligence that has been at the heart of the American experience. Daniel Calhoun attempts to assess the contribution of education to the intelligence of nineteenth-century Americans in his brilliantly original *The Intelligence of a People* (Princeton, N.J.: Princeton University Press, 1973). For Sydney Smith, see John Clive, *Scotch Reviewers: The Edinburgh Review, 1802–1815* (Cambridge, Mass.: Harvard University Press, 1957) and Lawrence Patrick Mannon, "Sydney Smith: A Study of His Writings on Education" (doctoral thesis, State University of New York, Albany, 1976).

For Abraham Lincoln's reading and schooling, see M. L. Houser, *Lincoln's Education and Other Essays* (New York: Bookman Associates, 1957). For Lincoln's larger education, see Carl Sandburg, *Abraham Lincoln* (6 vols.; New York: Harcourt, Brace & Company, 1926–1939). For the mythic Lincoln, see David Donald, "The Folklore Lincoln," in *Lincoln Reconsidered: Essays on the Civil War* (New York: Random House, 1961).

For the transnational influence of American culture, via missionaries, traders, soldiers, and exhibitors, on the one hand, and via deliberate seeking on the part of those influenced, on the other hand, see Halvdan Koht, *The American Spirit in Europe: A Survey of Transatlantic Influences* (Philadelphia: University of Pennsylvania Press, 1949); Max M. Laserson, *The American Impact on Russia—Diplomatic and Ideological—1784–1917* (New York: The Macmillan Company, 1950); Merle Curti, "America at the World Fairs, 1851–1893," in Curti, *Probing Our Past* (New York: Harper & Brothers, 1955), pp. 246–277; G. D. Lillibridge, *Beacon of Freedom: The Impact of American Democracy upon Great Britain, 1830–1870* (Philadelphia: University of Pennsylvania Press, 1955); Frank Thistlethwaite, *The Anglo-American Connection in the Early Nineteenth Century* (Philadelphia: University of Pennsylvania Press, 1959); Sigmund Skard, *The American Myth and the European Mind: American Studies in Europe, 1776–1960* (Philadelphia: University of Pennsylvania Press, 1961); David H. Finnie, *Pioneers East: The Early American Experience in the Middle East* (Cambridge, Mass.: Harvard University Press, 1967); Carl J. Friedrich, *The Impact of American Constitutionalism Abroad* (Boston: Boston University Press, 1967); James A. Field, Jr., *America and the Mediterranean World, 1776–1882* (Princeton, N.J.: Princeton University Press, 1969); Clifton Jackson Phillips, *Protestant America and the Pagan World: The First Half Century of the American Board of Commissioners for For-*

eign Missions, 1810–1860 (Cambridge, Mass.: Harvard University Press, 1969); Vincent M. Battle and Charles H. Lyons, eds., *Essays in the History of African Education* (New York: Teachers College Press, 1970); Eugene R. Huck and Edward H. Moseley, eds., *Militarists, Merchants, and Missionaries: United States Expansion in Middle America* (University, Ala.: University of Alabama Press, 1970); Edward H. Berman, *African Reactions to Missionary Education* (New York: Teachers College Press, 1975); and Henry Blumenthal, *American and French Culture, 1800–1900: Interchanges in Art, Science, Literature, and Society* (Baton Rouge: Louisiana State University Press, 1975).

H. J. Habakkuk, *American and British Technology in the Nineteenth Century: The Search for Labour-Saving Inventions* (Cambridge, Mass.: Cambridge University Press, 1967) and Douglass C. North, "Capital Formation in the United States During the Early Period of Industrialization: A Reexamination of the Issues," in Robert William Fogel and Stanley L. Engerman, eds., *The Reinterpretation of American Economic History* (New York: Harper & Row, 1971), pp. 274–281, provide an excellent context for considering Nathan Rosenberg, ed., *The American System of Manufactures: The Report of the Committee on the United States 1855 and The Special Reports of George Wallis and Joseph Whitworth 1854* (Edinburgh: Edinburgh University Press, 1969).

EPILOGUE

The essays in David Potter, *The South and the Sectional Conflict* (Baton Rouge: Louisiana State University Press, 1968), particularly the three grouped together in the section entitled "The Nature of Southernism," portray the seeming paradox of regional nationalisms with insight and sensitivity. Avery Craven, *The Coming of the Civil War* (2d ed.; rev.; Chicago: University of Chicago Press, 1957) and *The Growth of Southern Nationalism, 1848–1861* (Baton Rouge: Louisiana State University Press, 1953); David M. Potter, *The Impending Crisis, 1848–1861,* completed by Don E. Fehrenbacher (New York: Harper & Row, 1976); Clement Eaton, *Freedom of Thought in the Old South* (Durham, N.C.: Duke University Press, 1940) and *The Mind of the Old South* (Baton Rouge: Louisiana State University Press, 1964); Eric Foner, *Free Soul, Free Labor, Free Men: The Ideology of the Republican Party Before the Civil War* (New York: Oxford University Press, 1970); Merle Curti, *The Roots of American Loyalty* (New York: Columbia University Press, 1946); Howard K. Beale, *A History of Freedom of Teaching in American Schools* (New York: Charles Scribner's Sons, 1941); Sydney E. Ahlstrom, *A Religious History of the American People* (New Haven: Yale University Press, 1972); Charles C. Cole, Jr., *The Social Ideas of the Northern Evangelists, 1826–1860* (New York: Columbia University Press, 1954); H. Shelton Smith, *In His Image, But . . . : Racism in Southern Religion, 1780–1910* (Durham, N.C.: Duke University Press, 1972); and John Rollin McCarthy, "The Slavery Issue in Selected Colleges and Universities in Illinois, Ohio, Kentucky, and Indiana: 1840–1860" (doctoral thesis, Florida State University, 1974) document the role of education in the coming of the war.

The phenomenon of *Uncle Tom's Cabin* has fascinated historians for a century. Harriet Beecher Stowe, *Uncle Tom's Cabin,* edited by Kenneth Lynn (Cambridge, Mass.: Harvard University Press, 1962), is a convenient edition. J. C. Furnas, *Goodbye to Uncle Tom* (New York: William Sloan Associates, 1956) is the fullest treatment to date of the extraordinary circulation of the work. I have profited considerably from the readiness of Robert L. Cohen at Columbia University to share with me the research on his forthcoming dissertation on *Uncle Tom's Cabin* as a public opinion phenomenon.

Emerson David Fite, *Social and Industrial Conditions in the North During the Civil War* (New York: The Macmillan Company, 1910); E. Merton Coulter, *The Confederate States of America, 1861–1865* (Baton Rouge: Louisiana State University Press, 1950); and Emory M. Thomas, *The Confederate Nation, 1861–1865* (New York: Harper & Row, 1979) are the best comprehensive treatments of the impact of the war on institutions in general and educational institutions in particular. George M. Fredrickson, *The Inner Civil War: Northern Intellectuals and the Crisis of the Union* (New York: Harper & Row, 1965); Carl Degler, *The Other South: Southern Dissenters in the Nineteenth Century* (New York: Harper & Row, 1974); Drew Gilpin Faust, *A Sacred Circle: The Dilemma of the Intellectual in the Old South, 1840–1860* (Baltimore: The Johns Hopkins University Press, 1977); and James H. Moorhead, *American Apocalypse: Yankee Protestants and the Civil War, 1860–1869* (New Haven: Yale University Press, 1978) deal with the sense of crisis the war engendered in intellectuals on both sides. James O. Henry, "The United States Christian Commission in the Civil War," *Civil War History*, VI (1960), 374–387; Herman Norton, "Revivalism in the Confederate Armies," *ibid.*, 410–424; Robert W. Lovett, "The Soldier's Free Library," *ibid.*, VIII (1962), 54–63; O. L. Davis, Jr., "The Educational Association of the C.S.A.," *ibid.*, X (1964), 67–79; Robert H. Bremner, "The Impact of the Civil War on Philanthropy and Social Welfare," *ibid.*, XII (1966), 293–303; Walter I. Trattner, "Louisa Lee Schuyler and the State Charities Aid Association," *New York Historical Society Quarterly*, LI (1967), 233–248; and Wayne Flynt, "Southern Higher Education and the Civil War," *Civil War History*, XIV (1968), 211–225, deal with particular effects of the war on education. Henry Steele Commager, ed., *The Blue and the Gray: The Story of the Civil War as Told by Participants* (2 vols.; Indianapolis: The Bobbs-Merrill Company, 1950) is a splendid collection of documents.

John Hope Franklin, *Reconstruction: After the Civil War* (Chicago: University of Chicago Press, 1961) is a useful comprehensive history. E. Merton Coulter, *The South During Reconstruction, 1865–1877* (Baton Rouge: Louisiana State University Press, 1947) focuses on the South. Walter L. Fleming, ed., *Documentary History of Reconstruction: Political, Military, Social, Religious, Educational & Industrial, 1865 to the Present Time* (2 vols.; Cleveland: The Arthur H. Clark Company, 1907) is a useful collection of source material. Robert C. Morris, *Reading, 'riting, and Reconstruction: Freedmen's Education in the South, 1861–1870* (Chicago: University of Chicago Press, in press) and William Preston Vaughn, *Schools for All: The Blacks & Public Education in the South, 1865–1877* (Lexington: The University Press of Kentucky, 1974) are the most comprehensive discussions of educational programs for the freedmen; both have excellent bibliographies. Henry Lee Swint, *The Northern Teacher in the South, 1862–1870* (Nashville: Vanderbilt University Press, 1941); Richard B. Drake, "The American Missionary Association and the Southern Negro, 1861–1898" (doctoral thesis, Emory University, 1957); Joseph Norenzo Patterson, "A Study of the History of the Contribution of the American Missionary Association to the Higher Education of the Negro—With Special Reference to Five Selected Colleges Founded by the Association, 1865–1900" (doctoral thesis, Cornell University, 1956); William S. McFeely, *Yankee*

Stepfather: General O. O. Howard and the Freedmen (New Haven: Yale University Press, 1968); and Forrest E. Keesbury, "Radical Republicans and the Congressional Abandonment of the Mixed School Idea, 1870–1875" (doctoral thesis, Lehigh University, 1971) are illuminating specialized studies. There was an extraordinary burst of college founding during the immediate postwar era that has been insufficiently noted by scholars. Frank Luther Mott, *American Journalism, 1690–1960* (3d ed.; New York: The Macmillan Company, 1962) is the basic source for developments in the press.

A useful guide to the "new generation" of school and college leaders that came to the forefront after the Civil War is the list of those who signed *A Statement of the Theory of Education in the United States of America* (Washington, D.C.: Government Printing Office, 1874). That the statement was drafted by William T. Harris, the youthful philosopher-superintendent of the St. Louis public schools, is indicative of the esteem in which he was held. Kurt F. Leidecker, *Yankee Teacher: The Life of William Torrey Harris* (New York: The Philosophical Library, 1946) is the sole comprehensive biography. Brian Holmes, "Some Writings of William Torrey Harris," *British Journal of Educational Studies,* V (1956–57), 47–66, is an incisive review of Harris's ideas. Bernard J. Kohlbrenner, "William T. Harris, Superintendent of Schools, St. Louis, Missouri, 1868–1880" (doctoral thesis, Harvard University, 1942) deals with Harris's career in St. Louis. Henry Ridgley Evans, "A List of the Writings of William Torrey Harris," in *Report of the Commissioner of Education for the Year 1907,* I, chap. ii, is standard, though incomplete. The principal collection of Harris papers is at the Library of Congress.

INDEX

Aaron, Daniel, 568
Abbott, Frank C., 551
Abbott, Jacob, 270
Abbott, John S. C., 65, 374
Abelard, Peter, 294
Abell, A. S., 196
Academy, 67, 389, 427–428
Academy of Natural Sciences of Philadelphia, 80, 325
Acklon, Morely, 570
Adair, Douglass, 544
Adams, Evelyn C., 582
Adams, Francis, 578
Adams, Henry, 524
Adams, John: views on education, 103–104, 249–250; views on Indians, 233; quoted, 126; mentioned, 19, 115, 121, 125
Adams, John Quincy: views on education, 126, 127; views on Smithsonian Institution, 282, 284–286, 287; mentioned, 142, 453, 501
Adams, Samuel, 115
Adams Female Academy, 399
Addison, Joseph, 392
Afro-Americans: discordant education of slaves, 218–228, of free blacks, 228–230; educational dilemmas of race, 242–243; household, 377–378; church, 385–386; education in Sumter District (S.C.), 429–432; education of freedmen, 518–519; writings on, 559–561, 593–594. *See also* Lowery, Irving E.; Magee, James Henry; Stroyer, Jacob
Agassiz, Louis, 408
Agricultural Museum, 339
Agricultural societies, 327–329
Agriculture, study of: proposals concerning, 249, 277, 279, 284, 286; in agricultural societies, 337–338; via agricultural press, 339–342. *See also* Morrill Act
Ahlstrom, Sydney E., 524, 529, 532, 558, 576
Albion, Robert Greenhalgh, 586

Alcott, Abigail May, 86, 90–91
Alcott, Abby May, 90
Alcott, Amos Bronson, 13, 74, 83–91, 374, 540–541
Alcott, Anna Bronson, 86–87
Alcott, Elizabeth Sewall, 86
Alcott, Louisa May, 33, 86, 91, 514
Alcott, William Andrus, 259–260, 565
Alcott House, 84, 89
Aldrich, Frederic D., 570
Alexander, James Waddel, 170
Alexander, Samuel Davies, 29n
Alger, Horatio, 260, 565
Alien Acts, 190
Allen, Gay Wilson, 569
Allen, James B., 542
Allen, William Francis, 561
Allmendinger, David F., 535, 582
Almshouse, 68
Almy, William, 348
Altick, Richard D., 572
American Academy of Arts and Sciences, 122, 126, 250
American Academy of Fine Arts, 325
American Annals of Education, 176
American Anti-Slavery Society, 206, 509
American Bible Society, 58, 59–63, 304, 535
American Board of Commissioners for Foreign Missions, 58, 234, 242, 476, 500–502, 535
American Colonization Society, 243, 501
American Education Society, 58–60, 61, 401, 535
American Farmer, 339–340
American Home Missionary Society, 47, 58, 59–63, 401, 535
American Institute of Instruction, 175, 398
American Journal of Education (1826–1830), 176
American Journal of Education (1855–1881), 176

American Lyceum, 175, 312–318
American Missionary Association, 519
American Museum, 322–323
American Museum of Natural History, 326
American Philosophical Society, 4, 79, 121–128, 250, 369
American Society for the Diffusion of Useful Knowledge, 309
American Sunday-School Union: organization, 58, 59–63; publications, 68, 69–73, 227, 304, 305, 306; writings on, 535, 537
American Tract Society, 58, 59–63, 68, 69–73, 227, 304, 535
American Women's Education Association, 146
Americanization, 244–245, 376–377, 384–385, 438–440, 564
Amherst College, 156, 165, 265–266, 270–271, 500
Ancient languages, 118, 249, 250, 264, 271, 404–405. *See also:* Greek, study of; Hebrew, study of; Latin, study of
Anderson, Frank Maloy, 555
Anderson, John, 314
Anderson, Quentin, 568
Andersonian Institution, 314
Andover Theological Seminary, 273, 363, 500
Andrew, John, 564
Andrews, J. Cutler, 556
Angell, James B., 520
Appleton, Nathan, 352
Appleton Corporation, 416
Apprenticeship: in agriculture, 336–337; in domestic manufacture, 343; in shops and factories, 344–352; in the professions, 353–366; in the education of John McAuley Palmer, 466–467; in the education of William E. Dodge, 473–474; writings on, 573–574
Architecture, study of, 279
Aristotle, 404, 487

Fenning, Daniel, 262
Fenno, John, 189
Fenton, William N., 563
Ferguson, Adam, 27, 29, 115
Ferguson, James, 20
Fessenden, Thomas Green, 340
Fickling, Susan Markey, 586
Field, Alexander James, 552
Field, James A., Jr., 591
Filler, Louis, 547, 560
Fine arts, study of, 111, 249
Finegan, Thomas E., 551
Fineman, Helene H., 564
Fink, Rychard, 565
Finkelstein, Barbara Joan, 397, 554, 578, 581
Finley, Samuel, 115
Finney, Alfred, 234
Finney, Charles Grandison: compared with Lyman Beecher, 36; life and educational thought, 39–44; on preaching styles, 52; on Methodist preachers, 56; compared with Horace Bushnell, 65; mentioned, 100, 305; writings on, 531
Finnie, David H., 591
Fischer, David Hackett, 203, 555, 557
Fisher, Mary L., 561
Fisher, Samuel H., 576
Fishlow, Albert, 180n, 553, 555
Fisk University, 519
Fiske, Nathan W., 270
Fitch, John, 22
Fite, Emerson Davis, 593
Fitzhugh, George, 559
Flanders, Robert Bruce, 542
Fleet, Frederick, 513, 514
Fleischmann, Charles Lewis, 284–285
Fleming, Donald, 567
Fleming, Walter L., 593
Fletcher, Robert Samuel, 531
Flexner, Eleanor, 547, 584
Flower, Elizabeth, 523, 529, 541
Flynt, Wayne, 593
Fobes, Philena, 454–455
Fogel, Robert William, 592
Foner, Eric, 557, 592
Foner, Philip S., 528, 543
Forbes, W. A., 512
Ford, Emily Ellsworth Fowler, 566
Ford, Paul Leicester, 543
Fordham University, 446
Foreman, Grant, 562
Forman, Sidney, 576
Forsyth, John, 281
Foster, Ashley, 545
Foster, Charles I., 533, 534, 535
Foster, Charles Robert, 531
Foster, Claudia Christie, 561, 587
Fowle, William B., 176
Fowle, Zechariah, 300
Fox, Feramorz Y., 542
Fox, George, 56
Fox, Sanford J., 581
Franklin, Benjamin: on a national seal, 17; and deism, 23; as president of American Philosophical Society, 122; influenced by Adam Smith, 130; later life and educational thought, 253–261; compared with Noah Webster, 264; compared with Ralph Wal-

Franklin, Benjamin: (cont'd) do Emerson, 294; influence on printers, 299, 300; as author of didactic literature, 304, 314; as founder of Library Company of Philadelphia, 308, 311; mentioned, 72, 476, 503; writings on, 564–565, 570–571
Franklin, F. G., 526
Franklin, John Hope, 526, 560, 593
Franklin College, 508
Fraser, James, 577
Fraser, James Walter, 530
Fredrickson, George M., 559, 593
Free Academy: See College of the City of New York
Free School Society: See Public School Society
Freedmen's Aid Society, 519
Freedmen's Bureau, 516
Freeman, Maurice, 579
Frelinghuysen, Theodore, 59
French, study of, 111, 118, 249, 250, 271, 394
Freneau, Philip, 189
Fretageot, Marie Duclos, 79, 82
Friedel, Frank, 524
Friedrich, Carl J., 591
"Friends of Education," 175–178, 495
Frierson, John, 460–462
Froebel, Friedrich, 389
Frothingham, Octavius Brooks, 541
Fruitlands, 89–91
Fuess, Claude Moore, 566
Fuller, Edmund, 564
Fuller, Wayne E., 556
Furnas, J. C., 510n, 592

Gabert, Glen E., 552
Gabriel, Ralph Henry, 563, 567
Gaffield, Gary, 556
Gale, George W., 40
Gallagher, Ruth A., 563
Gallaudet, Thomas, 144
Gambrell, Mary Latimer, 576
Gardiner, John Sylvester John, 250
Gardiner (Me.) Lyceum, 341
Garfield, William H., 216
Garrettson, Freeborn, 53
Garrison, William Lloyd, 510
Garth, Thomas R., 554
Gartner, Lloyd P., 552
Gates, Paul W., 551, 573
Gaustad, Edwin Scott, 379n, 524, 534
Gedike, Fredrich, 391
Geiger, Maynard, 580
Geltner, Sharon Ordman, 549
Geneva College, 306
Genovese, Eugene D., 560, 561, 573
Geography, study of: proposals concerning, 110, 120, 144, 249, 279; in schools and colleges, 181, 393–394, 404
Geology, 3, 277, 279, 281, 404, 405
George, Carol V. R., 561
German, study of, 111, 116, 118, 250, 271
German-Americans, 180, 376–377, 384–385
Getzels, J. W., 584
Geyer, Carl Ludwig, 438–439
Gibbs, Josiah Willard, 408
Gibson, John M., 535

Gideonse, Hendrik D., 549
Gifford, John Walter, 551
Gilbane, Brendan Francis, 574
Gilman, Daniel Coit, 280
Gilman, William H., 568
Gilmer, Francis, 112
Gilmore, Al-Tony, 560
Gintis, Herbert, 552, 554
Gist, Noel P., 558
Gitelman, H. M., 585
Glahe, Fred R., 546
Glasco, Lawrence Admiral, 579
Glasgow Mechanics' Institution, 314
Glazer, Walter S., 213n, 558
Goddard, Harold Clarke, 530
Godfrey, Thomas, 308
Goethe, Johann Wolfgang von, 294, 296, 506
Goffman, Erving, 423
Gold, Harriet, 243
Goldstrom, J. M., 533
Good, Harry G., 545
Goode, George Brown, 567
Goodman, Nathan G., 544
Goodrich, Samuel Griswold, 257, 301, 302–303, 393–394, 569
Goodsell, Willystine, 548
Goodwin, Albert, 528, 557
Goody, Jack, 591
Goodykoontz, Colin Brummitt, 535
Gordon, Mary McDougall, 552
Gossett, Thomas E., 559, 562
Gould, James, 359–360, 576
Grammar: See English grammar; Greek, study of; Latin, study of
Grant, Ulysses S., 331–332
Grant, Zilpah Polly, 398–399, 582
Graves, John, 470
Graves, William W., 563
Gray, Asa, 408
Gray, Lewis C., 573
Greathouse, John S., 465–466
Greaves, James Pierrepont, 89
Greek, study of, 111, 281, 394, 404
Greeley, Horace: life and educational work, 196, 197–200; as printer, 345, 352, 412; as lyceum speaker, 422; influence on other editors, 436; as public figure, 486; antislavery position, 509; mentioned, 449, 572; writings on, 557
Greene, Maxine, 568
Greenough, Horatio, 497
Gregorie, Anne King, 586
Gregory, Francis W., 575
Gregory, Winifred, 556
Greven, Philip, 536
Griffin, Clifford S., 534–535
Griffin, Edward D., 231
Grimké, Angelina, 144
Grimké, Frederick, 214, 218, 242, 559
Grimké, Sarah, 144
Grimm, Dorothy Fear, 570
Grinnell College, 387
Grinstein, Hyman B., 586
Griscom, John, 58
Grob, Gerald N., 537
Grund, Francis, 369, 483n, 577
Guralnick, Stanley M., 583
Gurowski, Adam G. de, 370, 483n, 577
Gutek, Gerald Lee, 540